AMERICAN POWER
AMERICAN PEOPLE

VOLUME 1

Pre-Columbian America to Reconstruction

John Moretta • Graham Cox • Angela Murphy • Robert Buzzanco

Nunn McGinty
PUBLISHING

Cover Photos: Courtesy of Library of Congress, Prints & Photographs Division
Cover Design: Sarah Syah
Project Management: Brielle Matson

Printed in the United States of America

10 9 8 7 6 5 4 3 2 1

nunnmcginty.com

Nunn McGinty
PUBLISHING

ISBN 10: 1-60803-009-1
ISBN 13: 978-1-60803-009-5

Contents

Chapter 1

NEW WORLD, OLD WORLD

No group of people originated in the New World. The ancestors of all the inhabitants of the Western Hemisphere migrated at some point in history from the Eastern Hemisphere—the so-called Old World. Modern scholars have pointed to two large migrations of New World immigrants. The first of these is made up of Asian peoples who crossed the Bering Strait thousands of years ago from Siberia into what is now Alaska. These migrants were the ancestors of the various groups that make up our present day "Native American" or "American Indian" population. The second major wave of migration was made up of Europeans and their African slaves. This migration began at the end of the fifteenth century during what is known as the European Age of Exploration. This second wave of migration brought the Old and the New World together in a profound way that reshaped human societies and the natural world they lived in on both sides of the Atlantic. On the four continents on either side of the ocean—North and South America, Europe and Africa—life would forever be transformed, and with time these transformations would affect the rest of the world. The coming together of the Old World and the New during the fifteenth and sixteenth centuries makes this period one of the most significant epochs in human history.

Early Migrants

For many years scholars believed that the first Americans were migrants from Asia who crossed over an ancient land bridge, an isthmus that they named *Beringia,* that existed over the Bering Strait during the last Ice Age. These migrants crossed into the New World around 15,000 years ago in search of game and then dispersed through-

out the Americas from this northern location. By 8,000 B.C.E.[1] they had reached the Southern tip of South America. When the land bridge receded as the glaciers melted at the end of the Ice Age, scholars conjectured, this wave of migration ended and the New World was cut off from the Old. Recent archeological discoveries, however, have complicated this picture. New evidence suggests that there may have been earlier and later settlers who came by sea to the Americas from Asia, island hopping across the ocean to the Pacific coastline or crossing the Bering Strait by boat after Beringia was covered by water. Genetic studies have also muddied our understanding of the earliest inhabitants. Because of the biological similarities between the modern American Indian population and modern Siberians and Mongolians, scholars agree that ancestors of migrants from Asia came to dominate the Western Hemisphere during the pre-Columbian period, but new studies of DNA indicate that there may be other populations that arrived early on in the Americas. While debates about the meaning of this new evidence continue, most experts do agree that most of the earliest Americans arrived from the Asian continent thousands of years ago and that they spread throughout the Americas creating diverse cultures as they adapted to different regions and climates.

Scholars also agree that the earliest Americans formed hunter gatherer societies. As they migrated into the Americas, they found many large mammal species: mammoths and

---

[1] B.C.E. refers to "Before the Common Era" and C.E. refers to "Common Era," the preferred modern terminology for "B.C." and "A.D." respectively. Dates not followed by any acronym can be assumed to be C.E.

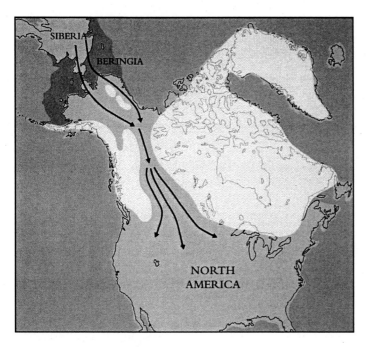

Migration to the Americas during the Last Ice Age

Americans remained migratory, moving around seasonally in search of a food supply. Members of these foraging societies might gather nuts on the plains in autumn and move towards the rivers in winter to hunt deer and migrating birds. In the spring they might rely on fishing and in the summer harvest wild plants. They did not deplete natural resources. Because they did not settle in one place, they had no way of storing excess supplies, and they instinctively kept a balance between their group's population and the natural resources available to them, sometimes going so far as to practice infanticide (the killing of infants) or geronticide (the killing of the elderly). Because of this balance, these societies were slow to evolve. There was no incentive for the early Americans to change the way they did things as long as their lifestyle worked for them. Foraging societies thus dominated the Americas for many centuries, as long as natural resources were relatively abundant.

mastodons, large bison and giant sloths, and even camels and horses. Clovis spear points, named after the site of their first discovery in Clovis, New Mexico, have been found at numerous sites throughout North America along with the remains of the large animals the early Americans hunted. Excavations of these sites indicate that these early Americans were migratory communities made up of several dozen people from the same kinship network. They kept hunting camps and moved around them for several-hundred square miles in search of game.

The large mammals that sustained the first Americans eventually became extinct sometime around 9000 B.C.E., most probably due to climate change. Overhunting may have also contributed to their extinction. Hunter gatherer, or *foraging,* societies continued, however, focusing on smaller game. Early

In time, in some parts of the Americas, the human population began to face a scarcity of resources. This scarcity led them to search for new ways of providing for their communities, and in order to do this they gradually turned to agriculture. The first farming societies of the New World emerged in Northern Mexico. The inhabitants of this region domesticated corn, or *maize*, thousands of years ago and eventually learned to plant beans and squash along with it in a combination that kept the soil fertile while providing people with needed nutrients. From Northern

Mexico corn cultivation diffused throughout the Americas east and west, north and south, and agriculture spread throughout the New World. This turn to farming encouraged settled societies and population growth. Agriculture laid the foundation for the more complex societies that emerged in Central America, Peru and in some parts of North America between 4000 and 1500 B.C.E..

These North American societies were experiencing what scholars call an *agricultural revolution*. Although some contest the term "revolution" because the shift took place very gradually over a long period of time, the turn to farming was indeed revolutionary because it fundamentally changed the way in which people ordered their societies.

Scholars have noted similar changes that occurred all across the world with the rise of agriculture. As agriculture developed, people became more sedentary in order to tend their crops. As stationary societies arose, people then developed new sources of food, clothing, and shelter. The types of dwellings that people lived in became more permanent. Pottery came into use as societies began to store goods for the future. Populations grew and individuals were freed from the constant need to search for material resources. Because farming is an on-going activity, there was a greater need to plan ahead. Settlers thus developed new ways to measure time. Societies also became more territorial. As men and women recognized the productive value of the land, there was a greater desire to control more of it and to protect it from those who might encroach. There was thus a need for defense, and land disputes could lead to outbreaks of war.

Specialization of labor emerged as the production of food became less labor intensive, freeing some members of the community to do other things. Cultural, political, and social development took place, and more elaborate religious ideologies emerged as more leisure time appeared and members of society had time to think about things beyond survival. A hierarchy arose within these societies as some held positions with higher status than others, and some were able to command the labor of others. In most areas, a division of labor based on gender also emerged—males doing one kind of work and females doing another. The agricultural revolution laid the ground work for modern society.

Pre-Columbian America

The ancient Aztec, Incan, and Mayan civilizations of Central and South America were the most complex societies that arose in the New World during the *Pre-Columbian Era*, the era before the New World was discovered in 1492 by Christopher Columbus. Their dominance can be attributed to their early adoption of agriculture. These societies built great cities and established empires with elaborate trade networks. They developed systems of religion, produced art, made architectural developments, studied the world around them, and respected a hierarchy of social class within their communities. When Europeans arrived to the New World, the Aztec and Incan civilizations were great empires that dominated portions of Central and South America.

Further north, early Americans developed less elaborate social orders. In general, the communities that emerged north of Mexico were smaller, more scattered, and they relied on foraging for a longer period of time. Some early agricultural civilizations did develop, however, and by the time of European arrival many of the northern groups had *mixed economies*—they relied on both foraging and farming. In the two thousand years before Europeans arrived in the New World, societies that were not as elaborate of those of Central and South America but still sophisticated in their own way rose and declined throughout the North American continent.

In the present day American Southwest, sites exist that reveal the ancient civilization of the Anasazi, ancestors of the Pueblo Indians. Like the settlers in Northern Mexico, the Anasazi began to plant and rely on corn. They settled near rivers and created elaborate irrigation networks in order to nurture their crop. The Anasazi built their dwellings near the cornfields that nourished the community. At Chaco Canyon in New Mexico, remains of an Anasazi village that existed between 900 and 1100 C.E. have been preserved by the dry desert climate. The site includes a large communal dwelling that contains over six hundred rooms. Another Anasazi ruin has been preserved at Mesa Verde, Colorado, where the Anasazi settlers created multistoried houses carved into cliffs that they inhabited between 1200 and 1300 C.E.

The Anasazi were sophisticated societies. Their ruins reveal religious shrines that they built into their homes, evidence of their astronomical observations, and hints of complex road and communications networks that linked Anasazi villages. For a time the

Anasazi cliff dwelling at Mesa Verde National Park in Colorado
Image courtesy of the National Park Service

Anasazi societies flourished, but each of the settlements eventually declined and dispersed. Scholars believe that draught and possibly attacks by nomadic tribes that entered into the area—the ancestors of the Navajos and Apaches—led them to abandon their larger settlements. The Anasazi scattered into smaller bands throughout the southwest. The Pueblo tribes that emerged from this dispersal continued many of the Anasazi traditions, however, like the planting of corn and the reliance on communal dwellings.

Further east, ancient burial mounds dot the American landscape from the Mississippi River over to the Atlantic coastline. Scholars who have studied these sites have determined that mound-building societies existed in the eastern part of the present-day United States for a long-ranging period, from about 1500 B.C.E. until just before the arrival of the first European settlers in the region. The last of the mound-building societies, the Mississippian Civilization, existed between 1000 and 1500 C.E. Members of Mississippian communities built these mounds in honor of their dead, and they practiced a religion that was based on deference to their ancestors. They had a mixed economy—relying on both farming and foraging to provide for their communities. Again, the cultivation of corn was important. Some of the mound-builders that settled along the Mississippi River established large towns with stately public buildings, but many lived in small villages. Cahokia, a mound-building community located near present-day St. Louis, Missouri was the largest of these towns. Archaeologists estimate that at its height in 1150 C.E., the city had between 10,000 and 20,000 inhabitants, and many satellite communities grew up around it. It served as a center of trade that dominated the region. Sites of other major towns have also been excavated in Alabama and Georgia. These

communities built up trade networks with one another, but they also experienced conflict that at times caused them to go to war. Skeletons found at the various mound sites indicate a number of violent deaths, and excavations reveal that larger towns built defensive structures to protect from invasion. The Mississippian societies began to decline in the thirteenth century, most probably due to the spread of disease in the congested communities. Warfare also may have played a role. As was the case with the Anasazi communities, people began to leave the villages and cities and disperse into smaller bands in the nearby countryside. As they did so, they brought elements of their culture, including the farming of corn and beans and the impulse to establish trade networks with surrounding tribes. Some of the small mound-building communities survived into the early sixteenth century, but epidemics brought by early European traders and explorers led to their final collapse.

When European colonists began to settle the area of the present-day United States in earnest, they would not encounter these more sophisticated civilizations. What they generally found as they arrived along the Atlantic coastline were smaller, scattered tribal societies with subsistence economies. These societies were just beginning to experience the agricultural revolution. They had mixed economies, and they were semi-nomadic. They planted small gardens and included corn among their crops. They relied heavily on the hunt, however, and they moved the location of their gardens frequently. Thus tribes were relatively small and their settlements less permanent.

The tribes that lived along the Atlantic seaboard, the Eastern Woodland Indians, would be the natives with which most of the early European settlers of North America would become familiar. The Eastern Woodland

Indians were made up of two general languages groups, the Iroquois and the Algonquian, but they were actually a diverse lot made up of many tribes with important cultural differences. These tribes did, however, have certain elements in common. The Eastern Woodland Indians generally held land cooperatively—the whole tribe claimed ownership and not individuals. They subsisted off of agriculture, fishing, hunting, and gathering. Their religions were diverse, but they all were *animistic,* which means that they worshiped elements of the natural world on which they were so dependent. Tribes chose leaders who made decisions for the community and managed trade and diplomacy with other groups. Gender roles were specialized. Women did much of the farming, gathering, meal-preparation and child-rearing while men hunted and protected the tribe from enemies.

The Eastern Woodland Indians traded with one another, but they also at times waged war. Some of these tribes formed alliances that were quite powerful. On the eve of European arrival on the Atlantic Coast, however, disease brought by the earliest European traders and warfare among the tribes had depopulated the Eastern Woodland Indian tribes, leaving them in a weakened state. While some of the groups that encountered the first Europeans who settled along the Atlantic Coast were able to hold their own against the settlers for a time, they were not strong enough or united enough to contest the European domination of the region in the long run as more and more and more Old World settlers arrived.

European Society and the Age of Exploration

Before the fifteenth century some Europeans ventured into the New World, but their forays were short-lived. Around 1000 C.E. Norsemen who had first colonized Greenland traveled to lands further west and spent time in present-day Newfoundland. Led by Leif Eriksson, they explored the coast of North America, and when they returned home they spoke of the abundant grapes they found on the shores of this western land, which they named "Vinland." Permanent colonization did not take place, however. Norse resources would not support distant colonies. Furthermore, Leif Eriksson's discoveries did not become common knowledge in Europe. The population of Europe was in decline at this time, the continent had little wealth, and European society was disorganized. It was a period of time in Europe that has become known as the *Dark Ages.* For centuries Europeans remained unaware of the existence of the Americas, and there was little incentive for inhabitants of the decentralized continent to look outward.

It was not until the mid-fifteenth century that Europeans began to think of exploring and expanding out into the world. Throughout the Dark Ages, Europe had remained divided into many small realms. In the mid-fourteenth century, the bubonic plague, or Black Death, had spread from the east into the continent and had depopulated much of Europe. Between one quarter and one third of the European population succumbed to the illness, leaving European society depressed and in disarray well into the next century. Only a few large cities existed, and most Europeans lived in small rural villages. Farming was important in most of Europe, but throughout the continent many Europeans also relied heavily on hunting and gathering. Most Europeans spent their time providing for their day-to-day needs. They had little time to think of exploring the world around them.

The early peoples of Europe were thus not that dissimilar to the early peoples of North America, but certain important cultural differences emerged. Two of these differences would generate significant conflict when Europeans eventually encountered the peoples the New World.

First, Europeans widely practiced private, rather than communal, ownership of land. A hierarchy emerged in the kingdoms of Europe based on who controlled the land. The social system that arose as a result is called *feudalism*. Feudal lords controlled large estates, and they lived off the labor of the peasant population who worked their lands. They demanded the obedience of these peasants, who were required to pay tribute in crops to the feudal lord. At the top of the hierarchy were monarchs who ruled the kingdom and raised armies to protect their power. They demanded deference from the feudal lords. In some areas, these lesser lords formed governmental bodies, like the English House of Lords and the French *parlements*, that checked the supreme power of the monarch and guarded their interests. Even so, by 1450, the power of some monarchs grew as they made alliances with a growing merchant class and asserted themselves over more territory. Larger, more powerful states began to emerge. When Europeans who were accustomed to the idea of individual ownership of land and a hierarchical society based on land wealth encountered American peoples who lived communally, this difference in their values became a major source of conflict.

Another way in which Europe was distinct was in the religious ideology that dominated the continent. Before the rise of Christianity, many Europeans held beliefs that were similar to early Americans, focusing on the spirituality of the natural world. In time, these animistic religions were supplanted as the Christian religion spread throughout the continent. The Roman Catholic Church unified Christendom in Western and Central Europe, and in the fifteenth century it was the most powerful entity on the continent.

The Christian religion was fundamental to the worldview of most Europeans. Christians were monotheistic, believing in one God, and central to their ideology was their belief that God sacrificed a son, Jesus Christ, for man's sins. Although Christian ideology emphasized love, community and fellowship among men, Catholic leaders and many of the church's Christian followers were intolerant of those who did not adopt their system of belief. Believing that Christianity was the one true religion, Catholics actively challenged and persecuted non-believers. During the Crusades of the twelfth and thirteenth centuries, armies were raised to challenge the dominance of Islam in the Arab world. Within Western Europe "pagans" who held on to old animistic religions, Jews who did not accept the divinity of Jesus Christ, and others who questioned Christian beliefs were persecuted, expelled, and, at times, put to death. When Europeans later arrived in the Americas, they met a population that was entirely unfamiliar with their religion, and earlier patterns continued as they strove to dominate and convert those that they could and as they alienated those who would not accept their ways.

Europeans eventually arrived in the Americas because of a number of related developments that arose in Europe during the fifteenth century that led to an *Age of Exploration,* which lasted from the mid-fifteenth until well into the seventeenth-century. By 1450, Europe was beginning to recover from the effects of the Black Death. The European economy improved, and European states were becoming stronger and more cohesive. A number of revolutionary changes came to European society at this time that led Europeans to look outward, seeking new economic opportunities, spreading their religious ideology, and expanding their influence into new regions.

First, and most central to the changes that would take place, was a *commercial revolution*. Economic recovery and population growth led to a greater desire for trade, and Europeans experienced an expansion of commerce that stimulated the development of markets, towns, and a new wealthy merchant class. Europeans of the fifteenth century were particularly interested in luxury goods from Asia: dyes, cloths, gems, precious metals, and most especially spices like pepper, ginger, nutmeg, cinnamon and cloves, which made European foods more appetizing. The long, overland journey to Asia was arduous and dangerous, however, and Islamic Arabs controlled many of the trade routes. Products from Asia were thus very limited and expensive. During this period, Italian ports served as trade centers where Mediterranean, North African, and Asian products came into Western Europe. Italian city-states established monopolies over the Mediterranean trade, raising prices and making expensive goods even more difficult to afford. These monopolies and the high prices that resulted from them led other groups in Europe to seek out new markets and alternative routes to Asia that would bypass Italian and Arab middlemen.

Second, powerful new nation states arose in Portugal, Spain, France and England as monarchs consolidated power over these regions. These more centralized states were in part a result of the commercial revolution. Monarchs made alliances with the rising merchant class, promising to protect their interests. Rulers of these new consolidated states were able to control more resources, which they put into both expanding and defending their power. They were eager to gain more wealth for their nations, which would make them even stronger. They thus sponsored explorations of new territories and the development of technologies that would help them to reach new markets and allow them to exert their influence in new parts of the world.

Third, during the fifteenth century there was a renewal of interest in learning and artistic expression in many parts of Europe. This movement was known as the *Renaissance*, an Italian word that references the "rebirth" of interest in the old classical Greek and Roman civilizations. The Renaissance originated in Italy, where the commercial revolution had encouraged the rise of a prosperous class of people who could spend money and time pursuing knowledge and cultivating the arts. They looked to recover the teachings of the classical past as well as to seek out new knowledge. Economic and political leaders provided financial support for many thinkers, writers, artists, and musicians during this era, and a rich period of cultural and intellectual development took place and spread throughout the European continent. The impulse to seek out new ideas helped to spark an interest among Europeans in understanding the world around them, and it fostered a wave of innovation as Europeans developed new, more sophisticated ways of doing things.

This intellectual energy helped to lead to a fourth development, the adaptation and refinement of Arab technologies and the creation of new ones that allowed for safer long-distance travel from home. Before the fifteenth century, Europeans lacked adequate instruments and navigation techniques to safely venture far from their coasts. Compasses had been used since the thirteenth century, but they were of limited value in the open ocean where readings could vary at different points on the globe. Most sailors used measurements of latitude—lines that determined distances north and south on the globe—in order to find their destinations, but calculating latitude was imprecise as well. Early on, sailors determined latitude by observing the stars, but in the fifteenth century they adopted and improved upon an Arab instrument called the *astrolabe*, which made determining latitude easier. In addition, new types of ships that were better suited to the open ocean, *caravels*, were created. The caravel was developed by studying Arab ships and improving upon them. Caravels were longer, narrower, and higher than the ships previously used, and were therefore more maneuverable on the high seas. New sails were added to the ships in order to capture the wind from a number of directions and give sailors more control over their navigation. Finally, new maps and navigation charts were produced in the fifteenth century that gave sailors a more accurate idea of where they were going. As Europeans ventured out into more territories, these maps became more and more detailed.

The Portuguese in Africa

Portugal, a state along the western coast of the Iberian Peninsula, was at the forefront of the Age of Exploration. The city of Lisbon, on the Portuguese coast, was an important port that brought trade from the Mediterranean into Western Europe, and the country became dependent on that trade. Portugal was at the center of many of the maritime scientific developments of the era, largely because of the efforts of Prince Henry the Navigator, the son of Portugal's King John I. Henry wanted to challenge the hold Arab and Italian middlemen had on the eastern trade, and he sought to make Portugal a significant maritime power. He established a school for geographers and navigators in the early fifteenth century that allowed the Portuguese to come up with many of the nautical developments of the era and to harness their power so they could expand outward into the world. In particular, the Portuguese were interested in exploring the west coast of Africa. They hoped to both establish new markets along this coast and to find a new route to Asia, which would allow them to gain a share of that trade. The Portuguese also expressed an interest in spreading Christianity among the African peoples in order to counter the influence of Islam, which had spread into the continent from the north.

Beginning in 1420, the Portuguese sent ships along the coast of West Africa. As they pushed further and further south, they explored regions that formerly had been unknown to them. They had not previously sailed so far from home, for legends abounded about the treacherous nature of the unfamiliar parts of the Atlantic Ocean. Europeans thought that sea monsters, or worse, the devil, inhabited the waters far from home.

The Portuguese sailors pushed on anyway, exploring the African coastline. Henry the Navigator died in 1460, but the trips to Africa were renewed under the leadership of his father's successor, King John II. Under his rule, the Portuguese sponsored the voyage of Bartholomeu Dias, who sailed around the southernmost point of Africa, the Cape of Good Hope, in 1487 and 1488. Ten years later, Vasco da Gama went all the way around Africa and sailed up the Indian Ocean coastline to India,

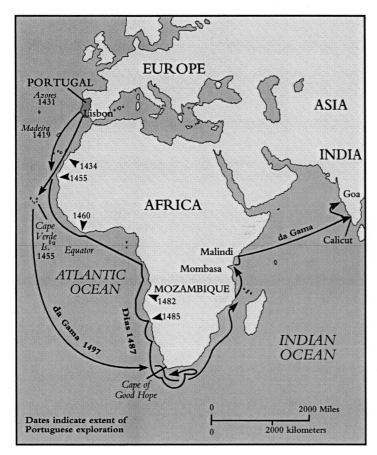

Portuguese Explorations of Africa

explorations and encountered new groups with whom they could trade.

The Portuguese did not colonize West Africa because the societies along the coast were too powerful at this time to be conquered and because Europeans were susceptible to African diseases. Instead they built trading posts along the coast that they called *factories,* and they paid tribute to those in power in each region in order to establish trade relationships with them. In Africa, the Portuguese established a lucrative trade in gold, spices, ivory, and, most significantly, slaves.

The Initiation of the Atlantic Slave Trade

opening up an alternative, but time-consuming, route to the east. The Portuguese could now bring products from Asia directly into their ports by sailing around the African continent.

It was not just the Asian trade, however, but the new markets they opened up in Africa that enriched the Portuguese. Groups that dominated the North and Northwestern part of Africa had long traded with Europeans and Arabs, sending goods across the Sahara Desert and into Mediterranean ports further north, but the Portuguese were able to open up new trade centers along the Atlantic coastline as they pushed southward with their

During the 1440s the Portuguese began to buy slaves on the West African coast. Other European powers would soon join in on this trade, and it would affect the economic and social order of the entire western world. After Europeans arrived in the New World, the slave trade expanded from Africa across the Atlantic Ocean, and it become crucial to the economic development of European colonies in the Americas. This Atlantic slave trade lasted for four centuries and brought millions of Africans into the New World as bound laborers, but it did more than simply transfer a population from one continent to another. The slave trade would help to enrich Europe, impoverish Africa, and shape new economic and social structures in the Americas. It set up power relationships that would resonate through history, all the way to the present.

Slavery existed in Africa before Europeans set up factories on the continent, but it was of a different nature than the form of slavery that would evolve as a result of the European trade with Africa. Slaves in Africa were usually acquired by leaders of one community as a result of warfare with another. Captives were taken and brought into the new tribe. Wealth in Africa was largely determined by the labor one controlled, so slave ownership was an indicator of status and power. Under the African system, slaves were allowed to marry, their condition was not inherited, and their living circumstances were much the same as the rest of the tribe members. Numbers gave communities power, so the taking of slave captives among Africans was largely a way in which to weaken rivals or to bring outsiders into a society.

As trade with the European powers emerged and their demand for slaves grew, the conditions of enslavement would change. Europeans began to use slaves as laborers in large plantations that they established as they colonized new parts of the world, and African traders along the coast began to purchase more and more slaves from the interior as they realized the European demand for bound labor. Much of Africa was transformed into a violent and unstable place as many Africans abandoned other economic pursuits to fill the needs of the slave trade and as more and more battles were fought in order to obtain captives to supply this trade. In addition to warfare, kidnappings took place in order to acquire slaves. Further and further into the interior of the continent, an ever increasing number of Africans were captured and sold into slavery. The African trade in slaves with Europeans

thus transformed both African society and the nature of the slave experience. Centuries later, when Europeans attempted to colonize Africa, the disunity and lack of economic development that resulted from the African dependence on the slave trade left African peoples vulnerable to European imperialists.

Between 1440 and 1500, the Portuguese bought slaves for use at home as domestic laborers. The Spanish soon began to participate in this trade as well. Domestic slavery had existed for many centuries in Europe, as it had in many parts of the world, but the use of slaves had significantly declined in most of Western Europe by the fifteenth century. Slaves were regularly employed as domestic laborers in some regions around the Mediterranean, but they were few in number. With the opening of the African slave trade, however, Europeans would find a new way to exploit the labor of slaves.

Both the Portuguese and Spanish began to purchase slaves in ever larger numbers to work on new sugar plantations that they established on Atlantic islands that they discovered and colonized during the first outward thrusts of the Age of Exploration. In Madeira, the Azores, the Canary Islands and elsewhere off the African coast, Europeans seized control and plantations emerged during the fifteenth century. Initially, the Portuguese and Spanish enslaved native inhabitants to provide the labor to produce sugar, but this labor force soon declined in number as the natives perished under the harsh conditions of their enslavement. They were replaced by slaves purchased in Africa.

On these plantations, slaves were used to perform the arduous labor that was necessary in order to produce sugar cane. They endured back-breaking work from sun-up to sun-down and were not adopted as members of a larger community. The need for labor on these plantations transformed the nature of the slave experience, and the use of African slave labor on these plantations provided a model for colonists as they expanded into the New World, establishing more sugar plantations. Eventually a new slave system arose in which African slaves provided most of the labor on large plantations established throughout the New World that provided Europe with high-demand crops like sugar, coffee, tobacco, rice, and in time, cotton.

This new form of slavery, *chattel slavery*, treated the slave as property—a commodity that could be bought and sold. Under the system of chattel slavery, not only was one enslaved for life, but children inherited slave status from their parents. Because this arrangement evolved out of the trade in Africa, this new system grew into a race-based one. It was taboo to enslave other Europeans as chattel slaves, and with time Europeans began to associate the blackness of the African peoples with slave status. Thus both an oppressive labor system and a racial ideology was born that would be central to the development of new societies that emerged in the New World as a result of the Age of Exploration.

The slave trade that had been established by Europeans in Africa played a large role in the transformation of the societies on both sides of Atlantic after the New World was colonized. When Europeans arrived in the New World, the slave trade expanded from the Old World across the Atlantic Ocean, and it become crucial to the economic development of European colonies in the Americas. This Atlantic slave trade lasted for four centuries and brought millions of Africans into the New World as bound laborers, but it did more than simply transfer a population from one continent to another. The slave trade would help to enrich Europe, impoverish Africa, and shape new economic and social structures in the Americas. It set up power relationships that would resonate through history, all the way to the present.

Before it ended in the nineteenth century, the slave trade was responsible for the forced immigration of as many as 11 million Africans to North and South America and the Caribbean. Indeed, until the late eighteenth century, the number of African immigrants to the New World was higher than that of Europeans; an astounding ration of 6 to 1. The movement of Africans across the Atlantic to the Americas represented the largest forced migration in human history.

As noted, the Portuguese had been the first Europeans to trade for and exploit Africans as slave labor. Moreover, the Portuguese traders found it considerably more efficient (and less dangerous) to leave the procurement of slaves to Africans, who were willing to sell captives in exchange for European commodities, such as guns and metallurgical products, which the Africans particularly valued. Thus by the 1450s, a small but regular traffic in slaves had been established between Europe and Africa. The Portuguese brutally exploited their African slaves, often working them to death on the large sugar plantations they had created on their island colony of Madeira, off the coast of northern Africa. The Portuguese did not think twice about inflicting upon their slaves such harsh work, for profits were high and replacement costs low. Sugar and slaves had become synonymous since the fourteenth century when Italian merchants first imported sugar cane from West Asia and set up the first sugar plantations on islands in the Mediterranean. For the sake of sweetness, Europeans subjected Africans to the suffering of slavery.

After the Portuguese established the slave trade in Africa, the Spanish followed them into this trade. Spanish colonists used African slave labor in the New World soon after Columbus' voyages (discussed below), establishing sugar plantations throughout the Caribbean, during the sixteenth century. At first they attempted to capture and enslave the native populations of the islands they conquered and claimed, but disease and warfare quickly reduced that potential labor force. Thus, by the middle of the sixteenth century the Spanish too had turned to the enslavement of Africans on their island plantations in the Caribbean. So desperate for such labor were the Spanish, that they granted their rival, Portugal, an *asiento* (license) to bring slaves to their possessions directly from Africa. In the late sixteenth century, the Portuguese, with the help of Dutch financing, extended sugar production to northeast Brazil, which became the model of the efficient and brutal exploitation of African labor. By 1600 some 25,000 enslaved Africans worked on the sugar plantations of Hispaniola and Brazil.

In the seventeenth century, the Dutch, skilled at finance and commerce, greatly expanded the European sugar market. They could produce so much for such little cost with African slave labor (in Brazil, which they took from the Portuguese in 1630), that sugar by the middle of the century ceased to be a luxury item. It was a product readily available for mass consumption by all classes of Europeans. Along with other addictive tropical commodities such as tobacco, coffee, and tea, sugar became what one historian called "a proletarian hunger-killer," helping to sustain people through increasingly long working days. Not to be left out of this sugar boom, both France and England established "sugar islands" in the Caribbean as well. The French first developed sugar plantations on the small island of Martinique, and then they

A late nineteenth century engraving reconstructing a scene on a colonial sugar plantation

seized the eastern half of Hispaniola from the Spanish, creating a sugar colony called St. Dominque (present-day Haiti). By the close of the seventeenth century, sugar and slaves had come to define the European colonial system in the West Indies.

West African Society

The overwhelming majority of Africans sold into slavery and brought to the New World came from West Africa, from long established societies and local communities. In the sixteenth century more than a 100 different peoples lived along the coast of West Africa from Cape Verde south to Angola. In the north were the Wolofs, Mandingos, Hausas, Ashantis, and Yorubas; to the south were the Ibos, Sekes, Bakongos, and Mbundus. Regardless of region, all shared a similar existence centered on the local community, which was organized along hierarchical kinship lines. In each village clan leaders and village chiefs decided what was best for the good of all inhabitants, ranging from food distribution and production to whether or not villagers should defend their territory or flee to a safer place. Local tribunals of elders arbitrated internal disputes. Men usually took second and third wives, creating a marriage system known as polygyny, in which large composite families with complex internal relationships developed. Restrictions on sexual relations, however, saw West African women bear fewer children than the typical European woman, and many enjoyed considerable social and economic independence as tradeswomen.

Economically, West African societies were agricultural, cultivating the land with techniques used for thousands of years. Farmers grew sorghum, millet, and rice on the grassy savannahs and fruits, root crops, and other vegetables in the tropical forests that straddled the equator. West Africans made iron tools and other implements, but because the region's soils were rather thin and poor, they had no use for iron plows. Africans practiced *shifting cultivation*, a mobile system of farming similar to that used by some the early North American tribes. They cleared land by burning, used hoes or digging sticks to work in the ash, rich in nutrients, and when the land ceased to be fertile, they let the old fields lie fallow and moved on to virgin soil. Men worked at clearing the land, while women worked at cultivation and the sale of surpluses at West African markets. West Africans produced enough food and commodities not only to sustain their respective tribes but to trade with other Africans as well. Although West Africa remained largely a collection of autonomous villages and rural communities, some large kingdom-states developed, complete with sophisticated, flourishing urban centers. Along the upper Niger River, where the grassland gradually turns to desert, sat the city of Timbuktu, one of Africa's most legendary trading centers for several centuries. Timbuktu was one of the Old World's greatest market places, where goods from all over the continent and the Mediterranean world were traded, and from where caravans traversed the great Sahara Desert carrying West African metal goods, gold, ivory, textiles, and slaves to the Muslim empires of North Africa and the Middle East.

The more powerful tribes competed with each other for control of this trade, and in the process created a succession of military empires, the most extensive of which became the Mali Empire, whose greatest ruler, the Muslim Mansa Musa (1313–1337), transformed Timbuktu into a leading academic and intellectual as well as commercial center.

Indeed, during his reign, Timbuktu became a capital of world renown. When the Portuguese first arrived in the fifteenth century, the most important state in the region was the powerful Muslim kingdom of Songhai (today the African nation of Mali). The Songhai had built one of the largest cavalries and armies in the Old World, with which they controlled the trans-Sahara trade. There were many lesser states and kingdoms along the West African coast, and it was with these African communities that the Portuguese first bargained for slaves.

The Africans had practiced slavery for centuries and had been involved in a slave trade network with the Muslim empires of the Middle East and south Asia for at least three hundred years by the time they engaged the Europeans in such an enterprise. Most enslaved men and women were war captives or had been condemned by their tribe or village to servitude as punishment for criminal acts or for other transgressions against the community or another individual. However, African slavery was not a permanent condition; most slaves were eventually incorporated into the families they served or were set free after a certain amount of time, either when the tribe or master believed the individual had sufficiently atoned for his or her behavior, or if they were captured in war, proved worthy of assimilation into the community. They were allowed to marry and their children were born free. "With us they [slaves] did no more work than the other members of the community, even their master," remembered Olaudah Equiano, an Ibo captured and shipped to North America as a slave in 1756, when he was a boy of eleven. "Their [the slaves] food, clothing, and lodging were nearly the same as the others, except that they [the slaves] were not permitted to eat with those who were born free." Most African slave traders believed such would be the treatment and condition of the first slaves they sold to the Portuguese; that European slavery would be similar to that practiced in Africa. How wrong the African traders were.

The Impact of the Slave Trade on Africa

Down to the present day, West Africa in particular, still suffers from the legacy of four centuries of the trade in human flesh. Little did sixteenth century Africans realize when they began the slave trade, first with the Portuguese and then over the subsequent centuries with the other European powers, that six centuries later their continent would still be affected economically, politically, ecologically, and environmentally from such an exchange. The long-range impact of the slave trade was unforeseen, and to this day its deleterious remnants can be seen throughout those countries whose political leaders engaged in the trade for several centuries. To put it simply, the slave trade and the labor of slaves allowed Europeans in both the Old and New World to grow stronger while weakening Africa.

In the short term, the slave-trading kingdoms on the coast increased their power at the expense of the interior states. Thus the West African state of Songhai gave way to the Gold Coast state of Akwamu. In the Niger delta the slaving states of Nembe, Bonny, and Kalabari arose, and to the south the kingdom of Imbangala drew slaves from central Africa. These coastal states however, soon discovered that they too would eventually be adversely affected by prolonged engagement in the slave trade; that the European New World demand for slaves was so great that it would only be a matter of time before the supply to meet that demand would come from their own states. In short, European and American slavers did not care from whom or from where they got the slaves to meet the New World's demand for such labor; the trade was simply too profitable to worry about African sensibilities, protocol, or any other civilized niceties. After all, to both European and American slavers, all Africans were the same—an inferior race that was allegedly suited for enslavement. As King Dom Affonso of the Kongo, whose country had been involved in the slave trade with Portugal, wrote to the Portuguese king John III in the sixteenth century, "[Your]Merchants [slavers]daily seize our own subjects, sons of the land and sons of our noblemen, they grab them and cause them to be sold, and so great Sir, is their corruption and licentiousness that our country is being utterly depopulated."

The loss of millions of men and women over the centuries caused the West African economy to stagnate, as essential labor for farming and other productive activities was either captured and enslaved or required to help sustain the slave trade in various capacities. West Africa began the sixteenth century self-sufficient and independent, able to adequately produce its food and other products. Participation in the slave trade ended such autonomy, as West Africans increasingly became dependent on the European slave traders for their finished goods, such as textiles and metalwares, which they previously manufactured on their own. African slave traders were expert at driving a hard bargain, and for several centuries they gained an increasing price for slaves—the result of rising New World demand and increased competition among European slavers. Even when they appeared to get the best of the transaction, however, the ultimate advantage lay with the Europeans, who in exchange for mere consumer goods got human capital—wealth-producing workers.

For every man or woman taken captive, at least another died as a result of chronic slave trading. Many of the new West African states that emerged as a result of participation in the slave trade became little more than sources for supplying captives to the European traders. A *gun-slave-cycle* pushed neighboring tribes into destructive arms races and endemic warfare, causing further population contraction and thus the decreasing ability to remain self-sufficient. Indeed, one of the most serious ramifications of the slave trade became regional starvation and even famine. The slave trade took so many people out of West Africa that in many areas there was not sufficient population left to grow food. The resulting political and cultural demoralization prepared the way for the European conquest of Africa in the nineteenth century. As the Nigerian poet Chinweizu writes, those West African leaders during the centuries of slave trading "had been too busy organizing our continent for the exploitative advantage of Europe, [they] had been too busy with slaving raids upon one another, too busy decorating themselves with trinkets imported from Europe, too busy impoverishing and disorganizing the land, to take thought and long-range action to protect our sovereignty." The continent of Africa was thus transformed as a result of the Atlantic Slave Trade that was initiated during the Age of Exploration.

Christopher Columbus

The European Age of Exploration began with the Portuguese expeditions along the African coast, but thanks to Italian mariner Christopher Columbus, Europeans found new continents to explore and exploit across the Atlantic Ocean. Columbus was not looking to discover a "New World." His motivation was the same one that drove the Portuguese efforts to sail around Africa. He wanted to find a new route to the rich markets of Asia, and he believed that he could reach these markets by sailing directly west across the Atlantic from European shores. Other Europeans had discussed the possibility of such a journey before, but most believed that the trip was impossible due to the distances it would involve. Columbus, however, believed that previous estimates of the world's circumference, which the Ancient Greek astronomers had put at around 24,000 miles, were flawed. He thought that that the circumference was actually closer to 18,000 miles and that he could reach East Asia in a voyage that would be long and difficult, but not impossible. The actual circumference of the earth is approximately 24,900 miles, making the Ancient Greek estimate more accurate, but Columbus's error would lead him to make his mark on history as the European who "discovered" the New World.

Columbus first approached King John II of Portugal about financing his Atlantic journey in 1484, but the Portuguese were more intent on their African explorations at that time. The Portuguese also had serious doubts about the feasibility of Columbus's plan. If his estimate of the distance he needed to travel was wrong, and the likelihood of this was great, Columbus would run out of provisions before he could reach Asian shores. No one expected that he might reach another great landmass before he reached Asia. King John thus declined the opportunity to sponsor his voyage, and Columbus took his plan to Ferdinand and Isabella of Spain, where he had more success in gaining support. Ferdinand and Isabella initially were as doubtful about

Columbus's plan as the Portuguese had been, but he eventually convinced them to outfit his voyage across the Atlantic. The financing of Columbus's voyage was a gamble for the Spanish monarchs, but it was one that would bring high rewards for Spain.

Spain was just emerging as a strong nation state at the time that Columbus appealed for aid. Early in the fifteenth century the area on the Iberian Peninsula that would eventually become Spain had been divided into a number of smaller kingdoms. The marriage of Ferdinand of Aragon and Isabella of Castile in 1469 brought two of these kingdoms into an alliance. When Ferdinand and Isabella inherited their respective thrones, they began the process of unification that would produce one of the strongest of the European nation states of the late fifteenth century. As they unified the various regions of Spain, the two monarchs also completed the *reconquista,* a centuries-long battle to expel Islamic peoples who had settled in Western Europe. The Spanish captured the last Islamic stronghold, Granada, in 1492, the same year that Columbus embarked on his first voyage. With the capture of Granada, the Spanish rulers launched the *Inquisition*, a movement sanctioned by the Catholic Church, in an effort to either convert or expel Jews and Muslims who remained in Spain. Thus, they united the Spanish peoples into a strong nation-state built largely on a common Christian religious identity.

Hoping to bring in more wealth for Spain and desiring to spread the Catholic Church's authority into new regions, Ferdinand and Isabella showed interest in exerting influence and establishing markets around the world. When the Portuguese made forays into Africa, Spanish merchants had followed in their wake, hoping to gain a share of the African trade. Spanish competition, however, led Portugal to appeal to the authority of the Catholic Church, which the Christian nations of Europe all recognized as supreme. In 1455, the pope gave Portugal sole possession of the lands in Africa. The Spanish thus were motivated to look outward across the Atlantic in search of new trade routes, since the Portuguese were granted this African monopoly. The Spanish monarchs chose to finance Columbus's trip in the hopes that he would be able to open up a new trade route to Asia, allow the Spanish to occupy lands found on his journey, and help to spread Christianity in new parts of the world.

In 1492, Columbus began his famous voyage with three ships, the *Niña*, the *Pinta*, and the *Santa Maria*. He journeyed first from Spain to the Spanish-controlled Canary Islands, and then he set a course west into the Atlantic Ocean. He reached landfall on October 12, just over two months after leaving Spain. Columbus named the stretch of territory he landed upon San Salvador. From there he explored the island he called Hispaniola (present day Haiti and the Dominican Republic), the Bahamas, and Cuba. He did not realize that he had stumbled into a "New World" when he arrived in these Caribbean waters. As he explored the region, he believed that he was in "the Indies" and that he had made it to Asia. Thus he named the peoples he came upon on this journey, the Taino inhabitants of the Caribbean islands, "Indians," a name which has been applied to the vast variety of peoples found throughout the Americas.

Columbus, who would take three more trips across the Atlantic, never realized the full significance of his discovery. In fact, he died in 1506 still believing he had opened a route to the Indies. As more and more Europeans made the trip west, however, others recognized that the land across the ocean was not part of Asia. In 1499, Amerigo Vespucci of Florence traveled to the Caribbean and drew up a map of the region. He was the one who first labeled the area as a *Mundus Novus*, a "New World." The continents found in the New World would eventually bear the name "America" in honor of this map-maker.

The Spanish in the New World

Columbus left behind a group of men on Hispaniola on his first trip across the Atlantic, establishing a Spanish presence in the New World. He returned to Spain with goods he found on the islands, stories about the region, and a number of Indians that he kidnapped in the Bahamas. Although he had found no substantial riches on this first trip, gold ornaments worn by some of the Taino people sparked his, and other Spaniards', hopes that they may find more gold in the newly discovered territory. Columbus believed that the Taino would provide an effective labor force to help to search for it and exploit this resource. Upon his return to Spain, he informed Ferdinand and Isabella that he deemed the Taino peoples fit to be enslaved, as they had no weapons that could stand up to those of the Spanish.

A burst of energy followed Columbus's discovery. Columbus took additional trips across the Atlantic along with other Spaniards interested in the New World, and colonists would begin to settle the islands of the Caribbean. After Columbus's discovery, Ferdinand and Isabella immediately appealed to the Catholic Church to sanction Spain's control of the areas he had explored. Pope Alexander VI confirmed Spanish control of the region, and he set up a north-south line in the Atlantic Ocean to help to determine Spanish and Portuguese spheres of influence. Basically the pope was dividing the non-Christian world among two powerful Christian nations who would control their respective regions in order to foster the spread of Christianity. West of the line he established, the Spanish would hold dominion, and east of it the Portuguese would maintain control. This would effectively give Spain authority in the New World and the Portuguese control of Africa. The Portuguese protested this arrangement, however, and in 1494 the *Treaty of Tordesillas* moved the line of demarcation further west, giving Portugal a stake in New World territories. Because of this treaty, Portugal would be able to colonize Brazil, which bulged east out of the South American continent, when it was discovered in 1500. The Portuguese settled in Brazil, establishing sugar and coffee plantations and importing African slaves to provide labor. With the exception of Brazil, however, the Treaty of Tordesillas gave the Spanish control over the Americas. This dominion over so much of the New World gave Spain a great amount of power, both abroad and at home, and the Spanish created an enormous, wealthy empire.

Spain's colonization of the New World began in the region first discovered by Columbus. In 1496, the Spanish founded the city of Santo Domingo on Hispaniola, which would serve as their first seat of government in the Americas. From there the Spanish spread into Puerto Rico, Jamaica, the Bahamas, and Cuba. On these islands, the Spanish enslaved the natives, forcing them to search for gold and using them as a labor force on new sugar plantations that were created. In time the population of Caribbean natives disappeared as the peoples of the islands were annihilated by European diseases and the violent treatment of the colonizers. When this happened, African slaves were brought in to serve as laborers in the Caribbean, and the Spanish pushed further west in search of new sources of labor and wealth.

The age of the *conquistadores* had begun. Conquistadores were Spanish adventurers who

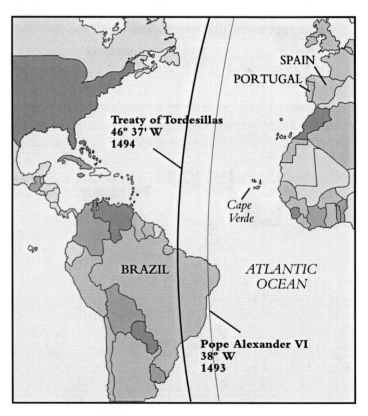

In 1493, Pope Alexander VI created a Line of Demarcation that indicated which territories could be controlled by Portugal and which could be controlled by Spain. This line was moved further West in 1494 with the Treaty of Tordesillas.

came to the New World in search of instant wealth. They did not wish to colonize the area permanently. Instead, they wanted to extract riches from the region as quickly as possible, by violent means if necessary, and to return home as rich men. In 1519, one of the most successful of these adventurers, Hernando Cortes, arrived with an army of six hundred men in present-day Mexico, where he set out to conquer the powerful and wealthy Aztec empire. Cortes was successful in this effort not only because the Spanish possessed weapons that the Aztecs lacked and because they carried diseases to which the natives had no immunity, but also because he was able to make alliances with other peoples of the region who resented Aztec power. In time he was able to control the vast area that the Aztecs had controlled, and from there Spanish power spread throughout Central America. In 1531, Francisco Pizarro led a similar effort against the Inca Empire in Peru, spreading Spanish authority along the Pacific Coast of South America. Both Cortes and Pizarro were able to quickly establish control over these vast territories because of the centralized, hierarchal nature of the civilizations that they conquered. By controlling the leaders of the communities, the Spanish could gain control of the entire society. In areas where less centralized societies held sway, it took the Spaniards a longer time to gain control. Still, Spanish power spread further and further throughout Central and South America, enriching Spain as the conquistadores seized gold, silver and other riches from those they conquered and transported these goods back to Spain.

When they had exhausted these readily available resources, the Spanish found new avenues of wealth. They began to plant crops, establish ranches, and to find ways to extract precious metals from the land. Spanish settlers in the Americas were granted *encomiendas* by the Spanish government in order to give them command of labor to generate this wealth. Those receiving these grants, *encomenderos*, agreed to convert natives to Christianity and protect those that converted. In return, the Spanish government upheld their right to demand tribute from the natives in the form of either goods or labor. The encomenderos thus controlled native communities in a system that was reminiscent of feudalism. The Spanish justified this system as an appropriate way to convert a population of non-Christians, and one of the duties of the encomendero was to provide missionary priests for the religious instruction of the villagers. If natives resisted conversion, the Spanish were harsh. Upon encountering new peoples in a territory, the Spanish read an announcement called a *requirimiento*, "a requirement", aloud to them in Spanish. The requirimiento demanded that natives accept Spanish rule and the Christian religion, and it proclaimed that if they did not do this, then they forfeited any property they held and they could be enslaved or even killed.

Although the Spanish settled mainly in Central and South America, they explored, and thus nominally controlled, much of the land further to the north—land in the present-day United States. During the sixteenth century, a number of explorers ventured into this territory seeking wealth. Francisco Vásquez de Coronado led an expedition into present-day New Mexico and explored as far north as Kansas in 1540 and 1541. Juan Rodriguez Cabrillo explored the California coastline and claimed that region for Spain in 1542. Both of these explorers were disappointed in their search for riches, however, and so there was little interest in settling these regions immediately after they were explored. It was only at the end of the sixteenth century that small settlements would emerge in New Mexico, and California was not colonized by the Spanish until late in the eighteenth century.

The first permanent European settlement north of Mexico was established by the Spanish at St. Augustine in Florida in 1565. This settlement was meant to be a military outpost for Spain that would establish the Spanish presence on the Atlantic coast of North America and help to provide protection for Spanish ships carrying cargoes back to Spain. Because few Spaniards wished to settle in this region, the Spanish sought to convert natives of the area and extract pledges of loyalty to Spain from this population. In this way they could establish Spanish control over Florida with few Spanish settlers. This approach was successful. For many years, St. Augustine remained a small outpost on the Spanish frontier with a population made up of a few Spanish missionaries and soldiers and a large majority of Hispanicized Indians (Indians that had adapted to Spanish culture).

The Spanish established other early settlements in present-day New Mexico. In 1598, Don Juan de Oñate arrived in this region with five hundred men, and he claimed the land for Spain. He set up a colony among the Pueblo Indian settlements, granting encomiendas to Spaniards that would allow them to extract tribute from the native population. These colonists founded the town of Santa Fe. They established sheep and cattle ranches throughout the region, and converted many of the Pueblo Indians to Catholicism. Santa Fe, like St. Augustine, remained a small outpost on the Spanish frontier for many years.

The region north of Mexico did not attract many Spanish settlers because of the nature of the North American environment. Explorers had failed to find ready sources of wealth as they had further south, and there was thus less

interest in venturing into the region. Also, North America lacked large empires like the Aztecs and Incas. With no central command structure to control, the Spanish would have had a difficult time pacifying the natives of the North American continent. Thus, although Spain claimed the southern part of North America and areas along the North American Pacific coast, they did not send many colonists there or build up any type of infrastructure to easily connect the frontier outposts to the more populated Spanish settlements to the south. As Spanish colonists poured into the Americas, they were attracted to the more developed areas of the empire.

By the end of the sixteenth century the Spanish had founded around two hundred cities and towns throughout Central and South America. The Spanish Empire encompassed the Caribbean, Mexico, portions of North America, and present-day Peru, Argentina, and Chile in South America. Spanish colonists set up printing presses, established universities and constructed churches in the places they settled. Around 200,000 European emigrants, mostly from Spain, had settled in the New World during this century, and another 125,000 Africans had been transported to the Americas to work on the Spanish plantations of the Caribbean as well as on the Portuguese plantations in Brazil. The New World had forever been changed because of Columbus's arrival on American shores. The Old World was changed as well.

The Columbian Exchange

The contact among Europeans, Africans and Native Americans that resulted from the Age of Exploration changed the cultural and the physical environment of both the Old and the

New World in a multitude of ways. Over the centuries, because of their isolation from one another, two separate ecological environments had evolved in the Eastern and Western hemispheres. The ships that crossed the Atlantic after Columbus's discovery of the New World would end this period of isolation. New animals, plants, diseases, technology, and cultural ways traveled back and forth across the ocean with far-reaching consequences. This process of biological and cultural exchange has been dubbed the *Columbian Exchange*, after the man who set it in motion in 1492.

New animals arrived in the Americas with the first European ships that crossed the Atlantic. Columbus himself brought with him pigs, sheep, and cattle to Hispaniola. Later European colonists imported more livestock from home to use as a source of food and to provide material for clothing. Unlike Africans and Europeans, most Native Americans had not raised livestock as part of their lifestyle, relying on hunting instead. They were generally unfamiliar with domesticated animals, so their appearance was a novel thing. Among the new animals brought over from the Old World were cattle, sheep, pigs and chickens. Some Native Americans adopted the practice of raising pigs and chickens for food after the Europeans arrived. Others kept sheep so that they could produce high quality woolen cloth. Horses, long extinct in the Americas, were also brought over by the Spanish for transportation. Horses gave the Spanish an advantage in their efforts to conquer Native American groups as they allowed for swift movement from place to place. In time, some of these Spanish horses made their way to the North American plains, where they prospered and were widely adopted by the tribes of the region. They transformed the cultures of the Plains Indians, making them more mobile and

giving them the ability to hunt large game like bison more easily.

There was, however, a downside to the arrival of all these new animals in the Americas. Europeans often allowed their livestock to roam free. Cows and pigs trampled native fields, overgrazed on native plants, and spread diseases that had not been present in the New World before their arrival. They also brought seeds of Old World plants that they had ingested. They spread these seeds through their excrement after they landed on American shores, and many of them grew into aggressive weeds that overtook the native plants of the region. The landscape was forever transformed.

Diets were also transformed as new crops arrived in both the Old and the New World. *Staple crops,* crops that make up a large portion of a society's diet and thus become central to a society's agricultural output, were exchanged across the Atlantic. Native Americans had relied on corn and, in South America, potatoes as their staple crops. Corn and potatoes were introduced to Africa and Europe after 1492, transforming the way people in those continents ate. Because the New World staples could be grown more efficiently than many of the European grains, in time Old World peasants began to widely adopt these crops. Malnutrition declined, and the population of Europe boomed. On the other end of the exchange, grains brought to the New World on European ships included wheat, rice, barley and oats. Colonists cultivated these products along with the corn they found in the Americas.

Other foods were exchanged as well. Before the Europeans arrived, Native Americans were unfamiliar with foods like turnips, peaches, pears, onions, grapes, bananas and citrus fruits. Europeans also brought new crops to the plantations they set up in the New World. Most important among these were sugar cane and, to a lesser extent, coffee beans, luxury crops that became so important in Europe as a result of colonial production that they became staple crops in their own right. Crops from the Americas that arrived in Europe included sweet potatoes, tomatoes, pineapples, squash, peppers, pumpkin, peanuts, tomatoes, beans, cacao and vanilla. Tobacco was a New World plant that was eventually transformed into a staple crop after American colonists learned to grow forms of it on New World plantations that appealed to European tastes.

One of the most devastating elements of the Columbian Exchange for Native Americans was the spread of Old World diseases in the Americas. Smallpox was the most deadly microbe that was brought by Europeans, but colonists also brought other diseases like the measles, chicken pox, whooping cough, diphtheria, influenza and the bubonic plague. Native Americans lacked immunity to these afflictions, and so the progression of new diseases annihilated much of the Native American population as they spread. Whole tribes were eliminated in some areas, and others were depopulated and weakened, making them vulnerable to European dominance. Illness arrived with the very first European traders and settlers, and the diseases spread more rapidly through the Americas than the colonizers themselves. Because of their swift spread, European diseases left some parts of the New World sparsely inhabited, giving the colonists the upper hand when they began to arrive in large numbers. Scholars disagree on the numbers of Native Americans that existed before and after European arrival, but most agree that millions of them died as a result of the Old World diseases that spread throughout the Americas beginning in the late fifteenth century.

Technology was also exchanged between the New and the Old World. Europeans learned some new technologies from Native Americans. European fishing, for example, was aided by the use of canoes and fishing weirs that were adopted from native societies. European technologies brought to the New World, however, assisted Europeans in their imposition of power over the new societies they encountered. The ships on which they traveled across the ocean were, of course, one such technology, but Europeans also brought with them firearms, gunpowder and iron tools. As the conquistadores marched through Central and South America, their weapons produced panic among the natives they encountered who had no experience with them. Firearms greatly aided the Spanish in their ability to control the peoples they encountered. In North America, as other European nations arrived to colonize the New World, many of the Eastern Woodland tribes entered into a vigorous trade with Europeans in order to procure firearms for themselves, for the tribes that had access to this resource would have an advantage in conflicts that erupted with other groups. Thus, European weaponry brought to the Americas proved a source of power for the colonists in both their power to control and in their ability to attract trading alliances.

Finally, the Columbian Exchange involved an exchange of language, knowledge and culture. Peoples in both the Old World and the New encountered new political and religious systems, new economic ideologies, and new ways of organizing society. At times this cultural exchange involved conflict, as Europeans imposed their ways on Native Americans and on African slaves and suppressed attempts to resist this process, but at other times it involved accommodation. Many peoples merged elements of both Old and New World to create new blended cultural ways as Europeans and Africans came to America in ever larger numbers. Still, the uneven nature of the Columbian Exchange gave the Europeans, led by the Spanish, an advantage in establishing dominance in the New World as well as the Old.

North American Explorations

While the Spanish grew rich off of its American empire, other strong nation-states were emerging in Europe. As leaders in France, the Netherlands, and England consolidated their power; they began to look outward, hoping to establish new trade routes and colonial outposts. North America became an object of interest to these nations. Europeans had learned that the American continents blocked sea routes straight to Asia, but some sought a mythical *Northwest Passage,* a waterway through the North American continent that would allow Europeans to make their way to Asian markets by sea. In addition, as various nation states grew in power in Europe, they hoped to strengthen themselves further by setting up their own colonial outposts. Spain had gained a huge advantage, however, with its early start in colonizing the New World. Other European states were forced to look to areas where the Spanish had not already established control—a further reason to focus on North America. These nations would not establish significant settlements in North America until the beginning of the seventeenth century, but they did begin looking for opportunities in the area during the century before.

French interest in the New World at first centered on the search for the Northwest Passage. In 1534, King Francis I sponsored the trip of Giovanni da Verrazano, an Italian sailor, who was to search for a water route to China through North America. He did not succeed, and in 1534, Jacques Cartier was dispatched with the same goal. Cartier also failed to find such a route, but he was able to discover the St. Lawrence River. He traveled up the river to the location of present-day Montreal, but the harsh winters of the region drove him home in 1542. Decades later, in 1608, Samuel de Champlain returned to the area that Cartier had explored, and he established the first colonial French settlement of Quebec. From this settlement French traders fanned out through North America, initiating a fur trade with the natives and bringing Catholic missionaries to evangelize them. Because they sought trade, their relationship with the natives was one of more give-and-take than that of the Spanish. The French traders had to adapt to Indian ways in order to successfully do business with them. Although French settlement was sparse, the French developed a strong presence in North America because of the wide-ranging trade networks they set up. During the seventeenth century, the French would establish a strong foothold in Canada. They spread out along the northeastern waterways and down the Mississippi River, where they would eventually colonize Louisiana.

The Dutch, residents of the Netherlands, also sought a Northwest Passage to Asia. The Netherlands had been controlled by Spain in the sixteenth century, but in time the Dutch rebelled, and in 1581 they declared their independence from the Spanish monarchy. The Netherlands became a great trading nation, growing to dominate the trade in the Baltic and Black Seas. By 1600 the Dutch city of

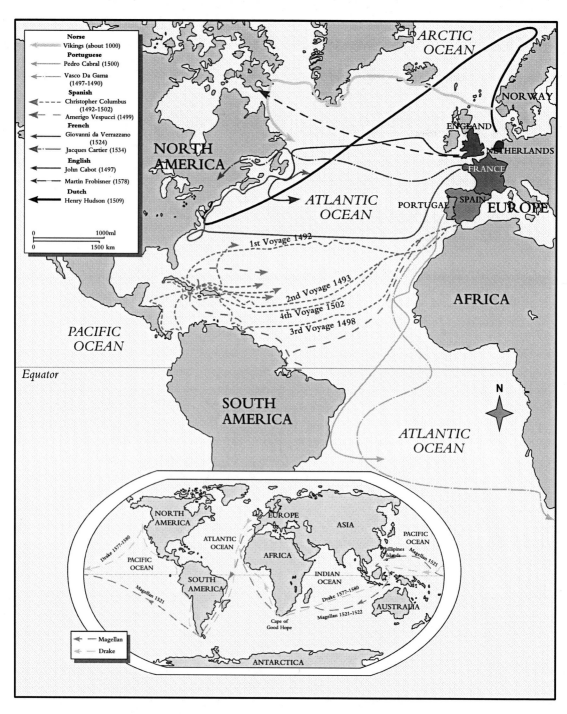

European Explorations of the New World

Amsterdam was at the center of European commerce, and the Dutch were looking to expand and trade in new regions. The Dutch East India Company was set up to coordinate this Dutch trade. In 1609, the company commissioned Henry Hudson, an English explorer, to search for the Northwest Passage to China. Like those who explored before him, he found no such passage, but he did discover the Hudson River near present-day New York. The Dutch established settlements along the Hudson and other nearby rivers, naming their colony New Netherland. They also created a new company, the Dutch West India Company, to coordinate the Dutch trade in the New World. Until the Dutch lost this colony to the English in 1664, they used this New World outpost as a base for a lucrative trade in furs with the native population. Unlike the French, who went to the tribes in search of trade, the Dutch did most of their trading from their settlements in New Netherland. Thus, they had a more geographically limited presence in North America than that of the French.

Although the English were the last to establish colonies in North America, England funded one of the earliest efforts to find the Northwest Passage. In 1497, just a few years after Columbus's first voyage, the English sponsored an Italian sailor named Giovanni Caboto, whose Anglicized name was John Cabot, to sail to across the Atlantic in search a pathway to Asia. Cabot found no such path, and he died during his second voyage in search of it. His journey was not unproductive, however. Cabot was the first European of the era to discover mainland North America, sailing up the eastern coast of the continent to Newfoundland.

Although Cabot had discovered a vast new region in his explorations, the English did not show much interest in colonization at this time. During the fifteenth century, England had been divided by war. Henry VII, the first Tudor monarch, unified the English people during the first years of the next century, but he remained too distracted in his efforts to maintain authority at home to have much concern with overseas expansion during his reign. Religious conflict would besiege the Tudor rulers that succeeded him throughout much of the rest of the sixteenth century, but by the century's end, England would be strengthened under the reign of Queen Elizabeth I, who ruled between 1558 and 1603. The nation would become strong enough during her time in power to eventually challenge the dominance of Spain in both the New World and the Old.

The Protestant English and Catholic Spain

During the sixteenth century a number of changes came to England that transformed the nation's place in the world and would eventually lead to English interest in New World colonies. The backdrop of many of these changes was the *Protestant Reformation*, which began in 1517 when a German priest named Martin Luther challenged the authority of the Catholic Church. Luther complained that the church had become too corrupt and had placed too much distance between Christians and their god. He was excommunicated from the Catholic Church for his criticisms, and he and like-minded Christians set up their own congregations. They became known as *Protestants* because they protested the dominance of the Catholic Church over Christian affairs. Other European theologians built on Luther's ideas, and new congregations emerged throughout the continent.

One of the most influential Protestant theologians of the sixteenth century was Swiss-born John Calvin. Calvin emphasized an all-powerful, all-knowing god who had chosen certain people, the *elect*, as predestined for salvation. Calvin emphasized the importance of doing good work in the world in order to honor God, for a good life was a sign that one might be a member of the elect. Calvin also called on Christians to follow God's higher law, even if they had to challenge those in authority in the existing social order.

During the sixteenth century, then, Europe became divided along religious lines, Catholic and Protestant. With some of these new Protestant denominations challenging existing hierarchies, they became a grave concern to the pope and the Catholic monarchies of Europe.

England became one of the strongest Protestant nations during this period. Protestantism flourished in England largely due to the so-called *English Reformation*. The English Reformation, however, was more about politics than spiritual beliefs. When King Henry VIII, the son of Henry VII, failed to produce any male heirs with his Spanish-born wife, Catherine of Aragon, Henry petitioned the pope to allow the dissolution of his marriage. The pope refused this request, so Henry broke with the Catholic Church in 1529. He divorced Catherine of Aragon and proclaimed himself to be the head of the Church of England. Unlike many of the Protestant sects spreading through Europe, the Church of England generally adhered to the structure and teachings of the Catholic Church. The English Reformation was essentially a political maneuver to give the king more control over religious affairs.

This maneuver, however, left a legacy of religious conflict in England that kept it looking inward through the first half of the sixteenth century. The Church of England held sway under Henry and his son, Edward VI, but its authority would soon be challenged. When Henry's Catholic daughter Mary, the daughter he had with Catherine of Aragon, became queen upon Edward's death, she re-established Catholic dominance and persecuted English Protestants. After her death in 1558, her Protestant half-sister Elizabeth I ascended to the throne, and the Church of England once again was ascendant. Meanwhile, followers of John Calvin's theology emerged in the country, and they set out to purify the Church of England, which they felt had retained too many of the corrupt vestiges of Catholicism. They referenced their goal in the name they took—*Puritans*.

During Elizabeth's reign, then, she faced challenges both from the growing Puritan population, from the alienated Catholic population of England, and from Catholic nations abroad. Of the threats faced by Elizabeth, concerns about Catholicism predominated. Catholic Spain had become a dangerous enemy in the years since Henry VIII had divorced Catherine of Aragon, and competition with Spain dominated foreign affairs during her reign.

One of Queen Elizabeth's big concerns was the presence of a large Catholic population in Ireland, off of the English coast. She worried that Spanish and French Catholics might be able to unite with the Catholic Irish population and use that island as a base from which to invade England. Thus, after she took the throne Elizabeth encouraged wealthy English Protestants to colonize Ireland and subdue the Catholic Irish. This they did, and the English experience in Ireland helped to provide a model for the nation's future New World colonies. When English colonists arrived in North America during the next century, they would treat the American Indian groups they encountered in much the same manner as they had the Catholic Irish— seizing their lands and maintaining a strict division between English and native societies.

English power increased during Elizabeth's reign, and the English began to successfully challenge Spanish supremacy in both the Old World and the New. England's commercial economy grew, and English leaders built up a strong navy. During this era, English pirates and smugglers often preyed upon Spanish ships transporting goods from American shores back home. Europeans of this time believed in a concept called *mercantilism*. This concept was based on the idea that there was a finite amount of wealth in the world—that people, and nations, could only become rich at the expense of one another. A nation's power therefore rested in extracting as much wealth from foreign lands as possible and in keeping that wealth from one's competitors. English piracy of Spanish ships was encouraged in order to enrich England, and thus promote the nation's power, at the expense of Spain. During the fifteenth century, the English government authorized privateers like Sir Francis Drake to plunder foreign ships and bring goods seized back to England.

English piracy contributed to the outbreak of war between England and Spain during the last decades of the sixteenth century. The relations between Spain and England had grown increasingly hostile during Queen Elizabeth's reign. The English queen had aided the Dutch, fellow Protestants, in their rebellion against Spain, and she had been responsible for the persecution of Catholics in England. The Spanish considered the Protestant English to be heretics, and they resented English attacks on their ships and challenges to their power.

Thus, with the blessing of the pope, King Philip II of Spain planned an invasion of England, hoping to dethrone Elizabeth I and establish Catholic rule in the nation. To accomplish this task, Philip sent the *Spanish Armada*, a great fleet carrying approximately thirty thousand men, from Spain to conquer the island nation.

The Spanish invasion, however, was an enormous failure. King Philip expected to overwhelm the English with the numbers of soldiers brought by the Spanish Armada, which was made up of over 130 converted merchant ships. His plans were foiled. The primary purpose of the ships in the fleet was transport, and they proved no match for the smaller, more modern and maneuverable ships of the young English navy. In addition, the English had become aware of the Spanish plans to invade and were able to initiate attacks on the Spanish Armada before it arrived in English waters. Finally, the Spanish met with bad weather, unfortunate luck which led to further losses. The English destroyed a large portion of the Spanish Armada in several skirmishes, and the fleet returned to Spain with about half of the numbers that it had embarked with, a devastating financial loss. The war between England and Spain lasted until 1604, but the defeat of the Spanish Armada in 1588 was a major turning point in European history, signaling the decline of Spanish and the rise of English power in the western world.

England and the New World

In addition to contesting Spanish power in the Old World, the English also began to take an interest in establishing colonies in the New World. Several developments would contribute to the colonizing impulse in England.

First, during the sixteenth century changes in the English economy led to a large landless population, and English leaders hoped that expansion overseas might provide a safety valve for those that had been displaced by economic change. Responding to an increase in demand for wool in the global marketplace, many English landowners of the era converted their agricultural lands to pastures for the grazing of sheep, a process called *enclosure*. They expelled peasants from their holdings as they made this shift to a less labor intensive operation. A large landless, impoverished class of people arose in England as a result, and the more prosperous classes of the nation worried that they would become a permanent source of instability. In addition there was a decrease in the food supply needed to feed the growing English population due to the shift from farming to grazing. Colonies would provide a way to clear England of some of its surplus population, open new markets through which to acquire food, and rid the country of some its more unruly elements.

Second, the principles of mercantilism motivated the English during the sixteenth century. Because the strength of a nation was believed to rest both on extracting as much wealth from foreign lands as possible and on avoiding a reliance on other nations for necessary products, mercantilist thought led to an increase in competition for colonies among European nations. England, like other European nations, looked to exploit the wealth of the colonial environment in order to help provide necessities for the homeland. This impulse grew more pressing for England after the 1550s when the world market in wool declined. The English hoped that colonies would provide new sources of wealth, and they sought to develop a lucrative colonial commerce that would allow England to acquire products that they had previously been dependent on purchasing from foreign nations like Spain.

Third, religious dissent provided a motive for colonization. Throughout the sixteenth century the number of Puritans grew in England, the most radical of which were *Separatists* who gave up on efforts to reform the Church of England. Instead they separated from the church and formed their own congregations. Both the Puritans and the Separatists became more and more alienated from the established church, and many of them began to feel like outsiders in England. By the early seventeenth century, many members of these congregations were looking for places outside of England where they could set up new religious and social systems in accordance to their own beliefs.

Thus England became more outward looking during the sixteenth century. Several explorations to the New World were sponsored during Queen Elizabeth's reign, and by the beginning of the seventeenth century the colonizing impulse had ripened.

At the behest of the English government under Queen Elizabeth, between 1577 and 1580 the privateer Sir Francis Drake became the second man to lead an expedition that would circumnavigate the globe. He followed the path of Portuguese explorer Ferdinand Magellan, who had led the first successful circumnavigation beginning in 1519, around South America. His reputation as a pirate grew on this voyage as he looted Spanish ships and settlements along the way. Drake traveled up the Pacific Coast of North America on this trip, naming the area New Albion, but he did not settle any colonies in the region. He returned to England a hero, collected a large reward from the Queen, and continued to harass the

Spanish in the years after his voyage. He also participated in the naval battles that led to the defeat of the Spanish Armada in 1588.

Sir Humphrey Gilbert and Sir Walter Raleigh were the first English explorers to come to the New World with the intention of setting up English colonies. Queen Elizabeth had authorized them to explore and colonize any lands occupied by "heathens" that had not already been claimed by a European power. In 1578 and 1583 Gilbert, who was a veteran of the English colonization effort in Ireland, sailed across the Atlantic in order to try to colonize Newfoundland. Lacking adequate funds, he failed to successfully settle the region, however, and his ship went down at sea during his second voyage. The first English colony was therefore established by Raleigh, his half brother, who landed in 1585 on Roanoke Island, off of the present-day North Carolina coastline. From this island, Raleigh explored the mainland, naming the region "Virginia," after the unmarried Queen Elizabeth, who was known throughout Europe as "The Virgin Queen."

Raleigh left a group of colonists to stay in Roanoke and returned to England to recruit more settlers after he explored this region. These first colonists stayed for a year before abandoning the colony, returning home to England on a ship commanded by Sir Francis Drake. In 1587, Raleigh transported a second group of colonists to Roanoke. Hoping the make this settlement permanent, he returned to England in order to marshal supplies for the colony. The supply ship was delayed, however, by the turmoil associated with the invasion of the Spanish Armada. When a ship with provisions for the colonists finally arrived in Roanoke in 1590, the colony had vanished. All that was found at the site of the settlement was the word "CROATOAN" carved in capital letters into a tree and a few belongings. The lost Roanoke settlers were never found, but some believe that they amalgamated with the Lumbee Indians, for Croatoan was the name of a Lumbee village on an island, present day Hatteras, sixty miles south of Roanoke. This is just a guess, however. No one is certain what happened to these first English settlers, and Roanoke has gone down in history as the "Lost Colony."

Despite the failure of the Roanoke colony, the English were not deterred. In the early seventeenth century, the English crown chartered two *joint stock companies* to encourage new colonization efforts. Through these companies, shares would be sold to investors in England, and the funds raised would be used to sponsor colonists who could find ways to make the colonized territories profitable for the investors. Two rival joint stock companies emerged. One was made up of a group of London merchants who acquired charter rights for Virginia from Sir Walter Raleigh. Naming themselves the Virginia Company, they decided to initiate a new effort to colonize the territory that Raleigh had explored. A rival group of merchants from Plymouth, England, calling themselves the Plymouth Council, also emerged. They hoped to sponsor the settlement of colonists further north on the Atlantic Coast of North America. In 1606 James I, who had succeeded Queen Elizabeth, issued a charter that divided America between the two groups. The Virginia Company would hold the rights to colonize the lands to the south known as Virginia. The Plymouth Council would be able to colonize areas to the north. Through the efforts of these joint stock companies, the first lasting English colonies would be established in the regions known as Virginia and as New England.

The Atlantic World

During the seventeenth century Europeans and Africans would arrive in the Americas in ever larger numbers, and it was during this century that the English planted permanent colonies on the Atlantic coast of North America. By this time, the Atlantic Ocean, which had once been a barrier to humans, had been transformed into a thoroughfare between two worlds. Societies in the Americas, Europe, and Africa that had evolved in isolation from one another now became connected, and they exchanged people, physical resources, and cultural ways. Historians of the American colonial period have recognized the importance of these connections in understanding the development of American society. More and more scholars have placed their considerations of early American history in the context of the *Atlantic World*. They recognize that in order to understand the cultures of the variety of American peoples and the power relationships that emerged among them over time, one needs to understand the way they were shaped by the exchanges that took place across the ocean as the Old World and the New collided.

Suggested Readings

Brian M. Fagan, *The Great Journey: The Peopling of Ancient America*, rev. ed. (2004).

Hugh Thomas, *Rivers of Gold: The Rise of the Spanish Empire, from Columbus to Magellan* (2004).

Alfred W. Crosby, *The Columbian Exchange: Biological and Cultural Consequences of 1492* (1972).

David J. Weber, *The Spanish Frontier in North America* (1992).

Patrick Collinson, *The Birthpangs of Protestant England* (1988).

Karen Ordahl Kupperman, *Roanoke: The Abandoned Colony* (1984).

Chapter 2

THE SOUTHERN COLONIES

In the aftermath of the Roanoke disaster, English enthusiasm for overseas colonization diminished. More pressing issues confronted England, such as war with Spain, whose attempted 1588 invasion of the English mainland became known as the *Armada*. To the surprise of all of Europe, the English defeated (with help from Mother Nature in the form of heavy storms) the supposedly invincible flotilla. After vanquishing the Spanish, England entered into the Elizabethan Golden Age and along with such prosperity, stability, and security, came a renewed interest in overseas expansion. Moreover, even before the *Armada,* as witnessed by Sir Walter Raleigh's personal investment in the Roanoke enterprise (it was estimated that Raleigh lost some 40,000 pounds sterling in the gambit), there had emerged in England a wealthy, entrepreneurial, moneyed merchant/capitalist class, willing by the early 17th century to once again look across the Atlantic and resume the effort to establish permanent English colonies in the New World. Motivating such individuals and their respective consortiums, was the desire for monetary gain, which they believed the New World could provide them, for they were certain the area contained untold wealth in the form of precious metals and rich, abundant land, all there waiting for them to exploit for themselves (first) and for the greater glory of king and country. Perhaps more important, beginning in the early 17th century, it would be the members of this class in particular, who would become the vanguard of English colonization and subsequent imperialism; it would be these individuals and the private companies emerging out of their ambitions that would one day deliver to England an empire upon which the sun never set. However, the road to empire did not begin very auspiciously. Indeed, as this chapter will discuss, many of the new efforts at colonization were very much like the earlier, failed ones: private ventures, with little planning or direction from the English government; small, fragile enterprises led by people unprepared for the hardships of life in the wilderness. Unlike the Roanoke experiment, they survived but not before enduring several years of "starving times" which almost brought to an end English presence in North America. Nonetheless, by the early years of the 17th century it appeared that the lures of the New World—the presumably vast riches, the abundant land, the promise of religious freedom, the chance to begin anew—were too strong to be suppressed for very long.

Four dynamics in particular shaped the character of these English settlements. First, the colonies were mainly business enterprises, and thus their main purpose was to produce a profit for either their company or proprietary sponsors. Second, and perhaps most important, because the colonies were only at best loosely tied to the English government through the agency of the Crown, they began at their inception, to develop their own political and social institutions, which over time (as will be seen in subsequent chapters), not only led to tensions with the English government but the emergence of a uniquely colonial or "American" identity. Third, as witnessed in Ireland, there were few if any efforts by the English colonists to "blend" their society with that of the indigenous peoples. Indeed, the English tried to isolate themselves from their Native American neighbors and create insulated communities that would remain purely English "transplantations." And fourth, as will be seen in this chapter, almost nothing worked out as they had planned.

Early 18th Century North America

By the early 18th century, numerous English colonies populated the eastern seaboard, while the French had established their own presence to the north and west.

The Early Chesapeake Colonies: Jamestown (Virginia) and Maryland

To avoid the mistakes made by Raleigh as well as personal ruin, a group of London merchant capitalists formed a joint-stock company, the London Company, (renamed the Virginia Company in 1609) through which they launched England's second attempt at establishing a permanent colony in North America. This nascent form of the modern corporation sold stock to small investors to raise the essential funds for their venture. After successfully procuring the necessary capital, the money was turned over to an elected thirteen-man "board of directors"—a council, charged with investing, disbursing, and most important, establishing the company's mission. The first step was to petition the king, James I, formerly

James VI of Scotland of the House of Stuart and Elizabeth's cousin, who inherited the English throne in 1603 from Elizabeth who had died without an heir, for she never had married. Thus began the reign of the Stuart dynasty in English history; a monarchy under whose auspices, England established its presence on the North American continent. It will also be under the Stuarts that England experienced some of its most tumultuous and momentous political upheavals and changes, many of which directly impacted the nation's North American colonies.

The company had little difficulty persuading James of the merits of their enterprise. First, the king charged the company a hefty free for his approval (which was the customary process in the procurement of royal charters for whatever the private undertaking was to be, both at home and abroad). Moreover, James was happy to oblige the company for it served the Crown's purposes while not putting the monarchy at any financial risk. From the beginning, the Crown, not Parliament, was involved in overseas expansion, and thus the Crown was reluctant to extend itself financially to support such endeavors, for the Stuarts knew Parliament would not be willing to come to their monetary rescue if such ventures failed. Colonization also appealed to the monarchy because it provided another potential source of royal revenue via taxation and from duties leveled on trade. National pride also motivated the king, for James did not want England to be left out of the race for empire in the New World, allowing England's rivals to have such an advantage. Finally James as well as his heirs hoped the establishing of New World colonies would help relieve England and the Crown of potential social, religious, and political problems by providing "a dumping ground" to where they could send indigents and dissidents.

For these reasons, James and later Stuart monarchs were willing to grant charters and concessions to individuals and companies to risk their funds on the New World. The first 12 of England's North American colonies, and all its West Indian island colonies, except Jamaica, were founded by private enterprise.

With charter in hand, the London Company in early 1607 had recruited 144 men to send to North America. However, unwisely the Company did not solicit the proper settlers—skilled artisans, craftsmen, and experienced farmers; rather the majority on board the three ships—the *Susan Constant, Discovery,* and *Godspeed*—were members of the aristocracy or gentry, individuals with no skills or experience in wilderness living. They simply were able to pay for their "ticket" to the New World and were ready for an "adventure," a Grand Tour of North America, similar to what their fathers would send them on in Europe as part of a "gentleman's education." An enterprise composed of such English humanity was destined to suffer most egregiously if not fail completely.

Only 104 survived the journey. After a few weeks of scouting, the reconnaissance party decided on a marshy island in the lower Chesapeake on which to establish their colony, Jamestown, in honor of their benefactor, King James I. The site chosen proved to be a poor selection; the area was low and swampy and subject to outbreaks of malaria. It was surrounded by thick woods, which made land cultivation difficult. Moreover, it bordered the territories of powerful local Indians. The result could not have been more calamitous. Compounding trying to survive the harsh environment, complete with infectious diseases such as malaria, the colonists also had to endure the relentless pressure from the London Company to make Jamestown a habitable and profitable colony. Indeed, company demands all but set the colonists up for certain failure. The council established that the colonists' main responsibility was to turn a quick profit for company investors. Thus, the colonists had no real incentive to make Jamestown a long-term success for themselves since they simply worked to advance the interests of their absentee stockholders. They were not allowed to own any private property and since the land was not theirs, they saw no reason to cultivate the soil, not even for their own sustenance. Moreover, since the majority of settlers were "gentlemen," the idea of working to survive rarely entered their minds. Indeed, of the original 104 colonists only ten were "skilled" artisans—jewelers, gold refiners, and a perfumer!; hardly occupations essential for survival in the wilderness.

They were no carpenters, blacksmiths, or masons among the original settlers. Such a situation proved disastrous for both the stockholders and the colonists; the former lost their profits, the latter their lives. In short, the colonists were to spend their time looking for instant wealth, such as gold, which both the settlers and the company initially believed was in Virginia, for if the Spanish could find such riches in their part of the New World then of course the precious metal was everywhere. When the colonists realized there was no gold in Virginia, they then turned their efforts to exporting lumber, pitch, tar, and iron but these were not the type of products the company wanted from the colony; these could be fabricated in England or imported more cheaply from other European countries. The result of such endeavors was that the colonists failed to establish any type of community that could sustain itself by producing necessary provisions, such as their own food sources, which forced them to rely on their Native American neighbors to survive. They thus purchased rations from those Indians willing to engage them and keep from starving to death. Despite Indian help, many died from diet-related sicknesses, for the English were unaccustomed to the native food provided. Others died of malaria. After six months only 53 of the original 104 settlers had survived; by January 1608, when ships appeared with additional men and supplies all but 38 colonists were dead.

At this juncture, with Jamestown on the verge of extinction, a 27-year-old soldier of fortune and famous world traveler, Captain John Smith, took charge of the colony and thanks to his efforts the settlement survived and with its survival, England would eventually have an empire in North America, that by 1763 stretched from the Atlantic seaboard to the Mississippi River, including all of eastern Canada to the Great Lakes. There is a good possibility that such preeminence would not have occurred if John Smith had not emerged in 1608 and taken charge of Jamestown. Had Jamestown failed, who knows how long it would have taken the English to rebound and try again and in the interval, other European powers might have gobbled up the rest of North America and "Americans" today might be speaking French or Spanish instead of English! Indeed, England owed a great debt of gratitude to John Smith, for he saved them an eventual empire.

When Smith took control of the colony he immediately imposed a harsh regime of work and order on the community. He also made contact with the 20,000 Algonquin living in the area, establishing an uneasy but mutually beneficial trade relationship that would last for several years. Powhatan, leader of the Algonquin Confederacy, had mixed feelings towards the English. He already had suffered at the hands of the Spanish, who earlier had attempted to establish an outpost nearby only to bring conflict and disease, which killed hundreds of his people. However, Powhatan hoped that the English would be different and that the Algonquin could establish an effective trading partnership that would benefit both parties; he found a willing Englishmen in John Smith. Powhatan also hoped to use the English as an ally against rival tribes, helping the chief to subjugate them, thus furthering his dominion in the Chesapeake area. Powhatan hoped to accomplish such objectives by simply providing the colonists with food, making them dependent upon his largesse for their survival. When Smith took control of the colony he was aware of Powhatan's stratagem but had little choice but to accept the chief's "generosity." By 1609, however, Smith and his men came to resent being at the mercy of a "-savage" and began organizing raids on nearby Indian villages, stealing food and kidnapping natives either for ransom or to enslave as workers. Powhatan responded to Smith's depredations by cutting off the settler's food supplies and killing off the livestock recently brought over by another 300 colonists, which included some women and children. Smith had returned to England in the summer of 1609 and during his brief tenure as colony leader, fewer than a dozen colonists in a population of about 200, had died. However, the majority of the colonists were glad to see Smith leave, for they resented his forced discipline and martinet behavior. Despite the presence of fresh colonists and a new leader, Jamestown's ordeal was not yet over.

Powhatan's reprisals kept the colonists barricaded within their palisade. Cut off from their food supply, the settlers lived off what they could find behind their fortress: "dogs, cats, rats, toadstools, horsehides," and even the "corpses of dead men," as one survivor

recalled. The winter of 1609–1610 became known as the "starving time" in the settlement, as 440 out of 500 colonists perished from starvation. In May 1610, a ship that had been bound for the colony the previous spring but had run aground in Bermuda, finally arrived and seeing the pitiful condition of the settlers, took the 60 emaciated survivors onto their vessel, abandoned the settlement, and sailed for England. However, as the refugees proceeded down the James, they met another ship coming up the river, bringing fresh folk, ample provisions, and the colony's first governor, Lord De La Warr. The departing colonists agreed to return to Jamestown. New relief expeditions with hundreds of colonists soon began to arrive, and the effort to find a profitable venture in Jamestown resumed.

Success At Last: The "Discovery" of Tobacco

Under the leadership of its first governors—De La Warr and then Sir Thomas Dale—Virginia not only survived but expanded and eventually prospered, but too late to save the Virginia Company from going under. Both De La Warr and Dale imposed strict order on the colony, at times making Smith's regimen seem like a vacation. Indeed, Dale went so far as to march the inhabitants off to work to the beat of a drum. Both men also sent military expeditions against the local Indian tribes in order to protect the new settlements, which began lining the river above and below Jamestown. In the process, Dale kidnapped Powhatan's young daughter Pocahontas. Several years earlier Pocahontas had played a role in mediating differences between her people and the English, and according to legend, intervened with her father to save John Smith, who was captured after one of his raids on a village for food, from death. Interestingly, Powhatan refused to pay Dale the ransom for her return. Pocahontas was now forced to live among the English and adapted to many of their ways. She converted to Christianity and in 1614 married John Rolfe and visited England with him. Suffice it to say when Rolfe arrived in England with a "native" wife who spoke English and had become a Christian, the couple no doubt raised many eyebrows of either disdain or fascination. Those who were captivated by her graciousness believed she was testimony that Native Americans could indeed be "civilized." Pocahontas died shortly before her return to Virginia. Although both governors promoted and secured expansion while continuing to stabilize the colony, Jamestown had yet to turn the profit long desired by the Virginia Company and its shareholders. However, a series of events would combine to turn this barely functioning outpost into the first step in the founding of an empire. The colonists' discovery of tobacco as a marketable cash crop proved to be the most important factor in saving Virginia and thus perhaps English presence in North America.

Europeans had become aware of tobacco soon after Columbus' return from his first voyage to the New World. It was on the island of Cuba where Columbus first saw natives smoking small cigars (*tabacos*), which they inserted in the nostril. Over the next century the smoking of tobacco in pipes or as cigars, and as fashions changed, consumed as snuff, became one of the most popular crazes ever to hit the European continent, especially among the upper classes, and those who provided the "jovial weed" as the Englishmen Sir Francis Drake referred to tobacco, realized substantial profits from growing and curing the plant's

leaves. Until tobacco cultivation in Virginia occurred, Englishmen imported their "weed" from the Spanish West Indian colonies, thus enriching one of England's most bitter adversaries. However, in 1612, the Jamestown planter John Rolfe, (soon to be famous for his marriage to Powhatan's daughter, Pocahontas in 1614, to be discussed later in this chapter), developed a hybrid of tobacco by crossing an imported West Indian strain with that of the local grown Indian variety. As Rolfe and others quickly discovered the Chesapeake area's climate and soil was perfectly suited for tobacco cultivation. As more and more "Virginians" engaged in tobacco planting, territorial expansion occurred commensurately. Tobacco growers needed large areas of land upon which to grow their profitable crops; and because tobacco exhausted the soil very quickly, the demand for land increased rapidly. As a result, English planters began pushing deeper and deeper into the Virginia interior, isolating themselves from Jamestown, while penetrating farther into Native American domain.

In 1617, Virginia tobacco planters shipped their first cargo to England, finding it fetched a relatively high price in the London market, three shillings per pound. By the time of the first shipment, many in English society considered the smoking of tobacco a "sinful indulgence" which only added to its growing popularity. Even the king's (James I) condemnation of tobacco smoking as "loathsome to the eye, hateful to the nose, harmful to the brain, and dangerous to the lungs," could not prevent Englishmen from smoking. James' detesting of smoking was so great that even tried to persuade Parliament to ban the weed's importation but to no avail; smoking had become too popular of a "vice" and pastime in English society to prohibit. Moreover, the Virginia Company successfully lobbied

Parliament to prevent such an act by convincing its members that a ban on tobacco importation would bring about Virginia's financial ruin as well as that of the company.

Thanks to tobacco, Virginia could now sustain itself; the colony had established its financial viability. Tobacco cultivation had taken off and was growing like the weed itself. The tobacco craze became so great in Virginia that colonists were even planting it in the streets and marketplace of Jamestown and in 1618 they planted more tobacco than corn and other food sources. By 1618 Virginia tobacco had captured the English market, with exports to England reaching over 50,000 pounds. By 1624 exports and reached 200,000 pounds and by 1638, over three million pounds of the "jovial weed" had been shipped "home." Tobacco became to Virginia in the 1620s what sugar was to the West Indies (to be discussed later in this chapter) and silver to Mexico and Peru. In London men joked that Virginia was built on smoke. Suffice it to say, tobacco transformed Virginia almost overnight into a different sort of society and economy originally envisioned by the Virginia Company.

Tobacco and the Changing Nature of Virginia Society and Labor

A tobacco planter first had to clear the field of trees, often only girdling them Indian-style and cultivating amid the dead trunks. Then, separate from the main fields, a rich bed had to be prepared for the tobacco seeds, taking care to protect the tender plants once they sprouted from the frost covering them with cloths or leaves. Using a heavy hoe, the planter then cultivated the actual fields, mounding the soil into small hills—again Indian fashion—arranged in rows; when the weather was warm enough—usually late spring, early summer—the slips from the seedbed were transplanted to the hills. Then fields had to be vigilantly maintained, especially from weeds taking over, or worse, protected from tobacco worms, green-horned little monsters with voracious appetites, which had to be picked off the maturing tobacco plants. Secondary shoots called "suckers" grew from the base of the stalks, and these had to be cut away else they steal nutrients from the parent plant. Toward the end of the summer (usually late August), the full-grown stalks were cut and hauled to curing barns to be dried, and after the proper amount of curing, the leaves were picked off and carefully packed into wooden barrels called hogsheads, that when fully loaded, weighed over 500 pounds. The whole process took about 10 months, February-November, with each step requiring tedious labor and exact timing, for to be off schedule by a few weeks or even days, could lead to the complete ruin of a crop, both in quantity and quality. Tobacco cultivation placed a premium on both menial labor and agricultural skill. Successful planters, understanding the role their skill played in producing a profitable crop, grew in self-confidence and optimism, increasingly sure of their ability to make decisions about a wide range of human activities.

The success of tobacco cultivation led to increasing demands for labor. In the first decades of the "tobacco craze" the Virginia Company attracted new workers to the colony by establishing what was called the "headright" system. Since the Virginia Company had more land than money, it offered land as dividends to its stockholders. Headrights were fifty-acre land grants given to each individual who came from England and established a tobacco "farm." Those who already lived in the colony received two headrights if they planted tobacco. This system was especially designed to attract family groups to migrate together, for the more family members who came, the more land the family would receive. In addition, anyone who paid for the passage of immigrants to Virginia would receive an extra headright for each arrival, an incentive to the already established planters to import new laborers. As a result of the headright initiative, some colonists were able to amass over several years, thousands of acres of land. Indeed, two of colonial Virginia's most legendary families, the Carters and Byrds, whose ancestors came to Virginia at this time, together came to own over 400,000 acres and several plantations by the end of the colonial era in the 1770s. In initiating the headright system the company was taking an important step in the direction of private enterprise, away from the corporate, company-directed economy of the early years.

The company also realized the importance of economic diversification and greater colonial self-sufficiency, thus the sending to Virginia of ironworkers and other skilled craftsmen to provide tobacco farmers with what they needed to sustain the tobacco boom. To keep those males in the colony from returning to England after making money from tobacco, the company in 1619, sent over 100 Englishwomen to Virginia (which was still overwhelmingly male) to become the wives of the male colonists. Perhaps the most important "enticement" the company offered to keep settlers in Virginia was to end the strict and arbitrary ruled imposed by De La Warr and Dale. English common law replaced martial law, guaranteeing all male colonists the full rights of Englishmen. The company (much to the English government's subsequent dismay) even

allowed the colonists greater rights to self-government than were enjoyed by those who lived in England at the time. In 1619 the company granted the colonists the right to form a legislative assembly, the House of Burgesses, a representative body to be elected by every free adult male colonist. The colony's government now consisted of a governor (appointed by the company) six counselors chosen from the House's members, and 22 elected delegates from the colony's various communities. On July 30, 1619, the House of Burgesses assembled for the first time in Jamestown, marking the first meeting in the New World of an elected representative government.

The company's concessions attracted 3,500 new settlers to Virginia in three years, three times as many as had come in the last ten years. By happenstance more than planning, by the beginning of the 1620s the Virginia Company appeared to have found the formula for establishing a successful colonial enterprise. Indeed, it became a model that all the other colonies would generally follow: colonists would have to be offered greater opportunities to make money and greater political freedoms and rights than they would have at home. These changes came too late however, to save the Virginia Company from bankruptcy. Although tobacco profits were substantial by the 1620s, years of having to financially sustain the colony while it struggled through hard times, including protracted Indian wars, proved too much to overcome. In 1624 James I dissolved the company and declared Virginia a royal colony, directly under the Crown's control. At this juncture, James also should have disbanded the House of Burgesses, which would have made it clear to the colonists that their government was in England in the form of King in Parliament. By allowing the House to remain in existence

James, as well as his heirs, were inviting future disaster for England. By not dismissing the Burgesses, James was allowing the colonists to believe they had been granted the *right to self government,* which they had received from the company not the Crown. Since the company no longer existed and the colony was now under royal control, James could have easily abrogated the company's concession and simply reestablished a more arbitrary form of government directly under a crown-appointed royal governor, which James did implement but allowed Virginians a voice in that government via the House of Burgesses.

As will be seen later in this chapter as well as in the next several chapters, over time the colonists grew very attached to their respective colonial assemblies, and in the process came to believe that *from the beginning* (Jamestown) they had been granted the right to have such institutions. Such was never the case but simply assumed. Neither the Crown nor Parliament effectively established their political hegemony over the colonies, allowing the colonists to develop under the illusion that they had the right to self government, and thus any attempt to take away that right was met with a determined colonial resistance. As will be seen in the chapter on the American rebellion and war for independence, this became the critical issue between the colonists and the British government. After the French and Indian War, when a financially desperate England needed to more effectively control the colonists, Parliament threatened the colonists with the most serious of reprisals if they did not comply with the new order: the dissolution of their respective colonial assemblies, which by the 1760s the colonists regarded as sacrosanct institutions; bastions of representative government and the protectors of their individual and collective liberties. It was this issue that became the fundamental cause of the American rebellion and subsequent declaration of independence. Perhaps that conflict could have been avoided or at least postponed had James I in 1624 dissolved the House of Burgesses, making it clear to the colonists that the government to which they owed obedience and allegiance was in England not in Virginia, or in any other colony. Sadly for England, James possessed neither the interest nor the personal sagacity to have realized such a portent; at the time all he cared about was his share of tobacco revenue he would now receive instead of that money going to the company. James's shortsightedness in 1624 eventually cost England an empire in North America.

Toward the Destruction of the Native Americans

The English discovery of tobacco dramatically and rapidly changed the relationship between the Chesapeake Algonquians and the English settlers; indeed the dynamic had completely reversed by the early 1620s. As noted earlier the tobacco craze saw the colonists begin to encroach on Indian farmland and as more settlers came, such "trespassing" occurred on both sides of the James River and further up its tributaries, and thus deeper and deeper into Native American territory. Moreover, at the same time, the various Algonquian tribes became increasingly dependent on English trade goods, especially metal tools. Perhaps impacting the tribes the most was the loss of their most important trade item: food, which the English were now growing for themselves and thus they were no longer dependent on the Indians for such sustenance. In short, the

Indians had become more dependent on the English for certain commodities, having lost their once dominant position in the exchange; they had lost their economic upper-hand, thus becoming more vulnerable to English reprisals and depredations.

Such was the situation confronting the tribes at the time of Powhatan's death. Succeeding the chief was his more militant brother, Opechancanough, who was determined to rid the Chesapeake of the English interlopers. On the morning of March 22, 1622, tribesmen called on the white settlements as if to offer goods for sale; then they suddenly attacked, eventually striking at all the plantations along the James River, and over the course of several days of raiding, killed 347 whites of both sexes and ages,(about one-third of the colonists), including John Rolfe. The reason for the uprising was tribal revenge for the English murder of Nemattanew, one of Powhatan's war captains and religious prophet. The devastating attack bankrupted the Virginia Company. The second Powhatan-Anglo war lasted for ten years and marked the turning point in English-Native American relations. Although some white Virginians admitted that they had provoked the uprising by "our own perfidious dealing," the majority of the surviving colonists concluded that the tribes could not be trusted nor converted to the English way of life. Thus began the policy of extermination of the Native Americans in United States history. Indeed, John Smith was euphoric when he heard the news of the attacks, for he had longed believed that the tribes had to be eliminated from the area if the colony was to progress. "It will be good for the Plantation," Smith declared of the massacre, "because we now have just cause to destroy them by all meanes [sic] necessary." Bolstered by instructions from the company to "root out [the Indians] from being any longer a

people," the Virginians conducted ruthless annual military expeditions against the native villages west and north of the settled areas. In most instances the English attacked and killed tribes that had nothing to do with the original 1622 assault on the plantations. Prior to the insurrection, the English were careful only to plant tobacco on the Indians' unused farmland. They now seized territory regardless of Indian ownership. In only 15 years' time the English and Native Americans in Virginia and eventually elsewhere along the Atlantic seaboard, had become implacable enemies. The poet John Donne referred to these wars as "the flood of blood."

With the tobacco economy booming and as settlers continued to pour into the colony, plantations continued to spread across the Chesapeake to the Eastern Shore and as far north as the Potomac. By the early 1640s the English had made it clear to the Native Americans that they had become obstacles to be removed from the path of English settlement. The aged Opechancanough determined to save his people from annihilation, struck again on April 18, 1644, killing 400 English settlers and taking many prisoners. Thus began the Third Anglo-Powhatan War. Uneasy truces were established in the aftermath of the first two conflicts, with the tribes still tenuously holding on to their lands. The third war ended however, in the Indians' total defeat two years later. English firepower and general ruthlessness if not outright savagery and butchery, proved too much for the tribes to resist. The Indians had fought to punish the English for their transgressions not to wipe them all out; the English, by contrast, went to war to annihilate the Native Americans, for in their new frame of reference "the only good Indian" became a "dead one." During the third war, Opechancanough was captured and killed.

The English took complete possession of the land between the James and York rivers. Henceforth no Indian was allowed to enter this area without wearing a special jacket signifying he was merely bringing a message from the chief *werowance*. Any English person found providing refuge for a Native American was executed. The land north of the York River was to be "Indian territory," making the region the first Native American "reservation." However, given the settlers' perpetual need for fresh acreage because tobacco quickly exhausted the soil (usually completely depleted after five years of cultivation), the English moved into that area as well. It would not be the last time that English colonists violated a treaty with the Indians.

Proprietary Maryland

By the time Virginia had achieved commercial success in the 1630s, another colony on the Chesapeake had been established, the proprietary enterprise called Maryland, named in honor of Charles I's Catholic queen, Henrietta Maria. The owner or proprietor of Maryland was an English nobleman, George Calvert, whom James I honored with a peerage, Lord Baltimore. Calvert was also a Catholic, and thus in all but the Stuart court, which was throughout the dynasty's reign, sympathetic toward Catholics, was persona non grata among the majority of the English aristocracy who were devoutly Anglican. In 1628, Baltimore received from Charles I, son of James I, who died in 1624, a huge land grant in Newfoundland to serve as a sanctuary for English Catholics, who although not physically persecuted any longer, nonetheless could not practice their faith openly and were in general a disenfranchised people. Calvert, however, did not find Newfoundland that inviting and thus

Charles I granted him a more hospitable domain, 10 million acres in what became the colony of Maryland. The charter given to the Calvert family was remarkable not only for the extent of territory granted—an area that encompassed parts of what is now Pennsylvania, Delaware, and Virginia, in addition to present day Maryland—but also for the powers given to the Calverts: the family would have "true and absolute" control over the province for as long as they desired to keep their "gift" from the king. Their only obligation to the Crown was to pay his majesty an annual fee. As will be seen in the next chapter, only one other North American proprietor received a more generous grant than Baltimore: William Penn. Suffice it to say, Baltimore found the king's offer much more to his liking and thus Maryland became the first proprietary colony, that is a "plantation" that was owned literally by an individual and his heirs. As noted earlier, Virginia was originally a charter colony one that was held by a group of private shareholders. Unlike royal colonies, in charter and proprietary enterprises, both financing and management were the sole responsibilities of either the proprietor or shareholders. George Calvert, the first Lord Baltimore died in 1632 but his son, Cecilius, the second Lord Baltimore, continued his father's efforts to establish a colony in the Chesapeake region.

Lord Baltimore appointed his brother Leonard Calvert to serve as the colony's first governor. In March 1634, two ships—the *Ark* and the *Dove*—carrying Leonard Calvert and about 300 other colonists, entered the Potomac River, turned up into one of its eastern tributaries, and established a settlement, St. Mary's, on a high, dry bluff. Fortunately for the settlers the surrounding Native American tribes, once part of Powhatan's confederacy, had no desire to engage in warfare with these latest English arrivals. Indeed, the Indians befriended the colonists, providing them with temporary food and shelter. Unlike their Virginia compatriots, the early Marylanders experienced no Indian assaults, no plagues, and no starving time. Although the colony did not suffer any hard times, as noted above, once a proprietor received his charter from the king, the latter had no responsibility for what then took place in the colony unless events or conditions affected the Crown directly. Thus, in order to economically survive—for proprietors could not go to the monarchy for money—the Calverts needed to attract settlers to Maryland as quickly as possible to offset expenses already incurred. Although established as a sanctuary for Catholics, the Calverts had no choice but to encourage or allow Protestants to emigrate to Maryland as well as their fellow English Catholics. However, much to their disappointment few of their Catholic brethren came to their safe haven while plenty of Protestants found Maryland to their liking. Thus the Calverts soon realized that Catholics would always be a minority in the colony so they wisely adopted a policy of religious toleration of all Christian denominations; that is to all those who professed a belief in Jesus Christ. Such became law in Maryland with the passage of the 1649 Act of Toleration. The act's primary purpose was to guarantee toleration by the majority Protestants of the minority Catholics! Although toleration was restricted to Christians only, Maryland nonetheless became one of the most religiously tolerant places in the world at that time. Moreover, this right was explicitly extended to women as well as men.

Although granted extensive powers ranging from dispensing land to making laws, Cecilius Calvert was no autocrat, perhaps because he knew he would have to compete for settlers with Virginia, which already had a representative government. Thus he wisely agreed in 1635 for the creation of a representative assembly—the House of Delegates—patterned after both Parliament and the Virginia House of Burgesses. Calvert relinquished much of his political power and prerogatives, particularly exclusive law-making rights, to the assembly but retained absolute authority to distribute land as he wished. Initially he granted large estates to his relatives and other English aristocrats, both Catholic and Protestant. Calvert kin received 6,000 acres and lesser non-family aristocrats 3,000 acres. Baltimore envisioned transforming Maryland into a replication of England's manor-dotted countryside, with huge estates owned by a gentry class and the land worked by peasant-like tenants. For a few years Baltimore's vision appeared to becoming a reality but by 1640, fewer family-members and English gentry were willing to come to Maryland. Moreover, a severe labor-shortage had developed in the colony, forcing Calvert to modify his original plan. Like Virginia, Maryland adopted the head-right system— a grant of 100 acres to each male settler, another 100 for his wife and each servant brought over, and 50 for each of his children. Despite such "generosity," by 1650, a distinct upper class of primarily large land-holding Catholics had emerged, who remained powerful even as the commoner population grew larger and more diverse. Like Virginia, Maryland became a center of tobacco cultivation; and as in Virginia, planters worked their land, first with the labor of indentured servants imported from England and then, beginning in the late 17th century, with slaves imported from Africa. Although it would be a number of decades before Maryland's population increased substantially (in 1650 it had a population of only 600), the familiar political economy emerged early. As in Virginia, attracting colonists required greater opportunities and freedoms—of self-government and or religion—than they had in England. Lord Baltimore recognized this reality early on and thus granted these concessions. Unlike their Virginia counterparts, Marylanders maintained generally peaceful relations with the local Native American tribes up through the 1670s. However, despite Baltimore's discernment, Maryland politics remained plagued for years by tensions, and at times violence, between the Catholic minority and the Protestant majority.

The on-going rancor and acrimony between the Catholic Calverts and their minority following (about one-fifth of the overall population) and the majority Protestant tobacco planters and other settlers (about four-fifths of the population) finally escalated into open rebellion in 1689. In that year the third Lord Baltimore (Charles Calvert), who apparently was not as conciliatory toward the Protestants as his father had been, nor as inclined to make further political concessions to the House of Delegates, decided it was time for his family to assert their full rights and powers as the "true and absolute proprietors" of Maryland. Such a decision proved disastrous for the Calverts, for it was much too late in the colony's political and religious development to assume such prerogatives. Exacerbating tensions was the decline in tobacco, which planters looked to Baltimore to help remedy by lowering export duties, revenue which still went directly to the proprietor, not the Crown. The colony's best land also remained in Catholic hands and much of it lay fallow as if the Calverts and their Catholic associates still hoped to transform the Maryland landscape into beautiful non-productive English manors. Protestant planters protested Baltimore's high-handed measures and attitude, and the proprietor responded by imposing a property qualification for voting and appointed increasingly dictatorial governors. According to the Anglican Reverend John Yeo, the Church of England was openly disparaged in the colony by the Catholic minority; even Quakers, whom Anglicans and other Protestant sects had long despised, were allowed greater religious freedom and protection. Naturally, Yeo accused the Catholic minority of all manner of moral laxity, looking the other way if not condoning debauched and dissipated behavior. "The province of Maryland is in a deplorable condition, for want of an established [Anglican] ministry. Here are ten or twelve counties, and in them at least twenty thousand souls, and but three Protestant ministers of the Church of England. The priests [Catholic] are provided for; the Quakers take care of those that are speakers; but no care is taken to build churches in the Protestant [Anglican] religion. The Lord's day is profaned; religion is despised and all notorious vices are committed; so that it is become a Sodom of uncleanness and a pest-house of iniquity."

When news of the Glorious Revolution, which deposed the Catholic James II (to be discussed in greater depth in the next chapter), reached Maryland in 1689, a group disgruntled dissidents, led by a former Anglican minister turned militia officer, John Coode, took over the government, proclaimed loyalty to the new Protestant monarchy of William and Mary, and got the new king and queen to revoke Baltimore's proprietorship, transforming Maryland into a royal colony in 1691. In 1702 Anglicanism became the colony's official, established faith to which all were to tithe. Religious toleration was still in effect but only for Protestants; Catholics no longer controlled the colony in any capacity; they once again became persona non grata even in what was to

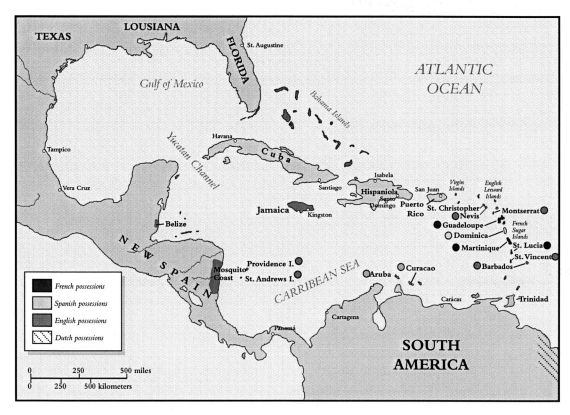

Principal Caribbean possessions of the major 17ᵗʰ century European powers.

have been their own refuge. Coode's rebellion brought an end to Maryland's experiment with religious toleration.

The Caribbean Colonies

Throughout the first half of the 17ᵗʰ century, the islands of the Caribbean and the Atlantic way station of Bermuda, were the main destinations for English immigrants to the New World; not the Chesapeake nor, as will be seen in the next chapter, New England. These Caribbean societies, most of which were colonized before their North American counterparts, developed close ties with England's mainland settlements, particularly influencing their socio-economic orientations and trading patterns.

The West Indies

Prior to the Europeans' arrival in the late 15ᵗʰ century, substantial native populations lived on many of the Caribbean islands. However, beginning with Columbus' arrival in 1492, and accelerating after 1496 when the Spanish established their first permanent colony on Hispaniola, the Amerindian population was all but wiped out by European epidemics. The Spanish were only interested in colonizing the largest Caribbean islands—Cuba, Hispaniola, Jamaica, and Puerto Rico, leaving the area's smaller islands up for grabs, even though the Spanish had claimed the entire West Indies as "theirs." By the early 16ᵗʰ century, English, French, and Dutch adventurers and traders thus began settling on some of these smaller islands but these fledgling colonies were always vulnerable to Spanish. attack and occupation. In 1621, the West Indies' geopolitics changed, the result of war between Spain and the Netherlands, which distracted the Spanish navy, allowing the English and the French in the Caribbean to pursue colonization without fear of Spanish reprisals. By the 1650s the English had established several important settlements on the islands, most notably on Antigua, St. Kitts, Jamaica (seized by an expedition led by Admiral William Penn, father of the future proprietor of Pennsylvania), and Barbados.

The English colonists on these islands initially tried cotton and tobacco cultivation but for a variety reasons could not sustain production sufficiently enough for profitability. They soon discovered however, what would become the most lucrative cash crop of the New World: sugar, for which there was a substantial and growing European market. Unlike other staples, sugar cultivation was labor-intensive and since European diseases had ravaged the native population, English sugar planters found it necessary to import workers from the homeland in the form of indentured servants. But the arduous work and the enervating tropical climate proved too much for these white laborers, most of who died within months after their arrival from England. Thus, rather rapidly, English West Indies sugar planters, like their Spanish counterparts, began importing Africans, as slaves, to work their plantations. These individuals brought in so many slaves, that the majority population on the English Caribbean islands was black not white, with African slaves outnumbering the English settlers by better than four to one. Those Englishmen who came to the islands quickly evolved into a tough, aggressive, and ambitious breed. Some became enormously wealthy from sugar and since their livelihoods depended on their work forces, they quickly put in place one of the harshest, cruelest, and rigid slave systems found anywhere in the New World.

Masters and Slaves

Since the majority of the population on the English sugar islands were African slaves the small white population lived in constant fear of slave rebellion. They thus imposed on their bondsmen a brutal and harsh regimen, laws and practices that ensured them complete control over their black laborers. As a result, the English planter elite treated their slaves with little regard for their physical or mental well being. Since sugar was so profitable, many planters concluded it was cheaper to import more slaves than to take better care of the ones they already owned, and thus many of these Englishmen became notorious for literally working their slaves to death. On some plantations, the average life expectancy for slaves was no more than three years after their arrival from Africa; few African workers survived more than a decade in this callous work environment. Even whites, who worked far less strenuously, often succumbed to the unsparing climate; most died before the age of 40, often from tropical diseases to which they had no immunity.

Establishing a stable society and culture in such severe, even deadly conditions, was extremely difficult. Most of the planter elite were only interested in making quick fortunes in sugar and then returning to England as wealthy men. They thus had no-long term commitment to the islands. Those who returned to

England left their estates to be managed by overseers, many of who were even more brutal in their treatment of the African laborers than the plantation owners, for they had been instructed by their employer to squeeze as much profit out of sugar cultivation as possible. Many overseers received a percentage of the profits as an incentive; a reward which resulted in slave foremen often working slaves to death. A large proportion of the European settlers either died or left at a young age, and thus the white population remained a distinct minority on the islands. Consequently, European society in the West Indies became very transient, dictated and controlled by sugar production and maintained by a rigid slave system, with few if any stable institutions being established such as those transplanted in the North American settlements—church, family, community. England's Caribbean colonies were governed by a small white planter elite ruling over a much larger African and native population.

Despite their brutal treatment and low life expectancy, African slaves managed to create a community and culture of their own. They started families (although many of them were broken up by death or the slave trade); they sustained African religions and social traditions (and resisted Christianity); and within the rigidly controlled world of the sugar plantations, they established patterns of resistance. As the North American settlements developed the ties between the English West Indies and the mainland grew, becoming part of the Atlantic trading network in which many American colonists participated and profited from. As will be seen in this chapter, once the North American southern tobacco and rice planters turned to African slavery to solve their labor needs, the Caribbean islands became their main suppliers of African bondsmen. Moreover, since their West Indian English brethren had

adopted slavery much earlier, southern mainland planters looked to their Caribbean counterparts to provide models of a successful slave system to be replicated in North America.

Toward African Slavery: White Indentured Servitude in the Chesapeake

Chesapeake society in the first half of the 17th century was shaped by four dynamics: the tobacco market, the availability of land, the demand for labor, and weak government. Neither Virginia's royal governor nor his proprietary-appointed counterpart in Maryland had any real political control in their respective colonies. Emerging in both settlements was a wealthy planter oligarchy, which wielded the real power. Motivated by profit, they operated without restraint while the rest of the colonists were forced to try to survive as best they could with little redress of their grievances from the planter elite. While planters profited wildly, for those unable to acquire sufficient land to engage in tobacco cultivation or the requisite skills for such enterprise, a marginal existence of despair and poverty became their daily reality. Artificial distinctions such as social status counted for little in comparison to willpower, physical strength, and ruthlessness. In this environment the political economy of slavery took root.

As discussed in the earlier part of this chapter, the growing and selling of tobacco affected nearly every aspect of life in the Chesapeake. Tobacco required a great deal of human effort to grow, and planters had to devise a labor system to provide and control the essential work force. For the first four decades of intense tobacco cultivation, Chesapeake planters used white indentured servants from England. These workers made possible the tobacco boom of the mid-17th century that finally proved the region had a viable economic future. However, as will be seen later in this chapter, indentured servitude had inherent flaws as a labor system, and overtime serious socio-political tensions in Virginia arose between freedmen (ex-indentured servants) and the planter elite, escalating by the mid-1670s into one of the most devastating rebellions to occur in American colonial history. As a result of that insurrection, Chesapeake planters began shifting to African slaves to solve their labor issues. By 1700, black slaves came to dominate the labor market, changing forever the South's future.

As already seen, the Chesapeake tobacco boom produced an incessant demand for labor, which the colonial English population could not provide, for it had not grown rapidly enough to meet labor demands. The Native Americans, understandably unfriendly and with their numbers decreasing rapidly because of disease and warfare, provided no ready source of labor. Although aware of slavery, including African and Indian bondage, Chesapeake planters associated slavery with "backward" Mediterranean and Catholic societies like Spain and were determined not to succumb to such "inhuman" practices, even though their Caribbean brethren were already well on their way to human bondage. Moreover, there was no need yet to ponder the possibility of slavery because England could supply the planter's with the labor they needed. Sustained population growth and an agricultural revolution (enclosure) that had forced hundreds of thousands of English peasants off the manors, had created a surplus population which the planters could employ on their Chesapeake estates. Thousands of such individuals had migrated to England's burgeoning cities searching for work,

but few of them had the requisite skills to be reabsorbed into the urban workplace; they were an agricultural people equipped to work only the land. Thus thousands of young men and women saw several years of labor in the Chesapeake as an acceptable hardship to bear in order to obtain their own land and a chance to make a better life. The lack of economic opportunity in England was severe enough to cause young workers to leave the world they knew and risk disease, overwork, potential abuse, and perhaps death in a strange new place. It was to this population that Chesapeake planters turned to solve their immediate labor needs.

From 1630–1680 about 75,000 of such individuals, including women, and children went to the Chesapeake to start a new life; about three-fourths of them came as indentured servants, individuals and families who had their transportation paid for by a Virginia or Maryland planter and in return for passage now became the "indenture" of that particular landowner for an agreed upon number of years until the debt for the crossing had been paid. The number of years owed was determined by the servant's age, gender, and skills. Although recognized as a legal agreement between master and servant with the servant guaranteed certain basic rights, the planter could set his servant to work at any task he chose until the cost of indenture had been paid off. There was no negotiation between master and servant over the amount of time to be served; masters solely determined the period of servitude and those workers willing to "contract" on this basis had little choice but to accept the terms or be thrown in jail for violation of contract. Tobacco profits in these years were substantial enough that most planters could repay the cost of investment in a servant in two years or less. However, contracts usually lasted from five to seven years and thus from year three on, indentured servitude proved to be a most profitable labor source.

For many indentured servants life in the Chesapeake was worse than they could ever have imagined in England. Death from disease was endemic, with many dying within months of their arrival and certainly before many fulfilled their contractual obligations. The work was unremitting and tiring, with ruthless and unprincipled planters taking hard advantage of them. Indeed, many servants were worked to the point of death. Servants might be beaten so severely that they died, or they might find their contracts sold from one master to another. In England custom and law provided servants with some basic protections but In Virginia, working conditions were brutal. Such was the existence of Richard Freethorne, a young servant who wrote to his parents in England that "I have nothing to comfort me, nor is there nothing to be gotten here but sickness and death. I have nothing at all—no, not a shirt to my back but two rags, nor clothes but one poor suit, nor but one pair of shoes, but one pair of stockings, but one cap." "With weeping tears," Freethorne begged his parents to send food. "We must work early and late for a mess of water gruel and a mouthful of bread and beef." Climatic extremes—infernally hot and muggy summers and bone-chilling winters— unfamiliar, deadly snakes and insects; loss of contact with friends and loved ones back in England, led to an existence filled with loneliness, isolation, despair, all manner of illnesses, and death. The vastly uneven sex ratio (the majority of servants were young men, teenagers, who outnumbered women 4-1 for the first two generations), aggravated by the paucity of roads and resulting isolation, meant that many indentured servants, even after gaining their freedom, could never find a spouse and gain the comfort and sense of home that a marital partner and children can provide. One result was limited population growth, which of course perpetuated the need to import servants to labor in the tobacco fields.

Before 1660, those indentured servants who survived their obligation, could expect upon gaining their freedom, to purchase land, plant tobacco for themselves, and begin sharing in the prosperity of the tobacco boom. If they lived long enough after their servitude they too could even afford to buy the labor of new indentured servants and obtain additional head rights. With more land and tobacco profits the former servants could even begin to move up the social ladder. As long as land along the waterways (the tidewater regions) remained plentiful and cheap, it was possible for at least some former servants to make the transition from servant to freeman to planter. Even those who were unable to rise to such status came to own small farms of modest homes with dirt floors and unglazed windows but homes nonetheless on their own land—an existence few could have obtained back in England. Clearly the more prosperous planters who were importing indentured servants and acquiring more land were in the process of creating a gentry class, separate from the masses of farmers, and service as a local justice of the peace or on the vestry reinforced their sense of community leadership and provided them with the reputation to solidify their status. The economic difference between the wealthy planters and the middling farmers was less than it would ever be again. This relative equality of social condition among Chesapeake whites and near universal involvement in a tobacco culture would eventually create a white solidarity that would shape Southern society for three centuries.

Comparatively few white indentured servants attained such an existence in the

Chesapeake. Many died before gaining their freedom, and of those who did survive, few had the skill, luck, good health, or ambition necessary to succeed. Since tobacco was such a boom-bust economy, beginning freemen could not sustain themselves through the learning curve that tobacco cultivation required. The margin of error was tiny, and one miscalculation or an unfortunate illness or a fire could doom a beginning farmer to failure. Once failed, few had the heart or desire to try again, and thus to survive, many had no choice but to become a tenant farmer or wage laborer. Many of such individuals and their families came to have an existence of almost unimaginable deprivation.

The Chesapeake of the mid-17th century hardly fits the popular stereotype of the Colonial South, with magnificent brick mansions lining the James and York rivers, their interiors filled with beautiful furniture and staffed with a retinue of black slaves. Not only were blacks few in number in 1650 (only about 1,000 in the entire Chesapeake at that time), but white planters lived a life far below what visitors to 18th century colonial mansions envision. Most so-called planters were in reality large farmers who lived in unpretentious houses or perhaps two ground-floor rooms that were sparsely furnished with furniture made by someone on the farm and the several indentured servants slept in a large attic or in a lean-to attached to the main house. The servants probably took their meals with the planter and his wife, if he were lucky to have one, though, if present, a servant woman would do most of the cooking. On smaller farms, women did very little field work, even if they were indentured servants. On larger plantations, white servant women did work in the fields, for tobacco was hoe cultivation not plow. Most women however, devoted the bulk of their time and energy to gathering, washing, and preparing vegetables and fruits for meals, which was extremely time-consuming. A farmer's wife may have spent as much as two hours a day grinding corn with a pestle and mortar to make meal. Often cider was brewed, and dairying— milking the cows, churning the butter, making cheese—took hours. Men usually slaughtered the hogs and beeves, but women finished the process by rubbing the meat with salt and then smoking the pork in the chimney and pickling the beef in barrels of brine. Laundry and housecleaning were also strenuous tasks, even though 17th century ideas of cleanliness would be considered appalling by today's standards. The making and mending of clothes occupied most evenings. The farmer's wife supervised the servant girl, if there was one, but performed most household chores herself. Certainly the farmer himself supervised the field work of male servants but he also worked in the field beside them. Homes were small, usually one room, 16x20 feet, with practically no furniture except a table—no chairs, few dishes, no bed but a mattress of sorts laid on the floor at night. Creature comforts were far less and certainly more spartan in the mid-17th century Chesapeake than poor farmers would have had back in England. In short, many indentured servants served their time only to find that scarcity of cheap land deprived them of the upward mobility for which they had come to the New World. Freedom meant still more years working for someone else as a tenant farmer or hired hand; finding a spouse was still difficult. Wasn't life after servitude supposed to mean more than poverty, despair, and loneliness? These freemen were understandably restless, frustrated, and alienated from the emerging planter elite and farmers who had gobbled up most tidewater land. Many of the small and middling farmers were also angered at what they considered exorbitant taxation, for which they blamed both the planter oligarchy and the royal governors.

Bacon's Rebellion

It was only a matter of time before the tensions between the planter elite and the freedmen would escalate into a violent confrontation between the two. Too many issues, too much resentment, had evolved over the decades that could not be ameliorated through compromise or conciliation. All that was needed by the 1670s was an individual willing to only lead such an insurrection but also one who could exploit and articulate the freedmen's grievances and unite them around a common cause. That person was Nathaniel Bacon, an upstart newcomer to the Chesapeake. Bacon proved to be an unscrupulous, power-hungry young aristocrat, who inflamed not only the white colonists' general fear of the "red men" into a frenzy of hatred but also manipulated for his own aggrandizement, the widespread animosity and poor white discontent with the political-economic establishment controlled by the planter elite. Without question the most serious repercussion of Bacon's Rebellion was that the event brought about the end of indentured servitude as a plantation work force and moved the Chesapeake colonies rapidly toward the enslavement of Africans as a permanent plantation labor force.

Compounding the growing tension between the Tidewater planters and the freedmen as well as between the established tobacco elite and their "backcountry" counterparts, were the policies of Sir William Berkeley, the imperious royal governor of Virginia, who served in that capacity for over 30 years. Over that time, Berkeley came to dominate the colony's politics. Assuming the governorship in 1642 at

the age of 36, over the course of his tenure, Berkeley pursued an aggressive expansionist policy, opening up Virginia's interior all the way to the Blue Ridge Mountains. Suffice it to say, the governor's ambitions led to constant conflict with the Native Americans, whom the colonists crushed in a series of wars during the 1640s. By the 1650s, the defeated Indians had agreed to treaties ceding most of the territory east of the mountains to the English and establishing a boundary west of which white settlement would be prohibited. As a result of white population growth in the colony in subsequent decades and concomitant shortage of land in the settled areas, by the 1670s English settlers had violated the treaty, establishing three counties in the territory set aside by the treaty for the Indians. Not surprisingly, there were frequent clashes between natives and whites in the area.

In the meantime, Berkeley expanded his own powers. In Virginia's early decades, voting for delegates to the House of Burgesses had been open to all white men, however by the 1670s, Berkeley had ramrod through the assembly bills restricting the franchise to landowners only, setting the amount of property owned high enough to exclude all but a minority of wealthy Tidewater planters. Elections were rare, and the same burgesses, representing the established eastern planters (the Tidewater elite) of the colony and subservient to the governor, remained in office year after year. The more recent settlers, especially those on the frontier (in the western and southwestern regions of the colony) were underrepresented in the assembly or not represented at all. Resentment of the governor's power and the tidewater aristocrats grew steadily in these newly settled areas (often referred to as the "backcountry").

By the 1670s, the greatest issue for the majority of freedmen was the shortage of land in the settled areas of the Chesapeake, forcing increasing numbers of such individuals to wander further to the west and southwest of the colony in search of virgin land for either tobacco cultivation or for general farming and stock-raising. Regardless of the purpose, what was left of the Native Americans in the area, such as the Doegs and Susquehannocks, were not about to let any more Englishmen take their land. Thus as the freedmen entered into native land, the inevitable occurred: red-white reprisals and killings. As the death toll among white settlers on the frontier increased, appeals went out to Governor Berkeley for a swift and effective response. Berkeley responded by persuading the House of Burgesses to establish a line of forts manned by militia recruited from the Tidewater to protect the settlers but not to exterminate the Indians, which was exactly the policy the frontier folk wanted Berkeley and the legislature to implement. Berkeley and many of the Tidewater planters who dominated the legislature believed that friendly Indians benefited the colony in a variety of ways, most important of which was that they provided a sort of "natural" boundary that kept colonists from wandering too far afield, thus preventing Berkeley and his associates on the Governor's Council and in the legislature from controlling the settlers, whom the elite did not want to be out of their purview, especially causing "expensive" trouble with the Indians. It must be remembered that Indian uprisings cost money to put down and the funds for such initiatives came out of the pockets of the gentry not out of the common folks' purses.

Out of this cauldron of fear, hatred, and vengeance toward both Native Americans and the planter oligarchy, emerged Nathaniel Bacon, who, ignored Berkeley's and the legislature's prohibition against making all out war against the Indians, and formed his own ragtag army of about 1,000 men from among the disgruntled and Indian-hating frontier settlers. Led by Bacon, this force proceeded to make war against all Indians indiscriminately. Berkeley condemned Bacon's actions, declaring him a rebel and traitor for having usurped both the governor's and the assembly's rightful authority to determine colonial policies. Much to Berkeley's and his supporters' chagrin, Bacon had become a rather popular leader and agitator among not only dispossessed freedmen but also among frontier planters as well, who despite Berkeley's official remonstrations, continued to lead his motley army against the hapless Indians. Backcountry planters complained that their taxes went into Berkeley's and his clique's pockets rather than being used for frontier defense. To Berkeley's and the gentry's surprise and outrage, once Bacon's force believed they had slaughtered enough Indians, Bacon then declared against the planter elite and the governor, calling upon men of every class to plunder and put back in their proper places those who had prospered at the expensive of the common folk. A small-scale but vicious civil war broke out between Bacon and his followers and Berkeley and those members of the planter elite who supported him. Both sides offered freedom to indentured servants and blacks slaves belonging to their enemies. Bacon's mob killed not only Indians without hesitation but the gentry as well, especially those they considered to be Berkeley's allies. The rebellion's climax occurred on September 19, 1676 when Bacon's forces burned Jamestown to the ground. Fortunately for Berkeley and the planter elite, a little over a month later Bacon died of dysentery and without his leadership the revolt petered out, for it had no focus beyond killing Indians, planters, and aggrandizing Bacon's ego. Moreover, a few months after Bacon's death, 1000 English troops had arrived at Berkeley's behest, ready to put down the rebellion with whatever force necessary and at the king's demand, for Charles II had no intention of allowing rebellion in his colonies, particularly in one as profitable to the crown as Virginia. As a result of the insurrection, 23 rebel leaders were executed and Berkeley was removed from office. According to Berkeley's estimates, at the insurrection's peak, some 14,000 Virginians had backed the rebel leader, but after his death that support quickly dissipated. As far as the area's Native Americans were concerned (at least among those who were still alive in the aftermath of Bacon's rampages), new treaties were reluctantly signed that opened new lands to white settlement.

Bacon's rebellion was significant for several reasons. For one, it illustrated the ongoing struggle between Indians and whites to define their respective spheres of existence and influence in the Chesapeake. It also revealed the bitter competition for place and power among rival elites, especially between those of the Tidewater and their backcountry counterparts. More important, the insurrection revealed the antipathy between landholders and the colony's large population of free, landless men, the majority of whom were former indentured servants. These men formed the bulk of Bacon's followers during the rebellion. Their hatred of both Native Americans and the planter elite drew them to Bacon, who, ironically, was a member of the colony's landed gentry. Although many backcountry landholders initially supported Bacon's cause, especially against the Indians, after he turned his plain folk's rage against the Tidewater elite, many withdrew their support, for they saw in that phase of the rebellion the potential for social unrest from below, which they feared just as much as their brethren to the east. The result was that the landed elites of both eastern

and western Virginia developed a bond of common interests, especially in their mutual desire to limit tobacco cultivation to themselves as well as reclaim and retain their political control of the colony. In the aftermath of Bacon's rebellion it became clear to the planter elite that if they hoped to avoid another insurrection in the future it was time to move away from the use of indentured servants as their principle labor force to an alternative form of labor, one which would never become free and thus not be inclined to rebel against the status quo. It was time to transition to African slave labor. African slaves, unlike white indentured servants, did not need to be released after a fixed term and thus did not threaten to become an unstable, landless class. By the time the English began to import African slaves into their colonies in the latter 17th century, the Spanish and Portuguese had been using enslaved Africans as plantation laborers for well over a century. The English were entering into a global economy that already had come to rely on slave labor.

The Rise of Slavery in the Chesapeake Colonies

As already established in this chapter, Chesapeake Englishmen, for a variety of reasons, avoided the use of African slaves on their plantations for several decades after their respective founding. As long as there was a plentiful supply of white Englishmen available in the mother country, there was no reason to shift to the most foreign servants of all—Africans. Moreover, to review, those Englishmen coming to the New World already felt they were venturing into the unknown and they wanted to hold on to as much of their English ways as possible; blacks from Africa seemed to them the strangest of people; some Englishmen even questioned their humanity. In short, the ethnocentric English, connoting evil and inferiority to *black* people, did not want themselves surrounded by workers who not only had a different skin color, but spoke incomprehensible languages and behaved in "strange" ways. Of course, the fact that the Africans were not Christians only added to their alleged inferiority in English eyes. Finally, transportation costs made the use of African slaves prohibitive. The great distance from West Africa to the Chesapeake along with the insatiable demand for black slaves in the West Indian sugar islands drove prices beyond what Chesapeake tobacco planters could afford to pay to import Africans. Indeed, the initial cost of black slaves was significantly higher than the price of white indentured servants. In short, cheaper, more familiar, available white servants became the laborers of choice for Chesapeake tobacco planters until after Bacon's Rebellion.

That is not to suggest that there were no Africans in the Chesapeake colonies prior to Bacon's Rebellion; quite the contrary. By 1660 there were approximately 1600 blacks in Virginia and Maryland, whose legal status varied widely. Some were clearly slaves for life, while others (the majority) were indentured servants, bonded in the same capacity as their white counterparts, who gained their freedom if they lived long enough. A few even arrived from either Africa or the West Indies as free. Some native-born blacks of mixed parentage were declared free by laws establishing legal status according to the status of the father (in Maryland for a few years) or the mother (in Virginia). Still other blacks earned enough money to purchase their freedom or were granted such status for good conduct or outstanding service. Until the 1670s, free blacks

had all the same rights as white colonial Englishmen; they could own property, testify in court against whites, vote, serve on juries, pay taxes, borrow money and extend credit to others, be fined and win court decisions against whites, even for a while own black and Indian slaves and the indentures of whites. The rights extended to free blacks in the first 50 years of their presence in the Chesapeake contrasts sharply with the racial mores of later centuries. Indeed, most white Chesapeake inhabitants paid relatively little attention to their being black, whether they were slave, indentured, or free, all were considered simply additions to the overall population or to the lower-class work force. Race or color was not yet the salient marker for identity that it would later become.

This uncertainty about status is not surprising. Since the English had no experience with slavery at home, a rigid caste system took time to crystallize. When Hugh Davis was whipped in 1630 "for abusing himself to the dishonor of God and shame of Christians, by defiling his body in lying with a negro," his transgression may have been sodomy rather than miscegenation. The record is unclear. Fifty years later when Katherine Watkins, a white woman accused John Long, a mulatto, of raping her, the neighbors (both men and women) blamed her, not him, for engaging in seductive behavior, which they described in lurid detail. Showing similar ambiguity was the case of Elizabeth Key, a mulatto, a Christian, and the bastard daughter of Thomas Key. In 1655 when Elizabeth claimed her freedom, her new owner fought to keep her enslaved. William Greensted, who had fathered two children by her, sued on her behalf, won, and then married her. One settler had no qualms about keeping her in bondage because of her dark skin, despite the known wishes of her deceased father. Another—Greensted—fell in love with her.

Also in the pre-Bacon Rebellion decades, because white servants were less expensive than African slaves, they were often worked harder than their black comrades; their skin color did not spare them from the most arduous labor. In fact, white servants and black slaves usually worked together at the same tasks, suffered similar discipline, ate the same food, slept in identical quarters, were subject to the same diseases, played and caroused together, and ran away together. Masters considered both a troublesome lot that needed constant monitoring and disciplining. Black and white laborers tended to regard one another as equals; fellow sufferers and friends. Many Africans became quite Europeanized in the mostly white society. These comparatively benign racial relationships not only between white servants and black servants/slaves but between white masters and black servants/slaves, continued as long as the black population remained small; that is as long as there were sufficient numbers of white Englishmen to fulfill Chesapeake labor needs and as long as those laborers presented no social or economic problems.

Helping Chesapeake whites to embrace the idea of enslaving Africans was English chauvinism, which became especially inflated after the Elizabethan era, which saw one of its manifestations become an aversion to non-English cultures and people. Sixteenth-century Englishmen disdained virtually everyone—the Irish, Spanish, the Native Americans, and certainly were prejudiced against those most foreign of all—the Africans. Throughout most of Western Europe, white Europeans had come to associate the color black with evil and terror, and thus in the English mind, the Africans' skin color made their vast differences from the English more pronounced. Indeed, Englishmen claimed Africans were unattractive, with "dispositions

most savage and brutish;" a "people of beastly living," who, "contract no matrimonie, neither have respect to chastity." Northern Europeans considered African women particularly distasteful, sexually promiscuous, and neglectful of their children. One 16th century traveler to Guinea thought that African men and women were almost indistinguishable. They "goe so alike, that one cannot know a man from a woman but by their breastes, which in the most part be very foule and long, hanging down like the udder of a goate." Yet, such an automatic predisposition to denigrate Africans was more of an abstract, superstitious dislike of the unknown and the different—a generalized and passive prejudice—than a systematic racism that informed every black-white interpersonal relationship. Although these views were not used to justify slavery, they formed the basis for the racism that would develop along with the slave system. In short, this predilection surely made easy the acceptance of perpetual slavery for Africans. Nonetheless The Chesapeake planters who bought blacks from the Caribbean or directly from Africa justified their actions as purchasing people already in bondage; they were not guilty of enslaving men and women but were merely changing the location of their labor. For almost a half-century, the Chesapeake's handful of blacks were not perceived by the white majority as threats nor were they considered unassimilable and different as to activate the passive prejudice into pervasive racism. That would occur in the aftermath of Bacon's Rebellion.

Even before Bacon's insurrection, the Chesapeake colonies enacted laws reflecting a desire to categorize black slaves differently from anyone else in the society, and the initial changes in one fashion or another all involved slave women. In 1643 a Virginia law declared that slave women (along with slave men and white male indentures) to be tithable, that is taxable property, while white women servants were considered dependents and were not so taxed. Another issue addressed before the 1670s was the increase in miscegenation, especially when one of the partners was a black slave. In 1662 Virginia legislated that henceforth all children born of a "mixed" relationship would have the legal status of their mother; thus if the mother was a black slave women and her partner was either a free black or white, the children would nonetheless be slaves for life or until manumitted by their master. Maryland passed a similar statute in 1664, declaring that the children of slave women were to serve for life, and those of white servant women who married black slave men would themselves serve as slaves for their husbands' lifetime, and any offspring would likewise be slaves. Racial intermarriage was not yet made illegal. In practical effect, these laws established that the status of children born of a slave mother—regardless of their father's status—was that of bondage. Thus began the association of slavery with race, with the implication that slavery was the *natural* corollary of being black. Slavery, in other words, was becoming fundamentally a matter of race.

Further pushing Chesapeake planters toward African slavery was the decrease in the supply of readily available potential white indentures of the desired age and gender: young men in their teens or early twenties. By the 1660s the two-hundred year population growth spurt England had experienced came to an end. Exacerbating this general drop in population was the Great Plague that struck England in the mid-1660s. The combined result was a labor shortage, which in turn led to an increase in wages for those who had survived and were healthy enough to work. Also job opportunities opened up in London, especially

in construction, in the aftermath of the Great Fire of 1666 that leveled a huge area of the city. As a result of these factors there were simply fewer young English people desperate for work and thus willing to come to the Chesapeake. Moreover, colonial expansion in the 1670s and 1680s, which saw the establishment of the colonies of the Carolinas and Pennsylvania, presented the Chesapeake with strong competitors for the decreasing numbers of willing white migrants. Servants thus became harder to procure and when they were, masters, unlike in previous decades, had to grant previously unheard of concessions to their servants in order to entice them to the area, such as shortening their time of service, effectively raising the price of indentured servants. By the 1670s the labor shortage in the Chesapeake became so acute that land-hungry tobacco planters lowered their qualifications and accepted as servants virtually anyone they could find or who was willing to come to the region; individuals they would have rejected wholesale a decade or so earlier—younger males, more women, Irishmen, the almost totally unskilled laboring poor, and finally, even convicts. In their desperation, they even reconsidered enslaving Native Americans. As these individuals proved to be not at all suitable for tobacco plantation work, increasingly, in their despair for appropriate laborers, planters turned to the enslavement of Africans as their only labor alternative if they hoped to keep their plantations as viable and profitable enterprises.

Helping planters to move in this direction was the chartering in 1674 of the Royal African Company, a joint-stock company authorized by the Crown to engage in the slave trade. The company was given a monopoly on all slaves brought into the empire, whether to the West Indies or to North America. Interestingly, although granted a monopoly on the slave trade, the actual price for slaves imported directly from Africa to the North American mainland dropped sufficiently enough for mainland planters to be able to buy directly from Africa as opposed to having to purchase slaves from the West Indies, even though many mainland planters continued to purchase slaves via the Caribbean. In 1698, the Royal African Company's 26-year monopoly on the exclusive right to import slaves directly from Africa to the North American mainland was ended by a parliamentary act. By that time however, numerous individual enterprising merchants in England, the Caribbean, and even in North America, had built their own fleets of smaller vessels and picked up where the company had left off, either going to Africa or to the West Indies to bring slaves back to the mainland. Most of these smaller slave traffickers went from plantation to plantation in the Chesapeake with their "merchandise" and over time came to dominate the trade and helped to push slave imports to the region to flood-tide proportions. Planters still preferred white indentured servants but since few were available, planters turned increasingly to the inexpensive African slaves.

In the decades following Bacon's Rebellion, as the cost for white indentured servants increased because demand exceeded supply, planters increasingly turned to African slaves to solve their labor needs. Not only did Africans become less expensive to purchase but profitable as well, especially if the slave lived a comparatively long, productive life, which planters increasingly realized was essential to help promote to guarantee a better return on their investment. Thus early on slave life expectancy was much higher in the Chesapeake than in the Caribbean, for mainland planters tended to take better physical care of their slaves than their more ruthless compatriots in the West Indies. Buying slaves came to be seen

not just as a necessary resolve to a labor shortage but economically advantageous as well. As planters made the offspring of their bondsmen slaves as well, they automatically increased their ready supply and thus were less dependent on continued importation. Moreover, slaves never became free to compete for land or grow tobacco independently and further depress the price. Slaves came involuntarily and did not have the opportunity to choose the colony to which they would come: they represented a steady source of labor. An added benefit was that many Africans had prior tobacco cultivating experience, for the weed had been introduced into Africa by the Portuguese who had brought it from Brazil in the 1550s. Out of fear of another rebellion as well as the result of economic and demographic factors beyond their control, Chesapeake planters inadvertently seemed to have found in African slavery a solution to many of their socio-economic problems. Beginning in the aftermath of Bacon's Rebellion (the late 1670s), slave imports shot upwards, increasing with the passage of years. More were imported between 1695 and 1700 than during the preceding 20 years, and more were imported between 1700 and 1705 than during the preceding 81 years. Within a decade, 1690–1700, the Chesapeake became a slave economy with enormous repercussions for everyone involved. As will be seen shortly, by 1700 other regions in the South were also developing a similar labor system, though based on a different staple crop.

The Procurement of Africans

Contrary to popular myth, not until the late 18th century did European slave traders penetrate the West African interior and procure slaves directly. The image of Europeans, hauling chained retinues of captured Africans to the coast to be transported on ships bound for the New World, was not reality. From the beginning of this particular African-European exchange of "goods," to the late 18th century, Africans controlled the slave trade; the Europeans were not allowed into the African interior, so slaves were brought by the African traders to designated trading posts along the West African coast for sale. Indeed, only the most audacious of Europeans would venture into the African interior searching for slaves, for few would escape such a foolish endeavor alive; the Africans involved in the trade were determined to protect their "interests" in this most profitable enterprise. From present day Guinea to Angola, the African kingdoms involved in the slave trade established trading posts along this 2300 mile coastline, and at these flourishing slave marts, "open for business" two or three times a year (and later on a more regular, year-round basis), native chieftains brought large numbers of blacks, most of whom were prisoners of war (some were criminals of sorts, or individuals whom the tribe had ostracized for various transgressions), out of the forests and to the ports. Sometimes large armies launched massive attacks, burning whole towns or villages and taking hundreds of prisoners. More common were smaller raids in which small bands of armed men attacked at nightfall, seized everyone they could before the rest of the village awoke, and then escaped with their captives. Kidnapping, or *panyaring*, in the patois of the slave trade, was also common. One seaman, ashore while his slave ship awaited its cargo, amused himself by peeking at a young African woman bathing. Suddenly two African raiders jumped from the bushes and dragged her off. He later saw them carry her on board and sell her to his ship's captain, no questions asked. Those Africans not involved in the slave trade were not reticent to condemn their fellow African participants. "I must own to the shame of my own countrymen," wrote Ottobah Cugoano, who was sold into slavery in the mid-18th century, "that I was first kidnapped and betrayed by those of my own complexion."

As the slave trade peaked in the middle of the 18th century, the European forts or trading entrepots gave way to small coastal clusters of huts where independent European traders set up operations with the cooperation of local headmen or chiefs. The breakdown of formal exchange opened the door for smaller operators, such as the New England slavers, who

An 18th century print of a slave coffle. As the demand for slaves increased, raiding parties penetrated deep and deeper into the West African interior. Tied together with forked logs or bark rope, men, women, and children were marched hundreds of miles toward the coast where their African captors traded them to European slavers.

entered the trade in the early 18th century. Often bartering rum, guns, or salt fish for human beings, these Yankees (many of whom came from righteous Puritan ancestry), earned a reputation for shrewd dealing, which they came by honestly. "Water your rum as much as possible," one New England slave merchant instructed his captain," and sell as much by the short measure as you can." Initially Yankees from Massachusetts dominated the North American component of the trade, but after 1750, the majority of New Englanders involved in the purchasing of human beings operated out of Rhode Island. Regardless from which colony they came, many a Yankee fortune was built from profits in the slave trade.

In the journey from the interior to the coast, approximately 10 percent of those captured died. Until they arrived at the coast, many had never seen a white man or the ocean, and both terrified them. On the coast European traders and African raiders assembled their captives. Those about to be purchased waited in dark dungeons or in open pens called barracoons. Families were split up as well as ethnic groups in order to minimize the potential for collective revolt. Most traders gathered their human cargo from a variety of regions, each with a different language, to make sure the captives could not communicate with each other and foment rebellion. Traders also had to be careful not to bring together antagonistic groups who might fight each other. Captains carefully inspected and then selected only those men and women they deemed physically capable for not just labor in the New World but of surviving the trip across the Atlantic as well. Suffice it to say, the selection process was often lewd, invasive, and humiliating, as all about to be enslaved, were naked and exposed to the beating sun, the whip, and rough and groping hands. Those chosen were then

branded on the back or buttocks with the mark of the buyer. Olaudah Equiano remembered that "those white men with horrible looks, red faces, and long hair, looked and acted in so savage a manner; I had never seen among any people such instances of brutal cruelty." Equiano's narrative, written during the 1780s, after he had secured his freedom, is one of the few that provide an African account of enslavement. Equiano and his fellow captives were convinced that they had "got into a world of bad spirits" and were about to be eaten by cannibals. A French trader wrote than many prisoners were "positively prepossessed with the opinion that we transport them into our country in order to kill and eat them."

The Middle Passage

Although being captured or kidnapped for eventual enslavement was undoubtedly brutal and traumatic, for slaves the worst was yet to come: the "Middle Passage" as English slavers and sailors in the 18th century called the middle part of a triangle from England to Africa, Africa to America, and America back to England. After captivity in forts and barracoons, those slaves selected were rowed, chained, in small groups, to the waiting ships. They were then packed into "shelves" below deck only six feet long by two and a half feet high. In most slave ships these shelves were tiered one top of the other several deep, sometimes as many as six shelves. "Rammed like herring in a barrel," wrote one observer, slaves "were chained to each other hand and foot, and stowed so close, that they were not allowed above a foot and a half for each in breadth." People were forced to sleep "spoon fashion" and the tossing of the ship knocked them about so violently that skin over their elbows sometimes was worn to the bone from scraping

The Trans - Atlantic Trade Network

By the beginning of the 18th century the various "triangular trade" systems developed during the previous century between Europe, Africa, the West Indies, and North America, had become quite complex and multifaceted in the types of goods being exchanged between the regions. Nonetheless, the most profitable commodities remained, sugar, rum, and slaves.

on the planks. With such little space between the platforms (at most on some ships, four and a half feet), the Africans could not stand up, nor because they were packed so tightly could they move from side to side. Enterprising captains filled every space available with their human cargo, even the smallest spaces by filling them with children. It was on board these ships that Africans were transformed into slaves. Men and women were kept separate,

their portions of the decks divided by partitions. Male slaves were shackled and confined below for most of the trip, other than time allowed for "exercise" on deck a few times a week (to be discussed shortly). The women were left unshackled, but their relative freedom left them prey to the sailor's lust.

Slavers debated the efficacy of packing strategies, with some arguing that additional room lessened mortality and thus increased profits. Others asserted that because demand was so great for slave labor in the New World, especially by the mid-18th century, and because the cost of transporting slaves across the Atlantic so high (accounting for three-quarters of the price of a slave), that "tight-packing" should prevail, even if scores of slaves were lost because of such confinement. One ship designed to carry 450 slaves regularly crossed the Atlantic with more than 600, and even if one-fourth to one-third were lost because of tight-packing, a profit was nonetheless made at the other end. The English were particularly efficient, carrying twice as many slaves per crew member and half again as many slaves per ship as the other nations, thereby increasing the profits. Their hold filled with human cargo, the ships headed toward Cape Verde to catch the trade winds blowing toward the Americas. A favorable voyage from Senegambia to Barbados might be accomplished in as little as three weeks, but a ship from Guinea or Angola, not able to pick up the trade winds and forced to make way in calm waters or be driven back by storms, might take as much as three months.

Monotonous, daily routine defined the slaves' existence on board. In the morning the crew opened the hatch and brought the captives on deck, attaching their leg irons to a great chain running the length of the bulwarks. After a breakfast of beans or gruel, or whatever starch-type food on board they could prepare easily for mass consumption, it was time for "exercise" or the ritual known as "dancing the slave." While an African thumped an upturned kettle or plucked a banjo, the crew ordered men and women to jump up and down in a bizarre session of calisthenics, for the slavers did not want the slaves who survived to lose "muscle tone," for

they would fetch a lesser price at auction if they appeared to be physically unfit for work. A day spent on deck was concluded by a second bland meal and then the slaves were stowed away for several days before they came on deck again for the same routine. Although "on deck time" was necessary to prevent muscles from atrophying and to clean out and sanitize the hold and bring out the dead and toss them overboard, captains were nonetheless reluctant to allow too much of such "freedom," for many slaves would jump over board the moment they were brought up. To prevent such suicides, captains stretched netting around their ships to catch the slave after he jumped into the water. According to one seaman, nightly he could hear "a howling melancholy noise, expressive of extreme anguish." Down in the hold the groans of the dying, the shrieks of women and children, and the suffocating heat and stench combined to create in the words of Equiano, "a scene of horror almost inconceivable."

Inadequate sanitation conditions were without question the most appalling of horrors to be endured on board the slave ship. There were "necessary tubs" set below deck, but Africans "endeavoring to get to them, tumble over their companions," one 18th century ship's surgeon wrote, "and as the necessities of nature are not to be resisted [urinating, defecating, even vomiting from seasickness], they ease themselves as they lie." Some captains, concerned for their cargoes well-being relative to profit, ordered crews to scrape and swab the holds daily, but so sickening was the task that on many ships it was rarely performed and thus the slaves were forced to lie in their own excrements. When first taken blow deck, the boy Equiano remembered, "I received such a salutation in my nostrils as I had never experienced in my life," and "became so sick and low that I was not able to eat." Atlantic sailors said you could "smell a slaver five miles downwind." Suffice it to say, many slaves sickened and died in these conditions. Among the most common afflictions contracted was "the flux," dysentery, which often reached epidemic proportions on board many slave ships. As one ship's doctor reported, the slaves' deck "was so covered with the blood and mucous which had proceeded from them in consequence of the flux, that it resembled a slaughterhouse." Frequent shipboard bouts of smallpox, measles, and yellow fever also decimated slave cargoes. Historians have estimated that during the Middle Passage of the 18th century at least 1 in every 6 Africans perished; the result of suicide or death from the various diseases noted above.

It is never to be concluded that these unwilling voyagers resigned themselves to their captivity or were too bewildered or traumatized by the ordeal; quite the contrary. The captives offered plenty of resistance. As long as ships were still within sight of the African coast, hope remained alive and the danger of revolt was great. One historian has found references to 55 slave revolts on English and American ships between 1699 and 1845. With resistance from the enslaved the norm rather than the exception, ship captains used all manner of terror to maintain order. Flogging—a punishment also used on sailors for infractions—was common. Some captains did not hesitate to torture or maim unruly slaves, using such devices as the thumbscrew, "a dreadful engine, which if the screw be turned by an unrelenting hand, can give intolerable anguish." Whipping and torture was not only used on the disobedient but to strike fear in the hearts of their companions. That was surely the intent of the captain and crew

of the *Brownlow* after some of the Africans on board rebelled. The captain ordered his crew to use axes to dismember the rebels, "till their bodies remained only like a trunk of a tree when all the branches are lopped away." The slaves' severed heads and limbs were then thrown at the other slaves, who were chained together on the ship's deck and watched as their brethren were murdered in such a gruesome manner.

Such fear of slave rebellion hardened captains and crews of slave ships. Few sailors signed onto a slave ship if they had better options. Thus, only the most desperate or destitute, or most unsavory seamen often signed aboard a slave ship. Indeed, one captain of a slaver described his crew as the "very dregs of the community." Although coming from backgrounds of ill-repute, the captain of such a motley crew could count on such individuals to mete out any harsh punishment he deemed necessary to keep the enslaved in line. The life of a 17th or 18th century sailor was hard enough; service on a slave ship—a floating prison—was even harder. Yet aboard, even the lowest crew member was superior to the Africans in the hold. Consequently, even though many were dark-skinned men from Asia, the Caribbean, or India, at sea, they were all considered "white people," and thus not only superior to their cargo but at liberty to treat the slaves any way they wanted; as kindly or as cruelly; however they might "fancy" at the moment. After repeated voyages both captain and crew became practiced in the ways of ruthlessness. Silas Todd, apprenticed to a slave ship captain at the age of 14, believed he was headed down such a barbarous path, and would have someday become a captain of a slaver had he not been "saved" during a Great Awakening revival in 1734. Todd was certain he would have become, after several years and voyages with the captain, "as eminent a savage" as the man under whom he had served.

Arrival in the New World

As the ship approached its destination, the crew made their cargo presentable, preparing the slaves for auction or for their single purchasers. All but the most rebellious of Africans were freed from their chains and allowed to wash themselves and move about the deck; all such activities of course, under the watchful eyes of armed crewmen. One account describes the ship's surgeon plugging captives' rectums with clumps of hemp fiber to prevent potential buyers from seeing the bloody discharge, a symptom of the flux. To impress buyers, slavers sometimes paraded Africans off the ship to the tune of an accordion or beat of a drum, but not until after first making them as "presentable" as possible, whether that entailed simply rubbing them with lotions to make their skin shinier and thus supposedly healthier, or force feeding them to make them appear less emaciated. Slavers also clothed the Africans (both men and women) and for many it was the first clothing they had worn since their capture, having spent most if not all of the Middle passage naked. They (both men and women) were simply given loin cloth to cover their "private parts;" for some women that meant only their lower torsos and thus their breasts remained bare. But the toll taken by the Middle Passage was difficult to disguise, no matter what ruse or cleaning up was used. One observer described a disembarking group as "walking skeletons covered over with a piece of tanned leather.

Some cargoes were destined for a single wealthy planter, such as those on Caribbean sugar islands who often bought several hundred at one time. The majority of slaves, however, were handed over to merchant middle men, who either bought the entire cargo from the ship's captain at "wholesale, thus becoming the "retailer" of such "merchandise," marking up the price either at auction or to those whom he knew were in the market for slave laborers, or bought the slaves on "consignment;" that is, splitting with captain on a prearranged percentage, the profit from the sale of the slaves at auction. In some cases the slave ship's captain sold his cargo directly to purchasers, eliminating all middlemen, thus garnering all the proceeds from the slaves' sale. To ensure his crew's continued loyalty and diligence, a smart captain would give his shipmates a small percentage of his profits as a bonus. Purchasers, whether at auction or as individuals who had bought the entire cargo, painstakingly examined the Africans, once again subjecting them to the indignity of probing eyes and poking fingers. Those slaves not sold immediately, and until they were bought, were kept in holding pens, which were almost as awful as the ship's hold they just left. If they were found to be too sickly or "deficient" for whatever reasons and thus unlikely to ever be purchased, they were frequently killed. South Carolinian planters/slave owners, engaged in an interesting method of slave procurement called the "scramble," an activity similar to the "calf scramble" seen at modern rodeos. In the slave scramble, standard prices were set in advance for men, women, boys, and girls. Once the prices were established, the Africans were then "driven," like a herd of cattle into a corral, and at a signal, the buyers would rush into the corral, grabbing or roping around the neck, their pick of the lot. Sometimes, to make this

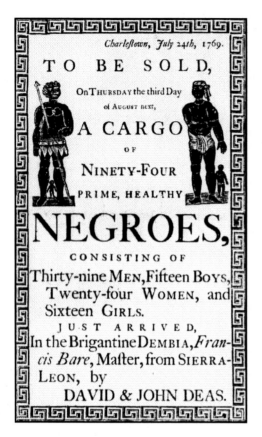

The announcement of the arrival of a consignment of slaves in Charleston, South Carolina, in 1769, where the most method of slave sale was by auction. Man and women alike were subjected to intimate inspection before the bidding began. Buyers were quite interested in the slaves' tribal origins but gave little concern to keeping family members together.

particular manner of slave acquisition more fun or entertaining, the slaves were allowed to run away from their prospective captors. No doubt such a game was designed to further dehumanize the Africans, making them appear to be no different than the beasts of burden, which,

ironically,(as will be seen in later this chapter), many Carolina slaves tended as their main task for the farmer or planter who had "grabbed" or "lassoed" them in the scramble.

Establishing A Slave Society in North America: The Slave Codes

As noted earlier, before Bacon's Rebellion and up to the 1700, the number of blacks in the Chesapeake and Carolina (whose founding, along with that of Georgia will be discussed later in this chapter) was quite small and scattered among a working class of white indentured servants, who, like their white counterparts, often worked side by side with their owners. Although there was a general English predisposition to view blacks—indeed anyone not English—as inferior, a surprising degree of harmony existed between blacks and whites. As long there were relatively few blacks in the region, and those that were there appeared to be acculturated, the potential for racism was mitigated. Although statues containing delineation of blacks as "different" and "separate" were passed prior to the 1670s, they were few in number compared to what was legislated in the Southern colonies by 1700. Overall, lower-class white workers and black slaves interacted with apparently little racial consciousness and their respective owners treated all workers—indentured or chattel— essentially the same. This 17th century harmony however, was short-lived as the denigration of blacks, racism, and white supremacy accelerated in the decades after Bacon's Rebellion. Prompting this dramatic turn of events was the rapid increase in slave imports, which began in the 1690s and reached a torrent by 1700 both in the Chesapeake and the Carolinas. Not only were there more slaves, but they were directly coming from Africa rather than the West Indies from where the majority of previous slaves had spent some time before coming to the mainland and had been somewhat acculturated. The new imports, directly from Africa, seemed far stranger to the whites and were beginning to dominate the work force. These exotic African slaves were called "outlandish" to distinguish them from the acculturated, American-born slaves whom whites called "country-born."

As a result of increased slave imports into both the Chesapeake and the Carolinas, by 1710, black slaves outnumbered whites in many Tidewater counties in Virginia and Maryland and in South Carolina as a whole. Blacks now appeared threatening, and the English predisposition to see slaves as vastly inferior, perhaps even subhuman, went into full force. The result was a spate of laws, the Slave Codes, passed between 1690 and 1715 in both slave regions that significantly altered the slaves' legal status. By law, slaves were no longer seen as individual co-workers but as indistinguishable members of a degraded and despised work force. The codes stripped the slaves of all humanity, relegating them to the status of property. This hardening racial atmosphere made it easier for whites to treat slaves with a harshness and an impersonalism almost unthinkable in the mid-17th century. Slavery came to be seen as the natural, almost biologically determined status of blacks. Virtually no whites understood that their ideology of race was more a social construct than a biological reality.

All forms of slavery have certain common elements: perpetuity, kinlessness, violence, and the master's access to the slave's sexuality. First, slavery is a lifelong condition. Second, a slave has no legally recognized family rela-

tionships, and because kinship is the basis of most societal and political relationships, a slave is socially "dead" outside the bounds of the larger society. Third, slavery rests on violence or its threat to keep the slave terrified and oppressed at all times and thus under his master's complete control. Finally, and related to violence, was the master's sexual access to the slave, sustained by law because the slave was his "property" and thus slaveowners had the right at any time to have sexual relations with their slave women (or men) and the slave had no protection from such abuse. In effect, unharnessed personal power characterized the Southern colonies' slave codes, which varied in specifics from one colony to another, but displayed underlying similarities. For example, in the Chesapeake colonies as well as in South Carolina and ultimately Georgia, slaves were forbidden to wander off their plantation without a "ticket" from their owner or overseer. They were never allowed to congregate in large numbers, carry clubs or arms, or strike a white person; this particular offense was punishable by instantaneous whipping, maiming or dismemberment, even death. Masters had license to "correct" (discipline) their slaves as they deemed necessary and if the slave died during punishment, the master was immune from legal prosecution. All white persons were bound to help in the apprehension of runaways or any "Negro unable to give a satisfactory account of himself." If a white person failed to cooperate with this particular code or were found to be harboring any such "fugitives," he or she could be fined and incarcerated. In areas of heavy slave concentration, such as in South Carolina, white men were required to serve in the slave "patrols," which were supposed to protect the community from possible slave insurrection as well as track down and punish runaways. Slaves committing felonies were tried in specially constituted courts, typically consisting of a justice of the peace and two slaveowners. Slaves convicted of a felony saw their punishment range from a "specific number of stripes [lashings from a whip] well laid on," all the way, occasionally, to burning at the stake. In short, a slaveowner might lash his slaves unmercifully, in full confidence that he was carrying out an obligation to society—and he had the written law to prove it.

Southern colonial/ American slavery added several other dimensions. First, slavery in all the Americas was hereditary, passed on from a mother to her children. Second, compared to other slave systems, including that of Latin America, manumissions—the freeing of slaves–was quite rare in the American South. Finally, Southern slavery was completely racial; a condition reserved for Africans, some Indians, and their children, even if the father was white. The line between slavery and freedom was one of color, and it was this line that the slave codes defined. In short, the creation of the slave codes reflected the symbiotic relationship between the law and slavery. The codes defined what it meant to be a slave while protecting the master's right to his slave property. The slave codes developed piecemeal in the Chesapeake, over the course of the 17th century, with the earliest "distinction" by statue passed in Virginia in 1640, which decreed that "masters are required to arm everyone in their household except Africans." Chesapeake lawmakers defined slavery as a racial institution, designed exclusively for Africans and protected this construct with a series of laws, which, in the process, also elevated all whites, regardless of their status in the general white community. Although the codes were intended to discipline and keep the black slaves oppressed at all times, from another perspective, they were also aimed paradoxically at regulating white behavior as well. In effect, the codes told whites, not blacks, what they must do in order to keep blacks segregated, suppressed, denigrated, and thus inferior to all whites, regardless of status, at all times. According to the codes it was the white man who was *required* by law to punish runaways, prevent slaves from assembling, enforce curfews, sit on special courts, and ride the patrols. Southern colonial legislators, most of whom were slaveowners, attempted to enforce slave discipline by the only means available, by forcing owners, individually and collectively, to keep their slaves under control. The slaveholding gentry were coerced as individuals by the popularly elected assemblies to maintain a private tyranny which was conceived to be in the general white community's best interest.

Thus by the beginning of the 18th century when both the Chesapeake and other Southern colonies had firmly entrenched slave systems, protected and guaranteed by law, the sustaining of such an order depended on the mass consent of the respective white communities, especially on the widespread agreement among masters that they had to maintain effective control of their slaves at all times. Master vigilance became the order of the day and to be derelict in any capacity of such a mandate could lead to racial unrest. In the slaveowners' minds, the codes bolstered the necessity and nakedness of their personal power. The codes thus became public dialogues among masters and among white men in general, as a way to confirm white superiority and black inferiority. In short, the codes were designed to promote and sustain a sense of white solidarity, inculcating in all whites, but especially in the mind of the non-slaveowning lower classes, that despite their status, they were above blacks and that to associate with the slaves in any capacity would be to degrade themselves. Thus one of the main purposes of the slave codes was to help transform all whites, but especially lower-class whites into racists, who, despite at one time, having much in common with their black counterparts, now came to view such individuals as a despised and servile people. Now, in the minds of all whites, to be black was to be a slave and if one was a slave they were inferior and consequently were to be shunned, segregated, and kept at all times subservient to whites. By the early 18th century the Southern colonies had put in place a slave society, which over the course of the next several decades would come to define and inform much of "the Southern way of life."

Carolina: A Barbadian Colony on the Mainland

With the success of the Chesapeake colonies, other Englishmen began looking at the territory southward from Virginia to the northern boundary of Spanish Florida. However, the expansionist desire was momentarily eclipsed by the English Civil War of the 1640s (to be discussed in the next chapter) and thus not until the 1660s and the Restoration (the return of the monarchy in the personage of Charles II), was England again prepared to engage in colonizing activities, both to the north and south of Virginia. Leading the initiative to establish a colony south of Virginia were several influential royal supporters, led by Sir John Colleton, an already wealthy Barbadian sugar planter and his court friend, Sir Anthony Ashley Cooper, later Lord Shaftesbury. Charles too was interested in enlarging the empire and thus to reward Cooper's and Colleton's as well as six other's for their

support of the Crown, the king granted to these men a huge expanse of land named Carolina, in Charles's honor. The king was most generous in his bequeathment, allowing the proprietors complete political control of the colony. The proprietors were quick to take advantage of the king's munificence, issuing a Concessions and Agreements that promised virtually complete self-government to the colony by means of an elected assembly, religious freedom (matched at the time only by Rhode Island), and a most generous land policy, granting to every settler 150 acres and the same amount for each dependent they brought to Carolina. Despite the proprietor's largesse, they simply could not attract sufficient numbers of settlers to get their enterprise off the ground. After several years of trying to entice colonists, by the close of the 1660s (the proprietors had received their charter in 1663) the "outpost" of what would become South Carolina, was a habitat of only a handful of settlers barely surviving. Dreams of establishing another Virginia seemed delusional.

However, in 1670 Ashley Cooper (Lord Shaftesbury), advised by his close friend John Locke, decided that to try to further recruit colonists solely from England or the British isles would be senseless; perhaps it would be better to look to already established English colonies in the New World for settlers, individuals or groups already "seasoned" and experienced in New World living and perhaps ready for a new adventure and opportunity if given the right incentives. For such individuals, the proprietors, led by Cooper, turned to the island of Barbados, that miniscule English island in the Caribbean that by the mid-17th century was producing vast quantities of sugar. Settled in 1627, within a decade Barbados had become a major source of the world's sugar. The island's tropical climate and disease-ridden environment had discouraged white servants, and the wealth produced from sugar production made possible the purchase of slaves. Almost from inception, the Barbadian labor force became African. In 1650, 15,000 slaves were there; by 1660, the number had climbed to 34,000 and zoomed to 52,000 by 1670. African slaves outnumbered the white population by over 10,000. By the end of the 17th century Barbados had become England's most profitable and productive colony, where per person (white) income was higher than in England. Most important, because of its African majority, Barbados became England's first slave society, where conditions for African slaves were brutal. As in their other slave societies, the English magnified the differences between themselves and Africans to enhance the distinction between landowners and slaves. Indeed, Barbadians were the first to portray the Africans as beasts, revealing a most intense racism responsible for the harshest slave codes in the Atlantic world. These laws prescribed that male slaves convicted of crimes could be burned at the stake, beheaded, starved, or castrated.

By 1670, the island's economy was dominated by a handful of wealthy sugar planters, who owned practically all the land, squeezing off the island smaller farmers and white servants who had served "out their time." It was to this population that the proprietors looked for settlers to come to Carolina, along with individuals from the older English colonies to the north (the New England colonies to be discussed in the next chapter), as well as Huguenots from France. Not all Barbadians coming to Carolina had been displaced by the sugar planter elite; also coming were some prosperous planters in search of new opportunities, and most important, they brought their African slaves with them. Sugar production had become so lucrative by the 1670s

that planters had ceased growing foodstuffs, finding it cheaper to import all they needed, including food, from elsewhere. Thus Cooper and the other proprietors believed they could transform Carolina into a profit-making endeavor by providing food and lumber products to their Barbadian brethren. In short, the proprietors' initially envisioned their "new" Carolina enterprise as a colony of a colony, and that they would profit by supplying Barbadian sugar planters with basic necessities grown or produced in Carolina.

The first colonists arrived at Charles Town (renamed Charleston in 1783) in 1670. Most of the original settlers were poor, small white farmers and ex-indentured servants from Barbados, with a smattering of similar migrants from Virginia, New England, England, and even France (mostly Huguenots), seeking opportunity or religious freedom. As noted above, some wealthy Barbadian planters also came, few in number, but a portent of the future in that they came with their slaves, and most important, a ready acceptance of the idea of a slave-based economy. Indeed, in many ways, Carolina was born a slave society in principle; unlike Virginia there was no gradual, evolutionary process of acceptance and eventual entrenchment. However, for the first decade and a half, most Carolina whites could not afford to purchase slaves and there was no lucrative, dominant staple such as tobacco requiring a large labor force. Until such an export crop existed, producing significant income for its cultivator, the necessary wealth required to purchase many slaves was not there.

The colony grew slowly at first but the settlers never experienced any "starving time" as had their Virginia brethren. Initially the pioneers experimented with a variety of exotic, Mediterranean-type products such as silk, olives, grapes, and citrus fruits, but all failed, as did surprisingly, early attempts at cultivating rice and indigo. The settlers then set their sights on simply growing mundane foodstuffs such as corn and peas and raising hogs and cattle, all of which proved profitable because they were sold to provision-starved Barbados, which was the proprietors' original intention. Carolina also had bountiful forests, from which Carolinians developed a lucrative extractive industry, producing lumber, shingles, pitch, tar, turpentine, and barrel staves, all of which found ready Caribbean markets. However, the early Carolinians most remunerative endeavor was the deerskin trade with the area's Native American tribes. As occurred frequently when Europeans entered a region, Indian tribes competed to trade with them, and rival groups of Europeans challenged each other to dominate the exchange. In the colonial period Indian wars usually pitted one group of Europeans and their Native American allies against another group of Europeans and their native allies, with the Indians doing most of the fighting. Such conflicts became extensions of Europe's expanding market economy as Native Americans fought for access to European goods while the Europeans struggled with each other to monopolize certain Indian products, most notably furs. In Carolina during the late 17th century the English settlers faced no competition with other Europeans for control of the fur trade, and thus within little more than a decade, more than 50,000 deerskins annually were being exported to England. Before rice and indigo, Carolina fortunes were made on the skin of the whitetail deer.

The fur trade also introduced the Carolinians to another, even more profitable "commodity:" Indian slaves. Indeed, until about 1690, enslaved southeastern Native Americans were the most valuable product produced by the colony. One raid against Spanish mission Indians (Native Americans who had converted to Catholicism) brought back 5,000 captives, comparable in size to a slaving foray in West Africa. In part, this magnification of the Indian slave trade, which had been miniscule in the 17th century, was the result of the extensive deerskin trade network noted above. By the early 18th century, trade connections were made through friendly local Indians to Native nations as far away as the Mississippi River, and most of the enslaved Indians came from regions far west of present day South Carolina. Some Indian deer hunters came to realize that slaves fetched a higher price than pelts, so raids were made against enemy tribes for captives, especially women and children to sell into bondage; the men were simply killed. So lucrative for awhile was the Indian slave trade that Carolina traders quickly established their control over the entire Southeast, driving out the Spanish, French, and even their fellow Englishmen in Virginia. In the 1680 Westo War, the Carolinians sent their Indian allies, the Savannahs, to destroy and capture the Westos, who were the Virginians' partner in the Southeastern deerskin trade. The Carolinian marauders, in conjunction with other Indian allies, succeeded in driving the Spanish out of the region as well, destroying the last of their missions in the area and enslaving their natives. Because Indian slaves were dangerous as long as they were near their homelands, most were shipped off to other colonies, most notably New England and the Caribbean.

By the close of the 17th century, the Carolinians had come to dominate both the Indian slave and fur trades. They had eliminated all European competitors, including their neighbors the Virginians, and with the alliance of a few tribes brought the rest of the Native Americans of the region under their control. The Carolinians hegemony, however, did not last long. One of their closest, most loyal trading partners for 40 years, the Yamasees, grew weary of being cheated out of their land and having their women and children enslaved, revolted in 1715, taking the Carolinians by surprise and recruiting other Indians in their cause. The Yamasees got within 12 miles of Charles Town before they were stopped. They might have been able to penetrate Charles Town had their Indian allies not abandoned them along the way. The Yamasee War (1715–1716) claimed the lives of 400 white South Carolinians (a higher proportion of the population that was lost in King Philip's War in New England in the late 1670s), forced the Carolinians to vacate their frontier settlements, and revealed the precariousness of the entire South Carolina settlement.

As the Carolina economy began to prosper, the result of trade in deerskins to England and food and livestock to Barbados, the increased need for laborers exceeded the supply of white immigrants from England and elsewhere. The same demographic developments in late 17th century England that affected the Chesapeake also impacted Carolina, especially the decrease in the supply of potential indentured servants. Although as noted above, Carolinians enslaved Native Americans, there were not enough of them to solve the colony's labor needs. Thus, as occurred in Virginia and Maryland, increasingly Carolinians shifted from a servant economy to a slave economy in the 1680s and 1690s. However it was not until the 1720s and the rice boom of that decade did Carolina become, like the Chesapeake colonies, a slave society. Prior to that time, Carolina was a society with slaves, who were set to work in

the more open conditions of a mixed economy. Slaves worked with whites of various origins at a variety of tasks: growing food for export to Barbados; cutting timber in the forests for lumber, shingles, barrel staves, working in the infant naval stores industry providing pitch and tar for English shipping, and herding cattle in the woods and rounding them up in cow pens for the beef market at home and in the West Indies. African slave herdsmen may have been the South's first "cowboys." In this diverse economy of Carolina's pioneer days, blacks and whites worked together and socialized together not as equals but with a greater degree of harmony than they would for the next two-and-a-half centuries.

From the beginning, the Carolina proprietors had hoped to become rich by discovering a bonanza crop like tobacco or sugar that could be grown there and profitably sold in England. Although the colony was thriving by the close of the 17th century, the result of the various enterprises noted above, it was not until rice and indigo cultivation was pursued aggressively did Carolina become the lucrative colonial venture its proprietors had envisioned. After several years of experimenting with different cultivation techniques and rice seeds, did rice farming becoming profitable. By 1700, Carolina rice planters had exported 400,000 pounds of rice; by 1710, they were exporting 1.5 million pounds, and by mid-century, 50 million pounds were being shipped annually. Increased rice production saw the "natural" corollary of increased importation of African slaves. Initially, as in the Chesapeake, rice planters purchased most of their slaves from the West Indies, but the clamor for slave laborers became so great by the 1720s that the islands could not keep pace with such high demand. Carolina planters thus bought their slaves directly from Africa and much to their delightful surprise, many of the Africans they purchased (accidentally at first then by planter preference subsequently) came from West Africa's Grain coast, with expertise in planting and growing rice, helping to expand Carolina's rice production and profitability, which in turn allowed planters to buy even more slaves. Thanks in large part to African expertise, the rice industry matured and became more efficient, shifting from dry-land cultivation to fresh water, swampy regions for irrigation to flood the fields and kill the grass, and finally, after mid-century it shifted once more to tidal-swamp areas in the low country. Rice production required tremendous start-up and maintenance costs, and the necessary labor was back-breaking, and only blacks were thought capable of performing such work.

Another important crop was added to Carolina's economy in the 1740s, when Elizabeth Lucas Pinckney, a young South Carolina woman, successfully adapted West Indian indigo to the low-country climate. It is likely here as well, that the assistance of Caribbean slaves, skilled in indigo culture was crucial. The indigo plant, native to India, produced a deep blue dye important in textile manufacture. Rice best grew in the lowlands, but indigo could be cultivated on high ground. In addition, the two staples had different seasonal growing patterns thus the two crops harmonized perfectly. Rice and indigo production rose steadily over the next 30 years and by the 1770s they were among the most valuable commodities exported from Great Britain's mainland North American colonies. Indigo production was as labor intensive as rice production, and as with rice, Carolina indigo planters believed it was work suitable only for blacks and the profits from both were enormous. By the rice boom of the 1720s, gone

from South Carolina was the old mixed economy with a degree of white-black equality in the workplace. Coastal Carolina resembled England's Caribbean sugar islands, where black slaves on manorial-sized plantations greatly outnumbered whites and slaves were assigned almost exclusively to agricultural tasks. Moreover, the Carolina slave codes, enacted in the 1690s, were the harshest on the North American continent, reflecting the Carolinians "Barbadian connection." Before the importation of slaves to the United States ended in 1808, at least 100,000 Africans had arrived at Charleston. One of every five ancestors of today's African Americans passed through that port on his or her way to the rice and indigo fields. Carolina, like the Chesapeake in the early 18th century, had become a full-fledged slave society. Politically, as in the Chesapeake, the largest, wealthiest indigo and rice planters came to dominate and controlled the colonial legislature, dictating to both the governor and the Carolina plain folk how the colony should be run, which was always to be to their benefit, with everyone else in the colony (whites only of course) only marginally involved in the decision-making and legislative process.

The Northern Portion of Carolina: North Carolina

As can be seen from the above discussion of the development of present-day South Carolina, the Carolina proprietors paid little to no attention to settle the northern portion of their land, the region between Virginia and Cape Fear or the future colony/state of North Carolina. Various factors contributed to this neglect: an inhospitable coastline for shipping, with shifting sand bars and shallow inlets with no natural harbors such as that of Charles Town; perceived soil and climate not conducive to staple crop production; and unfriendly Indians such as the Tuscarora. This lack of attention meant that northern Carolina developed with little proprietary assistance, and although the area was sparsely settled until about 1725, thereafter it developed through a rich stream of migration from Europe, persisted in an increasingly profitable mixed economy, and by 1790 was second in white population among the Southern states only to Virginia.

Even before the Carolina proprietors received their grant from Charles II, Virginians from Norfolk had penetrated northern Carolina around Albermarle Sound, searching for virgin tobacco land. Indeed, one such intrepid individual, Nathaniel Batts, established a home on the western shore of the sound in 1655, becoming the first permanent white inhabitant in all of Carolina. Batts traded with the Indians for deerskins, but word soon spread that the area was perfect for tobacco cultivation and Virginians began coming to the territory, setting up tobacco farms. As a result, by the 1660s the region around Albermarle Sound was more tied to the tobacco economy of the Chesapeake than to the provisioning trade and later rice industry of southern Carolina. In effect, the Albermarle area had become a colony of Virginia, settled by small farmers and servants who had fulfilled their indentures, coming in search of inexpensive if not free land. Suffice it to say, such "usurpation" by Virginia upset the Carolina proprietors who now took serious interest in the northern portion of their grant.

Although initially hoping to profit from tobacco, the Albermarle settlers realized that because of the absence of deep-water harbors tobacco proved to be not as profitable as hoped because it could not be exported directly to England but through Norfolk, Virginia first. Thus, north Carolinians were less committed to trade with England and developed a more diverse local economy. Tobacco was grown as a money crop, but farmers also learned to grow peas, corn, beans, raise cattle and hogs, even poultry for their own food and for trade either to Virginia, the rice farmers to the south, or especially to the West Indies via shallow-drafted boats not suitable for transatlantic commerce. The burgeoning economy saw increases in population and by the 1690s more counties were organized beyond the Sound. Also helping to promote population growth was the development as in southern Carolina, of the naval stores industry, which complemented tobacco and food production, all of which brought hitherto unknown prosperity to northern Carolina. Of course, prosperity and a thriving, diverse economy attracted more settlers.

Another lucrative, individualistic enterprise north Carolinians engaged in for about a decade was trade with and harboring some of the most famous (or infamous) Caribbean pirates of the era. The islands of the colony's Outer Banks provided the perfect hiding place and striking point from which the buccaneer's swift, shallow-drafted vessels could attack England's larger, cumbersome, oceangoing ships laden with valuable goods. For about a decade (1710–1720), these independent maritime opportunists, loyal only to themselves and to their fortunes, plied the waters of the Outer Banks, not only raiding the cargo ships of any nation, but also trading with north Carolinians, who were more than happy to purchase or barter with their corsair friends for all manner of exotic goods. Indeed, north Carolinians welcomed the pirates, not only providing them a safe sanctuary, but often publicly advertising when their ships were to arrive with their latest booty. Of course, when asked by English officials trying to apprehend these outlaws, north Carolinians would declare they never saw such people nor did they know where they were "hanging about." No more colorful and legendary group ever roamed the coastal waters of North America than these sea brigands, whose names are recognized to this day; men such as the brute Edward Teach, alias "Blackbeard," or Stede Bonnet, the "the gentleman buccaneer," who, as a well educated and wealthy retired British army major, set up his freebooting headquarters along the Carolina coast. The British navy finally captured them both, hanging Bonnet in 1718 and killing Blackbeard after a fierce battle the same year. Much to the disappointment of north Carolinians, the heyday of Carolina pirating had ended.

News of northern Carolina's flourishing economy not only brought English settlers from neighboring Virginia and from the homeland but also other Europeans to the region as well, most notably French Huguenots, Swiss merchants from Bern, and Palatine Germans. These three groups, along with the English gave northern Carolina a rich ethnic and religious diversity along with a devotion to a diversified economy that neither the tobacco region to the north nor the rice-growing region to the south could claim. In short, northern Carolina became a place economically and socially unlike its northern and southern neighbors. It was in effect a pluralistic society and although many north Carolinians owned slaves, particularly those engaged in tobacco cultivation, northern Carolina did not become a slave society. Indeed, compared to Virginia and South Carolina, African slavery was virtually absent in northern Carolina; as late as 1712, when Carolina was divided into North and South Carolina, there were only approximately 800 slaves in the region—a decade after the Chesapeake and South Carolina had become slave societies. Northern Carolinians produced their own foodstuffs and everything else they needed; they were in effect subsistence farmers; some also produced pitch and tar for the naval stores trade when crop needs did not require their attention. They profited by selling surplus corn and livestock to tobacco and rice planters and to hungry Barbadians. They were even known later to drive herds of cattle, hogs, and turkeys northward to Baltimore and Philadelphia. Thus, in the "middle" of two slave societies there existed the antithesis; a white community ethnically and economically diversify and tied only in a most marginal and peripheral sense to commercial production and the larger Atlantic trade network. In many ways, colonial northern Carolinians became the prototype for the future "American" independent, non-slaveholding yeoman farmers, exalted by Thomas Jefferson as the "essence" of the great democratic, republican experiment called the United States.

The Founding of Georgia

With the founding and flourishing of the Carolinas, especially South Carolina, England worried that its two European rivals, Spain and France, would find English presence so close to their respective territories threatening and thus do all they could to drive the English out of the Carolinas. Interestingly, of the two nations, by the early 18th century, France, not Spain, had become the greater potential menace to English interests in the southeast. The unprecedented French encroachment on the Gulf Coast (to be discussed later in this chapter) alerted the Carolinians to a potential threat surely as it spurred the Spanish in

Mexico to respond. The French had also established garrisons at Mobile, Natchitotoches, Natchez, and then Fort Toulous in central Alabama, all of which clearly endangered the Carolinians lucrative deerskin trade with the Indians all the way to the Mississippi River. Further alarming Carolinians was the French establishment of New Orleans in 1718 near the mouth of the Mississippi and the seizing of Pensacola from the Spanish in 1719. These French initiatives convinced the Carolinians and England that the French planned to connect their Gulf Coast settlements with their fur trading empire in Canada. Carolinians thus saw the possible end to one of their most lucrative trading enterprises, and there was always the possibility that Spanish Florida could be reinforced and become more aggressive. Such fears came to fruition during the Yamasee War (discussed earlier in this chapter), which Carolinians believed the French and Spanish helped to instigate in order to drive the English out of Carolina. Although the Carolinians defeated the Yamasee, they nonetheless continued to feel vulnerable to French and Spanish reprisals. Carolinians thus became convinced that steps had to be taken to establish a buffer between their communities and the enemy, prevent the Gulf and French Canadian settlements from being linked, and safeguard the Carolina fur trade routes to the west. All these purposes could be served by establishing another English settlement between South Carolina and Spanish Florida, which would not only prevent further potential Spanish encroachments but those of the French as well from the west.

The English government took seriously the Carolinians' entreaties, but all attempts at establishing a defensive barrier between Carolina and European rivals failed. Interestingly, not until the military exigencies of such

an endeavor combined with the reform desires of a group of English philanthropists did England successfully establish its 13th colony in North America, Georgia. The individuals most responsible for the founding of Georgia were Sir John Perceval, James Ogelthorpe, and Dr. Thomas Bray, all of whom were committed to reforming England's penal system, especially as it pertained to debtors. After heading a Parliamentary investigative committee charged with uncovering abuses in the penal system, Ogelthorpe became convinced that England needed to establish a charity colony for the poor rather than putting such individuals in prison. Ogelthorpe also believed such a colony in North America could serve as a place to proselytize among slaves and Indians while providing a place of redemption for the deserving poor. Perceval, Ogelthorpe, Bray, and other men of such ideals formed a group called the Georgia Trustees and petitioned the king, George II for a charter to establish their charity colony. Their request was granted in 1732, with the king's authorization to govern the colony for 21 years, after which it would revert to the Crown. Originally to be a refuge for debtors, Georgia also became a haven for many other economically dislocated Englishmen, "worthy" poor, who through no fault of their own had become unemployed: farmers, artisans, and tradesmen. Georgia came to be seen as a way of providing all these unfortunates an opportunity for a new life.

Ogelthorpe came with the first colonists, arriving with the just over 100 hopefuls at Charles Town in mid-January 1733. Although never officially named governor by either his fellow trustees or the king. Ogelthorpe's natural abilities and forceful personality made him the leader of the experiment. After landing at Charles Town, the colonists eventually made their way to present-day Savannah, which became Georgia's first settlement. There was illness and death the first summer, but supplies were sent by the trustees, and friendly Indians, the Yamacraws, helped provide provisions as well. Ogelthorpe treated the Yamacraws and other local natives fairly, in fact, he became a good friend to Tomochichi, the Yamacraw chief, who helped the Georgians secure peace with the larger Creek confederacy of Native Americans. There was no "starving time" and thus the colony proved a success, which attracted more impoverished but "worthy" men and women but ironically, very few debtors. Georgia's reform image spread throughout Europe, and within a year, others seeking a new chance in life requested to come. Coming to Georgia in 1734 were 100 German Lutherans from Salzburg, Austria, driven out by the Catholic Church. After a few years of hardship and disease the Salzburgers began to prosper, and their presence attracted additional European settlers—some transient, most permanent—to Georgia. By the mid-18th century, this gave the colony a substantial German-speaking population and cluster of German folkways. Sensing the need for citizen-soldiers who could both farm and fight, the Georgia trustees recruited a group of Scottish Highlanders, known to be aggressive defenders of their property and way of life— with the result that by 1741, several hundred had come, most of them settling in Darien, at the mouth of the Altamaha River, the accepted boundary between English and Spanish authority. In less than a decade, Georgia's stability and prosperity, along with a reputation for openness to European victims of oppression and poverty, had attracted to the colony people from England, Germany, Switzerland, Wales, Scotland, Ireland and even a handful of Jews, who established one of the nation's ear-

liest Jewish communities in Savannah. About fifty arrived from Eastern Europe in the summer of 1733, and although they had no rabbi, they founded a synagogue, called Mickva Israel, and practiced their faith free from any harassment or persecution. Georgia thus became known for its religious pluralism and toleration, even of non-Christians.

The early Georgians, their numbers increasing, soon felt secure enough to begin to protest Ogelthorpe's paternalistic leadership and restrictive policies. Safe from danger, the colonists began to think about their long-term prosperity. The trustees wanted to keep Georgia a charitable preserve for the worthy poor and objected to the idea of individual farmers wanting huge blocks of land for themselves. The trustees somewhat compromised, parceling out land in small amounts to individual farmers that they could hold for their lifetimes; the land could not be sold and could be conveyed only to their male heirs. If there were none, the land reverted to the trustees. In 1735, the trustees also issued decrees prohibiting African slavery in Georgia as well as the use of rum and other strong drinks, and restricted trade with the Indians. In the trustees mind, Georgia was to be a moral experiment to where they transported persons in unfortunate circumstances, to be trained in the ways of thrift, sobriety, and morality, so they would become upstanding citizens. Such an experiment required the prohibition of alcohol, which they believed if they allowed their colonists to imbibe, would lead to intemperance and abuse, and disallowance of slavery, which was immoral in and of itself and also tempted slaveowners with idleness, licentiousness, and a hunger for extravagant profits. Good relations with the Native Americans were necessary for security reasons and a sense of fairness hence trade with the Indians had to be closely monitored. Much to the trustees' disappointment, by the 1740s, the majority of Georgians chafed under these restrictions. They had come to the colony to have a freer life, and thus for many colonists the trustees' mandates were impinging upon their right to have a better, more bountiful existence.

The trustees believed that Georgia's climate and soil was similar to that of the Mediterranean and thus products like wine, olives, and silk could be produced. When it became obvious to Georgians that neither their colony's climate nor topography was conducive to the growing of such commodities, Georgia farmers wanted to adopt the hugely profitable system of rice cultivation pioneered in South Carolina. Recognizing the strenuous work involved in setting up rice fields, those Georgians wanting to engage in such an enterprise and seeing the wealth slavery was bringing to South Carolina, wanted an end to the prohibition of slavery. Ogelthorpe and his fellow trustees were loath to end the ban on slavery so Georgians sought ways to circumvent the law, often leasing slaves for 99 years from South Carolina "owners" and paying them the entire 'rent" in advance. Others simply bought slaves in flagrant disregard of the law. So intense did the opposition to the law become that in 1750 the trustees were forced to revoke the 1735 prohibition. Never able to realize a colony of small, contented farmers, the trustees surrendered Georgia back to the Crown a year early, in 1752. With Ogelthorpe's laws repealed— from outlawing alcohol to land restrictions to the prohibition of slavery—Georgia by mid century resembled the plantation society of South Carolina. Savannah became a little Charleston, with its robust civic and cultural life, and its slave markets as well. By 1750 Georgia had transformed itself from a fragile new settlement, a buffer between South

Carolina and vague enemies to the south and west to a prosperous colony that was producing a profitable agricultural export for the world market. It had ceased in its noble experiment to become and remain a place of charity for the worthy poor, who would not only find personal redemption from an impoverished or dissipated past, but could reclaim their lives and start anew in a land of guaranteed opportunity for all. Georgia, while remaining open to Europeans fleeing from oppression and destitution, was now enslaving black Africans as fast as she could afford them. The colony was no longer a reformer's ideal of small independent farmers but a booming plantation society, not much different from its northern neighbors in South Carolina and the Chesapeake.

The Latin South

Colonial American history is often thought of as the progress of English settlements across a vast continent occupied only by decreasing numbers of Indians and the presence of French and Spanish settlers is only sporadically discussed as a prelude to the Louisiana Purchase and the later Anglo-Texan revolt (highlighted by the battle at the Alamo) against Mexican authority and the subsequent controversy over Texas annexation to the United States. Yet the cultures of Spain and France left a deeper imprint on the region from Florida to Texas than the passing mention of their presence most United States history texts devote to the printed page. European wars and rivalries affected Spanish and French attempts to establish mainland colonies as much or more than homeland problems did, and in fact, these Old World antagonisms shaped the timing of both the beginning and the end of Spanish and French control of large portions of the present-day South. By contrast, England, except for the *Aramada* of the late 16th century, and a few other brief forays into continental geopolitics in the early 17th century, wisely remained detached from European affairs and thus Englishmen during the 17th century could devote more time and energy to developing and expanding their New World colonial enterprises.

Initially the Spanish in Florida were little bothered by the English colony at Jamestown. By 1607, Florida had become for the Spanish merely a way-station for its ships still carrying silver and gold from Mexico and a mission field for the Franciscans whose series of mission outposts at Indian towns swept across from San Agustin (present-day Saint Augustine, Florida) to the northernmost Sea Islands of Georgia, called Guale after a local Indian chief. Westward the Franciscans had pushed their missions all the way to present-day southern Alabama, and by 1674 had established 32 missions in Florida ministering to more than 13,000 officially Christian Indians. Beginning in the 1670s however, Spanish security and hegemony over the region suddenly became threatened by the English presence in South Carolina. As noted earlier in this chapter by that decade the Carolinians had begun developing a lucrative fur trade with the area's Native Americans, gaining influence over the Indians, who found it hard to resist British goods. English and French pirates also raided the isolated missions in coastal Guale, forcing the Spanish to abandon Georgia and retreat into Florida and to try to hold on to their missions there. Carolinian-armed Indian allies periodically marauded the missions, eventually attacking them full force in 1702 and 1704, when expeditions led by South Carolina governor James Moore invaded Florida with a combined Indian-Carolinian army, devastating the missions near San Agustin and the Apalachee

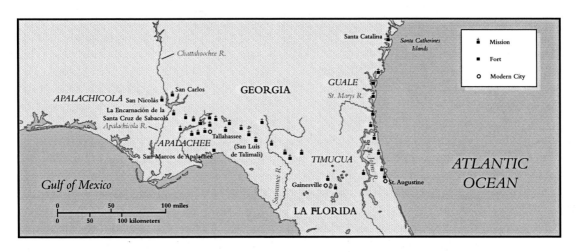

Spanish Missions in the Southeast. In order to secure their northern Florida frontier from possible English and French incursions, the Spanish established a string of missions and presidios, stretching from San Augustine, Florida all the way to central Alabama. Their purpose was not only defensive and strategic but also altruistic: they hoped to convert as many Native Americans as possible to Catholicism, and in the process, to Spanish allies.

region; neither the missions nor Spanish authority ever completely recovered in Florida. At the same time that the English were challenging Spanish territory in the east, another European rival, France, had begun to threaten Spanish presence from the west.

As noted in Chapter 1, although the 16th century Spanish conquistadors/explorers Cabeza de Vaca, Hernando de Soto, and Francisco Coronado, had traveled through Alabama, Mississippi, Louisiana, Texas, and elsewhere, most notably the Great Plains, they were all searching for gold and with no intention or interest in establishing any sort of permanent settlements in these areas; Spain used their sojourns for wealth only to claim the territory. At the western periphery of this tenuous empire, the Spanish in the late 16th and into the 17th century attempted to bring Christianity to the Native Americans, planting as they had in the southeast a string missions, with the first of such outposts established near present-day Santa Fe, New Mexico in 1598 and in the decades of the next century built more near the upper Nueces River and in the Edwards Plateau region of Texas; the oldest permanent settlement in Texas began in 1681 at the mission site at Ysleta near present-day El Paso. Except for these smattering of missions, which had little success in converting the Plains tribes of the area (the Apaches, the Comanches, the Wichitas, and the Kiowas, to name but a few), who were simply too nomadic and war-like to embrace the Franciscans' proselytizing, Spain neglected the entire region from the Rio Grande to the Escambia River in West Florida, seeing neither a military nor an economic reason to become more involved. Then France entered the arena, and the entire geopolitical situation changed.

Not until the 1670s did France become a threat to Spanish suzerainty in the old south-west. Prior to that decade the French empire in Canada seemed too far away to affect Spanish interests. However, beginning in the 1670s and over the course of the next several decades, into the early 18th century, the French expanded out of Canada, led by their intrepid fur traders and explorers, seeking not only to extend the reach of their fur trade deeper into North America, but also to find a warm-water river route southward from Canada. In 1673, the Jesuit, Father Marquette and Louis Jolliet, had come down the Mississippi River all the way to where it joined with the Arkansas River, and nine years later, in 1682, Rene Robert Cavelier, Sieur de La Salle, floated all the way to the Gulf via one of the Mississippi's several mouths, staking a French claim to the region. La Salle just showing up would have been provocation enough for the nervous Spanish, but when he returned from France with an expedition intent on expanding France's empire into the southwest, the Spanish became apoplectic with fear. Fortunately for the Spanish, La Salle's attempt to establish a permanent French colony at the mouth of the Mississippi failed, largely because he had miscalculated where that mouth was and landed on the Texas coast at Matagorda Bay. There, near the Lavaca River, La Salle built a small garrison named Fort Saint Louis but that soon dissolved and La Salle decided to return to Canada for reinforcements but was killed by his own men in eastern Texas in an argument over how to share the sparse food supply. While La Salle was gone the Indians finished off the remnant of the French forces at Fort Saint Louis. Thus ended the French attempt to extend their North American empire to the Gulf Coast, a chimerical empire at best.

La Salle's Texas venture, exaggerated by the Spanish into an "invasion" of the Texas coast, helped to force the Spanish out of their complaisance relative to their borderland possessions. Already harassed in the east by the English, and now being attacked at their center by another European rival, the Spanish now put forth more concerted efforts to defend their empire from English and French interlopers. By the time Spanish forces arrived at Fort Saint Louis, the garrison had been abandoned and destroyed by Indians. The Spanish Governor Alonso de Leon of Coahuila led the Spanish contingent and when he arrived a band of Tejas Indians from eastern Texas (from whom the name Texas came), to De Leon's shock, asked the Spaniard to establish a mission for them, which he agreed to do. In the next few years two Catholic missions were located in east Texas, but disease, food shortages, and the Indians general lack of interest, doomed the two missions to failure; they were abandoned by the Spanish in 1693. With the French threat apparently gone from Texas, for the next two decades, Spain once again forgot about this particular borderland province until the French once more appeared on the scene.

Although foiled in their first attempts to establish a presence along the Gulf Coast or at the mouth of the Mississippi River, the French renewed their efforts in the late 1690s when Louis XIV authorized another expedition to try to lay claim to the region, now called Louisiana after the great "Sun King." To lead this new venture, the king and his ministers chose two French-Canadian explorers, the brothers Le Moyne, Pierre, Sieur d'Iberville, and his brother Jean Baptiste Le Moyne, Sieur de Bienville. Their mission was to establish a settlement somewhere at the mouth of the Mississippi and from there perhaps other outposts along the Gulf Coast. The brothers sailed from France in October 1698 and reached present-day Mobile three months later. Pierre left the bulk of his force at Mobile

and he and his brother continued westward until they found what they believed to be the mouth of the Mississippi and made their way up stream, all the way to present-day Baton Rouge, Louisiana. After attempting to establish settlements along the southern portion of Mississippi, all of which failed, the le Moyne brothers decided to bring all settlers to one location, present-day Mobile, Alabama, officially founded in 1711. Believing it was important to erect a barrier against Carolina fur traders and trappers, the French in 1717 established Fort Toulouse at the juncture of the Coosa and Tallapoosa Rivers, just north of the present city of Montgomery, Alabama. From their base in Mobile, the French over the course of the next decade established several other settlements in Louisiana. Setting up both forts and trading posts, both to buy furs from the Indians and to stymie the Carolina traders, who were ranging far to the west by this time, The French placed trading centers at Natchitoches in northwest Louisiana in 1714, near the Texas border; Fort Rosalie at the site of Natchez, Mississippi in 1716, and the colony's first town, New Orleans, on the bank of the Mississippi south of Lake Pontchartrain in 1718. The economy depended on exchanging cheap European goods with a variety of Indian groups for valuable deerskins; the French displayed little interest in developing any sort of significant agricultural enterprises.

This strong French presence surprisingly did not alarm the Spanish until a group of French traders, led by Louis Juchereau de St. Denis, showed up at a Spanish mission and presidio (garrison) on the Rio Grande, asking to open trade between French Louisiana and Spanish Texas. Because there was now peace between the two nations in Europe (the War of the Spanish Succession had just ended on the continent), St. Denis saw no obstacles that would prevent such an endeavor that would benefit both countries colonial settlements. At first the Spanish were hostile toward the idea and St. Denis, but the wily Frenchman convinced the viceroy in Mexico City of the merits of this proposal and St. Denis next found himself leading a Spanish expedition to northeast Texas to establish a string of six Franciscan missions and a presidio near present-day Nacogdoches and San Augustine, with the last one, Los Adaes, actually located across the Sabine River in Louisiana. Unfortunately a year after these settlements had been established (1719), a French force, hearing that war had resumed in Europe between France and Spain, attacked the Spanish mission at Los Adaes, causing the entire Spanish population to flee east Texas, all the way to the presidio at San Antonio, established in 1718. Surprisingly the French did not move into the vacated region, which allowed the Spanish to return in 1721 and reclaim the area. Los Adaes became the Spanish capital of Texas for the next 50 years, even though it was actually in Louisiana. This half-century marked the heyday of Spanish Texas. The economy of the entire Spanish Borderlands (which included present day California, New Mexico, Arizona, parts of Nevada, Utah, and Colorado) was not based on agriculture but rather on livestock—hogs, mustangs, and especially cattle. In the Southeast particularly, Spanish breeds of cattle and hogs later interbred with English stock. In the late 19th century, descendants of the original Spanish mustangs were the mount of choice for Texas ranchers—those Western icons, the cowboys.

Interestingly, thanks in large part to the French "threat" to their dominions, the Spanish during the 18th century took the settlement of their borderlands seriously, especially Texas, which by the 1760s had close to 2,500 inhabi-

tants permanently settled in three main locations: Nacogdoches, San Antonio, and La Bahia (Goliad). The largest concentration was in San Antonio. Spanish place names, ranching techniques and terms, the concept of a homestead law that exempts a person's property from seizure for debt; the idea that a husband and wife jointly share their property—these and other facets of the Spanish heritage left a permanent legacy and imprint on Texas culture, language, customs, even food. In 1762 France, as a result of defeat in the Seven Years' War with Great Britain, ceded Louisiana to Spain, removing once and for all the French threat that had worried Spain for close to a century. With the French menace gone, the Spanish abandoned their presidios and missions from eastern Texas (even Nacogdoches temporarily) and relocated everyone to the area around San Antonio. In that vicinity a string of missions were built, and today five of them are maintained by the National Park Service, visible reminders of the Spanish heritage of the Latin South. For the next 50 years, occasional explorers, promoters, pioneers, and scoundrels from Louisiana and the eventual United States came to Texas and settled there, all the while tensions simmered between the *tejano* population and the assortment of Anglo-Americans and other non-Mexican groups. As will be seen in a later chapter, one of the biggest mistakes the Spanish then Mexican government in Mexico City made was open Texas' door to immigration, which in the end cost Mexico all of its borderland territory.

While the Spanish controlled Louisiana and New Orleans, two disastrous fires in 1788 and 1794 destroyed the original French buildings of the Crescent City. The presently existing Vieux Carre was rebuilt by the Spanish, which explains why the "French" Quarter largely exhibits Spanish architecture. Otherwise,

French culture persisted in Louisiana. Spain later was forced by Napoleon Bonaparte to give Louisiana back to France, which, as will be seen in a later chapter, he promptly sold the territory to the United States in 1803. That episode as well as the history of the Hispanic Southwest belongs to another part of the American story.

Conclusion

As reflected in this chapter, although England came late to the New World, once fully engaged in overseas expansion, the English, despite initial setbacks born of stupidity, arrogance, and greed, rapidly developed in their Southern colonies commercially successful and profitable enterprises, based on the production of staple crops cultivated by slave labor. Interestingly, had it done been for the perseverance of Captain John Smith and the relationships he established with the local Native Americans, Jamestown would have gone the way of Roanoke and England might not have ever returned to North America. Equally fortuitous were the Virginians' "discovery" of tobacco; had they not found such an immediately lucrative cash crop, the Jamestown settlement might have economically languished indefinitely, ultimately failing, and again the potential end of empire for England.

Southern colonial prosperity and permanency was founded first on the blood, sweat, tears of indentured servants, mostly from England then on the backs of brutally enslaved Africans, the latter to the amount of over 11 million captured and forcibly brought to New World in chains over the course of two-and-one-half centuries. Indeed, one of the great paradoxes of mainland Southern colonial history was that initially tobacco, rice, and indigo planters wanted to avoid African slavery at all costs, but as this chapter revealed, over time and because of homeland demographic factors beyond their control, staple crop planters not only turned to African slavery to solve their labor needs, but once they embraced the notion, they put in place, sanctioned by law, a completely segregated black and white society, stripping the black slaves of all humanity into valuable chattel. Simultaneously, these black codes elevated lower class whites while denigrating the slaves, thus turning whites, who once had much in common as laborers with their black brethren, into racists. Thus one of the more insidious purposes of the slave codes was to inculcate a racist mentality in all Southern whites, whether or not they actually owned slaves. Although in retrospect, Southern planters of cash crops would have turned to African slavery sooner or later, it was the inherent flaws of indentured servitude, culminating in the Chesapeake with Bacons" Rebellion, that accelerated the process toward the adoption of African slavery. By 1700, the Chesapeake colonies of Maryland and Virginia, South Carolina, and ultimately Georgia by the 1740s had become full-fledged slave societies.

The Native American tribes of the Southeast were also rather quickly dispensed with once the English required their land for tobacco cultivation in the Chesapeake or the Indians themselves for slaves as in the Carolinas. Unlike the Spanish or even the French to a lesser degree, the English had no desire to convert the Native Americans to Christianity. Indeed, early on in the English frame of reference the only "good Indian was a dead Indian," and the English displayed this mentality and implemented such a disposition ruthlessly and without hesitation. Thus, by 1700, gone from the Chesapeake were the major tribes that inhabited the area when the English first arrived in 1607. In the Carolinas the Native American peoples lasted a bit longer, primarily because of the lucrative deerskin trade that developed between the Carolinians and the region's Native Americans.

By the middle of the 18ᵗʰ century, the American colonial South was well on its way to becoming a rather distinct region, especially compared to the colonial North, which as will be seen in the next chapter, developed much differently socially, economically, and politically, over roughly the same time period. Indeed, by the time of the American revolt against British authority in the mid-1770s, two rather distinct colonial America's had emerged and as will be seen in this volume, the differences between North and South only continued to grow more pronounced in subsequent decades. In effect, many of the foundations for American sectionalism had been put in place by the end of the colonial period.

Suggested Readings

Wilcomb E. Washburn. *The Governor and the Rebel: A History of Bacon's Rebellion in Virginia* (1957). Explores the causes and consequences of the 1676 uprising in Virginia.

Edmund S. Morgan. *American Slavery, American Freedom: The Ordeal of Colonial Virginia.* (1975). The seminal study of the evolution of African slavery in Virginia.

Sidney Mintz. *Sweetness and Power: The Place of Sugar in Modern History.* (1985).

A global history of the significance of sugar in the making of the modern world.

Allan Kulikoff. *Tobacco and Slaves: The development of Southern Cultures in the Chesapeake, 1680-1800.* (1986). Explores how the rise of slave-grown tobacco affected Chesapeake society.

Ira Berlin. *Many Thousands Gone: The First Two Centuries of Slavery in North America.* (1998). The most extensive study of the origins and development of colonial slavery.

Winthrop Jordan. *White Over Black: American Attitudes Toward the Negro, 1550-1812.* (1968). A detailed look at how ideas about race developed over time in England and the American colonies.

Peter H. Wood. *Black Majority: Negroes in Colonial South Carolina from 1670 through the Stono Rebellion.* (1974). Examines how the expansion of rice production affected the slave system and lives of South Carolina slaves.

Frederic W. Gleach. *Powhatan's World and Colonial Virginia: A Conflict of Cultures.* (1997). A Study of Indian culture and the impact of European colonization upon it.

David Price. *Love and Hate in Jamestown: John Smith, Pocahontas, and the Start of a Nation.* (2003). Presents the reality and legend of John Smith, Pocahontas, and early Virginia.

Alan Taylor. *American Colonies.* (2001). A comprehensive survey of the history of the North American colonies from their beginnings to 1763.

Chapter 3

THE NORTHERN COLONIES

During the 17th century many of the same socio-economic pressures within England that led to the establishment of the Southern colonies were also responsible for the colonization of the regions north of the Chesapeake, or the Northern Colonies, which came to be the main settlements of New England, Pennsylvania, and after 1664, New York. Also included in this area of English North America were the smaller, colonial entities of New Jersey and Delaware, the latter an "outgrowth" of Pennsylvania. In New England, a similar process occurred, as the colonies of Connecticut, Rhode Island, and New Hampshire all evolved out of their original "parent" colony of Massachusetts, which was considered the center of New England life and polity. Most important, and a dynamic largely missing in the founding of the Southern colonies, was religion, which initially was the main impetus for the settling of both New England and Pennsylvania. Indeed, neither Massachusetts nor

ENGLISH SETTLEMENT IN NEW ENGLAND, ca. 1640

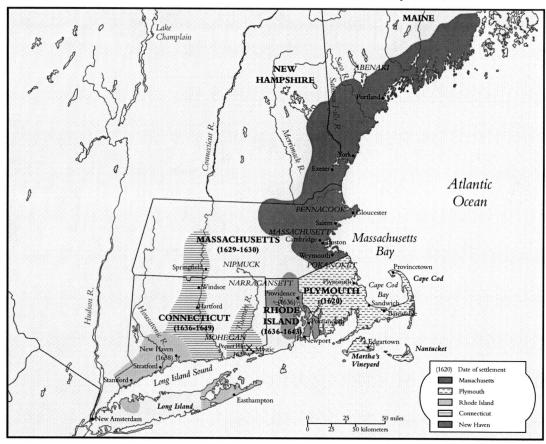

By the mid-seventeenth century, English settlement in New England had spread well inland and up and down the Atlantic Coast.

Pennsylvania, both of which had become by the middle of the 18th century two of Great Britain's most commercially successful North American colonies, would have existed had it not been for the Puritans and Quakers, the persecuted religious dissenters who originally established them as safe havens for their respective followers.

The Founding of New England: Plymouth and the Massachusetts Bay Colony

The Puritans

No discussion of the founding of the New England colonies is complete without an understanding of one of the most important of the Protestant faiths to emerge out of the 16th century Reformation: Calvinism, and its English manifestation, Puritanism. As noted in Chapter 1, the Protestant Reformation, ignited by Martin Luther and completed by John Calvin, dramatically changed forever the face of European Christianity. Those Europeans embracing the new Protestant faith, found spiritual succor and nourishment in either Lutheranism or Calvinism, with the latter becoming especially appealing to Reformation Englishmen. However, with the Elizabethan settlement of the 1570s, the Church of England, created by her father, Henry VIII, with the monarch the head of that institution, had become a "compromise" church; that is a house of worship that combined Protestant and Catholic doctrines and ceremonies.

Although the majority of Englishmen accepted the Elizabethan Settlement, relieved to be rid of the rancor, divisiveness, and violent persecution that the Reformation had visited upon England during the reigns of her predecessors (especially during the years of her fanatical Catholic sister Mary, alias "bloody Mary," for her brutal executions of Protestants for "heresy"), there remained groups who believed that the Church of England had not gone far enough in purging from practice, ritual, and structure, Catholicism. Indeed, the "reformed" church's ecclesiastical structure of bishops and archbishops remained Catholic except for the substitution at the top of the king for the pope. Indeed, the king appointed and commanded close to 9,000 clergy, from the archbishop to parish priests. Those opposed to such a system came to be known as "Puritans," for their desire to purify the Anglican church of *all* appearances and manifestations of lingering "popery." To these hardcore English Calvinists, it was their duty to God and to their country to rid the nation's church of the last remnants of its Catholic past.

Equally important to the Puritans was England's social and political well-being, which they believed was also in danger because of the power of the Crown to use the Anglican Church to promote political as well as religious conformity and obedience to the monarchy, exclusive of Parliament. Church and state were united in England with the law demanding that everyone support the official Church of England with taxes and regular attendance. Because the monarch was head of the official church, religious dissent, especially during the Stuart dynasty, as will be seen shortly, became symbiotic with treason, not just heresy. One Anglican clergyman declared that "no subject may, without hazard of his own damnation in rebelling against God, question or disobey the will and pleasure of his sovereign." The Stuarts used their position as head of the church to extort revenue and punish dissidents. The early Stuarts often ordered bishops to instruct parish priests to extol in their sermons particular Crown policies. Charles I dictated that the clergy preach that Parliament sinned when it denied new taxes demanded by the monarch. Thus the Puritans became not only the champions for religious purity, but in the process also became some of the most outspoken of the Crown's political critics, defending Parliamentary rights and personal liberties against an increasingly arbitrary, despotic, and alleged "papist" monarchy. In short, the Puritans wanted to change both the Church of England and the body politic, which they saw as one in the same; to serve and praise God and to be at all times reflections of His righteousness and will on earth.

The Puritans believed that a truly reformed Protestant church should be one that reflected the original simplicity and purity of the church of Jesus Christ and his apostles. In should be a place of worship where individual souls could nurture a more direct relationship with God. Rejecting the intercession of priests administering ceremonial sacraments, the Puritans believed that God's Word, as revealed in the Bible was the starting point for a life of righteous living along with prayer groups and heeding learned and zealous ministers who delivered evangelical sermons. Physically Puritan churches were to be austere, drab and colorless places, stripped of all Catholic "idolatry"—statues, paintings, gold chalices—all were nothing more than distractions and manifestations of a lavishly corrupt medieval institution called the Catholic Church. There was no need for an elaborate, prolonged Mass, filled with formulaic prayers uttered in an unintelligible, foreign, and "popish" language called Latin; no need to venerate saints, praying to them for help or guidance by lighting candles to solicit their

"attention." Puritan catechism even relegated the Virgin Mother to obscure importance and prayers to her were not going to win God's or Jesus' forgiveness. God's saving grace and thus salvation was determined solely by God and only He knew who was saved or damned. No amount of devout supplication, moral living, reading the Bible, or obeying to the letter a minister's preaching, could guarantee one salvation. God alone determined one's fate and He saved selectively and arbitrarily, rather than universally or as a reward for good behavior. It was this particular article of Calvinist theology, that of predestination, that the Puritans believed defined the essence of their faith. Moreover, the Puritan's God was the wrathful, vengeful, omnipotent Jehovah of the Old Testament, and mankind was nothing more than a collection of innate sinners, "a stench in God's nostrils," whose only hope for redemption was to prostrate themselves before the Lord and beg for his forgiveness and grace, and if inclined, He might grant it.

In seeking reform, Puritans divided over the details. Most remained within the Anglican Church, relentlessly agitating for its "purification," while others, the more radical Puritans, believed the institution beyond redemption, and thus it was time to completely separate from such a venal and corrupt entity. These "Separatists" determined immediately to withdraw to their own independent congregations. Without any larger authority to enforce orthodoxy, the many autonomous Separatist congregations steadily splintered in their beliefs and practices, overtime forming many distinct Protestant sects.

The Puritans were incorrigible doers, devoted to God's Word as revealed in the Scriptures, perfecting their morality accordingly. Their prodigious energy reflected their conviction that righteous activity was a sign that they had been elected for salvation. Puritanism reinforced the values of thrift, diligence, and delayed gratification, asserting that men honored God and proved their own salvation by working hard in their occupation—their "calling" bestowed by God. As one Puritan declared, "God sent you unto this world as unto a Workhouse, not a Playhouse."

Puritans strove to live in the world without succumbing to worldliness. Although believing God monetarily rewarded the diligent and godly, a potential sign of one's "election," Puritans nonetheless scorned conspicuous consumption and covetousness, certain that individuals who pursued such self-aggrandizement would fall prey to carnal temptations, thus losing sight of the ultimate purpose of human life: preparation for salvation in the next world. Yet, these saints could never escape worldly temptation because Puritan virtues helped them to accumulate money. Thus within every devout Puritan male there existed this demanding tension of how to reconcile individual prosperity with a faith that condemned personal acquisitiveness and displays of material success. However, as will seen later in this section, those Puritans born in North America and with the passing of each generation, the 'temptations" that abounded in the wilderness proved too overwhelming resist, and thus by the close of the 17th century the progeny of many of New England's original Puritan settlers had transformed into shrewd, prosperous, and some of the most self-indulgent merchant and professional elites in the British empire.

The Puritan's zeal and over-bearing righteousness dismayed most English people, who preferred Anglicanism and the traditional culture characterized by church ales, Sunday diversions, ceremonial services, inclusive churches, and deference to the monarch. In short, for the moment, the majority of Englishmen were satisfied with the House of Stuart, and were more than happy with their church, which they believed represented the best of both of England's religious traditions and thus they saw no need for further anguish and public rancor over whether or not the Anglican Church needed further reform or "purification." That issue had been settled long ago for most Englishmen and to continue agitate for a further cleansing of the church of its alleged Catholicism was completely unnecessary to the majority of Englishmen. Thus many Englishmen were beginning to see the Puritans as troublesome zealots.

Suffice it to say Puritan agitation alarmed the Stuart monarchy, which wanted a united and quiet realm of unquestioning loyalty. James I recognized the subversive potential in Puritanism's insistence on the spiritual equality of all godly men and on their superiority to all ungodly men—who in Puritan eyes included most of the king's bishops, ministers of state, if not the monarch himself. James announced that if the Puritans did not conform to his authority and that of the church, he threatened to "harry them out of the land." Fortunately for James and for England, the majority of Puritans were not ready or willing to challenge the king's authority or the church's supremacy, at least overtly; surreptitiously they did both and James reluctantly tolerated their clandestine activities to undermine both his power and that of Anglican church. Although James would have liked nothing better than to "harry them" out of England, purging the pulpits and courts of Puritans was difficult, for the crown depended upon propertied and educated men to keep and preach order in the counties, and such men were often Puritans.

James' reluctant accommodation with the Puritans collapsed completely in 1625 upon the accession of his son Charles I as king. Married to a Catholic princess, Henrietta Maria of France (which did not sit well with the majority of Englishmen not only because of her faith but also because of Anglo-French rivalry), Charles hoped to reconcile English Catholics by restoring some church ceremonies previously suspended to mollify the Puritans. It was actions such as these that infuriated the Puritans, causing them to suspect Charles of being at the very least a "closet" Catholic. Charles also elevated the High Church Anglican and court favorite William Laud, to bishop in 1628 and to archbishop in 1633. In return for such status, Laud and his allies preached that it was the Christian duty of Parliament and taxpayers to submit to the king. In effect, Charles had no intention of pursuing his father's conciliatory policies; he was determined to enforce strict conformity, to change the Anglican Church anyway he deemed appropriate, and most egregiously, he was a firm believer in absolutism, an idea that both Puritans and most Englishmen agreed to resist.

During the late 1620 and early 1630s Laud and most other bishops enforced the new Anglican orthodoxy, which increasingly reflected a Catholic revival. They dismissed Puritan ministers who balked at conducting the high church liturgy while church courts prosecuted growing numbers of Puritan laypeople. Laud censored all Puritan tracts and publicly denounced those opposed to the new regime as heretics, raising in the Puritan mind, (and in the mind of non-Puritan Englishmen), the specter of Bloody Mary and a Catholic revival with mass persecutions complete with torture and execution via burnings at the stake or decapitations. Such fears became reality when Laud had pilloried, mutilated, and branded three Puritans who illegally published their opposition treatises.

Puritan hopes of securing a redress through Parliament dissipated after 1629 when Charles dissolved that body and proceeded to rule arbitrarily for the next eleven years, bringing to fruition his absolutist designs. As will be seen later in this chapter, Charles' many mistakes, ranging from alienating the Puritans to trying to rule England as an autocrat without Parliament, eventually plunged England into several years of bloody civil war, ultimately costing Charles not only his throne but life as well. Charles usurpation of power and his apparent desire to return England to the Catholic fold convinced many despairing Puritans that it was time to emigrate across the Atlantic to a "New England", where they would establish the true church and a godly community; a "city upon a hill," for all to behold and serve as an inspiration for their brethren back home to rise up and throw out the anti-Christ Charles, purify the church, and restore God's grace upon England. However, before these particular saints came to North America in 1630, ten years earlier, a group of Separatists, known in American folklore as the Pilgrims, established the first Puritan settlement in North America, Plymouth "plantation" on the south shore of Massachusetts Bay.

Plymouth Colony

Not all Puritans believed the Church of England could be redeemed from its corruption and popery. For these particular saints, if the church was beyond further reformation then there was no reason to remain in such a sinful and venal environment. Indeed, the Separatists believed Satan had begun "to sow errors, heresies, and discords" in England. Consequently, in 1608 several hundred Separatists fled to the Netherlands, a country known for its religious toleration and plural-ism. However, within a decade of their arrival, to the Separatists' dismay, the Netherlands proved just as inhospitable as England, for Dutch toleration allowed for not only all Christians, including Catholics, but was a safe haven for European Jews as well. Being devout Calvinists, the Separatists concluded they could no longer live in such an "ungodly" place, fearing that their children in particular would be drawn into and "corrupted" by the surrounding open and tolerant culture. Thus a small group of the more rabid Separatists decided to emigrate to Virginia, obtaining per-mission to do so by a London Company still in desperate need of settlers for their Jamestown colony. Carrying 150 colonists and crew (among them many non-Puritans called "Strangers" by the Pilgrims), the *Mayflower,* in September 1620, sailed from Plymouth, England bound for Virginia. There were originally two ships in the expedition, the *Mayflower* and the *Speedwell,* but the lat-ter leaked so badly that it had to turn back, while the *Mayflower* continued on its voyage to Virginia. Blown off course, the Pilgrims landed not in Virginia but hundreds of miles to the north, on Cape Cod. Here the 102 sur-vivors established the first Puritan community in New England, Plymouth.

Interestingly, these Puritan emigrants had followed French and English mariners, fish-ermen, and fur traders who had visited the New England coast during the summers. In 1607 some English promoters had estab-lished a small settlement at the mouth of the Kennebec River on the Maine coast but Native American hostility and the hard winter demoralized the colonists who eagerly sailed home the following year. Their reports labeled the region frigid and inhospitable. Determined to improve that image, Captain John Smith (of Jamestown fame) explored the coast in 1614, naming it New England because he claimed the climate and soil resembled that of the mother country. Smith published promotional literature, proclaiming that the land was "so planted with Gardens and Corne fields that I would rather live here than any where. Here every man may be mas-ter of his own labour and land and by indus-try grow rich." Such inviting descriptions greatly intrigued Puritans disgruntled with their Anglican rulers. Although "New England" was not the Pilgrims' original des-tination, it was for the thousands who fol-lowed them a decade later.

Before landing the Pilgrim leaders drew up the Mayflower Compact, a response to the non-Puritan single men—the "Strangers" the company had hired—who worried about Pil-grim authority. To assuage these men's fears that they would have no voice in the colony, William Bradford, who had assumed the lead-ership of the Pilgrims, drafted the above document, guaranteeing that all men of the expedition would be subject to "just and equal laws" enacted by representatives of their own choosing. The signers also agreed to "covenant and combine [themselves] together into a civil body politic," thus formally creating the first document of self-government in North Amer-ica. Although much has been made about the importance of the Mayflower Compact, upon closer examination of its immediate purpose and design, it becomes clear that, despite all the subsequent nostalgic ballyhoo about its alleged democratic and egalitarian principles, the compact was simply an agreement made among the colonists to obey the decisions of the majority, an essential precaution in a colony with uncertain legal status.

By the time the Pilgrims landed, hun-dreds of European fishing vessels had been operating along the New England coast for decades, not just fishing for mainly cod, but also landing and trading with the various tribes. Unfortunately these fishermen not only brought trade goods but diseases as well, most notably smallpox, but a more current theory suggests that viral hepatitis, spread by spoiled food, had caused the decimation of the Patuxet and Pokanoket tribes, who lived where the Pilgrims established Plymouth colony. Indeed, so recently had the Indians inhabited the area that when the epidemic hit, the Pilgrims were able to supplement their

Signing of the Mayflower Compact as depicted by J.L.G. Ferris

meager supplies by rummaging Indian graves, homes, and hidden stores of grain. Nonetheless, half of the colonists died, reducing their number to around 50 by the beginning of spring. The remaining colonists only survived through the help of local Indians, notably with the assistance of a Patuxet warrior named Squanto, who with 20 other Indians, had been kidnapped and brought to Spain in 1614 by the English explorer Thomas Hunt, who planned to sell them as slaves.

Rescued by a local priest, Squanto somehow made his way to London, where he learned English. He returned to Massachusetts in 1619 only to find his tribe had been wiped out by the recent epidemic. He served as interpreter for the Pilgrims, taught them where to fish and how to plant corn, and most important helped in forging an alliance with Massasoit, leader of the once-powerful Pokanokets. Massasoit and his surviving fellow tribesmen had come under the dominion of the Narragansetts, to whom they were now paying tribute. Squanto persuaded Massasoit that the

English might prove effective allies against the Narragansetts.

Squanto's and Massasoit's assistance to the Pilgrims was not born of altruism but rather an initiative reflecting shrewd diplomacy. For both Squanto and Massasoit, the survival and liberation of their tribe from the Narragansetts was paramount and if that could be accomplished by helping the English to pull through while forming an alliance with them to ensure both of their continued existence, then the Native Americans were willing to engage in such negotiations. By the time Squanto died from fever in 1622, he had helped secure the future of Plymouth colony. In the autumn of 1621, the Pilgrims invited their Indian allies for a thanksgiving feast to celebrate that year's harvest.

By 1630 Plymouth plantation numbered about 1500. Most important, by that time they had earned enough money to pay off their London creditors, which in turn allowed for their political independence from the company; they were now free to implement their

Mayflower Compact to whatever democratic or restrictive degree they collectively chose. Until 1627 all land was held in common but after that year it was divided among the settlers, who established over the course of the next decade flourishing farms, selling their surplus crops to their fellow Puritans flooding into Massachusetts during the Great Migration. Plymouth survived as an independent colony until 1691 when it became part of its larger, more influential neighbor to north, the Massachusetts Bay Colony. Plymouth demonstrated that New England could be inhabited by Europeans but the key to their longevity was to establish mutually beneficial relations with the local Native American peoples.

The Great Migration and the Establishing of the Massachusetts Bay Colony: The Bible Commonwealth

In 1630, a much larger Puritan migration began, subsequently called the "Great Migration," which saw over a ten-year period, about 14,000 English Puritans come to New England. Although certainly significant for the peopling of New England, this migration did not represent the greatest wave of Englishmen crossing the Atlantic to North America. Indeed, the departure represented only about 30 percent of all the English coming to England's various New World colonies during the 1630s. Surprisingly, many more emigrated to the Chesapeake and the West Indies. Also, the majority of English Puritans remained at home, waiting to see how God would treat both the mother country and the New England experiment. Finally, the Great Migration was brief, as Puritan emigration declined to a trickle after 1640, amounting to 7,000 for the rest of the century. Consequently, colonial New England became populated primarily by the descendants of the great surge of emigrants who came during the 1630s.

Similar to their Separatist counterparts, those Puritans coming to New England during the 1630s sought a distant refuge, where they could live apart from sinners and far from a persecuting government and church. However, unlike the Separatists, this main body of Puritans was not coming because they believed the Church of England was beyond redemption; quite the contrary. Most important, the expedition's leaders wanted neither their peers nor posterity to see them as frightened refugees, fleeing England in search of a safe haven from persecution or God's wrath, which many believed was about to descend upon England because it had become such a sinful place. Rather, the Puritans of the Great Migration, convinced themselves and hopefully others, especially those who stayed behind in the mother country, that they were coming to North America on an "Errand into the Wilderness" for God, to establish a purified church and godly community, which would inspire their countrymen in England to reform and save the nation; rising, if necessary, in righteous rebellion against Charles I and throw out the anti-Christ and deliver England up to the Lord. Once that was accomplished, the Puritans would return to England, having fulfilled their mission for God.

The Puritans believed God held them to far higher standards than other, less godly people yet at the same time they were God's favored people. Indeed, they considered themselves the heirs of the ancient Israelites of the Old Testament. Like their ancient forebears, if they honored God's wishes, He would bestow health and abundance upon them in this world.

But should they deviate from His will in any way, God would punish them as rebels—more severely than He chastised common pagans, like the Indians. Consequently, Puritan authorities did not hesitate to punish or exile people who seemed bent on the devil's work of destroying New England: sinners, dissidents, and witches. Otherwise God would withdraw his favor and permit Satan the temporary triumph of vanquishing New England. At a minimum, retreat across the Atlantic might save the saints from the divine punishments gathering against the wicked English nation. Indeed, as the colony's leader John Winthrop concluded, God had designated New England as "a refuge for manye, whome he meant to save out of the general destruction." At the same time, Winthrop exhorted his fellow colonists to remember their "errand," which was to make Massachusetts a "City upon a Hill [where] the eyes of all people are upon us. So that if we shall deal falsely with our God in this work we have undertaken, and so cause Him to withdraw his present help from us, we shall be made a story and a by-word through the world." In other words, foremost in the Puritan mind should be their mission for God, which was to establish Massachusetts as a beacon of reformed churches and virtuous communities conspicuous to the mother country.

Not all Puritans supported emigration, particularly given its high costs, grave dangers, and uncertain consequences. Moreover, as of 1630, most Englishmen who had migrated to the New World were already dead in either Chesapeake or West Indian graves, and those who had survived had established in those places the most profane societies, at least in the Puritans' view. Many Puritans thus questioned whether New England would turn out any better. As a result, most English Puritans regarded the migration as premature and dangerous, a foolish weakening of the reform cause at home. As Robert Reyce told his friend John Winthrop, "The Church and Commonwelthe heere at home hath more needs of your best abilitie in these dangerous tymes than any remote plantation."

Historians have long debated the Puritans' motivation in coming to North America. Some have asserted that the impetus for migration was purely economic while others have contended that devotion to their faith prevailed over all other factors. More than likely it was a combination of both dynamics. Thus motivating Puritans to come to the New World was the opportunity to serve God while simultaneously improving themselves, which they believed God wanted them to do because such activity pleased Him and he would reward them with salvation for having lived such a virtuous, productive life.

Despite the opposition of many Puritan leaders to migration, in 1630, under the leadership of the genteel lawyer John Winthrop, the Great Migration began. Winthrop, along with a group other wealthy and influential Puritans, formed a joint-stock company, the Massachusetts Bay Company, and to the surprise of many, fairly easily obtained a royal charter. It appeared that by this time, Charles I was more than glad to rid himself and England of the troublesome Puritans, whom, as will be seen later in this chapter, not only challenged him religiously but politically as well through their defense of Parliamentary rights. At the moment Charles simply wanted as many of them gone from England as he could "encourage" by granting them a most generous gift: he allowed them to take their charter, capital, and records to New England, which in effect gave them complete autonomy from the king's authority. Thanks to Charles' haste, the Puritans were able to convert their commercial charter into a self-governing colony 3,000 miles away from bishops and king. Once in Massachusetts, the company leaders established the most radical government in the European world: a quasi-theocratic republic, where Puritan men elected their governor, deputy governor, and legislature (known as the General · Court). Until his death in 1649, whether elected governor or not, John Winthrop remained the single most powerful Puritan in the colony.

Beginning with a settlement named Boston, Winthrop's Puritans established the Massachusetts Bay Colony on the coast north of Plymouth. After a hungry winter in 1630–31, the colonists raised enough food to sustain themselves and the numerous new settlers coming to the colony during the decade. In New England the starving time of adjustment proved far shorter and less deadly than in the Chesapeake.

New England attracted an unusual group of settlers: the sort of skilled and affluent people who ordinarily stayed at home rather than risk their lives in a hazardous transatlantic crossing and the uncertainties of life in the North American wilderness. As noted in the previous chapter, most 17th century English emigrants were poor, young unskilled single men who had limited opportunities in the mother country. Seeking regular meals in the short term and the prospect of land in the long, they indentured themselves to Chesapeake or West Indian planters, with many dying before they had completed their contracts. In sharp contrast, most of the New England colonists could pay their own way and emigrated as family groups. In 1631 a Puritan boasted that the majority of his brethren were "endowed with grace and furnished with means." New Englanders also enjoyed and benefited from a more balanced gender ratio; at mid-century the New England male to female ratio was 6 males for every four females, compared with 4 males for 1 female in the Chesapeake. Such a balanced sex ratio created a more stable society and faster population growth. Moreover, since the New England climate and topography were unsuitable for staple crop production, there was thus no need for laborers in the form of indentured servants. Less than one-fifth of New England emigrants came as indentured servants during the Great Migration. Again, in contrast to the Chesapeake and the West Indies, where the majority of servants came in large numbers as single individuals for sale upon arrival to new masters, almost all of the New England servants came with their Puritan families, generally one or two per family. Over time servant numbers declined in the colony for most New Englanders could not afford to buy replacements. Those servants who came during the Great Migration became free once their term expired and they acquired their own land. By the end of the 17th century, servants amounted to less than 5 percent of the New English population.

With a climate and soil not conducive to cash crop production, the Puritans had little need not just for indentured servants, but for African slaves as well. Although slavery was allowed in New England and some Puritans owed an African slave or two for use as house servants or farmhands, slavery never took hold of the region; not because of Puritan humanity and opposition to human bondage, but rather because New Englanders could not grow in their rocky soil the requisite staple crop. Thus in 1700 less than 2 percent of New England's inhabitants were slaves, compared with 13 percent for Virginia and 78 percent for the English West Indies. Indeed, compared to the rest of the empire, New England possessed an unusually homogeneous colonial population and culture: free, white, transplanted English.

Land and Labor in New England

Since neither African slavery nor indentured servitude informed New England's workforce, the Puritans relied instead on the labor of family members, most notably sons and daughters, to sustain their farms. The comparatively healthy climate and good diet allowed for prodigious Puritan families, on average six to seven children, who all reached maturity. By age 10, boys worked with their fathers in the fields and barn, while daughters assisted their mothers in the house and garden. Most sons did not marry until their middle or late twenties, thus remaining on the family farm, providing continuous, essential labor, mitigating the need for servants or slaves. Moreover, since arable land was scarce in New England and competition for property thus keen, by staying at home many sons were ensured that upon their father's death, they would inherit the estate. They would not have to worry about competing with other males in the community for town lands.

Initially, land in the Massachusetts Bay Colony was owned collectively; that is it belonged to the town community to be distributed among its inhabitants as equitably as town leaders deemed essential for the welfare of the commonweal. The Puritans desired to replicate in New England their homeland lifestyle, and since the majority came from small towns in southeastern England, they brought with them that culture in attempt to transplant in the New World as much of the old and familiar that was possible. They even named the majority of their new hamlets after the villages they had left in England. Since the Puritans were a communally-oriented, corporate people, the New England town came to define their environmental and demographic existence rather than the dispersed settlements and large estates seen in the Chesapeake. In short, Puritan leaders favored relatively compact town settlements to concentrate people sufficiently for defense, to support public schools, to promote mutual supervision of morality, and most important, to sustain a convenient and well-attended local church.

Depending on a town resident's social status, each household received between 10 and 50 acres; the latter amount given to individual's such as ministers or other heads of household's responsible for the village's general well-being. As the 17th century progressed land allotments increased, with some families acquiring between 100 and 200 acres of farmland. Although meager in comparison to some Chesapeake plantations, compared to landholdings in England, New Englanders owned significant amounts of land. During the 17th century over half the men in England possessed no land at all while those that did consider themselves "rich" if they owned 50 acres. New England farmers also owned their land outright, a freehold, while in England most land "owned" by the common folk was actually leased to them by a larger landholder. Also absent from New England was the paying of quitrents, an annual fee for the land charged to landowners either by the proprietor (as will be seen in Pennsylvania) or the crown. More than likely Charles I would have imposed such a payment on the Puritans had they not wisely taken their charter with them to North America.

New England farming was labor-intensive with all work done by hand labor, ranging from the clearing of forests to the building of

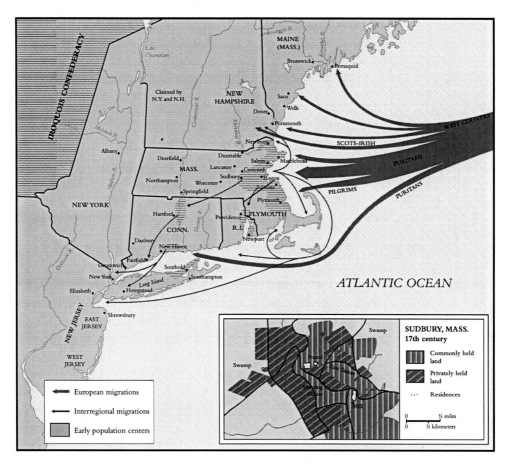

Early New England. Despite some variety among emigrants to New England, the region remained relatively homogeneous and stable with everyday life centered in small towns like Sudbury (located to the west of Boston). Most families lived close to one another in houses clustered around the meetinghouse, in contrast to the decentralized plantations of the South. The privately held farm lots were mixed together as well, so that neighbors worked and lived in close contact with one another.

houses and barns to plowing and planting fields to the harvesting of crops. Such work was more demanding in cold and rocky New England than in the flatter, warmer, and fertile Chesapeake. New England farms also generated little profit; most were subsistence entities and none, as noted above, because of climate and topography, produced the colonial staples in greatest demand in Europe, tobacco or sugar. Instead, New England farmers raised a northern medley of small crops—wheat, rye, maize, potatoes, beans, and garden plants. Because of similar climate, all these foodstuffs (except corn) were grown in England, thus the Puritan farmers did not have a profitable export market to the mother country.

The New England family farm also tended to a modest but essential herd of livestock—commonly two oxen, five other cattle, a horse, two sheep, and six pigs. Because livestock needed grazing land, the New England farm had large pastures and hayfields but small grain fields. The farm families consumed most of their own crops and butchered animals or traded them for the goods and services of local artisans, principally carpenters, blacksmiths, and shoemakers. Since New Englanders were largely self-sufficient subsistence farmers, diversified in their agricultural output and not cultivating staple crops for an external market, they were much less vulnerable, if at all, to the boon-and-bust cycle that affected their Chesapeake cash-crop producing counterparts.

Although economically the New England environment demanded more labor and while returning smaller rewards, in contrast to the Chesapeake, it provided longer and healthier lives. The Chesapeake, with its long, hot, humid summers and low topography, was a natural breeding ground for malaria and dysentery that afflicted the region's inhabitants on a regular basis. By contrast, New England was a northern and hilly land with a short growing season and faster-flowing rivers and streams which were less hospitable environments for such diseases. In New England, people who survived childhood could expect to live to about 70; in the Chesapeake, only a minority survived beyond 45. This healthier, longer-lived, and more gender-balanced society sustained rapid growth through natural increase, whereas in the Chesapeake, the West Indies, and in the other Southern colonies, only continued human imports sustained growth. Beginning with the Great Migration in 1630 through the end of the century, New England received only 21,000 emigrants, a fraction of the total of 120,000 (including

African slaves) that went to the Chesapeake. The West Indies received even more human beings, both black and white, about 190,000 during the 17th century. However, in 1700, New England's total population of 91,000 exceeded the 85,000 whites in the Chesapeake and the 33,000 whites in the English West Indies. Although not the wealthiest English colonial region, New England was the healthiest, the most populous, and the most egalitarian in property distribution.

Although wealth did equal power in New England as it did in the Southern colonies, neither was as concentrated in the hands of the few as was the case in the Southern colonies or the West Indies. In New England towns the larger landholders did dominate local politics, but their property holdings were not significantly more substantial than the local average. Such was true for the region's major seaport cities—Boston, Salem, and Newport—where there congregated a wealthy elite of merchants and professionals, but their collective political power was much less than that of the South's great planters, the result of New England's system of many nearly autonomous towns which saw political power dispersed throughout the countryside. Because New England had the most decentralized and popularly responsive form of government in the English empire, royalists denounced the region as a hotbed of "republicanism." As will be seen later in this chapter, James II attempted to destroy such "radicalism" but in the end the Puritans prevailed, keeping intact their cherished autonomy and representative government.

Puritan Family Life

The two most important institutions for Puritan New Englanders were the church and family. Indeed, Puritans thought of the family as a microcosm of the larger society; "a family is a little Church, and little commonwealth." In short, in the Puritan frame of reference, there was no sharp distinction between home and the wider world. It took a family to establish and maintain a farm and English culture expected all adults to marry and divide their labors into gender-specific responsibilities. Men did the heaviest work, including clearing the land, constructing the house and barn, tending the livestock, harvesting the hay, and cultivating the grain crops. It was incumbent on women to maintain the home and garden, care for the numerous children, make clothing and soap, prepare the meals, and preserve foods. When a husband was away or incapacitated, the wife also had to assume his labors as well, becoming a "deputy husband" until he returned or recovered. In all these roles and expectations the Puritans simply replicated the gender hierarchy of the mother country.

However, the Puritan faith, especially as it evolved in New England, allowed women greater authority, protection, and respect than that enjoyed by their sisters in the Chesapeake or old England. Although there was never any doubt about who was "the man of the house," and such was reinforced my Puritan ministers, the clergy nonetheless took equal pains to remind men to behave kindly and generously relative to Puritan females. Although distrusting of the passion of love because they thought it could lead to impulsiveness and disorder, Puritanism nonetheless preached that love and mutual respect were the foundations of a Christian marriage. Puritans greatly respected the natural affection that grew between a husband and wife over the course of their years together. Indeed, New England Puritans celebrated the sexual expression that took place in marriage. Courting couples were even allowed to lie in bed together with their lower bodies wrapped in an apron, a custom known as "bundling," free to caress and kiss each other. In the words of an old New England ballad: *She is modest, also chaste/ While only bare from neck to waist/ And he of boasted freedom sings/ Of all above her apron strings.*

Unlike in the Chesapeake or in England, where civil or religious authorities rarely intervened in domestic disputes, in New England, both magistrates and ministers and church congregations routinely protected women from insult and abuse. New England women could also more easily obtain divorce when abandoned or when their husbands committed adultery. As one historian of the Puritan family has concluded, the Puritan effort "to create the most God-fearing society," tended "to reduce the near-absolute power that English men by law wielded over their wives."

New England Prosperity: Fish and Ships

The influx of thousands of Puritan newcomers during the Great Migration allowed for the original settlers to prosper by selling to the new emigrants, at inflated prices, the goods they needed to survive in the wilderness. Consequently, when the Great Migration ended in 1640, economic depression set in, causing many in England who had opposed migration, including the quintessential Puritan leader, Oliver Cromwell, to write New England off as "poore, cold, and useless." Determined not to fail, during the 1640s the Puritans innovated, turning to the sea and developing enterprises that transformed their once largely subsistence economy into one of the most diverse and profitable economies in the empire.

The process began during the 1640s, which saw the development of the cod fishing industry by the residents of coastal towns such as Marblehead and Gloucester. Interestingly, their main customers were the Catholic countries of Spain and Portugal to whom the New Englanders sent their better quality cod. The inferior grades of fish went to the West Indies to feed sugar plantation slaves. In 1641, New England fishermen caught 600,000 pounds of fish, a catch that grew tenfold to six million pounds in 1675. By that decade, New England fisheries employed 440 boats and more than 1,000 men.

Few New England fishermen were devout Puritans, even Puritans at all, and because fishing was hard, cold, dirty, dangerous, and poorly-paid work, few "respectable" Puritans (those of the middling-sort) left their farms to catch cod. Thus in New England as in old, fishing attracted hard-drinking and hard-swearing, property-less, desperate men. In contrast to the Puritans, who came primarily from southeastern England, most fishing folk originated in the English West Country and came to New England with previous experience in the waters around Newfoundland. By promoting the fishing trade, the Puritans took their first step toward economic prosperity but at the cost of having to tolerate the presence, albeit limited, of the sort of unsavory and defiant folk whom they had hoped would have stayed in England. Suffice it to say, Puritan magistrates were constantly hauling fishermen into court, charging them with public drunkenness, assault and battery, blasphemy, Sabbath-breaking, and fornication.

Although important to New England's economic resuscitation, cod fishing never became to New England what tobacco had become to the Chesapeake or rice to the Carolinas: a staple that determined prosperity or ruin. New Englanders wisely refrained from

dependency on any one product for their survival, and thus cod was one of many diverse commodities Puritans exported abroad. Although the majority of New England farmers raised crops for family consumption or for local markets, some generated small surpluses, which they sold to merchants to obtain West Indian and Chesapeake produce as well as manufactured goods imported from England. Puritan frugality or austerity was a fine virtue initially, but as successive generations became more prosperous and less pious and less fearful of incurring God's wrath for their desire for a better material life, imports of sugar, rum, tobacco, cloth, tools, and even fineries such as silk, wine, and chocolate, could be found in increasing numbers of Puritan households.

It became readily apparent to New Englanders engaged in the fishing trade that the West Indies represented their best market, not just for cod but potentially for all their products. Thus early on, a close trading partnership emerged between the West Indies and New England. By the 1650s, New England seaport merchants packed and exported agricultural surplus along with lumber and fish, to the West Indies to help feed and house the indentured servants and slaves working the sugar plantations. In return, West Indian planters exchanged molasses, rum, and sugar, some for Puritan consumption but most for carrying to other markets in the Chesapeake or Southern colonies and Europe. Interestingly, as the 17th century progressed and New England's carrying trade accelerated, more New England products found their way to the West Indies than to England, for the mother country did not need what New England produced but did demand West Indian products which New England vessels increasingly began carrying to England. During the 1680s about half of the ships servicing the English Caribbean came from New England.

As noted briefly in Chapter II, by the beginning of the 17th century New Englanders began participating in the Triangular Trade, bringing slaves directly from Africa to the English Caribbean and trading for molasses or sugar and then taking those products back to New England to be processed into rum, which the Yankees would then trade with the West African slavers for slaves. This particular trading system proved very profitable for New Englanders, for it was a network that left out the mother country, benefiting mainly the British West Indies and New England Yankees. In effect 17th century New Englanders and their English counterparts in the West Indies developed in tandem a mutually beneficial and profitable trade in which New England freedom depended on West Indian slavery.

Both the fishing industry and the carrying trade demanded ships, and thus by the close of the 17th century, New Englanders developed their third most lucrative enterprise, ship building. Not only by the end of the century were Yankees building almost all of their own vessels but ships as well for a growing number of English merchants. In many ways, ship building was a natural and logical endeavor for New Englanders, for they possessed in abundance all around them the most important ingredient: dense forests full of high-quality timber. The plethora of trees more than compensated for the higher cost of colonial labor, enabling Yankees to produce ships at half the cost of London shipyards. Between 1674 and 1700, New England shipyards built more than 1200 ships, totaling 75,000 tons. By 1700 Boston alone had 15 shipyards, which produced more ships than the rest of the English colonies combined. Indeed, by the beginning of the 18th century, after London, Boston had

become the second-largest shipbuilding center in the empire. Equally important for New England was the boon to the region's job market that the shipbuilding industry provided. The construction of a 150-ton vessel required up to 200 workers, most of them skilled artisans. Related industries were also stimulated such as sawmills, sail lofts, smithies, iron foundries, rope walks, barrel shops, and taverns. Even New England farmers benefited from the enterprise, providing food for the various workers, victualing the ships, and supplying the timber to build the vessels.

Endowed with quality ships and skilled mariners, New England merchants developed profitable and extensive transatlantic trading networks of growing complexity. Yankee-made ships with Yankee sailors on board were seen in every major port-of-call in the empire, earning incredible profits carrying goods they neither produced nor consumed. New England's aggressive foray into the carrying trade not only brought the area into direct competition with the mother country, but the region also was not performing the preferred colonial function of producing (as was the case in the Southern colonies) profitable agricultural staples for the homeland. Under the policy of mercantilism (to be discussed in greater detail later in this chapter), colonies were at all times to be subordinate to the needs of the mother country, providing essential raw products, which were not only high in value but also ones that could be transformed into finished products for both domestic and overseas consumption. At no time or in any capacity were colonial establishments to be competing with the mother country, which, by engaging in fishing, shipping, and shipbuilding, the New Englanders were precisely doing. In short, by 1700, New England had become a competitor rather than a complement to England's economy.

Suffice it to say, English fishermen, merchants, and shipbuilders protested the activities of these Yankee interlopers as they lost markets to them. As Josiah Child warned the Stuart monarchy, "Of all the American Plantations his Majesty has, none are so apt for the building of Shipping as New England, nor none more comparably so qualified for the breeding of Seamen, not only by reason of the natural industry of the people, but principally by reason of their Cod and Mackeral Fisheries: and in my poor opinion, there is nothing more prejudicial and in prospect more dangerous to any Mother-Kingdom, than the increase of Shipping in her Colonies, Plantations, or Provinces." As will be seen later in this chapter, New England's reputation in the mother country as a den of Puritan heretics and hypocrites was destined to incur not only the wrath of homeland merchants and other economic interests, but the monarchy as well, as both called for an end to New England's virtual autonomy within the empire.

Dissension in the Puritan Ranks

Being so far from England and persecution, compounded by the inherent tensions within the Puritan movement, inevitably led to polarization within the Puritan community. Many Puritans had always had difficulty finding a balance between emotion and intellect, between the individual and the community, between spiritual equality and social hierarchy, between anxiety over salvation and the self-satisfaction of believing one was saved. In New England the absence of oppression intensified division. Their migration to a new and strange land, populated by people they thought of as savages, as well as the pressure of thinking that the whole world was watching them, only increased the Puritans' desire to maintain strict order. Thus, Puritan magistrates rarely hesitated to invoke the power of government to punish sinners, believing it their duty to protect the commonweal from God's wrath if they did not.

Inspired by the Old Testament and reinforced by English common law, the Puritan colonies criminalized immorality, including the breaking of the Sabbath, worshipping idols, blasphemy, and practicing magic. The most sensational cases involved male sex with animals. In 1642 New Haven authorities suspected George Spencer of bestiality when a sow bore a piglet that resembled him! He confessed and they hanged both Spencer and the poor sow. New Haven also tried, convicted, and then executed the unfortunately named Thomas Hogg for the same offense.

The Puritans were especially hostile toward those individuals who publicly promoted an alternative form of Protestantism; that is those who challenged Calvinist orthodoxy. The Puritans had come to New England to establish the true church and their own ideal of a godly society. They were not even remotely interested in promoting or sanctioning religious toleration and pluralism. Puritans denounced liberty of conscience as an invitation to heresy and anarchy, and ultimately to divine anger and punishment. New England was to be a bastion of orthodox Calvinism and those who did not subscribe to such beliefs had better not come to New England. Catholics, Anglicans, Baptists, and especially Quakers were all considered persona non grata and had better stay away. In virtually all the Puritan colonies (except Rhode Island) dissenters were prosecuted, tried, convicted, and exiled. After being banished, those who dared to return risked death.

The greatest disputes and discontents came from within the Puritan community. As noted above without an overbearing church and state to struggle against, Puritans quickly discovered their many differences, ranging from church organization, to who was or who could be saved, to how the Bible should be interpreted, to complete separation from the Church of England. All these issues came to the forefront within a few years of the Puritans' arrival in Massachusetts. The majority of Puritans condemned such ideas as heresy, fearing that any concession to unorthodox notions would surely damn them as individuals while incurring God's retribution upon their commonwealth. The individual who had to deal with such challenges was Governor John Winthrop, who soon realized that his most difficult task in trying to keep community and church unified was to keep his more radical brethren from not only undermining Puritan orthodoxy, but upsetting the body politic as well. Winthrop initially feared that trouble would come from the true believers, who in their zeal would become too doctrinal and oppressive. However, much to his surprise, the most troublesome lot were the unexpected and unforeseen radicals, who emerged early in the Bay Colony, and who wanted to take the Puritan faith and church in completely different directions; down paths that Winthrop and the majority of Puritans believed would destroy the all-important consensus of beliefs and behaviors that had God's blessing.

Roger Williams and Toleration

The first individual to upset Puritan conformity and harmony was Roger Williams, a brilliant and obstinate young minister. No sooner had he landed than he announced, to the dismay of Winthrop and others that he was really a Separatist and would not minister to any congregation unless the commonwealth repudiated all ties to the Church of England. The colony was already suspect in England, for many there saw the Puritans at best only paying lip service to English laws and rejecting the English way of life. Winthrop and other magistrates believed any repudiation of the Church of England, no matter how corrupt its current state, was not only a disavowal of their "errand" but also an act of political suicide. Puritans were certain English royalist officials were looking for any excuse to rescind their charter; they were right as will be seen later in this chapter.

Without a church of his own, Williams began preaching to anyone who would listen to his separatist sermons. Not only did Williams challenge the Puritans' "errand," but also the legitimacy of their charter, claiming that the king had no right to grant land owned by the Indians. He further angered Puritan elders by advocating a strict separation of church and state as well as segregating those who had been saved from those who remained unconverted; that is those Puritans who had yet to have the conversion experience, a sign from God that they had been "saved." The final straw for the Puritan establishment was Williams' call for religious toleration, with each congregation or sect governing itself free from state interference. In effect, Williams was propagating the end of the Bay colony's quasi-theocratic regime. Needless to say, Winthrop and other Puritan leaders believed Williams' ideas to be heretical and when he violated an order to stop preaching his unorthodox views, the magistrates decided to ship him immediately to England, where he might be imprisoned or even executed for his religious notions. Winthrop, however, saved Williams from possible death by warning him of his potential fate, giving him time to flee to Narragansett Bay, which was outside of Massachusetts Bay's jurisdiction. Some of Williams' faithful followed him to the area where they established the new colony of Rhode Island, which received a royal charter in 1644. The colony soon became a refuge for dissenters of all sorts, although the Puritans of Massachusetts referred to it as "the sewer of New England." Although despising their wayward brethren who had fled to Rhode Island, dismissing them as a den of heretics, the colony nonetheless provided Massachusetts and later Connecticut and New Haven (both founded by dissenters but not for the same reasons that Williams had established Rhode Island), with a place to where they could banish their nonconformists. In effect, Rhode Island became a "dumping ground" for discontents who would otherwise have festered in their midst, thus helping Massachusetts, Connecticut, New Haven to maintain orthodoxy.

Anne Hutchinson and the Equality of Believers

No sooner did Winthrop and the orthodox Puritans of the Bay Colony rid themselves of Williams, than an even more controversial and divisive individual emerged in the form of Anne Hutchinson, whose religious beliefs were even more radical than those of Williams. Hutchinson was just over 40 when she, her husband, and their 12 children followed the Reverend John Cotton from England to Massachusetts Bay. Cotton was a popular preacher who believed that the doctrine of predestination defined the essence of Puritanism. Hutchison pushed that tenet to its logical, if disturbing conclusion. She claimed that she had experienced several direct revelations from God, one telling her to follow Cotton to Boston. Hutchinson shared her revelation and other notions with her fellow Puritans by holding informal Bible discussion meetings at her Boston home. At these sessions Hutchinson challenged the Puritan precept of "preparation," by proclaiming that if God had truly chosen those whom he would save, it was unnecessary for such individuals to prepare themselves for saving grace by leading sin-free lives. To Hutchinson, neither good behavior nor prosperity, were reliable signs that one had been saved. It was not that Hutchinson was advocating any sort of nihilism; she simply believed that her neighbors were deluding themselves into thinking that their good works would save them. Hence, she accused them of the heresy of Arminiansim. By claiming that the Holy Spirit spoke directly to her, Hutchinson opened herself up to charges of another heresy, antinomianism, which asserted that faith alone was all that was necessary for salvation. Since she had obviously been saved because of her revelations, Hutchinson believed she was exempt from having to adhere to Puritan social or religious strictures.

To the magistrates' despair, Hutchinson's parlor Bible studies attracted a significant number of attendees and genuine followers. Her popularity and self-righteousness emboldened her to claim that certain ministers were "fakirs;" that is, in her view, they were unconverted. Needless to say, such an accusation did not sit kindly with either the clergy or secular authorities who began an intensive campaign against her and her allies. Indeed so powerful and influential had Hutchinson become, that by the time of the 1637 gubernatorial election, opposition leaders moved the election site out of Boston to ensure the return of John Winthrop to that position. Many were certain that had they not ordered a change of venue, whomever candidate Hutchinson supported would win. Winthrop had opposed Hutchinson's radicalism from the beginning but was not governor at the time of her ascendancy to such influence. Winthrop reclaimed the governorship and from the moment he took office he made the censuring of Anne Hutchinson his first priority of business.

Winthrop and company began their assault on Hutchinson by banishing from Massachusetts some of her strongest ministerial allies. With such individuals gone there was no one left strong enough to buffer Hutchinson from the Puritan wrath about descend down upon her. She was put on trial for slandering the ministry. Although certainly unduly critical at times of some Puritan clergymen, she probably would have been acquitted had she not claimed that God had revealed to her that he would punish her persecutors. Apparently at this precise moment in the history of the Bay Colony, many of Hutchinson's followers believed that they were truly following a saint, even though the veneration of the saints was not part of Puritan orthodoxy. Her announcement changed the whole purpose of her trial; slander was bad enough but to assert that in effect God spoke directly to her, such a proclamation to orthodox Puritans was plain heresy, for the Puritans believed divine revelations had stopped during biblical times. Hutchinson was convicted of heresy and ordered to leave the colony. Followed by 80 families, she and her family found temporary refuge in Roger William's Rhode Island. Eventually Hutchinson moved to the Dutch colony of New Netherland, where she was killed in an Indian war.

What so alarmed the Puritan establishment was that such heresy had come out of the mind and mouth of a woman, which in their view no woman, unless she was possessed by the devil, would dare speak about let alone challenge the sanctity of Puritan orthodoxy.

Indeed, Winthrop was so nonplussed by Hutchinson's assertions, that he suggested that she might be a witch. Without any evidence at all of sexual misconduct, ministers claimed that Hutchinson's words and actions as well as those of her followers reflected women motivated by lust and that unless they were punished, it would lead to communal living, open sex, and the repudiation of marriage. Neither Anne Hutchinson nor any of her followers, male or female, were motivated by carnal pleasures; rather, their banishment revealed the deeper fissures within the Puritan community beginning to come to the surface, caused by the determination of men like Winthrop and others to keep their saintly commonwealth rigidly controlled at all times.

In the mind of men like John Winthrop, if the radicalism of an Anne Hutchinson was allowed, God would surely be displeased and would no doubt punish not just the heretics such as Hutchinson but the whole community as well. What is perhaps most revealing about the Hutchinson controversy as well as that caused by Roger Williams, was that once in the New World, even the most devout Puritans saw a wilderness not just for their material taking, but a place where they would be free to express themselves without fear of reprisal. Unfortunately for both Hutchinson and Williams, such a notion proved delusional; the arm of Puritan authority was even longer than that of England's in the Bay Colony. In both instances, Winthrop and his fellow magistrates made it clear that all had to obey the brand of Puritanism they had established in Massachusetts; that dissent in any form would not be tolerated and those who questioned the sanctity of those tenets with their radical notions would be banished accordingly. Thus one of the great paradoxes or contradictions of New England Puritanism is the assertion that the Puritans came to North America seeking religious freedom, yes, true, but exclusively *for themselves*. Massachusetts was never to become a refuge for anyone but the right sort of Puritan; certainly not for Separatists such as Williams or "heretics" such as Anne Hutchinson. They wanted the liberty to follow their own religion but actively denied that opportunity to others, even among their own "kind." Puritans insisted on their right to keep out nonbelievers—anyone who did not embrace their brand or Calvinism. John Winthrop stated his colony's policy succinctly: "No man hath the right to come into us without our consent."

Massachusetts' Puritan leaders were certain that the criticism of dissidents would ruin the colony's reputation at home, for the presence of nonconformists' represented in the orthodox mind, a failure to create the inspirational, godly commonwealth that all English Puritans and citizens in general were to behold and emulate. That was the whole reason for the Bay Colony's existence. However, news of such suppression and ostracism played into the hands of English critics, who denounced New England as a land of religious hypocrites, seditious Separatists, and petty despots. In 1652, an English Puritan warned his colonial friends that, "It doth not a little grieve my spirit to hear what sad things are reported daily of your tyranny and persecutions in New England. . . . These rigid ways have laid you very low in the hearts of the saints, while the enemies [the Anglicans] of the Lord were gloating."

Such chastisement from English Puritans surprised and dismayed Massachusetts Puritans. Indeed, by mid-century a strain had developed in the transatlantic relationship as English Puritans began to favor religious toleration for all Protestants; a policy New England

Puritans would never accept no matter how politically and religiously necessary it might be for the welfare of all English subjects, regardless of their location. This was precisely what occurred in the aftermath of the English Civil War, and New England Puritans, instead of rejoicing Parliament's victory over the crown and the eventual execution of Charles I, felt betrayed by the very English Puritans who had led the crusade against Charles' autocracy and popery. Instead of initiating the final cleansing of the Anglican Church, which New England Puritans believed would occur once Charles was gone, English Puritans, led by Oliver Cromwell, not only left the Anglican Church as it was, but proceeded to grant religious toleration to all English Protestants, no matter how radical or unorthodox their theology might be. As a result, New England Puritans concluded that they had failed in their "errand" for God and thus were now stranded and forsaken in the New World. If New England was now to become their permanent home then it was time to turn away from England and create a way of life that still honored God but simultaneously enhanced their material well being, which as noted above, the Puritans did by developing the fishing, shipping, and ship building industries. Believing they had been abandoned by England also helped accelerate the transformation from Puritan to Yankee. However, none of these momentous changes would have occurred in New England without the English Civil War of the 1640s and the ensuing Cromwellian Protectorate and dictatorship of the 1650s.

England in Turmoil

It was only a matter of time before the Stuart monarchy would find itself in conflict with Parliament. Beginning with James I and cresting during the reign of his son Charles I, tensions had been developing between the two institutions. Causing the antagonisms and eventual polarization were the two overlapping issues of sovereignty and religion. As noted earlier in this chapter, both James and Charles Stuart were high-church Anglicans and vigorously opposed any concessions to Puritanism. Moreover, both monarchs believed in absolutism and tried to impose such a system of government on a most recalcitrant Parliament. Although James I believed in limited checks on his power, his son Charles believed he was accountable to no one but God, and thus believed he had the "right" to rule England without Parliament's participation. Moreover, Charles was determined to impose religious conformity within England and Scotland—that of high-church Anglicanism, which many Englishmen, especially the Puritans, believed was code for the ultimate return to Catholicism. In 1630 Charles I marched troops into Parliament and dissolved it, and for the next ten years ruled England as an autocrat.

In the meantime, the Archbishop of Canterbury, William Laud, moved the Church of England increasingly toward a visibly more Catholic orientation in ceremony, liturgy, and structure, which of course infuriated the Puritans, many of whom were also vocal and powerful members of Parliament. Charles responded heavy-handedly to all opposition to him, but was especially harsh on the Puritans. In 1640, largely as a result of attempting to force the Presbyterian Scots to accept his religious reforms, the Scots revolted, leaving Charles no choice but to summon Parliament in order to raise money to put down the Scottish rebellion.

Parliament convened but before they would vote Charles the funds for war, they issued a Petition of Right, which henceforth Charles had to agree to abide by if he hoped to repel the invading Scots. The petition reasserted those freedoms Englishmen held dear, including no taxation except by act of Parliament, no arbitrary arrests or imprisonment, and no quartering of soldiers in private homes—all rights Charles had violated with impunity during his ten-year autocracy. Charles agreed to "consider" the petition, and that promise for the moment was good enough for Parliament and the funds requested by Charles to put down the Scottish rebellion were given. However, Charles had no intention of accepting any limits on his powers, especially ones dictated to him by Parliament. For two years Charles equivocated and procrastinated on signing the Petition of Right. Finally, Parliament's patience wore thin and when it became clear Charles had no intention of signing the document, Parliament rebelled in June 1642. For the next five years, bloody civil war engulfed England.

From the moment the conflict began, those Englishmen who sided with Parliament became rebels, and rebels carried the stigma of treason. The habit of loyalty to God and king remained strong and Parliament had the difficult task of building the machinery of war upon unconstitutional foundations and of convincing a doubtful nation that God and justice were on its side. Initially it appeared that God favored Charles, whose royalist forces inflicted several crushing defeats on Parliament's unorganized, undisciplined, and untrained army. However, the right man at the right time emerged to save Parliament from defeat in the form of the fanatical Puritan MP, Oliver Cromwell, who took charge of the army and in short time forged the New Model Army, and infused it with a passionate devotion to cause and victory. At the decisive Battle of

Naseby in the summer of 1645, the New Model Army routed Charles' forces. For the next two years, Charles was more or less a king in exile in his own country, still monarch but without any real power.

In 1647 the military, led by Cromwell took control of the government by coup d'etat. Charles made one more attempt at regaining power by rallying to his cause fellow Scots, who suddenly remembered that, after all, he was a Stuart and a Scotsman, and conservative Parliamentarians who had been driven out of Parliament by the extremists and the military. In August 1648 at the battle of Preston Pans, Parliament's soldiers of righteousness routed Charles forces. In the year 1648–49 the tempo of constitutional change attained revolutionary proportions. In January 1649 the House of Commons declared itself to "have the supreme power in this nation," and whatsoever it enacted "hath the force of law, although the consent of the king or the House of Peers [Lords] be not had thereunto." The newly sovereign House of Commons then declared kingship to be "unnecessary, burdensome, and dangerous," and thus ordered the execution of Charles I, which was carried out on Sunday, January 30, 1649. A week later the House of Lords disappeared from England's body politic, joining the episcopacy of the Church of England, which had been abolished three years earlier.

Charles' execution and the inability of the House of Commons to govern England effectively eventually brought to power Oliver Cromwell, who although wisely granting religious toleration to all Protestants but not "papists," imposed on England a moralistic military dictatorship. From 1649 to 1660 England officially became a Puritan republic, although for much of that time Cromwell dictated national policy. In 1654 Cromwell declared England to be a Commonwealth and himself Lord Protector. As Cromwell's regime became more arbitrary and oppressive, increasing numbers of Englishmen longed for the restoration of the ancient constitution—king in Parliament—which they believed would safeguard property and assure to "the natural rulers of society"—the aristocracy and gentry—their control of local and national government. In 1658 Cromwell died and when his son and successor proved an inept leader, Parliament, with the military's blessing, restored the monarchy in the form of Charles II, Charles I's son, who had been in safe exile in France since the civil war began. In the same room at Whitehall where his father had waited eleven years before to walk out upon the scaffold, Charles II was acclaimed as monarch by Parliament. King, Lords, and Commons were united in their determination to turn back the clock to 1641. The skeletons of war, rebellion, and regicide were firmly and securely shut into the closet of forgetfulness. All in attendance at the coronation pretended that 20 years of treason never existed. Two decades of civil war and Cromwellian dictatorship became an Interregnum, a limbo between periods of legality. With peace and stability at home, England could once again devote attention and energy to expanding and regulating its North American empire.

New Colonies, New Patterns

In the first half of the 17th century, the English developed two distinct clusters of settlements along the Atlantic seaboard: the Chesapeake to the South and New England to the north. Until the 1660 Restoration, England had neglected the area in between Virginia and

Maryland and the Massachusetts Bay Colony, the Mid-Atlantic coast. Its temperate climate proved far healthier than both the Chesapeake and New England, and its fertile soil was especially promising for cultivating grain, raising livestock, and reproducing people. The region also possessed three navigable rivers that reached deep into the interior: the Susquehanna, Delaware, and Hudson. English dismissal of the area allowed the Dutch and Swedes to establish their own small colonies: New Netherland in the Hudson Valley and New Sweden in the Delaware Valley. Although upset by this "usurpation" of land they believed belonged to them, until after the Restoration there was little England could do, beset as it was with two decades of civil and religious strife. Moreover, the Dutch and Swedes were fellow Protestants and allies in the European wars of religion during the early 17th century— The Thirty Years' War, 1618–1648.

However, from 1660 to the end of the century, as the geopolitics of both Europe and North America changed and as the English grew in power and ambition, the later Stuarts, Charles II and his brother, James, Duke of York, pursued aggressive expansionist policies. They intended to not only extend English presence in North America, but in the process, augment the crown's preeminence at home as well. Along the way they also hoped to consolidate the empire as much as was possible under royal control. The Stuart brothers also possessed a violent envy of Dutch wealth, from whom they also learned of the connection between overseas colonies, commercial expansion, and national power. By conquering New Netherland, Charles and James meant to strengthen England's commerce by weakening its principal rival, the Dutch empire. The acquisition of New Netherland (which had annexed New Sweden) would also end the

geographical void between the Chesapeake and New England, promoting their mutual defense against other empires and the Indians. Finally a conquest also promised increased crown control over its own fractious colonies.

Prior to the Restoration, unlike their Spanish or French counterparts, the English monarch exercised little power over his colonists. Moreover, during the early 17th century the English crown simply did not have the financial resources to launch and administer distant colonies. Relying on the proprietary or company system of colonization also affected the political relationship between colonists and the English government, initially indirectly but overtime most discernibly. The colonists compelled their distant and weak proprietors to share political power. The proprietors appointed the governor and council, but men of property elected an assembly with power over finances. Throughout the empire, propertied Englishmen believed legislative control over taxation to be their most fundamental liberty. Proprietors were not overjoyed at having to relinquish so much power to colonial assemblies but they had little choice if they hoped to attract and retain men of means, who were essential to the colony's economic development and thus critical to the proprietor's revenues.

By the time of the Restoration, the liabilities of the proprietary system had become apparent to the new Stuart regime which had greater imperial ambitions. Noting increasing colonial population growth and prosperity, imperial officials sought tighter control, the better to regulate and tax colonial commerce. Officials also worried that rival European powers might attempt to take possession of England's scattered, distinct, fractious, but wealthy North American colonies. Indeed, the colonial arrangement seemed ripe for foreign picking; for many separate surrenders rather than for collective defense. In a showdown with another empire, one English colony could appeal for help from the others, but because of already bitter inter-colonial rivalry, assistance was unlikely. Many imperial bureaucrats thus concluded that the proprietary colonies should first be converted into royal colonies and then consolidated into an overarching government like the Spanish viceroyalty of New Spain. During the second half of the 17th century, crown officials gradually converted a few proprietary colonies into royal colonies. This transformation simply meant that the king, rather than the proprietor, appointed the governor and council, for the crown felt obliged to retain the elected assemblies. The crown's first initiatives in this direction occurred in those colonies producing the greatest revenues: tobacco-rich Virginia and the sugar colonies of Barbados, the Leeward Islands, and Jamaica. As will be seen the crown was much slower to reorganize the New England colonies not only because they lacked a lucrative staple beneficial to royal revenue, but also because they knew the region's Puritan majority would make any imperial attempt to command the saints' greater obedience a costly and difficult endeavor.

The Dutch Empire

The Dutch colony on the Hudson River was actually nothing more than a frontier trading post and a relatively minor enterprise compared to the rest of the Netherlands' colonial possessions, which by the middle of the 17th century literally spanned the globe. Dutch ascendancy to both military and economic might was not only remarkably rapid but out of all proportion to its confined geography and small population of 1.5 million (compared with 5 million English and 20 million French). By the early 17th century the Netherlands had become the nexus of northern European commerce, dominating the carrying trade of Northern and Western Europe, the North Sea fisheries, and Arctic whaling. In 1670 the Dutch employed 120,000 sailors on vessels totaling 568,000 tons—more than the combined shipping of Spain, France, and England. By the middle of the 17th century, the great Dutch city of Amsterdam (and its port of Rotterdam), had come the center of European shipping, banking, insurance, printing, and the textile industries.

Contributing significantly to Dutch commercial preeminence was the nation's liberal government, which promoted and guaranteed all citizens intellectual freedom and religious toleration; such sagacity was unique in 17th century Europe. While the Netherlands' neighbors proceeded down the paths of centralized, authoritarian monarchies, the Dutch opted for a federal republic dominated by wealthy merchants and rural aristocrats. The seven provinces comprising the Dutch federation enjoyed domestic autonomy but the most populous and prosperous province, Holland, usually determined the nation's military and foreign policies. The Netherlands also became the safest haven in Europe for a multitude of both religious and intellectual refugees. While the other European powers forced religious conformity upon their countrymen, causing dissidents to flee from persecution, many found safety in the Netherlands, as the Dutch welcomed all such outcasts—Jews, Catholics, and Huguenots, benefiting from their talents and investments. European intellectuals also gravitated to Amsterdam because the Dutch were more open to new ideas, especially if they helped to improve both the quality and quantity of Dutch life. The great 17th century philosophers Rene Descartes, John Locke, and Benedict de Spinoza all emigrated to escape censorship in their own countries.

Beginning in the 1620s and over the course of the next 30 years, the Dutch embarked on aggressive overseas expansionist agenda, often engaging in war against either the Spanish or Portuguese in their pursuit of empire. In the Far East the Dutch took from the Portuguese Indonesia and Sri Lanka, allowing them to supplant the Portuguese as the primary carriers of the especially valuable spice and silk trade from Asia to Europe. To protect that trade route, in 1652, the Dutch established a small colony at the Cape of Good Hope at the southern tip of Africa, the future Capetown, South Africa. However, the most lucrative enterprise the Dutch usurped from the Portuguese was the export of sugar from New World plantations and the transportation of slaves from West Africa to cultivate that sugar. In 1637 the Dutch captured Elmina Castle, the principal Portuguese fortified trading post on the west coast of Africa. Beginning in 1640 and for the next 20 years the majority of the slaves sent to the Americas arrived on Dutch slave ships. As noted in Chapter II, in the 1630s the Dutch seized the northeastern sugar production area of Portuguese Brazil and as a result, by 1650, the Dutch were refining most of the sugar consumed in Europe. To prosecute their attacks and build their empire, the Dutch developed the most formidable fleet of warships in Europe. In the navy's most spectacular raid, a Dutch flotilla, led by Holland's most legendary privateer, Piet Heyn, intercepted and captured the entire Spanish treasure fleet homeward bound from the Caribbean in 1627. The loss of the ships and 200,000 pounds of silver virtually bankrupted the Spanish crown while enormously enriching the Dutch.

However, the Dutch spread themselves too thin in their haste to become a great European and imperial power. Their European rivals watched with envy and noted that commerce, colonies, naval might, and national wealth were all interrelated. By mid-century, the Dutch faced attacks from their former allies against Spain: the French and the English. Their targets included the Dutch colony along the Hudson River, New Netherland, which was a minor operation on the fringes of an overextended empire with wealthier assets and higher priorities to defend elsewhere in the world.

From New Netherland to New York

The Atlantic and North America also attracted the Dutch, although never as strongly as did the East Indies. In 1609, Henry Hudson, an Englishmen in Dutch service, sailed up what the Dutch called the North River (the English renamed it the Hudson) and claimed the whole area for the Netherlands. New Netherland extended from the trading town of Albany (which 17th century ships could ascend for 160 miles, a greater distance than was possible on any other river on the Atlantic seaboard), down the Hudson River to the island city of New Amsterdam (the future New York City). In 1614, Lutheran refugees from Amsterdam built a fort near modern Albany to trade with the Mahicans and Iroquois for furs but they did not occupy the site on a year-round basis. In 1621, the Netherlands' governing body, the States General granted a charter to a group of wealthy burghers to form the Dutch West India Company, giving it jurisdiction and monopolistic commercial control over all Dutch interests and enterprises in the

New World. Thus colonizing New Netherland in North America became the company's responsibility. The first permanent settlers arrived in 1624, and dispersed throughout the 160 mile-long river valley. The Company's plan was to first fortify the river's entrance at New Amsterdam, which became the colony's most populated town, major seaport, and government headquarters. In the lower Hudson valley, the Company promoted agricultural development, awarding huge tracts of land to individuals called "patroons." The company hoped these vast estates would produce grains, cattle, and lumber to supply the fur traders at Fort Orange (Albany) as well as ship such goods to the West Indies to feed the slaves on the sugar plantations. In effect, New Netherland became a bifurcated colony with a small fur trading outpost upriver and larger agricultural settlements on the lower river.

This interesting system of settlement led to different Indian policies in the two halves of the valley. Upriver the Dutch were too few and too dependent on trade to intimidate their native neighbors, the formidable Iroquois Five Nations (primarily the nearby Mohawk). Terrifying as enemies but invaluable as trading partners, the Iroquois determined the success or failure of the trading post. Fort Orange became as much a Mohawk as a Dutch asset. The Dutch thus forged a commercial alliance with the Iroquois, who occupied a strategic position between the coast and the interior, and through Dutch hands the Iroquois sought to channel their furs.

The Dutch did not extend the respect shown for the Iroquois to the downriver Algonquian-speaking bands. Compared with the Iroquois, the Algonquians of the lower Hudson contributed little to the fur trade and their warriors were fewer and less well supplied with firearms. Downriver Dutch, who were mostly farmers, regarded the Algonquians as a nuisance, to be removed as quickly as possible. On the lower Hudson the Dutch inherent ethnocentrism became readily apparent, while such sentiments had to be restrained when dealing with the Iroquois.

Once armed by the Dutch, the Iroquois

The arrival of Hendrick Hudson in the bay of New York, September 12, 1609. Popular Graphic Arts Collection, Library of Congress.

engaged in a series of military adventures known as the Beaver Wars. They invaded the territories of neighboring tribes, and in the late 1640s they attacked and dispersed the Hurons, who had long controlled the flow of furs from the Great Lakes to the French in Montreal. As a result of these wars, the Dutch trading system extended deep into the continent's interior. Assisted by the Iroquois, the Dutch on the lower Hudson in a series of brutal wars beginning in the 1640s, succeeded in driving the Algonquians out of the area, further into the interior, opening the way for further Dutch expansion. In 1655 the Dutch succeeded in overwhelming a small Swedish colony on the lower Delaware River, incorporating that region into their sphere of influence as well.

Dutch Colonists

Although extending to all who came to New Netherland religious toleration (even to Jews and Catholics), the West India company was not nearly as magnanimous when it came to the colony's governance. Dutch republicanism remained at home. The Company appointed the governor and an advisory council of leading colonists but did not allow for an elected assembly. Governors rarely consulted the council and were legendary for being contentious, arbitrary, and mostly incompetent; again reflecting that in the grand scheme of the Dutch empire, New Netherland persisted to be an afterthought. Although governed by petty despots, the Company nonetheless welcomed all religious dissenters from both Europe and other North American colonies. Officially, only the Calvinist Dutch Reformed Church could hold public services, but New Amsterdam burghers looked the other way as "private meetings" for worship proliferated throughout

the settlement among the mix of Puritans, Quakers, Lutherans, and Jews. Indeed, Jewish colonists enjoyed more freedom in New Netherland than in any other colony. Thanks primarily to religious toleration, New Netherland became the most religiously and ethnically diverse colony in North America. Indeed, the Dutch were a minority in their own colony. New Netherland attracted emigrants from Belgium (Flemish and Walloons), France (Huguenots), Scandinavia, and especially Germany. The non-Dutch whites composed nearly one-half of New Netherland colonists. Many had migrated first to Holland to live and work but then were recruited by the Company to come to New Netherland. As in New England, the emigrants came as family groups of modest means of farmer or artisan status; few were unmarried young men and even fewer were indentured servants. One-fifth of the New Netherlanders were Puritan dissenters who relocated from New England to settle on Long Island. About one-tenth of the population were enslaved Africans, mostly owned by the Dutch West India Company and residents of New Amsterdam, where they constructed wharves and buildings and served as longshoremen. The company rewarded favored slaves with a status called "half-freedom," which permitted free movement within the colony and the right to marry and own private property in return for an annual payment in grain, furs, or wampum.

Despite an appealing location and a comparatively tolerant society, the Dutch colony failed to attract sufficient settlers to compete with its ever-expanding English neighbors. In 1660 New Netherland had only 5,000 inhabitants—better than the 3,000 in New France, but far behind the 25,000 in the Chesapeake and the 33,000 in New England.

Why did New Netherland fail as a viable colonial enterprise? In part, the colony had difficulty attracting settlers because of its reputation for arbitrary government and Indian wars. In addition, the vast and rich Dutch empire, especially its colonies of Ceylon, the East Indies, and Brazil, were much more alluring to Dutch emigrants than the Hudson River valley. However, the main reason for New Netherland's failure to thrive was that the mother country simply had a much smaller pool of potential colonists with fewer incentives to leave, compared with the more numerous and discontented English. Blessed with a booming economy and the highest standard of living in 17th century Europe, the Dutch had much less reason to emigrate than their English counterparts. Moreover, the Dutch were not suffering through any painful economic transition or bitter religious strife. The Dutch also lacked the masses of roaming poor who became indentured servants in the English tobacco and sugar colonies in the Chesapeake and West Indies. Finally, the tolerant Netherlands did not generate a disaffected religious minority such as the Puritans who founded New England.

Beginning in the early 1650s with Oliver Cromwell and over the course of the next two decades, England and the Netherlands fought three wars—1652–54, 1664–67, and 1672–4, to determine commercial primacy worldwide. Primarily naval engagements and fought to a draw, England in the end nonetheless prevailed, supplanting the Dutch as the greatest naval and trading power in the world; a title England held for over two hundred years. It was during the Second Dutch War, 1664–1667, that England conquered New Netherland. Charles II's objective in seizing New Netherland was to eliminate New Amsterdam as a base for Dutch shippers who traded with Virginia, to capture the valuable fur trade of the upper Hudson, to intimidate the wayward

Puritans, and to erase New Netherland as an obstruction between the Chesapeake and New England colonies. Charles used the pretext that New Netherland obtruded on land previously explored and claimed by England. But as the Duke of Albermarle stated bluntly, "What matters this or that reason? What we want is more of the trade the Dutch now have."

Thus in 1664 an English fleet sailed into Manhattan harbor and forced the surrender of New Amsterdam without firing a shot. Aided by Puritans from Long Island, the English forces appeared to have the upper hand and thus the Dutch believed resistance would be futile. The next year, England declared war on the Netherlands, a conflict that lasted until 1667. Only five years of peace transpired before a third and final war broke out. These Anglo-Dutch wars marked the beginning of the end of Dutch commercial supremacy and England's ascendancy.

Charles named his brother James, Duke of York, proprietor of New Amsterdam. James renamed it New York in his honor; New Amsterdam became New York City and the upper Hudson trading posts of Beverwyck and Fort Orange became known as Albany. Victory secured to the English the entire Atlantic seaboard between Florida and Acadia. Otherwise the English government did little to disturb the existing order, preferring simply to reap the benefits of this profitable and dynamic colony. With settlers of various ethnic backgrounds, speaking many different languages and accommodating a wide range of religious sects, New York became the most heterogeneous colony in North America. In 1674 the colonists were granted the status of English subjects, and in 1683, after persistent appeals, James approved the creation of a representative assembly. The Delaware Valley communities of mostly Swedes and Finns, with a spattering of Germans and Dutch, became the proprietary colony of New Jersey in 1665. New Jersey was initially owned by Sir George Carteret and Lord John Berkeley, but a consortium of wealthy Quakers led by William Penn purchased a portion of the colony 1676 to provide a safe haven for their persecuted brethren.

William Penn and the "Holy Experiment" of Pennsylvania

As noted above, in 1676 a group of wealthy Quakers, known as "Weighty Friends" in Quaker parlance, purchased a portion of New Jersey (West New Jersey) as a prelude to eventually establishing a full-fledged Quaker refuge in North America. Even more so than the Puritans before them, the Quakers became one of the most persecuted Protestant sects in Restoration England, which saw not only the return of the monarchy but concomitantly a resurgence of an even more intense and oppressive Anglicanism. Along with English Catholics, the Quakers became one of the Church's favorite targets for proscription. After several decades of enduring persecution, the Quakers, in the early 1680s, led by William Penn finally concluded that in order to save their followers from Anglican scorn and punishment, that it was time to leave England and establish a "holy experiment" in North America; "an example and standard to the nations" of the world of an ideal Christian community.

Similar to the New England Puritans, who believed their colony of Massachusetts was a special place, Penn referred to Pennsylvania in equally righteous terms: it was a "holy experiment." However, in stark contrast to Puritan Massachusetts, Pennsylvania had no tax-supported established church, not even for Friends. Penn certainly wanted his colony first and foremost to be a refuge for persecuted Quakers but he spoke in universalistic terms, of "a free colony for all Mankind that should go hither." Penn thus welcomed (much to the dismay of many Friends) both non-Quakers and non-Britons, promising all equal rights and opportunities.

The Quaker Faith

Founded in 1640 by George Fox, The Society of Friends (derisively named Quakers because they allegedly shook or trembled when experiencing a union with the Lord), was just one of the many sects that emerged in England after the dismantling of the Church of England soon after Charles I' execution. The son of a humble weaver with only the bare rudiments of formal education, Fox nonetheless became one of England's most legendary religious voices and leaders. Fox appealed to so many of the religious and spiritually disillusioned because he rediscovered in the Christian faith what the Protestant reformation had lost—its inner core of mysticism. The essence of Fox's belief was that people's souls communed directly with God, who revealed Himself to the faithful through an "Inner Light," which was the Holy Spirit, who potentially dwelled within every person. How was one to discover their Inner Light and thus find and know God? Fox asserted that the awakening of this Spirit could come about only by a mystical experience, by an emotional and spiritual exchange and ultimate union between believer and God. Anyone truly awakened by that Spirit could thereafter live in sanctity, for he or she was filled with God's living grace and constant love.

The Artist who sketched this Quaker meeting called attention to one of that sect's most controversial practices by placing the woman at the center of his composition. Women were allowed to speak in Quaker worship services and to preach and proselytize at public gatherings of non-Quakers. The Puritans roundly condemned this liberty as contrary to the teachings of St. Paul.

The Quakers took to an extreme the Puritan condemnation of elaborate ritual and church hierarchy, rejecting all sacraments, liturgies, and paid intermediaries—ministers as well as bishops—for all interfered with the direct communion between the human soul and God. Renouncing formalized worship of any sort, including prayers and sermons, Quakers met together as spiritual equals and sat silently until the divine spirit inspired someone, anyone, to speak. A Quaker service thus consisted of potentially long periods of silence interspersed with brief fits—the "quaking"—of testimony or revelation as a member or several members simultaneously experienced that mystical awakening of their Inner Light. Meetings often lasted several hours and ended when no one felt further compelled to speak.

Although professing to be Christians, the Quakers attenuated the concepts of original sin and salvation through Christ; their Jesus was a living symbol of salvation but not a necessary agent, and he certainly did not rank on a Trinitarian par with God. This notion led more orthodox Christians to accuse, condemn, and promote the persecution of Quakers for being Unitarians—those who believed in the humanity of Jesus rather than his divinity, and thus denying that God the Father, Jesus the Son, and the Holy Spirit were one sacred personage. Although the charge was not completely true, the Quakers' Christ was nonetheless not part of the same trinity of both Catholic and Protestant orthodoxy. Moreover, the Quaker's God was not the wrathful, vengeful, omnipotent Jehovah of the Old Testament, which the Puritans claimed He was because of mankind's inherent depravity and sinfulness. To Quakers, since man was inherently good or at least predisposed to do good rather than evil, especially after accepting God's grace, God must be a forgiving and loving deity who expected the best, not the worst, from mankind, his most perfect creation.

Quakers also believed they were to be practicing, activist witnesses and examples to their faith in their daily lives. Humble sobriety was not for Sunday alone; it ought to be part of the daily regimen, along with plain dress and the use of plain, familiar if archaic language—the use of "thee" and "thou"—with all people, regardless of their social status, including the king. Deference was not a part of Quaker vocabulary, even when it came to something as customary as doffing one's hand in the presence of a supposed social superior. In the Quaker faith, only God warranted such submission. Such behavior only reinforced the suspicion that the Quakers were dangerous radicals, intent on subverting the social order.

Christ had preached the brotherhood of man, thus Quakers refused to make war. God had warned against false swearing, so Quakers refused to take oaths of allegiance or for testimony. An honest man's word, they insisted, was as good as his oath anyway. In a society that perceived all Europe to be a potential military threat and which regarded all dissidents as subversives, a group that refused military service and rejected loyalty oaths was naturally suspect. Finally, Friends accepted and promoted the democratic implications of their faith. The concept of the Inner Light meant that all men *and women* were equal before God, and thus all should have the same rights and privileges not only within the Quaker community but in the larger society as well.

Had the Quakers been content to practice their faith quietly, behind closed doors, they might have been tolerated, although their refusal to swear oaths automatically excluded them from government service, politics, and the universities. Unfortunately for their well-being, they could not remain quiet or passive. True evangelists, they believed God called upon them to spread His word. Their peculiar mannerisms drew attention and aroused suspicion, resulting in physical assaults on many a Friend. The previously persecuted Puritans, both in England and in North America were the most brutal in their treatment of Quakers. Massachusetts in particular treated Quakers most atrociously. There, in towns such as Salem, Friends' ears were lopped off, bodies whipped, tongues bored, fines levied, and people imprisoned. Boston's hostility was almost psychopathic with its cored whips and starvation of prisoners. One Quaker was encased in irons and whipped; when he refused to recant he was taken out and beaten until the flesh of his back and arms became jelly. Others were stripped to the waist, lashed to the back of a cart, and whipped out of town. In 1658 Boston passed an act against the "pernicious sect," making it possible to arrest them without warrant, imprison them without bail until tried, and if found guilty, banish them, and if they dared return they would be put to death.

Fortunately for the Quaker cause, the son of one of England's most celebrated naval war heroes, Sir Admiral William Penn, became a Quaker and because of his father's connections with the Stuarts (both Charles II and his brother, James, Duke of York) was able to obtain a charter to establish a North American colony to be a refuge for his persecuted brethren. Since his "convincement" in 1667 at the age of 23, devotion to his faith as well as to liberty of conscience for all Englishmen, consumed the life of William Penn Jr. Penn often traveled to the continent on behalf of the Society of Friends, winning converts and recruiting potential settlers in the Netherlands and Germany. In England he was jailed several times for his alleged scandalous and blasphemous speeches and treatises, all of which simply attempted to explain the Quaker faith and prove to fellow Englishmen that the Quakers were not subversives. In the 1670 Penn-Meade trial, which began as another attempt to imprison Penn for having supposedly violated the various acts under the Clarendon Code (a series of laws passed in the early Restoration that forced religious conformity), the proceedings quickly turned on another, more important issue, that of a judge's right to compel a jury to reconsider its verdict. Penn believed a judge could not; that a trial by a jury of one's peers was sacrosanct in English common law, and thus a jury's verdict was to be honored. Naturally the jury had ruled in Penn's favor; that he was not guilty of violating the Clarendon Code. In a landmark decision, a higher court vindicated Penn.

For years Penn had believed the Quaker's Truth could transform England. By 1680 Penn no longer had such delusions. Friends must now look elsewhere for their own safety. Like the Puritans of Massachusetts Bay, he decided that if the forces of the old order proved intractable in England, then it was time to turn to virgin territory for construction of the model Christian society. Thus in June 1680, William Penn formally appealed to the king for a land grant west of the Delaware River between Lord Baltimore's Proprietary in Maryland and Duke James' proprietary in New York.

No doubt the audacity of Penn's request shocked Charles' court, for Penn was one of England's most notorious dissidents and ex-convicts. At the same time Penn was soliciting the Crown for a colonial charter, Charles and imperial authorities were attempting to consolidate the empire under tighter royal supervision. As noted earlier in this chapter, Massachusetts was beginning to attract royal attention for its recalcitrance and thus the Crown was in the process of implementing a plan to deprive the Bay Colony of its charter. Neither Charles nor his advisers wanted to make the same mistake Charles' father had made in 1630 of letting any future charters leave England; he wanted no more Massachusetts in his empire. That either Charles or Parliament would permit another religious visionary to set up a social experiment in the American wilderness seemed highly unlikely.

Penn was fully aware of the controversial nature of his request. He thus had to find some face-saving approach for Charles that would allow the king to give Penn his land without causing a political uproar. Penn's tactic lay in the large sum of money—16,000 pounds—the Crown owed Admiral Penn for services and outright loans. Penn thus suggested a deal in which the king would make restitution for money owed the Admiral with a land grant to William Penn Jr. Since Charles was chronically short of money, the idea of paying a debt with currently worthless wilderness land that might eventually bring profit to the Crown attracted the king's attention.

To convince his hardcore Anglican Tory court opposed to any concessions to nonconformists such as the Quakers, Charles argued that he would be ridding his realm of troublesome fanatics much the same way his father had relieved himself of the Puritan nuisance. Perhaps the most important issue relative to Penn's grant was strategic. The area requested by Penn was inland from the coast, encompassing lands once held by the Susquehannas, and standing athwart the ancient Iroquois warpath to the south. The new colony would be in position to help New York with frontier defense, and it would act as a buffer zone for the Maryland-Virginia frontier. The colony required someone who had experience as well as integrity, and Penn was the ideal choice.

When finally approved in April 1681, Penn's charter was generous. It declared Penn the "True and Absolute Proprietor" of an empire of 45,000 square miles to whom the colony's inhabitants were to render total obedience. No private citizen in English history had ever possessed as much land nor as complete control of all the resources that went with such ownership. Penn was given the power to govern in conjunction with an assembly, and together they would make the colony's laws. The king could not impose trade duties without the proprietor's or the assembly's consent. Penn could also appoint all magistrates and establish a judicial system. In all cases (excluding murder and treason), Penn was the ultimate source of appeal, not the king. Penn also had the power to make war on enemies, levy customs, and dispose of lands as he saw fit. Finally, and most important, Penn was given the right to grant religious toleration to *all* Christians, even Catholics in his colony.

More thought went into the planning of Pennsylvania than into the creation of any other colony. Twenty drafts survive of Penn's First Frame of Government, his 1682 constitution for the province. Through revision after revision, the document, changing names with new versions, metamorphosed from a liberal document, the Fundamental Constitutions of Pennsylvania, to the final, more conservative Frame of Government, in which power was firmly under the proprietor's appointee, the governor, who ruled in conjunction with a council chosen from among the colony's wealthy elite. Governor and council would appoint all officials, including judges, and draft the laws. Although concentrating ultimate power in the hands of the few, in all other areas Penn's Frame of Government was far more progressive than his critics were willing to admit. Inviolably secure was the cornerstone of religious toleration, the driving obsession of Penn's life since his convincement. Indeed, to Penn, his colony was first and foremost a "holy experiment" in religious toleration. The government would make no effort to dictate matters of conscience. However, Pennsylvania was not to be a prototype for total religious freedom; it was to be a safe place for *all Christians,* including Catholics, but especially for persecuted Protestant sectarians. Penn granted permission to worship or not to worship as one pleased.

Also firmly established were an enlightened judicial system and penal code. All courts were to be open and conducted in the English language, and a person was allowed to plead his own cause. Naturally, trial by jury was guaranteed, so was bail except in the case of capital offenses, and anyone wrongfully imprisoned was entitled to double damages against the informer or prosecutor. Prisons were to be workhouses and inmates were provided free lodging and food. Only two offenses were subject to capital punishment: treason and murder. Penn's charter gave him the power to pardon and abolish all crimes except murder and treason so he eliminated the death penalty on all others. At the time, England still had a long list of crimes punishable by death other than treason and murder: piracy, arson, burglary, highway robbery, horse stealing, rape, and kidnapping.

Settlers had been arriving in Pennsylvania for a year when Penn landed in 1682 with his first Frame of Government, and on the surface the colony appeared to be well on its way to becoming the profitable and righteous enterprise Penn envisioned. Indeed, between December 1681 and Penn's arrival, 23 ships had brought over 2,000 colonists to Pennsylvania. A year later, 20 more ships brought another 2,000 emigrants. By 1686, Pennsylvania's population exceeded 8,000.

The first settlers were a varied lot— yeomen from Wiltshire in southern England, artisans from Bristol in the west, tradesmen from London, and gentry from Ireland and Wales. The majority of colonists were naturally Quakers but because Penn had guaranteed religious toleration to all Christians, the colony also attracted English Anglicans, German Pietists, Dutch Calvinists, and even a smattering of English and Irish Catholics. Like the New England Puritans—but unlike the Chesapeake colonists—most early Pennsylvanians came in freedom as families of middling means with a deed of sale, paid for in England, for a freehold in the unchartered expanses of the new "Promise Land" of Pennsylvania. Persons of great wealth were few, and about one-third were indentured servants, bound for a period of service to individuals in better circumstances. Most settled as farmers in the many rural townships but some lingered in the "instant city" of Philadelphia as artisans and merchants. Whether rich, middling, or poor, word of the new Quaker settlement in the valley of the Delaware had sparked yet another wave of European migration to the New World.

Timing also favored Penn's colony, for it was far easier to develop a later rather than an earlier colonial enterprise. Learning from their predecessor's mistakes, Quakers came with no golden delusions and thus did not suffer any of the "starving times," which afflicted their Chesapeake counterparts in the early 17th century. The Pennsylvanians also benefited from having sufficiently developed colonies as neighbors, who could provision them until their farms and trades became self-sustaining and productive. When Pennsylvania farmers did produce surpluses, they could sell livestock and grain to the large West Indian market, which the older mainland colonies had stimulated into a profitable commercial network by the 1650s. Moreover, Pennsylvania's healthier and more temperate climate, which Penn had touted in his promotional pamphlets, proved to be a great boon in the colony's economic development and population growth. It was warmer than New England's and certainly more salutary than the hot, humid, malarial Chesapeake. The invigorating conditions, abundant economic opportunities, and relatively even gender divisions combined to encourage early marriages and numerous children. In 1698 a visitor reported that he seldom met "any young Married Woman but hath a child in her belly, or one upon her lap." Although immigration slowed during the 1690s, natural increase sustained a population that nearly doubled from about 11,000 in 1690 to 18,000 Pennsylvanians by 1700.

In the 75 years of English colonization of North America, no Englishman did more to pre-establish the structure and functioning of government than William Penn. No other compact compared in comprehensiveness to Penn's 1682 Frame of Government. Yet, for all the preliminary work done in England, Pennsylvania first years were not marked by political order and stability, but rather by constant tension and hostility between sections, groups, and individual, forcing Penn to alter several times over the next 20 years his original Frame of Government. Even before returning to England for the first time in 1684, Penn had to grant the Assembly a greater role in colonial governance. Moreover, from the beginning there had been resentment toward Penn for allowing the Free Society of Traders (a group of wealthy Quaker merchants) to pretty much govern the colony as well as dictate its economy. Penn in effect, became an absentee proprietor, staying away from Pennsylvania for decades at a time. In his absence anti-proprietary factions emerged, constantly challenging his authority and demanding that Penn give his colonists greater political autonomy; to have the right of complete self-governance. Several factors contributed to his brethren's incessant clamor for greater freedom, but it was the Quakers' inherent anti-authoritarianism that became the single most important cause of this ongoing tension. Indeed, even before leaving England, the Quakers were perceived as litigious, uncooperative, and thus ungovernable.

Despite their disclaimers, Quakers exhibited less respect for government authority and for its necessary place in human affairs than any other Englishmen, regardless of religious affiliation. No doubt prompting Quakers to adopt such an attitude was the fact that they were the most persecuted of all

Dissenters in Restoration England, suffering at the hands of government more consistently and more intensively than any other religious group. As far as they were concerned, the reality of Restoration government blatantly and cruelly negated the notion that governing authority was the word of God himself and thus was to be obeyed when exercised justly and only passively and respectfully disobeyed on other occasions. To the Quakers, government was the enemy, creating and enforcing ungodly laws, twisting laws and acting arbitrarily, and depriving them of the goods and services that governments supposedly had been created to safeguard. Quakers had difficulty believing that governments that ruined them or left them to rot in jail were agents of divine authority.

That Quakers would opposed a government, created in conjunction with one of their own, is perplexing, especially when Penn pledged himself to justice in government and his laws were voted on by elected representatives, all of whom were Quakers. Two factors mitigated these considerations. First, and probably most frustrating to Penn, was the inability of his Pennsylvania brethren to separate his government from England's and to accept his authority as distinct from that of the Crown. Penn compounded this particular issue by sending his colonists mixed messages regarding their allegiance to him and to England. As Penn became increasingly authoritarian (because of his colonists refusal to obey his mandates), he went so far as to contend that his powers as feudal lord of both the land and the government of Pennsylvania was greater than those of the English king. Such audacious declarations demanding obedience caused many Pennsylvania Quakers to view Penn no differently than they viewed the distrusted (if not detested) English authorities, including the

king. To many North American Friends, Penn became a disappointing, and thus an alienating manifestation of governmental power; simply another suspect authority.

Penn had hoped that once Quakers were safely tucked away in their own colony, free from fear of harassment and persecution, they would no longer feel the need to be combative and litigious, behavior Penn believed Quakers assumed in order to better protect or insulate themselves in an openly hostile environment. However, much to Penn's chagrin, transplanting did not affect any change in his brethren's attitude toward authority, even though government officials were of their own choice and religious persuasion. New World Quakers carried with them to Pennsylvania a residual anti-authoritarianism, and were just as inclined to "scurvy quarrels that break out to the disgrace of the Province;" and as irritatingly consonant with their Old World counterparts in questioning every manifestation of civil authority.

The second reason for Penn's troubles with his colonists was that neither he as a famous "Public Friend" nor the weighty counterparts he appointed to the Council could awe or intimidate the rest of the Quaker colonists into submission. Penn either naively or presumptuously believed that his exalted position within the Quaker community, as well as his title as "True and Absolute Proprietor" of his own colony, warranted his fellows' obedience. Quakers believed all individuals were equal in God's eyes and thus no one, not even the king, and certainly not one of their own, was to be respected any differently than the lowliest of society.

In exasperation, Penn appointed a Puritan and former Cromwellian soldier, Captain John Blackwell as governor in 1688. Penn's choice of a Puritan to manage his colony did not sit well with the majority of his brethren. Still fresh in the Quaker historical memory was the brutal treatment meted out by Puritans, especially in Massachusetts. Such an affiliation did not bother Penn, who was more impressed by Blackwell's proven abilities in affairs of government, finance, and administration. As he told Thomas Lloyd, one of the ringleaders of the anti-proprietary faction, "Since no Friend would undertake the Governor's place, I took one that was not, and a stranger, that he might be impartial and more reverenced." Penn instructed Blackwell to "inspect the animosities, to use some expedient; And if no way else, authoritatively to end them, at least suppress them. Rule the meek meekly, and those that will not be ruled, rule with authority." Blackwell was to collect all rents owed Penn and other proprietary revenues without further delay, and most important, to silence the Assembly's demand for greater powers. In Penn's mind, here was an individual, stern but devout, who hopefully would be able to establish obedience, harmony, and stability in his colony.

Blackwell lasted 13 months, resigning because Penn believed he had treated the Quakers too harshly! When push came to shove Penn cratered to his colonists' cries of tyranny and prejudice. Penn's gamble with Blackwell proved disastrous, convincing even more Quakers that Penn was an unsympathetic and estranged proprietor. The utopian hopes raised by Penn led to spreading disillusionment, for they elevated hopes to a level that could never be fulfilled.

Instead, Quakers, in their constant battling with one another and in their disregard for Penn's authority, proved they were no different than all the others who had come to the New World; indeed, they became just as land-hungry, just as aggressive in their pursuit of personal wealth; and just as covetous of political power

and autonomy as the rest of their North American counterparts. Ironically, because Pennsylvania Quakers were free from persecution, which in England had bonded them in mutual defense, they now no longer needed such unity and self-protection. Persecution had provided coalescence in the Quaker community; it provided an important annealing force in their daily lives. In Pennsylvania, the absence of oppression intensified division in the Quaker community.

These same problems affected other American colonies but not as intensely as they did in Pennsylvania. The Quaker as a social type was in many ways an exaggerated manifestation of his Puritan counterpart. Quakers, however, differed from New England Puritans in their failure in the crucial first decades to develop a means of getting rid of their more troublesome peers. Although John Winthrop witnessed the splintering of the Massachusetts Bay colony into "a hundred earnest little Utopias," he and other Puritan leaders maintained a degree of stability absent in Pennsylvania, by either ostracizing dissidents or allowing them to leave the fold. By contrast, neither the Pennsylvania Quakers nor Penn would have ever sanctioned the casting out of even one, let alone several of their fellows, no matter how disruptive they became. That simply was not the Quaker way. Indeed, such individuals were not even allowed to leave of their own volition. Regardless of all the tension and rancor caused by such rebels, Quakers believed *all* the faithful must be kept tightly within their loving community, for only within the confines of Quaker fellowship could such a "problem" be resolved.

In the end, much to Penn's disheartening realization was the reality that his Quaker brethren could not resist the vast opportunities for individual accrual his colony provided. Continued adherence to Old World creeds would gain only a modest existence in a land of plenty, while the development of more profane standards was better suited for conquering the wilderness. Penn had assiduously planned a godly utopia, delicately balanced between democracy and deference, deeply religious yet utterly tolerant. Sadly, he lived to see his holy experiment vanish in a quarrelsome, commercial metropolis controlled by a self-serving, acquisitive group of former saints. Indeed, Pennsylvania became one of the most instantly commercially and financially successful colonies in the history of the British Empire. By 1700 the colony was well established in the Caribbean trade as an exporter of wheat, dairy products, and livestock. Quaker families were thriving and the colony's policy of religious toleration attracted thousands of outsiders, much to the chagrin of the original Quaker settlers. It was Penn's faith-inspired vision of creating in the wilderness of North America a place where all who came would be guaranteed fundamental human rights that no one should be denied because of their skin color, gender, or religious beliefs. Over time, as the American character and identity evolved, it became apparent that of all the European people who came to North America in the 17th and 18th centuries, it was the Quakers and their leader William Penn, who had left the most enduring imprint on the shaping of the American creed, which to this day cherishes and espouses the liberties William Penn first established in Pennsylvania.

The Northern Colonists and Native Americans

As seen in the previous chapter, within less than two decades of their arrival, the English in the Chesapeake were at war with the area's Native American peoples, largely the result of the Britons insatiable demand for land. In the Chesapeake it was Indian land upon which to grow tobacco. In New England the same motivation precipitated a series of conflicts with Native Americans; in the Puritan case however, confrontation with local tribes occurred much earlier and with more immediate devastating effects on Native Americans.

Native Americans and Property

In English society, men gained status by accumulating property through market transactions, rather than by redistributing property as did the Indian chiefs. In the wild plants and animals of New England, the colonists saw potential commodities as particular items that could be harvested, processed, shipped, and sold to make a profit. Consequently, New Englanders disdained the Native Americans as "Lazy Drones who love Idleness Exceedingly." Puritans insisted that the Christian God meant for them to enjoy the land in reward for their godly industry and to punish the Indians for their pagan indolence. Puritan righteousness and arrogance dictated how much land the Indians needed, which shrank with every passing year. The 1640 resolves of the town of Milford, Connecticut, summed up the Puritan view of land ownership rather succinctly: "Voted that the earth is the Lord's and the fullness thereof; voted that the earth is given to the Saints [the Puritans]; voted, we are the Saints."

Perhaps out of guilt, the Puritans felt compelled to "legitimize" their land titles by buying tracts of Indian land, offering trade goods in return for their marks on paper documents called "deeds." To the English a signed deed represented a legal transaction, protected by the law in which the signatories gave up their right to the land and had to move out; to the Native Americans, who had no concept of private property, they believed they had signed a piece of paper as a gesture to *share* the land with the colonists. The natives thus expected to continue to hunt and fish on the land and use portions of it as their needs dictated. Suffice it to say, the Indians were surprised and offended when Puritan "property" owners shot at them or arrested them for "trespassing" on the settler's land. When the Indians responded with their own reprisals, the colonists saw themselves as innocent victims obliged to protect themselves against dangerous and perfidious brutes who could not keep their bargains.

As the New Englanders cleared the forests with a vengeance, they destroyed in the process, the Native Americans' entire ecosystem—the habitat for the wild animals and plants critical to the Indians diet and clothing, making the natives' land more alien and hostile. The settlers also introduced pigs and cattle that ranged far and wide, beyond an individual's property, into the forests and the Indian cornfields, destroying the natives' food sources. When the Indians reacted by killing and eating the offending livestock, the colonists demanded that the culprits stand trial in their courts for theft.

Tribute

In the early 17th century, the arrival of colonial goods, diseases, and people dramatically changed the power relations between rival Indian groups. Welcoming opportunities to trade, the Native Americans competed to co-opt the newcomers in order to make them allies in their conflict with native enemies. As noted earlier in this chapter, during the early 1620s

the Wampanoag Indians had hoped to incorporate the Plymouth colonists into a mutually beneficial network of exchange and alliance. However, much to the Wampanoag's dismay, the Pilgrims regarded their treaty as Indian submission to English domination. As a result of the Great Migration, which augmented English presence and strength, the Puritans of Massachusetts Bay and Plymouth allied, and with force of arms bullied the local natives, demanding their formal submission and payment of tribute in wampum—beads and shells Native Americans used as "currency" in their trade relations with other tribes. Although wampum had little to no value in England, it was "as good as gold" when it came to the fur trade with the Abenaki Indians of Maine, who cherished the seashells of Long Island sound, which the Puritans forced local tribes to make into wampum. In effect, the New Englanders extorted wampum from the southern New England Indians and then shipped it to Maine to procure furs for shipment to England. In many ways, the Puritans ran a protection racket that forced local tribes to purchase peace with wampum. The colonists also collected wampum as court fines levied upon individual Indians convicted by colonial courts for such transgressions as killing pigs that had demolished native crops. Between 1634–1664 New Englanders extorted more than 21,000 fathoms of Indian wampum (nearly seven million beads), worth between 5,000 and 10,000 pounds once converted to furs. This swindling financed the steady expansion of settlements that dispossessed the natives of their lands.

The Pequot War

The first major conflict between the Puritans and Indians erupted in 1636, as the Saints engaged in aggressive expansion into the

Mystic River valley of southeastern Connecticut where the Pequot lived. Colonial leaders demanded that the Pequot pay a heavy tribute in wampum, give up several of their children as hostages, and turn over suspects accused of killing an English trader. The Pequot naturally refused such egregious demands and in retaliation the combined militias of Connecticut, Massachusetts, and Plymouth, in conjunction with Narragansett and Mohegan warriors attacked the Pequot. As a reward for their assistance, the Puritans promised their Indian allies that they could have as many Pequot prisoners as they wanted. This appealed to both tribes because they needed to replenish depleted numbers. In May 1637, Narragansett and Mohegan warriors led the Puritan forces deep into Pequot territory to surprise a palisaded village beside the Mystic River. The settlement contained about 70 wigwams and 400 inhabitants, mostly women, children, and old men. Apparently there was another Pequot fort in which the warriors resided, but after consulting with their chaplain, who probably told them to remember Saul and Amalekites, the Puritans, commanded by Captains John Mason and John Underhill, chose the village with the women and children, and set it ablaze. The Pequot died either in the flames or were shot by the Puritan militia as they attempted to flee the inferno. Only about five inhabitants survived by breaking through the surrounding circle of guns and swords; the godly had their own uses for terrorism.

The annihilation of one's enemy, especially of women and children, was not the Native American way of warfare. Attacks on enemy tribes were for punitive reasons only; for transgressions or insults made or to establish boundaries or protect sacred grounds. Very few on either side were killed and rarely were women and children the victims; more were usually captured than killed because prisoners of war were one of the ways tribes replenished their population, especially by taking women and children. Thus the Puritan slaughter of the Pequot appalled the Narragansett and Mohegan, who had expected to capture and adopt the women and children. They condemned the Puritan mode of war as "too furious and slays too many people." Naturally the Puritans dismissed their allies' humanity, declaring that the Indian mode of war was "more for pastime than to conquer and subdue." A veteran of European warfare, Underhill sarcastically noted that "they [the Indians] might fight for seven years and not kill seven men." If so, on a single day, Underhill helped to destroy the equivalent of nearly 400 years of Indian warfare. Regarding war as a test of their godliness, the Puritans interpreted their especially bloody victory as a sign of God's blessing upon them.

Unable to unite (although the Narragansett sachem Miantonomi attempted such a Pan-Indian movement in 1642, but his proposal foundered as the Puritans adeptly played one tribe off against another), the various Indian bands became shrinking minorities in a land dominated by increasing numbers of Englishmen. In 1670 the 52,000 New England colonists outnumbered the Indians of southern New England by nearly 3 to 1. Many Indian bands divided over how best to deal with the powerful and aggressive colonists. Should they fight to remain autonomous or should they accept subordination as Puritan wards? Did safety and survival lie in resistance or submission?

Praying Towns

The Pequot slaughter distressed many Puritans, especially those who believed that it was time to bring God's Word to the Indians. Thus began among some Puritan clergy a movement to evangelize the Native Americans who were left in southern New England. Beginning in the late 1640s, the Reverend John Eliot along with the Mayhews, Thomas and Thomas Jr., took the lead, often over opposition from their fellow colonists, who preferred simply to wipe the Indians away. The missionaries sincerely wished to rescue the Indians from future, certain annihilation while saving their souls from damnation. However, as Eliot and the Mayhews quickly learned, the missionary effort demanded that Indians surrender their own culture as the price to be paid for their physical survival. Because the English could not conceive of permitting Indians to remain independent and culturally autonomous peoples, they had to convert or die.

The Mayhews were more successful than Eliot, although he received the greater fanfare for his efforts. The Mayhews worked with local sachems and only took exception to the tribal powwows, which allowed for prophets or medicine men to perpetuate "pagan" rituals and beliefs. The Mayhews encouraged Indian men to teach the settlers of Martha's Vineyard and Nantucket how to catch whales, an activity that made them a vital part of the settlers' economy without threatening their identity as males. Eliot, by contrast, attacked the sachems' authority as well as the powwows, challenged the traditional tribal structure, and insisted on turning Indian men into farmers, a female role in Indian society. Despite his heavy-handedness and disregard for native folkways, Eliot, by the early 1670s had established more than 1,000 Indians, nearly all of them survivors of coastal tribes that had been decimated by disease, in a string of seven "praying towns," and Eliot was busy organiz-

ing five more among the Nipmucks of the interior. In permanent, compact "praying towns" the Indians could be kept under close surveillance and under more constant pressure to change their behavior and appearance. In praying towns they could also be removed from friends and relatives who refused to change their traditional ways. Restricting Indians to fixed settlements also freed up additional lands for English acquisition. Although less impressive than the Spanish Franciscan or French Jesuit missions, the Puritan proselytizing effort was a vast improvement upon the completely negligible effort at such an endeavor in the Chesapeake.

By 1675 about 2,300 Indians, perhaps one-quarter of all those living in southeastern New England, were in various stages of conversion to Christianity. But only 160 of them had achieved the kind of conversion experience the Puritans required for full church membership. The Puritan missionaries required from the Indians a thorough conversion, manifest in virtually all aspects of their behavior. They had to give up their Algonquian names and take new English names, and they had to give up wearing body grease, playing traditional sports, and killing lice with their teeth. The missionaries forced Indian men to cut their hair very short, in the Puritan fashion, for the Saints considered long hair as a sign of vanity and pride, sins they were quicker to detect in others than themselves. Short hair and English attire also set the praying Indians apart from their traditionalist brethren. Most important, Indians did not embrace the Puritans sense of sin. Nor could they grasp why their best deeds made no difference in God's eyes; in other words they could not fathom predestination. Comfortable in their own culture, most Indians rejected converting to English ways and beliefs.

The praying towns did appeal to small and weak bands, like the Massachusett, Nipmuck, and Pennacook, all of whom had been especially devastated by the English invasion. These tribes hoped to find in Christianity a way to make sense of their recent catastrophes. They worked to stabilize their world by seeking new supernatural guides, superior to their shamans, who had failed to stop the epidemics, cattle, hogs, and settlers. In the impressive technology and apparent disease immunities of the English, these Indians detected a transcendent form of supernatural power that they desperately hoped to tap for their own use, seeking in the new faith a capacity to recover their numbers and power. Although the missionaries were pleased with the progress of their converts, most lay Puritans continued to distrust the praying Indians as treacherous savages with a dangerous veneer of insincere Christianity. In 1675–76 a brutal war would put to the test the sincerity of both Indians and Puritans.

King Philip's War

One of the bloodiest Anglo-Native American conflicts in American colonial history took place in New England in the years 1675–76. Leading the native uprising was the Wampanoag sachem Metacom, son of Massasoit, who had celebrated the first thanksgiving feast with the Pilgrims. To the Puritans, Metacom became known as King Philip, in reference to one of England's most despised enemies, King Philip II of Spain. For over a year Metacom had been quietly preparing for a war that he considered inevitable. The Wampanoag, one of the larger, more autonomous bands, had resisted the Puritans' evangelizing, believing that if they succumbed to Puritan proselytizing they would lose their whole way of life. Moreover, by 1675, the Puritans were once again engaged in an aggressive land acquisition movement and Metacom was determined to resist this latest English attempt at taking more native land. Metacom was also tired of seeing his people blamed for everything that went wrong in the colony and being punished for their slightest transgressions of English laws they did not understand nor believe fair. Such was the incident that precipitated the conflict. In the spring of 1675 the Plymouth colonists provoked the confrontation by seizing, convicting, and executing three Wampanoag for allegedly murdering a praying-Indian preacher and possible spy for the English, John Sassamon. The hanging of their brothers incensed young Wampanoag warriors, who took it upon themselves to avenge their tribesmen's death by attacking isolated Puritan homesteads, looting and burning.

To the Puritans' surprise and horror the rebellion spread with deadly effect during the summer and fall 1675 as initial Wampanoag victories encouraged other bands with their own grievances to join in. Indiscriminate Puritan counterattacks on neutral Indians created additional enemies, including the Narragansett. Numbering about 4,000, the Narragansett were the largest, most powerful tribe in the region. Although the Puritans were quick to label Metacom the evil mastermind behind the uprising, in truth, each band fought spontaneously under its own leaders; all however, were united by a simmering, combustible hatred for the Puritans and their years of self-righteous oppression, duplicity, and perfidy.

Remembering their easy victory (slaughter) over the Pequot a generation earlier, the Puritans initially believed they would be able to dispense with this latest "savage" uprising with similar facility. They were quickly proven wrong. Since the 1630s, the Indians had acquired firearms and perhaps more important, they had built forges to make musket balls and repair their own weapons. They had even become marksmen with the smooth-bore musket by firing several smaller bullets instead of a single musketball with each charge. The settlers, by contrast, were still poor shots, even though many had gotten better with a musket since arriving in North America and having to hunt or kill Indians. However, most of the time, the Puritans usually paid the Native Americans to hunt for them. Moreover, in the tradition of European armies, the Puritans discharged volleys without aiming, which usually resulted in a few kills but mostly misses or maybe a fortunate wounding of the enemy.

To the Puritan's shock, the Indians not only proved effective riflemen but were organized, purposeful in attack and battle, and most horrifying to the colonists, willing to engage in total war, which saw the brutal slaughter of scores of English men, women, and children; lessons in warfare they had learned from their Puritan nemeses. During the summer and fall of 1675, the Indian rebels assailed 52 of the region's 90 towns, destroying 12 and killing in the process entire colonial families, including women and children. When one settler boasted that his Bible would save him from harm, the Indians disemboweled him and stuffed the sacred book in his belly. When the Puritans counterattacked, the Indians took refuge in the swamps, repelling their foes and inflicting heavy losses. Or they surprised and ambushed the Puritans who were unfamiliar with the paths through forests. Indian victories bolstered their confidence while shocking and demoralizing the Puritans. Frontier towns were abandoned as hundreds of Puritans fled to the coastal cities for safety. It also became increasingly difficult to recruit men to fight for what appeared to be a losing war.

For decades the colonists had labored to remake the New England landscape by constructing churches, houses, fences, and barns, and unleashing their livestock. To reverse their land's alienation, the Indian rebels systematically burned, killed, mutilated, and desecrated all of those symbols of English civilization. The Indians regarded every dying colonist, every burning farm or defiled church as accumulating evidence that the English God was no match for their own revitalized spiritual power. Indeed, altogether, by war's end, the Indians killed about 1,000 settlers.

Naturally the Puritans transformed the war from one caused by their own treachery and cruel treatment of the Indians and general disdain for native culture into a sign from God that they had sinned and thus were being punished by the forces of Satan for their transgressions. Such were the sentiments of Increase Mather, a prominent Boston minister, who warned that no victory would come until New England repented and reformed. At first the Massachusetts General Court agreed, blaming the war on young men who wore their hair too long, on boys and girls who took leisurely horse rides together, on people who dressed above their station in life, and of course on the blaspheming dissidents among them. In reality, what Mather feared and what he railed about was that by the 1670s, much to his dismay, the "old-school," hardcore Puritanism of the first generation of emigrants was fast fading way, losing its appeal and thus hold on succeeding generations born in the New World. In effect, New England society was becoming more secular, less devoted to the original Puritan message and purpose, and thus in Mather's view, New England was becoming a sinful place, just waiting for God's retribution, which had finally come in the form of Metacom.

To vindicate their God and prove their own worthiness, the Puritans believed it essential to annihilate once and for all their Indian enemies. Thus, for the Puritans their struggle to put down the Indian uprising became a holy war, a righteous crusade against the forces of evil and darkness, in which e very dead Indian and burned wigwam manifested the resurgent power of the Puritan God and his renewed approval of his chosen people, the Puritans. Unfortunately, in the passion of their jihad, Puritans typically ventilated their rage by attacking and killing Indians who had nothing to do with Metacom and his followers. Among the first victims were the praying town Indians, whom the Puritans regarded as insidious spies and covert raiders. To protect the praying Indians from the wrath of blood-lusting Puritans or from joining Metacom's forces, colonial authorities relocated them to two cold and barren islands in Boston harbor, where hundreds died from exposure, malnutrition, and disease (or were stolen by slavers) during the hard winter of 1675–1676.

In early 1676, the desperate Puritans realized that they could not win without the assistance of Indian allies, principally the Pequot and Mohegan. The Puritans also recruited praying town Indians but required each to prove his loyalty and conversion by bringing in two scalps or heads taken from the enemy. About one-third of the natives in southern New England assisted the colonists, and thus King Philip's War became a civil war among the natives. The Puritan's recruitment of Indian allies proved a smart move, for by the summer of 1676 the tide of war turned in the Puritan favor. The Indians taught the allies how to avoid ambushes and how to track down and destroy the rebels in their refuges. Wise colonial commanders abandoned completely inappropriate European military tactics, based on masses of men engaged in complicated maneuvers to deliver volleys of fire. Instead, they adopted the Indians' "skulking way of war"—stealth, ambush, and small party terrorist raids and individual marksmanship. As summer approached the Indian rebels had run out of food and ammunition, just as they faced a revamped, augmented, and more resolute enemy. Driven from their villages and fields, Metacom's forces were on the run, desperately hungry and often sick. Unable to make guns and gunpowder, they became even weaker. Moreover, the war had cut off their access to colonial traders. Also aiding the Puritan cause was the entry on the Saints' side of the powerful Mohawk Indians of New York (one of the Iroquois Five Nations), whom Governor Edmund Andros of that colony allowed to participate, even though he had no great love for the Puritans. (Andros was a devoted Stuart royalist and high-church Anglican). With such overwhelming forces arrayed against them, Metacom's rebels' days were numbered.

By the close of summer 1676, the Indian resistance had collapsed, as one demoralized group after another surrendered. In August, Metacom died in battle, shot by a praying town Indian who served with the Puritan militia. The English cut off his head for display on a post atop a brick watchtower in Plymouth. The bitter and bloody war devastated the Puritan settlements buts especially the Indian villages. The conflict killed about 3,000 Indians, a quarter of their population in southern New England. Rather than treat the captives as prisoners of war, the Puritans declared the Indians traitors, executing the chiefs while selling the rest of the survivors into West Indian or Mediterranean slavery. Some of the defeated Indians escaped northward, seeking a safe haven among fellow Algonquians, the Abenaki in northern New England and New France. The refugees carried with them a bitter hatred for New Englanders. As will be seen in a later chapter, in a long series of wars between 1689 and 1760, the remnants of Metacom's rebels and their descendants guided French raids that repeatedly devastated New England's frontier settlements.

Indian Strategies of Survival

In some ways, America became as much a new world for Native Americans as it did for the European emigrants. European cloth, muskets, hatchets, knives, and pots, were welcomed among the Indians and spread far into the interior, but they came at a price. Indians who learned to use them gradually abandoned traditional skills and became increasingly dependent on trade with Europeans, a process not complete until the 19th century. Alcohol, the one item always in demand, was also dangerous. Indian men drank to alter their mood and achieve visions, not for sociability. Drunkenness among Native Americans became a major, if intermittent social problem.

Settlers who understood that their future depended on the fur trade, as in New France, tried to stay on good terms with the Native American peoples in their region. The Dutch West India Company put New Netherland on such a course, and the English governors of New York after 1664 followed such initiatives. Edmund Andros, governor from 1674–1680, cultivated the friendship of the Iroquois League, in which the five member nations had promised not to wage war against one another. In 1677 Andros and the Five Nations (the Mohawk, Oneida, Onondaga, Cayuga, and Seneca) agreed to make New York the east-ernmost link in what the English called the "Covenant Chain" of peace, a huge defensive advantage for a lightly populated colony. Thus, while New England and Virginia fought bitter Indian wars in the 1670s, New York avoided conflict. The Covenant Chain later proved flexible enough to incorporate other Indians and colonists as well, all able to live in peace along the Hudson River Valley for several decades.

Without question, the most successful Englishman to develop not only peaceful relations with Native Americans, but bonds that proved profitable and mutually beneficial was William Penn. By the time of the Quaker's arrival in Pennsylvania, the major Algonquian tribe in the area was the Lenni Lenape (numbering about 5,000), who had already been involved for decades in trade relations with the Dutch and the Swedish settlers, who predated the Quakers. Moreover, by the time of the Quakers' arrival, the Lenni Lenape possessed more land than their reduced numbers could use, and thus welcomed the opportunity to sell some for coveted trade goods. There is little doubt that Penn's sincere yet shrewd policy of cultivating Indian goodwill contributed significantly to Pennsylvania's rapid growth and financial success. Penn's approach allowed his colony to enjoy prolonged peace with the local tribes, avoiding the native uprisings that had devastated Virginia, New England, and New Netherland, as well as South Carolina.

In his first meeting with the natives, Penn laid the foundation for peaceful relations with the Lenni Lenape, telling the tribe that "The King of the Country where I live, hath given me a great Province but I desire to enjoy it with your Love and Consent, that we may always live together as neighbor and friends and not devour and destroy one another but

William Penn concluding a treaty with the Delaware Indians, by Benjamin West 1681.
In this exchange, Penn presents the Indians with cloth, one of the European trade goods
most in demand by Indians.

live soberly and kindly together in the world."
In this single statement Penn disassociated
himself from the entire history of European
colonization in the New World. In contrast to
the violent intimidation, deception, and fraud
often perpetrated on Native Americans by previous colonial leaders, Penn acknowledged the
Lenni Lenape as the land's legitimate owners,
and he publicly treated their culture with
respect.

Penn was keenly aware of the disintegra-
tive effects two generations of contact with
the Finns, Swedes, and Dutch had had on the

Lenni Lenape. Unlike most of his contemporaries, who asserted that the interaction with
"civilized" white Europeans had "benefited"
the "savage," Penn contended the opposite:
that it was the treacherous Europeans who
were corrupting Native Americans. "The
worst is that they are worse for the Christians,
who have propagated their vices and yielded
them tradition for ill and not for good things."
Penn believed that if the Lenni Lenape had not
established relations with the Europeans they
would have been better off, for their inherently "blessed equable temperament" and

simple life would not have been adulterated. As Penn noted, "They care for little because they want but little, and the reason is, a little contents them. In this they are sufficiently revenged [better off than] on us: if they are ignorant of our pleasures, they are also free from our pains. We sweat and toil to live; their pleasure feeds them—I mean their hunting, fishing, and fowling."

Penn also observed the effects of the European "luxury" that had "filled them with anxieties" and "had raised their passions"— alcohol. Penn was certain "the drinking of strong spirits" was insidiously destroying their idyllic, simple life. "Sober they are extraordinary, sensitive people of high integrity; drunk they are helpless dupes," exchanging for rum, "the richest of their skins and furs." Penn believed Native Americans' addiction to alcohol was not just another manifestation (or confirmation) of their alleged inherent, barbarous nature. To Penn it reflected something deeper: a need for relief from the intolerable tensions created by the conflict of cultural values in which they were caught.

By the late 17th century, Penn's peaceful policy so impressed Native American tribes that Indian refugees began migrating to Pennsylvania, fleeing from abuse and internecine warfare in other colonies. Penn's government welcomed Shawnees from South Carolina, the Nanticoke and Conoy of Maryland, the Tutelo from Virginia, and some Mahicans from New York. As a Conoy explained to the Quakers, "The People of Maryland do not treat the Indians as you & others do, for they make slaves of them & sell their children for Money." Welcoming the refugees was shrewd as well as benevolent. The exiles were relocated along the Susquehanna River, replacing the Susquehannock, thereby giving Pennsylvanians a security screen to the west of their settlements in the Delaware Valley. The outlander's villages provided a buffer, especially against the French and their Indian allies, who became particularly menacing (as will be seen in the next chapter) in the late 1690s. By that decade England was at war with France, and typically the conflict spilled across the Atlantic to North America. The English government called on its colonies to do their part, expecting them to provide men and arms in defense of the empire. Fortunately, the Quakers' perspicacity in locating the fugitive tribes along their western pale relieved them of having to compromise on their avowed pacifism as their native clients bore the brunt of any frontier warfare. Behind a western rampart of Indian allies, Pennsylvanians enjoyed peace and prosperity until the 1720s, when their desire for land encroached upon their Indian friends, bringing to an end what was perhaps the longest, most amicable relationship between Europeans and Native Americans.

Mercantilism, the Navigation Acts, and the Redefinition of Empire: The Dominion of New England

By the Restoration mercantilism had come to define English imperial policy. Indeed, even before the founding of Jamestown, this economic theory had become the driving force behind English overseas expansion. Mercantilism rested on the belief that the world's wealth was finite, that one person or nation could grow rich only at the expense of another, and that a nation's economic health depended therefore, on extracting as much wealth as possible from home. The principles of mercantilism spread throughout Europe in the 16th and 17th centuries and increased competition among nations. Every European state was trying to find markets for exports while trying to limit its imports. One result was the increasing attractiveness of acquiring colonies, which would become the source of raw materials and a market for the colonizing power's goods. In effect, colonies were to become the providers of raw materials for the mother country while absorbing both the mother country's excess finished goods and surplus humanity; in short colonies were to become the "dumping grounds" for both "commodities." Perhaps most important, at all times, colonial economic needs were to be subordinate to those of the mother country; that is, colonies existed for one single purpose: to enhance the wealth and power of the mother country. At no time were they to compete with the mother country, nor were they to produce goods that did not benefit either the empire or the mother country directly. Thus, the European imperial powers all believed colonial trade and other enterprises had to be closely regulated and monitored in order to ensure that colonial wealth, whether personal or collective, advanced not the individual or community, but the interests and power of the sponsoring nation state and empire as a whole. Suffice it to say, mercantile theory was anti-capitalist and opposed to individual accrual, especially at the state's expense.

Although the Restoration's new royalist Parliament rescinded all legislation passed during the Commonwealth, these Cavaliers promptly reenacted and extended the original 1650s Navigation Act in a series of new measures. The 1660 Navigation Act required that all colonial trade be transported on English made ships manned by a crew, including the captain that was three-fourths English. The act also created a category of "enumerated" goods, of which sugar, tobacco, timber, and eventually naval stores, were the most important, that could only be shipped directly to England; the intent being to give England a monopoly over the export of major staples from every English colony to Europe and to the rest of the world. The colonists were allowed to export un-enumerated products to other English colonies, so the act did allow for a substantial degree of inter-colonial trade within the empire. In 1663 Parliament passed the Staple Act requiring that all goods sent from Europe to the colonies pass through England on their way, where they would be subject to English taxation. By passing this particular measure, England ensured its monopoly on all colonial trade by guaranteeing that it controlled *all* products sent to the colonies, even those not "made in England." In effect, English merchants were setting themselves up as middle men, marking up the price on all exports to the colonies, regardless of place of origin. Naturally such a procedure forced the colonists to pay higher prices, especially for non-English goods. Finally an act passed in 1673 imposed duties on the coastal trade among the English colonies as well as providing for the appointment of customs officials to enforce the Navigation Acts. These mandates, with later amendments and additions, formed the legal basis of England's mercantile system in America for a century.

The Dominion of New England

Before the Navigation Acts, all the mainland colonial governments (excluding Virginia, a "royal colony" with a governor appointed by the king) had operated largely independently of the crown, with governors chosen by the proprietors or by the colonists themselves and with powerful representative assemblies. London officials recognized that to increase their control over their colonies they would have to create a body in London to reign in and monitor the independent minded colonial governments, which were unlikely to enforce the new laws.

In 1675 Charles II created a new government agency, the Lords Committee of Trade and Plantations, or simply the Lords of Trade. This body, a permanent committee of the Privy Council, was to enforce the Navigation Acts and administer the colonies. Although Virginia was the oldest royal colony, the West Indies became the focus of most of the new policies, simply because the Caribbean remained a much more important theater of international competition. The instruments of royal government first took shape in the islands and were then extended to the mainland and obstreperous Puritan Massachusetts became the first of the mainland colonies to come under the new royal yoke. In 1679 Charles II stripped the Bay Colony of its authority over New Hampshire and chartered a separate royal colony there whose governor he would himself appoint. Charles also began seeking legal grounds for revoking the colony's corporate charter and making Massachusetts itself a royal colony. He soon became convinced he had found reasons when the Massachusetts General Court declared that it would not abide by the Navigation Acts because Parliament did not have the power to legislate for the colony. Such an assertion and usurpation of both royal and Parliamentary authority incensed both the king and Parliament and thus in 1684, with Parliament's blessing, Charles revoked Massachusetts' charter.

Matters for the Massachusetts Puritans only got worse with the ascension of Charles' brother to the throne as James II in 1685. A devout Catholic and consumed with hatred for the Puritans (it was the Puritans after all, who had executed his father), no sooner did James become king than he punished Massachusetts further by incorporating *all* of New England—New Hampshire, Connecticut, and Rhode Island and later New York and New Jersey—into a consolidated super-colony called the Dominion of New England. Modeled on a Spanish viceroyalty, the Dominion extended from the Delaware River to Canada. James dissolved the assemblies in all the respective colonies, administering the Dominion through a governor-general assisted by a lieutenant governor and an appointed council. The new arrangement dramatically and abruptly halted the momentum colonials had been gathering toward greater colonial autonomy defended by powerful elected assemblies dominated by wealthy elites. For governor-general, the king appointed Edmund Andros, previously James' imperious New York governor. Francis Nicholson became lieutenant governor, carrying out his duties in New York, while Andros and his Dominion council presided in Boston. Interestingly, allowing James to implement his consolidation agenda as well as to prorogue Parliament, and thus not have to depend on that body for income, was the substantial revenue pouring into the royal coffers from the American colonies. By the time of James' reign, the colonies had become cash cows, providing James with enough income to fund his more authoritarian regime.

Arbitrary and centralized, the Dominion regime shocked New Englanders. Reorganizing the courts and the militia, Puritan judges and officers were replaced with Anglican newcomers. On instruction from James, Andros destroyed Puritanism by defunding it, forbidding the Puritan clergy from drawing their salaries from town taxes. Moreover, the Dominion was far more expensive than the old charter governments, requiring unprecedented levels of taxation. A good portion of the increased cost of administration covered Andros' lavish salary of 1,200 pounds, an amount that exceeded the entire annual outlay to maintain the former Massachusetts government. Andros also brought along two companies or regular troops, whom he expected the colonists to provision. To raise revenue, Andros levied new taxes without an assembly and without even the support of a majority of his own council, composed largely of merchants. The Dominion regime also vigorously enforced the Navigation Acts by establishing in Boston a new vice-admiralty court, which operated without juries. The new court greatly depressed the port's business, seizing six merchant ships for violating the acts in the summer of 1686. With their incomes in contraction, New Englanders were hard pressed to pay Andros' increased fees and taxes. Andros' rigid enforcement of the Navigation Acts and his brusque dismissal of the colonists' claims to the "rights of Englishmen" made him quickly and thoroughly unpopular.

The Glorious Revolution

James II was not only losing friends in America but also alienating powerful Englishmen at home as well by attempting to Catholicize the country and rule, as his father had tried, as an absolute monarch. By 1688 his popular support had all but evaporated, and Parliament, determined to avoid another civil war at all costs, invited his Protestant daughter Mary, and her husband, William of Orange, ruler of the Netherlands, to assume the throne. James II (perhaps remembering what had happened to his father, Charles I) offered no resistance and fled to France. As a result of this bloodless coup, which the English called the "Glorious Revolution," William and Mary became joint sovereigns.

When news of James' overthrow reached Boston, Puritans were jubilant and quickly moved to overthrow his unpopular viceroy in New England. Andros was arrested and imprisoned. To the Puritans' joy they were not reprimanded for their actions by the new monarchy; quite the opposite. The new sovereigns accepted Andros' removal and quickly abolished the Dominion of New England, restoring all the colonies to their independent status and granting them all the right of self-government. They did not however, recreate them exactly as they were. In 1691, they combined Massachusetts and Plymouth, making it a single, royal colony; Massachusetts Bay Colony no longer existed has it had since 1630; it was now a royal colony under the king's sovereignty. The new charter restored the General Court but the king now appointed the governor. It also replaced church membership with property ownership as the basis for voting and office-holding.

In New York, the Glorious Revolution had a different impact. Andros had been governing the colony through a lieutenant governor, Francis Nicholson, who enjoyed the support of the province's wealthy merchants and fur traders. Other, less favored colonists—farmers, mechanics, small traders, and shopkeepers—had a long accumulation of grievances against Nicholson and his allies. Leading the dissidents was Jacob Leisler, a German emigrant and prosperous merchant.

He had married into a prominent Dutch family but had never won acceptance as one of the colony's elite. In May 1689, when news of the Glorious Revolution in England and Andros' fall in Massachusetts reached New York, Leisler raised a militia, captured the city fort, drove Nicholson into exile and proclaimed himself the new head of the New York government. For two years he tried in vain to stabilize his power in the colony amid fierce factional rivalry; the established elite saw him as nothing more than a rabble-rousing parvenu. In 1691, when William and Mary appointed a new governor, Leisler briefly resisted. Although he soon yielded, his hesitation allowed his many political enemies to charge him with treason. He was convicted and executed. Fierce rivalry between what became known as the "Leislerians" and "anti-Leislerians" dominated New York colonial politics for many years thereafter.

England's Glorious Revolution of 1688 touched off uprisings, mostly bloodless, in several colonies. Under the new sovereigns, the representative assemblies that had been abolished were restored and the scheme for colonial unification from above was abandoned. However, much to the disappointment of many colonists, the Glorious Revolution in America proved no vindication of Americans' resolve to govern themselves. In New York and Maryland in particular, the uprisings had more to do with local factional and religious divisions than with any larger vision of the nature of the empire. While insurgents did succeed in toppling the authoritarian regime of the short-lived Dominion of New England, ironically Massachusetts Puritans lost their previous autonomy and came under greater crown scrutiny. As the first century of English settlement in America came to a close, the colonists were becoming more a part of the imperial system than ever before.

Witchcraft, Witches, and the Salem Witch Trials

By the 1690s it appeared to many old-line Puritans that the majority of their brethren had become wayward saints; that they had lost sight or had forgotten completely the original purpose of the Puritan migration to the wilderness of North America. Such refractory behavior, if not outright disdain for Puritan traditionalism was especially rampant among the younger generations, all of whom had been born in the New World and were thus a generation or two removed from Puritan hardships and suffering both in England and in North America. To them, the "errand" had no meaning or purpose anymore, for they had known only the good life in New England and none of the ordeal of their forebears. As a result of such perceived wantonness among so many, Puritan clergymen feared that it was only a matter of time before God's wrath would descend down upon New Englanders for their manifold transgressions. To try to bring back the fold, many New England clergymen began delivering a new genre of sermon knows as the "jeremiad," named after the grim Old Testament prophet Jeremiah. A jeremiad catalogued the sufferings and sins of New England: Indian wars, the Dominion of New England; earthquakes, fires, storms, all sent by God to punish a region wallowing in immorality and irreligion. Finding the present generation wanting, a jeremiad exhorted listeners to reclaim the lofty standards and pure morality ascribed to New England's founders.

The jeremiads not only warned audiences of impending or continuing cataclysms if righteousness and godliness did not return, but also that God would cease to protect them from Satan, and thus send among them his most perfidious and insidious agents, witches. A rebellious and fallen angel, Satan recruited humans to sign their name in blood in his book. In return the signers received from the devil supernatural and magical power, to use for themselves for whatever self-servicing or evil purposes. In exchange for such temporal power, the individual's soul became Satan's upon death for eternity. Since New England's founding, whenever cattle and children sickened and died, Puritans suspected that some in their midst practiced satanic magic. For the community's safety, witches had to be identified, prosecuted, and neutralized. The authorities pardoned witches who confessed and testified against others, but persistent denial consigned the witch to public execution by hanging. Contrary to popular myth and previous European practice, the New England Puritans did not burn witches at the stake.

That a pre-modern, deeply religious people as the Puritans would believe in magic and witches made perfect sense, for they lived in an unpredictable and often deadly natural world beyond their control. Seventeenth-century life in the North American wilderness was rife with all manner of inexplicable (to the Puritans) natural calamities—sudden fires, floods, windstorms, droughts, crop blights, and livestock diseases. Especially disturbing were periodic epidemics of measles, influenza, and smallpox that proved especially fatal to children. Since the Puritans had no scientific understanding of the causes of such maladies or natural phenomenon, they naturally called out for an explanation, some attribution of cause, that might protect people from further suffering, or at least console them with resignation to God's will. No Puritan wished to believe that misfortune was purely random and without supernatural meaning, whether the event be a sign from God or Satan, for that would confirm their helplessness and isolation in a world without God. Puritan New England was certainly more anxious about witches than the other English colonies, which hosted very few trials and probably no executions. New England's chief distinction was that the Puritans continued to prosecute and execute witches after 1650, when such proceedings virtually stopped in old England. Puritanism kept New England behind the times in supernatural belief.

The Salem Witch Trials

Several factors contributed to the most legendary outbreak of witchcraft hysteria in the early 1690s in Salem, Massachusetts. As briefly noted above, many perplexing and anxiety-inducing issues had coalesced by the early 1690s to create the perfect environment for such frenzy. For one, the Puritans were without an effective government because they had not yet received their new charter. The opening battles of King William's War had just begun with the French Catholics of Canada and their Algonquian Indian allies raiding settlements on the northern and eastern frontiers. Slaves reported that the French were planning to recruit New England's Africans to join a force of Indians and French soldiers. Internally, land scarcity by the decade had also become a significant factor, particularly as increasing numbers of young men had no opportunity to inherit their fathers' estate as had been the case in previous decades. Frustrating such individuals was the fact that many widows were in possession of vast amounts of acreage, just holding on to them until they passed. Thus, one of the targets of the witch-hunts that began in Salem, were elderly, widowed women, whose land young men coveted. By accusing such a person of being a witch or by consorting with the devil or engaging in the occult or black magic, young men hoped that such women would not only be convicted of witchcraft but as punishment lose their land as well, which they would then have access to.

Igniting the delirium in late 1691 were several adolescent girls who, one day, sponta-neously, in the middle of play and conversation, threw themselves to the ground writhing in fits and all manner of bodily contortions, and allegedly speaking in tongues and then awakening at night with nightmares. The girls proclaimed they had been taken over by evil spirits, that there were witches in the community that had cast such spells upon them. Hysteria spread throughout the town, and hundreds of people (most of them women) were accused of witchcraft. Since the only way to avoid prosecution was to confess and name others, accusations of witchcraft began to snowball. By the middle of 1692, hundreds of Salem residents had come forward to accuse their neighbors for a variety of reasons, most of which reflected old scores to be settled within the Salem commu-nity. Others accused neighbors, friends, even relatives out of a desire for property or other material aggrandizement. By the time the investigation and trials ended, 156 people had been jailed and 20 executed by hanging with one man pressed to death (crushed under the

WITCHCRAFT AT SALEM VILLAGE.

1876 illustration of the courtroom of a Salem witch trial. The central figure is usually identified as Mary Walcott.

weight of stones) for refusing to enter a plea. As in previous witch-hunt hysterias, most of the accused were women past the age of 40, and most of the accusers were women in their late teens or 20s, along with in Salem, young men in roughly the same age group. The girls who had been the original accusers later recanted and admitted that their story had been fabricated.

In many ways the Salem witchcraft mania reflected the last-ditch, desperate effort by old-school Puritans to redeem a perceived fallen people and society and return both indi-viduals and community to the halcyon days of godliness and morality; in effect to the years prior to 1650 when all Puritans seemed to be unified in their purpose in having come to North America. However, the witchcraft panic also reflected a New England society and a Puritan faith in significant transition if not transformation. Indeed, many old-line Puri-tans feared that Puritanism, especially in its original form, had died in the wilderness of New England and along with the faith, the Puritan way of living as well. Whether they liked it or not, life in the wilderness had indeed changed many a New Englander from Puritan to Yankee, and as this new species of New Englander entered the next century, he became even less Puritan and more Yankee.

Despite the taint of the Salem witch hunts, the Puritans have left a prodigious and enduring legacy for English-speaking North America. Compared with other colonial regions, New England was a land of relative equality, broad (albeit moderate) opportunity, and thrifty, industrious, and entrepreneurial habits that sustained an especially diverse and complex economy. The region's large, healthy families, nearly even gender ratio, and long life expectancy promoted social stability, the steady accumulation of family property, and its orderly transfer from one generation to the next. Nowhere else in colonial America did colonists enjoy readier access to public worship (except perhaps in Pennsylvania), and nearly universal education. That those ideals remain powerful in our own culture attests to the enduring importance of the Puritan legacy.

Conclusion

After a period of considerable instability, by the beginning of the 18th century, almost all of England's North American colonies had developed societies that they would maintain until the American Revolution; some would not change until after the Civil War. For the most part, the colonies were prosperous, with a large white middle class. The efforts to replicate a European hierarchical order had largely failed, although manifestations of that system prevailed in the Southern colonies. Each region had found a secure economic base: farming and shipping in New England; mixed farming in the middle colonies, and staple crop production in the Southern colonies. The Southern colonies had become slave societies, although slavery was allowed and practiced in every colony. All the colonies had more or less figured out how to control their own populations, whether by granting them—in the case of the Europeans—increased opportunity and political rights, or by exercising tighter control, as was the case for enslaved Africans. These strong economic foundations, when combined with political stability, were the preconditions for the 18th century's rapid population increase, when the mainland English population would far surpass that of the French and Spanish colonies. Indeed, as will be seen in the next chapter, by 1750, mainland Spanish and French colonies were still little more than frontier outposts, although both nations still maintained imperial visions for North America. Native Americans remained a strong presence, especially west of the Appalachian Mountains, but the competition among European powers—and even individual colonies—for the tribes' loyalty, their trade, and their land, remained a source of conflict.

Suggested Readings

Victoria D. Anderson. *New England's Generation: The Great Migration and the Formation of Society and Culture in the Seventeenth Century.* (1991). A careful study of emigration from England to New England.

Patricia Bonomi. *Under the Cope of Heaven: Religion, Society, and Politics in Colonial America.* (1986). Traces the interrelationship of religion and politics and the rise of religious diversity in the colonies.

William Cronon. *Changes in the Land: Colonists and the Ecology of New England.* (1983). A path-breaking examination of how English colonization affected New England's natural environment.

Stephen Innes. *Creating the Commonwealth: The Economic Culture of Puritan New England.* (1995). Explores the economic development of the New England colonies and its impact on Puritan society.

Edmund S. Morgan. *The Puritan Family* (1944). An early but still considered one of the best assessments of family life and gender relations in colonial New England.

Carla G. Pestana. *The English Atlantic in an Age of Revolution, 1640–1661.* (2001). Analyzes how the English Civil War and Restoration reverberated in the American colonies.

Bernard Bailyn. *The Peopling of British North America.* (1986). A brief survey of European migration across the Atlantic to North America.

Jill Lepore. *The Name of War: King Philip's War and the Origin of American Identity.* (1998). An examination of the cause and consequences of one of the most important colonial red-white conflicts.

John A. Moretta. *William Penn and the Quaker Legacy.* (2007). Best brief but comprehensive biography of the founder of Pennsylvania and the impact the Quaker faith had upon the development of the American creed.

Mary Beth Norton. *In the Devil's Snare: The Salem Witchcraft Crisis of 1692.* (2002). The most recent study of the witch trials, place them in the context of anxieties over Indian warfare on the Massachusetts frontier.

Chapter 4

TOWARD REVOLUTION

During the eighteenth century Europeans would continue to settle throughout North America and compete with Native Americans for space. Due to the prosperous conditions described in chapter three, the English colonies grew much faster than the Spanish and French colonies. Even so, all three empires continued to seek influence and space in the New World, and in many cases they tried to use alliances with the Native Americans to gain the upper hand. Of course, Native Americans had plans of their own. As North Americans, both immigrant and native, competed for land and resources, major changes in the intellectual climate of Europe also began to influence the colonists' attitudes toward their home government. The tensions between the colonists and Native Americans would lead to conflict that would reverberate back to England and France and embroil the two empires in a war that spread across the Old and New Worlds alike. The consequences of this war would

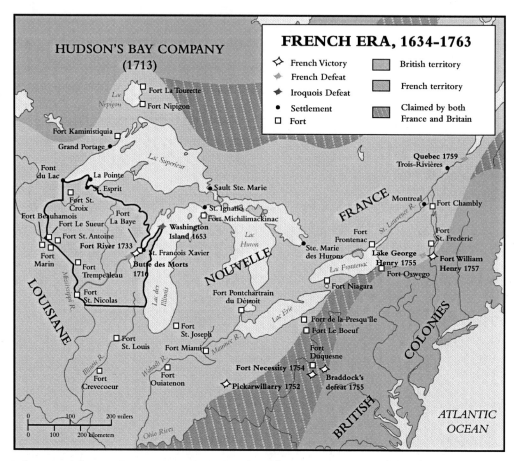

This map shows the territorial claims of New France and of British North America. As the British colonists moved westward and the French colonists moved south the two groups began to compete for space.

ultimately put an end to both the French and the British claim to North America.

Competing Empires

North America in the eighteenth century continued along much the same path as described in chapters two and three. Europeans continued to migrate to the New World, but as late as the 1750s they remained outnumbered by Native Americans. As we saw before, Britain dominated North America, but France and Spain remained a presence in the area.

Though they had claimed North American land along the St. Lawrence River and Great Lakes, the French remained most concerned with their West Indian colonies until the late seventeenth century, at which point they were able to concentrate more on their colonial efforts in Quebec and Louisiana. Embroiled in religious wars within their own country, the French only made halfhearted efforts to colonize North America before the 1670s. After that point, however, a new minister, Jean Baptiste Colbert gained power and began working to centralize the country's imperial efforts. In his vision, the plantation agriculture of the West Indies and the fur and fishing trades of North America would bring wealth to the home government through the same mercantilist system that was enriching Great Britain. Central to his plan was tight control from Paris, and he worked hard to transcend the distance and control life in Quebec. He developed subsidized emigration plans and tried to encourage settlers to marry and reproduce by offering government paid dowries. While his emigration plans largely failed because few French adults were willing to relocate, the colonial population did begin to expand due to natural increase once agriculture took off.

Quebec's main contribution to the French empire came from trading furs with Native Americans, primarily the Algonquians. They guarded this trade jealously, building outposts and forts to intercept any British efforts to establish a fur trade of their own. Generally the French would trade guns, ammunition, knives, alcohol, tobacco, or cloth for the fur. This trade, however, was in some ways as much about politics as it was about trade goods. Essentially, the French wanted to establish a presence in North America before Britain claimed the whole continent. Moving southward from their Quebec base, they established forts along the Mississippi in present-day Louisiana and Mississippi. These forts included Louisburg, Forth Niagara, Fort Toulouse, Fort Biloxi, and the most important of all, New Orleans.

Control of the Mississippi River region gave the French an important strategic advantage. For one thing, it allowed them to cut the Spanish North American empire in half by dividing Texas and Florida. It also allowed them to keep British westward settlement in check, and the Native Americans of the region, including the Choctaws and Chickasaws, appreciated that fact and made important alliances with the French.

The most important colony in this area, Louisiana, started slowly, and its early days almost mirror the situation in Jamestown. It was controlled by private investors as much as by the state, and a disproportionate number of early settlers were men, largely military personnel. As in Jamestown, the area was unattractive to settlers, partly because of the difficulties in growing food. Like the English did in many of their North American colonies, then, the French began colonizing criminals in a forced settlement scheme to make up for the lack of interest among the general population. Even with the new source of settlers, the colony refused to thrive in its early days and, like Jamestown, the settlers were forced to turn to their Native American neighbors for food and other assistance. To help grow food and perform the labor needed to make the colony thrive, the French government approved the importation of African slaves in 1719, and by 1727 the colony had a black majority. Even this did not help, though, and the colony still failed to develop any significant cash crops, remaining primarily a frontier post where Europeans, Indians and Africans met to exchange goods. As a result, the home government did not offer Louisiana the level of protection it offered the others and the settlement was left to its own devices for the most part. Because of its position at the nexus of exchange between Europeans, Native Americans, and Africans, Louisiana developed a unique culture which included a high level of intermarriage. Finally, the colony remained heavily populated by Native Americans.

As the French were trying to gain a tighter hold over Quebec and generally ignoring Louisiana, their Caribbean colonies were thriving. In these colonies, which included Martinique, Guadeloupe, and Saint-Domingue, most of the natives had died off and had been replaced by slaves imported from Africa. Slaves greatly outnumbered whites on these islands, and a large percentage of slave imports into the New World were directed here. These slaves were busy growing a very valuable cash crop—sugar. Another important crop of the region was coffee.

As we saw in chapter two, the Spanish had claimed relatively small pockets of land in what is now the United States and had been working hard to defend these settlements from French and English encroachment. One of these settlements was at St. Augustine, Florida. This settlement, like the English settlement at Jamestown and the French settlement at New Orleans, started off slowly. Indeed, at one point the Spanish considered abandoning it, but British settlement of the Carolinas made this colony important as a strategic outpost. It also became a haven for many runaway slaves from the British colonies, and this caused a great deal of tension between the two empires, especially once the Spanish began to actively encourage the runaways. Eventually escaped slaves would even create their own settlements in Florida, the most famous of which was called Santa Teresa de Mose. Because Spain offered freedom to slaves who escaped British settlements and came to Florida, this settlement was actually founded by people who were technically free and thus became the first free black community in North America.

Other Spanish settlements in North America were much farther to the west in the colony of New Mexico. There the settlement of Santa Fe served as an outpost for Spanish North America and, like Florida, the colony's main importance was as a buffer, in this case against the French rather than the English. Many of the settlers were Franciscan priests who established a number of missions in New Mexico, hoping to spread the Catholic religion among the native groups. Though they could not legally enslave the natives because it was forbidden by Spanish law, the Franciscans did much harm to the religion and culture of the Pueblo peoples they encountered in the region. In addition to the Franciscans' meddling with Pueblo culture as they tried to force them to accept Catholicism, some Spanish settlers broke the law by enslaving the Indians outright. Elites associated with the Spanish government, such as Governor Juan de Onate and his lieutenants, were able to use the *encomienda* system to exploit native labor. Under this system, Spanish settlers were granted land and given the title *encomendero*, which allowed them to force the Indians who lived on that land to pay them tribute. For many, the form of tribute demanded was labor. This system upset the entire social order among the region's native populations because the Pueblo had been accustomed to selling their surplus crops to the Navajos and Apaches, and those groups had come to count on being able to buy the food they needed from the Pueblo.

When the Spanish demands for Pueblo labor left them unable to fulfill the demands of their native neighbors, those neighbors began to take what they needed by force. In response the Pueblo turned to their native gods for comfort and were then punished by the Spanish for abandoning Catholicism. The result was Pope's Revolt. Led by a medicine man named Pope, the various Pueblo groups united to oust the Spanish in what was the most successful Native American revolt in North American history. After forcing the Spanish from Santa Fe in 1680, the Pueblo managed to keep them away for 13 years. In the long term the revolt had a number of consequences. For one matter it taught the Franciscans to use gentler methods of conversion. It also led to the end of the *encomienda* system and put a stop to much of the exploitation once the Spanish did manage to return to their colony.

Society in this Spanish colony was highly stratified. At the top were the nobility, made up of a hereditary aristocracy that included government officials. Members of this group took pride in their "pure" European ancestry, seeing their white skin as evidence of superiority. Of course, this did not prevent them from seducing and raping Native American women and creating illegitimate children. Many of those children found themselves in the second strata of society, among the *mestizos*. This group was half Spanish and half Native American and made up of landed peasants who valued the Spanish side of their heritage. Under this group were the Pueblo who lived in their own communities. Finally, the bottom layer of society was made up of other Native Americans, generally those who had been enslaved or had moved to the settlements after being sent away from their own groups.

Trouble began to brew in this region by the turn of the eighteenth century. On the one side were the Spanish and their Pueblo allies. On the other were the French from Louisiana, who had started to arm different groups of Native Americans to harass the Spanish. Their newly-armed allies included the Comanche, the Wichita, and the Pawnee.

Indeed, alliances with the French and Spanish led to major changes in the lives of the Native Americans who, by this point, had migrated to the Great Plains. One of the first major changes was the introduction of the horse. This was due to the Spanish, who left hundreds of horses behind after being expelled by the Pueblo. These horses found their way into the hands of all of the Plains Indian groups by the mid 1700s, and this development drastically changed their lives. Coupled with the guns traded to the Indians by the French, the Plains groups were then able to hunt buffalo more effectively, and this left them better fed and better clothed. It also meant more hides for better houses. As European settlement spread westward, eastern Indian groups such as the Sioux, the Creek, the Arapaho, the Cheyenne, among others, were pushed westward where they joined the original Great Plains groups.

Of course, the arrival of better transportation, guns, and more and more groups of Native American settlers onto the Great Plains led not only to better living conditions but also to increased warfare. One group known especially for its ability to dominate the others was the Comanche. This group did a particularly effective job of terrorizing the Spanish settlements within New Mexico. In response to the growing attacks, the Spanish built a number of settlements in present-day Texas to serve as a buffer and protect Santa Fe.

Of course, the English did not appreciate the encroachment of either France or Spain into North America, especially as their own settlements were growing and expanding westward. As both natural increase and immigration led to larger populations in the English colonies, more settlers began seeking a new start beyond the Appalachians. At the same time, society within the eastern settlements was changing, and their importance within the larger Atlantic community was increasing rapidly.

Changes in Colonial Society and Economy: A Population Boom

One of the most significant developments in eighteenth century British North America was the population explosion that took place between 1700 and 1750. This population growth, which saw the number of colonists go from 250,000 at the beginning of the century to more than a million by midcentury, was fueled by both natural increase and immigration. The growth in natural increase was the largest source of the population explosion, and it was due largely to improvements in the mortality rates of both children and adults in the colonies. Women were more likely than before

to marry, and they married much earlier in the colonies than in Europe, often in their late teens and early twenties. These earlier marriages led to more babies, with many women giving birth to seven or eight children. Thanks to the healthier climate and better standard of living six or seven of these children would make it to maturity. Like white women, enslaved women gave birth to an average of six to eight children, but the mortality rate was higher in the slave quarters. Although 25–50 percent of slave children would die before reaching maturity, the North American slave population's ability to reproduce itself was unmatched in other parts of the New World.

The immigrants who came to the British North American colonies at this time included those who ventured to the colonies voluntarily to seek their fortunes as well as those who were transported by force. Indeed servants, whether indentured or enslaved, made up 90 percent of the immigrants to Britain's colonies before 1775. A significant development after the turn of the century was a major change in the origins of colonial immigrants. Whereas the earliest colonists had originated mostly from England, those who came later hailed from Northern Ireland, Scotland, Wales and Germany, and a growing number were of Jewish heritage.

The largest of these immigrants groups was the Scotch-Irish. After starting out in Scotland, these Presbyterian settlers had moved first to Northern Ireland to escape famine and then to the British colonies to escape the religious persecution they faced in Great Britain's Anglican society. Massachusetts was the first to welcome these settlers, who generally emigrated in family groups, but once their numbers started to swell (as many as 250,000 came to the colonies, all told) they changed their minds. As a result, most Scotch-Irish settlers ended up heading to the southern and middle colonies.

Germans made up another large immigrant wave. Over 100,000 settlers came from Germany, and most headed to Pennsylvania. Like the Scotch-Irish, they also migrated in family units. More religiously diverse than the Scotch-Irish, the German immigrant population included Catholics, Lutherans, Quakers, Mennonites, and Amish. Most of these settlers were skilled farmers, and they contributed to the prosperity of the colonies in which they settled.

In addition to these groups of Europeans who were voluntarily migrating to seek a fresh start, there were many unfree European migrants who came to the colonies in the eighteenth century. Some were indentured servants. Many of these were English and Welsh men between the ages of 18 and 25. As many as 50,000 were British convicts. Like the indentured servants, they were sold upon arrival for specified periods of service to those who needed laborers.

Of course, indentured servants and convicts were not the only bound laborers brought to North America. The slave population increased dramatically from the mid seventeenth century, when there were fewer than 3,000 persons of African descent in mainland North America, to the mid eighteenth century, where there were more than 300,000. Most of this increase was in the southern colonies, most notably South Carolina which had a black majority as early as the 1720s. This population growth was a product of a slave trade that had become very well-organized and quite profitable.

While indentured servants and English convicts faced a humiliating sale on the auction block, African slaves endured so much more. Many slaves were war captives, but some were children who had been captured by raiding parties or, in some cases sold by their own families who were desperate to survive themselves. Two famous slaves who were kidnapped and sold into slavery and later wrote about their fate were *Olaudah Equiano* and Ottobah Cugoano. Both men later produced narratives that told of the horrors they faced after being captured and sold to slavers. Looking back upon their enslavement, both men told of the horrors of being captured, enduring a forced march to the coast, where they saw the sea for the first time, and being held in a holding pen while they awaited the ship that would take them across the ocean. As many as 10 percent of those captured died before reaching the coast, and those who survived waited in terror to be loaded into the ships that would take them into slavery. This was a terrifying period for all slaves. They did not know what to expect, and many heard rumors that they were being sold to cannibals who planned to eat them. Once they were loaded onto the ships they faced the horrors of what is known as the "*middle passage*," or the trip across the Atlantic Ocean. For this trip, slaves were packed into the ships as closely as possible. In fact, they were packed so tightly together that some suffocated, if not from the close quarters then from the lack of clean air. In many cases they were left to lie for long periods in their own waste. Due to these conditions, anywhere from 10–20 percent of those packed onto the ships died along the way.

Changes in Colonial Society and Economy: Capitalism and Overseas Trade

Once the colonies were established they began to see tremendous economic growth, becoming vital components in a capitalistic trans-Atlantic trade network. People in the colonies not only produced for this growing market, but they played important roles as consumers. It fact, it was at this time that North America, or at least British North America, became a consumer society. Naturally, along with this development came the emergence of clear classes. Merchants in the towns and plantation owners in the countryside became increasingly wealthy while the poor in both town and country became poorer, inching toward absolute poverty. Most who managed to amass a fortune at this point did so through agriculture or shipping, and they often depended on the actual labor of others. This was particularly true in the plantation south where landowners sold crops like tobacco that were grown by slave labor, made a nice profit, and used the money to purchase more land and more slaves so they could repeat the cycle.

Middle class families worked together as units, whether on the farm or in town. Women and children played important roles in this collective effort. On the farm women were in charge of feeding the family, from growing vegetables and collecting dairy products to preparing the meals. They also made the family's clothing, starting with raw material such as wool and turning it, step by step into wearable goods. They also took care of the children. In that role they also served as teachers and nurses, and some of the hardest moments were when they were unable to save a sick child. Men cleared the land, built the homes and barns, raised market crops, and took those crops to market. Children also worked, doing such things as milking dairy cows, tending sheep, or helping in the gardens. In short, the whole family worked together.

Of course, class was not the only factor that determined how a particular person would make a living. There were also important regional differences. The wealthiest region was the South, which by this point had a number of major cash crops to sell on the world market. Indeed, southern cash crops made up 60 percent or more of all exports from the colonies, and most of this was tobacco. Other important southern cash crops included rice, which became a major crop in South Carolina after white settlers learned from their slaves how to grow and cultivate it, indigo, and corn.

These crops were all grown by slaves who worked in one of two systems—task or gang labor. Gang labor was prevalent on tobacco farms. Under this system, slaves were divided into groups, or gangs, and worked in units under the watchful eye of an overseer. The image many people have of groups of enslaved women and men standing in a row hoeing weeds or harvesting crops is an image of gang labor. This system led to closer bonds among many of the slaves, whose teamwork led them to rely upon each other and to form strong ties. One serious disadvantage, however, was the constant close supervision and pressure to keep up a certain work pace. Task laborers, on the other hand, generally worked with crops like rice and were assigned specific jobs. Given quotas on how much work to complete each day, slaves who worked in this system were not supervised as closely, and they were allowed to use whatever free time they had left after completing their assigned task for the day. This type of work did not foster the close bonds that gang labor did, but it allowed slaves much more free time to do things like plant their own gardens, raise their own chickens or hogs, fish, or hunt. These activities all allowed them to supplement their own diets as well as sell surplus produce to earn a little money. In many cases, they used the extra money to buy their own freedom or the freedom of their family members.

Like southerners, middle colony residents also made their living primarily through agriculture. There were, however, major differences. For one thing, while there was slavery in the middle colonies, it did not play nearly as large a role there. Part of the reason for that was that the middle colonies did not include the plantation size landholdings. Farmers here grew wheat and other grains to sell on the market, but they did not amass the huge farms and slave labor forces of their southern counterparts. Instead they relied upon a mix of family members, indentured servants, slaves, and tenants, known as cottagers, who rented a portion of the farmer's land and worked it in exchange for wages. Overall, this region had the most even distribution of wealth, and most people here were middle class. In addition to successful farms, the middle colonies held most of North America's best ports—Philadelphia, New York, and Baltimore. The ports became important commercial and manufacturing centers. More than any other, this was the region that was known for its diversity. Especially after the Scotch-Irish and German immigrants arrived it was known for diversity of population. The mixed farming and industry ventures gave it a diverse economy, and the mix of cultural and religious backgrounds of its residents gave it a sense of cultural diversity.

Like the other two regions, New England was made up primarily of farmers. But residents here relied even less on outside labor than their counterparts in the Middle Colonies. Here most of the labor was done by male family members, and most of the produce was consumed by the family. The abundance that was sold on the market generally went to the West Indies, but this region did not rely primarily on agriculture to make its money. Instead, New England developed a manufacturing base and a diversified economy of grain, fishing, ranching, lumbering, shipbuilding, and shipping. Of all of these ventures, shipbuilding was of particular importance because it provided a key base for many other ventures, from lumbering to fishing, to shipping goods across the Atlantic. The shipping business fueled the growth of colonial ports and helped to create a strong and prosperous merchant class in the port cities.

A Consumer Revolution

The colonies played an increasingly important role in the world economy as demand for such luxury goods as sugar and tobacco skyrocketed in both the old and new worlds. What was once only available to the wealthy fell into the grasp of middle class consumers as production increased and new markets were sought. Take tea for example. It was once a luxury of the highest social order, but by the mid eighteenth century so much of it was produced in Asia and imported into England and the colonies that it became cheap enough for most people to afford. With the increasing use in tea came a corresponding increase in the demand for sugar. With the increasing demand for sugar came greater demand for slaves to grow the sugar. As planters acquired more slaves and grew larger and larger sugar crops, the price of sugar decreased in the search for new consumers. Through this means, both tea and sugar became part of life first for the middle class and then for the lower classes.

As more and more colonists made their fortune by selling these luxury crops to a growing consumer market, they were then able to turn around and use that money to buy finished goods from Britain. One good example would be nice porcelain cups from which to drink their sweetened tea. As more and more colonial middle class families began buying nice tea sets, they began to use these sets to serve tea to their friends and neighbors, who in turn felt the need to buy nice sets of their own. This was the beginning of conspicuous consumption as more and more people made enough money to buy goods that they felt would display their social status. Clothes also fit into this category, especially after the British textile revolution began to take off.

This conspicuous consumption led to a more genteel lifestyle in Britain as well as in the colonies, and this only served to reinforce growing class distinctions. People who had the means to purchase the proper clothing and household goods to fit into the gentility became increasingly snobbish toward those who did not, and they looked down upon them as their social inferiors. Hoping to escape such scrutiny and enter the genteel class themselves, more and more working class and poor began to strive to purchase items they would not have considered important before—from fancy clothing to china to silverware to mirrors. This trickle-down effect that left even those who could barely afford it buying consumer goods is what is known as a consumer revolution, and it is the basis of capitalist development. It also set the groundwork for the Industrial Revolution, which will be discussed in depth in a later chapter.

Early Urbanization

Colonial cities began to grow considerably during the eighteenth century. At the turn of the century Boston was the largest city with 7,000 people. By 1750 it had grown to 12,000. Philadelphia was not far behind with 10,000, and New York had about 7,000. These remained the major cities in the North America, but some new cities, including Lancaster, Pennsylvania, Albany, New York, Baltimore, Maryland, Salem, Massachusetts, and Savannah, Georgia, emerged on the colonial scene. By the time of

the American Revolution, Philadelphia would eclipse Boston with 30,000 residents to Boston's 16,000. New York trailed Philadelphia, but not by much, with 25,000. The main thing all of these cities shared in common was that they were ports.

Class divisions emerged and then quickly grew in these cities. The upper class was made up government officials, professionals, and merchants. They increasingly indulged in the type of conspicuous consumption described above. Their lifestyle was much like that of the European upper classes and included social clubs of various types such as hunting clubs and lavish parties and dances. Urban associations like the Masons and various types of self-improvement societies played an important part in their social lives. Middle class urbanites were often craftsmen and mechanics who made comfortable enough livings to support their families. Sometimes they were able to take on apprentices. At the other end of the spectrum were the urban poor. They spent their days laboring for the basic necessities. During the course of the eighteenth century this poor class grew substantially and the almshouse became another important urban fixture. Indeed, the growth of the pauper population led many colonial cities to resemble London, a European city known for having a large impoverished population.

The cities had a number of places where the people would meet and interact on a daily basis. One center of life was the tavern, where people of all classes, but especially the working class and poor, met with friends and family to socialize but also where they met with possible employers. The upper class also had a number of voluntary associations and social clubs they could join and take part in. In addition, cities contained churches, theaters and newspapers. For most people church was more than simply a place of worship. It was a place where they could interact socially with friends and family and meet potential mates. Similarly, theaters brought people together, allowing them opportunities to wear their fancy clothing and to learn about all the latest trends. Finally, newspapers served important functions in the cities by keeping residents abreast of the latest happenings and discussing the political and social events of the day.

One final group of city dwellers was African Americans. Some of these black residents were enslaved, but a growing number had managed to gain their freedom. Relations between black and white residents were often tense, and as the black population grew the resulting tension led to a number of rumors of revolt. The most famous example was New York. A 1712 revolt in this city left nine whites dead and led to terrifying reprisals against the slave community that included the execution of eighteen people convicted as rebels. Three were burned at the stake, another was tortured by the medieval technique of being broken on the wheel, and another was starved to death. Several killed themselves to avoid such torture. In 1741 the mere rumor of another revolt led to the hanging of eighteen blacks and four whites. To make a clear statement, officials burned a dozen more at the stake. Of course, both of these revolts caused concern in other colonial cities, and Philadelphia officials, for example, tried to prevent the same thing from happening in their city by imposing import duties on slaves.

Life in the Countryside

Of course, not everyone in the colonies moved to the cities. The majority remained on the farms. Indeed the population growth in rural

areas led to significant overcrowding, especially in the areas where over farming pressured the land and left it less fertile, such as the tobacco areas of the Chesapeake. In New England, large farming families ran out of land to pass down to their sons after several generations of dividing their landholdings up among their sons. This led to outmigration of grown children to newer areas, and this meant that parents had less control over the choices and behavior of their grown children. Some of the sons of this generation managed to acquire land in frontier regions, some migrated to cities, and others entered into agreements to farm the land of others. For many of the children of the mid to late eighteenth century, the lack of land opportunity meant later marriage—in the early to mid twenties rather than the late teens to early twenties.

Slavery in the countryside was woven even more tightly in the social fabric than it was in the cities. Chesapeake planters were especially known for creating plantations that closely resembled English country estates. They also sought to lives the lives of English gentry, relying on the work of others to line their pockets as they dominated the social and political lives of their colonies. They had the money and the power to earn the loyalty of lesser whites in their region by lending them money, helping them market their goods, and promising them social and political protection. In the lower south planters also reigned supreme but the task-oriented labor system, along with a higher rate of absentee ownership of the plantations, led to greater social and cultural independence for the slaves. There the slaves were more able to maintain more of their own customs, including religion, and they developed unique languages such as the South Carolina Sea Island dialect known as Gullah. This dialect combined a number of different African and European languages to create a unique creole language that lives to this day in some areas.

Slave revolts were rarer than may be expected, but one famous revolt did occur in South Carolina in 1739. Known as the *Stono Revolt* or *Stono Rebellion*, this uprising was the bloodiest one seen in the North American mainland colonies. Twenty slaves who had been brought to the colony directly from Africa managed to murder a store owner and take weapons and ammunition that they then used to kill other whites as they headed toward St. Augustine, Florida, where they hoped to find freedom under Spanish jurisdiction. The fighting lasted for over a week, and the drama did not end until the final rebel leader was captured three years later. As in New York, authorities responded by torturing the rebels and making life even harsher for slaves in general. As in Philadelphia, colonial leaders also placed large duties on slave imports.

While the colonists were building their own consumer societies in North America, Europe was being transformed by a major intellectual current known as the *Enlightenment*. Put simply, the Enlightenment was an 18th century intellectual movement that believed in the possibility of improvement of humankind through reason, scientific investigation, and experimentation. The human mind, Enlightenment thinkers believed, had the capacity to figure out the secrets of the universe. Enlightenment thinkers shared faith in reason and belief in progress and perfectibility (otherwise known as the idea of history as progress). They also had confidence that man could discover the causes of all natural phenomena, and they believed that set principles governed nature, man, and society and that empiricism and observation made it possible to discover these laws.

They also shared a willingness to challenge authority, in both government and religion. This led to a call for toleration of religious differences and a belief that there were no absolutes. There were two main strains of Enlightenment thought—the scientific and the political.

The Scientific Revolution and the Age of Enlightenment

The 17th and 18th centuries (1600s and 1700s) saw huge changes throughout the Western world. A "Scientific Revolution" occurred and science began to dominate most intellectuals' thoughts. This started in the late 16th century and spread and grew throughout the 17th and 18th centuries. Major changes that led to this revolution included the development of new methods of observation and data collection and advances in printing which made it easier for scientists to share their work. Empiricism became the buzzword as more and more people began to agree that things must be observed in order to be understood.

Many fields of science were transformed by this growth in empiricism, beginning with astronomy. Discoveries in this field led people to question religion first and then government. This began in 1543 when Nicolas Copernicus showed that the earth was not the center of the universe. The old belief, based on the theories of Ptolemy and Aristotle, was that the earth was the center and was surrounded by perfect crystalline spheres which contained the moon, the sun, the planets, and the stars. After the last sphere was the realm of God and angels. This system fit perfectly with church teachings because the universe was well-ordered and man was at the center.

The new system introduced by Copernicus, however, did not fit with church teachings. Copernicus showed that the sun was at the center of the universe, and he was able to use math to help figure out the basic rules of astronomy with calculations that began to make sense. Galileo then invented the telescope in 1609 to help test Copernicus's new ideas, and what he found really destroyed the Ptolemaic system by showing that the universe is totally subject to mathematical laws. Scientists saw this as proof that nature was inherently logical and regulated mathematically to the tiniest detail.

The conclusion was that all science could be reduced to mathematics. *Francis Bacon* took it all further by advocating the idea of *"empirical induction"*, or learning through observation alone. Experimentation and observation became honored over inherited theories, and calls for innovation and change began to replace the middle age concept of further refining known truths. The conclusion was that the peak of human learning was not in ancient Greece and Rome but lay ahead in the future. *Isaac Newton* then applied the use of empiricism and logic to establish a new basis for physics. He introduced the belief that all objects in the universe were moving through "mutual attraction." In short, he discovered gravity. After Newton, the natural universe became a realm of law and regularity. Spirits and divinity were no longer necessary to explain the universe's operation.

This rise in scientific thinking led to an attack on superstition in general. The Salem Witch Trials serve as evidence that belief in, and fear of, witches was common in Europe and the colonies. This started to fade out around 1700 as people became less likely to believe in witches or supernatural phenomena of many kinds. The Salem trials occurred in 1692 and they were the last serious incident of this type. The accusers could not prove scientifically that the people were witches and more and more people began to want scientific proof and were less willing to rely on traditional methods of investigation. Also, some enlightenment thinkers, namely Cesare Beccaria of Italy, began to call for an end to cruel punishment and focus on reform over capital punishment.

The scientific ideas of the Enlightenment affected the colonists in many ways. One example involves the field of medicine. First, Boston minister Cotton Mather read about a technique that involved exposing people to a small amount of the smallpox virus so that they would build up immunity and thus be safe from the disease afterward. His slave Onesimus confirmed that the practice was used in his native region of Africa, and Mather worked hard to develop this idea of inoculation, or immunization, and to bring the technique to the colonies. Another development in the medical field occurred in 1751 with the building of the Pennsylvania Hospital at the behest of Benjamin Franklin. Similarly, the Eastern State Mental Hospital was created in 1773 to rehabilitate the mentally ill.

The ideas of history as progress and the perfectibility of life led the colonists to a number of efforts to reform and improve society. Benjamin Franklin was central to many of these efforts. He fought to create a colonial equivalent to the Royal Society of London, a group that met to discuss the newest innovations in scientific and technological developments. This debating society later became the American Philosophical Society. As an editor and publisher of the *Pennsylvania Gazette* and *Poor Richard's Almanack* he also did much to publicize and spread new ideas, theories, and attitudes associated with the Enlightenment.

Similarly, he played a central role in establishing the colonies' first lending library, the Library Company of Philadelphia, the first fire company, and the academy that later became the University of Pennsylvania. Interestingly, this was the only colonial college that was founded for secular, rather than religious, purposes.

Benjamin Franklin was the best example of an Enlightenment figure in North America. Among his inventions were bifocal glasses, the rocking chair, and the Franklin Stove, a device that allowed people to cook food and heat their homes at the same time. He was also instrumental in creating the first library and the first hospital, and he is perhaps best known for his experiments with electricity. He was also an important publisher and statesman.

Deism and the Great Awakening: The Enlightenment and Religion

The Enlightenment affected religion in several ways. Even among the intellectual elite, very few questioned the presence of God, but many, especially the French intellectual Voltaire, began to argue that religion as it was just caused wars and hatred. Most sought, however, not to do away with religion but to use scientific observation to understand God and the universe they still believed he had created. Harvard became the colonial center of a new more liberal theology, and religious conservatives created Yale to train ministers in traditional Calvinist doctrine. Along with the growth in the more liberal religious ideas came a new emphasis on *Arminianism*, or the belief that the individual could help ensure his or her own salvation with good works.

Among the most liberal of the new ideas was a more "scientific" religion called *Deism*. Deism stemmed from the idea that everything functions according to natural laws and orderly systems. Deists believed that God created the universe and everything in it, like a skilled clock maker creates a perfect clock, but then, like the clock maker, stepped back to let it all work on its own. Natural laws, such as those discovered by Newton, were what allowed it to all work out without God's intervention. Deists believed that studying nature helped people appreciate God's work. Is this Christianity? Not exactly. The system described by Deists leaves no room for a miracle in which a virgin gives birth to the savior of the world. Also, if God stepped back and let it all work out on its own, would he have sent his son to save the world? No. Deists saw God as rational and scientific, just like they were trying to be themselves. The God they believed in did not interfere in people's day to day lives and there were no miracles. Many of the "Founding Fathers," including Benjamin Franklin, Thomas Jefferson, James Madison, and Thomas Paine, were Deists, and this point is an important one given the prevalence of assertions that America was "founded as a Christian nation." It is not that simple. Some of the colonies were founded as "Godly societies" based on Christianity (New England and Pennsylvania especially), and many colonies had "established" churches (churches supported by state collected taxes from the people), but this was starting to change.

Deism was a belief system shared by many colonial intellectuals, but the average person was more affected by another religious movement known as *The Great Awakening*. This movement, which was actually a series of highly-emotional religious revivals, occurred at a time in which most colonies supported one of the main "established" churches—Anglican, Presbyterian, or Congregational—and those churches fought hard to maintain their monopolies. In this atmosphere, any type of questioning or religious dissent was strongly discouraged. Then, beginning in 1734 and lasting until 1745, all of this changed dramatically as travelling, or "itinerant," preachers began to travel throughout the colonies and introduce new ideas. These *evangelical* ministers sought converts to their cause by claiming that official ministers were often out only for their own good and insisting that the real key to salvation was "rebirth" in both conviction and behavior. This "new birth" was signaled by a sudden and intense emotional episode, or moment of conversion. This new movement was the first popular movement that spread throughout all of the colonies and reached out to all classes.

The Great Awakening appealed to the younger generation, many of whom sought the leadership of preachers who had less formal education but a greater ability to reach out to their audiences on an emotional level. One of the most famous of these ministers was *George Whitefield*, an Anglican minister from England who travelled throughout every one of the colonies preaching about the sinfulness of humans and the forgiveness of God. Using biblical stories to create simple script-based sermons which he acted out dramatically, Whitefield reached out to the rich as well as the poor, men as well as women, the young and the old alike, and even the enslaved. His use of drama and emotion appealed to those who had little or no formal education themselves. What appealed even further was his emphasis not on a reasoned and educated assessment of the scriptures themselves but on a dramatic and emotional conversion experience that all followers thought they could participate in.

The focus on conversion led to a challenge of traditional ministerial authority. Revivalist ministers criticized traditional ministers for their traditional focus and lack of conversion. In response, traditional ministers criticized the itinerates' emotionalism. Some congregants then became curious about the new style, and attendance at the revivals grew. Many were attracted to what they saw as a more democratic fellowship, especially since revivalist ministers called upon people to look inward rather than to outward hierarchies for guidance.

Some historians have seen this phenomenon as a backlash against the more rational

GEORGE WHITEFIELD.M.A.

Elisha Gallaudet   *Sculp.s N.York.1774*

Known as the "Great Itinerant," George Whitefield traveled throughout the North American colonies spreading the zeal of the Great Awakening to people of all classes. He focused on the importance of an emotional conversion experience rather than on a rational reading of scriptures. He gained the status of an icon within his own lifetime and colonists traveled for long distances to hear him speak.

appeal to emotion and emphasis on conversion, the Awakening could indeed easily be seen as a backlash against Enlightenment rationalism. On the other hand, the assertion that the Awakening was a way for the less educated to use reason to understand God has merit. After all, the assumption that only the educated can reason is false.

The Great Awakening had a large impact on education in the colonies, primarily because the competing denominations created their own colleges to educate their ministers. Princeton University, which started out as the College of New Jersey, was founded by Presbyterians in 1746, followed by Columbia University, which started out in 1754 as the Anglican King's College. The College of Rhode Island was founded by Baptists in 174; it is now Brown University. Rutgers was founded as Queens College in 1766 by the Dutch Reformed, and Dartmouth, a Congregationalist school for Indians, was founded in 1769.

Ironically, though they may seem at odds on first glance, the Great Awakening and the Enlightenment both helped fuel the push for the later constitutional guarantee that the church and the state would be separated. On the one hand, intellectuals who followed Enlightenment ideas would come to believe that religion was a matter of personal conscience and that no state should be able to dictate choices in this field, or force people to pay taxes to support churches

religion of the intellectual elite, but others have insisted that the awakening actually stemmed from the efforts of everyday people to use their own reasoning ability to understand God on their own terms. With its

they were not part of. On the other hand, those who chose to follow the various new denominations would insist that it was their right to do so and that no government should be allowed to force them to pay taxes to support other churches. In that sense, the religious developments were a major source for freedom and democracy.

Four Stages of Progress: Political Science and the Enlightenment

In addition to science and religion, the Enlightenment had an important political impact. By this point politics had already changed drastically, and the Enlightenment led to further changes. As European governments had evolved up to the 1600s, they generally fell into one of two categories—absolutist or constitutionalist. The most notable example of an absolutist government was France under Louis XIV, while England and Holland were good examples of constitutionalist governments.

Absolutism meant certain things. First, leaders ruled under an idea that they had a "divine right" to rule and only had to answer to God. They believed that God had given them their positions as leaders, so they did not have to answer to the people they ruled. Under this system, religious sects were strongly regulated. Instead of being kept in check by the church, feudal nobility, and financial limitations, absolutists used these factors to rule. For example, instead of bargaining with nobility for money, they created bureaucracies and new ways of raising money that did not rely upon the cooperation of their subjects. Under this system, the king appointed people to bureaucratic positions and gave them jobs. Those people then owed him for giving them their jobs. They collected money (taxes) for the crown, not for themselves, and they were paid a salary by the king. The king sometimes managed to bypass the nobility and limited their power by giving these jobs to the middle class instead. Absolutist kings also maintained permanent standing armies and interfered with the private lives of their subjects through the use of secret police. Basically, under absolutism the king *was* the state.

Constitutionalism was quite different. Basically, under this system the government was limited by the law. The authority and power of the government was balanced by the rights and liberties of the subject, and those rights and liberties were protected by a constitution. The constitution could be written or unwritten. England's was mixed, which meant that some parts were written and some were based on tradition. What mattered was that the government admitted that its power was limited, and it acknowledged that it must abide by the higher law.

Constitutional governments can be either republican or monarchial, but either way the sovereign power rests in the electorate (the voters) and is exercised by those they elect to represent them. Under a *republic*, there is no king and all representatives are elected by voters. Under a *constitutional monarchy*, the monarch (who is not elected but gains his or her position through inheritance) maintains a degree of power, but ultimately the bulk of the power is held by the elected representatives. What this essentially means is that the king remains the head of the government, and he rules under the idea that he is at the top because God put him there, but he must work with a representative body of legislators chosen by the people. In England's case, this body was called *Parliament*. It must be understood, however, that "constitutional" and "democratic" governments are *not* the same thing. The difference is a matter of who can vote. In the case of England, elites held the bulk of the power, and they had to have land and wealth in order to vote.

The way in which England came to have this system is a long and complicated story. After 1200 or so, elites managed to get power and keep the king in line. For one thing, the king at that time was militarily weak. Also, the bishops had begun exerting power and insisting upon having input regarding who would be named archbishop. At the same time, an efficient civil service made it almost possible to run the country without a king. In 1215 barons took over London and forced the king (John) to sign the *Magna Carta*. This document established a committee of 25 barons who could meet and overrule the king on some matters, serving as a representative body. This body became the precursor to the parliament that later developed and became crucial to England's constitutional system. The Magna Carta also guaranteed the freedom of the English church and gave judicial rights to courts. This was really a very limited document, but by the 1700s it began to take on mythical traits in the minds of many people, especially the North American English colonists.

Indeed by the time settlers began moving in large waves to the North American colonies, an image of the English government had developed that celebrated that nation as one of the most enlightened and representative in the world. Between 1588 and 1689 England had transformed from royal absolutism to a constitutional monarchy. Elizabeth I had great personal power and was very well respected by the people, but she also respected certain limits to her rule. After she died, however, her Scottish cousin James took her place on the throne in 1603 and tried to rule through absolutism.

There were a number of problems with this. First, he did not play the role of monarch as well as Elizabeth had, and he did not have the knack for working with the people that she did. He also had a Scottish accent that did not go over well with the people he sought to rule because it made people see him as "foreign." He also ignored traditionally-respected rights of the people and made it clear that he wanted to rule over aspects like personal liberties and property rights without due process, ignoring the Magna Carta. He expressed these ideas to the House of Commons, the group which, by that point, was in charge of the nation's funds. Furthermore, the country was in debt but James lived lavishly, and his extravagant court offended people. Finally, he publically flaunted his male lovers, and that offended many of his subjects. At the same time, the House of Commons knew its own power and wanted to use its control of the purse to gain more influence in the governing of the country. They wanted a voice in how the money was spent, how foreign affairs were conducted, and what religious reforms were allowed. Basically, a social revolution had made these people more wealthy and powerful, and they wanted more power.

Social changes in England put more power in certain people's hands and fostered constitutionalism by changing the outlook of those who served in the Commons. Henry VIII, Elizabeth's father, had dissolved the monasteries when he separated England from the Catholic Church. Those who managed to get their hands on the confiscated land were able to sell it and become rich. Also, the land in general had become more productive as wasteland was drained, fertilizers were used, and common lands were enclosed for raising sheep. The flocks and herds of livestock were increased and improved with careful breeding. Those profiting from all of these developments had to start keeping precise accounts, and record keeping began to improve as new middle-class business-related occupations such as bookkeeping and accounting emerged.

There were also new commercial ventures for people to invest in. The textile industry began to really take off, partnerships and joint stock companies developed, and a number of foreign enterprises were available for British capitalists to invest in. This led to both the growth of capitalism and increased social mobility, and people began to invest profits in the new businesses and emerging economic ventures to make even more money. At the same time, incomes began to rise faster than prices. A "new money" set emerged, made up of people who became wealthy from commerce rather than heredity, and their wealth was in business and other forms of capital rather than land. These were generally the people who served in the House of Commons, and with this rise in "new money" the House of Commons ended up richer than the House of Lords, which was made up of those who gained their wealth from land and inheritance. Greater wealth led to better educational opportunities for Commons members and their families. Many studied law and used their legal knowledge against the king.

The House of Commons was willing to tax itself if it had influence in how taxes were spent and a voice in the creation of state policies. The Stuart kings (James I and his son Charles I) thought the Commons were overstepping their bounds and posing a threat to the idea of divine right. Charles tried to circumvent Parliament and rule without them, but he ended up needing money to fund a war, so he appealed to the Commons. After being called, Parliament met and managed to pass a number of laws that limited the monarch's power and made arbitrary government impossible. They also passed a law that Parliament would meet every three years. As all of this was develop-

ing, a civil war broke out. To make a really long story short, in 1649 the king was executed, and that really undercut the notion of divine right.

From 1649–1660 England was under a military dictatorship, but Charles II (son of Charles I) was brought back in 1660 and Parliament was restored in what is known historically as "The Restoration." Though both houses of Parliament were restored, no resolution was reached as to the constitutional position of the king. Even so, Charles II and Parliament got along fairly well. For one thing, Charles developed a cabinet to work between him and Parliament. Also, there was an agreement that he would call Parliament and they would approve his requests for money. Parliament, however, did not vote him enough money so he basically accepted a bribe from the French to relax laws against Catholics, slowly bring Catholicism back to England, support the French against the Protestant Dutch, and convert to Catholicism. Word of this agreement leaked out, and the Commons passed a bill to deny the throne to Catholic successors, but Charles dissolved Parliament before the law was passed. James, his successor, appointed Catholics to important positions in the army, universities, and the government. He then granted a general indulgence giving religious freedom to everyone. His wife then produced a male heir to the throne, and this was the proverbial last straw. Parliament (or, at least some members of Parliament) asked James' Protestant daughter Mary and her husband, William of Orange, to come take the throne and they did.

In 1689 William and Mary were crowned king and queen in what is known as the *"Glorious Revolution."* This was the final move in the destruction of divine right monarchy in England, once and for all. By removing one king and choosing his successors, Parliament showed itself to be above the monarch. William and Mary showed agreement by signing the English *Bill of Rights*. This document is seen by many as the cornerstone of English liberty. It said that law would be made in Parliament and that the monarch could not suspend law. It also said that Parliament must be called regularly and that the crown could not interfere in elections or parliamentary debate. It provided that the king could not remove judges and that there would be no standing armies in peace time. It also said that the monarch must always be Protestant. Even though this was a major development, this was not a democratic revolution. Parliament essentially represented the upper classes and most people could not vote.

Of those who could vote, one relatively new group was the rising middle class. This group did not hold the vote due to traditional standards of land ownership, but they were coming into their own as a class, and they paid enough taxes to be included in the franchise. Motivated by commercial interests, this group began calling for freedom from state regulation and for fewer restrictions on their commercial efforts. This was a start toward a call for free trade as mercantilism began to come under fire. The middle class was also growing in confidence and willing to question things more. Their growing wealth gave them a sense that they were entitled to input in how the country was governed, and the more power they got, the more they wanted. Since literacy was spreading, especially through the middle class, more and more people were exposed to Enlightenment ideas that corresponded nicely with the needs of this emerging class.

The Glorious Revolution, then, created a three-part government with the representative body dominant. This system included checks and balances, the people were represented by elected leaders, Parliament's sovereignty was guaranteed, and constitutionalism was ensured through a written Bill of Rights. Building on this, a number of British thinkers developed political views that fit the Enlightenment system.

Thomas Hobbes had become very alarmed at the chaos of England's Puritan Revolution (not the Glorious Revolution—one that came before it and ushered in a dictatorial system). In 1651 he wrote *Leviathan* in an attempt to apply the scientific method to politics and create a "political science." In other words, he was trying to use reason to understand politics. He concluded that "the life of man is nasty, brutish, and short" and to ensure the welfare of all, the state must have tight control and keep the people in line. Therefore, according to Hobbes, absolute power is needed for good leadership, and he called for a tightly-ordered commonwealth ruled by law and order for the good of all.

Another political thinker, *John Locke*, opposed Hobbes but also wanted to use science and natural laws to understand and perfect government. He justified the Glorious Revolution as a defense of man's natural rights and called for *religious toleration*. His ideas became the basis for the belief in the need to maintain separation of church and state. According to his philosophy, man is rational and born with a clean slate ("*tabula rasa*"). Thus, since everyone is born with a clean slate, everyone is born equal. He also believed that people are motivated by pleasure and the avoidance of pain and that government should educate people and make them better but also mould behavior by using pleasure and pain. This theory of government says that man's natural state is equality and harmony; government's function is to regulate society and keep it peaceful by providing law and

An important philosopher of the Enlightenment era, John Locke greatly influenced British intellectuals in both the mainland and the North American colonies. His ideas of toleration led to an American emphasis on the notion that the church and the state should be kept separate, and his ideas of natural rights and the contractual nature of government would lend a great deal of support to the American colonists in their quest for independence from Great Britain.

judges; people make a *contract* with the government to protect their rights; and people have a natural right to oppose governments that do not hold up their end of the contract. His theory of rights and equality says that all people are born with the natural rights of life, liberty, and property. Keep in mind, though, that his version of equality means equality *before the law*, not social equality.

Adam Smith took Locke's ideas a step further and also applied them to economics. He called for the government to take a "hands off" role in economics ("*laissez faire*"). In essence, he tried to apply the natural liberty idea to economics. His idea was that what is good for the individual will be good for society because laws of supply and demand will work out naturally through an "*invisible hand*." He argued that government has a place in the judiciary, the military, and the policing system but not in the economy. A less-studied, though also important, aspect of Smith's thinking was his view of history and his attempt to apply scientific observation to history. He and others in the Scottish leg of the Enlightenment came up with the idea that history progresses in four distinct stages: 1) hunting 2) pasturage 3) agriculture and 4) commerce. They believed that societies progressed through these stages as they grew in population and needed to find new ways to subsist. The catch, however, was that once they reached the final stage, decay and decadence became inevitable. Finding American Indians in the first 3 stages helped to reinforce this theory, and by the time of the Revolution many Americans began to see breaking away from England as a way to avoid the decay and decadence stage and preserve a really good overall political system.

Many of these ideas spread from Britain to France, where intellectuals often gathered in salons to discuss them. Other Europeans, especially the French, really liked the new empiricism and the idea of English liberties embodied in the Bill of Rights. One French intellectual, *Voltaire*, tried to spread empiricism and religious toleration further. He introduced the idea that most inhumane crimes are

Adam Smith is best known for his economic theories of laissez faire, which stated that an "invisible hand" regulates free market economies and that the government should not interfere with the natural workings of this system. He also contributed the idea that societies progress through four stages—hunting, pasturage, agriculture, and commerce.

committed in the name of religion, and he ridiculed superstition and the French witch trials. He spent time in England and fell in love with its political system, especially the idea of freedom of speech. Another French intellectual, *Montesquieu*, also greatly admired the English government after the Glorious Revolution. His favorite aspect was its balance of executive, legislative, and judicial powers ("balance of powers" with "*checks and balances*"). Finally, *Jean Jacques Rousseau* focused on the idea of society as corrupting and said that people lived under a *social contract* and needed few social constraints. He also said that law should be made by the "general will" of the people.

By the time of the Glorious Revolution, the British had had colonies in North America for about a generation. Events of this revolution played out in America too, as we saw in chapter three, and by the mid eighteenth century the North American colonists had started to evaluate their home government based upon the ideas of men like Locke, Smith, Montesquieu, and Rousseau. Locke's ideas of natural rights, which included the rights to preserve life and liberty and the right to protect property, were of particular significance. Under his belief system, people enter voluntarily into a social contract in which they create governments to protect these rights, and when the government fails to do so, the people have a right to break that contract. Colonial elites like Thomas Jefferson believed strongly in this social contract theory, and their perception of the home government's failure to protect colonial rights would play a major role in leading them to ultimately fight for independence, as we will see in the next chapter. Also, many colonial elites came to believe strongly that British society had clearly reached Smith's fourth stage of development, and by the time of the American Revolution many colonial intellectuals had concluded that the period of decadence was at hand. Along with that societal decay, American intellectuals began to see signs of corruption in the home government, insisting that the king and Parliament were out to enslave the colonists and force them to fund and fight in wars of empire to enrich the home governments. To what extent was that true? The best way to evaluate this question is by examining the relationship between the home government and the colonies in the years leading up to the American Revolution.

English Administration and Salutary Neglect

While the home government was busy experiencing the upheavals and revolutions of the seventeenth century, it was basically ignoring the colonies. After the Restoration of the Stuart dynasty in 1660, however, the government began to experiment with new plans of governing the colonies. Even so, the colonists remained largely in charge of their own affairs, and this led them to develop a strong sense of their rights as part of the British system.

As we saw in an earlier chapter, the main reason for the very existence of the British colonies was so that the home government could reap financial rewards, and one of the main ways this was governed was through a system known as *mercantilism*. This system is based on the idea that the supply of wealth in the world, based on precious metals like gold and silver, is fixed. What changes, then, is how much of this fixed amount of wealth is claimed by each nation. One nation can only gain wealth if another loses wealth. To remain on the winning end of this equation, leaders must closely regulate all aspects of a nation's economy. Imports must be kept to a minimum so money is not sent to other countries to pay for goods. As a result, manufacturing must be encouraged, so that the goods people need can be purchased from local sources and thus money will be kept in circulation within the nation. Sometimes subsidies and monopolies would be used to help develop and protect a nation's manufacturing and shipping industries. In this system colonies were important sources of raw goods, but they also provided important markets for the home country's finished goods.

Also, for the system to work as planned, the government had to keep tight reins on all shipping. England lost this edge briefly during the 1640s while it was preoccupied by civil war. The distraction allowed the Dutch to step in and take over trade with the British colonies, but after the war, the British government regained the trade through *Navigation Acts*. The first of these acts required that all goods imported by England or the English colonies had to arrive on English ships managed by English crews. These acts were expanded during the Restoration. The first changes, which were applied in 1660, included the provision that certain products not produced by the mother country, such as tobacco, cotton, and sugar (all colonial products) could only be shipped from the colonies to England or to other English colonies. This was expanded further in 1663 with the requirement that all ships carrying goods from Europe to North America stop in England and pay a duty there before proceeding to the colonies. Finally, a 1673 act added the requirement that every captain loading certain listed ("enumerated") articles in the colonies pay duties on those articles. These acts were meant to allow the British government to make the most out of its colonies. As we saw in chapter three, however, they provoked anger and distrust among the colonists and led ultimately to the annulment of the Massachusetts charter and the creation of the Dominion of New England.

After the Glorious Revolution William and Mary strengthened the Navigation Acts and the regulation of trade with the American colonies. In 1696 another Navigation Act added a requirement that governors in the colonies enforce the previous acts. The provision that offended colonists the most, however, allowed customs officials to use general search warrants called "writs of assistance" to search suspected smugglers. These writs were very open-ended and did not specify what was to be searched, leaving broad latitude to those doing the searching. The act also stated that those accused of violating the Navigation Acts would be tried in *vice admiralty courts*. These courts did not have juries, so the cases were decided by royally-appointed judges. The rationale was that colonial juries had generally been lenient and refused to convict smugglers. The new monarchs also created a new body to oversee the Navigation Acts and colonial trade—the Lords Commissioners of Trade and Plantations. The goal of this overhaul was to strengthen the administration's control of colonial trade. The problem was, however, that the regulations were not applied in a steady and uniform manner, and the colonists became accustomed to disobeying them without consequence.

By the time of the Glorious Revolution colonists were accustomed to the home government leaving them largely to their own devices. This lack of interest in the day to day workings of colonial governance is known as *salutary neglect*, and it left the colonists free to do pretty much as they pleased, including ignoring the Navigation Acts. For the most part, the colonists reserved their loyalty for their local governments.

The local, or colonial, governments were like miniature replicas of the home government. By this time most of the colonies had Crown-appointed governors. (The exceptions were Connecticut and Rhode Island, where governors were elected.) These governors were the chief executives of the colonies and had some powers that even the monarch did not have. For example, they held the power of absolute veto over the colonial assemblies.

They also had the power to appoint and remove officials and grant pardons, and they were commanders of the colonial militias. In many ways, each governor was like a king of his colony. Similarly, the colonies included elected assemblies that in many ways resembled Parliament. The lower houses were chosen by popular vote. Because most believed the notion that men who "held a stake in society" would be most likely to act (and vote) on the society's best interests, voting rights were restricted to male property holders, but property ownership was so widespread in the colonies that more people could vote in the English colonies than anywhere else in the world at the time. These elected assemblies held great power because they controlled the budget since they had to approve taxes and expenditures. They also had the power to introduce legislation. Throughout the eighteenth century they managed to increase their powers and they and their constituents came to see self-government not as a privilege but as a basic right. Importantly, most colonists came to see these governors and assemblies as their real governing bodies and the king and parliament as interlopers.

Westward Settlement and the Native Americans

Another thing most colonists claimed as a matter of right was the right to spread westward. Of course, this brought them into conflict with Native Americans. It also brought them into conflict with other European powers, namely the Spanish and French. The conflicts over North American land were actually part of larger tensions between the major European imperial powers.

Conflict with the Native Americans began soon after Europeans began colonizing the New World. As we saw in chapters two and three, a number of wars broke out between the Indians and the settlers throughout British North America. The common factor among those wars was that the Indians were generally not united and the settlers played upon the situation to use the divide and conquer tactic. Of course, it was not only the English who were encroaching upon Native American land. As we saw earlier, the Spanish and the French were also claiming parts of North America. What this equated to was a cauldron of tensions stewing in North America and spilling over into Europe. The English settlers had started out along the eastern seaboard but had been progressing westward almost from the beginning. At the same time, the French had started out in the far north but had been moving southward, and the Spanish had started out in Florida and had been harassing and trying to infringe upon British settlements to their north. All the while, Native Americans were losing land little by little due to each of these movement patterns.

Tensions between the home governments in Britain and France over North America began to take off after the Glorious Revolution. William of Orange was a Protestant, and his ascent to the British throne put England in alliance with other Protestant nations and in opposition to the Catholic France in the War of the League of Augsburg (1689–1697), which was known as King William's War in the colonies. This war was just the beginning. It was followed by the War of the Spanish Succession (1702–1713), which was known in the colonies as Queen Anne's War; the War of the Austrian Succession (1744–1748), known in the colonies as King George's War; and, most importantly the Seven Year's War (1754–1763), which was known in the colonies as the French and Indian War.

The ongoing conflict with other nations and their colonies meant a number of things for the colonists. For one thing, the constant warfare cost the colonial governments a fortune. The wars had to be funded by taxes, and this caused tension when colonial legislatures started to resent the amount of money they were expected to raise. This particularly affected Massachusetts, where royal governors, who owed their allegiance to the Crown, pushed colonists to contribute much to the war efforts. This contribution extended beyond funding to manpower, and many colonial men were forced, in one way or another, to join the British forces. This led to resistance and rioting as early as the 1740s. Colonial civilians were also directly affected by the wars as they faced property loss at the hands of plundering armies, both enemy and friendly. This resulted in tensions that would not be resolved until well after American independence. Of course, the British government came out of the wars with a large debt as well, and they would then expect the colonies to raise taxes to help pay the debt. As we will see in the next chapter, this would be a major factor in causing the American Revolution.

French and Indian War

The most famous of all of these wars was the French and Indian War. The events leading to this war began in 1750 when settlers from Virginia, who had been granted land beyond the Allegheny Mountains in the Ohio River valley by King George began to survey their new land and to try to establish trade with the Indians in the area. The French did not appreciate this incursion into what they considered their land, so they built a number of forts in the area. The governor of Virginia sent a young militia officer named George Washington to warn the French to back off, but they did not heed his warning. As a result the governor sent Washington and a small militia force back to the area where they and their Iroquois allies were to build a fort at the conjunction of the Monongahela and Allegheny Rivers. When they arrived, however, they learned that the French had beaten them to this strategic location and built Fort Duquesne. Virginia militia responded by ambushing the French, killing ten soldiers and capturing twenty one, while only one managed to escape. The Iroquois scalped

several of the wounded soldiers as Washington watched in stunned silence. This was the beginning of the *French and Indian War*. Sadly and ironically, the Virginians learned only after the attack that the French were on a mission to peacefully discuss the disputed area. After the ambush, Washington and his men retreated to Great Meadows, where they built Fort Necessity, which was soon attacked by a large force of French soldiers angry at the brutal fate of their friends. The battle only lasted a day. All of the Virginians' horses and livestock were killed and 300 men (one third of the Virginia forces) were killed or wounded.

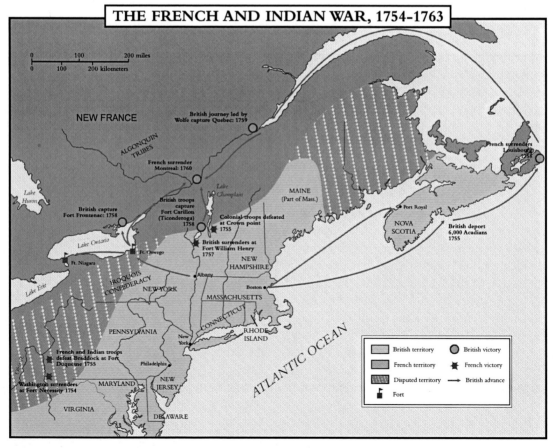

This map shows the major battles and skirmishes of the French and Indian War.

From these colonial beginnings a world war was launched. First, the British responded by expelling most of the French population from Nova Scotia, forcing about 6,000 Acadians to French Louisiana, where they became known as "Cajuns." The two powers then clashed all along the American/Canadian frontier for about two years. At that point, other European powers became involved as Austria, Russia, Saxony, Sweden, and Spain aligned with the French and Prussia and Hanover aligned with the British. As in most conflicts of the time, the British were able to use their superior navy to blockade their enemies, preventing French supplies and reinforcements from making their way to the New World. This was particularly troublesome for the French because the supplies included important trade goods they hoped to use to keep the allegiance of their Indian allies.

The turning point of the war occurred in 1758. At that point Fort Louisbourg in Canada fell to the British, who then marched to the original scene of attack—Fort Duquesne. Outnumbered, the French burned the fort and fled. The British later built Fort Pitt in this location, which is now the city of Pittsburgh, Pennsylvania.

In 1759 a battle at Quebec proved decisive. Here the British were commanded by General James Wolfe, who led his troops up the St. Lawrence River where they spent two months trying to subdue the French forces under General Louis-Joseph de Montcalm. On September 12–13 the British finally found a way up the cliffs that surrounded Quebec and attacked in the battle that led to the death of both generals but also put an end to French power in North America once and for all. The fighting continued until 1763, especially among the Native Americans, and the British continued to engage the Spanish in battles throughout the New World, but the events at Quebec were what ultimately mattered. After Quebec but before the official end of the war, the British king, George II, died and his grandson, George III took his place. This was an event of long-term consequence because the new monarch would take a much more active role in colonial matters that his predecessors had.

The Seven Years War ended with the *Treaty of Paris of 1763*. It officially put an end to all French power in North America and gave Britain all of France's North American land east of the Mississippi, except New Orleans. It also gave Britain Spanish Florida. Spain ultimately received New Orleans and the rest of Louisiana, which included all of France's former land west of the Mississippi, to make up for the loss of Florida. This arrangement left France with no North American territory.

The Indians who had aligned with the French could not believe that they lost their land through an agreement that they were not part of. Just as bad, the British did not trade with them and give them the gifts they were accustomed to receiving from the French. In what is known as *Pontiac's Rebellion* the Indians fought back by capturing a number of British forts around the Great Lakes and in the Ohio River valley. They also raided British settlements throughout Virginia, Maryland, and Pennsylvania, killing thousands of settlers. During one Native American attack upon the new Fort Pitt, the British troops responded by giving them blankets and handkerchiefs that had been infested with smallpox. Colonists decided that the only way to deal with Indians was to remove them, but the British government negotiated. They came to an agreement that the Indians would give the forts back in exchange for renewed trade and a promise of gifts from the British. The Indians also insisted that they retained their lands despite what the Treaty of Paris said.

Conclusion

At the end of the French and Indian War, Britain dominated North America, the Spanish retained land west of the Mississippi, and the French waited for a chance to seek revenge. The Native Americans jealously guarded their rights to land west of the Appalachian Mountains, but the British settlers continued to help themselves to that land. Finally, the British government had a new king who was much more interested in colonial affairs than previous monarchs had been. Collectively this was a recipe for disaster, and it would erupt in a war that would spell the end of the British North American Empire.

Suggested Readings

Fred Anderson, *Crucible of war: The Seven Years' War and the Fate of Empire in British North America, 1754–1766* (2000).

Richard Bushman, ed., *The Great Awakening: Documents on the Revival of Religion, 1740–1745* (1989).

Ramon A. Gutierrez, *When Jesus Came the Corn Mothers Went Away: Marriage, Sexuality, and Power in New Mexico, 1500–1856* (1991).

James Pritchard, *In Search of Empire: The French in the Americas, 1670–1730* (2004).

Peter Silver, *Our Savage Neighbors: How Indian War Transformed Early America* (2007).

Stephanie E. Smallwood, *Saltwater Slavery: A Middle Passage from Africa to American Diaspora* (2007).

Serena Zabin, *Dangerous Economies: Status and Commerce in Imperial New York* (2009).

Richard White, *The Middle Ground: Indians, Empires, and Republics in the Great Lakes Region, 1650–1815* (1991).

Chapter 5

THE WAR FOR INDEPENDENCE

Before the French and Indian War, the English North American colonies had enjoyed a relatively peaceful relationship with the motherland. Although they were valuable colonies whose very existence was supposed to support the prosperity of the empire, they were allowed a degree of independence unimaginable in the Spanish colonies. While the Spanish colonies were controlled closely through local governors known as viceroys, the English colonies were often able to alter or ignore rules and regulations from the King and Parliament.

At the same time, the English system of government was known for the impressive freedom and liberty it gave its subjects, both at home and in the colonies. The King was the head of the system, but he had to answer to a strong Parliament in England. Similarly, governors provided the top tier of leadership in each colony, but they also had to rule in cooperation with colonial assemblies. Both Parliament and the colonial assemblies were made up of representatives elected by the people. Landowners in England voted for parliamentary representatives, and colonial landowners voted for representatives in their assemblies. In short, most American colonists were proud British subjects who were happy with the representative system that allowed them to elect their own colonial representatives and gave them an unprecedented level of self-rule.

English subjects, whether on the mainland or in the colonies, enjoyed a level of representation almost unique in the world, and they were very proud of that fact. They had developed a tradition of jealously guarding their rights as English subjects. For many, to be "English" meant to be "free," especially as they compared their system to that in France. It was no democracy, but almost nobody would have wanted a true democracy. There

was a general belief in the idea that certain people had the right and duty to rule, or at least to represent, others. There was also a general fear of the masses. These issues are important when considering whether the American Revolution was radical or conservative—a major debate among historians.

In addition to appreciating the English political system, most colonists were also grateful that the home government had come to their rescue against the French and the Indians, and they felt a strong sense of cultural and familial ties to the rest of the empire. This all began to change drastically, and by 1776 most colonists were calling for independence. Most of the reasons for this stem from changes the English government made in response to the debt they occurred during the French and Indian War.

British Colonial North America: Salutary Neglect and the Colonial Governments

The Glorious Revolution had established Parliament's supremacy, and colonists thought it gave them the same rights to self-government that it gave subjects in the mainland. They saw it as vindicating the right of self-government in general, which by extension included colonial assemblies. For the most part, the home government never gave a clear or definitive answer on the issue of whether self government was a right or privilege shared by the colonies. Why did this become an issue in the colonies?

There were two major reasons for colonization. Some colonies were economic ventures founded specifically to make a profit. Some of these were founded by joint stock companies. Take, for example, the southern colonies that were founded to bring money to investors and ended up doing so through the cultivation of cash crops like tobacco, rice, indigo, and sugar. Similar yet with a key difference, some colonies were proprietary colonies founded to make money for the king specifically. The question that arose pertaining to these colonies was that if they were for the monarch to make money, then who was actually in charge—the monarch or Parliament. Still other colonies were founded as religious ventures. The goal of those colonies was not to make money but to create a place where people could implement religious ideas or plans. As we saw earlier, the Puritans and Quakers were the best examples of these types of colonists. The Puritans founded the New England colonies, and the Quakers founded Pennsylvania, each hoping to create a model religious society. Both groups were offshoots of the Protest Reformation.

What is important is that both types of colonies ended up developing various forms of self government. Every colony had a charter from the king that guaranteed settlers retained their rights as English subjects. Those established as business corporations turned these business charters into constitutions. One example would be the way Virginia used its charter to create a representative governing body, the House of Burgesses. When trying to attract more settlers, Virginia publicized and emphasized the fact that settlers had a degree of influence in the local government. Church-based colonies developed governments as well. The most famous example was the *Mayflower Compact,* which took a covenant to make a congregation and turned it into a constitution for a civil government in New England.

As a result, every colony also had a popular assembly that looked like a miniature Parliament. Most of these actually exercised more real power than Parliament in London. The colonies, then, were like miniature republics. In fact, political participation was even greater in the colonies because most colonials, unlike most English subjects at home, owned property. As a result, about 50 percent of adult white men could vote, making the colonies the most democratic polities in world history.

This situation led colonists to develop an even stronger sense of pride in their "English liberties" than the people in England itself had. They began to see political participation as their right, and property rights in the colonies took on an even stronger meaning than in England. Hostility to taxation also became even stronger in the colonies than in England. The idea of "deference," which made most English subjects accept their place in society, did exist in the colonies but it was different. There was no colonial nobility, so the natural deference to nobility did not develop. Also, property ownership was widespread so a large portion of men could vote and even aspire to office.

Even though this is a clear difference from England, since there was more opportunity and a more level playing field, it still does not mean that everyone in the colonies was equal. Conditions were just different enough that a greater percentage of adult men could vote, and this led to a growing feeling of equality, at least among propertied white men. Still, however, there were poor people who did not own land and who worked for others. There were also indentured servants, slaves, and women, who did not have a political voice. The colonies may have been more democratic but they were nowhere near what we today consider democratic, and colonials, like the English, did not want a real democracy because they believed that some people were naturally better at leading and making decisions for others. They also generally feared the masses.

Another difference was that in the colonies there was no disdain for business or "new money" as there was in England, where "old money" was seen as more honorable.

This situation of a growing sense of freedom and natural rights of self government was reinforced by "*salutary neglect*." This basically meant that the home government in England had left the colonists to govern themselves to a large degree. This worked well for about 70 years after the Glorious Revolution. In the 1680s, some colonial charters were revised to put a crown-appointed governor over the assemblies, but while this caused friction it did not make a huge problem because the assemblies kept the power of the purse.

There was friction also as the main goal of the whole colonial system was for the mother country to be self-sufficient through "*mercantilism*," a system in which a country tried to sell more goods than it bought from other countries. Under this system, colonies had two main functions, to produce raw materials and to buy manufactured goods from their own mother country. The *Navigation Acts* played a part in this by at least theoretically ensuring that the colonies would buy from England. Under these acts, only English ships could import and export goods to the colonies, and only English subjects could trade with the English colonies. Goods produced in the colonies could only be sent to England. This system sounds restrictive but it was not a large problem because England was at war in Europe and was thus preoccupied. Therefore, smuggling was widespread, but the government just let it go unchecked. For example, there was a good deal of trading between the English colonies and other countries' colonies in the Caribbean, and this was very prosperous for the colonists. It gave them

money to buy English goods, so the home government was even more likely to ignore it. This hands-off approach is what was known as "salutary neglect." This atmosphere of salutary neglect changed after the French and Indian War, and this was a major factor that led to the American Revolution.

There were a number of links between the French and Indian War and the American War for Independence. First, before and during the war fear of a French invasion from Canada had kept colonists loyal to England because they needed British military power to protect them. This changed once the British drove the French from the area. Second, during the war New England and New York merchants continued to trade with the French West Indies, even though it made it much more difficult for Britain to conquer those islands. This disloyalty made more people in England agree that tighter controls were needed to be kept over colonial trade. Third, the war was very expensive and the English government had to raise taxes to pay off war debt. Even though this war was fought largely to protect the colonies, English taxpayers at home were being forced to pay much more in taxes than colonists were. For example, English taxpayers generally paid twenty-five shillings a year in taxes, while the typical colonists only paid two percent of that. The English government needed the colonists to pay their share of the war debt, so they tried to raise taxes in a number of different ways. As we will see, this attempt to raise colonial taxes became the most important factor that would lead to revolution. Fourth, as if the war debt were not enough, Britain now had to employ about ten thousand English soldiers to protect the American colonies on an ongoing basis from the Spanish, French, and, most importantly, Indians. Of course, the British believed the Americans should help pay for this defense with taxes, and this added to the taxation pressure.

Each of these issues presented an important challenge that needed to be dealt with creatively yet firmly. Part of the problem was that the current monarch, *King George III* was not up to the task. He was a deeply religious and conscientious man, but he lacked the

King George III will forever be known throughout history for two things—for losing the American colonies and for going insane. The third Hanoverian monarch of England, he was the first of his line to be born in England and to speak English as his first language. He was one of the most cultured English monarchs and one of the first to study science. He reigned for nearly 60 years, the second longest monarchy in British history

ability to deal with the situation. Ultimately he ended up relying too heavily upon a series of advisors whose advice was often inadequate. For many of these advisors, matters in England itself took precedence over colonial matters. This led to an inconsistency of leadership that went from over conciliation to rigid inflexibility.

One final issue that created tension between the government in Britain and the colonists was the matter of westward expansion. The western boundaries set for the colonies by the Treaty of Paris overlapped with the Ohio River Valley lands claimed by the Indians. Preparing for an influx of white settlers, and resentful that the French had signed away their land rights without consulting them, the Indians in this region launched a series of assaults on British settlements along the Great Lakes and in the Appalachians. Led by an Ottawa chief named Pontiac in what is known as *Pontiac's Rebellion*, the Indians managed to wipe out every British post in the Ohio River Valley except for Fort Pitt and Fort Detroit. Hoping to ease tensions with Native Americans and to control westward expansion, George III had issued the *Royal Proclamation of 1763*. This act promised that all land west of the Allegheny Mountains would be left for the Indians. The Native Americans, however, remained skeptical and the rebellion continued into 1766. Even after the fighting ended, their concerns remained valid as white settlers continued to move into Indian land.

The goal of the Proclamation of 1763 was to prevent another war with the Indians, but it upset colonists for a number of reasons. For one thing, many wealthy colonists were land speculators who had hoped to carve up and sell the land that the government was now telling them to stay off of. Westward expansion brought land dealers much revenue, and that was now cut off significantly. Also, some settlers had already moved into the area west of the mountains and were now living in forbidden territory. These colonists still feared another Indian attack, and the Proclamation did nothing to address those fears. Finally, this Proclamation was the first indication that Parliament could, and would, override the colonial constitutions. Thus, an idea emerged among colonists that Parliament was ignoring the constitution and the basic rights and liberties of English subjects. This notion became the basis of one of the major ideological arguments in support of the American Revolution.

This was all complicated by the Enlightenment ideas we discussed in chapter four. As we saw, new ideas on science, religion, and politics were circling the globe. People were thinking science could be applied to understand basically everything, including politics, and central to this was a belief in a set of universal laws that could be discovered. Many saw America as the perfect testing ground for the new ideas that were emerging. Although people throughout the world saw England as the leader in, and best example of, the political innovations that were leading to an expansion of liberty, many began to worry about the implications of Adam Smith's theory of progress. In short, many began to believe that Britain had reached the fourth stage of societal progress and that decay was inevitable.

The Road to Independence: The Specific Causes of the War

There were two main intellectual currents that fueled the events that caused the colonies to eventually seek independence from Great Britain. First was *"Republican Ideology."* In England there were two main parties, the *Tories* ("court" party) and the Radical *Whigs* ("country" party). The Whigs were the ones who were worried about the idea of the fourth stage of development and the inevitable decay and corruption that was to follow. They developed a political ideology known as "republicanism." Their dislike of the idea of inherited aristocracy and its privileges led them to conclude that the "court" was indicative of luxury and vice. Instead of believing that inherited status gave some people the natural right to rule others, they insisted that an individual's character was what determined his ability to lead. They believed that one characteristic, *"civic virtue,"* was essential to good leadership. This concept basically referred to the ability to put the good of the whole ahead of personal desires. They believed that men must volunteer to serve their country (either in politics or war), not for profit and personal gain but for duty to society. They also insisted that people must avoid luxury and ostentation. Finally, they believed in something called *Commonwealth Ideology*, which was essentially the idea that power would naturally corrupt and should thus be kept in check. This group greatly influenced the American colonists, and their ideas were widespread in the colonies, especially among the colonial political and intellectual elite (many of whom are now referred to as the "Founding Fathers"). Republican ideology, then, was a "country" ideology which stressed simplicity and feared corruption and a concentration of power.

The other intellectual current was *"Political Liberalism."* Put simply, it was a belief in self rule based on John Locke's and Jean Jacques Rousseau's ideas. Political liberals believed that government was a social contract and that leaders could be overthrown when they were not ruling in the people's best interests. Along with this there was a belief that in exchange for consenting to be taxed, people deserve to be represented in the government. Under this belief, colonists believed that England could impose tariffs and regulate trade in the empire through such means as the Navigation Acts, but internal taxes should be left to colonial assemblies because the people in the colonies were directly represented in the colonial assemblies but only indirectly, or virtually, represented in Parliament. In other words, Parliament could put tariffs on goods but they could not directly tax colonists. In this intellectual climate a number of events occurred which led the colonists first to fight for their rights as English subjects and then, later, for independence.

As we saw earlier, changes that followed the French and Indian War drastically altered the relationship between England and the North American colonies. In addition to the King's proclamation to stop westward expansion, the colonists faced a series of efforts to tighten and enforce a number of tax-collection measures. First, enforcement of the Navigation Acts was tightened. The acts themselves were not new and had existed for a long time as an important part of the mercantilist system. Under the acts, goods traded with other countries were taxed, and this encouraged colonists to trade only with England, the mother country. Until the French and Indian War, however, these acts had been loosely enforced. After that war the English government tightened up the enforcement to help pay off war debt. The government began this process by using open-ended search warrants called *Writs of Assistance*. In 1761, Massachusetts lawyer James Otis unsuccessfully argued that these writs violated the colonists'

constitutional rights, but the British government said that they were tightening the laws to raise money to pay for colonial defense. Colonial trade with Britain was not hurt at all, and the tighter enforcement only made more restrictions for trading with other nations. From this point the situation gained intensity after the King appointed a new chief minister, George Grenville. Grenville was charged with the task of funding the country's skyrocketing defense costs while also paying off government debt.

Two new revenue acts passed by the English government in 1764 only made matters worse. The *Sugar Act*, also called the "Revenue Act," was intended to raise money for colonial defense. It actually lowered the duty on foreign molasses by half, but it raised taxes on refined sugar, textiles, wine, and coffee. A similar tax had existed before, but it was heavily evaded so enforcement of this act was strengthened in 1764, and this led to a great deal of tension. One reason for the tension was that the colonists were using French molasses to make rum, especially in Rhode Island. Thus, even if the tax was actually lowered its strict enforcement would put many out of business in New England. The *Currency Act* was another measure. Colonial planters were heavily in debt to London merchants, and colonial assemblies made their own currency and used it to repay the debts. The only problem was that they inflated the value of their currency and thus cheated the creditors. The Currency Act thus barred the colonists from printing their own currency.

Colonists responded to all of these measures by boycotting British merchandise, and things continued to escalate throughout 1765. The *Quartering Act* played a large role in increasing the tensions. After the French and Indian War, the king created a standing peace time army in the colonies to protect them from possible invasion by other European powers and Indians. The troops, however, needed somewhere to stay while in the colonies, so the Quartering Act was passed to require people to let soldiers stay in their private homes. The New York legislature refused to enforce this act; however, so the king gave up.

Another act passed that year, the *Stamp Act*, required people to buy stamps to place on licenses of all sorts, newspapers and other publications, official documents of all types, and even playing cards and dice. This was not the best idea because the government angered newspaper publishers and lawyers, the very people who controlled and influenced public opinion. The act angered colonists for many reasons. To begin with, the Stamp Act was a *direct tax* and they continued to insist that direct taxes fell solely under the jurisdiction of colonial assemblies. This was where the taxation issue really began to emerge. Parliament had placed this tax on colonists but colonists said they had no representation in Parliament. Instead, colonists argued that they were represented directly in colonial assemblies and, as a result, only colonial assemblies could place direct taxes on them. Another major point of contention was that violators were tried in *vice admiralty courts* which had no juries. Finally, many saw the act as a deliberate attempt to weaken the colonies.

The Stamp Act tensions led to a number of events. First, the *Virginia Resolutions* were passed in 1765. They said that the General Assembly of Virginia was the only one that could tax Virginia, and that the Crown had always recognized Virginia's right to govern its own internal affairs before. Also, a new group, the *Sons of Liberty*, formed in response to this act. Led primarily by colonial brewer Samuel Adams, this group was formed to

prevent the enforcement of the Stamp Act, sometimes even tarring and feathering revenue agents and stamp collectors. Their terror tactics were so successful that all of those who had been appointed agents quit before the act went into effect.

Even more importantly, the *Stamp Act Congress* met from October 7-25, 1765. At this congress colonial leaders got together and decided how to fight the act. *John Dickinson*, a Pennsylvania moderate, proposed 14 resolutions in a "Declaration of Rights and Grievances," which claimed that the colonists had all the rights and liberties of the king's subjects in Great Britain. The resolutions said that the colonists could not be taxed without their consent or the consent of their representatives, that the colonists were not represented by the House of Commons, and that only colonial legislatures could constitutionally tax the colonies. They also called out strongly against the use of vice admiralty courts.

Colonial boycotts played a large role in resistance to the Stamp Act. Merchants in New York, Philadelphia, and Boston got together and refused to buy European goods until the act was repealed. As a result, business in the colonies was pretty well suspended because people refused to buy the stamps, and courts everywhere refused to use the stamps and closed instead. (The exception was Rhode Island, where the governor himself refused to enforce the stamp law.) Before the end of the year, business returned to normal but without the use of stamps, in direct violation of the law. The decline in British exports to the colonies led merchants in many British towns to petition Parliament to repeal the tax because the boycotts were destroying British businesses. Indeed, a quarter of all British imports had gone to the American colonies and half of all shipping was devoted to American trade.

The boycotts put this all to a halt and many British workers faced lay-offs.

Meanwhile, the King continued to shuffle his ministers in ways that unintentionally affected colonial affairs. First he appointed a new minister, the Marquis of Rockingham, after dismissing Grenville for matters unrelated to the turmoil in the colonies. Even so, the change in ministers proved beneficial for the colonists and the situation overall. Rockingham was a leading Whig and was thus more sympathetic to the colonial situation. As a result he hoped to end the tensions, and the first step he took was to repeal the Stamp Act in 1766. He could not simply repeal the act without affirming Parliament's authority over the colonies. To get around this issue Parliament passed the *Declaratory Act,* which declared that Parliament had full authority to make laws for the American colonists.

Following this act, another round of tension developed in 1767 after the King appointed yet another new minister. Charles Townshend, the new Chancellor of the Exchequer, imposed a series of new taxes collectively known as the *Townshend Acts*. He made sure all of the taxes were external taxes, with new import duties on glass, white lead, paper, paints, and tea. He also worked to ensure efficient collection, affirming the power of the superior courts to issue writs of assistance, establishing new vice-admiralty courts, and setting up an American Board of Commissioners of the Custom in Boston. One major problem, however, was that the Townshend duties hurt British manufacturers because they placed taxes on goods that were exported from England. Another problem was that the taxes had to be collected in the colonies, and this led to an increased collection cost. Finally, they fostered further colonial discontent because Townshend intended to pay the salaries of officers and royal governors with the revenue they generated. Why this mattered to the colonists was that governors had been paid by the colonial assemblies, and that had left them dependent on the legislative bodies. This new system freed the royal representatives from the checks placed on them by elected officials.

The immediate colonial reaction to the Townshend Act included a revival of the boycott through a *"nonimportation"* movement. Colonial leaders issued a list of items they encouraged citizens not to buy, and there was a general effort to increase the production of colonial manufactures. Women played a large role in this effort. Calling themselves the *Daughters of Liberty*, they worked day and night to produce "homespun" cloth, often holding spinning bees in which women from different communities competed with each other to produce the most cloth.

Further resistance to the Townshend Act came when John Dickinson wrote a series of letters (collectively called *"Letters from a Pennsylvania Farmer"*) for the *Pennsylvania Chronicle*, basically declaring the acts unconstitutional. Also, the Massachusetts General Court said that the acts violated the concept of "no taxation without representation." It also argued that the acts were an attempt to make colonial governors independent of the assemblies by taking away their power of the purse, thereby taking power out of the hands of the people. (Remember, the king appointed the governors, and the colonists who were eligible to vote elected the assemblies.) Samuel Adams then sent a letter to other colonial assemblies to get them to join the resistance, and the Massachusetts governor declared the letter seditious and dissolved the General Court. Even so, other states responded to Adams's call and endorsed the General Court's actions.

Samuel Adams, known mainly as the leader of the Sons of Liberty, played the leading role in the early stages of colonial resistance. Though he was a distant cousin to the wealthy and refined Boston lawyer John Adams, he brought a more popular influence to the resistance. Running his family brewery into bankruptcy soon after inheriting it, he was known for his passion for politics rather than material profit. Indeed, he could often be found in local taverns debating political issues of the day with stevedores, sailors, and roustabouts. Described by the royal governor as the "most dangerous man in Massachusetts," he wrote impassioned newspaper articles and letters, and he organized many protests. He worked tirelessly to make sure the colonists were aware of the illegality of Parliament's efforts to tax them. He also played a large role in enforcing the boycotts.

As Adams fought to keep the resistance going, the British learned that another of their colonial enemies, *John Hancock*, was smuggling wine into the colonies. Hancock was a known smuggler who had even locked up a customs official so he could unload his cargo without paying the tax. The British decided they had had enough, so they seized Hancock's ship, the *Liberty*. An angry mob then assaulted customs officials, forcing them to flee to an island in the harbor and call for troops. The British responded by sending troops to Boston.

Opposition continued to grow. New York and Boston barred goods covered by the Townshend Acts. By 1769 only New Hampshire was not participating in some type of boycott of British goods. Another set of Virginia Resolves was passed, reaffirming the argument that only the Virginia legislature could tax Virginians. It also condemned the idea that those who broke the law would be taken to England for trial. Other state assemblies also took nonimportation measures, and again, the boycotts hurt British business so British businessmen called for modifications to the Townshend Acts. Fighting actually broke out in January of 1770 at the *Battle of Golden Hill*. New York Sons of Liberty leader Alexander McDougall was angry that the state assembly appropriated funds for the Quartering Act after earlier refusing. Citizens and soldiers then clashed in a riot, and there were several injuries, though none were fatal.

The next major event, and one of the most famous, was the *Boston Massacre*, which occurred in March of 1770. Troops had arrived in 1768, and from that point on minor clashes had erupted between citizens and soldiers. When they were not on duty, soldiers needed jobs, and the job competition created much tension because colonists needed the jobs themselves. Colonists also resented the presence of a standing army in peace time. As a result, citizens harassed the soldiers and often threw snowballs (which were, in reality, hard ice chunks) at them. The soldiers would sometimes fire into the air to make them stop. In one particular instance, however, when the soldiers fired they hit several people. Five, including a runaway mulatto slave and sailor named *Crispus Attucks*, were killed and eight were wounded. Six soldiers and a captain were arrested and put on trial in the colonies, where they were defended by John Adams. Five were acquitted, and two were found guilty of manslaughter.

The Townshend duties were also repealed. For one matter, Townshend died and was replaced by Frederick, *Lord North*, who wanted to repeal the acts but not look weak. As a result, North repealed all but the tea duty. He also promised no new taxes. At the same time, the Quartering Acts expired and were

The Boston Massacre gave colonial radicals an important rallying point in their effort to pull moderates into their cause. In this engraving Paul Revere portrays the British Grenadiers attacking the citizens in a regular volley, but in reality both sides would have been belligerent and unorganized during the incident. Revere also changed the color of Crispus Attucks, the first martyr to the American cause. While this image shows the dead man to be white, Attucks was of mixed ancestry and his death during this incident made him the most famous black man to participate in the revolution.

not renewed. As a result, the colonies' nonimportation agreements collapsed. Though this skirmish gave the colonists their first martyr to the cause, many colonists actually saw the British reaction as fair and reasonable since the King allowed the soldiers to be tried in the colonies rather than taken back to Britain. This bolstered the Tory cause, at least for a time, and peace ensued temporarily.

Even so, colonial radicals wanted to keep the agitation going and leaders in Boston were still trying to get the colonists to resist even the tea tax. At the same time, the customs schooner *Gaspee* ran aground near Providence, Rhode Island, and colonists attacked and burned it. Also, there was still irritation that the Massachusetts governor and judges were getting their salaries directly from the crown instead of the colonial assembly. *Committees of Correspondence* were formed in Boston to communicate with other communities and foster inter-colonial cooperation. This effort was successful, and by 1774 only North Carolina and Pennsylvania did not have such a committee.

The next major events centered around the *Tea Act* of 1773. Parliament, in an effort to revive the near-bankrupt East India Company, gave the company a tax exemption on its overstocked tea. This meant that tea would now be imported into the colonies at the lowest cost ever. Despite the low cost, the act was resisted because it was seen as an effort by the government to financially ruin the merchants and smugglers who were leading the resistance movement. Colonial merchants were also upset about the idea of monopoly. Knowing about the unrest, New York harbor pilots were warned not to bring any tea ship to port. The Sons of Liberty branded all tea importers "enemies" and called for a boycott that December. In Massachusetts, Governor *Thomas Hutchinson* was determined to beat the resistance and insisted that the tea be unloaded and the duty paid. In response, a group of colonials, led by Sam Adams and John Hancock, disguised themselves as Mohawk Indians and boarded three ships that collectively held 342 chests of tea. They threw the tea overboard in what is known as the *Boston Tea Party*.

The final steps to war took place in 1774 and 1775. First the *Coercive Acts* were passed to punish Massachusetts for the Tea Party as well as the other problems the Sons of Liberty had caused. They included several provisions. First, the Boston Port Bill said that no ship could be loaded or unloaded in Boston Harbor until customs was paid for the tea party damage. The only exceptions were military goods, food and fuel. Second, the Administration of Justice Act protected crown officials in Massachusetts from major suits before hostile provincial courts by transferring trials to London. Third, the Massachusetts Government Act annulled Massachusetts' charter and replaced the elected House of Representatives with a council appointed by the crown. It also let the governor fill all judicial positions, all the way down to the justices of the peace and banned all town meetings, except for one annual election session, without the prior consent of the governor. Fourth, the Quebec Act extended the boundaries of Quebec, giving it territory claimed by Massachusetts, Virginia, and Connecticut. It also provided religious toleration for French Catholics, and this greatly upset Protestant Americans. Finally the New Quartering Act extended the earlier quartering act.

In response to the Coercive Acts, the colonists called the *First Continental Congress* from September 5 to October 26, 1774 to discuss the provisions of reconciliation and develop non-violent methods of rebellion. The group included men of various political views who were representing all of the colonies except Georgia. Radicals at the Congress included Samuel and John Adams and Patrick Henry. George Washington was more moderate but committed to protecting what everyone still saw as the fundamental liberties guaranteed to them as British subjects. Conservatives included Joseph Galloway of Pennsylvania and John Jay of New York.

The central question facing all delegates was just how tough a stance the Congress should take toward the King and Parliament in resistance to the Coercive Acts. The radicals thought that well-organized resistance could make the King and Parliament back down a third time. The radicals dominated the proceedings. They insisted that Americans should prepare for war in case Britain refused to back down again. To push Congress in their more radical direction, Samuel Adams and his political allies in Massachusetts had stirred people at home. On September 9, 1774, a convention of citizens in Suffolk County (the county Boston is in) met and adopted a set of resolutions written by Dr. Joseph Warren, a friend of Adams. These are known as the *Suffolk Resolves*, and they called for support of American rights as British subjects, a complete economic boycott, and the thorough training of the colonial militias in case they had to fight. Congress took a major step in preparing for possible military confrontation by approving the Suffolk Resolves.

To address the boycott aspect, the Congress also created what became the *Continental Association* and called for both non-importation of British goods as well as nonexportation of colonial goods (raw materials) to England if Parliament did not back down within a year. They also decided to refuse to pay debts to English creditors. Finally, the association called upon each colonial community to create a *Committee of Observation and Inspection* to make sure all colonists participated in the boycott. Colonists who did not promise loyalty were derisively called "tories," but most historians now call them "loyalists" (the term they used themselves).

Even as they approved these radical measures, Congress did have proposals for conciliation. Three American political theorists introduced a *Dominion Theory*, which stated that the American colonies were separate realms ruled by the monarch rather than Parliament. *James Wilson*, a Pennsylvanian, started this process by arguing that the king, and not Parliament, had authority over the colonies in his *Considerations on the Nature and Extent of the Legislative Authority of the British Parliament*. Thomas Jefferson then introduced *Summary View of the Rights of British America* which appealed to George III to listen to the arguments of the colonists. John Adams's *Novanglus Letters* followed and laid out clearly the dominion theory. Finally, *Joseph Galloway*, Pennsylvania's Speaker of the House, wanted to keep imperial ties because he feared a lack of order, so he offered a Plan of Union. Under his plan, America would have a central government over all provincial assemblies. This would give Americans a greater voice in the British government's decisions affecting the colonies (more direct representation). The British Empire would later use such a plan in India and other colonies of the Second Empire, but Americans of the more radical sort said such a plan at the moment would divert everyone from the real task of fighting the Coercive Acts. (Galloway would later be attacked as a loyalist and forced to seek British protection.)

When the Congress adjourned in late October 1774 it called for defiance over submission. Importantly, however, it still did not seek independence. The group's last act was to call for a *Second Continental Congress* to meet in Philadelphia in May 1775 unless Britain took back the Coercive Acts in the meantime.

At the same time, New Englanders began to prepare for war. British troops were sent from Boston to Charlestown and Cambridge, Massachusetts, to seize the province's cannon and powder. Thousands of militiamen flocked to Cambridge in response. Hostilities did not break out, but the Massachusetts House in Salem named itself a Provincial Congress and created a Committee of Safety to be led by John Hancock. This committee had the power to call out the militia, and special militia groups called "*minutemen*" were told to be ready for a call at any time.

The Formation of the Continental Army and the Beginning of Hostilities

Officials in England basically ignored the Congress's work. At this point they had had enough of the colonials' recalcitrance. Fed up with the agitation, they wanted to teach the Americans a lesson. Furthermore, the King had started to see colonial complaints as a push for independence. This view was very inaccurate, but the perception made the King angry enough to fight.

The fighting began in the winter of 1774-75. Lord North wanted to offer the colonies a conciliation plan, but Parliament rejected the idea and declared Massachusetts to be in a state of rebellion. It then passed the *New England Restraining Act*, which forbade the colonies of New England from trading with anyone other than Britain and the colonies of the British West Indies. It also banned New Englanders from the North Atlantic fisheries after July. Once Parliament learned that New Jersey, Pennsylvania, Maryland, Virginia, and South Carolina had joined the Continental Association, these colonies were also included in the act. Commander-in-chief of British troops in North America, General *Thomas Gage*, sent warning to London that the colonists gravely resented the presence of the British troops and asked for additional troops to be sent for added security.

The King and his ministers began to prepare for a brief demonstration of their military force, confident that such a show would put an end to the rebellion. The King sent secret orders to tell General Gage to round up and arrest the ring leaders like Adams and Hancock. Gage was also to do whatever he had to to end the unrest in Massachusetts. In February of 1775 the King and Parliament authorized funds for a large force of regular troops in America and sent 3 high-ranking generals, William Howe, Henry Clinton, and John Burgoyne, to Boston. They also declared Massachusetts to be in a state of rebellion. This made it acceptable for British soldiers to shoot suspected rebels if they had to. All of this would later be applied not just to Massachusetts but to all 13 colonies.

Gage was not so sure about all of this. Because he was actually in America he could see that the colonials were not so weak and would not be so easy to put down. He had long urged caution but now had to act because he was under orders. Fighting officially broke out on April 19, 1775 when British troops tried to march 20 miles from Boston to *Concord* to seize the colonial militia's supply and destroy it. The Boston Committee of Safety heard of the plan and sent Paul Revere

and William Dawes to alert everyone that "the British are coming." The minutemen harassed the British along the way, and fighting broke out at *Lexington*. In these skirmishes, the British lost 73 men and 200 were wounded. The Americans lost 49 and 39 were wounded. Although the fighting had begun, the colonists were not yet calling for independence. In retrospect the "shot heard round the world" at Lexington is considered the first skirmish of the Revolution. Even so, independence was not yet the goal. (Remember, this is April of 1775, not July of 1776).

After Lexington and Concord, within days, thousands of colonists joined the militia stationed near Boston. Most colonists, however, still thought the ministry would come to its senses and give colonists their rights as British citizens. Little did they know the government had finally decided enough was enough.

The *Second Continental Congress* met in Philadelphia in May of 1775. Still, very few delegates were calling for independence at this point. New Englanders like Samuel and John Adams were starting to think that way, though. Most, however, still hoped things could be resolved. By the summer, two factions had emerged in Congress. New Englanders and some followers were calling for a Declaration of Independence. Moderates, mostly from the middle colonies and led by men like John Dickinson of Pennsylvania, still wanted to work it all out. The moderates remained dominant into the spring of 1776.

Congressional debates centered on a number of issues, but two issues really stood out. First, there was a debate over whether or not they should create a *Continental Army*. In June of 1775 delegates listened to New Englanders and agreed to make the militia forces currently around Boston into such an army. They asked other colonies to supply troops to contribute to this army and unanimously named *George Washington* the commander-in-chief. He had experience in the French and Indian War and was from Virginia. That was important because most of the people who remained loyal to the Crown lived in the South, and Congress hoped that Washington's appointment would win over more southern support. Essentially, this was still mainly a New Englanders' war, and they needed to get all colonies on board.

The second debate was whether or not they should fight for independence or for their rights as British subjects. New Englanders obviously wanted independence. Moderates on the other hand, though very much concerned with American rights, feared separation. They generally were very wealthy and feared a loss of law and order without the stabilizing force of British rule. They also felt that a weak, independent American nation would not make it very long because it would not be able to compete with stronger European countries. They thus tried to keep communications open. One example, John Dickinson, wrote the *"Olive Branch Petition"* asking King George to intercede with Parliament and find some way to protect the English liberties of Americans. This petition was approved by Congress in July 1775 but basically ignored by Britain.

Meanwhile, the fighting continued to spread. On May 10, 1775 a group of citizen-soldiers seized a fortress in upstate New York at the southern end of Lake Champlain— *Ticonderoga*. They managed to capture more than 100 useable artillery pieces to help drive British forces out of Boston. This was led by *Benedict Arnold* and *Ethan Allen*.

Also, many hoped the province of Quebec would become a fourteenth colony and thus wanted to lure Canada into the fight. Congress approved an invasion in the summer of 1775, and there was a two-pronged attack led by General Richard Montgomery and Colonel Benedict Arnold. The plan was for the two leaders to meet in, and capture, *Quebec City*. This attempt to seize part of Canada failed, in part because of an outbreak of smallpox among the Americans, but it was an aggressive effort and made it hard to support the claim that colonists were just defending their home and hearth until differences with Britain were worked out.

In Boston, Gage resumed the offensive against the "troublemakers" in New England. On June 17, 1775 he attacked rebels at Breed's Hill in a fight known as the *Battle of Bunker Hill*. Citizens watched from nearby rooftops as the British made three separate charges before managing to dislodge the rebels, who were running out of ammunition. This was the bloodiest engagement of the entire war. The British lost 1,054 men (40% of those engaged), and the Americans lost 411 (30%). On the one hand it dampened the enthusiasm the colonists gained from the events at Lexington and Concord. On the other hand, however, the redcoats made a drastic mistake by not pursuing the fleeing rebels, so it was not as bad as it could have been.

By the end of 1775 fighting erupted in the South as well. In Virginia, the last royal governor, *Lord Dunmore*, had angered the colonists by dissolving the assembly in 1774, when they voted to fast and pray in support of the Bostonians. As a result, Virginia's planters (the leading men in Virginia society) began meeting in provincial conventions as if royal authority no longer existed. Dunmore called upon British subjects still loyal to the King to help him bring these elites back to their senses, but very few came to his aid. Therefore Dunmore decided to appeal to slaves. On November 7, 1775 he issued what we now call *Lord Dunmore's Proclamation*, offering freedom to slaves who would leave their masters and join the British forces. About 2,000 responded and served in Dunmore's "Ethiopian Regiment." Due to insufficient training they were beaten badly at a battle at *Great Bridge* in December of 1775.

The main importance of Dunmore's Proclamation, in terms of its overall role in the war, was that it upset southern planters, even many who were loyal up to that point. Slaveholders lived in constant fear that their slaves would rise up against them, and the royal governor had indeed tried to get them to do just that. This was so upsetting that Thomas Jefferson even alluded to it in the first draft of the Declaration of Independence by accusing the King of fostering servile insurrection. To keep slaves from joining, many planters spread a rumor that Dunmore was really just trying to coax slaves away and sell them to the West Indies sugar plantations (a much more brutal form of slavery in many ways). The defeat at *Great Bridge* ended all appearance of royal authority in Virginia.

These events in Virginia were an example of what was occurring all over the colonies as the fight began to move toward independence. Starting in the summer of 1775 one colony after another ended royal government, and Massachusetts asked the Continental Congress for permission to create a more permanent government based on a written constitution. New Hampshire ousted its royal governor and followed suit. Congress, forced to act, said that colonies could develop their own governments but they would operate only until the dispute with England was settled. Moderates realized that new state governments looked even more like independence than forming a colonial army had. They did everything they could to stop fellow Americans from completely rejecting British authority. Provincial assemblies in Pennsylvania, New York, Delaware, Maryland, and South Carolina kept protesting an irrevocable split with England.

Events of 1776, however, overwhelmed the moderates. In January a recent migrant from England named *Thomas Paine* published a pamphlet called *Common Sense*. An instant best seller, this pamphlet attacked congressional moderates for being timid and denounced the British monarchy. This pamphlet played perhaps the lead role in rallying most colonists to the independence cause. In February, loyalists and patriots battled in North Carolina at *Moore's Creek Bridge* and the Patriots won. North Carolina's provincial congress then agreed that delegates could discuss independence and vote on a plan of national government. Soon after, Virginians, furious about Dunmore's proclamation, gave similar instructions to their provincial congress. In May, Rhode Island leaders grew tired of waiting on everyone else and declared independence on their own. On June 7, 1776 Virginia's *Richard Henry Lee* urged independence and presented congress with resolutions that called for the creation of a national government and the formation of alliances with foreign nations to support the war effort.

Days after Lee's presentation, Congress formed two committees. One, chaired by John Dickinson, was asked to produce a plan for a central government. The other, chaired by Thomas Jefferson, was to prepare a statement on independence. Though Dickinson continued to argue against independence, twelve states (all but New York) voted in support of

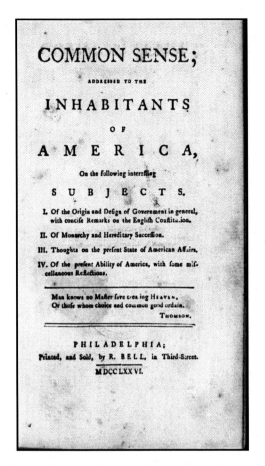

COMMON SENSE;

ADDRESSED TO THE

INHABITANTS

OF

AMERICA,

On the following interesting

SUBJECTS.

I. Of the Origin and Design of Government in general,
with concise Remarks on the English Constitution.

II. Of Monarchy and Hereditary Succession.

III. Thoughts on the present State of American Affairs.

IV. Of the present Ability of America, with some mis-
cellaneous Reflections.

Man knows no Master save creating HEAVEN,
Or those whom choice and common good ordain.
THOMSON.

PHILADELPHIA;
Printed, and Sold, by R. BELL, in Third-Street.
MDCCLXXVI.

Published anonymously in 1776, the pamphlet *Common Sense* became an instant best-seller. Later attributed to Thomas Paine, this essay called for an immediate declaration of independence, and it stirred the colonists to break from England rather than fight for their rights as British subjects. It is known as perhaps the greatest piece of American propaganda to date and the final spark that ignited the American Revolution. Paine followed up on this effort with a series of pamphlets called *The American Crisis* during the Revolutionary War, and he later gained further fame with *The Rights of Man* and *The Age of Reason*.

Lee's resolutions. This is the point at which independence was declared (on July 2). On *July 4, 1776* Congress adopted the *Declaration of Independence* after making a few changes.

After the Declaration, the military buildup then escalated on both sides. In England those who directed the war effort were King George, Lord North, and Lord George Germain (the American Secretary). Their main job was to put together the Campaign of 1776. Germain played a key role, and his plan was to concentrate as many troops as possible on the port of New York since many loyalists still lived there. He hoped they could then use the surrounding countryside for food and supply bases and that the loyalists would rebuild the royal government while British soldiers destroyed the rebel army. The goal was to break American will because the longer the rebellion lasted the more likely it could succeed. Germain hoped it would only take one campaign season.

Their second job was to get a military force together. The middle classes were exempt because they were seen as important and productive members of society. The rank and file were used instead, and they came from two sources. First, the poorer, less productive citizens in the British Isles would be recruited, but army life was brutal so it was hard to get even the most destitute to sign up. So, to find more troops the King and his advisors turned to a second source—Germany. They basically paid the heads of state of German principalities for soldiers, called *"Hessians."*

Another important task was to assemble good military leadership. The King saw Gage as too timid and too respectful of the Americans, so he recalled him in October 1775.

William Howe was then sent to replace him as commander-in-chief. His brother, Admiral Lord Howe, was put in charge of the naval expedition to get the troops to America. These men, however, were not hard-hitting attackers either. They sympathized to a degree with Whig leaders in England who saw the American cause as based on legitimate grievances, and they planned to move carefully and use the presence of the large army to scare Americans into signing loyalty oaths and renouncing the rebellion.

The Americans faced some unique challenges in putting together their army. First, they had the question of whom the army belonged and answered to. It had started out as a Massachusetts group and others had just added to it. Also, people were joining through colonial militias, so the question was whether each militia should worry about its own colony first before considering the needs of the group as a whole. The solution was that Washington decided to answer to the Continental Congress first, putting the whole over the state. They were the ones who chose him, and he decided to answer their requests before local requests. Even so, the issue was never totally resolved and continued to cause problems throughout the war.

There was also confusion within Congress itself as to how to deal with army issues such as strategy and supplies. They finally established a congressional Board of War in 1776, but there was still relative chaos over these issues. Perhaps the most unique problem of all was that Americans were laboring under a world view that focused on the importance of the *citizen soldier* and saw the professional standing army as evil. The ideal fighter, Americans believed, was a common man who was defending his home (in other words, fighting on the defensive, not on the offensive or for personal gain). To Americans, soldiering was a duty, not a career, and soldiers should fight for a specific goal and then go home. This was very different from a standing army.

At the same time, the Americans faced some of the same challenges shared by most armies. There were issues over officers and their ranks. At first the Congress issued commissions to officers, creating four major generals (Artemas Ward of New England, Israel Putnam and Philip Schuyler of New York, and Charles Lee) and eight brigadier generals. One of the most famous of the brigadier generals was Rhode Island Quaker Nathaniel Greene, who had studied manuals on the art of war and became the most important of his rank. Almost immediately, however, there was contention over status and rank. In 1777 Congress tried to settle this with the Baltimore Resolution, which said that when choosing generals the factors to be considered would be line of succession, personal merit, and number of troops raised by each state. There were also supply issues, and they were made worse by Congress's chaos. Basically, the problem was one of how to supply an army with no central government and bureaucracy. Another challenge involved discipline. These were not trained soldiers like the British had in their standing army. They were "citizen soldiers." These people were also coming from a background of fighting for their rights, and they were very individualistic and lacked much regard for hierarchy or authority.

Washington's first task, then, was to turn these citizen soldiers into trained and disciplined fighters. Militia training usually involved getting together on the occasional

African Americans played a number of roles in the American Revolution. General George Washington opened the door for black soldiers in 1777 by allowing recruiters to include free blacks among the ranks, and a year later he approved an entire regiment of enslaved blacks. Both free and enslaved blacks fought on both sides of the war. Some slaves gained their freedom through such service. One of the most famous was James Armistead, a slave who was freed by Lafayette for providing valuable scouting and intelligence during the war. Here both men are depicted, with Armistead holding Lafayette's horse.

weekend and drilling informally. It also usually involved drinking and goofing off. Those days has to end if they hoped to beat the British, and Washington had learned this lesson through his work in the French and Indian War. The militia members also were accustomed to enlisting for short terms and then going home. That also had to be fixed. Washington could not abandon the militia tradition, however, because of the fear of standing armies and the love of citizen soldiers, so he had to work from within the system. He and his advisors decided to modify the system by using the militia on the periphery but developing a core of trustworthy regulars. Thus, he used both amateurs and regulars. After deciding how to tackle the job of putting the army together, step one was instilling camp discipline. He used general orders and court martial and began flogging soldiers caught drunk or asleep (things that had been overlooked in the past). He also came down on unsanitary camp conditions and insisted on clean kitchens and proper waste disposal. By late fall he thought he saw progress.

Like the British, the Americans faced challenges in finding soldiers. After 1776 the rank and file of the Continental Army, like that of the British, was made up of the poorest citizens, as well as many who were unfree. Most of the long term soldiers were young (early teens to mid 20s). They came from the ranks of the landless and unskilled. There were also many indentured servants and slaves sent as substitutes for their masters to fight under the promise that if they fought they would be freed at the end of the war. Massachusetts and Rhode Island allowed free and unfree blacks to enlist in 1777, and Maryland and Virginia eventually followed.

After the Declaration of Independence was issued the nature of the war changed, and what had started as a war to gain rights as British subjects became a "revolution" to break away from the mother country once and for all. At that point it became more important than ever for colonists to choose sides. From the beginning, popular opinion had been divided into three camps. On one extreme end were Whigs, or Patriots, who had been radical from the beginning and were the first to call for independence. On the other end were the Tories, or Loyalists, who remained loyal to the Crown. In the middle were most colonists. Generally indifferent, they were swayed by events to side with either of the other two groups. After the Declaration of Independence, the uncommitted were often forced to choose sides. Most who remained loyalists lived in seaport cities and the South. Ultimately they were forced to side with the Patriots or flee to British lines for protection, often leaving behind all of their wealth and possessions. In many cases, the war played out much like a civil war where colonial Tories and colonial Whigs battled violently for the future of the colonies. By the end of the war, about 100,000 colonists, three percent of the overall population, had fled to the British and ultimately left the new country for Britain or Canada. This also applied to black loyalists, most of whom ended up first in Nova Scotia and then in Sierra Leone.

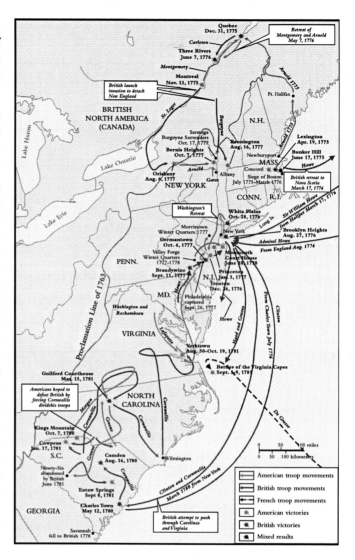

This map shows the major battles and campaigns of the American Revolution.

The Revolutionary War

The best way to follow the main events of the revolutionary war is to look at each theater of battle separately. Much of the action occurred in the mid-Atlantic area, in what were the middle colonies, because the capital, Philadelphia, was located in this region. Significant battles also took place in the northern and southern colonies as well.

Battles of the Middle Colonies

The first major campaign after the Declaration of Independence was the campaign for New York. General Washington and his men had driven British troops under William Howe out of Boston by placing the cannons they had captured at Ticonderoga on *Dorchester Heights*, which overlooked the city. They then harassed and bombarded the British until they left. At first, Howe took his men to Halifax, Nova Scotia, Canada, but he soon moved them back down to Staten Island, New York. By August he had about 43,000 soldiers, including seamen, in New York. In contrast, Washington had about 28,000 on his rolls but only 19,000 were present and fit to fight. These ready and able soldiers lacked good weapons and needed more supplies. Also, they had not been well trained or disciplined yet. The Continental Congress, however, insisted that Washington defend New York, so he did. British control of the sea left them able to attack either Manhattan or Long Island, so Washington decided he had to defend both areas. The British managed to break through and surround much of Washington's army, but they failed to follow up, so Washington managed to get all but about 250 troops out. The Continental Congress allowed Washington to withdraw from New York at that point. After the Battle for New York, Washington retreated through New Jersey, and Howe chased him but never quite caught up.

In early December, Washington took what was left of his army across the Delaware River to Pennsylvania. Spirits were low, and hundreds of men deserted. They were half-starved and battle-weary. Others became ill, and many were suffering from battle wounds, so they were left along the way in hopes the British would treat them decently. Howe felt he had basically destroyed the Continentals, so he ordered his troops into winter camps. He then returned to New York City, figuring he would finish them off in the spring. He knew he had more troops and outnumbered the rebels and that his troops were more organized and professional, so he was confident that all would be well until he decided to resume fighting.

Washington spoiled Howe's plans by refusing to give up and deciding to launch a bold counterstrike at *Trenton*, New Jersey. His muster rolls only included 6,000 troops, and he broke them up into three groups to re-cross the icy Delaware River and attack the British front lines. This attack was a "do or die" situation. Success would save his army and the revolutionary cause, while defeat would cause the remaining troops to either be captured or give up. These front lines the Continentals were attacking were those Howe had left when he went back to New York. They were made up of Hessians.

The important thing about Trenton was that Washington used the element of surprise. It was winter and it was not customary to attack in the snow and ice. It was also Christmas night, so the Hessians were still groggy from celebrating. Many had hangovers. This was the first real American victory of the war, and it helped to restore American morale. Within an hour, the battle was over with 22 Hessians and the British commander (Colonel Rall) dead, 98 wounded, and almost 1,000 in custody as prisoners. Only four Americans were wounded.

On the night of December 25, 1776, George Washington took his troops across the Delaware River to attack the British and Hessian troops at Trenton, New Jersey. This image was painted by Emmanuel Leutze in 1851 depicting the famous crossing. Of course, as with all artistic renderings, this image is not completely accurate. First and foremost, Washington and his men crossed at night during very bad weather. Also, there would have been ice sheets floating in the Delaware that would have hit the boat and made it impossible for the men to stand on the boat as depicted here. Finally, the flag shown in this image would likely have not been used at the point of this crossing. Even so, this painting has become an icon of American revolutionary history.

Even so, the Americans were still basically losing the war overall. France was giving Americans covert assistance in the form of cash gifts and loans, because the Continental Congress had sent three delegates, including Benjamin Franklin, to enlist their aid. Everyone was waiting for a big American victory to prove to the French that the cause was worthy and winnable so that the French would give more direct assistance. Thus, the Americans needed to win something even more impressive than Trenton.

As fighting resumed in the spring of 1777, Howe decided to alter the overall game plan and seize Philadelphia. He had been told to march up the Hudson to meet up with Burgoyne, who was coming down from Canada, and cut off New England in the "Hudson Highlands Strategy." The goal was to isolate New England, the seedbed of the rebellion. Howe, however, had been knighted by this point and was feeling smug and arrogant, so he decided to change the plan. He decided to go after and destroy Washington's army. He tried to lure Washington into battle, but Washington refused to take the bait. Howe then decided to lure Washington out by seizing Philadelphia. He figured Washington would try to protect the capital and he could get the Continental Army then. Washington took the bait this time and the two armies ended up fighting on September 10-11, 1777 at *Brandywine Creek*. After desperate hand-to-hand fighting, the British won, but they did not manage to destroy Washington's army. The British then moved in and took Philadelphia. The Americans attacked, trying to get the British out of the capital, resulting in the *Battle of Germantown*. It was a confusing mess because of a very heavy fog, and the Americans ended up shooting at each other. Howe then attacked, and the Americans had to withdraw. The English were thus able to capture Philadelphia. This was a huge psychological victory for the British, but it was a hollow victory militarily. The Continental Congress had already managed to move to York, Pennsylvania. Even so, it was a huge psychological loss for the Americans.

After Philadelphia, Washington took his men to winter camp at *Valley Forge*, Pennsylvania, 25 miles west of the capital. There, Washington's 11,000 troops camped from December 19, 1777 to June 19, 1778. For many, Valley Forge symbolized the heroism of Washington's troops because conditions were horrible yet most held on. This particular winter was extremely harsh, and the men were poorly clothed, poorly fed, and housed in poor conditions. As a result, 2,500 died. Toward spring, things began to look up for the Americans, though. Friedrich Wilhelm Ludolf Gerhard Augustin, Baron von Steuben arrived in late February to help train the troops. This led to much better-disciplined, more professional troops. Other important foreign volunteers

were *Marquis de Lafayette* and Baron de Kalb. Another important change occurred when Nathaniel Green took over as Quarter Master General and solved the supply issues. Finally, an official alliance with France was announced in May of 1778. As the newly-trained troops left Valley Forge, they engaged the British at *Monmouth*, New Jersey.

Battles of the Northern Theater

It was action in this theater that made the alliance with France possible. When the Revolutionaries had tried to invade Canada earlier in the war, the British learned the importance of securing the Mohawk Valley and upper Hudson River to prevent such action in the future. In the summer of 1776 Sir Guy Carleton tried to get together a fleet to gain control of Lake Champlain. He assembled a large force of three large York vessels, 20 gunboats, over 200 flat-bottomed transports, 700 seamen and gunners, and an army of 12,000 men. Benedict Arnold was in charge of repelling this invasion, and he had three schooners, two sloops, three galleys, eight gondolas fitted out with 70 guns, and whatever seamen and gunners he could get together. Carleton's goal was to retake Ticonderoga, and basically all Arnold could hope to do was harass the British. The first battle between the American and British fleets resulted in October of 1776 with the *Battle of Valcour Bay*. This battle stalled and delayed the British, leaving them able to take Lake Champlain but not Ticonderoga.

A few other battles occurred here, but the most important by far was the *Battle of Saratoga*. It occurred at roughly the same time that Howe was taking Philadelphia. Indeed, Howe was supposed to be heading up there instead of provoking Washington at

Philadelphia. The plan was for three columns to converge on New England and seal off the area for the Campaign of 1777. Burgoyne kept up his end of the deal. Strengthened by hundreds of Native Americans who joined the fight hoping to stop the Americans from settling westward and taking tribal lands, he was able to move south from Canada in June. He drove the rebels from *Ticonderoga* after pushing into Lake Champlain in July. Colonel Barry St. Leger also kept up his end of the deal. He went up the St. Lawrence River to Lake Ontario and then to the Mohawk Valley as planned. The goal was to serve as a diversionary force. The two groups were then to meet in Albany, New York, but after seizing Ticonderoga, Burgoyne faced harassment by the Americans, who had blocked paths by cutting down trees, destroying bridges, and bouldering up streams. Thus the British advance was slowed to less than a mile a day. At the same time, the diversionary force under St. Leger, made up mostly of Iroquois Indians, fell apart as the Americans beat them at the *Battle of Oriskany*. The Americans then engaged Burgoyne's Hessians at *Bennington*, Vermont and won.

In all of this chaos, *Benedict Arnold* displayed great skill and brilliant leadership on the field that inspired the Americans to win in two separate battles on September nineteenth and October seventh. Burgoyne then surrendered to General Horatio Gates on October 17, 1777 at *Saratoga*. The whole situation can be blamed largely on Howe's refusal to cooperate with the Hudson Highlands strategy.

The true importance of *Saratoga* was that it convinced France to commit publicly to the American cause. Essentially, the battle showed that the cause was practical and that the rebels could win. France then granted diplomatic recognition to the American

nation. They also committed themselves as allied to the Americans, and in June of 1778 France and Britain officially went to war. The entry of France turned this into a world war. Spain then joined the fight in an effort to regain the Rock of Gibraltar. Britain and the Netherlands also ended up at war over Caribbean islands, which had been a source of war supplies for the Americans.

Battles on the Western Frontier

Native Americans, particularly the Iroquois, played important roles in the fighting that took place in the western theater, along the Great Lakes and the Ohio River Valley. Here, at Fort Niagara and Fort Detroit, British leaders encouraged loyalists and Native Americans to raid the western settlements and bring back the scalps of colonists. In response George Rogers Clark took his forces to engage the British and their allies in a surprise attack at *Kaskaskia*, in present-day Illinois. Another major battle in this region occurred when Clark and his men captured the British garrison at *Vincennes* in present-day Indiana.

Even with Clark's successes, loyalists and Iroquois continued to harass settlers in western Pennsylvania. Washington responded by sending 4,000 men under General John Sullivan to the region to not only beat but to "destroy" the Indians. They achieved this order by burning as many as 40 Native American villages in an all-out push to put an end to the Iroquois Confederacy once and for all.

Battles of the Southern Theater

The change in the nature of the war after France entered the scene led the British to rethink their war plan, and they devised a new "*Southern Strategy.*" The assumption was that British troops could no longer be concentrated against the Americans but would have to be spread throughout the globe. Howe was replaced with a new general, Sir *Henry Clinton*, who was made the new North American commander. The forces in North America were reduced, and Clinton was told to withdraw from Philadelphia. The idea was to avoid major battles with Washington's army in the north while getting ready to concentrate on the south, where the British leaders expected to find a large number of loyalists. They hoped to use bands of armed loyalists to supplement their forces and subdue the rebels. They planned to start in Georgia and go North, reintroducing royal government as each region was conquered. Ultimately, they hoped to subjugate the south first and then the north. They thought that all they would need to do would be to wait patiently and carefully cultivate and nurture loyalist sentiment.

This new "Southern Strategy," which began in late 1778, appeared to begin well. *Charleston* fell in 1780. Lord Cornwallis, the British commander in charge of the region, then hoped to take his troops through the back country of the Carolinas to rally the loyalists and raise a loyalist militia. This effort was fairly successful. The British then defeated the American forces at *Camden* in August of 1780, and it was looking as if the British had managed to gain control of South Carolina. As a result, Cornwallis prepared to march north.

The tide began to turn, however, in the fall of 1780. In October the patriot militia defeated Patrick Ferguson and his group of loyalists at *King's Mountain*. Ferguson had been patrolling the North Carolina countryside with over 1,000 loyalists in an attempt to "pacify" the area when 1,200 North Carolina, Virginia, and South Carolina militiamen gathered to stop his forces. Ferguson heard of the large group gathering and decided to move back closer to Cornwallis and the main body of forces. The militia found out where he was headed and chased him. Realizing the militia was about to overtake him, Ferguson organized a defense on top of King's Mountain, a wooded hill with a clear top. The militia arrived at the base and surrounded the mountain. They then began climbing up, and they had an advantage because the slopes of the mountain were wooded, giving them plenty of cover to hide in. The summit, however, was not wooded, so Ferguson's men were exposed and thus an easy target. Ferguson and 157 loyalists were killed, 163 were severely wounded, and 698 were captured. The patriots only lost 28, with only 62 wounded.

Francis Marion, also known as the "Swamp Fox," was also campaigning against the loyalists in the South Carolina low country at this time, and Thomas Sumter was focusing on the South Carolina up country. At the same time, the American forces in this theater were given a new commander—*Nathaniel Greene*. Greene split his army to make a wider sweep through the Carolinas. Fearing the loss of South Carolina, Cornwallis sent troops to deal with these patriot bands, and a number of encounters resulted. The British lost many of these encounters, one of which was the *Battle of the Cowpens*. It began when Cornwallis sent Colonel Tarleton to seek and destroy General Morgan's patriots. Morgan had 600 experienced soldiers from the Continental Army and the Virginia Militia, as well as 500 inexperienced militiamen. Morgan coordinated efforts with Washington, and together they captured the entire British force. The British lost almost 1,000 men with 110 being killed and 800 taken prisoners. All of the

British supplies were also captured by the Americans, who lost only 73 people—12 killed and 61 wounded.

Another encounter occurred at *Guilford Courthouse*. Here Morgan and Greene, aware that Cornwallis would be seeking revenge for Cowpens, engaged the British. Morgan wanted to stay and keep charge of the prisoners and supplies he took at Cowpens, so Greene took his army and Morgan's troops and headed north as a diversion. He was able to delay Cornwallis all the way, leading him on a cat and mouse chase into Virginia. To catch up, Cornwallis burned his supplies and then found himself exposed and without supplies, so he began withdrawing southward. Greene and the Americans then followed him, and at Guilford Courthouse Greene decided it was time to fight. The British technically won this battle, but at great cost. Cornwallis's army was now in tatters, having lost nearly a third of its force, including some of its best officers. Green then turned to the task of taking the British fort at a town called *Ninety Six*, South Carolina. He never managed to take it, but the British ended up abandoning it in July of 1781. The fighting at Ninety Six signaled the end of British control of the interior. It was also the end of the Southern Campaign.

The final battle was the *Battle of Yorktown*, on October 6-19, 1781. After Guilford Courthouse Cornwallis, though ordered to protect the British position in the Carolinas, decided to march north to Virginia and take command from Benedict Arnold, now a general for the British. At the same time, Washington and the French were planning to attack New York. The British knew of the plan so they did not send Cornwallis's reinforcements and they ordered Cornwallis to New York. Cornwallis did not listen and instead stayed in Yorktown. Washington's French aid Marquis de Lafayette saw what Cornwallis was doing and told Washington. Washington then changed plans, and he and French General Rochambeau, with 2,500 Continentals and 4,000 French troops, marched toward Philadelphia rather than New York. British General Clinton saw that the Americans were not going to New York, so he ordered the British fleet to Chesapeake Bay. On August 30th the French fleet arrived at Chesapeake Bay, and the British fleet from New York arrived on September 5th. The naval battle that resulted ended in a French victory. The 3,000 French naval troops then joined Washington's army, and together they attacked Cornwallis's troops. Cornwallis surrendered to Washington on *October 19, 1781*, ending the fighting in the American Revolution.

The Treaty of Paris

The *Treaty of Paris* was signed on September 3, 1783. This treaty provided that England accepted American independence. It also set the western boundary of the U.S. at the Mississippi River. It had limits, though. First, the British had promised they would look out for the interests of the Indians who had helped them, but they did not. Also, the British told the Americans to restore the rights and property of former loyalists. The Americans said they would pass this agreement on to the states, but the states largely ignored it. Finally, the Americans promised not to impede any efforts British merchants made to collect the pre-war debts owed to them.

Suggested Readings

Fred Anderson. *Crucible of War: The Seven Years' War and the Fate of Empire in British North America, 1754–1766* (2000).

Edward Countryman. *The American Revolution: Revised Edition* (2003).

Samuel Griffith. *The War for American Independence: From 1760 to the Surrender at Yorktown in 1781* (2002).

Ray Raphael. *A People's History of the American Revolution: How Common People Shaped the Fight for Independence* (2002).

Theodore Savas and J.David Dameron. *A Guide to the Battles of the American Revolution* (2010).

Gordon S. Wood. *The American Revolution: A History* (2003).

Chapter 6

BUILDING A NATION

After breaking from Britain, Americans had to come up with a government of their own. In 1774 colonial delegates had met in Philadelphia at the First Continental Congress. In 1775, three weeks after Lexington and Concord, this group met again in the Second Continental Congress. This was the body that issued the Declaration of Independence and then became the first national government of the United States. Once the Americans decided to break away from the Crown they had to come up with a viable system of governance first to keep the colonies together during the war and then to create a new nation after the fighting ended. The Continental Congress had served well since 1775, so that body continued to coordinate war efforts and to govern in the immediate post-war years. The plan of government they came up with, the Articles of Confederation, faced a number of serious problems, most notably the inability to tax or to regulate trade between the new states. Indeed, the state governments created during and after the revolution held much more power than this loose federal organization.

By 1787 the problems with this system became serious enough that leaders were demanding revision. That year they met in the convention that is known to historians as the Constitutional Convention. Before examining the Constitution that emerged and the government it created, we should consider a number of important questions. For example, the Americans boasted that their revolution was to create an entirely new system of government, known as a republic. What exactly is a republic and how does it differ from what the colonists had under England? What exactly were the Articles of Confederation and why do most historians say they were inadequate? What were the major changes brought about by the government that was later created by the U.S. Constitution? Finally, just how different was life under this new system for the average person?

The American Experiment in Republicanism

As we saw before, the ideas of the Enlightenment greatly influenced the colonists' decision to fight for independence. These same ideas influenced the decisions they made when creating their new government. The government they had revolted against was a constitutional monarchy that included a king or queen who ruled through hereditary succession as well as a representative body (Parliament) voted on by landowners. This system allowed, to some extent, a set of checks and balances. Collectively this system and the Bill of Rights protected individual liberty. The Americans, however, wanted to expand the representative aspect of this system, so they turned to a form of government used in Classical Greece and Rome—Republicanism.

Republicanism is a system whereby elected officials are chosen by voters and then expected to rule for the greater good of the people and the country as a whole. The idea of putting one's own best interests aside and acting for the good of society overall was known as *civic virtue*. In a republic this trait is essential not only for the leaders but also for the voters. This ideal, however, is hard to live up to, so leaders faced a bit of a conundrum. They wanted to do away with the monarch and to rely solely on representative government but they realized that this plan could only work if the citizens—both voters and leaders—remained able and willing to act upon the greater good.

While looking to the republics of Greece and Rome for guidance, the founders of the American republic also incorporated the newer ideas of the Enlightenment. From John Locke and Jean Jacques Rousseau they borrowed the idea of natural rights and contract theory. They also included Locke's concept of toleration, which became the bedrock for the idea of separating the church and the state once and for all. Another major influence was Baron de Montesquieu, whose ideas of checks and balances led to the American focus on separation of powers. This separation of powers was two-tiered. First, within the federal government distinct branches—the executive, the legislative, and the judicial—would counterbalance each other's power. Second, the individual state governments would keep the federal government in check.

The state governments played an important role in this system. In fact they were initially much stronger than the federal government. This was partially because the state governments were created first. As soon as the fighting began, the governors and other Crown officials left the colonies and the assemblies took over. They often expelled any loyalists, assumed the role of provincial congresses, and turned their colonial charters into constitutions. These constitutions set up the state governments. They replaced the appointed governors and councils with elected governors and senates. In most cases they included clear separation of powers that gave more strength to the legislatures and less to the governors, and they generally included a bill of rights.

Under this system the states basically had all of the authority. Only they could adopt laws binding individual citizens, and only states could levy taxes. States were also in charge of all matters of domestic concerns or internal policing. In essence, it was left to the states to create what we actually think of as governments. The states, then, were like miniature republics.

The Articles of Confederation: Their Weaknesses and Their Strengths

The new national government, which was set up under the *Articles of Confederation*, (also known as the Articles of Confederation and Perpetual Union) was much weaker than these state governments. It was created between June of 1776 and November of 1777 by a committee within the Second Continental Congress that was led by John Dickinson. It took effect on March 1, 1781. Before the Articles took effect Congress directed the war and turned to state governments to implement its resolutions, recommendations, and requisitions.

Under the Articles of Confederation, all that existed on the national level was a unicameral Congress made up of delegates who were appointed by state legislatures. (This was still a representative system because voters chose the state legislators who appointed the congressional delegates.) These delegates had no power to levy taxes and had to rely upon the states to honor requests to forward funds. It had no power to enforce its ordinances and resolutions, and there were no courts to support the legality of its measures. It did have responsibility enough to settle disputes between the states and was in charge of Indian affairs, the postal service, and the coinage of money. It also had jurisdiction over war matters and other foreign affairs issues. Delegates were appointed for single-year terms, and regardless of the number of delegates each state sent, states were only given one vote. Most representatives did not actually stay the full term, instead choosing to come and go as their personal circumstances allowed. Also, delegates often had a hard time agreeing on how to use the state's single vote, and there was no effective system in place to solve disagreements between delegates, whether they were from the same state or different states.

This Congress had a number of problems to deal with, beyond those involving the delegates. The most significant was the fact that the new state legislatures held most of the power and were hostile toward the idea of creating a strong central government. This left Congress unable to regulate commerce between the states or with foreign countries. Also, there was no administrative head of the government, and most actions required almost unanimous support. For example, any matters pertaining to war, the armed forces, treaties, and finances had to be approved by nine states, and it required unanimous approval for Congress to be able to pass tariffs on foreign goods, their only means of funding beyond voluntary state contributions. Any amendments to the Articles of Confederation also had to be unanimously ratified by the states. Because there were no federal courts, it was also hard to settle disputes. This weak federal government faced a number of problems as it tried to get the new nation on its feet.

To begin with, the new government had foreign affairs matters that had to be resolved. For one matter, the Americans had promised in the Treaty of Paris to return Loyalist property and to guarantee immunity to Loyalists for the next year so that those who had left could return to the U.S., sell their property and otherwise handle their final affairs. Congress had also agreed to have the states return property confiscated from Loyalists. Despite these

promises, Loyalists were being persecuted and, in some places, lynched even after the war had ended. This issue would not be resolved until 1783, when some Loyalists were finally able to return to their estates and resume their lives. Only in 1787 did all of the states remove laws .discriminatory to Loyalists.

The new nation also faced a number of boundary issues with both Britain and Spain. Ignoring the boundaries that had been laid out in the treaty after the revolution, both of these countries continued to keep illegal military posts and soldiers on what was now American soil. British soldiers remained out west, and the Spanish kept forts in lands that were above their northern boundary, which was now the U.S. southern boundary. Both of these countries were also stirring the resentment of Native Americans in the region and arming them. Finally, the Spanish closed the port of New Orleans to Americans, and this hurt American settlers in the west because they needed access to goods and markets. As a result, Congress sent John Jay to negotiate with the Spanish, but he was largely unsuccessful. Similarly, the British were barring American ships from the Great Lakes, because Americans had not paid back prewar debts to British businessmen or returned property they had taken away from Loyalists during the war. All of this agitation left Americans vulnerable to Native American attacks, and Joseph Brant, a Mohawk Indian leader who had sided with the British during the war, used the situation to try to get Indians to band together and fight American settlement in the west. This was basically a powder keg waiting to explode. Finally, the different states claimed territory in the west, and this led to disputes over land claims and deeds.

In addition to all of these problems, Congress also had to deal with issues of supplying

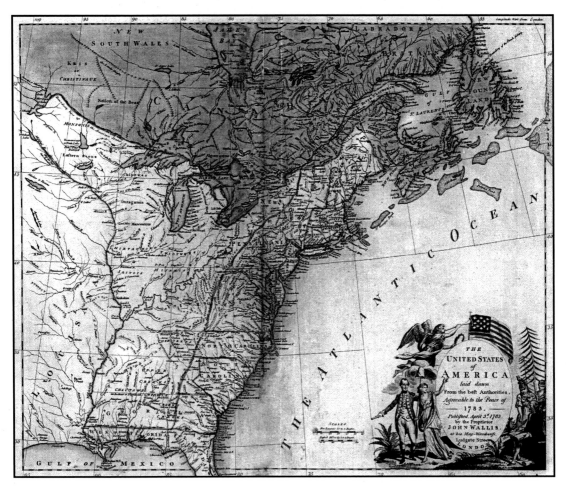

This map shows the boundaries that were set for the new United States by the Treaty of Paris in 1783. Even though the treaty clearly set the western and southern boundaries of the U.S., Great Britain and Spain continued to test the young nation's power by maintaining military bases on what was clearly U.S. soil.

the army and demobilizing. This became a major issue in 1783 as disenchanted soldiers and officers who had not been paid for many years began to plan what is known as the *Newburgh Conspiracy*. Essentially, the army had remained camped at Newburgh, New York, for two years after the war ended to keep an eye on British troops still there. They needed food, clothing, supplies, and wages, but Congress was having trouble paying wages for their wartime service, much less keeping them provided for in the post-war period. The soldiers had been promised half pensions for life, but Congress had no clear avenue through which to get the money to fulfill this promise. Officers began to protest not being paid, and they would have revolted but for the intervention of George Washington. Some leaders of state governments, like Robert Morris, Gouvenor Morris, and Alexander Hamilton used this situation to call for national power to tax, but such a change would have required strengthening the Articles of Confederation.

Financial problems extended well beyond the matter of supplying the army. The national government was also in debt from the war but Congress had no power to raise the money to pay off the debt, which included an estimated $10 million owed to other countries and $40 million owed to Americans. During the war Congress had amassed this debt because their only means of funding was to turn to the states, but the states did not contribute enough, so they turned to France and to American businessmen and merchants. They also turned to American farmers for provisions to feed the troops. To pay this debt, Congress asked for an amendment to the Articles of Confederation that would provide for a national import duty of five percent. Amending the Articles, however, required a unanimous vote, and though they tried for five years Congress never managed to get the necessary approval.

At the same time, the new nation's economy was on very shaky footing. Trade between the states was just starting to become established, especially as small-scale manufacturing was just starting to take off in the U.S. This internal trade, however, faced a number of problems most because of the different trade regulations in each state. Foreign trade dropped significantly as the British government closed off the West Indies to the U.S. The British also initially significantly cut trading with the U.S. because England favored trading with its colonies and when the U.S. gained its independence it lost its favored trade status. At the same time, currency was depreciating.

To resolve these problems Congress turned to Robert Morris, the richest man in America, to come up with a plan. Morris, who as Superintendent of Finance was the closest Congress had to an executive leader, had a number of ideas for solving the new nation's financial distress. First, he issued a currency to replace the worthless Continental currency. Called "Morris Notes," this currency was backed by his own private credit. He also planned to establish a Bank of North America to be funded by private subscriptions and incorporated by Congress. He was trying to restore public credit and make Congress less dependent on the states for funding. (Remember, only states could levy taxes.) His ideas were sound, and Alexander Hamilton would later use a similar plan to save the government as the nation's first Secretary of the Treasury. At the time, however, Morris's plan did not work because it depended upon the national government having a secure income and the only way to ensure such an income would have been to amend the Articles of Confederation. Amending the Articles required unanimous approval of the states, and this was impossible to achieve. As a result the Confederation government was never able to get its finances in order and the new nation's debt grew from $10 million to $28 million as Congress ran a deficit each year.

Stemming from these efforts to raise money to pay the debts, a conflict emerged between rural and urban interests over matters of public debt and finances. Morris's Bank of North America drew a great deal of criticism. It managed to profit, but it did so by only lending money to people who were good credit risks. This selective lending caused resentment among artisans and farmers who argued that it was only benefitting a commercial elite and not them. At the same time, tensions developed between creditors and

Captain Daniel Shays, shown here with one of his co-conspirators named Job Shattuck, led a rebellion in 1786 in response to the repressive monetary and taxation policies that prevailed in the young United States following the Revolution. Four rebels were killed in the uprising and some of the oppressive taxes were eliminated. The larger effect of the rebellion, however, was that it bolstered the movement to create a stronger national government.

up having to sell their land and livestock to pay back taxes. Those whose land and livestock did not bring in enough money to pay the taxes were jailed when they could not come up with the tax money. People were being jailed for small debts and many lived in constant fear of losing their farms. In this climate farmers began to demand reform. When they did not get the reform they called for, some protested through military means.

The final result of this unrest was *Shays' Rebellion.* This occurred in 1786 when the Massachusetts legislature adjourned without addressing the needs of the farmers, who had become desperate by that point. Led by Captain Daniel Shays, a war veteran turned destitute farmer, a band of about 1,200 men formed an army and closed the courts in order to prevent farm foreclo-

debtors. The government needed to pay back the people who had lent money for the war effort, and many state governments imposed taxes to repay war bonds in full. This benefitted the wealthy because they had bought the most war bonds. Also, rich speculators who had the money had bought war bonds that had been originally held by farmers and artisans at a fraction of what they were worth, but they were now being paid full value. This made the farmers who sold the bonds feel cheated, and they began to argue that state governments were showing favoritism toward the commercial interests. The taxes raised to pay the bonds back made it worse, because many farmers could not pay the taxes, so they ended

sures. Their main goal included a more flexible monetary policy which would allow them to use their crops, primarily corn and wheat, as money. They also wanted taxes to be postponed until the agricultural depression that had gripped the country after the war abated. Their rebellion was ultimately crushed by the state militia. Four rebels died, but their deaths were not completely in vain. The uprising forced the new state legislature to finally address the crisis by eliminating some of the taxes that were so oppressive to the farmers.

Most historians have portrayed the Articles of Confederation as basically useless, but there was at least one real victory under them. The government under the Articles did manage to get the states to give over their claims to western land to the federal government. The government then sold those lands to raise revenue through a series of ordinances such as the Land Ordinance of 1784, the Land Ordinance of 1785, and the *Northwest Ordinance* of 1787. These plans allowed the national government to hire surveyors to organize the western land into clear grids, to establish clear boundaries, and then to sell the land to raise funds to pay off debts. They also provided for the settlement of the western lands and the organization of that land into new territories and, eventually, new states. Initially the new territories would be governed by a governor, a secretary, and three judges, all of whom would be chosen by Congress, but when a territory reached a population of 5,000 free men, those men would choose their own assembly that would govern in tandem with a governing council appointed by Congress. Once a territory reached 60,000 free inhabitants it could create a constitution and apply for statehood. Finally, this ordinance provided for the exclusion of slavery from the Northwest territories. The first state to enter the union through this process was Ohio. Those that followed included Indiana, Illinois, Michigan, and Wisconsin.

The Northwest Ordinance was one clear success under the Articles of Confederation, but it was not enough. Some leaders, especially those who had a direct financial stake in the new country's solvency, had already begun calling for a stronger central government. The unrest made so evident by Shays' Rebellion helped fuel this growing cry as self-interested middle and upper class men began to fear the masses more than they feared centralization of power. Some leaders, especially James Madison and Alexander Hamilton, who had served together in Congress in 1782–83, began to call for a national convention to meet in Philadelphia in 1787 and revamp the federal system. They argued that no effective national government could keep relying on state governments to implement its policies and decisions, and most realized they needed a more genuine national congress. If they were going to keep the lower orders in line, the new congress would need the power to pass legislation that individuals would be required to follow, rather than mere resolutions that were only recommendations to the state governments. They also knew that a truly effective national government would need to look more like the state governments, with executive, legislative, and judicial branches. They also needed national laws and the power to enforce them. They knew that not everyone would agree, so they decided to hold a closed meeting to work this all out. This resulted in the *Constitutional Convention* of 1787.

The Constitutional Convention

Those who met in Philadelphia on May 25, 1787 actually started out with the stated goal of simply revising the Articles of Confederation. Fifty-five men attended this meeting at one point or another and thirty-nine ultimately signed the document. Some of the more famous delegates include George Washington, Benjamin Franklin, George Mason, Gouverneur Morris, James Wilson, and James Madison. They wanted to increase the power of the national government by giving it the power to tax and to regulate interstate commerce. They also wanted to give the national government all "necessary and proper" powers needed to deal flexibly with issues that would arise in the future.

James Madison was the leading figure behind this movement. He was joined by a group of delegates, mostly from Virginia and Pennsylvania, who agreed on the need to replace, rather than revise, the Articles of Confederation. The result was what some historians refer to as the "Revolution of 1787," but it could also be seen as a counterrevolution that shifted power away from the people and into the hands of a governing elite. This second revolution radically changed the new country by creating a strong national government. These "nationalist-minded" men met first in Benjamin Franklin's home on May 16, and the presence of Franklin and George Washington gave this group a sense of legitimacy. Most of the intellectual leadership, however, was provided by Madison (now known as the "Father of the Constitution"), Wilson, and Morris. Paradoxically, these men wanted a government that would represent the people, yet they feared the masses.

These nationalists presented a new plan, known as the *Virginia Plan*. They proposed this plan right after the convention opened because they had already met and worked it out. This plan called for a bicameral (two branch) national legislature with representation in both houses being based on population. The representatives in the House would be elected by the people, while the Senators would be chosen by the state legislatures. A powerful national executive and a judicial branch would be chosen by the national legislature. This plan revealed a fear of true democracy because only the lower house of the legislative branch would be chosen by the people. Those in the other branches and upper legislature would either be appointed or indirectly elected. These nationalists were careful to keep a low profile so that states' rights advocates, most notably Patrick Henry, would not realize what was going on. Though Henry was elected a delegate to the convention to amend

the Articles, he stayed home because he did not realize that they were going to redo the entire system. Thus, in the absence of opposition, on May 30, just three days after the convention started, six of the eight states present agreed to the need for a national government with three branches—legislative, executive, and judiciary. Even after most agreed that they needed a new government altogether, there were still a number of disagreements.

One major problem was the apportionment of representation in Congress. Delegates from large populous states like Pennsylvania and Virginia agreed that representation in both houses of the legislature should be based on population. Those from small states, however, disagreed. They wanted equal representation for each state. To solve this problem, William Patterson presented the *New Jersey Plan*, which called for a unicameral (single house) legislature in which each state would have one vote. They also wanted a more "federal" than "national" government. The debate was solved by the *Connecticut Compromise* (also known as the Great Compromise). Under this compromise, representation in the lower house was apportioned by population. Each state would get equal representation in the upper house. Many, including Madison, saw this as too much compromise, but overall it was seen as the best solution.

Slavery posed the strongest point of disagreement. By 1787 slavery in America was on the decline. It remained significant in five states, but only South Carolina and Georgia argued for its expansion. Still, there were issues that arose pertaining to slavery. One question was whether or not slaves were "residents" who should be accounted for when determining representation or simply "property" and thus not eligible to be counted. This was resolved by the *Three Fifths Compromise* that said each slave would be counted as three fifths of a person. Another question revolved around the future of the international slave trade. South Carolina and Georgia insisted it be allowed to continue. The other representatives compromised and agreed that Congress would not prohibit the importation of slaves from Africa for 20 years (until 1808) but would be able to tax slave imports at $10 per person. Finally, there was an issue surrounding the fate of escaped slaves, and it was decided that those who escaped slavery and sought refuge in other states would be returned under a fugitive slave clause. Despite all the heated discussion of slavery, the delegates somehow managed to avoid using that word in the document itself.

After coming to agreements on these two larger issues, the delegates set to work laying out the actual structure of the new government. One point of debate involved the powers of the presidency. Some wanted a strong executive, but others feared that this would be too much like the monarchy from which they had revolted. What resulted was an executive that would face re-election every four years, could recommend legislation but had to gain Congress's approval, and would have to report annually on the state of the nation. He could also veto acts of Congress, but that veto could be overridden by a two-thirds vote in each house of Congress. He was commander-in-chief and could also make treaties, but the treaties would have to be approved by two-thirds of the Senate. He could also appoint judges and diplomats, but, again, his appointments had to be approved by the Senate. Even with these checks on his power, the president of the U.S. actually had much more influence than the British monarch.

But the delegates were sure to limit the president's power in a number of areas. For example, the president could not declare war,

and he could not make peace. These powers were given instead to Congress. Unlike the British monarch, the president could be impeached, or removed from office by the House for treason, bribery, or unstated "high crimes and misdemeanors." Once impeached by the House, he would face the Senate which would then decide whether or not to remove him from office. This would require a two-thirds vote. This would make the president accountable but in constant danger of being removed for small issues.

Another debate that centered around the presidency was how the chief executive would be elected. Some thought the executive should be elected by the state legislatures or state governors. Others, such as James Madison, Alexander Hamilton, and James Wilson wanted the president to be popularly elected in order to make him more independent. The Electoral College was created as a compromise. Under this system, the people of each state would choose presidential electors who would then cast their votes for the president. The number of electors each state would have would be determined by the number of members each state had in the Senate and the House combined.

The final task of the delegates was to set up the third branch of government, the judicial branch. They created a Supreme Court that included a Chief Justice and other judges, but they left it to Congress to decide how many judges would be included. The Supreme Court would operate under implied powers to ultimately review federal and state laws.

The new government created clearly provided for the Enlightenment ideals of a separation of powers and a system of checks and balances. Separation of powers is embodied in the three branches of the government as well as the combination of state and national government. Checks and balances can be

This scene depicts the signing of the United States Constitution. A number of American leaders are represented in this painting, but perhaps the most easily identified is Benjamin Franklin. One of the last acts of his long life was to sign the Constitution and ask Americans to follow his lead in supporting the new government. Fully aware that the document was less than perfect, he thought it was better than the Articles of Confederation and that it would be improved in the years ahead.

seen in the President's veto power, Congress's power of impeachment, and the Senate's power to oversee treaties and appointments. It is perhaps best exemplified in the Supreme Court's power of judicial review.

After all of this haggling, 39 of the 42 delegates signed the new Constitution. Benjamin Franklin devoted the last major speech of his life to calling for the delegates to support the new government and adopt it despite its faults, so they did. After the convention ended, delegates made the new Constitution public and proposed it to the people on September 28,

1787. The next step was *ratification*, a process through which each state was asked to pass, or approve, it. Of course, not everyone agreed with the changes. At this point, those who supported the Constitution began to call themselves *Federalists*, and those who opposed it were called *"Anti-Federalists."*

The main Anti-Federalists were Virginia governor Edmund Randolph, Virginia delegate George Mason, and Massachusetts delegate Elbridge Gerry. Revolutionary hero Patrick Henry was another. In general, Anti-Federalists were from rural areas and were not involved in the market. They were also more likely to have served in the militias than the regular Continental Army during the revolution. In short, they were less likely to be of the wealthy leadership class to which the new government owed money. These men opposed the Constitution for a number of reasons. They said the Constitution gave too much power to the national government, and they said this power would be too easy to abuse and would open the possibility of a dictator or a president who would abuse his position. They also said the power to tax would be abused and that the Senate would become aristocratic and elitist like the House of Lords in the English Parliament. They also feared the Constitution would create a standing army, and they did not like the fact that it neglected to provide for individual rights such as freedom of speech or press. Finally, they added that the Federalists wrote the Constitution too quickly and with too much secrecy and that Americans should give the Articles of Confederation another chance.

They wanted a second convention so they could all go home, take a break, and come back and go over it one more time. They wanted a larger House of Representatives and a Bill of Rights as well. Most were prepared to support the Constitution once it was amended. In general, people who were called "Anti-Federalists" also wanted greater separation between the executive branch and the Senate, a clear statement that all powers not granted specifically to Congress be left to the states, constitutional protection for trial by jury, and other specific protections such as "due process of law." They also wanted a promise that Congress would only impose direct taxes when they could not get enough money from import duties, excise taxes, and other sources. In other words, they wanted to make sure that only state legislatures could pass direct taxes for the most part and

that the federal government could only step in if the state failed to send its share of the revenue. They also were uncomfortable with what is known as the *"necessary and proper clause"* which gave the national government unstated powers to deal with issues that might arise in the future. Opponents argued that this gave the government too much broad power and made its boundaries unclear. It is important to remember, however, that Anti-Federalists were not necessarily against the Constitution. They just wanted it made better.

After the Anti-Federalists presented their arguments, the Federalists defended the Constitution through a number of counter-arguments. These men had, for the most part, come to believe that all people were motivated by self-interest, and they had started to doubt the notion that civic virtue alone would lead most people to act on the greater good. Thus, they insisted that the Articles of Confederation were just too weak and had too many problems to be fixed. What was needed, they argued, was a stronger government that could keep citizens in line and protect liberty. They maintained that the national government's increased power would not be abused because of the checks and balances between the three branches. They also said that the government's power would not be corrupted because the United States is such a large, diverse country that no one faction could ever take over and become dominant and abuse the others. They argued that because the convention was calm, thorough, and deliberative, it was not hasty. To support this claim, they pointed out the number of compromises. They also pointed out that the Federalist position was supported by patriotic men such as George Washington, Benjamin Franklin, John Adams, and Thomas Jefferson, all men of virtue and patriots who had played key roles in the revolution. Finally, they promised to add amendments to protect individual freedoms once the Constitution was ratified.

The Federalists presented these arguments to the public through a series of pamphlets and newspaper articles known as the *Federalist Papers*. These were written by James Madison, Alexander Hamilton and John Jay. Madison was born on a large Virginia plantation and attended the College of New Jersey (now Princeton). He was a member of the Virginia delegation to the Continental Congress and a strong supporter of complete religious freedom and separation of church and state. He is known for being the most active delegate at the Constitutional Convention and a close ally of Thomas Jefferson. By contrast, Alexander Hamilton was born out of wedlock in the British West Indies, and his enemies would often make a fuss about his illegitimacy. John Adams called him the "bastard brat of a Scots pedlar" and Thomas Jefferson called him "that foreign bastard." He came to the colonies to study at King's College (now Columbia University) in New York, and many of the ideas he would have throughout his life would be modeled after British ideas. He fought in the revolution and impressed George Washington, who chose him as his private secretary and confidential aide. He had served in the Continental Congress as a delegate from New York. Finally, John Jay was born in New York and also went to Columbia, where he studied law. He served in the Second Continental Congress and was one of the signers of the Declaration of Independence. He was chosen by the Continental Congress to be in charge of foreign affairs and, as we saw earlier, was sent to negotiate with the Spanish. It was his difficulties during those negotiations that convinced him that a stronger central government was needed.

Born out of wedlock and never allowed to forget his origins, Alexander Hamilton played a significant role in ensuring the passage of the Constitution. He, along with James Madison and John Jay, contributed to a series of essays known as the *Federalist Papers*. These essays convinced Americans to accept the new Constitution. After the new government was created, George Washington, chosen as the first president of the U.S., selected Hamilton as his Secretary of the Treasury.

In the end, the Constitution was accepted by a vote of 11-2, with only North Carolina and Rhode Island rejecting it. Some states which passed it only did so by a small margin. For example, the Virginia legislature voted 89-79; New York's vote was 30-27; and the Massachusetts vote was 187-168. The

Congress that had been ruling under the Articles of Confederation then began to prepare to surrender power to the newly-created government. It chose New York City as the new capital and set the date for the elections.

The new government met in March of 1789 in New York City, but it was a month before enough representatives were present to make a quorum. Once that happened, the Senate's presiding officer was able to certify that *George Washington* had been elected president with 69 electoral votes and John Adams vice president with 34 votes. The choice of Washington for president was crucial in the ultimate success of the new government. To many he was the very embodiment of civic virtue. Washington then chose his advisors, which included Thomas Jefferson as Secretary of State, Alexander Hamilton as Secretary of the Treasury, and Edmund Randolph as Attorney General. These men made up what would one day become the presidential cabinet. The new president also chose John Jay as the first Chief Justice of the Supreme Court.

After the Constitution was adopted and the new government set in place, the Federalists kept their promise and added the *Bill of Rights*, a set of amendments to the Constitution which protected individual liberties. Some examples included the First Amendment which ensured the separation of Church and State, guaranteed freedom of worship, and guaranteed freedom of speech, press, and assembly. The Second Amendment provided for a well-regulated militia, and the Fourth Amendment guaranteed the right of privacy against unreasonable search and seizure by police. The Fifth Amendment guaranteed due process of law, protecting people from testifying against themselves, and the Sixth Amendment gave the accused the right to trial and the right to defense council. It is the basis for the idea of "innocent until proven guilty." After the passage of these amendments, Federalists gained popularity because they kept their promise, and North Carolina and Rhode Island then accepted the Constitution. At that point the Anti-Federalist movement disappeared.

George Washington, former leader of the Continental Army, was chosen as the first president of the United States after winning 69 votes from the electoral college. His win was no surprise. Indeed, many historians have argued that the men who drafted the Constitution had Washington in mind when they created the executive branch. To his peers he embodied the ideal of "civic virtue."

A Social Revolution?

The American Revolution brought in significant change in terms of the government, first with the Articles of Confederation and then with the Constitution, but was it all that revolutionary in social terms? In some ways there were cultural changes of significance. One major area of transformation involved religion. Before the revolution, most Americans had tolerated religious dissent, but many colonies still had official established religions that were supported by taxes. For example several states supported the Anglican Church. Before the war was even over, however, all states except Virginia had done away with tax support for the church. Virginia followed suit soon after. At that point religion lost all state support in the new nation. Those who wrote the Constitution took this a step farther by not directly mentioning God. Determined to protect religious freedom, they included the promise in the First Amendment that Congress would "make no law respecting an establishment of religion or prohibiting the free exercise thereof." This made the United States unique at the time since most nations had established religions that were supported by taxes. In response, the churches had to regroup and develop new structures of their own. The first national church structures emerged at this time, beginning with the Methodists in 1784. The Anglican Church was too closely associated with England, so American Anglicans renamed themselves the Episcopal Church in 1789, the same year the Presbyterians held their first national meeting.

The churches were not the only forces influenced by a new national outlook, but the sense of nationalism that grew in the U.S. was influenced strongly by a sense of divine destiny. This was a carryover from the Puritan and Quaker missions, but it was enhanced by a new belief that America was now somehow a beacon of liberty and equality for the rest of the world to look to as an example. The extent to which this was true should be evaluated by looking at what the revolution ultimately meant to most Americans, not just the new leadership class.

In one sense it could be argued that the spirit of equality affected people of all social orders in the early days. Indeed, the notion of deference that had permeated colonial society did start to weaken during the revolutionary years, and that trend continued after the war. In a theme common throughout U.S. history, men who participated in the war gained a new sense of their own strength and equality and translated this into broadened participation in politics after the war. Most of the new state governments expanded the franchise significantly as property qualifications were lowered. In some states, such as Pennsylvania, Delaware, North Carolina, and Georgia, any male taxpayer could vote. Not only did more men vote, but more were able to run for office and serve in the state legislatures which, unlike the colonial assemblies, had a fairly broad base of participation. Even so, those hoping to hold office did have to meet stronger property requirements than those who only planned to vote. While participation was broadened on both of these levels it is still important to remember that no state adopted universal male suffrage, and women were left out. One important thing to note, however, is that most state constitutions did not include the word "white" so black male property holders and tax payers could vote in many places in these early years.

Even with this expanded franchise, however, it could be argued that the revolution was hardly revolutionary for the common person, especially after the Articles of Confederation gave way to the Constitution. At first, it appeared that the participation of African Americans, Women, and Native Americans during the war would translate to long-term gains, but the leadership ultimately allowed their fears of the masses to lead them to keeping the lower orders in check.

As we saw before, slaves and free African Americans played a number of different roles in the war, and in some ways their lives changed as a result. In New England and the Middle States the revolutionaries offered freedom to slaves who had participated in the revolution by spying, building fortifications, serving as nurses or cooks, or fighting on the battlefield. Indeed, the revolutionary rhetoric included a number of ideas that supported opposition to slavery. For example, colonists said they did not want to be made slaves by the British, and this made it hard to then defend keeping others in bondage. Also, some leaders, most notably Thomas Jefferson, realized that slavery was wrong and even publically admitted it. Of course, sometimes their concern was selfish, because they realized that freedom was something they were willing to fight for, and they started to fear that blacks would fight for their freedom too. This fear of revolt was widespread, and as we saw earlier, Lord Dunmore's Proclamation made it worse.

Thomas Jefferson voiced his fear-based opposition to slavery in the rough draft of his Declaration of Independence:

> We hold these truths to be [sacred and undeniable] self evident, that all men are created equal and independent; that from that equal creation they derive in rights inherent and inalienable, among which are the preservation of life, and liberty and the pursuit of happiness; that to secure

these ends, governments are instituted among men, deriving their just powers from the consent of the governed; that whenever any form of government shall become destructive of these ends, it is the right of the people to alter or to abolish it, and to. institute new government, laying its foundation on such principles and organizing its powers in such form, as to them shall seem most likely to affect their safety and happiness. Prudence, indeed, will dictate that governments long established should not be changed for light and transient causes: and accordingly all experience hath shewn that mankind are more disposed to suffer while evils are sufferable, than to right themselves by abolishing the forms to which they are accustomed. but when a long train of abuses and usurpations, begun at a distinguished period, and pursuing invariably the same object evinces a design to [subject] reduce them to arbitrary power, it is their right, it is their duty, to throw off such government, and to provide new guards for their future security. —

He then went on to criticize the king for forcing slavery upon the colonists:

> he has waged cruel war against human nature itself, violating its most sacred rights of life and liberty in the persons of a distant people who never offended him, captivating and carrying them into slavery in another hemisphere, or to incur miserable death in their transportation hither. This piratical warfare, the

opprobium of infidel powers, is the warfare of the Christian king of Great Britain. [determined to keep open a market where MEN should be bought and sold,] he has prostituted his negative for suppressing every legislative attempt to prohibit or to restrain this execrable commerce [determining to keep open a market where MEN should be bought and sold]: and that this assemblage of horrors might want no fact of distinguished die, he is now exciting those very people to rise in arms among us, and to purchase that liberty of which he had deprived them, by murdering the people upon whom he also obtruded them: thus paying off former crimes committed against the liberties of one people, with crimes which he urges them to commit against the lives of another.

While some of the passages above were stricken from the final copy of the Declaration, they reveal an unease with slavery, if for no other reason than because it put whites in danger. It was this concern that led all states except Georgia to put an end to the importation of African slaves after the war. (South Carolina later changed its mind and reopened the trade.)

One idea that did remain in the final draft was the notion that all men were "created equal." African Americans heard the rhetoric of slavery and liberty and realized this contradiction too, so they fought hard to make sure that "all men" would include black men. Many reasoned that the participation of blacks in the war meant that they should gain equal access to the freedom and liberty offered by the new government. Many earned land for their efforts in the war, and some took it a step farther by petitioning the state governments to ask that their rights be respected. In one of the most famous examples, Prince Hall from Massachusetts, led the effort that presented the following petition in 1777:

The petition of A Great Number of Blackes detained in a State of slavery in the bowels of a free & Christian County Humbly sheweth that your Petitioners apprehend that they have in Common with all other men a Natural and Unalienable Right to that freedom which the Grat Parent of the Universe that Bestowed equally on all menkind and which they have Never forfeited by any Compact or agreement whatever— but that wher Unjustly Dragged by the hand of cruel Power and their Derest friends and sum of them Even torn from the Embraces of their tender Parents from A populous Pleasant and Plentiful country and in violation of Laws of Nature and of Nations and in Defiance of all the tender feelings of humanity Brought here Either to Be sold like Beast of burthen & Like them Condemned to Slavery for Life Among A People Professing the mild Religion of Jesus A people Not Insensible of the Secrets of Rational Being Nor without spirit to Resent the unjust endeavors of others to Reduce them to a state of Bondage and Subjugation your hononuer Need not to be informed that A Live of Slavery Like that of your petitioners Deprived of Every social privilege of Every thing Requisite and render Life Tolable is far worse than Nonexistance.

Thanks to leaders like Hall, along with white antislavery sympathizers, some progress was made toward abolition at this point. Quakers in Pennsylvania and New Jersey had been calling for abolition for quite a while before the revolution even began, and this movement began to spread. In this context the first abolitionists emerged. These early antislavery proponents were called "*gradualists*" because they thought slavery should end gradually, only after slaves were "prepared" to be productive citizens. The most famous gradualist group was the *Pennsylvania Abolition Society* (PAS), led at one point by Benjamin Franklin. Gradual abolition triumphed in the northern and middle states, and it looked like it was going to take off in Virginia and Maryland.

Slavery was ended throughout the northern states by three main avenues. First was legislative. The assembly in Pennsylvania was the first to pass a gradual abolition law in 1780. It said that children born to slaves after a certain date would be free when they turned 28. The second avenue was judicial. Slavery was ruled unconstitutional by the Massachusetts supreme court in 1783 because the state constitution had said that "all men are free and equal" and slaves like a man named *Quok Walker* and a woman named Elizabeth Freeman but more popularly known as *Mum Bett*, petitioned that this meant slavery could not exist in the state. They won. Finally, some states took a constitutional route. Vermont, for example, ended slavery by banning it outright in the state constitution. As northern states ended slavery, southern slaves heard about the emancipation efforts and the growing free black communities, and many ran away to join them. Historians have estimated that as many as 100,000 slaves took this route.

Support spread for abolition in parts of the South too, especially Virginia and Maryland. Thomas Jefferson provides a great example of the dilemma people in this region faced. They knew slavery was wrong but their wealth depended upon bound labor. Jefferson once said slavery was like "having a wolf by the ears." This quote embodies the fear he expressed in the rough draft of the Declaration. Slave owners were scared that slaves would revolt but they were also scared to live with free blacks. For some, the best idea was to relax manumission laws. This was most prevalent in upper south states like Maryland and Virginia. For states further

Elizabeth Freeman, more popularly known as Mum Bett, was a slave who gained her freedom through the American court system. Enslaved in Massachusetts, she claimed that the state constitution offered liberty to everyone, and she managed to use this argument not only to earn her own freedom but also to help end slavery in her state.

south, however, this seemed impractical. For one thing, slavery was losing profitability in the tobacco areas, but it was gaining profitability in states that relied on crops less likely to leach the soil of its minerals. Another problem, especially for South Carolina, was the size of the black population. In that particular state, slaveholders had imported so many slaves that blacks actually outnumbered whites.

Many who lamented the size of the black population in the U.S. thought that if they did free the slaves they would need to send them out west to unsettled land or back to Africa. Indeed, this idea became popular throughout the U.S., and an organization called the American Colonization Society (ACS) would eventually be formed to end slavery and send blacks "back" to Africa. Some blacks supported this idea, either through the ACS or independently, believing that if blacks could create their own societies beyond the bounds of American racism they could prove their equality and gain respect in the U.S. One of the earliest black Americans to support the idea of African colonization was *Paul Cuffe*, a Massachusetts sea captain and shipbuilder.

This fear of the effects of emancipation was fueled by a number of factors. For one matter, the French followed the American lead and revolted against their monarch beginning in 1789. Their revolt, however, came to embody the image of the radical masses overthrowing authority and ushering in a period of anarchy. This image terrified U.S. leaders who generally feared the unruly masses. More specifically in terms of slavery, the French Revolution spawned another revolt that terrified American slaveholders. This occurred when slaves in the French colony of Haiti took advantage of the upheaval in the home government to secure their own freedom. Led by

Toussaint L'Ouverture, they revolted in 1791 and eventually created their own independent republic. This was the only successful slave revolt in the western hemisphere, and it led many Americans to cool their revolutionary zeal and seek instead a stabilizing force before matters escalated to that point in the U.S.

Women of the era faced a similar situation. Their wartime support led to some benefits, but ultimately they remained subservient to men and excluded from the public sphere. Because of a principle known as *coverture*, married women could not own property and thus could not vote. They also could not enter into contracts, and it was almost impossible to obtain a divorce. Single women could own property, but they could not vote either, and in most cases women in general could not preach or hold office, and very few were able to obtain formal educations. During the war women did a number of things to help the cause. Many took care of family farms while their husbands and sons were off fighting. Others participated in the boycotts and enforced them by harassing people they saw violating them. Still others supported boycott efforts by making goods that Americans would otherwise have bought from the British. Some became "camp followers" and did the cooking, sewing, nursing, and cleaning for the soldiers. Others became spies, and some even pretended to be men and fought on the battlefield.

After the war some women called for a degree of change in their lives, but very few wanted to completely transform their existence. A good example is Abigail Adams. While her husband John was serving in the Continental Congress, she wrote to him to ask him to "remember the ladies" when developing "the new code of laws" he and the other leaders were developing. She only wanted the new lawmakers to "be more generous and favorable" to the ladies than their ancestors had been. "Do not put such unlimited power in the hands of the husbands," she implored, asking him to "Remember, all men would be tyrants if they could." What she wanted was for men to give up "the harsh tide of master for the more tender and endearing one of friend" and regard their women "as being placed by Providence under your protection, and in imitation of the Supreme Being make use of that power only for our happiness." This was no call for equality. Rather it was a request for protection so that women could stay safely within what was traditionally seen as their feminine sphere. Even this mild request was ridiculed by the leaders of the time. Abigail's husband John, for example was determined to maintain the status quo. "Depend upon it," he replied, "we know better than to repeal our Masculine systems." Thomas Jefferson agreed, insisting that women should not bother with politics.

After the war the idea did begin to spread that women should be educated due to a new emphasis on the idea of the "Republican Citizen." Simply put, in a Republic citizens have to have special character traits. Because they can vote, they have to be educated so that they may take this privilege seriously. They also have to learn the traits associated with civic virtue, the republican requirement we discussed earlier. Naturally, children's first teachers are their mothers, so more and more people began to argue that mothers had to be well educated in order to teach their sons the basic traits of republican citizenship. This concept is called "*Republican Motherhood*." Of course, this education was much more rudimentary than that offered to men, and it was geared toward making women better wives and mothers, not intellectually independent. Indeed, women who were seen as too intellectual were often referred to as "women of masculine minds."

Some women, most notably *Judith Sargent Murray*, did dare to challenge the prevailing notions about gender roles. Murray wrote a series of essays collectively called *The Gleaner*. This work supported female education on the grounds that women should be able to support themselves if their husbands died or if they never found a husband. Of course, this notion of women not needing male support was quite radical for the time. In her essay "On the Equality of Sexes," Murray argued that women had talents beyond the domestic realm and were capable of excelling in other areas of life, but few would have supported this assertion. Most women themselves would have argued that their proper place was in the home. Thus, for the most part, women did not reap any large benefits for the revolutionary zeal for egalitarianism. In general, when they married women continued to give up control of their property, and women gained no political rights from national independence.

Like African Americans and women, Native Americans also played a number of roles in the revolution and saw a number of changes in their lives afterwards. Many, especially the Mohawks, made the fatal error of seeing the British as their best hope for fair treatment and siding with the British against the colonists. Those who made this choice faced heartbreaking disappoint at the end of the war when they learned that the British surrender included the surrender of Native American lands to the revolutionaries. Others, such as the Oneidas, sided with the colonists, and many others remained neutral. During the war, the Continental Congress promised its allies protection and fair treatment after the war, but once the fighting ended and their assistance was no longer needed the U.S. leaders forgot their promises.

Ultimately what happened was that after the war Native Americans continued to lose territory and their situation grew increasingly worse. One important result was the disintegration of the Iroquois League, one of the few forces that had helped keep the Native Americans organized in their fight against white encroachment. After the revolution the Iroquois were forced to surrender land in Pennsylvania and New York to the U.S., and the Cherokees handed over their claims in the Carolinas and present day Tennessee and Kentucky. The Ohio groups also lost most of their lands. The Creeks did try to resist efforts Georgia made to take their land, even going so far as to enter war with Georgia in 1786 with the help of the Spanish from Florida. They ultimately lost their land but at least managed to wrestle some trade concessions with the U.S. government.

Conclusion

When it came time to create a new nation, the former colonial leaders faced a dilemma. Their revolution had focused on ideas of liberty and universal equality, but experiences under the Articles of Confederation made the leaders of the new nation question just how much liberty and equality they wanted for the new country. Growing increasingly suspicious of the lower orders and of too much democracy in the hands of "the people," especially after the Haitian Revolution and Shays' Rebellion, many of these leaders began to rethink the system they had created. What resulted could be called a counterrevolution that ushered in a new level of elitist rule through the Constitution. The issues that arose between debtors and creditors and rural and urban interests would continue to plague the new nation under the Constitution throughout the period known as the Federalist Era.

Suggested Readings

Douglas Bradburn, *The Citizenship Revolution: Politics and the Creation of the American Union, 1774–1804* (2009).

Linda K. Kerber, *Women of the Republic: Intellect and Ideology in Revolutionary American* (1980).

Gary Nash, *The Forgotten Fifth: African Americans in the Age of Revolution* (2006).

Cassandra Pybus, *Epic Journeys of Freedom: Runaway Slaves of the American Revolution and Their Global Quest for Liberty* (2006).

Charles Royster, *A Revolutionary People at War: The Continental Army and American Character, 1775–1783* (1979)

Alan Taylor, *The Divided Ground: Indians, Settlers, and the Norhtern Borderland of the American Revolution* (2006).

David Waldstreicher, *In the Midst of Perpetual Fetes: The Making of American Nationalism, 1776–1820* (1997).

Gordon S. Wood, *The Creation of the American Republic, 1776–1787* (1969).

Chapter 7

THE EARLY REPUBLIC AND THE FEDERALIST ERA, 1789–1800

Almost by acclamation George Washington became the nation's first president. Washington and his closest advisors (soon to be called Federalists) believed that the delicate balance between power and liberty had almost tipped toward anarchy during the "Critical Period" of the Confederation years. As expressed in the previous chapter, the purpose of the writing of the Constitution was redress this "imbalance" and restore power to the Revolutionary elite, many of whom had retreated from public service in the aftermath of the War for Independence believing that if they had taken power at that moment, they risked the horrors of counterrevolution. The Founding Fathers wisely did not and thus by 1787 when the people had come to "their senses," realizing that they did not possess the republican requisite of public virtue, without which they could not govern a new nation effectively, the elite seized the opportunity to regain control of the republic, and in the process, counter the democratic excesses of the Confederation period. The elite came into national office determined to make the national government powerful enough to command respect abroad and to impose order and stability at home. For the most part they succeeded but in the process they engendered an equally resolute opposition who wanted to give back greater liberty and power to the common folk, via a more limited government. These self-styled Democratic Republicans (led almost from the beginning by Thomas Jefferson) were as devoted to the revolutionary ideals of limited government and the yeoman republic as the Federalists were tied to their agenda of an orderly commercial republic with a powerful national state. The rivalry and acrimony that emerged between the nation's first two political parties reflected in many ways the revolutionary conflict between liberty and power.

However, this time the struggle was purely domestic and within a backdrop of international intrigue and war between France (which began its own march toward republican revolution in 1789) and Britain. Only when this Age of Democratic Revolution ended in 1815 with Napoleon Bonaparte defeated could the Americans survey the kind of society and government that their revolution had brought forth.

Establishing the National Government

George Washington left his plantation estate, Mount Vernon, for the temporary capital of New York City in April 1789. In every city, town, or hamlet he passed throngs of people turned out to cheer and fete their conquering hero. Militia companies and local dignitaries escorted him from place to place, church bells marked his progress, and lines of girls in white dresses waved demurely as he passed. At Newark Bay he boarded a flower-bedecked barge, and surrounded by scores of boats, crossed to New York City. There the crowds were even larger and more energized and jubilant, as he made his way to the president's house. He arrived on April 23 and was inaugurated first president of the United States of America seven days later.

The "Republican Court" of George Washington

No sooner was he inaugurated than Washington found himself embroiled in controversy—what title should be bestowed on the office. Vice President John Adams wanted a title of honor for the president, one that would reflect the power of the new executive. The Senate rejected "His Excellency," for it reminded them of their colonial past when that was the term used to address royal governors and other British officials. After several proposals, ranging from "His Highness," to "His Mightiness," to "His Majesty," which the Senate debated for a full month, it became clear that none of titles would sit well with the more democratic House of Representatives, which in the end declared that it preferred the austere dignity of "Mr. President." Thomas Jefferson, not yet a member of the government, pronounced the whole affair "the most superlatively ridiculous thing I ever heard."

Although dismissing the whole debate title as "ridiculous," Jefferson would learn that much was at stake over what the president should be called. The Constitution provided a blueprint for the republic, but it would be George Washington who would be responsible for translating that vision into a working state. Washington knew his every action, behavior, and decision would be precedent-setting in numerous capacities. It mattered very much what citizens called their president, for that was part of the huge constellation of laws, customs, and forms of etiquette and protocol, that would give the new government either a republican or a more regal tone. Many of those close to Washington wanted to make the office as exalted as possible; to remove presidential power and prestige from the plebian localism and democratic excesses they believed had nearly killed the republic during the 1780s. Washington's stately inaugural tour, the high salaries paid to executive appointees, the endless round of formal galas and presidential dinners, the appearance of Washington's profile on some of the nation's coins—all were meant to promote the power and grandeur of the new government, especially its head of state. When Jefferson became Secretary of State and it was

incumbent upon him to attend official social functions, he chafed at all the pomp and circumstance and aristocratic pretensions that seemed to surround Washington. Jefferson felt isolated at such events "unless there chanced to be some democrat from the legislative Houses." It was a revealing episode in the arguments over how issues of power and liberty would be addressed in the new republic.

President Washington and his Cabinet

Washington's most immediate task was to divide the federal government according to various functions. Even though the Constitution does not explicitly state that there will be a cabinet, it does refer to executive branch departments. Based on his interpretation of the document, Washington initially divided the executive branch into three departments: State, Treasury, and War. A short time later two more departments were added, Justice and Postmaster General. Washington gave each department specific duties and appointed a cabinet secretary to head each one. For the positions Washington chose individuals he knew and trusted personally for their experience and expertise; they were not his close friends; that kind of nepotism or "spoils" would not occur until the Jacksonian era. Washington wanted the best and brightest among the elite to serve in his cabinet, and thus he chose as Secretary of State, fellow Virginian Thomas Jefferson and another Virginian Edmund Randolph as Attorney General. For Secretary of War, Washington bestowed that honor upon his old friend and fellow comrade-in-arms during the War for Independence, General Henry Knox. And finally, for the most important cabinet position, that of Secretary of the Treasury, he chose his brilliant aide-de-camp, Alexander Hamilton, who, as will be seen shortly, quickly emerged as the most powerful man not only in the Washington administration but perhaps in the country as well. As is customary today, all executive appointees at the cabinet level had to be confirmed by the Senate, which all were. Initially, Washington did not meet with his department heads as a group but gradually moved toward establishing the precedent that the president meet on a regular basis, if not every day, with his entire cabinet to discuss and formulate administration policy.

How did Washington view his responsibilities as president?dramatically different than modern presidents. Indeed, if we were to assess Washington's presidency by modern criterion, he would not be considered our second greatest president behind Abraham Lincoln. Washington believed it was not his job to govern the country on a daily basis; that was Congress' responsibility because they represented the people, and if the United States was a democratic republic then that branch closest to the citizenry should have the charge of governance, not the executive branch. Washington believed his most important role relative to governance was to administer and to uphold all laws passed by Congress, for in his frame of reference if a bill passed both houses of Congress, the people had spoken and were in favor of such a statute. In that context, Washington also believed that he could not negate the people's will by vetoing legislation passed by Congress. In effect Washington believed that his most important role as president was to bring honor, prestige, integrity, and power to the national government and he was confident that he could deliver such qualities through the executive branch because he himself possessed such attributes.

Although willing to relinquish power when it came to domestic policy, Washington

believed the president should be directly responsible for foreign policy and diplomacy. Even though that was to be the main focus of the State Department and its secretary, Washington nonetheless asserted presidential authority over foreign affairs (which at this time also included the country's relations with Native Americans), and as will be seen in this chapter, became his own Secretary of State, much to Jefferson's chagrin. Finally, Washington served two terms as president (even though he had grave reservation about serving a second term), thus establishing the precedent and eventual law that the president can only be elected to two four-year terms. Even though he was a "hands-off" president, especially when it came to domestic affairs, Washington during his tenure nonetheless laid the foundation for presidential conduct and expectation that would be adhered to by his generational successors. Not until the presidencies of John Quincy Adams and Andrew Jackson, both of whom were members of the post-Revolutionary generation, did executive leadership challenge the precedents for presidential behavior first established by George Washington.

The First Congress

"Father of the Constitution," James Madison of Virginia, came to dominate the nation's First Congress. Under his auspices Congress strengthened the new national government in a variety of capacities. First the gathering passed a tariff on imports, which would be the government's chief revenue source along with the sales of western lands. Congress then turned its attention to the amendments to the Constitution that had been demanded by the state ratifying conventions, even in those states that had ratified the document without any preconditions. They now all clamored for such addendums.

Madison initially proposed 19 constitutional amendments to the House of Representatives, however only 10 survived congressional scrutiny and given to the states to be ratified as the Bill of Rights. In some form or another, all ten amendments reflected the fears of a generation that had struggled both ideologically and ultimately physically with the idea of centralized power. The First Amendment guaranteed the freedoms of speech, press, and religion against governmental interference; these were to be liberties protected by the government as "inalienable rights" for all citizens. The Second and Third Amendments, prompted by the fears of a standing army, sanctioned the continuation of a militia of armed citizens, the republican ideal of a constabulary of virtuous citizen-soldiers, to maintain domestic peace and order as well as to defend the country if need be from foreign threats. The amendments also stated the specific conditions under which soldiers could be quartered in private homes. The Fourth through Eighth Amendments protected and defined a citizen's right in court when under arrest—rights whose violation had been central to the Rebellion's list of grievances. The Ninth Amendment stated that the enumeration of specific rights in the first eight amendments did not imply a denial of other rights; the Tenth stated that all powers not specifically relegated to the national government by the Constitution were reserved exclusively for the states and their citizenry to determine.

Madison, a devoted nationalist, had performed skillfully, shrewdly and craftily, assuaging his more states' rights colleagues' fears that the Constitution created an overpowering national government, which Madison assured his associates that the Bill of Rights would mitigate any and all potential for the central government to descend into tyranny. By brilliantly channeling their trepidations into the relatively innocuous area of civil liberties, Madison soothed their mistrust while preserving a strong national government. In short, Madison constructed the Bill of Rights to guarantee those personal liberties that the majority of American citizens believed the Revolution was fought for and that most directly affected their daily lives, while not weakening in any capacity the integrity and strength of the national government.

After creating the executive departments discussed above, Congress then created the federal courts that were demanded but not specified in the Constitution. The 1789 Judiciary Act established a Supreme Court with six members along with 13 district courts and 3 circuit courts of appeals. The act made it possible for certain cases to be appealed from state courts to federal circuit courts, which would be presided over by traveling Supreme Court justices, thus dramatizing federal power. As James Madison and his more nationalist congressional compatriots of the First Congress surveyed their handiwork, they could congratulate themselves on having augmented national authority in a variety of important capacities.

Alexander Hamilton and Hamiltonianism

Without question Alexander Hamilton was one of the most brilliant of the Founding Fathers, whom Washington entrusted with the herculean task of creating the new nation's economic and financial foundations. Hamilton had served as the General's aide-de-camp during the War for Independence, and in that capacity he and Washington became very close friends and confidants; indeed a filial relationship developed between the two men, which by war's end, saw Hamilton emerge as one of Washington's most favored officers. Thus few were surprised when the president named Alexander Hamilton as his Secretary of the Treasury. Since Washington made it clear to his cabinet that he would be in charge of the nation's foreign policy initiatives, thus relegating Thomas Jefferson as Secretary of State to minor cabinet status, such a scenario allowed for Hamilton to become as Treasury Secretary, the most powerful man in the Washington administration, if not the country. Indeed, more than any other cabinet member, and perhaps even more than Washington himself (he later referred to Washington's presidency as "my administration"), Hamilton directed the making of a national government. Because the president gave Hamilton carte blanche to get the country's economy stable and functioning, Hamilton used such license to create the economic system he believed best served the national interest while simultaneously increasing the power of the national government. To Hamilton, the relationship between the economy and the national government were inextricable and symbiotic and had to be if the great democratic republican experiment called the United States was to not only succeed but someday become the most powerful and emulated nation in the world. Hamilton believed that such was America's destiny and he was determined to put the country on the path toward greatness and power the moment he assumed his cabinet position.

Of all the revolutionary elite, perhaps no individual was more fanatically devoted to the government's success and the augmentation of the government's power than Hamilton. The New Yorker (and Columbia University graduate) greatly admired the British system of centralized government and finance and was a supremely arrogant and ambitious man.

However, his yearning was not purely personal; for Hamilton as well as for many other Founding Fathers, their fulfillment was tied to the nation's success; so if the Republic failed then they had faltered as well. It was if men like Hamilton saw the United States as organic extensions of their selves out of which emerged an often rabid, single-minded nationalism. Indeed, for many of the Founding Fathers, including Hamilton, that became their larger objective: to use the central government as an agency to inculcate fellow citizens with a sense of nationalism; to obviate the localism and parochial thinking they believed endemic at the time among the majority of Americans. Finally, and much to Hamilton's subsequent undoing, he was a non-pareil elitist; Hamilton simply disdained the common people, believing them wholly unfit to not only to participate in government but to have any input whatsoever in determining national policy. He dismissed the people as plebian rabble, certain that if they ever gained political power the United States would become a "mobocracy." The people were very aware of Hamilton's contempt for them, and despite Washington's unequivocal support for his secretary and his agenda, Hamilton became one of his generation's most reviled men in American popular politics.

A successful lawyer by training and profession, Hamilton read voraciously on a variety of topics, including Adam Smith's seminal work, *The Wealth of Nations,* as well as the works of the French physiocrats and the other political economists of the Scottish Enlightenment. Hamilton discerned from his reading that at the moment what was best for the country's nascent economy was a form of "mixed capitalism;" that is it was imperative to use the powers of the national government to help bring about a more balanced economy among trade, manufacturing, and farming. What worried Hamilton was that when he looked out at the nation's economic landscape, he saw a country in which 90 percent of its citizens earned their livelihoods with their hands in the dirt; they were farmers. Hamilton believed that as long as the United States remained such an overwhelmingly agrarian economy it would have to import from other nations, most notably Great Britain, all its other commodities, especially manufactured goods. In Hamilton's mind, the United States would in effect still be a colonial economy, dependent on a "mother country" for essential products and thus vulnerable to foreign market caprice and exigencies. That is not to say Hamilton wanted to tip the economic scales in the completely opposite direction; all industry and trade while curtailing agriculture. Hamilton knew that first and foremost a nation must have the ability to feed itself and if it could not and had to import food, that would be worse than having to depend on foreign nations for manufactured goods. He simply believed that no nation was truly politically independent until it had become economically self-sufficient and that goal became the overarching purpose of his economic agenda and vision for the United States. As will be seen shortly, his every program was designed with that larger objective in mind.

Hamiltonian Economics: The National Debt

In 1789 Congress asked Treasury Secretary Hamilton to report on the public debt. The debt fell into three categories, Hamilton responded. The first was that owed to foreign creditors, in the amount of $11 million dollars, with the lion's share of that money going to France but the United States also owed money to Spain and the Netherlands. The domestic debt was over double that of the foreign—$24 million—and this was money owed by the national and state governments to American citizens, who had supplied food, arms, and other resources to the Continental Army and to the independence cause in general. Congress agreed that the foreign debt was to be paid in full on a priority basis, for United States honor and credibility were at stake. Moreover, if countries that had loaned the United States money during crisis times would they not be even more inclined to make loans during times of peace and stability, especially if they had been paid in full—that is face value plus interest? In effect, the United States, by paying its foreign obligations was establishing itself as a good "credit risk" for the future. Thus with Congressional approval, Hamilton paid foreign creditors, liquidating the nation's foreign debt and positioning the United States for future loans. Interestingly a bit of controversy ensued because Hamilton paid foreign creditors in dollars; not in their respective currency—livre, guilders, or pesetas. At first the Dutch, French, and Spanish, were outraged, claiming that the dollar was a worthless currency. Hamilton agreed, stating that yes indeed it was in Europe, but in the United States, dollars were as "good as gold" where they would be redeemable at full face value. Here we see just a glimpse of Hamiltonian perspicacity, perhaps even a bit of guile. By paying them in dollars, foreign creditors had no choice but to spend their currency in the United States if they hoped for any return on their money. Such investment and spending would help stimulate American economic expansion, which from the beginning was Hamilton's principal objective in paying off the foreign debt.

Paying the domestic debt, however, raised troublesome questions. It was money owed to all those citizens—merchants, farmers, and soldiers—who had received government compensation during the war years for services rendered or for their contributions to the war effort. They were paid with paper script or bonds and we told at the time to keep all such "money" for they would someday be able to redeem their certificates at face value plus interest. However, during the Confederation period, hundreds of speculators went about the country and bought up at a fraction of their face value as many of the notes as they possibly could. It was relatively easy for these men to hoodwink the original holders out of their bonds, for many believed that they would never be compensated by the government, especially one as weak and chronically short of funds as the Confederation Congress. When news began circulating throughout the country that the Constitution would create a government likely to pay its debts, speculators and their agents coveted the bonds even more. By 1790, the overwhelming majority of the bonds hand wound up in the hands of Northeastern speculators, who had bought the notes for as little as 10 to 30 percent of their original value. If the "rumor" that the new government was ready to make good its obligations of full payment plus interest to all holders, the speculators stood to make enormous windfall profits.

Equally contentious were the war debts incurred by the individual states. Hamilton and his nationalist supporters wanted the central government to assume all state debts, combining them with the foreign debt as well as with the money owed to individual citizens holding war bonds, to create a large public debt. Such consolidation would fuse individual interests with those of national government, creating in the process a citizenry whose loyalty was first and foremost to the government and the nation, for they would see both as inextricable

entities. A public debt would also create the need for taxation to reduce the deficit while simultaneously expanding the government's civil service, for people would be needed to service the debt and collect the tax revenues. In short, the nationalists hoped to use the creation of a public debt as means to expand the power and presence of the national government deeper into Americans' daily lives. Similar to the issue with the government bonds, the majority of state certificates had also been purchased by speculators, who now stood to make twice as much, for they held both state and national paper. Especially upset by the "assumption" idea were local officials whose respective states had paid off most of their notes in the 1780s. Such was the case for all the Southern states except South Carolina. However, none of the Northern states had paid their obligations and thus if the federal government assumed the state debts and paid them off at face value, money would flow out of the southern, middle, and western states into the Northeast, whose citizens would hold fully four-fifths of the national debt.

The above scenario was exactly what Hamilton hoped would be the result of his funding and assumption proposal. He knew that the majority of the bonds had been bought up by mainly Northeastern speculators and he intended for his bill to make them very wealthy men but whose wealth and future self-interest would be tied directly to the interests of the national government. What Hamilton envisioned with his initiatives was to use the government as an agency through which would be created a capitalist/entrepreneurial class that would invest its new-found money to develop and grow the nation's manufacturing and commercial sectors. Hamilton believed that the only way such enterprises could ever be undertaken was if they had the assistance and the initial stimulation from the federal government who would provide the essential start-up capital. In Hamilton's view, such policies were imperative if the country was to become economically self-sufficient; viable manufacturing and commercial sectors had to be initiated and the only way for such enterprises to get started was with government assistance. If not, the nation's economy would languish indefinitely in an agrarian malaise and the United States would remain a weak, vulnerable country, dependent on foreigners for their economic survival. Such a scenario was an anathema to a super-nationalist such as Hamilton.

In his Report on Public Credit, Hamilton agreed that the foreign debt should be paid promptly and in full, but he insisted that the domestic debt be a permanent, tax-supported fixture of government. Under his plan, the government would issue securities to creditors and would pay them an annual interest rate of 4 percent. Hamilton's funding and assumption plans announced to the international community and to actual and potential government creditors that the United States would pay its bills. Politically, Hamilton's agenda was to create through his programs, a new financial elite, dependent on and thus loyal to the federal government. This coterie of wealthy financiers would not only become the capitalist vanguard of industrial entrepreneurs but would also become in the process the new ruling class as well; the privileged successors to the Founding Fathers who would ensure that power remained securely in the hands of the "best and the brightest," and not in the hands of the people. Indeed, Hamilton's worse nightmare was that after his generation had passed on, the common folk would seize power, and if that happened, the Republic's days were numbered. To prevent such a disaster, Hamilton believed his generation had to put in place programs and policies at the national level now that would ensure the orderly transfer of power from one generation of elite to the next. The national debt, in short, was at the center of Alexander Hamilton's plan for a powerful national state firmly under the auspices of the nation's upper classes.

Hamiltonian Economics: The Bank of the United States and Excise Tax

As part of his overall agenda and vision for the nation's economy, Hamilton believed it essential to establish a national bank, aptly called the Bank of the United States. According to Hamilton, the government would deposit its revenue in the bank and would supervise its operations, but the bank would also be a semi-private institution as well, under the daily charge of a board of directors drawn from the private sector and representing the bank's stockholders or investors. The Bank would print and back the national currency and would regulate other banks, much the same way the Federal Reserve System presently operates. Hamilton also made the bank's stock payable in government securities, thus adding to the value of the securities, giving the bank a powerful interest in the government's fiscal stability while binding the holders of the securities even closer to the national government. In short, Hamilton was again attempting to use the powers of the national government via his office, to create institutions and policies designed to ensure the elite's loyalty to the government, vesting their interests with that of the government's. In this particular case, private individuals would not only have a direct, controlling

A 1794 painting by Baltimore artist and sign painter Frederick Kemmelmayer depicting President Washington as commander in chief of the army dispatched to put down the Whiskey Rebellion

chapter, much to the surprise of the Washington administration, western farmers protested the measure, ultimately rising in a "Whiskey Rebellion," which the president had to threaten the use of force to quell the uprising.

Passed in April 1791, the national bank and the federal excise measures completed the Hamiltonian agenda. Taken separately, the consolidated government debt, the national bank, and the federal excise tax competently solved the government's immediate financial problems. Taken as a whole, however, they appeared to numerous Americans as a carbon-copy of Great Britain's treasury-driven government.

interest in a government institution, but would also be financially rewarded by the government for their participation in helping to secure and stabilize the nation's economy. One did not have to look too closely to see that Hamilton had replicated verbatim the Bank of England. The Bank would also be a source of loans for those individuals interested in starting manufacturing enterprises.

To fund the national debt, Hamilton called for a federal excise tax on wines, coffee, and alcoholic beverages in general, i.e. beer and whiskey. The tax on "spirits" would fall especially hard on frontier whiskey producers, who were mainly farmers who supplemented their incomes by using their excess grain to make whiskey. Hamilton's "whiskey" tax was not only to raise revenue but to establish as well the government's power to tax and to collect it even in the most remote regions of the republic. As will be seen later in this

The Rise of Opposition: The Birth of the First Party System

In 1789 every branch of government was under the auspices of the Constitution's most fervent supporters; the most radical anti-federalists found sanctuaries in the state governments or retired from politics altogether. Nearly everyone in the national government was committed to making the new government work. In particular, Hamilton and James Madison in the House of Representatives were certain they would be able to continue the personal friendship and amicable collaboration they enjoyed during the Constitutional Convention and during the ratification process. However, much to Hamilton's dismay, his old friend quickly turned into a most intransigent adversary, the result of his opposition to Hamilton's fiscal and economic policies. Joining Madison crusade in the House to defeat the Hamiltonian agenda was Thomas Jefferson, who was certain that Hamilton's programs were designed to dismantle the Revolution. By 1792 and the end of Washington's first term, the consensus of 1789 had completely unraveled, largely because of Hamilton's programs and the ideological debate they engendered, which quickly became bitter, divisive, and acrimonious. More than 25 years later, Jefferson still insisted that the battles of the 1790s had been "contests of principle between the advocates of republicanism and those of kingly government." In short, to the day he died, Jefferson believed that his war with Hamilton during the 1790s represented the quintessential conflict between the forces of reaction and elitism and democratic republicanism.

Hamilton challenged his opponents, declaring that his national debt proposal was a solution to specific problems of government finance and did not reflect in any way an attempt to establish a British-style state. In the House, Madison and his supporters (the majority of whom were fellow Southerners) asserted that the funding and assumption bill was unfair; that it concentrated wealth not only in the North, (to the South's disadvantage) from where the majority of speculators had originated, but also in hands of an elite, privileged few at the expense of the majority of citizens. These were men, Madison railed who benefited from government insiders to reap fortunes from notes bought at rock-bottom prices from soldiers, widows, and orphans— the common folk whom Hamilton mistrusted and despised. Madison branded Hamilton's plan "public plunder." Hamilton retorted that, regardless of who held the original bonds, when they sold them to speculators their actions reflected someone possessing little faith in the government to make good its obligations. Such people should not be rewarded for such fecklessness and infidelity.

Madison, Jefferson, and the other members of the opposition knew that Hamilton's argument not only had merit but it also had the support of George Washington, whom they knew would never challenge Hamilton on such policies because the president both favored his treasury secretary and believed in his agenda. Thus the opposition concluded that since they did not have the president's support or a majority in Congress, that perhaps it would be best to compromise with Hamilton. In exchange for accepting his proposals on the debt, they secured his endorsement for locating the nation's permanent capital at a site on the Potomac River. The compromise reflected the essence of American revolutionary republicanism. Hamilton intended to tie northeastern commercial interests to the federal government. If New York City or Philadelphia became the permanent capital, political and economic power would be concentrated there as it was in Paris and London—court cities in which power, wealth, and every kind of privilege were in league against a plundered and degraded countryside. Benjamin Rush, a Philadelphian but a hardcore republican, condemned the "government which has begun so soon to ape the corruption of the British court, conveyed to it through the impure channel of the City of New York." Madison and other agrarians considered Philadelphia and Boston to be just as bad, and supported Hamilton's funding and assumption bill only on condition that the capital be moved further south; in effect to pastoral northern Virginia. The compromise would distance the commercial power of cities from the federal government and would put an

Second Street Philadelphia. As the view of this busy street scene shows, social, commercial, political, and religious—"public" and "private"—life commingled on the streets of the early republic's cities.

end to the "republican court" that had formed around Washington. This radically republican maneuver ensured that the capital of the United States would be, except for purposes of government, a place of no importance.

A Clash of Titans: Jefferson versus Hamilton

Personalities rather than ideology and partisanship dominated American politics and the first two party systems during most of the antebellum era. Indeed, two of the most passionate and divisive of such personal feuds in United States political history occurred during this time. The first was the intense rivalry between Alexander Hamilton and Thomas Jefferson, which reached at times a bitterness and viciousness rarely ever

again seen in American politics. The other, very similar clash took place in the 1820 and 1830s between Henry Clay and Andrew Jackson, which will be discussed in a later chapter. The two conflicts reflected in many ways the 1960s adage that the "political is personal and the personal is political." The cliché perfectly defines the clash between Hamilton and Jefferson, whose antagonisms dictated and determined much of the history of the Republic's first decade.

It was during the Bank bill controversy that the ideological as well as personal antipathy between the two men first began. Jefferson opposed the bill on the basis of its constitutionality; that is he did not believe the federal government (Congress) had the right charter a bank and that if Congress created such an institution it would revive the popular fears of centralized despotism that had nearly defeated the Constitution's ratification. Jefferson, unlike Madison's earlier attacks on funding and assumption, in which he argued about the "unfairness" of such a measure, cleverly used a more sophisticated legal argument, that of the bill being unconstitutional, to stop the Hamiltonian legislative juggernaut. Interestingly, Hamilton agreed with Jefferson that the Constitution does not *explicitly* state that Congress or the government had the right to "incorporate" itself; that is to go into the banking business. However, Hamilton asked Jefferson to find in the document where it stated that the government *did not* have such power or authority *expressly stated*. Jefferson obviously could not but Hamilton asserted that the bank's creation—the expansion of federal power—reflected the application of the clause in the Constitution empowering Congress "to make all laws which shall be necessary and proper" to the performance of its duties. In other words, Hamilton argued that the creation of a national bank was "necessary and proper" for the country's present and future economic stability and security. President Washington and a majority in Congress ultimately sided with Hamilton.

The Hamilton-Jefferson contest over the bank reflected the larger issue of constitutional interpretation; that is should the document be interpreted verbatim or literally leaving no room for "elasticity" as domestic or foreign exigencies may demand? Advocates of such a view, led by Jefferson, became known as strict constructionists; insisting that the government had no powers beyond those specified in the Constitution. Jefferson expressed fears that Hamilton's policies were transforming the Constitution into a de facto document. Jefferson took exception to all of Hamilton's proposals, arguing not only against the bank but the federal excise tax and the funding and assumption bill as well. He was certain that the tax would arouse public opposition and that funding the debt would reward speculators and penalize ordinary citizens. Even more ominous, Jefferson asserted, Hamilton was using government securities and stock in the Bank of the United States to buy the loyalty not only of merchants and speculators but of members of Congress. Thirty Congressmen owned stock in the bank and many others held government securities or had close ties to men who did. Jefferson charged that his "corrupt squadron" of "paper men" in Congress was, in the classic fashion of evil ministers, enabling Hamilton to control Congress from his non-elective seat in the executive branch. In his every attack on Hamilton's programs, Jefferson portrayed his

rival as a pernicious Anglophile, working assiduously and clandestinely to bring about the end of republicanism and transform the United States into another European-style monarchy and aristocracy. Jefferson insisted that, "The ultimate objective of all this is to prepare the way for a change, from the present republican form of government to that of a monarchy, of which the English constitution was the model."

That Hamilton was an admirer of the British system there was little doubt; but to label him an outright Anglophile and to accuse him of possessing such pretensions and sentiments was purely partisan and false. Hamilton's alleged Anglophilia was born of his desire to make the United States a self-sufficient and powerful nation. Indeed, that passion was the driving force behind all of his programs and ideas. In the Hamiltonian frame of reference Great Britain was the undisputed power in the world, with a booming, industrializing economy second to none. Hamilton believed that it was in the United States' best interest to cultivate strong economic ties with England, for such a relationship would be of great benefit to the United States. Moreover, in Hamilton's view, if the United States hoped to someday become a great and powerful country, then it could learn much from the British system on how to achieve such status. In short, Hamilton believed the United States needed to maintain strong commercial ties with the former mother country in order to better develop its own economy and eventual economic and political independence.

Hamilton and his supporters, who by 1792 began to refer to themselves as Federalists, insisted that the centralization of power and a strong executive were necessary to the republic's survival. They pointed to the provincialism, selfishness, and disorder that plagued the nation during the 1780s, when revolutionary public virtue degenerated into democratic excesses and "mobocracy." They feared all such wantonness and dissipation would return if the Jeffersonians had their way and the Revolution would be destroyed. The argument drew its urgency from the understanding of both Hamilton and Jefferson that the United States was a small revolutionary republic in a word governed by kings and aristocrats, and that republics had a long history of failure; they all knew that it was still very possible for Americans to lose their revolution. Until late 1792 the Hamilton-Jefferson feud was largely confined to members of the government, including Congress. Hamilton and his supporters tried to mobilize the commercial elite on the government's side, while Madison and Jefferson struggled to hold off the perceived monarchial plot until the citizens could be aroused to defend their liberties; that is they were waiting for the perfect political time to take the issues directly to the people to rally them to their crusade against Hamilton's imperious policies. As both sides began mobilizing popular support, events in Europe came to dominate the politics of the American republican experiment, to place that venture in even greater jeopardy, and to increase the violence in American politics to the point that the republic almost failed.

The Republic in a World at War, 1793–1800

In late 1792 French Revolutionaries, led by the Parisian Jacobin clubs, rejected the idea of a constitutional monarchy and proclaimed the French Republic. To show the world that the ancien regime was dead in France, and that

there would be no going back, the radical Jacobins beheaded Louis XVI in January 1793, and executed by guillotine his queen, Marie Antoinette and as many members of the royal household as they could round up. The monarchy's death marked the beginning of the Reign of Terror, as radical republicans, in the name of the revolution, and the suppression of counter-revolution, would execute over the course of the next two years over 50,000 Frenchmen from all classes, not just the aristocracy. As the other European powers watched with horror the events in France, they became concerned that if not checked, French revolutionary passion and ideas would soon infect their countries. Thus in 1792, Austria and Prussia declared war on France, and a year later France declared war on conservative Britain, thus launching a war between French republicanism and British-led reaction that, with periodic moments of peace, engulfed the Atlantic world until France's defeat in 1815.

Americans and the French Revolution

That the French Revolution would reverberate across the Atlantic and affect the United States was a given. Coming back to haunt the new nation were the treaties signed by Ben Franklin with the French monarchy in 1778, pledging U.S. support if France should go to war. At the time Franklin had warned Congress of such a possible repercussion, but that body turned a deaf ear, for the country was desperate for the French alliance and thus was willing to mortgage the Republic's future security. However, the Washington administration, which by the beginning of the president's second term was becoming less apolitical and increasingly more Federalist, claimed the 1778 treaties were no longer binding; they became null and void the moment the king's executioner held up Louis' head for the crowed to cheer. In other words, the treaties were made with a government that no longer existed. This would become the basis of Washington's neutrality declaration.

When the revolution began in 1789 the overwhelming majority of Americans supported the cause, under the delusion that they not only had inspired the French to overthrow monarchial and aristocratic tyranny, but that the French would naturally adopt the same evolutionary processes toward republicanism prescribed by the Americans. For the first three years it appeared that was exactly what was happening in France. However, with the king's execution and the advent of the Reign of Terror, increasing numbers of Americans began to disassociate themselves from such a bloodbath, for even in its most violent days, the American Revolution never approximated the terror and blood-letting the French were inflicting on each other. The execution of thousands of citizens from all classes horrified Americans and when the French threatened the sovereignty of nations by declaring a war of all peoples against all monarchies, such a declaration proved to be the final straw for many American supporters. Indeed, the French people by 1795 had become fanatical revolutionaries, who saw their movement as even more righteous and momentous than what had occurred in America in 1776. To defend their country and revolution from foreign invaders they formed a true citizens army (of both men and women), ultimately comprised of hundreds of thousands of French citizens. The French, through their army saw themselves as the vanguard of revolutionary change for all of Europe and thus after repelling the Austro-Prussian forces, decided it was their duty to mankind to liberate all the rest of the oppressed European peoples in the name of the French Revolution. The French army, filled with a *rage militaire* and a *esprit d'corps* unprecedented in European military history, became an undefeatable juggernaut of revolutionary passion and commitment that rampaged its way across the European continent for the next several years, conquering other nations in the name of liberation. The argument between Jeffersonian republicanism and Hamiltonian centralization was no longer a squabble within the United States government. National politics was now caught up and subsumed within the struggle over international republicanism.

No sooner did all-out war begin in Europe, than President Washington declared American neutrality. The announcement outraged the French, who felt betrayed by the Americans, who in the French mind owed France their existence, for without French help in 1778 there might not have been a United States of America. Moreover, the French could not understand why a revolutionary people such as the Americans professed to be, would not come to their aid without hesitation, for the French were fighting for the same righteous and glorious purpose the Americans had fought for in 1776. Unfortunately for the French, by 1795, few Americans still believed the two events were even remotely similar.

Washington and most of his advisers realized that the United States was in no condition to fight a war. They also wanted to maintain peaceful relations with Great Britain. Ninety percent of American imports came from England, and 90 percent of federal revenue came from customs duties on those imports. In short the nation's economy as well as the government's stability and financial health depended on good relations with Great Britain. Moreover, Hamilton and his Federalist colleagues genuinely sympathized with the British in the war with France and believed that the conflict offered a golden opportunity for the United States to not only improve but strengthen ties with Great Britain, which they were convinced would prove to be of great economic benefit for the republic. The Federalists regarded the United States as a "perfected" England and viewed Britain as the defender of hierarchical society and ordered liberty against French homicidal anarchy.

Jefferson and his followers saw the French Revolution differently. They applauded the French for carrying on the spirit of the American Revolution as well as for being the harbingers of republicanism to Europe. The Jeffersonians condemned the Federalists' monarchial politics and their desire to keep the United States in a neocolonial status relative to Great Britain. The faction led by Madison and Jefferson wanted to abandon the English mercantile system and trade freely with all nations. They did not care if that course of action hurt commercial interests (most of which supported the Federalists) or impaired the government's ability to centralize power in itself. While they agreed that the United States should try to maintain neutrality, the Jeffersonians sympathized as openly with the French as their Federalist counterparts did with the English.

Maintaining Neutrality and Citizen Genet

Declaring neutrality and actually getting other countries to honor that position proved to be a very difficult status for the Washington administration to maintain. President Washington found that out soon after his announcement. As the president quickly discovered, neither belligerent—France nor England—had any intention of respecting American neutrality, for neither could understand how the United States could be detached from this war. The French

position and mentality has already been explained. As far as the English were concerned, the majority of Americans were not a Gallic people; they were Anglo-Saxons and thus they should support their "mother country." Because both sides had such views on American neutrality, as the years progressed, both Britain and France engaged in all manner of intimidation, harassment, even threats of war, to get the United States to abandon its isolationism and become an ally. In the end, as will be seen in the next chapter, the United States, to Europe's surprise, opted for war rather than succumb to continued economic and political extortion.

In April 1793, the French sent Citizen Edmond Genet as minister to the United States. Genet's ruling Girondists were the revolutionary faction that had declared war on all the monarchies; they ordered Genet to enlist American aid with or without the Washington administration's approval. After the president's neutrality proclamation, which Genet blatantly disregarded, the French proceeded to openly recruit American privateers to harass British shipping and enlisted Americans to become part of a filibustering expedition with designs on Spanish New Orleans. Genet then opened France's Caribbean colonies to American shipping, providing American shippers a choice between French free trade and British mercantilism. However, before Genet could do any more to undermine American neutrality, the Girondists fell from power in France in 1793. Learning that he would be guillotined if he returned to France, Genet decided to obtain asylum in the United States, which was granted. He eventually married a daughter of the old anti-Federalist governor of New York, George Clinton, and lived out the rest of his life as an American country gentleman. Although furious with Genet's underhanded activities,

Washington found the British's efforts of insulting and undermining American neutrality to be even more egregious and threatening to American security than those of France.

As soon as the British found out about France's free trade declaration, they immediately began seizing any ship trading with France's West Indian possessions. These Orders in Council resulted in 250 American ships falling into British hands. Even more outrageous, the Royal Navy began stopping and searching United States merchant ships, looking for alleged English deserters or for those English sailors who had "jumped ship" for safer, better-paying work in the American merchant marine. Inevitably, some American seamen were kidnapped or "impressed" into the British navy, a practice the Royal Navy had engaged in for years, especially during time of war when their manpower needs were the greatest; the impressment of foreign sailors was one way to ensure sufficient manpower. Suffice it to say, impressment infuriated the Washington administration, for it was a flagrant and contemptuous violation of American neutrality as well as an assault on American sovereignty. Meanwhile, to add insult to injury, the British, operating from Canada and from their still-garrisoned forts in the Northwest, began promising military aid to the Native Americans north of the Ohio River. Thus, while the French ignored United States neutrality, the English engaged in both overt and covert acts of war.

The Destruction of the Woodland Indians

Although many of the woodland tribes were still intact and still living on their ancestral lands in 1790, they were in serious trouble. The members of the old Iroquois Federation had been dismantled and confined to reservations in New York and Pennsylvania; those who refused to be relocated fled to Canada. The once-powerful Cherokees had been severely punished for having been British allies during the War for Independence and by 1790 had ceded three-fourths of their territory to the United States. Like the Iroquois, by this time they were nearly surrounded by white settlements.

In the Old Northwest, the Shawnee, Miami, and other tribes—with the help of the British who still occupied seven forts within what was formally the United States—continued to trade furs with the British and to attack encroaching white Americans. Skirmishes with frontier Americans however, brought U.S. government reprisals. In the Ohio country, expeditions led by General Josiah Harmar and General Arthur St. Clair failed to defeat the Indians in 1790 and 1791—the second engagement ending in a disastrous and humiliating defeat for the U.S. Army, which saw 630 soldiers killed. In 1794 President Washington sent a third army, under General "Mad Anthony" Wayne, which defeated the Indians at Fallen Timbers near present-day Toledo. The ensuing Treaty of Greenville forced the Native Americans to cede two-thirds of what are now Ohio and southeastern Indiana. It was at this juncture that the British decided to abandon their forts in the Old Northwest. Following the army's victory at Fallen Timbers, white settlers flooded into what remained of Indian lands. In 1796 President Washington, who had reluctantly sent the army on all three occasions because he respected Native Americans and wanted peace with them, not their destruction or removal, threw up his hands and announced that "I believe scarcely any thing, short of a Chinese Wall, or a line of troops, will restrain Land Jobbers and the encroachment of settlers upon the Indian

Major Indian Villages and Indian–United States Battle Sites, 1789–1800. During the first decade of existence, the new federal government struggled to assert control over the trans-Appalachian territories, claimed by Native Americans as their homelands and coveted by United States settlers and land speculators.

Territory." Five years later Governor William Henry Harrison of the Indiana Territory admitted that frontier whites "consider the murdering of the Indians in the highest degree meritorious."

Relegated to smaller territory but still dependent on the European fur trade, Northwest natives now fell into competition with settlers and other Indians for the diminishing supply of game. The Creeks, Choctaws, and other tribes of the Old Southwest faced the same problem: even when they chased whites out of their territory, the Anglo-Americans managed to kill or scare off the deer and other wildlife, thus ruining the old hunting grounds. When the Shawnee sent hunting parties farther west, they discovered that they were not welcomed by their western brethren. The Choctaws also sent hunters across the Mississippi only to find that the Osage and the other tribes of Louisiana and Arkansas considered them to be trespassers and drove them out. The Native Americans of the interior now realized that the days of the fur trade, on which they depended for survival, were numbered.

Faced with shrinking territories, the disappearance of game, and dwindling opportunities to be traditional hunters and warriors, many Indian societies plunged into despair. European epidemic diseases (mostly smallpox, measles, and influenza) ravaged people who were increasingly sedentary and vulnerable. Old internal frictions grew nastier. In the Old Southwest, full-blooded Native Americans came into conflict with "mixed bloods"—who often no longer spoke their native language and who wanted their people to adopt white ways. Murder and clan revenge plagued many tribes and depression and suicide became more common. The use of alcohol, which had long been a scourge on Indian societies, became more prevalent. Indian males spent more time in their villages and less on the hunt, and by most accounts they drank more and grew more violent. Although the Washington administration made peace with the Native Americans of the interior a priority, the president simply could not stop the white onslaught into the Old Northwest and Southwest during the 1790s, marking the beginning of the end

for the majority of the regions' native peoples and their way of life.

Western Troubles

Problems with Native Americans tribes were not the only issues confronting the second Washington administration on the nation's western pale. At the same time, frontier whites, sometimes with the encouragement of English and Spanish officials, grew increasingly angry at a national government that could neither pacify the Indians nor guarantee their free use of the Mississippi River. President Washington learned that 2,000 Kentuckians were armed and ready to attack New Orleans—a move that would have started a war between the United States and Spain. Meanwhile Georgia settlers continued to make forays against the Creeks, which could have easily escalated into a full-fledged Creek-U.S. conflict. However, to the Washington administration the most alarming "western disturbance" had nothing to do with Native Americans but rather with the president's own citizens: the refusal by western grain farmers to pay the excise tax on whiskey, which Washington considered to be a direct challenge to his administration and to federal authority. In western Pennsylvania western mobs tarred and feathered excise officers and burned the property of distillers who paid the tax. In July 1794 near Pittsburg, 500 militiamen marched on the house of General John Neville, one of the most hated of the federal excise collectors. Neville, his family, and a few federal soldiers fought the militiamen, killing two and wounding six before they abandoned the house to be looted and burned. Two weeks later, 6,000 "Whiskey Rebels" met at Braddock's Field near Pittsburg, threatening to attack the town. Faced with serious international and domestic threats to his new government, Washington was not about to let "mobocrats" make a mockery of either his presidency or federal authority or the sanctity of the Constitution, which gave the government the right to tax with the people's consent. Since the excise tax had passed Congress, in Washington's view it was law and his job as president was to enforce the nation's laws; a responsibility the general took very seriously. He was thus determined to end the Whiskey Rebellion with force if necessary. In September 1794, Washington ordered 12,000 federalized militiamen from eastern Pennsylvania, Maryland, Virginia, and New Jersey to quell the Whiskey Rebellion. Washington was so intent on upholding federal authority that he personally led the army out to western Pennsylvania. No doubt when the rebels saw "General Washington" leading the army they quickly laid down their arms and scattered, for they knew Washington would not hesitate to fire upon them if they did not disband. The president promised amnesty to rebels who pledged to support the government and obey its laws and prison terms for those who did not. As the army marched west from Carlisle, they found defiant liberty poles but no armed resistance. Arriving at Pittsburg, the army arrested 20 suspected rebels—none of them leaders—and marched them back to Philadelphia for trial. In the end only two "rebels," both of them feeble-minded, were convicted. President Washington pardoned them and the Whiskey Rebellion was over; federal authority and the office of the president had been vindicated.

Jay's Treaty

Although President Washington had success in dealing with Indians and frontier rebels, when it came to negotiating with the British,

the president found them to be a much more challenging adversary. By 1794 tensions between the United States and Great Britain over the violation of American neutrality, impressments, the reoccupation forts on American soil, and military aid to Native Americans on the warpath, had reached a dangerous level. Washington believed it was time for diplomacy to try to ease these perturbations before they reached the point beyond which they could be ameliorated. Above all, Washington did not want a war with Great Britain; a conflict he knew the country was not at all prepared for and would lose as a result. If defeated, Washington and other American leaders knew such a calamity would not only mark the end of the Republic but the possible reoccupation of North America by Great Britain as well. To avoid such a prospect, in 1794 Washington sent John Jay, chief justice of the Supreme Court, to Great Britain to hopefully negotiate some sort of rapprochement with Great Britain. Armed with the news of Wayne's victory at Fallen Timbers, Jay extracted a promise from the British to remove their troops from the Northwest Territory. However, that was the only concession Jay got from the British; on all the other tension-causing issues, Jay found British officials obdurate and incredibly supercilious, forcing the American to retreat and accept whatever the British meted out at the "negotiating" table. In the end, Jay brought home a "treaty" that made no mention of impressment or other violations of American maritime rights, nor did it refer to the old issue of British payments to Southern slaveholders for slaves carried off during the War for Independence. The treaty did allow small American ships back into the West Indies, but only on terms guaranteed to render a Senate rejection. In short, Jay's Treaty granted British trade a most-favored-nation status, and in exchange, the British agreed to abandon their northwestern forts. Washington knew that given Great Britain's overwhelming military power, this was the best Americans could expect. Indeed, even before Jay left for England, Washington had told his ambassador that he would .be operating from a position of weakness and that British officials would be in a most disrespectful and intractable mood and thus unlikely to consider any of America's issues. If that were the case, then Washington urged Jay not to push the British and if all he could get was a "promise" of no war in the immediate future, then so be it. The president, obliged to choose between an unpopular treaty and an unwinnable war, passed Jay's Treaty on to the Senate, which in June 1795 ratified the document by a bare two-thirds majority.

It was during the debate on Jay's Treaty that the public first became aware of the dissension that had emerged among Washington administration officials over a variety of issues; Jay's Treaty simply became the final straw, especially for the Jeffersonian "Republicans." The seaport cities and much of the Northeast reacted favorably to the treaty, for this section of the country was fast becoming a Federalist stronghold and increasingly dependent on British trade for their economic livelihood. The treaty ruled out war with England and cemented an Anglo-American trade relationship that strengthened both Hamilton's national state and the established commercial interests that supported it. Moreover, there was little enthusiasm for the French Revolution in the Northeast—particularly in New England, with its long history of colonial wars with France. The South, on the other hand, saw Jay's Treaty as a blatant British and Federalist designs to subvert republicanism in both France and the United States. It was becoming clear that the

South was fast becoming a Republican base. The Virginia legislature branded the treaty unconstitutional and Republican congressmen demanded to see all documents relating to Jay's negotiations. Washington responded by telling his fellow Virginians that their request could be legitimate only if the House was planning to initiate impeachment proceedings—thus tying approval of the treaty to the president's enormous prestige. Virginia promptly rescinded its demand.

Washington knew that Jay's Treaty was no treaty at all; that it was an American capitulation to British intimidation. However, it did avert a war, at least for the foreseeable future. To somewhat atone for the Jay Treaty mishap, Washington announced on March 3, 1796 the details of a treaty that Thomas Pinckney had negotiated with Spain. In this agreement, Spain recognized American neutrality and accepted the border between the United States and Spanish Florida on American terms. Most important, Pinckney's Treaty put an end to Spanish claims to territory in the Old Southwest and gave Americans the unrestricted right to navigate the Mississippi River and to transship produce at the Spanish port of New Orleans. Coupled with the victory at Fallen Timbers, the British promise to abandon their posts in the Northwest, and Washington's personal popularity, Pinckney's Treaty helped turn the tide in favor of the unpopular Jay's Treaty. With a diminishing number of hotheads willing to oppose Washington, western representatives joined their Northeastern counterparts and increasing numbers of southerners to ratify Jay's Treaty.

Washington's Farewell

Reluctant to run for a second term, Washington was adamant about not serving a third. He thus set the precedent of a two-term limit that was observed by every president until Franklin Roosevelt. As first president Washington could be proud of his accomplishments. He had presided over the creation of a national government; he had established U.S. control over the trans-Appalachian to the Mississippi River by ending British, Spanish, and Native American military threats and by securing free use of the Mississippi River for western farmers and their right of deposit at New Orleans. As far as the Native Americans were concerned, although forced to go to war against them three times, Washington nonetheless remains one of the few American presidents to have as his official policy not removal or extinction but rather respect for their culture and land and recognition of their rights as a free and independent people; as the legitimate residents of the United States with whom he believed he could live in peace. Unfortunately Washington's noble and sincere attempt at trying to establish peaceful coexistence with Native Americans was constantly challenged and undermined by his fellow citizens' complete disregard for Native American rights, forcing Washington to put down Indian uprisings, which he knew had been provoked by the white onslaught into Indian Territory. Those policies together with quelling the Whiskey Rebellion in western Pennsylvania made it clear that the government could and would assert its dominion over the nation's most distant regions. He had also avoided war with Great Britain—although not without overlooking assaults on American sovereignty on the high seas. Most important Washington gave the office of the president what it needed most: dignity, honor, integrity, prestige, respect, and power. In the end these contributions proved to be his most lasting legacy.

As he was about to leave government he wrote, with substantial help from Hamilton, his farewell address. In his speech, he warned against long-term "entangling alliances," with other countries; the United State, he said, should stay free to operate independently in international affairs—an ideal that many felt had been betrayed by Jay's Treaty. Washington also cautioned against internal political divisions, which by the end of his presidency were becoming less inchoate, vociferous, partisan, and acrimonious. Interestingly, he did not regard his own Federalist supporters as a "party" but rather they were simply "friends" of the government. Although personally ideologically in tune with the Federalists more than the Democratic Republican opposition, Washington nonetheless succeeded in remaining detached from the partisanship unfolding before him. He was not a "political" president or a politician; Washington saw himself and wanted posterity to regard him as a statesman, who had placed the nation's security and the government's success above all other interests. However, he did see the Democratic Republicans (the name by which Jefferson's allies called themselves by 1796), as a self-interested, irresponsible "faction," thus branding them, in the language of classical republicanism, as public enemies. Washington's call for national unity and an end to partisanship was in fact a parting shot at the Democratic Republican "party."

The 1796 Election

Washington's retirement opened the door to the fierce competition for public office that he had feared; in 1796 Americans experienced their first contested presidential election. The Federalists chose Vice-president John Adams of Massachusetts to be their standard-bearer, although Adams did not have Hamilton's endorsement because the former Secretary of the Treasury believed he was neither personally nor ideologically committed to the Federalist vision and agenda for the country. As will be seen, Hamilton was proven correct. The Democratic Republicans nominated Thomas Jefferson. According to the gentlemanly custom of the day, neither candidate campaigned in person; a president directly campaigning for office and fully engaged in the hustings would have to wait for new generation of political leaders to emerge. Jefferson stayed at home in Monticello while Adams retired to his farm outside Boston. However for the candidates' respective friends, relatives, supporters, newspaper editors, and even certain European dignitaries, all were free to engage in whatever partisanship they deemed essential for victory.

Since it was clear that Adams would carry New England and that Jefferson would sweep the South, the election would be decided in Pennsylvania and New York. Some states, most of them in the South, chose presidential electors by direct vote but the majority of states, including the crucial mid-Atlantic states, state legislatures selected the presidential electors. The 1796 election would be decided in elections to the legislatures of those states, and in subsequent intriguing within those bodies. John Beckley, clerk of the House of Representatives, devised the Republican strategy in Pennsylvania. He secretly circulated a list of prominent and respected candidates for the state legislature who were committed Jeffersonians. Discovering the Republican slate only when it was too late to construct a similar list, the Federalists lost the elections. In December Beckley delivered all but one of Pennsylvania's electoral votes to Jefferson. In New York, however,

there was no John Beckley. Adams took the state's electoral votes and won the national election. The distribution of electoral votes revealed the bases of Federalist and Republican support: Adams received only 2 electoral votes south of the Potomac, and Jefferson received only 18 (all but 5 of them in Pennsylvania) north of the river.

The voting was over but the intriguing was not. Alexander Hamilton, who since his retirement from the Treasury in 1795, had directed the Federalist party from his New York law office, was still one of the most powerful men in the country and the undisputed leader of the Federalist. Much to his chagrin, Hamilton knew he could not manipulate the independent and almost perversely upright Adams. Moreover, Adams was almost as apolitical as his predecessor, and consequently had no intention of becoming a Hamilton lackey or of engaging in the nitty-gritty of partisan politics. Hamilton was aware of Adams' mentality and thus secretly instructed South Carolina's Federalist electors to withhold their votes from Adams, which would give the presidency to Adams' running mate, the South Carolinian Thomas Pinckney, relegating Adams to the vice-presidency. (Prior to the 12th Amendment's ratification in 1804, the candidate with the majority of the electoral votes became president, and the second-place candidate became vice-president.) Like some of Hamilton's other schemes, this one backfired. New England electors heard of the plan and angrily withheld their votes from Pinckney. As a result, Adams was elected president and his opponent, who received the second most electoral votes, Thomas Jefferson, became vice-president. Adams narrowly won the election, but he took office with a justifiable mistrust of many members of his own party and with the leader of the opposition party as his vice-president! It was not an auspicious beginning for the second president of the United States.

Troubles with France

As John Adams entered office an international crisis was already in full swing. As a result of Jay's Treaty, France recalled its envoy and broke off all diplomatic relations with the United States. The French government interpreted the treaty as an Anglo-American alliance, which was incorrect but apparently the French were still smarting from the United States' refusal to join them in their revolutionary cause as an ally. Indeed, the French were so outraged by Jay's Treaty that they hinted they intended to do all they could to overthrow the Adam's administration, which they saw as a continuation of Washington's alleged anti-French disposition. They announced however, that they would postpone such action in the hope that their "friend of the Revolution," Thomas Jefferson, would replace that "old man in Washington" in 1797. In order to ensure Jefferson's victory, French privateers seized American ships trading with Britain, giving Americans a taste of what would happen if they did not elect an administration friendlier to France. When the election went to Adams, the French gave up on the U.S, and set about harassing British shipping as best they could in the Atlantic and Caribbean. In 1797 France expelled the American minister, refusing to reestablish relations until the U.S. addressed French "grievances," which was code for becoming a French ally. The French ordered that American ships carrying "so much as a handkerchief" made in England be confiscated without compensation and announced that American sailors serving in the British navy would be summarily hanged if captured.

President Adams of course wanted to protect American commerce from French depredations. He knew, as his predecessor had realized, that the United States could not win a war against the greatest military power in Europe at the time. So, like Washington in his dealings with England, Adams too had to play the diplomatic game. He thus sent to France, in hopes of negotiating a settlement of grievances between the two countries, three respected statesmen: South Carolinian Charles Cotesworth Pinckney, Virginian John Marshall, and the Boston Yankee, Elbridge Gerry. All three men of course were Federalists; in fact they belonged to the Hamiltonian faction within the party that called themselves the "High Federalists." By 1797 the reign of terror had been over for two years and because of international war, the revolutionary fervor of the earlier years had subsided at home; indeed, by the time of the American entourage's arrival, the revolution had begun its move to the right—the radical republicans, the Jacobins and Girondists, had been purged from power, with most of them executed by the increasingly more conservative middle class that had taken control of the government by 1797. By that year what was left of the aristocracy had also reclaimed much its earlier status and power. Nonetheless, the new government, the Directory—a committee of five men representing each of France's estates or classes—still believed the United States had betrayed their country by reneging on their 1778 treat agreements. Thus when the American emissaries arrived in Paris they were left cooling their heels in the outer offices of the Directory. At last three French officials (correspondence identified them only as "X, Y, and Z," and thus the ensuing diplomatic debacle later became known as the XYZ affair), approached the American officials and declared that France would "receive them"—open negotiations—if they paid a bribe of $250,000, arranged for the U.S. to loan $12 million to the French government, and apologized for unpleasant remarks that John Adams had made about France. The delegates obviously refused to succumb to extortion, telling the French, "No, not a sixpence," and returned home. There a journalist transformed their remark into "Millions for defense, but not one cent for tribute."

President Adams asked Congress to prepare for war, and the French responded by seizing more American ships. Thus began in April 1798, an undeclared, "Quasi-War" with France on the high seas but mostly the nation's ships exchanged their fire in the Caribbean. While the French navy dealt with the British in the North Atlantic, French privateers inflicted costly blows on American shipping. After nearly a year of fighting, with the British providing powder and shot for American guns, the U.S. Navy chased the French privateers out of the West Indies.

Crises at Home, 1798–1800

The troubles with France precipitated a crisis at home. The disclosure of the XYZ correspondence, together with the quasi-war with France in the Caribbean, precipitated a surge in popular antipathy for France and even clamors for all-out war. Just three years earlier the American public displayed a similar temperament and outrage toward England because of the Jay Treaty. In both instances cooler minds prevailed and a full-scale war was avoided. Of greater importance, the tensions with France produced serious political ramifications that the earlier Jay Treaty controversy did not. Pro-French Republicans, for example, incurred public hostility for their continued support for France. Many Federalists, (in particular the High Federalists) led by Alexander Hamilton, wanted to use the crisis to destroy their political opponents. Without consulting President Adams, the Federalist-dominated Congress passed a number of war-time measures, even though the country was not officially at war with either Great Britain or France. The first was a federal property tax—graduated, spread equally between sections of the country, and justified by military necessity, but a direct federal tax nonetheless. Congress then passed four laws known as the Alien and Seditions Acts. Designed by the High Federalists, these measures' purpose were to destroy the Democratic Republican party; in effect, by means of political proscription. The first three were directed at immigrants, who at this time were flooding into the United States, fleeing the war in Europe. The more politically-savvy Democratic Republicans were at the docks to greet them, hoping that when they became naturalized citizens and had the right to vote, they would remember who had first shook their hand and welcomed them to the United States. Thus the purpose of the Alien Acts was to curtail immigrant voting potential by extending the naturalization period from 5 to 14 years and empowered the president to detain enemy aliens during wartime and to deport those he deemed dangerous to the United States. The fourth law—the Sedition Act—set jail terms and fines for persons who advocated disobedience to federal law or who wrote, printed, or spoke "false, scandalous, and malicious" statements against "the government of the United States, or the President of the United States [note that Vice-president Jefferson was not included], with intent to defame or to bring them or either of them, into contempt or disrepute."

It was obvious to everyone that the Sedition Act was designed to censor Republican criticism of Federalist policies and ultimately by such acts of proscription, demolish the party, thus removing any challenge to Federalist hegemony of the national government. To the High Federalist sponsors of this bill, a Republican such as Thomas Jefferson in the White House (in which John Adams was its first occupant even though it was barely completed) would be disastrous for the nation, for they were certain he would give power back to the very "rabble' who almost destroyed the country in the 1780s. Thus to ensure the nation's future security and survival, the Federalists believed their Republican opponents had to be crushed here and now.

President Adams never used the powers granted under the Alien Acts. But the Sedition Act resulted in the prosecution of 14 Republicans, most of them journalists. William Duane, editor of the *Philadelphia Aurora,* was indicted when he and two Irish friends circulated a petition against the Alien Act on the grounds of a Catholic Church. James Callendar, editor of a Jeffersonian newspaper in Richmond, Virginia, was arrested, while another prominent Republican went to jail for statements made in a private letter, criticizing Federalist policy. Jedediah Peck, a former Federalist from upstate New York, was arrested when he petitioned Congress to repeal the Alien and Sedition Acts. Matthew Lyon, a scurrilous and uncouth Republican congressman from Vermont, had brawled with Roger Griswold, a Federalist in the House chamber; he went to jail for his criticism of President Adams, Federalist militarism, and what he called the "ridiculous pomp" of the national administration. It was obvious to most informed Americans and to the Republicans that not only were the Federalists out to obliterate their party but that they

A Brawl in Congress. The politics of the early republic were often rough. Here two congressmen (one of them later convicted under the Sedition Act) come to blows on the floor of the House of Representatives.

were blatantly violating the Bill of Rights, particularly the First Amendment rights of numerous citizens. It was time for the Republicans to counterattack, not only to defend their party and save it from possible extinction but the sanctity of freedom of speech and press guaranteed in the Bill of Rights. For Republicans this became their greatest concern in their fight against the Sedition Act.

The Virginia and Kentucky Resolves

In their counterattack Republicans turned to the states for help. Southern states, which had provided only 4 of the 44 congressional votes for the Sedition Act, took the lead. Jefferson provided the Kentucky legislature with draft resolutions, and Madison did the same for Virginia. These so-called Virginia and Kentucky Resolves reiterated the constitutional fundamentalism that had informed Republican opposition to the Federalists through the 1790s.

Jefferson's Kentucky Resolves reminded Congress that the Alien and Sedition Acts gave the national government powers not specified in the Constitution and that the Tenth Amendment made it clear that such powers are reserved for the states. He also argued that the Constitution was a "compact' between sovereign states, and that state legislatures could thus "nullify" federal laws they deemed unconstitutional—thus establishing the states' rights theories southern-ers would come to embrace as their gospel after 1830. Jefferson further warned that if the federal government proceeded to try to enforce a law after a state had nullified its application in that state, then that state could exercise its full sovereignty and secede from the Union. Perhaps most important, the resolves questioned the concept of the Union created by the Constitution. According to Jefferson and Madison, the Union was a uniting of independent sovereign states, (individual republics), that had voluntarily agreed, for their better collective security, to "compact" to form a country, (not necessarily a nation). However, they always retained their sovereignty and if that self-determination was ever violated by the federal government, then that state could withdraw from the compact or Union. In short, Jefferson and Madison were arguing in their respective resolves that the Union was not a union of people but of individual states. Such a disposition seems especially disingenuous for Madison, whose contributions to the writing of the Constitution were manifold, especially the preamble, which clearly affirms that the people, not the states, created the Union. Such rhetoric made it obvious that Republican leaders were willing to go to any extreme to not only save their party but to demonstrate to the people the gravity of the constitutional crisis at hand. Beyond such ominous, exaggerated, and misguided declarations, the Virginia and Kentucky Resolves had few

immediate effects. Opposition to the Sedition Act ranged from popular attempts to obstruct the law, to fistfights in Congress, and Virginia began calling up its militia. No other states however, went as far as Virginia and Kentucky in directly challenging the acts, and armed opposition to Federalist policies was limited to a few areas in the South. The acts became so unpopular that when they came up for renewal in 1799 President Adams vetoed both measures. A year earlier Adams had let the acts "pass" by simply not signing them. Interestingly Jefferson and Madison hesitated to challenge the Alien and Sedition Acts in the Supreme Court, both because the Court was dominated by Federalists and because they did not want to set a precedent for giving the Supreme Court the power to rule on the constitutionality of laws.

But the damage had been done, especially to the Federalist party, upon which the measures backfired. Instead of the acts destroying the Republicans, they ended up obliterating the Federalists, whom the people now regarded as the party of elitism, reaction, and oppression. Ironically, by passing such laws, the Federalist not only guaranteed their own elimination from power in the national government but made a Republican victory in 1800 a certainty, their worst nightmare come true. In short, the Alien and Sedition Acts proved to have been political suicide for the Federalist, who over the course of the next decade would slowly disappear from the nation's political landscape and bring about the end of the Republic's first party system.

The Politicians and the Army

Federalists took another ominous step by implementing President Adams' request that Congress create a military prepared for war.

Adams wanted a fortified navy, both because the undeclared war with France was being fought on the ocean and because he agreed with other Federalists that America's future as a commercial nation required a strong navy. Hamilton and other High Federalists preferred a strong standing army as well. At Washington's urging and against his own judgment, Adams appointed Hamilton inspector general, making the New Yorker the de facto commander of the U.S. Army. Congress authorized the creation of a 20,000 man army and Hamilton proceeded to raise such a force. Congress also approved funds for a much larger army to be called up in the event of a declaration of war. When he expanded the officer corps in anticipation of such an army, Hamilton excluded Republicans and commissioned only his political friends. The High Federalists made it known that they intended to use the standing army to enforce the Alien and Sedition Acts and to put down an impending rebellion in the South. Beyond that, there was little need for such a large constabulary. The quasi-war with France was a conflict at sea and most Americans believed that the citizen militia could hold off any land invasion until an army was raised. The Republicans, President Adams himself, and many other Federalists now became convinced that Hamilton and his High Federalist coterie were determined to destroy political opponents by force if necessary, enter into an alliance with Great Britain, and impose Hamilton's statist designs on the nation with the army ready to be used if necessary to effect such policies. By 1799 Adams and many of his Federalist friends were certain that Hamilton and his supporters were dangerous anti-republican militarists.

Adams was both fearful and angry. First the Hamiltonians had tried to rob him of the presidency, and then had passed the Alien and Sedition Acts, the direct tax, and plans for a standing army without consulting him. None of this would have been possible had it not been for the crisis with France. Adams, who had resisted calls for a declaration of war, began looking for ways to achieve peace. He decided that even though it would split his party and probably cost him reelection in 1800, it was time to try to reopen negotiations with France. He also procrastinated on creating Hamilton's army. At first the Federalist-dominated Senate refused to authorize the sending of an envoy to France but relented when Adams threatened to resign, which would leave the presidency to Thomas Jefferson, a prospect even the most progressive Federalists were not ready to accept. An emissary was sent to France and successfully achieved a rapprochement. The French released the United States from their 1778 treaty commitments but they refused to pay reparations for attacks on American ships since 1793—the very point over which many Federalists had wanted to declare war. Peace with France took the wind out of the sails of the more militaristic and repressive Federalists and intensified the growing rift in the party between the High Federalists and their more moderate counterparts, ensuring a split come presidential election time in 1800.

"The Revolution of 1800:" The Election of Thomas Jefferson

"Jefferson and Liberty" became the Republican campaign slogan for the 1800 presidential election. By this time, the Republicans had developed effective techniques for mobilizing voters, such as printing pamphlets, handbills, and newspapers, all of which contained information not only about their candidate but their

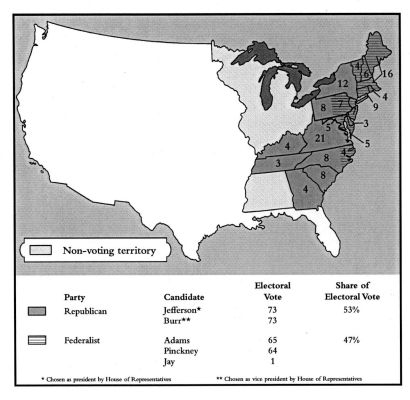

Party	Candidate	Electoral Vote	Share of Electoral Vote
Republican	Jefferson*	73	53%
	Burr**	73	
Federalist	Adams	65	47%
	Pinckney	64	
	Jay	1	

* Chosen as president by House of Representatives   ** Chosen as vice president by House of Representatives

Map of Election of 1800

party's platform and ideology as well. In many ways, the Republicans had become a modern political party machine, complete with staff workers at a variety levels to individuals who organized mass meetings and rallies to promote their cause. In four short years, Republicans had learned that if one wants political power in a democratic republic, they had to go out and convince the electorate that they were the people's party and would deliver what the people wanted once in power. The Federalists, meanwhile, continued to view mass politics and campaigning as beneath them, and thus they found it difficult to match their opponent's mobilization.

In their campaign speeches the Republicans charged that the Federalists' actions of the past four years were not only expensive, repressive, unwise, and unconstitutional but even more ominous, they reflected the classic means by which despots destroyed liberty. The Republicans presented themselves as the party of traditional agrarian purity, of liberty, and states' rights, of "government rigorously frugal and simple," in the words of Jefferson. They were optimistic, convinced that they were riding the wave of the future. Divided and bitter, the Federalists waged a defensive struggle for strong central government and public order, and resorted frequently to negative campaigning. They denounced Jefferson as an atheist, a Jacobin, and the father of mulatto children— the first two charges were without foundation, while the last was apparently true, according to results of DNA matching tests. The Federalists also warned that the election of Thomas Jefferson and his radical allies would release the worst horrors of the French Revolution onto the streets of American towns and cities. Each side believed that is defeat in the election would mean the end of the republic.

The 1800 presidential campaign marked the first time the Republicans and Federalists operated as two national political parties. Caucuses of congressmen nominated respective slates: John Adams and Charles Cotesworth Pinckney of South Carolina for the Federalists and Jefferson and Aaron Burr of New York for the Republicans. The balloting for presidential electors took place between October and December 1800. Adams took all the New England states while Jefferson captured the South and West. Party discipline was so effective that one of the provisions of the Constitution was shown to be badly outmoded. By this clause, the candidate receiving a majority of electoral votes became president and the runner-up became vice-president. However, to the Republicans shock and subsequent quandary, by casting all their ballots for Jefferson and Burr, Republican electors created a tie between the two men, with each receiving 73. Adams finished "second" with 65 and C.C. Pinckney third with 64. Such an outcome forced the election into the House of Representatives. Even though the Republicans had won control of the House, Congress was not set to reconvene until March 1801. Thus, the Federalist majority was given a last chance to decide the election, and if that were the case, then Alexander Hamilton, still the party's most influential and powerful member, would decide who would become the nation's third president. However, Hamilton did not intervene until after the House had cast 34 ballots. Finally on the 35th ballot, Hamilton decided it was time to break the impasse. Fortunately for the Republicans and the United States, if there was one individual Hamilton hated more that Jefferson, it was Aaron Burr, whom he could never allow to become president of the United States. Burr, he warned, was obsessed with power, "an embryo Caesar." Thus, on the 35th ballot, as a result of "instructions' from Hamilton, the House Federalists arranged with their opponents to elect Jefferson without having to cast a single vote in his favor; they all turned in blank ballots. Interestingly, prior to Hamilton's intervention, most of the Federalists had

supported Burr. To avoid a repetition of the crisis, Congress and the states soon adopted the 12th Amendment to the Constitution, requiring electors to cast separate votes for president and vice president. The election of 1800 also set in motion a chain of events that culminated four years later when Burr killed Hamilton in a duel, the crescendo of the hatred each man had had for each other for several years. No doubt Hamilton's intervention in the 1800 election, which cost Burr the presidency, contributed to the challenge that took Hamilton's life. Burr, while serving as vice-president, engaged in a filibustering plot to form a new nation in the West from land detached from the United States and the Spanish empire. Acquitted of treason in 1807, he went into exile in Europe, eventually returning to New York, where he practiced law until his death in 1836.

Before retiring the Federalist Congress got off one more shot at the Republicans. In January 1801, just as the session expired, Congress passed the Judiciary Act of 1801, which gave John Adams the power to expand the federal judiciary by appointing new judges, justices of the peace, attorneys, clerks, and marshals. Needless to say, he filled these positions with good Federalists, and then he left office.

The events of the 1790s demonstrated that a majority of Americans believed the common people had a right to play an active role in politics, express their opinions freely, and contest the policies of their government. His party, wrote Samuel Goodrich, a prominent Connecticut Federalist, was overthrown because democracy had become "the watchword of popular liberty." To their credit, the Federalists never considered resistance to the election result. Adams' acceptance of defeat established the vital precedent of a peaceful transfer of power from a defeated party to its successor.

Conclusion

The first decade of the federal government's existence had demonstrated that the love of liberty and the love for order and stability sometimes led in different directions, and they gave rise to very different visions of what constituted "good" citizenship. Democratic Republicans fumed at what they saw as the liberties Federalists had taken with the Constitution, and their willingness to abrogate civil rights in the name of order, stability, and security. Federalists were convinced more than ever that Democratic Republicanism was a dangerous scourge upon the land, tantamount to lawlessness, and itself, the greatest threat to the republic. The 1790s had witnessed a steady escalation of suspicion and mistrust, of which the Whiskey Rebellion, the Alien and Sedition Acts, and the Virginia and Kentucky resolves had been only the most striking illustrations. The political parties organized that fractious spirit, but they did little to defuse it. Meanwhile, even as Americans fought over the terms of the new republic's founding, those terms began to change.

Suggested Readings

Catherine Allgor. *Parlor Politics: In Which the Ladies of Washington Help Build a City and a Government.* (2000). The role of elite women in creating a national political culture.

Joanne B. Freeman. *Affairs of Honor: National Politics in the New Republic.* (2001). A brilliant analysis of political culture in the new nation.

Frederick Hoxie, Ronald Hoffman, and Peter J. Albert, eds. *Native Americans and the Early Republic.* (1999). This collection of essays counters views of Native Americans as passive victims of American westward settlement in the early Republic.

Jeffrey Pasley, etc. al., eds. *Beyond the Founders: New Approaches to the Political History of the New Republic.* (2004). Lively new perspectives on the founding era.

David Waldstreicher. *In the Midst of Perpetual Fetes: The Making of American Nationalism, 1776–1820.* (1997). The role of popular celebrations in creating American nationalism.

Phillip Ziesche. *Cosmopolitan Patriots: Americans In Paris in the Age of Revolution.* (2009). A very smart discussion of the way in which Americans understood their Revolution to be just like the French Revolution— and profoundly different.

Stanley Elkins and Eric L. McKittrick. *The Age of Federalism.* (1993). A detailed account of the politics of the 1790s.

Joyce Appleby. *Capitalism and a New Social Order: The Republican Vision of the 1790s.* (1984). Explores how the Jeffersonians sought simultaneously to expand economic enterprise and equality of opportunity.

John C. Miller. *Crisis in Freedom: The Alien and Sedition Acts.* (1952). Examines how the Adams administration sought to use the power of the federal government to stifle dissent and the free press.

Drew McCoy. *The Elusive Republic: Political Economy in Jeffersonian America.* (1980). An influential study of the economic and political outlook and policies of Federalists and Jeffersonians.

Chapter 8

JEFFERSONIAN AMERICA, 1800–1815

The Jeffersonians in Power

On the morning of March 4, 1801, president-elect Thomas Jefferson left his rooms at Conrad and McMunn's boarding house to *walk* to the half-built capital city of Washington to be inaugurated third president of the United States. He refused to ride in a carriage and was attired in the clothes and unpretentious appearance of the common people—pants, not knickers; boots not buckled shoes; a plain shirt and jacket; not a ruffled blouse and fancy coat, and perhaps most revealing no powdered, coifed wig; just his own reddish-brown hair which he wore almost down to his shoulders. There were military salutes along the way, but Jefferson forbade all the pomp and ceremony that had surrounded Washington's inauguration day. Accompanied by a few friends and escorted by a company of Maryland militia (and not by the professional army of which Hamilton had dreamed), Jefferson walked up the street and into the unfinished capitol building; the central tower and the wing that would house Congress were only half completed. Jefferson joined Vice-president Aaron Burr, other members of the government, and a few foreign diplomats in the recently completed Senate chamber where he took his oath of office, administered by the newly appointed Chief Justice of the Supreme Court, John Marshall, a distant relative and political opponent from Virginia.

In a voice barely audible to those at a distance, Jefferson delivered his inaugural address. Referring to the political contention that had brought him into office, he began with a call for unity, insisting that "every difference of opinion is not a difference of principle. We have called by different names brethren of the same principle. We are all Republicans, we are all Federalists." With that statement Jefferson hoped that he could eradicate the political animosity and factionalism that had almost brought the Republic down during the Alien and Sedition act crisis, and return to the consensus the elite appeared to have shared pre-1789. Most important, Jefferson was optimistic that within a short time the Federalist Party would simply dissolve, already having committed political suicide with their passage of the Alien and Sedition Acts. Jefferson believed he could speed up that process by inviting moderate Federalists into a broad Republican coalition, in which there would be no room for the statist designs of Alexander Hamilton and his High Federalist friends.

Jefferson went on to outline the kind of republican government he envisioned. Grateful for an Atlantic Ocean that separated the United States from "the exterminating havoc" of Europe and that his countrymen were the possessors of "a chosen country, with room for our

Portrait of Thomas Jefferson by the artist Gilbert Stuart

descendants to the thousandth and thousandth generation," he declared that Americans were a free and virtuous people, capable of sustaining republicanism and thus there was no need to build a national state based on European models. In such a statement Jefferson clearly was taking the Federalists to task for having so mistrusted the inherent rectitude of the American people and for having attempted to impose on them such an antithetical and anathematic form of government. A people blessed with isolation, bountiful resources, and liberty, needed only "a wise and frugal Government, which shall restrain men from injuring one another, shall leave them otherwise free to regulate their own pursuits of industry and improvement, and shall not take from the mouth of labor the bread it has earned. This is the sum of good government, and this is necessary to close the circle of our felicities."

Jefferson's "wise and frugal" government was code for his states' rights mentality. It also meant that he intended to shrink the government's expanse and presence in Americans' daily lives by cutting taxes, gutting the bureaucracy, paying its debts without incurring new ones, thus ending the need for taxation. Such a program would greatly curtail the burgeoning Federalist state. Jefferson also promised a national defense policy based on "a disciplined militia" that would fight invaders while regulars were being trained—thus ridding the nation of Hamilton's standing army. The "citizen's army" would protect republican liberties from domestic enemies and from the European nations. Most important, Jefferson promised to promote an agrarian republic, with "commerce as its handmaiden," which meant he would work assiduously to keep the United States an agricultural economy while attempting to dismantle as much as was possible the Federalist manufacturing and commercial

agenda. Beyond the fostering of an agrarian republic and reducing the size and expense of government, Jefferson promised very little else. He was fortunate that he became president at a most propitious time relative to European affairs. By the time of his inauguration, the French Revolution had come full circle; Napoleon Bonaparte, with the aid of conservatives, aristocrats, and monarchists, had just taken over the government by military coup d'etat and made the consolidation of his power at home a priority rather than continuing to expand France's empire on the continent. In effect, both of the main belligerents—France and England—were temporarily exhausted after eight years of war and thus there was momentary peace in Europe, which allowed Jefferson to implement his domestic agenda without having to worry about international events obtruding upon his initiatives. Moreover, Jefferson faced little to no opposition to his agenda at home, for the Federalist Party was becoming a leaderless and defunct organization, especially with the High Federalists becoming persona non grata within their own party. Jefferson was thus confident that he could bring about during his presidency the fulfillment of the republican ideals of 1776.

The unpretentiousness of Jefferson's inauguration set the social tone for his administration. As noted in the previous chapter, Jefferson despised the formality and aristocratic pomp and ceremony of the Washington administration and thus there were few elaborate balls, levees, and dinners. He sent his annual State of the Union addresses to Congress to be read by a clerk rather than delivering them in person, in the manner of English kings and his Federalist predecessors. He refused to ride about Washington in a carriage and instead, either walked or rode a horse when out on his errands. Abandoning the grand banquets favored by Washington and Adams, Jefferson preferred to entertain senators and members of the House at small dinner parties, where attendees sat at a round table without formal seating, a reflection of Jefferson's more egalitarian temperament. As noted above, Jefferson dressed in the common man's attire—old homespun and when not at work in the White House, and sometimes even when he was, he would have on his feet a pair of worn bedroom slippers. At his intimate dinners, brilliant conversation was the order of the day, a nicety Jefferson perfected while he was a diplomat and a visitor to the salons of Paris. The president's dinners set examples of unpretentious excellence through which this cultivated country squire hoped to govern the republic that he claimed to have saved from monarchists.

Purging the Government

As promised in his inaugural address, Jefferson made his first priority of business the curtailing of the size and expense of government. During his first administration, indeed, in his first year in office, Jefferson reduced the diplomatic corps and replaced officeholders who were incompetent, corrupt, or avowedly antirepublican. To the surprise and anger of many of his more fanatical and vengeful Republican compatriots, not all those purged from federal office were Federalists. Jefferson realized that to do so could cripple the government's daily functioning, for the Federalists had been running the government for eight years and to eliminate individuals with such experience and expertise because of their political affiliation would be foolish. Moreover, by keeping moderate Federalists in the bureaucracy, Jefferson was making good his inaugural promise of conciliation and unity. The replacements were not the vindictive revolutionaries that Federalists had warned against, but rather Republicans cut from the same elite cloth as the departed Federalists. Jefferson only slightly altered the status and politics of the federal bureaucracy; its size was reduced but its shape and content remained intact.

Jefferson made more substantial cuts in the military, which he feared more than a Federalist-laden bureaucracy. The Federalist had built a sizeable army and navy to prepare for war and, if necessary, to put down insurrections at home. Legislation passed in March 1802, reduced the army to two regiments of infantry and one of artillery—a total of 3,350 officers and men, most of whom were assigned to western frontier posts far from civilian population centers. Similar cutbacks were made in the navy. The goal, Jefferson asserted, was to rely mainly on the militia for national defense but to maintain a small, well-trained professional army as well. Interestingly, the same bill that reduced the army created the military academy at West Point. Jefferson also abolished all taxes except the tariff, including the hated whiskey of 1791 and property tax of 1798, and paid off part of the national debt, which fell during Jefferson's two terms from $80 million to $57 million. Jefferson also pardoned all those imprisoned under the Sedition Act and repaid with interest the fines that had been levied under them. Thus with a few deft strokes, Jefferson dismantled the Federalist state.

Republican Agrarianism

Jefferson brought to the presidency a clearly defined political philosophy, much more so than either of his predecessors. Behind all the events of his two terms and those of his successors in what became known as the Virginia Dynasty (James Madison, 1809–1817; James Monroe, 1817–1825), was an ideology that embodied Jefferson's interpretation of American republicanism.

Jefferson's years as American envoy to France in the 1780s greatly influenced his political thinking. Affected by the extremes of wealth and poverty he saw there, and the violent revolution such conditions unleashed, he came to believe that it was impossible for Europe to achieve a just society that could guarantee most of its citizens the "life, liberty, and pursuit of happiness," of which he had declared in the Declaration of Independence. Jefferson was equally disdainful of English industrialization, which produced in that nation's factory towns, squalor, poverty, and misery amongst the working classes, whom he believed would ultimately rise up in revolt not only against such an oppressive economic system but against the government that supported it as well. Such were the reasons why he opposed the Hamiltonian agenda, for he saw in Hamilton's initiatives the potential for the same kind of conditions to arise in the United States. In short, in Jefferson's mind, industrialization would only bring about bitter class division and ultimately class warfare because of the inequities and disparity of wealth inherent in such an economic orientation.

Jefferson believed that only America provided the fertile earth essential for the citizenship necessary to a republican form of government. What the U.S. had and Europe lacked, was an abundance of land, which he believed was republicanism's essential prerequisite. As long as there was room to grow, republicanism would flourish in America. In the Jeffersonian frame of reference, if the United States was to remain the bastion of republicanism, it was imperative for the nation's economy to remain predominantly agricultural. Jefferson thus envisaged a nation of small family farms clustered together in rural communities—an agrarian republic. He believed only a country of roughly equal yeoman farmers, each secure in his own possessions and not dependent on someone else for his livelihood, would exhibit the concern for the community good—public virtue—that was essential in a republic. In other words, only in a society in which the majority of its members (in the early Republic that meant white males only) believed themselves to be equals could republicanism flourish. In short, in the Jeffersonian equation, egalitarianism and republicanism were symbiotic. More romantically, Jefferson also believed that those who earned their livelihood from the soil were more in tune with the cycles and rhythms of nature—an important ingredient in the formation of the republican character. Indeed, Jefferson said that "those who labor in the earth are the chosen people of God," and so he viewed himself as one of the "chosen," even though his "farm" was the large slave-owning plantation of Monticello.

Yet another European event influenced Jefferson's thinking. In 1798, the Englishman Thomas Malthus published his seminal and deeply pessimistic *Essay on the Principle of Population*. Warning of an impending population explosion, Malthus predicted that the British population would soon outstrip the country's food supply. Unless population growth was checked, misery and poverty would soon engulf not just England and Europe but the United States as well. Malthus' prediction alarmed many Americans, who had taken great pride in having one of the fastest rates of population increase in the world, close to 40 percent per decade. Jefferson was not worried. He used Malthus to highlight the opportunity to avoid such a catastrophe America's vast land resources provided; Americans need not worry about Malthus' dire predictions because they had at their disposal millions of acres of land to where they could expand and cultivate.

Jefferson's vision of an expanding agrarian republic remains to this day one of our most compelling ideas about America's uniqueness and special destiny. Indeed, Jeffersonian agrarianism informed much of the American creed and became one of the most enduring ideological legacies in American history. However, as already seen in this volume, expansionism also contained negative aspects. The lure of western lands fostered constant mobility, restlessness, and dissatisfaction rather than the stable, settled communities envisaged by Jefferson. Expansionism caused environmental damage, in particular soil exhaustion—a consequence of abandoning old lands rather than conserving them and moving on to new ones. Finally, and perhaps most devastating, expansionism bred a ruthlessness toward Native Americans, who were violently pushed out of the way for white settlement or who were decimated by the diseases that accompanied Anglo-American advance. Jeffersonian agrarianism thus engendered some of the best and some of the worst traits of the developing nation.

Jeffersonians and the Courts: John Marshall and the Advent of Judicial Review

Although Jefferson succeeded in rolling back much of the Federalist agenda, he could not extirpate all of the initiatives, especially those pertaining to national authority and primacy.

Such was the challenge that confronted Jefferson in his battle with the federal court system, which at the time was dominated by the Federalists. Suffice it to say Jefferson and his party wanted to correct such an "imbalance" and believed the best way to accomplish that was to repeal the 1801 Judiciary Act, passed by the lame-duck Federalist Congress just before Jefferson's inauguration. Moreover, as noted in the previous chapter, just before leaving office John Adams had appointed and signed the commissions for a bevy of new judges, marshals, federal attorneys, clerks, and justices of the peace, all of whom were staunch Federalists, as well as expanding the number and levels of federal courts. It was if Adams was having a "Hamiltonian moment," attempting to preserve and protect the federal judiciary as a Federalist bastion from Republican revenge and retrenchment.

Republicans disagreed about what to do with a Federalist-packed judiciary. A minority distrusted the whole idea of an independent judiciary and wanted to pass legislation and an amendment to make all judges popularly elected. Such an idea was even too democratic for Thomas Jefferson, who surprisingly wanted courts shielded from popular control. However, all Republicans, including Jefferson deeply resented the fact that the entire judicial system was in Federalist hands. Jefferson was able to replace the new federal marshals and attorneys with Republicans as well as dismissing some of the federal justices of the peace, but judges were appointed for life and could only be removed by impeachment. Jefferson believed the best way to relieve his administration of these men was to simply abolish their jobs by repealing the 1801 Judiciary Act and thus did away with all of Adams' appointees.

Emboldened by repeal of the Judiciary Act, the Republicans next attempted to reduce the Federalist presence on the Supreme Court by impeaching Associate Justice Samuel Chase for alleged "high crimes and misdemeanors." The move was purely partisan and vindictive; Chase was a hardcore, vituperative, openly hostile anti-Jeffersonian High Federalist, who during the Alien and Sedition Act crisis prosecuted sedition cases with great relish, handing down the maximum sentences and fines the act allowed for its Republican violators. He also was incredibly, arrogantly impolitic, delivering anti-Jeffersonian diatribes from the bench. In short, Chase was an unpleasant, overbearing, and unashamedly partisan member of the bench. However, whatever his personal flaws, there was no legal or constitutional justification for his impeachment; he was a competent, knowledgeable, and upright; he simply could not keep his political thoughts to himself nor his antipathy for the Jeffersonians quiet. In their quest to impeach Chase, Democratic Republicans became loose Constitutional constructionists, a reversal of their earlier interpretations during the debate on the chartering of the Bank of the United States. In their defense of Chase, the Federalists became the strict constructionists, arguing that the power to impeach had been narrowly drawn and should be used only in cases of clear criminal behavior; Chase's outspoken partisanship was no criminal act. In the final vote, Chase was acquitted and the Supreme Court remained Federalist, 5 to 1. Jefferson's desire for a Democratic Republican court would have to wait for unforced vacancies in 1804 and 1807 and the creation of a new western circuit in 1807.

Of greater significance than the Chase controversy was the establishing of judicial review by the Supreme Court under the leadership of one that body's most outstanding chief justices of all time, John Marshall, a Federalist and Adams appointee, who was a firm believer in national supremacy. The Marshall Court's first landmark decision came in 1803, in the case of *Marbury v. Madison.* As noted earlier, on the eve of leaving office Adams had appointed a number of justices of the peace for the District of Columbia. Madison, Jefferson's Secretary of State, refused to issue commissions (the official documents entitling them to assume their posts) to these "midnight judges"—Adams' last-minute appointees. Four, including William Marbury, sued Madison for their offices. To the shock of his Federalist colleagues both on the bench and in the larger political community, Marshall declared unconstitutional the section of the 1789 Judiciary Act that allowed the courts to order executive officials to deliver judges' commissions. It exceeded the powers of Congress as outlined in the Constitution and was therefore void. On the one hand, Marshall proclaimed that the courts had a duty "say what the law is," thus unequivocally defending the independence of the judiciary and the principle of judicial review. On the other hand, Marshall conceded that the Supreme Court could not force the executive branch to appoint Marbury to a position that no longer existed. At first glance Jefferson's government appeared to have won the battle over Adams' last minute appointees. However, in the long run, Marshall established the principle that only the federal judiciary could decide the constitutionality of laws passed by Congress—a power known as "judicial review."

Seven years later, in *Fletcher v. Peck,* the Court extended judicial review to state laws. In 1794 a corrupt Georgia legislature (most of whom were on the payroll of the Yazoo Land Company) had given the company the right to purchase land in present-day Alabama and Mississippi claimed by Georgia. The company then sold the land to individual buyers, mostly New England speculators, for a huge profit. Two years later, many of the corrupt lawmakers were defeated for reelection and the new Georgia legislature rescinded the land grant and subsequent sales. The legislature also turned the land over to the federal government whereby Jefferson agreed to pay off the investor's claims with federal money. John Marshall however, interpreted the entire exchange differently. Whatever the circumstances of the legislature's initial action, according to Marshall, the Constitution forbade Georgia from taking any action that impaired a contract. Therefore the individual purchasers (the New England speculators) could keep their land and the legislature could not repeal the original grant.

Marbury v. Madison and *Fletcher v. Peck,* were vital steps in realizing the three-way balance of power among the branches of the federal government—executive (president), legislative (Congress), judiciary (courts)— envisaged in the Constitution. Equally important, during his long tenure in office (1801–1835), Marshall consistently led the Supreme Court in a series of decisions that favored the federal government over state governments, the sanctity of contracts, private property rights, and the protection of private enterprise from either state or federal encroachment. Under Marshall's direction, the Supreme Court established itself as a powerful nationalizing and unifying force.

The Louisiana Purchase

One of the greatest ironies of Jefferson's presidency involved his greatest accomplishment: the Louisiana Purchase, the result not of astute American diplomacy but rather the consequence of international events both in the Western Hemisphere and Europe that allowed for the largest acquisition of foreign territory in United States history to "fall into Jefferson's lap." Moreover, it was Jefferson's good fortune that Europe remained at peace during his first term, allowing Jefferson to not only successfully implement his Republican agenda, but as noted earlier, he did not have to be constantly looking over his shoulder to see what European event would soon be affecting the United States. As long as Europe was at peace, Jefferson could go far toward the realization of his republican vision. The one development that posed an international threat to the United States turned into a great triumph: the purchase of the Louisiana Territory from France in 1803.

The vast Louisiana Territory stretched from the Gulf of Mexico to Canada and from the Mississippi River to the Rocky Mountains. Ceded by France to Spain in 1762 as part of the reshuffling of colonial possessions at the end of the French and Indian War, Spain, according to the Treaty of Paris ending that conflict, was never to give the territory back to France. However, in the intervening decades power politics had changed dramatically in Europe so that by the beginning of the 19th century, France had emerged as the continent's greatest power while Spain continued its declension. By 1800 Spain was in no condition to reject or resist the French demand for Louisiana to be returned to its "rightful" owners. Napoleon's "request" was straightforward: Spain either gave Louisiana back to France or France would invade Spain. The Spanish king chose wisely; he ceded Louisiana back to France.

Napoleon wanted Louisiana back in order to resurrect the French empire in America with the sugar island of Saint Dominique (present-day Haiti and the Dominican Republic) at its center with the mainland colonies feeding

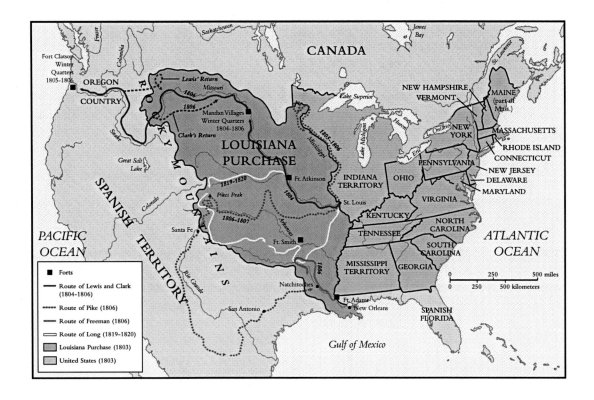

Louisiana Purchase. Although Lewis and Clark made the first exploration of the Louisiana Purchase, other explorers quickly followed. Among the most important were Zebulon Pike, who explored the Arkansas and Red rivers, and Steven Long, who explored the Arkansas and Platte rivers. Long described the plains as the "Great American Desert."

the islands and thus making the empire self-sufficient. Late in 1802, the Spanish, who had retained control of New Orleans, closed the port to American trade, giving rise to rumors that they would soon transfer the city to France. To forestall such a move, which could threaten the very existence of American settlements west of the Appalachians Jefferson dispatched envoys to France in early 1803 to offer to purchase the city from the French.

By the time the delegates reached Paris, French plans for a resurrected New World empire had collapsed. To Napoleon's utter dismay and humiliation, Saint Dominique slaves, led by Toussaint L'Ouverture, revolted against the French and defeated their attempts to regain control of the island, which the slaves had originally secured in the 1790s from the French and then later had defeated a British expeditionary force attempting to seize the island. At the same time, war between France and Great Britain seemed imminent. Napoleon—reputedly chanting "Damn sugar, damn coffee, damn colonies"—decided to bail out of

America and concentrate his resources in Europe. Needing money for such ambitions and with his dreams of American empire in ruins because of his inability to establish control over Saint Dominique, Napoleon astonished Jefferson's delegation by announcing that France would sell not only New Orleans but all of the Louisiana Territory to the United States for the bargain price of $15 million (the equivalent of perhaps $250 million in today's money); a purchase that would roughly double the size of the United States.

To the shock of his Republican colleagues, Jefferson initially hesitated to authorize the purchase, for he worried about the constitutional repercussions of his actions, for the Constitution did not give the president the power to buy territory; only Congress could sanction such a purchase and moreover, under the Constitution, the acquisition of foreign territory was considered a treaty between the United States and that foreign country and consequently, in order to be legal and binding, that treaty had to be ratified by the Senate. Suffice it to say, Jefferson faced an incredible dilemma. If he followed strict Constitutional protocol, it could take months for the purchase/treaty to be legitimized. If that were to become the case, there was no way Napoleon Bonaparte would wait around while the Americans debated his offer.

After pondering his options, Jefferson concluded that he did indeed have the *right* as president to authorize the purchase without first having to go through the appropriate Congressional channels. He found his rationalization in the necessary and proper clause of the Constitution, thus ironically paying homage to his old nemesis Alexander Hamilton, who had used the same argument during the Bank bill controversy. It appeared that Thomas Jefferson's devotion to strict constructionism had

been more political than principled. Once Jefferson overcame that particular ideological impasse he then concluded that the acquisition of Louisiana would be good for the United States on a variety of levels. It would assure Americans access to interior rivers; it would eliminate a serious foreign threat on the nation's western border; and it would give American farmers enough land to sustain the agrarian republic for centuries to come. Indeed, Jefferson believed that the republic had gained the means of renewing itself through time. Republican senators who had shared few of Jefferson's reservations, quickly ratified the Louisiana treaty over Federalist objections that the purchase would encourage rapid settlement, which would affect Native Americans, leading to more Indian wars, as well as incorporate into the country thousands of "foreigners"—Spanish, French, "new" Indians (the Plains Indians of the Mid-West), and whomever else had taken up residence in the territory over the past several decades. Such a motley assortment of people, the Federalist believed, would only increase backcountry barbarism and make it almost impossible to govern not only a country already too large, but one now inhabited by "strange" peoples totally unfamiliar with American ways. Despite Federalist protests, the purchase/treaty sailed through Congress, whose ratification met with overwhelming public approval.

The Lewis and Clark Expedition

Within a year of the purchase, Jefferson dispatched one the most important domestic expeditions in American history, that of Meriwether Lewis and William Clark. Both men were Virginia-born veterans of Indian wars in the Ohio Valley, and their assignment was to explore the new territory with the greatest attention given to detail. Their task was both scientific and commercial—to study the area's plants, animal life, native peoples, and geography and to discover how the region could be exploited commercially as well as agriculturally. Jefferson hoped his explorers would establish trade relations with western Indians and locate a water route to the Pacific Ocean—it appeared Jefferson still dreamed of the possibility of a Northwest Passage that could facilitate commerce with Asia.

In the spring of 1804, Lewis and Clark's 50-member expedition set out from St. Louis on their famous journey across half a continent. They spent the winter in the area of present-day North Dakota and then resumed their travels in April 1805. By this time they had been joined by some western Plains Indians, most notably a fifteen-year-old Shoshone Indian woman, Sacajawea, the slave wife of a French fur trader, who served as their interpreter. After crossing the Rocky Mountains, the expedition reached the Pacific Ocean in the area of present-day Astoria, Oregon, only to find that already there were a host of British, French, and even Russian fur traders and whalers. Indeed, they had been in the Oregon Country for several decades and apparently this area lay

Lewis and Clark at the mouth of the Columbia River

beyond the nation's new boundaries. Lewis and Clark returned in 1806, bringing with them a wealth of detailed information about the region—its landscape, topography, mountains, rivers, lakes, flora and fauna, and of course about the human beings who inhabited the territory, including the European fur traders who had established outposts on the Oregon coast. Although failing to find the mythical Northwest Passage (because it did not exist!), Lewis and Clark demonstrated the possibility of overland travel to the Pacific coast. To their surprise, they found Native Americans in the trans-Mississippi West accustomed to dealing with European traders and already connected to global markets. Their journey's success helped to strengthen the idea that American dominion was destined to reach all the way to the Pacific.

Although the Lewis and Clark expedition was without question one of the most important in American history, delivering invaluable information to the Jefferson administration, it also provided the president with some disappointing assessments as well. By far the most important in this category was their appraisal of the suitability of the land they traversed for farming. Unfortunately for Jefferson, Lewis and Clark dashed the president's hopes that he had purchased millions of acres of "green pastures" for farming. In Lewis and Clark's evaluation, the complete opposite was true; most of the territory was completely unsuitable for agriculture; indeed Lewis and Clark believed the entire Great Plains region to be a desert, for they had crossed the area in the summer when the heat and lack of rain turned the earth brown. In their Eastern frame of reference, such a topography reflected barren soil. Suffice it to say Jefferson was disappointed at hearing such news but somewhat relieved when told that the Oregon country was most green and fertile. Interestingly, on United States maps made after the expedition, the present-day Great Plains region was designated as The Great American Desert, and thus not until after the Civil War would Anglo-American settlers venture into the area, and then only because they were given free land via the 1862 Homestead Act. Not until the close of the 19th century did Jefferson's dream come true that he had purchased an agrarian paradise, "an empire of liberty," for his fellow citizens. By 1900 American farmers, (thanks to the "Hamiltonian" industrial revolution that produced the requisite machinery to cultivate the harsh land), had transformed the Great American Desert into the bread basket of the world.

As Jefferson stood for reelection in 1804, he could bask in his many accomplishments. Indeed, he could look back on an astonishingly successful first term. He had greatly calmed the bitter partisanship that had divided the country prior to his presidency; he had greatly reduced the national debt; he had ended the potential for militarism by curtailing the size and expense of the armed forces; he had cut taxes, and he had doubled the size of the Republic at remarkably little cost. Jefferson was more confident than ever that the Republic could preserve itself through peaceful expansion. The "wise and frugal" government he had promised in 1801 was becoming a reality.

The combination of international peace, territorial expansion, and inexpensive and unobtrusive government left the Federalists without a campaign issue in the 1804 election. They knew they were going to lose not only because they had nothing with which to attack the Jefferson administration, but because they were fast becoming a leaderless and ideologically irrelevant party, detached from the mainstream of popular politics and the people in general. Nonetheless they went through the

motions of nominating Charles Pinckney of South Carolina as their presidential candidate and then watched as Jefferson captured the electoral votes of every state but Delaware and Connecticut. Jefferson even took other Federalist "heartland" states such as Massachusetts, Vermont, and New Hampshire. As he began his second term in 1805, Jefferson could assume that he had ended the Federalist threat to the Republic.

The Republic and the Napoleonic Wars, 1804–1815

No sooner did Napoleon receive his "check" from the United States for Louisiana than he used the money to resume the war in Europe, determined to crush, once and for all "the nation of shopkeepers," Great Britain. This 11-year war, like the conflicts of the 1790s, dominated United States national politics. By this time the majority favored and supported neutrality and few Republicans championed Napoleon as they had defended the 1789 French revolutionaries, and none but the most rabid Federalists wanted to intervene on the side of Great Britain. However, as will be seen shortly, neither belligerent would permit U.S. neutrality. The Louisiana Purchase demonstrated that despite its vaunted isolationism from the Old World, the United States continued to be deeply affected by events throughout the Atlantic world. At a time when Americans still relied on British markets for their farm produce and British manufactured goods, European wars directly influenced the livelihood of American farmers, merchants, and artisans. Jefferson hoped to avoid foreign entanglements but he found it impossible as president from being drawn into European wars. Even as he sought to limit the power of the national government, foreign relations compelled him to expand it.

Interestingly, at the beginning of the conflict, because their rural economies had been exhausted by the previous eight years of fighting, both France and Great Britain encouraged Americans to resume their role as neutral carriers and suppliers of food. For a time Americans made huge profits. Between 1803–1807 U.S. exported foodstuffs and plantation staples rose from $66.5 million to $102.2 million. Re-exports—goods produced in the British, French, and Spanish West Indies, picked up by American ships and then reloaded in American ports onto American vessels—rose even faster, from $13.5 million to $58.4 million. However, in 1805, the result of geopolitical changes in the European war, both Great Britain and France ended their lax trade policies with the United States and resumed their harassment of American shipping. The British more so than the French because of their superior navy and because they had just won a great naval victory at Trafalgar, off the North African coast, where they devastated the combined French and Spanish fleets. However, France remained invincible on land; Napoleon's armies won a decisive victory over Austria and Russia at the battler of Austerlitz, which gave Napoleon control of Europe. The war reached a stalemate: Napoleon's army occupied Europe and the British navy controlled the seas.

At this juncture, in hopes of starving the French into submission, Great Britain decided that in order for such a plan to succeed, they could not allow any neutral countries to trade with France. Thus beginning in 1805 and the British blockade of France, the Royal Navy began once again seizing American ships engaged in the re-export trade with France. The

Jefferson administration decided it was time to get tougher with the belligerents and with the British in particular. In Jefferson's view the diplomatic approach of his predecessors had failed and thus Jefferson was willing to explore other means of getting the belligerents' attention and respect for American neutral rights. In the spring of 1806 an angry Republican Congress passed the Non-Importation Act, which forbade the import of British goods that could be bought elsewhere or that could be manufactured in the United States. With the passage of that measure it became clear Jefferson believed that the time for diplomacy had passed and now it was time for more drastic action such as economic sanctions. No doubt Alexander Hamilton, although dead as a result of his duel with Aaron Burr, was exultant in his grave, for this was precisely the scenario he believed his programs would have prevented; that is, an American economy unable to sustain itself without foreign trade. The Non-Importation Act hurt Americans across the nation because the U.S. was dependent on England in particular, for most of its manufactured goods. Moreover, Great Britain was still the United States' best trading partner, and thus if Americans could not trade with Britain, the economic impact on the United States, especially on New England, whose entire economy was commercially oriented, would be disastrous. The French issued decrees that, in conjunction with Great Britain's Order in Council, virtually outlawed all American commerce with Europe. The British also resumed the impressment of American sailors, and by the time of the War of 1812, an estimated 6,000 American citizens had been impressed into the Royal Navy. As in the past, Great Britain remained the most egregious violator of American neutrality and potentially the greatest threat to American security. By 1807 war with Great Britain appeared imminent as anti-British rallies and demonstrations took place in American cities and towns in which cries for war were heard constantly. Jefferson responded by barring British ships from American ports and American territorial waters and by ordering state governors to call up as many as 100,000 militiamen. The United States in 1807 stood at the brink of war with the most powerful nation in the world.

While dealing with the British, Jefferson also had to contend with other maritime issues, those caused by the "Barbary pirates" of North Africa, who had been harassing European shipping in the Mediterranean and the Atlantic for several years, by either attacking ships directly or by demanding tribute. In order to avoid being attacked, several countries paid the impost; to protect their vessels from the pirates. Until Jefferson's presidency, the United States had paid extortion as well. Jefferson however, refused demands for increased payments, and the pasha of Tripoli (present-day Libya) declared war on the United States. Jefferson ordered the U.S. Navy and marines to North Africa and after three years of fighting, the navy won a decisive victory in 1804 at Tripoli Harbor, bringing an end to the conflict. The defeat of the Barbary pirates demonstrated Jefferson's resolve to use force when necessary to defend American sovereignty and honor. However, Jefferson knew that war with either Great Britain or France would be a completely different conflict, one which the United States could easily lose. Thus, like his predecessors, he ignored the public clamors for war with Great Britain and continued to pursue neutrality. Indeed, Jefferson wanted to avoid war at all costs; war inevitably brings high taxes, government debt, the repression of dissent, and the creation of a bloated military and civil service—precisely the evils that Jefferson

had vowed to eliminate. Worse, war carried the danger of defeat and thus the possible failure of America's republican experiment.

Jefferson had one more card to play: He could suspend U.S. trade with Europe altogether, thus keeping American ships out of harm's way. At Jefferson's urging and browbeating, Congress in December 1807, passed the Embargo Act, which forbade American ships from leaving United States ports and denying all foreign vessels access to American ports and trade. In effect, the Embargo Act cut off all U.S. exchange with the outside world. What prompted Jefferson to push for such a drastic measure? For many years Jefferson had assumed that U.S. farm products and U.S. markets for imported goods had become crucial to the European economies. However, within less than a year's time it became clear that the United States was more dependent on foreign trade than either of the belligerents. Indeed, both France and England simply found new markets, which was relatively easy for them to do because they both had empires at their disposal for the products they needed but were previously obtained from the United States. When it became obvious that the Embargo Act had backfired, that it was devastating the American economy and commerce with little affect on the belligerents, Jefferson repealed the decree before leaving office in 1809, replacing it with the Non-Intercourse Act, which banned trade with only Britain and France but stipulated that if either side rescinded its edicts against U.S. shipping, commerce with that country would resume.

For the year and a half that it was in effect, the Embargo Act proved to be one of the most economically disastrous acts ever passed in American history. Before its passage American exports had stood at $108 million. By the end of 1808 they had dropped to $22 million.

The economy slowed in every section of the country, but the hardest hit area was of course New England, whose entire economic orientation was based on ship-building and shipping, and if such enterprises were shut down, the entire New England economy would feel the impact. While the ocean-going merchant fleets rotted at anchor, unemployed sailors, dockworkers, and other maritime workers and their families sank to levels of despair that had seldom been seen in British North America. New England Federalists were especially outraged, convinced that although Jefferson had not overtly sought revenge on them for the Alien and Sedition Acts during his first term, he was doing so now by economically ruining them, individually as well as collectively. The Federalists accused Jefferson of plotting an end to commerce and reversion to rural barbarism, and they often took the lead in trying to subvert the embargo through smuggling and other means. In short, the Federalists saw the Embargo Act as Jefferson's last attempt to destroy them once and for all.

As a result of the Embargo Act, the Federalists, who but three years earlier appeared to be a party on the brink of extinction, found themselves resuscitated. In the 1808 presidential election their candidate C.C. Pinckney of South Carolina, received 47 electoral votes to James Madison's 122. Madison, Jefferson's old ally, best friend, and Secretary of State, was the president's chosen successor. Four years earlier, Pinckney had received only 14 electoral votes to Jefferson's 162. Although the Republicans retained control of both Houses of Congress, Federalists made significant gains in Congress and won control of several state legislatures, especially in New England and the mid-Atlantic states—those commercial regions of the country that were the most adversely affected by the Embargo Act. Federalist opposition to the act, and to the supposed Southern, agrarian stranglehold on national power that stood behind it, was clearly gaining ground.

The Road to War: James Madison's Presidency

Only a handful of individuals in United States history became president during times of intense crises and James Madison was one of those men. At home as well as abroad, Madison had to contend with serious issues, unleashed by international events beyond his control and which he inherited from his predecessor. If not carefully and skillfully managed these tensions could escalate into war with a foreign nation with grave domestic consequences. Madison was aware of all such potential ramifications of his actions and made the avoiding of war with Great Britain a priority. However, as will be seen shortly, both international and domestic pressures proved too overwhelming for Madison to avoid a conflict of arms and thus he became the first president of the Republic to fight a "foreign war." To his credit, down to the eleventh hour, Madison did all he could to avoid a fight but to no avail. Neither the British government nor many of his own people would allow him any alternative but war.

When Madison took office in the spring of 1809, it was clear the embargo had failed to coerce the British into stopping their seizure of American ships and men. As noted earlier, the act had devastated the American economy and led to the loss of 90 percent of the government's revenue. The Non-Intercourse Act, which had replaced the Embargo Act, had proved equally ineffective, with neither

England nor France complying. Madison, determined to preserve peace, tried yet another "economic sanction": Macon's Bill No. 2, which passed Congress in 1810. The bill was a strange piece of legislation that rescinded the ban on trade with France and Britain but then authorized the president to reimpose non-intercourse on either belligerent if the other agreed to respect American neutral rights of trade. In September 1810 the wily Napoleon decided that he would lift his decrees against American shipping, hoping, that such a display of "magnanimity" would lead the United States into conflict with Great Britain, for he knew the likelihood of his enemy accepting anything short of American support for the British cause was remote. Madison accepted the French pledge, and then issued a proclamation that the British had three months to follow suit. Madison believed his position was "at least an extrication from the dilemma, of a mortifying peace, or a war with both the great belligerents."

In the end Madison's actions led to war. The British refused to revoke their Orders in Council and told the Americans to withdraw their restrictions on British trade. The United States would either have to obey British trade mandates (thus making American exports and the American merchant marine a part of the British war effort—a neocolonial status utterly repugnant to most Americans) or go to war. When Congress reconvened in November 1811, it voted military measures in preparation for war with Great Britain.

The Rise of the Warhawks

While Madison tried to avert conflict with Great Britain, he simultaneously faced the strident and at times insulting clamors for war in Congress. Leading the charge for war against Great Britain were a group of newly-elected super-nationalistic, jingoistic, expansionist young lions, mostly from the South and West. This new generation of political leaders had come of age after the winning of independence and thus their fervent nationalism. Their leaders included Henry Clay and Richard M. Johnson of Kentucky, the former elected Speaker of the House of Representatives in 1810; John C. Calhoun and William Lowndes of South Carolina; George M. Troup of Georgia, and Peter B. Porter of the Niagara district of New York. These were just a few of the more bellicose and chauvinistic members of the group. The War Hawks spoke passionately of defending national honor against British insults, but they also had more specific goals in mind, such as the annexation of Canada. "Agrarian cupidity [greed], not maritime rights," declared Congressman John Randolph of Virginia "urges the war. We have heard but one word, Canada, Canada, Canada!" Randolph exaggerated, for many Southern War Hawks were equally expansionist minded, agitating for the conquest of Spanish Florida, long a bane for Southern slave owners because it had become a haven for fugitive slaves. Members of Congress also spoke of the necessity of upholding the principle of free trade and liberating the United States once and for all from European infringements on its independence. Unimpeded access to overseas markets was essential if the agrarian republic were to prosper.

Aiding the War Hawks in their taking control of Congress were the many fissures in both the Republican and Federalist Party, especially among its older members, who divided on the issue of war. The Federalist minority, which was united against Madison, was joined on many issues by northeastern Republicans who followed the pro-British

Federalist line on international trade, and by Republicans who wanted a more powerful military than their other compatriots would allow. Also opposed to Madison were the self-styled Old Republican Southerners, led by John Randolph. Thus it was a deeply divided Congress that met the war crisis.

However under War Hawk leadership, especially that of Henry Clay, the Republican divisions disappeared as Clay and his fellow Hawks imposed order and unity on their congressional compatriots. As Speaker, Clay controlled debate, packed key committees with like-minded individuals, and worked tire-lessly behind the scenes to bring his colleagues together on the issue of war with Great Britain. In the winter and spring of 1811–1812, the War Hawks led Congress into a declaration of war. In November they voted military prepara-tions, and in April they enacted a 90-day embargo—not to coerce the British but to get American ships safely into port before war began. On June 1, 1812, Madison sent a war message to Congress. This was to be the first declared under the Constitution, and the presi-dent stayed out of congressional domain by not asking specifically for a declaration of war. He did, however, present a list of American grievances that could be interpreted in no other way: the enforcement of the Orders in Council, even within U.S. territorial waters; the impressment of American sailors; the use of spies and provocateurs within the United States; and the wielding of "a malicious influ-ence over the Indians of the Northwest Terri-tory." Madison concluded that war had in fact begun: "We behold on the side of Great Britain a state of war against the United States; and on the side of the United States, a state of peace toward Great Britain."

Congress declared war on June 18, 1812. The vote was far from unanimous, despite the War Hawks assiduous attempts to make it so. In the House, the vote was 79 to 49 and in the Senate, 19 to 13. All 30 Federalists voted no and so did one in five Republicans, nearly all of them from the Northeast, where anti-war sentiment was loud and strong. Thus the war became a Republican war, more particularly a Southern and Western Republican war, with the Northeast, whose commercial rights were supposedly the main issue, adamantly opposed to the declaration.

Native Americans and the Impending War with Great Britain

The growing crisis with Great Britain took place against a backdrop of deteriorating U.S.-Indian relations, especially in the West, which also helped put the United States on the path toward war. Thomas Jefferson had long advocated removing those Native Americans east of the Mississippi River who refused to cooperate in "civilizing" themselves. The Louisiana Purchase made Jefferson even more determined to pursue a removal policy. "The acquisition of Louisiana," he wrote, "will, it is hoped, put in our power the means of inducing all the Indians on this side [of the Mississippi River] to transplant themselves to the other side." In short, Jefferson wanted to completely eliminate, by removal, all of who were left of the native peoples east of the Mississippi River; to force them, in effect, to migrate to the territory west of the river. To put this pol-icy into action, Jefferson purchased as much land west of the Appalachian mountains as he could, hoping that such a scheme would allow the Indians the ability to move further west with their "money," buy land somewhere else and transform themselves in the process into "civilized" yeoman farmers. Such an expectation was delusional; few Native Americans understood the value of money or did they have any intention of buying land with that money, or of "settling" down and becoming simple farmers. Jefferson even encouraged traders to lend money to Indians in hope that accumulating debt would force them to sell some of their holdings, thus freeing up more land for "our increasing numbers." It was clear Thomas Jefferson believed the United States was for white people only and that all other inhabitants either had to adapt to Anglo-American ways or step aside and move somewhere else. Yet, at the same time, Jefferson's administration continued Washington's policy of promoting settled farming among the Indians. Benjamin Hawkins, a friend of Jefferson who served as American agent for Indian affairs south of the Ohio River, encouraged African-American slavery among the tribes as one of the "signs" that Native Americans in the region were becoming "civilized" by adopting one of white America's more salient manifestations of "property" ownership.

The Native American Response

By 1800, nearly 400,000 white American settlers lived west of the Appalachian Mountains. They far outnumbered the remaining Native American tribes. The Indians' seemingly irreversible decline in power and in numbers led some leaders to rethink their opposition to assimilation. Such sentiment was strong among the Creek and Cherokee, whose respective chiefs, the mixed-bloods, Major Ridge for the Creeks and John Ross for the Cherokee, enthusiastically supported the federal policy of promoting "civilization." Many mixed-bloods had established businesses as traders and slave

owning farmers with the help of their white fathers. Such a disposition was strongest among the various tribes of "mixed-bloods," who became increasingly more present as a result of white advancement into the Old Southwest. The mixed-bloods assimilationist views infuriated "nativists" who wished to root out European influences and resist further white encroachments on Indian lands.

The period from 1800 to 1812, was an "age of prophecy" among many Native American peoples. Movements for the revitalization of Indian life arose among some Creeks and Cherokees, Shawnees, Iroquois, and many other Northwestern tribes. However, most of these particular leaders were accommodationists, believing continued armed resistance to the white onslaught into their lands to be futile, and none advocated any sort of Pan-Indian movement as a way to better defend their rights. Handsome Lake of the Seneca, who had overcome an earlier addiction to alcohol, preached that Indians must refrain from fighting, gambling, drinking, and sexual promiscuity. He believed Indians could regain their autonomy without directly challenging whites or repudiating all white ways, and he urged his people to take up farming and attend school.

Tecumseh's Vision

A more militant and prideful message was propagated by two Shawnee brothers, Tecumseh, a chief, who had refused to sign the Treaty of Greenville in 1795, and Tenskwatwa, a "medicine-man" and religious prophet who called for the complete separation from whites, the revival of traditional Indian culture, and resistance to federal policies. White people, Tenskwata ("The Prophet") preached, were the source of all evil in the world, and Indians should abandon American alcohol, clothing, food, and manufactured goods. The Prophet was a mesmerizing, charismatic speaker, who acquired a huge following among several tribes in the Northwest, many of whom after hearing his exhortations, were ready to unite and repel the white invaders. His disciples became so numerous that a town, specifically for them and their leader, was built on the Wabash River in Indiana, appropriately name Prophetstown.

Tecumseh meanwhile traversed the Mississippi River Valley attempting to unite all the tribes of the region into a pan-Indian alliance, which he believed imperative if Native Americans had any chance of surviving the continuing white onslaughts. The alternative to resistance, Tecumseh declared, was extermination. "Where today are the Pequot?" he asked. "Where are the Narragansett, the Mohican, the Pocanet, and other powerful tribes of our people? They have vanished before the avarice [greed] and oppression of the white man, as snow before the summer sun." Indians, he proclaimed, must recognize that they were a single people and unite in claiming "a common and equal right in the land." He repudiated the accommodationist and assimilationist chiefs who had sold land to the federal government and who believed white America was willing to integrate Native Americans into their culture. To Tecumseh, all such hopes were delusional and in the end would lead to the complete annihilation of the Native American peoples. "Sell a country! Why not sell the air, the great sea, as well as the earth? Did not the Great Spirit make them all for the use of his children?" In 1810 Tecumseh, with British help—arms, money, and supplies—had succeeded in uniting several thousand Native Americans in the Mississippi Valley into a confederated alliance and with such a force began attacking white frontier settlements in the region. In November 1811, while Tecumseh was absent, American forces under William Henry Harrison, attacked and destroyed Prophetstown in the Battle of Tippecanoe.

The War of 1812: The "Second War of Independence"

In retrospect, it seemed remarkably foolhardy for a disunited and militarily unprepared nation to go to war with one of the world's two major powers. Moreover, with the expiration of the 1811 charter of the Bank of the United States and the refusal of Northern merchants and bankers to loan money because they opposed the war (with many outright sympathetic if not supportive of the British), the government found it difficult to finance the war. Before the conflict ended, the nation was essentially bankrupt. As will be revealed in the discussion of the war, the War of 1812 was one of those wars that should never had occurred but was inevitable!

The War Hawks had pushed the Madison administration into a war to defend American sovereignty and honor, to secure American western territory, and the maritime rights of the United States. However, no sooner did the shooting start, than they war they planned and fought reflected the not the larger issues noted above but rather the more chauvinistic interests of Southern and Western Republican expansionism. Federalists and their Northeastern Republic allies expected a naval war. After all, it was on the high seas that the British had committed their most egregious violations of American rights and sovereignty. Many remembered the U.S. Navy's successes in the quasi-war against France (discussed in the last chapter) and believed the U.S. Navy was capable of producing the same results in this conflict. The War Hawks, however, had a different view and purpose for this war. They saw the conflict as the perfect opportunity for American expansion, especially northward, with an invasion of Canada and subsequent annexing of that British province to the United States. If that was their priority, then the army, not the navy, had to be strengthened. Reasoning that no U.S. naval force could challenge British control of the seas then it was time to prepare for a land invasion of Canada. Federalist and the Old Republicans were outraged by this idea and charged Madison with having deceived them about the war's purpose. They accused Madison and the War Hawks of planning a war of territorial aggression. The Old Guard could protest all they wanted; the invasion of Canada was a given. The War Hawks believed Canada was ripe for the taking because it was lightly garrisoned and with a population of only half a million (many of them French and American émigrés, whose loyalty to England, the War Hawks believed, was suspect), made Canada seem the easiest and most logical place in which to hurt the British. It was also from bases in Canada that the British supplied Tecumseh's formidable Indian confederacy. Canada was both valuable and vulnerable, and American policymakers reasoned that they could take Canada and hold it hostage while demanding that the British back down on other issues.

As had occurred during the War for Independence, American ambitions for taking Canada quickly turned into fiascoes and humiliating defeat. First, the United States miscalculated overall British strength. True, the number of British troops in Canada was relatively small, but the Americans underestimated the number of Indian allies the British had at their disposal, which was several thousand. Moreover, American generals such as William Hull, governor of the Michigan

Territory took into Canada an invasion force of rag-tag militia and volunteers, not professional soldiers and they were easily defeated by the British and their Indian allies. The combined native-British contingent force not only drove the U.S. forces out of Upper Canada (Ontario) but proceeded under the leadership of General Isaac Brock, to invade the United States! The British and their Indian allies occupied many of the remaining American garrisons in the Northwest and transformed the U.S. incursion into a British occupation of the Northwest. Another U.S. foray from the east fared o better; its 6,000 man force of mostly New York and Ohio militia with a small contingent of U.S. regulars, were routed and slaughtered at the Battle of Queenston Heights in western Ontario, near where the Niagara River separates Ontario from western upstate New York. The Canadian invasion debacles was making it clear that Jefferson's beloved republican militia was completely incapable (as they had been in the War for Independence) of fighting outside of their own "backyards," and of standing toe-to-toe against trained, disciplined, professional soldiers, no matter how few in number they might be. As the winter of 1812 set in it was clear that Canada would not fall as easily as the Americans had assumed. Not only had they been militarily defeated and humiliated but much to their chagrin, a supposed apathetic Canadian population did not hail the American invaders as "liberators" but rather as uncouth, ramshackled, wild frontier misfits and interlopers. The American loyalist émigrés were not about to welcome the very people who had driven them from their homes in America in the aftermath of the War for Independence. Indeed, by the time of the war, the assortment of Tory expatriates, discharged British soldiers, and even American-born set-

Battle Campaigns of the War of 1812. The War of 1812 was largely a naval war, fought along the Atlantic coast, in the Gulf of Mexico, and on the Great Lakes. Several land campaigns proved important, however: the British ground attack that ended in the looting and burning of the capital, and Jackson's trek overland to New Orleans.

tlers who had migrated to Canada had become a self-consciously British-Canadian people who simply did not like Americans. Even the French Catholics of Quebec and Montreal viewed the Americans as invaders and did not come to their assistance. Indeed, for these particular *canadiens,* this was a war between two groups of *Anglais,* whom French Canadians saw as no different than all the rest of the English-speaking people around them.

Tecumseh's Last Stand

Like the War for Independence, the War of 1812 became a two-front struggle—against the British and against Native Americans. Tecumseh's Indian confederacy, bruised but not broken in the Battle of Tippecanoe, allied itself with the British in 1812. Tecumseh, who had married and English woman and who spoke perfect "King's English," was commissioned a general in the British army. On a trip to the Southern tribes Tecumseh found the traditionalist wing of the Creeks—led by prophets who called themselves Red Sticks—willing to join his pan-Indian alliance. The augmented confederacy provided stiff resistance to United States forces throughout the war. The Red Sticks chased settlers from much of Tennessee. They then attacked a group of settlers who had taken refuge in at stockade surrounding the house of an Alabama trader named George Mims. In what whites called the Massacre at Fort Mims, the Red Sticks (reputedly with the help of black slaves within the fort) killed at least 247 men, women, and children. In the Northwest, Tecumseh's warriors, fighting alongside the British, spread terror throughout scores of white settlements.

Although routed on land, U.S. forces ironically fared better on water against the nation reputed to have the greatest navy in the world. However, it must be remembered that until Napoleon's defeat in 1814, the British were forced to fight the United States with only those troops and ships already stationed in North America; they simply could not spare the manpower or ships, preoccupied as they were with defeating Napoleon, which to British policymakers and war strategists was their priority. They simply could not reinforce their army or navy in North America until Napoleon had been defeated. This of course proved a great boon to the United States' chances for victory. Such was the scenario that played out on Lake Erie, where an American naval victory over the vaunted British navy not only boosted American morale but proved to be one of the United States' greatest and most important triumphs in the war.

The barriers of Niagara Falls kept Britain's saltwater navy out of the upper Great Lakes, and on Lake Erie the British and Americans engaged in a frenzied shipbuilding contest through the first year of the war. The Americans won. In September 1813 Commodore Oliver Hazard Perry cornered the British fleet at Put-in-Bay and destroyed it. Control of Lake Erie enabled the U.S. to cut off supplies to the British in the Northwest, and as a result, a U.S. army under William Henry Harrison retook the area and continued on into Canada in search of Tecumseh's Indian forces, which they found on October 5, 1813 at the Thames River. In the ensuing battle, Tecumseh was killed and with his death, the pan-Indian alliance he had

The Taking of the City of Washington, an 1814 engraving produced in London, portrays the assault during which the British forces captured the undefended city and burned the White House, the Capitol, and several warships.

worked so hard to put together soon dissipated. Tecumseh's body was ravaged by American soldiers, with many taking as souvenirs pieces of his hair, clothing, and swatches of skin torn from his corpse. The following spring, in March 1814, General Andrew Jackson's Tennessee militia aided by pro-assimilation Choctaw, Creek, and Cherokee, defeated the hostile Red Stick Creeks at the Battle of Horseshoe Bend in Alabama. Although called a battle, the confrontation was a massacre of over 800 Creek Indians, many of whom were women and children. Apparently Jackson sought revenge for the Fort Mims attack

Fort McHenry is best known for its role in the War of 1812, when it successfully defended Baltimore Harbor from an attack by the British navy in Chesapeake Bay. It was this bombardment that inspired Francis Scott Key to write "The Star-Spangled Banner."

and thus showed no mercy on the Creeks. Jackson dictated the terms of surrender, requiring the Indians, hostile and friendly alike, to cede more than half their land, over 23 million acres to the federal government. With the Battle of the Thames and the Battle of Horseshoe Bend, the military power of the Native American peoples east of the Mississippi River was broken forever.

In 1814, having finally defeated Napoleon (at least for a year; he would return to power briefly in 1815 and in June of that year, would meet final defeat at Waterloo), thus ending the larger conflict of which the War of 1812 was a "sideshow," Britain could now concentrate their resources on the American war. They already had blockaded much of the American Atlantic coastline from Georgia to Maine and during the summer of 1814 began raiding the shores of Chesapeake Bay. Emboldened by the weak American resistance they met on their marauding forays, they decided to attack Washington, D.C., chasing the army and politicians out of town and then burning down the capitol and the president's mansion. The British sacking of Washington was more an act of retribution than the implementation of a scorched-earth policy. Earlier an American army had torched the Canadian capital of York (Toronto). The British then proceeded to attack the much larger city of Baltimore but they could not blast their way past the determined garrison that commanded the harbor, Fort McHenry. One of the battle's spectators, Francis Scott Key, was so inspired by American resistance that he wrote "The Star-Spangled Banner," a doggerel poem that was later set to music and chosen as the national anthem in the 1930s. By the close of 1814, the war had reached a stalemate: Britain had repulsed American attempts to conquer Canada and had blockaded the American coast, but neither side could take and hold the other's territory.

The British now shifted their attention to the Gulf Coast, in particular to the city of New Orleans, which they deemed of vital importance to the United States because it was the hub of the nation's trans-Appalachian trade and communication networks. Peace negotiations had begun in August 1814 in Ghent, Belgium so the British wanted to capture the city and hold it as a bargaining chip. However, waiting behind an impregnable fortification of cotton bales that he had palisaded around the city, Andrew Jackson was already at New Orleans, waiting for the British to attack. The British landed about 7,000 men at New Orleans in late December 1814, and for several days exchanged artillery barrages with the Americans. Finally, on January 8, 1815, the British launched their offensive, hurling 6,000 men in a frontal assault, across open ground toward 4,000 Americans concealed behind cotton bale breastworks. Suffice it to say, the British were slaughtered, cut down by the American's withering fire. The charge lasted half an hour and when the smoke cleared, 2,000 British soldiers lay dead or wounded. American casualties numbered only 70. Behind the American barricades, Jackson commanded a most interesting army: U.S. regulars, Tennessee and Kentucky militiamen, clerks, workingmen, and free blacks from the city, and about 1,000 French pirates under the leadership of the legendary Jean Lafite, who had become a close friend of Andrew Jackson. The war produced a number of heroes, many of whom parlayed their fame into prominent political careers, two of whom eventually became presidents of the United States: Andrew Jackson and William Henry Harrison.

By this time, with neither side wishing to continue the conflict, the United States and Great Britain signed the Treaty of Ghent in December 1814, ending the war. That was about all the accord did; none of the issues that had caused the war were addressed and would not be until years later. However, at that moment neither side cared; they just wanted an end to hostilities, especially the English who had been at war since the early 1790s and were exhausted. The Americans too were anxious for war's end for they too were tired of fighting even though they had only been in combat for less than 18 months! Considering that the war had not been a military success for the United States, the Treaty of Ghent was about as good an outcome as could be expected.

The End of the Federalist Party: The Hartford Convention

Jefferson and Madison succeeded in accomplishing what both men considered to be one of their paramount objectives: the extinguishing of the Federalist Party. As noted earlier in this chapter the war momentarily revitalized Federalist fortunes. With antiwar sentiment at its peak in 1812, Madison won reelection by the relatively narrow margin of 128 electoral votes to 89 over his Federalist challenger, the New Yorker DeWitt Clinton. Although losing the presidential election for the fourth straight time, many Federalists were nonetheless sanguine the war had rejuvenated their party to the point that victory in the next presidential election was a real possibility. However, the Federalists' party's penchant for self-destruction rather than continued resuscitation took over. In December 1814, a group of New England Federalists assembled at Hartford, Connecticut, to ventilate their party's long-standing grievances, especially the Republicans' economic proscription policies and the domination of the federal government by Virginia presidents and their own region's declining influence as new western states entered the Union. Dominating the gathering were what were left of the old High Federalists, many of whom had always been or had become in their later years abolitionists and thus the convention called for an amendment to the Constitution for the eradication of the three-fifths clause, which they rightly asserted strengthened Southern political power disproportionately and thus at New England's expense. They also advocated that a two-thirds vote of Congress be established for the admission of new states, declarations of war, and laws restricting trade. Contrary to later myth, the Hartford Convention did not call for secession or disunion. However, convention Federalists did affirm the right of a state to "interpose" its authority (nullify federal laws) if the federal government "violated" the Constitution—according to that state's interpretation. Adding to Federalist woes was the fact that during the war the New England states seldom met their quotas of militiamen for the war effort, and some Federalist leaders had openly encouraged resistance to the war. The British had encouraged that obstruction by not extending their naval blockade to the New England coast, and throughout the first year of the war, New England merchants and farmers traded freely with the enemy. Forty years earlier New Englanders were in the forefront of American colonial protest against alleged English tyranny; indeed New England was the epicenter of resistance and eventual armed rebellion against British authority. At the time many Southerners saw them as wild-eyed radical republicans. Times had obviously changed since the 1770s and early 19th century New Englanders, led by the Federalists, were now perceived by Southerners and Westerns as reactionaries bent on destroying republicanism either by proscription (the Sedition

Act) or by betraying the country by aiding and abetting its enemy.

The Hartford Convention had barely adjourned when news of Jackson's victory at New Orleans electrified the nation. "Rising Glory of America,' one newspaper exulted. In speeches and sermons, political and religious leaders alike proclaimed that Jackson's triumph revealed, once again, that a divine hand oversaw America's destiny. The Federalists' antiwar convention caused many Americans to believe them unpatriotic if not traitors. Within a few years their party no longer existed. Its stance on the war was only one cause of the party's demise. The urban commercial and financial interests the party championed represented a small minority in an expanding agricultural economy. Their elitism and distrust of the common people placed Federalists more and more at odds with the new nation's democratic ethos. Yet, in their dying moments Federalists had raised an issue—Southern domination of the national government—that would long outlive their political party. Ironically, as will be seen in the next chapter, at war's end and over the course of the next several decades, especially in the North, a profound social and economic transformation would occur that strengthened the very forces of commercial development that the Federalists had championed and the Republicans had disdained and feared.

Conclusion

A number of contemporaries called the War of 1812 "The Second War of American Independence." Despite widespread opposition to the conflict, it confirmed the ability of a republican government to conduct a war without sacrificing its institutions. Jackson's victory at New Orleans not only made him a national hero but also became a celebrated example of the ability of virtuous citizen soldiers to defeat the forces of despotic Europe.

The war also completed the conquest of the area east of the Mississippi River, which had begun during the Revolution. Never again would the Indians or the British pose a threat to American control of this vast region. The war also marked the end of Native American resistance to the white onslaught that would engulf the Old Northwest and Southwest in the years following the conflict's end. In the war's aftermath, white settlers poured into Indiana, Michigan, Alabama, and Mississippi, bringing with them their distinctive forms of social organization. "I have no doubt," Jackson wrote to his wife, "but in a few years the banks of the Alabama will present a beautiful view of elegant mansions and extensive rich and productive farms." Jackson did not mention that those estates would be built and the land cultivated by slaves.

Britain's defeat of Napoleon inaugurated a long period of peace in Europe, and as a result, Americans no longer had to worry about European affairs obtruding upon their daily lives, and thus Americans' sense of separateness from the Old World grew ever stronger in the decades after the war.

Perhaps the most important repercussion of the War of 1812 was its impact on Jeffersonian agrarianism. Indeed at war's end, Jefferson saw that he must sacrifice his dreams of agrarianism. Throughout this political life, Jefferson envisioned American yeomen trading farm surpluses for European manufactured goods—a relationship that would ensure rural prosperity, prevent the growth of cities and factories, and thus sustain the landed independence on which republican citizenship rested. Westward expansion, he had believed, would guarantee the yeoman republic for generations to come. However, by 1816 Jefferson sadly realized that he had deluded himself; that he had been naïve, for the war revealed the flaws of his agrarian ethos; his policies had made the United States vulnerable and weak, unable to sustain itself in times of crises. As Jefferson reflected and lamented, his own party was taking steps to atone for Jeffersonianism's shortcomings; measures that would help transform the yeoman republic into a market society and a boisterous capitalist democracy in the decades ahead.

Suggested Readings

Lance Banning. *The Jeffersonian Persuasion: Evolution of a Party Ideology.* (1978). A studious examination of Jeffersonian ideas, relating them to the ideological origins of the American Revolution.

Richard Hofstadter. *The Idea of a Party System: The Rise of Legitimate Opposition in the United States,* 1780-1840. (1969). A study of how Americans began by rejecting the idea of organized political parties and ended up accepting their legitimacy.

James P. Ronda. *Lewis and Clark Among the Indians.* (1984). An account of the most famous exploring party in American history.

Adam Rothman. *Slave Country: American Expansion and the Origins of the Deep South.* (2005). A pioneering study of how the United States secured control of what are now the Gulf States, opening the door for expansion of slavery.

Marshal Smelser. *The Democratic Republic, 1801-1815.* (1968). Still the best narrative history of the presidencies of Jefferson and Madison.

John Sugden. *Tecumseh's Last Stand.* (1985). Relates the rise and fall of the era's most prominent Indian leader.

Steven Watts. *The Republic Reborn: War and the Making of Liberal America, 1790-1820.* (1987). An examination of the causes and consequences of the War of 1812.

Gregory Evans Dowd. *A Spiritual Resistance: The North American Indian Struggle for Unity, 1745-1815.* (1992). Dowd argues for the emergence in Jeffersonian America, of a coordinated and militant resistance, led by prophets like Tenskwatawa, and his half brother Tecumseh, and expressed through a pan-Indian spiritual revival.

Peter S. Onuf. *Jefferson's Empire: The Language of American Nationhood.* (2000). Connects Jefferson's ideas about race to his idea about empire.

Robert W. Tucker and David C. Hendrickson. *Empire of Liberty: The Statecraft of Thomas Jefferson.* (1990). This exploration of Jefferson's political philosophy and foreign policy is an especially useful guide to the circumstances surrounding the Louisiana Purchase and the War of 1812.

Chapter 9

UNITY AND DIVISION IN THE EARLY REPUBLIC

In the decades after the War of 1812, Americans experienced a burst of activity and growth. Economic and geographic expansion helped to foster a new spirit of nationalism in the young republic, promoting a sense of unity among the American people. Advances in transportation and communication physically and intellectually linked Americans together in new ways, and industrial development helped Americans to create a new domestic marketplace. The American nation grew larger physically as new states and territories were added to the Union, and the population of the nation boomed as the United States received its first large influx of immigrants. For a time political factionalism receded. The Federalist Party went into decline after the end of the war, and the Democratic Republican party held sway over the executive and legislative branches. After the War of 1812, Americans entered into what many scholars have called an Era of Good Feelings.

At the same time, however, these same forces that helped to generate a sense of American unity also brought differences of opinion among Americans over the nature of the new republic. Bad feelings occurred alongside the good, as dissent and division erupted in American society over the many changes that were taking place.

The economic changes that came to the nation in the aftermath of the War of 1812 created a vigorous market economy that linked Americans together, but it also brought with it a new boom and bust cycle, which, during times of economic hardship, left many Americans questioning the nature of economic change. In addition, a sharper sense of class differentiation emerged. The new economy widened the gap between the rich and the poor, and it produced a broad middle class of Americans, many of whom sought to impose their values on the rest of the American populace.

Economic change also fostered the expansion of wage labor in the northeast, and with it came a new American working class whose members created a unique culture and sense of identity. Members of the working class sought ways to preserve their independence within the constraints of the wage labor system as well, and many formed groups that challenged economic leaders to meet their needs. A large part of this working class consisted of immigrants from places like Ireland and Germany, and their arrival became an additional source of conflict, as many Americans became concerned about how they would affect the American republic.

Economic growth also led to regional economic specialization, as the northern states increasingly became more industrial and reliant on wage labor and as the southern states became ever more dependent on staple crop agriculture and the slave labor system that was its engine. Divisions over slavery entered into American politics as the nation expanded. For the first, but not the last, time Americans were confronted with the need to find a political compromise concerning slavery that would keep the political power of the northern and southern states in balance as new states were added to the union.

Eventually, these divisive forces led to the revival of political factionalism in American society. A new party system began to emerge during the late 1820s that was defined largely by the attitudes Americans held concerning the changes that had come to the nation in the aftermath of the War of 1812.

The Rise of Manufacturing

Much of the change that came to American society was a result of the *Industrial Revolution*, a modernization process that began first in

England and then spread from there through the western world. During the last part of the eighteenth century and moving forward into the nineteenth, the English economy underwent massive change as a result of the Industrial Revolution. New sources of energy and techniques of manufacturing were developed during these years that allowed the production of man-made goods to become more extensive and efficient. A factory system arose in order to provide products that were in great demand in the world market. Especially central to the new factory system in England was the manufacturing of textiles. Machines were developed that could use water power to quickly spin cotton into thread and yarn that could then be woven into cloth.

Because of the efficiency of factories, England became an economic giant, providing most of the manufactured goods to nations in the Atlantic World, including the United States. The War of 1812, however, had stimulated American interest in developing more domestic manufacturing facilities. British goods had been cut off from the United States during the course of the war, and in the war's aftermath there was little desire to remain dependent on Great Britain for manufactured goods. Thus, in the decades after the War of 1812, Americans fostered their own industrial revolution.

Before the war, most manufacturing in America took place in households or in small workshops where artisans crafted various goods by hand. In the years after the war, Americans witnessed the rise of a factory system that was modeled on the one that existed in England. As in England, the first large American factories produced textiles.

Although Americans wanted to build textile factories like those that existed in England, it was not easy to gain the knowhow in order to make this happen. The English, hoping to hold a monopoly on the textile market, closely guarded their secrets regarding the running of factories. The English government had enacted laws forbidding the export of textile machinery, and it even went so far as to disallow the emigration of skilled workers from the nation in order to keep their knowledge from benefitting other countries. Over time however, through several incidences of industrial espionage, Americans were able to learn the secrets of the English system, which they copied and then improved upon.

The first American textile factory was actually created before the War of 1812. It would provide the foundation for the immense growth in the textile industry that would occur following the war. Samuel Slater, a British emigrant to America, established a textile mill in 1790 in Providence, Rhode Island. Slater, who had worked in a textile factory before he came to America, disguised himself as a farm laborer in order to emigrate from Great Britain to the United States. He had memorized British designs, and upon his arrival in Rhode Island he copied the English machinery from memory and built his own mill. As the British did, Slater used the labor of women and young children in order to keep the mill running. He employed entire families to do the work, giving men the most skilled positions and allowing children to work alongside their parents. At his factory, yarn was spun at the mill and then it was "put out" to home weavers who turned the yarn into cloth. This *putting out* system became characteristic of the early textile industry. In time, other Americans built their own mills, and they began to appear along the rivers of New England, where waterpower was readily available to keep the mills running.

Further innovations occurred in the American textile industry as a result of technology developed by Francis Cabot Lowell, a Bostonian who had toured an English textile mill on a visit across the Atlantic in 1810. Lowell asked questions during his tour and made sketches of the machines he saw from memory so that he could build his own mill in Massachusetts. He then improved upon this machinery with the invention of the power loom. This was an important development because it allowed finished cloth to be completed in factories rather than requiring it all to be spun in nearby homes. In 1814, with funding from a group of Boston investors known as the Boston Associates, Lowell opened up a mill using this technology in Waltham, Massachusetts. His mill was extremely efficient, producing a large amount of cloth at a relatively low cost, and the use of the power loom allowed American textile factories to compete more favorably with the British market.

In 1817, Lowell died at the age of 42, but his system lived on. The Boston Associates moved the factory to a new location, establishing a town they named Lowell in honor of the deceased inventor. At Lowell, a new type of industrial community was created. Because of available lands to the west in the United States, and the lure they held for young men, there was a labor shortage in New England at the time. The Lowell operators thus appealed to a new source of labor—young women from nearby farms who hoped to earn some money before marriage. There was some concern, however, about sending young women out into the world away from their parent's supervision. At Lowell, the mill owners responded to this anxiety with the creation a model factory town, where the women workers lived in boarding houses that were well-chaperoned. This close supervision allowed young single

Women use a Power Loom at the Lowell Textile Mills

women to maintain their respectability even as they left home to join the work force.

Although the Lowell work force was a unique one, it still is representative of what happened in northeastern American society as a result of industrialization. Young people left the support of their parents and their small communities to move out into the world in order to work in the new factories that arose. Individuals moved from farms, which were largely self sufficient, to become wage earners in an industrial environment. The rise of the factory system thus transformed not only the American economy but also the nature of work in the United States.

Regional Economic Development

A key figure in the Industrial Revolution in America was a man named Eli Whitney. Whitney would participate in the process of creating industrial innovations that would help to transform both the southern and the northern economies of the United States. He helped to introduce the use of interchangeable parts in manufacturing, a process that became known as the American System of Manufactures, in the Northeast. He also was responsible for the invention of the cotton gin, a machine that contributed to the expansion of the plantation system, and slave labor, throughout the South. His innovations, and the effect they had on the American economy in both the North and the South, remind us that the Industrial Revolution's impact was not limited to the manufacturing centers of the Northeast. It affected the South as well, but while it encouraged the growth of manufacturing and a new wage labor system in the North, in the South it prompted Americans to become even more committed to plantation agriculture and to the institution of slavery.

Whitney is perhaps best known as the man who invented the cotton gin, but his work with *interchangeable parts* was also very important in the development of the American economy. The concept of making items out of identical pieces that could be interchanged with one another originated among gun manufacturers. Before the use of interchangeable parts, each gun was unique. Therefore, if one part of the gun broke or failed, the entire gun had to be replaced. With interchangeable parts, a new part that was identical to the broken part of the gun could be ordered to make it operable. The idea of using this type of manufacturing to create guns originated in France, but because of opposition from French gunsmiths, whose livelihood the system would threaten, the process was never adopted there.

In the United States, however, American political leaders saw the benefit of producing guns made of interchangeable parts. If Americans went to war, it would make the provisioning of weapons more efficient, and the

hostilities that were brewing across the Atlantic during the last decade of the eighteenth century made war look more and more likely. In 1796, around the same time that the first textile mills were being established in the United States, the US government awarded Eli Whitney a contract to make ten thousand muskets for the army using the new methodology. He delivered on the contract in 1809, and in the process he became an outspoken promoter of the use of interchangeable parts.

In time the use of interchangeable parts became commonplace in producing American goods, so much so that it became known as the *American System of Manufactures*. In addition to firearms (including muskets, rifles and revolvers), other items like typewriters, sewing machines, and clocks were made using interchangeable parts during the course of the nineteenth century, and with time larger items like locomotives, bicycles, and automobiles were produced using the process. This American System of Manufactures promoted the growth of American industry throughout the nineteenth century and into the twentieth, and it helped northeastern Americans to become major producers of manufactured goods for the global economy.

Eli Whitney's cotton gin similarly helped to transform the southern economy of the United States. The *cotton gin*—"gin" is short for the word "engine"—was created by Whitney and introduced in 1793 in order to aid in the process of removing seeds from cotton. At the time of the invention, two types of cotton were grown in the United States. *Long-staple cotton* was one strain. This type of cotton had seeds that were easy to remove, but it could be grown only in the soil of the South Carolina and Georgia sea islands. It was thus, by necessity, a small crop in the American South. *Short-staple cotton* was more well-suited for the soil throughout much of the southern mainland, but its seeds were sticky and difficult to remove. It took an entire day for a person to clean a single pound of cotton by hand. More and more Americans wished to grow it, however, as the demand for cotton increased with the growth of the textile industry in Britain, and later, the United States. It was a very profitable crop and would become even more so if a labor-saving method could be developed in order to more easily process the cotton once picked.

Whitney responded to this demand with his device, which pulled cotton through mesh wire in order to easily remove its seeds. With it, up to fifty-five pounds of short staple cotton could be cleaned in a day. This innovation, combined with the enormous demand for cotton generated by the explosion of textile mills, encouraged planters throughout the South to grow cotton. By the time of the War of 1812, around sixty million pounds of cotton were produced in a year in the mainland portions of Georgia and South Carolina. As the money poured in, more and more southerners became cotton farmers. The plantation system moved west. Between 1816 and 1820, cotton planting expanded into Alabama, and during the next two decades it pushed further through Mississippi, across the Mississippi River, through Louisiana, and eventually into East Texas.

Along with the spread of cotton plantations came the spread of slavery. This labor system, which many had believed to be dying institution that would soon fade away, was invigorated and southerners became more committed to preserving it. Slavery had become instrumental to the prosperity of the region as cotton came to dominate the southern economy.

The changes brought by the Industrial Revolution thus helped to make regional economic differences between the North and South even more sharply defined. Wage labor, manufacturing, and the process of urbanization grew in the North, while the South remained committed to the plantation system and slavery. Cultural differences that already existed between the two regions were reinforced. At the same time, the two regions were economically interdependent, as the South provided much of the cotton for the textile mills of the North. Thus, the economic changes both joined and divided Americans in different regions of the United States. The tensions involved in this dichotomy would greatly influence the relationship between the regions in the decades to come.

A Revolution in Transportation

While the factory system and the expanding cultivation of cotton were important agents of economic transformation, developments in transportation also contributed to the process of change, promoting western expansion, regional economic specialization and a more interconnected economy. Many historians have noted the importance of the *Transportation Revolution* that took place in America during the first half of the nineteenth century. Innovations such as the steamboat, the building of canals, and, eventually, the development of a vast railroad system upon which steam powered locomotives could travel transformed the nation.

Before the Transportation Revolution, the maximum speed for overland travel in America, and throughout the world, was the speed of a horse. Water transport allowed for more efficient travel, so people throughout the world tended to cluster in settlements around rivers and coastlines, which allowed them to more easily connect with others. Most Americans rarely ventured far from home as travelling was a slow and arduous process, and economic exchanges usually took place within the community. Although a vast system of exchange existed across the Atlantic Ocean, allowing for the growth of a wealthy class of merchants in the eastern cities of eighteenth century America, most of the communities outside of the Atlantic port cities relied primarily on their local economic resources, as easy connections to a larger marketplace of goods had not yet been forged.

Americans recognized the desirability of a better transportation system as they began to expand further into the interior, and their first efforts at improvement consisted of the building of better roads. Roads in America during the eighteenth century were rough, rutted trails that were slow and uncomfortable to travel upon. Between the 1790s and 1820s there was thus a wave of road-building throughout the United States. Private companies and state governments erected *turnpikes,* paved roads that charged a toll to travelers who used them. The name turnpike refers to the barrier of sharp protrusions that would be turned aside at toll stops when a traveler paid his toll. These roads made for a swifter, more comfortable journey as Americans traveled and transported goods from one place to another.

The US government also became involved in the road-building process, using funds from the sale of public lands in the new state of Ohio, which entered the Union in 1803, to finance a *National Road* that would run from Maryland to Ohio. The road was begun in 1808 and eventually ran beyond the state of Ohio, all the way into Illinois by 1839. Towns sprung up along this road and grew rapidly, and the city of Baltimore, where the road terminated to the east, grew as trade

from the west poured in. The National Road, and other roads that were financed by individuals or state governments, eased the conditions of travel, but soon other developments would help to make travel and trade even more efficient.

During the same time that better overland roads were being constructed, Americans began to find ways to improve methods of water travel, using steam-powered shipping to move goods and people along the larger rivers of the United States. Before the steamboat was employed, barges were used to float goods down the Mississippi River to New Orleans, where they would then be shipped around to the Atlantic port cities of the nation or to Europe. Travel downstream was relatively swift, but the barges could not be floated easily back up the river. The steamboat solved this problem. In 1807 Robert Fulton constructed the first steamboat, the *Clermont,* which was used in New York, and later, in 1811, he constructed a steamboat that could navigate the swift waters of the Mississippi. Soon others created similar vessels, and steamboats appeared in rivers throughout the United States. The use of steamboats allowed for greater ease of upstream travel and for faster and cheaper trips overall.

Larger rivers thus became ever more important to Americans for travel and trade, but the roundabout route to coastal markets was still not ideal. What farmers and merchants really wanted was a way to ship goods directly to the Atlantic coastal cities from the west. The new roads that were created helped, but hauling goods over land was costly and slow. To solve this problem Americans built *canals,* man-made waterways that cut from western markets to the eastern ports. Canal transport still relied on horse power, using horses and mules along a towpath beside the canal to pull barges through the waterway, but a horse could pull more weight and make better time over long distances when the goods were pulled through water rather than over land.

Canals were expensive to build, so most of the financing was done by state governments. The first and most successful of the canals was the *Erie Canal*, which was financed by the state of New York in order to provide a waterway that would connect the Hudson River in New York to the Great Lakes. New York had a geographical advantage over other eastern cities in the construction of a canal because there was a break in the Appalachian Mountains along its route west. States south of New York had a formidable obstacle in the rugged mountain range. Even with the advantage of this gap in the range, however, the construction of the Erie Canal represented a monumental achievement. It was 363 miles long, and engineers had to deal with hills, valleys and streams that crossed its path along the way. The Erie Canal opened in 1825, and it was enormously lucrative for the state of New York. Tolls from canal traffic paid off New York's seven million dollar investment in the canal within seven years, and New York City arose as the center of American trade and finance as a result of the canal, which shifted trade away from the Mississippi River into the northern port.

The impact of the Erie Canal on the nation as a whole was profound. Not only did it contribute to the development of New York, but it also led to the rise of many prosperous towns along the waterway. The city of Chicago emerged as a major city as it became a western hub in the transportation network that

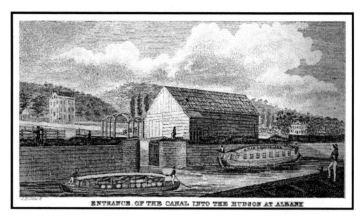

Entrance of the Erie Canal 1823, by James Eights

would develop as a result of the canal. The canal led to greater economic specialization throughout the northern part of the United States. Agriculture spread quickly west as a result of the new route, and the population of the Northwest increased. At the same time, agriculture declined in New England as it became cheaper to grow crops further west. As farming declined in the Northeast, the region became even more reliant on trade and manufacturing. The wave of western settlement had provided a new market for northeastern manufacturers who could now easily ship their products west.

Other states saw the economic advantages that New York had gained as a result of the construction of the Erie Canal, and many set out to build their own canals, even at the cost of having to push through the Appalachian Mountains. These states, however, never truly enjoyed the advantages brought by canals. They started their projects too late, and many were never completed. For by the mid-nineteenth century, another innovation in travel had appeared that proved more useful in creating an overland transportation and trade network—the railroad.

Railroads emerged in the 1820s as inventors produced steam powered locomotives that could be run along a system of tracks. The first public railroad was created in England in 1825. Americans soon followed suit, and in the 1830s track systems were built throughout the Northeast on which steam locomotives could pull train cars filled with people or with products. Railroad networks slowly grew in the 1830s, but in the decades that would follow there was an explosion of railroad construction throughout the nation that would serve to further knit the country together.

It is difficult to overestimate the impact of Transportation Revolution on American society. The innovations of the early nineteenth century created new markets that turned American attention away from the Atlantic Ocean and towards the western United States as a focus of trade. This, in turn, led Americans to feel less dependent on Europe. The innovations lowered the cost of doing business, and helped to contribute to economic growth. They also encouraged western settlement, and Americans poured in ever-larger numbers into the territories that had been added to the nation by the Louisiana Purchase. The Transportation Revolution helped to fuel an optimism among the American people as the nation grew. As we will see, however, the changes that it helped to bring about produced challenges for the American public as well.

A Revolution in Communication

Alongside the developments in transportation that took place in the early nineteenth century were developments in the ways in which people communicated with one another. It was not just products and people that could travel faster because of the technological innovations of the era. Information could as well. In addition to the other revolutionary changes taking place at this time, American society underwent a *Communications Revolution*.

Central to this revolution in communications was an invention created by Samuel F.B. Morse, the *telegraph*. Before the telegraph was invented, all information was passed through verbal or written messages delivered by one individual to another. The American Postal System was among the most efficient in the world at this time, but the rate of travel was still limited to the speed that a letter or newspaper could physically be transported from one point to another. Samuel Morse's invention changed this. He created a new system in which electric signals could be sent along a cable from one place to another to relay information instantaneously over long distances. To give meaning to these electronic signals, Morse created a new alphabet of dots and dashes, which became known as *Morse Code*. Telegraphs took hold in the United States by the 1840s, and telegraph lines were erected alongside the railroad tracks that spread through the country in the decades that followed. As more and more telegraph lines were erected, information could be relayed instantaneously over longer distances, linking Americans more tightly together. Personal and business information could be exchanged with little delay, and news developing around the nation was disseminated more rapidly, giving life a sense of immediacy that had not existed before.

Indeed, Americans became more informed about the world around them as the field of journalism underwent profound changes. As American newspapers took advantage of the telegraph in order to gain instantaneous access to the news from around the nation, several newspaper owners recognized the value in creating a clearinghouse for information, where the news could be shared cooperatively by wire and then circulated to news agencies throughout the country. In 1846, they formed the *Associated Press*, which was responsible for nationalizing and homogenizing America's news. That same year, the *rotary press*, a steam powered press, was invented, allowing newspapers to be reproduced more quickly and at a much lower cost. The invention of the rotary press ushered in the age of mass circulation newspapers. As newspapers could be sold more cheaply, more Americans purchased them and thus became better informed. A more knowledgeable and culturally connected public emerged as a result of the revolution in communications.

The "Era of Good Feelings"

After the end of the War of 1812, as America was beginning the process of all of this economic and technological development, the American political system changed as well. The first political party system collapsed as a result of the war. Although the diplomatic outcome of the fighting had essentially been a draw, Americans experienced a sense of triumph and a surge of nationalism at the end of the war. The United States had demonstrated that it could hold its own against Great Britain, and Andrew Jackson's victory at the Battle of New Orleans had made Americans feel like winners despite the fact that the war was a stalemate. Because of this surge of nationalism, the Federalist Party's opposition to the war effort made them a party of traitors in the eyes of many Americans. Thus, the Republican Party came to dominate the executive and legislative branches of the American

government after the War of 1812, as the Federalist opposition melted away. With the election of Republican candidate James Monroe in 1816, Americans entered into an era that has been referred to as the *Era of Good Feelings*, a term coined by a journalist of the time, because of the lack of partisanship. that existed and the sense of national unity that had emerged after the war. Monroe beat his Federalist opponent, Rufus King, in this election so handily that it signaled the death of that party. The president would run unopposed for his second term in 1820.

As the Republican Party rose to dominance in American politics, its character changed, moving away from some of the agrarian idealism that had been central to its ideology in earlier years. When President Madison stepped down from the presidency in 1815, he called for a more active federal government that would get involved in promoting industrial economic development. In 1816, the Republican Congress passed a major tariff to protect American manufacturing from British competition, it chartered a second Bank of the United States, and it approved the use of federal funds for the building of roads.

Ironically then, it was the small-government Jeffersonian party that ushered in this era of increasing government involvement in stimulating economic development. Why did this shift take place? It was largely a response to the tremendous growth that characterized the decades after the war ended. As the economy grew, many Americans wanted the government to help to protect American manufacturing. And as the nation grew physically, there was a hope that the government could help finance the improvements in transportation necessary in order to knit the expanding nation together. In time, factions would develop within the Republican Party over whether or not it was appropriate for the government to undertake these responsibilities, but it would take some time for these factions to shape themselves into a new, second party system.

John Marshall & the Supreme Court

Although the Republican Party controlled the elective branches of the US government, the old Federalist Party maintained its influence in the judicial branch. The chief justice of the Supreme Court, John Marshall, was a Federalist from Virginia who, during his time on the bench between 1801 and 1835, did much to expand the power of the federal government. As chief justice, Marshall strengthened the authority of the court, firmly establishing the process of *judicial review*. The concept of judicial review legitimized the court's power to evaluate the constitutionality of federal and state laws and to overturn laws that the court deemed to be in conflict with the Constitution. In addition to bolstering federal power, Marshall's court also did much to protect American business interests and nurture the growth of the modern American economy. A series of decisions made by the Supreme Court under Marshall's leadership during the decade after the end of the War of 1812 illustrate his influence on the American political system and economy.

Two important decisions were made by the court in 1819. One, *Dartmouth College* v. *Woodward*, asserted that all charters that were given to corporations by states were protected by the Constitution. The court case arose when the state of New Hampshire attempted to convert Dartmouth College, a private college that had been chartered during the colonial period, to a state university. The college

resisted this conversion, arguing that its original charter, made in 1769, was a contract that could not be broken. The Supreme Court agreed with this argument, and Marshall declared in his decision that any private corporation that received a state charter was protected by the Constitution. The charter could not be revoked by the state. This decision was far-reaching during this time of economic development, for state governments were issuing numerous corporate charters for the establishment of new factories and transportation companies. The court declared that the Constitution protected the new businesses, and the decision limited the power of states to regulate them or take away their rights as established in the original charters. The decision thus promoted the growth of the modern corporation and established the idea that the government had little power to direct or control private enterprise.

The other important decision in 1819, *McCulloch v. Maryland*, was the most significant ruling of the Marshall Court. It established the idea that there were "implied powers" that the Constitution gave to the federal government. The decision thus expanded the power of the federal government by allowing a broader interpretation of the Constitution, and it allowed the federal government to exert increasing authority over the power of the states. The case involved the decision of the state of Maryland to levy a tax on a branch of the Bank of the United States in Baltimore. Politicians in Maryland had established the tax because of their opposition to the bank and their feeling that it was unconstitutional. The tax was thus the state government's way of attacking the national bank's power. Marshall's court ruled on two questions: whether Congress had the constitutional right to establish a national bank and whether a state had the right to tax or interfere with a federal agency. Marshall referred to the idea of *implied powers* of the Constitution in his decision. He argued that, although the Constitution did not explicitly give Congress the right to establish a national bank, it did not deny Congress that right either. The establishment of the bank was legitimized by the clause of the Constitution that declared that the government had the right "to make all laws which shall be necessary and proper" for executing its duties. Because of this clause, Marshall argued, the federal government had implied powers that were not spelled out in the Constitution. The Bank was constitutional. On the second question, whether or not a state could tax a federal entity, the Marshall Court said no. The power to tax was also the "power to destroy," and the state governments had no right to attack the federal government in this way. This decision thus extended the constitutional authority of the federal government and promoted the idea of the supremacy of federal over state power.

In 1824, the court's ruling in *Gibbon v. Ogden* further increased federal power, ruling that the national government had a right to regulate interstate commerce. The ruling grew out of issues that came to light as a result of the Transportation Revolution. When Robert Fulton and his partner Robert Livingston created the first steamboat company, the state of New York had granted them a monopoly. They had the sole right to transport passengers on the Hudson River to New York City. In time, they extended their business, granting a man name Aaron Ogden the right to ferry passengers across the river to New Jersey. A competitor entered into the business, however. After obtaining a Congressional license, Thomas Gibbons opened his own ferry business. Ogden sued him for infringing upon his

territory and won in the New York courts. The Supreme Court, however, overturned this decision, declaring that the state of New York had no jurisdiction over commerce that involved another state. Congress had the power to regulate all interstate commerce. This case illustrates the issues that concerned the Marshall Court. It both extended the power of the federal government while encouraging the development of the national market economy.

The Expansion & Limits of American Power

Along with the economic development of the nation of the early nineteenth century there was a physical extension of American power. During the Era of Good Feelings, much of the political action was centered on the geographical expansion of the United States and the making of diplomatic agreements that would help to set new margins for the American nation.

After the War of 1812 ended, the Native American and British barriers to moving west had been removed, and Americans began pouring into western lands to the Mississippi River and beyond. Although new economic systems were developing in the east, most Americans were still farmers, and they were eager to seek out new fertile land where they could raise crops. In the South, plantations were established as Americans ventured further and further into the region's broad *black belt*. ("Black belt" refers to the area from Georgia to East Texas where there was rich, black soil suitable for growing cotton.) In the North, farmers sought out good lands for smaller farms that would produce much of the foodstuff of the American nation. An interconnected regional economic system, with cotton plantations in the South, industry and trade in the Northeast, and smaller farms that produced wheat and other foods in the Northwest emerged. During Monroe's presidency, five new states were admitted to the Union as Americans pushed west: Missouri, Illinois, Mississippi, Alabama and Maine. In addition Florida was purchased from Spain in 1819 at the price of $5,000,000.

The acquisition of Florida was a key development of the era. By the beginning of the nineteenth century Spain's control over Florida was weakening. Indeed Spain was suffering from internal discord at home, and Spain's hold over all of its Latin American colonies was loosening. During the first decades of the nineteenth century one Spanish colony after another overthrew Spanish rule and declared themselves as independent nations. US leaders sensed an opportunity in Spain's weakness.

The United States had already claimed West Florida by this time, and many southern Americans were now looking for an opportunity to settle in the rest of the region. Most Americans believed that the United States should be in control of all of the Atlantic Coast south of Canada. Spanish control of Florida dug at the nation's pride, and it proved problematic when Seminole Indian tribes would strike into Georgia, which they did with some frequency, and then retreat across the state border to Spanish protection. In addition, Florida was a haven for slave runaways from American plantations.

In 1818, President Monroe gave General Andrew Jackson the task of subduing the Seminole Indian population along the Georgia-Florida border, authorizing him to use any means necessary to pacify the region. Jackson interpreted his instructions as an authorization to invade Florida. He did so and quickly seized two Spanish forts at Pensacola and St. Marks. Jackson eventually ended this *Seminole War* by withdrawing from the Florida forts.

In Washington DC, there was much discussion about whether or not Jackson had overstepped his authority by capturing these Spanish forts, but John Quincy Adams, the son of second president John Adams who served as Monroe's secretary of state, saw an opportunity in Jackson's venture. In 1817, Adams had begun to negotiate with the Spanish minister, Luis de Onís, concerning the acquisition of Florida. In addition, he also wished to convince Spain to recognize the validity of the Louisiana Purchase and the American claims over that territory acquired from France. In order to pressure Onís into making an agreement favorable to the United States, he urged the US government to take responsibility for Jackson's actions. Jackson's invasion had illustrated how easy it would be for Americans to take Spanish territory by force. He hoped that this show of force would encourage Onís to agree to the sale of Florida as an alternative.

This he did. The Spanish were worried that if they did not make the sale, then the United States would take Florida and then move into Texas or other Spanish territory. In order to preserve some influence in North America, the Spanish agreed to the *Transcontinental Treaty*, also called the Adams-Onís Treaty, in 1819. By the terms of this treaty, the Spanish agreed to cede Florida to the United States for the price of $5,000,000. This money, however, did not go to Spain but instead went to American citizens who held claims against the Spanish government. In addition, Spain recognized American claims over the Louisiana Purchase territory and to lands in the Pacific Northwest above the 42nd parallel. In return, the United States agreed to not to dispute Spanish control of Texas.

In the aftermath of the War of 1812, no land had exchanged hands between the US and Great Britain, but there were still territorial issues to work out. Tensions remained high along the American-Canadian border in the immediate aftermath of war as both nations maintained troops in the Great Lakes region. In 1817, however, the *Rush-Bagot* agreement helped to demilitarize the border region. It limited the number of military vessels each nation could have on the Great Lakes, and eventually the border was fully demilitarized. In 1818, Great Britain and the United States agreed to the 49th parallel as the northern boundary of the American-controlled Louisiana territory, and it set up a system of joint control over the Oregon territory that would last at least ten years.

The Monroe administration thus worked to define new, expanded boundaries for the American nation in the aftermath of the War of 1812. Treaties were drawn up with European nations in order to ensure that there would be no encroachment on areas that Americans considered to be part of the United States. The Monroe Administration, however, also wanted to limit new European ventures in the New World as a whole.

As the Spanish empire crumbled throughout Latin America and new, independent republics were established, American leaders became concerned that Spain might try to regain these colonies. More so, however, they were anxious that other European powers might attempt to fill the power vacuum created by Spain's decline. They worried in particular that France might attempt to colonize these new, independent states. In addition Russian moves to extend its influence into Alaska from the Pacific ignited concerns. Thus, in December 1823 when President Monroe delivered his annual message to Congress, he included a statement about European colonization of the Americas in his speech. Monroe declared that the United States would resist any attempt of European powers to extend influence into the Western Hemisphere. At the same time, he promised that the United States would refrain from entangling itself in European affairs or interfering with colonies that already existed in the Americas.

In making this statement, which became known as the *Monroe Doctrine*, Monroe was exerting America's claim to a position of respect among the powerful nations of the world and announcing its intention to exercise power beyond its own borders in the Western Hemisphere if it felt it to be necessary. At the time, few Europeans paid much attention to the proclamation, and those that did expressed their contempt for American "bluster." For the

This cartoon from the early twentieth century depicts the mentality of the Monroe Doctrine and illustrates its long term influence.

most part, however, the European powers abided by Monroe's terms because they had little energy or ability at this time to exert influence over new colonies so far from home. In time, the Monroe Doctrine became an important precedent in American foreign affairs; for in later years, as Americans expanded their influence in various parts of Latin America, future administrations would refer to the Monroe Doctrine as a guiding ideology.

The Missouri Crisis

Although the economic and geographic expansion of the time often served to unify Americans and feed into a nationalistic spirit, the changes that came in the early nineteenth century fostered dissent and division as well. The political crisis that erupted when Missouri applied for statehood in 1819 exemplifies the ways in which the geographic expansion of the nation helped to contribute to rising tensions between the North and the South. At the center of this tension was the institution of slavery.

When Missouri, a portion of the territory that the US gained through the Louisiana Purchase, applied for statehood, slavery was already established in the region. Many of the settlers that had emigrated to Missouri had come from the South, and they had brought their slaves with them. It was thus a foregone conclusion that Missouri would apply to enter the Union as a slave state. Some Northern politicians, however, found this problematic. Up until this point, new states had come into the Union in pairs, preserving the balance in the Senate between the slave and the free states. The entry of Missouri would upset this balance in favor of the South. Furthermore, Missouri would be the first state besides Louisiana itself, which had been admitted as a slave state in 1812, to be created out of the Louisiana Purchase territory. There was concern that its admittance would set a precedent for the rest of the unorganized federal territories, over which there was no provision concerning slavery.

A congressman from New York, James Tallmadge, caused a stir when he responded to these northern concerns and attached an amendment to the Missouri statehood bill in February 1819. His amendment provided for a ban on the introduction of any new slaves in Missouri and it required the gradual emancipation of slaves that already resided there. This addition to the bill became known as the *Tallmadge Amendment.* The amended bill passed the House of Representatives, but the Senate repeatedly struck it down. Thus a political stalemate over the issue of Missouri statehood took place, and for the next year the nation debated what to do about the Missouri crisis. Many Americans from free states argued that Congress was within its rights to demand that slavery be abolished as part of the terms of statehood. A large number of Southerners disagreed. They argued that Congress had no such right, and that such a provision would attack the property rights of slaveholders. Furthermore, the South would be marginalized if slavery were banned from new states entering the union.

In 1820, politicians found a compromise that would ease the sectional crisis. The population of Maine, an area that had been part of Massachusetts up to this point, had submitted its own petition for statehood. If Congress admitted Maine as a free state, Missouri could be admitted with slavery, and the sectional balance in the Senate would be preserved. In February 1820, the Senate passed the *Missouri Compromise,* which provided for the admission of both of these states—Maine without slavery and Missouri with—to the Union.

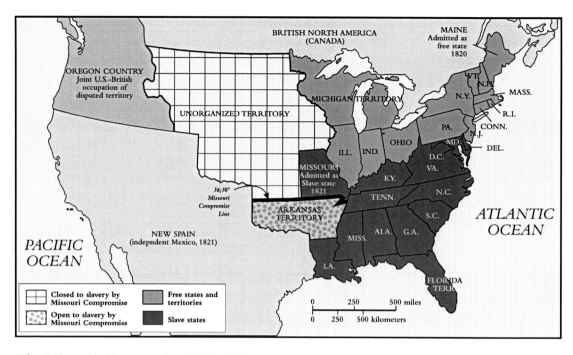

The Missouri Compromise, 1820–1821

In addition, an amendment was added to this compromise that prohibited slavery in the rest of the Louisiana Purchase territory north of Missouri's southern border, along the 36-30 line of latitude. While slavery was banned above that line, it would be allowed below it. At first the House of Representatives rejected this bill, but Speaker of the House Henry Clay was able to push through the major provisions of the compromise by breaking them down into three separate bills.

The Missouri Compromise eased sectional tensions for a time, but sectionalism would not disappear. The Missouri Crisis, Thomas Jefferson said, was a "fire bell in the night"—a warning that the issue of slavery was a dangerously divisive one for the American nation. Jefferson was right. The crisis was indeed a warning, for as Americans added new territories to the Union in later years sectional antagonisms concerning slavery and political representation would resurface, forcing Americans to search for new compromises regarding the place of slavery in the nation.

The Boom & Bust Economy

At the same time that the nation faced this crisis concerning slavery, Americans experienced the strains of their first national economic depression. After the War of 1812 ended, Americans had enjoyed a period of prosperity. During these years, because of the chaos created by the Napoleonic wars in Europe, there was a high European demand for American agricultural products, especially cotton. The high price that Americans received for their products stimulated western expansion as farmers sought new lands for cultivation, and with this expansion there was an uptick in the sale of western lands. American banks provided easy credit to settlers in order to fuel this westward surge, and more and more lands were opened to cultivation. The prosperity of this period helped to produce a widespread optimism in the American nation about the possibilities of the expanding American marketplace.

Americans would soon find, however, that this rapid growth had a downside. An economic bubble had been produced in the United States that would soon burst. In 1819, as Europe recovered from the Napoleonic wars, the demand—and thus the price—for American products fell. Farmers who had obtained credit with the expectation that the prices of their products would remain high found themselves unable to pay off their debts. Banks started calling in the loans that had fueled western expansion, and this led to many foreclosures. The lack of funds coming into the banks in turn caused widespread bank failures. Farmers were the hardest hit population during this downturn, but, because of the interconnected nature of the economy, its effects were felt throughout the nation.

These events ushered in a depression that would last for several years. Americans had experienced hardship before, but because the economy had become more interrelated after the War of 1812, this was the first depression that had such a widespread impact. Economists now know that modern market economies have a *business cycle*. A *boom* occurs when high prices can be obtained for products and the economy expands, but it is eventually followed by a *bust*, when those prices decline and the economy contracts. Americans at the time had no idea that they were entering into such a cycle, hence the name they gave to this economic downturn—the *Panic of 1819*.

Americans experiencing the hardship of depression indeed felt a panic, for they had no idea how long their suffering might last or, indeed, whether prosperity might return at all.

Prosperity, it turned out, would not return until 1823. This upturn led to a boom that lasted for a decade and a half until a second bust occurred in 1837. Recovery from this downturn began in 1843 and a third period of expansion took place, but it was of course followed by a third depression, which hit in 1857. During each economic panic many wage workers found themselves out of work, farmers lost their lands, and banks and businesses closed. Thus, while the new market economy fueled a degree of optimism about the wealth it could bring to Americans and to their nation, the roller coaster ride of the business cycle also produced heavy doses of anxiety about the economic hardship that it could produce.

Social Structures of the New Economy

The changing American economy brought other tensions as well; for economic shifts contributed to a reordering of American society. Although Americans had always had social divisions, economic change weakened old ideas about social rank, which had been relatively fixed. It created a hope for upward mobility among all white members of American society. Even with the boom and bust nature of the economy, the factory system and the increasingly interconnected markets contributed to a general increase in wealth for the American people, and all American citizens hoped to gain their own share of this increase. The ability to achieve upward mobility, however, was not guaranteed, and the wealth that was created during this era was not equally distributed. The growth of the American market economy benefitted some classes of Americans far more than others.

During the first half of the nineteenth century, the class stratification that resulted from the new economy was especially visible in the northeastern cities. As the merchants and factory owners of that region accumulated great amounts of wealth, many wage laborers who worked in their factories found upward mobility more difficult to achieve. Pay was low and work was unsteady. In cities like New York, the wealthy erected extravagant mansions, formed exclusive clubs, and developed the elaborate social rituals of high society. At the same time, urban poverty exploded in other sections of these cities. Slums like the infamous Five Points neighborhood of New York City appeared, where people crowded into dwellings, and many remained homeless, living on the streets. The divide between the rich and the poor became wider and more visible as these cities became increasingly segregated according to financial status.

The new economy also produced a growing middle class in the northeastern cities. New types of job opportunities arose, which allowed many Americans to make a living by providing the services necessary to keep the economy rolling—in trade, management, or in professions like law, banking, insurance, and accounting. In the cities, members of this middle class bought their own homes, less lavish than those of the rich but more substantial than those the working class crowded in, and they made their lives comfortable with the many new material possessions that the market economy provided. In the past, an American's wealth had largely been determined by the amount of land one held. As the American economy diversified and the urban middle class population increased, this tendency declined. Americans recognized that wealth could be manifested in ways other than land ownership—through control of labor and through the ownership of other types of assets.

Members of this expanding middle class created new cultural ways that were very influential in American society. They valued the comforts that the new economy could provide, and their focus on material gain and upward mobility led middle class leaders to promote habits that they felt would help them to reach these goals. Thus, values like hard work, sobriety, responsibility, and thrift were lifted up in the schools, churches, and in the literature of the day. At the same time, one's possession became an indicator of one's class. Middle class Americans worked to broadcast their status through fashion, items they displayed in their homes, and the acquisition of other material goods.

Middle class family life underwent substantial change as well, as work moved away from the home. The idea of *separate spheres*—a separation of the public world of work and the private world of family—emerged. This idea led to a specialization of family roles. Increasingly, the ideal was for the man of the house to enter the public world of the workplace, while the woman would take care of the needs of home and family. Social attitudes about appropriate male and female behavior materialized around the notion of separate spheres. While men were expected to provide for their families and take charge of their direction; women were to take care of the family's moral well-being, keep a comfortable home, refrain from public expression and remain submissive to their husbands.

As this new middle class value system took hold throughout the north, many Americans found that they could not live up to the middle class ideal. Working class Americans experienced a number of hardships as they sought the elusive goal of upward mobility. Although men were expected to support their families, it was difficult to find a job that would pay a *family wage*, a salary large enough to support a modest family. While women were expected to tend the home, many women found that they had to work in order to survive. When they did work, they made less than men, since it was assumed that they did not need to make a family wage. Men thus increasingly opposed female participation in the workforce, as they feared that having low-paid women work in their field would devalue their own labor.

In addition to financial hardship, working class Americans also faced the difficulties of adapting to the routines of wage labor. The rise of the factory system changed the rhythms of work. Before the age of industry, most Americans worked in or near their homes. Many lived on farms, where all members of the household had labored together to raise, process and market their crops. They worked hard, but they determined their own pace and their work remained task-oriented. People tended to intermix their day with both work-related and domestic tasks, not following a fixed schedule. In urban areas, the apprenticeship system predominated. Under this system, skilled artisans who crafted the products of the day by hand employed apprentices who learned their skill and then eventually opened their own shops. Their routine was similar to that of American farmers; for artisans lived close to their homes and apprentices were considered to be members of the household. Pre-industrial labor systems were less scheduled, their days less full, and their jobs less repetitive than what Americans would experience after the rise of the factory system.

The factory system changed the nature of work. It destroyed the apprenticeship system, as the tasks of making various items were divided up into discrete steps. Increasingly, the jobs available in manufacturing were *unskilled labor* positions—low-paid wage labor positions that demanded the performance of these repetitive tasks. As trade after trade shifted away from employing skilled artisans and started using unskilled labor, many artisans suffered a loss in income and position as a result. Former artisans and farmers that were hired in the new unskilled labor positions of the early nineteenth century found their workdays to be harsh and demanding. There was less flexibility than there had been with pre-industrial forms of work, and workers had to adjust to the regulation of their days as factory bells determined their schedule. The division of work and home was also an adjustment. Leisure time was no longer infused into the work day, and working class Americans worked long hours—ten or more hours a day, six days a week.

These changes in the nature of work led to concerns about the loss of independence that arose with industrialism and the wage labor system. Farmers and artisans, while their lives may have been full of hardship, were independent producers. Factories required that wage laborers be under the direction of another. Furthermore, their jobs were tenuous. Positions were often temporary, and during economic depressions they were apt to disappear all together.

American workers therefore created a number of organizations through which they could agitate for change. In Philadelphia, urban artisans and workers formed a Mechanics' Union of Trade Associations in 1827, and the following year a *Working Men's Party* was formed in the city. Similar organizations followed suit, and by 1833 Working Men's Parties existed throughout the nation. The goal

This work schedule for the Lowell Mills illustrates the regulated nature of the work day for wage laborers.

of these parties was to abolish the dependence engendered by wage labor. Members pointed to the inequalities of wealth brought by the rise of industry, complaining that workers received little share of the wealth created by the new economy. Wages were too low and the cost of living was too high to get ahead. In order to alleviate this problem, they demanded laws that would abolish banks, decrease taxes, and provide public education for the children of workers. These parties had some local influence for a time, but their real impact came after mainstream politicians began to espouse some of their ideas.

In addition to Working Men's Parties, some workers formed unions in order to agitate for higher wages from their employers, but employers usually responded by dismissing employees who joined such unions. During the panics that hit the American economy during the first half of the nineteenth century, efforts to unionize were upset further, for economic depression created a surplus of workers, which ate away at any bargaining power a union had. Unions received little support from the government at this time, and so efforts of laborers to unionize would not take hold for many decades. Even so, American politicians began to recognize the power of the growing population of working class Americans, and some of their concerns were eventually given voice in their political platforms as the American political system evolved.

Immigration

Before the 1830s, most of the wage laborers in the United States were native-born, but after that decade, wage labor positions were increasingly filled with immigrants who came to the United States from Europe. Most of these new immigrants were from Ireland and Germany, and they came to America in ever larger numbers, beginning with a trickle in the 1820s and building up to a massive wave by the 1840s and 1850s. Political unrest and poor economic conditions at home sent these people to the United States, where they hoped to find political freedom and upward mobility.

European immigrants had steadily arrived on American shores since the colonial period, but there was a surge of new arrivals during the first part of the nineteenth century. This influx was partially due to the rise of industry both in Europe and the United States. Industrialization had disrupted traditional social structures in Europe as it had in America, but in America there was a dearth of labor while in Europe there was a greater supply. Despite the low pay offered to unskilled laborers in the United States, American positions were more easily acquired and higher paid than those in Europe. Those running labor-starved industries and public works welcomed the arrival of new wage earners during periods of prosperity when labor was in great demand. In addition, some Europeans, especially the Germans, came to the United States hoping for a different type of upward mobility. America famously had much available western land, and some immigrants arrived hoping to acquire their own piece of property to farm. Finally, many of these immigrants arrived to American shores because of political unrest at home.

In Ireland, the Catholic Irish had long been subjugated politically and economically by the Protestant leaders of their country and their English allies. Irish Catholics began to immigrate into the United States in large numbers beginning in the 1820s and 1830s, but it was after 1845 that the real surge in Irish immigration took place. In successive years during the late 1840s, a great potato famine wiped out the potato crops on which much of the Irish Catholic peasantry was dependent for their food supply. Approximately one million Irishmen and women died as a result, and another million and a half left Ireland for other homes. Most of them came to the United States. These Catholic Irish immigrants, especially those who were dislocated by famine, were generally very poor. They came with little but the clothes on their back, and they

clustered in the northeastern seaport cities, seeking out unskilled labor positions. They also provided much of the labor for the public works of the era, like the building of roads, canals, and, later, the railroad.

German immigrants who came to the United States were, in the main, better off than the Irish. Although few were wealthy, they did arrive in America with some means. Many were small farmers or artisans who had lost their positions due to the rise of industrialization, but there were also a number of middle class liberals who were persecuted by authoritarian leaders at home for their democratic ideals. Germans began coming to the United States in significant numbers in the 1830s, but there was an increase in German immigration during the 1850s because of political persecution and an increase in the number of Germans who experienced economic dislocation. Although some settled in urban areas, many Germans settled in German agricultural communities that were established in rural areas throughout the nation. There they maintained many aspects of their German culture. They kept their language and customs and established German schools, churches and institutions that served to draw newer German migrants to these communities. A large German community, for example, was established in central Texas in the 1830s. Later migrants were attracted to these communities and helped them to grow, and aspects of the German culture are still evident in the German towns of that state.

The United States has traditionally been referred to as a nation of immigrants, as all Americans have ancestors that at one point in time came from somewhere else. This early nineteenth century wave of immigration, however, challenged many Americans' sense of themselves, for it was the first time since the

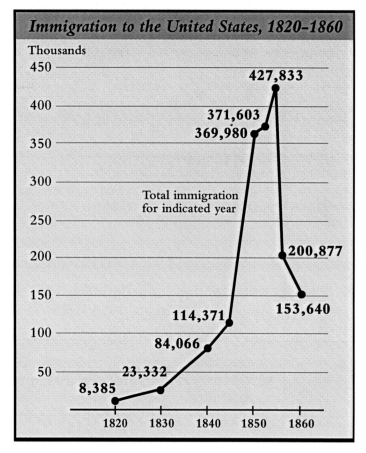

The immigrant influx of the first part of the nineteenth century.

nation's founding that a large wave of newcomers came to American shores.

With the rise of immigration came a rise in *nativism*—anti-immigrant sentiment. Although many Americans viewed immigration as beneficial to the United States because the newcomers contributed to the growing economy and provided a cheap labor force, others saw them as a problem. A number of concerns were expressed by nativists.

First, they pointed to the disorder that arose in the American cities as immigrants clustered into them. Poverty, crime, unsanitary conditions, and urban disorder had spread as the cities of the United States grew. Although the problems that arose were more associated with the numbers clustering in the city and the rapid growth of urban areas than with the background of the urban residents, immigrants became a handy scapegoat for the chaos associated with urban growth.

Second, nativists argued that immigrants from abroad did not have a proper education in democracy. They had not been raised, as Americans had, to be good republican citizens; yet after only a short naturalization period of five years, white immigrant men were given the vote. Nativists worried that the immigrant vote would corrupt the political system, and many urged that the period of naturalization be increased to twenty-one years.

Third, one of the largest concerns that nativists held concerned the influx of Irish Catholics. Despite the ideal of religious freedom that was so often espoused among Americans, most American citizens saw the United States as a Protestant nation, and they wished to keep it so. Anti-Catholic sentiment was actually the most profound strain of nativism that existed during the first half of the nineteenth century. Many Protestants viewed the Catholic Church at this time as anti-republican and authoritarian, and there was worry that Catholic citizens would hold their loyalty to their church above their loyalty to their adopted nation. This concern was unfounded, however, as

American Catholic leaders emphasized republican values and promoted loyalty to the American republic. Even so, sermons were preached against the Catholic menace, rumors circulated asserting that depravity existed within the Catholic Church, and, at times, anti-Catholic riots broke out in the northeastern cities.

The rise in European immigration, then, provided yet another source of conflict that challenged Americans during the first half of the nineteenth century. It sparked worries about how immigrants would affect the social, political, and religious structures of the nation as they crowded into American ports.

Revival of Political Factions

Although some of the changes brought by the modernization of the American economy, like the influx of immigration, did not fully flower in the United States until the 1830s and 1840s, Americans in the 1820s could see that their society was transforming. Attitudes about the changes that were taking place were reflected in the politics of the period, and they helped to contribute to a revival of partisanship during the late 1820s. As the market economy began to emerge, the Republican administration had become quite active in encouraging economic development. It had established a second Bank of the United States, passed tariffs in order to protect American manufacturing, and encouraged states to fund *internal improvements*—the building of roads and canals to link the nation together. While many Americans supported the government's intervention in the economy, others began to doubt that this intervention benefitted all members of American society.

Speaker of the House Henry Clay was one of the more active promoters of economic development. Hailing from the state of Kentucky, he wished to encourage prosperity for the West. He developed a plan that he called the *American System.* This plan would help to cement links between the manufacturing Northeast and the agricultural West by enacting higher tariffs to protect American industry and by providing federal support for internal improvements. Secretary of State John Quincy Adams agreed with Clay's promotion of a strong central government that would encourage a modern economy, for this would advance the economy of the industrial Northeast, the region he called home. It wasn't just regional loyalties, however, that drove these men. Both Adams and Clay were ardent nationalists who believed that a strong federal government and the promotion of the market economy were crucial to American strength and unity. Other politicians, however, were wary of this use of government power. Secretary of the Treasury William H. Crawford, from the state of Georgia, opposed the idea of the American System, arguing that it interfered with the rights of states.

As the presidential election of 1824 neared, these three men all sought to become the next president of the United States, and they were joined by Andrew Jackson, the hero of the Battle of New Orleans who had just been elected as a US Senator representing Tennessee. Before the election of 1824, presidential candidates had been nominated by Congressional party *caucuses* in which Congressional representatives for each party chose the candidate for their respective party. The Republican Party had nominated Monroe in 1820, and he had run unopposed. In 1824, the Republican Caucus chose William H. Crawford as the candidate. The Republican

Party was far from united behind this states' rights candidate, however, and many boycotted the caucus and supported other candidates. "King Caucus" was overthrown as state legislatures and mass meetings were held around the country to endorse rival candidates. Three additional candidates were nominated, creating a unique presidential ballot that contained four choices: William H. Crawford, John Quincy Adams, Henry Clay, and Andrew Jackson.

Because no party system was in place, the constituencies for these candidates were largely drawn upon regional lines. William H. Crawford drew much of his support from the South, John Quincy Adams from the Northeast, and Henry Clay from the West. The fourth candidate, Andrew Jackson, was a westerner like Clay, but his support fell less along regional lines. He had a more widespread appeal, and votes came in for Jackson from all across the nation. While it was unclear where he stood on the major economic questions of the nation at this time in his career, he was a popular candidate because of his status as a war hero, for his win at the Battle of New Orleans had become the stuff of legend. In addition, he held appeal because of his humble origins and plain-spoken ways. He became the candidate of the "common man."

This image was appealing to the masses of Americans who benefitted from the expansion of the *franchise*—the right to vote—that took place during the first decades of the nineteenth century. In the aftermath of the American Revolution, voting rights were still reserved to those of higher social rank in society in most places, and land-owners dominated the political system. In the 1810s, however, reformers began to push for the expansion of the vote. They used the democratic rhetoric of the American Revolution to

make their point and argued that it was not just land-holders who had a stake in how the republican government would be run. Gradually, many of the eastern states passed laws that broadened the franchise. As new western states were added to the union in the years after the War of 1812, they passed constitutions that set up a broad white, male franchise. With the expansion of the vote, the tone of politics began to change. Instead of electing elites to make decisions on behalf of other Americans, these new voters preferred simpler men who were more like themselves. By 1824, many of the American states had accepted universal white male suffrage or required only the payment of taxes or militia service as a requirement for the vote. Only a few states had property requirements for the vote still in place by the mid-1820s.

Jackson was the candidate that appealed to a large portion of this expanded electorate in 1824, and he won the most popular and electoral votes during the election. Because the votes were split among so many candidates, however, he failed to gain the majority of the electoral college votes needed in order to win the election. The decision of who would be the next president thus fell to the House of Representatives; for the Twelfth Amendment of the Constitution provided that the House of Representatives was to choose the president from among the three largest vote-getters when there was no clear majority. Henry Clay gained the fewest number of votes, disqualifying him from consideration. William H. Crawford had suffered a stroke during the election, and his medical condition put him out of the running. The House of Representatives thus had to choose between Andrew Jackson, who had received 99 electoral votes and John Quincy Adams who had received 84.

Henry Clay had been disqualified from consideration, but as Speaker of the House he held much influence over who would be chosen to be the next president. Clay threw his weight behind Adams. Because Jackson and Clay were both from western states, Jackson represented a threat to Clay's regional political base. In addition, Adams and Clay had similar ideals about the function of the federal government, and they promoted many of the same programs. Clay's support of Adams helped to sway the House of Representatives' vote, and Adams became the sixth president of the United States.

This election helped to revive political factionalism in the United States. Jackson's supporters believed that Adams had been illegitimately elected, and they argued that Jackson's plurality of both electoral and popular votes should elevate him to office. Jackson, in fact, had gained nearly the amount of popular votes as Adams and Crawford combined. His supporters argued that the House of Representatives had ignored the will of the people. After Adams was elected, he made matters worse when he named Clay as his secretary of state, a position that Jefferson, Madison, Monroe, and now Adams had held before rising to the presidency. It seemed to many who supported Jackson that Clay had swung the election towards Adams so that Adams could, in turn, place Clay in a position to succeed him in the presidency. Disgruntled supporters of Jackson asserted that a secret deal between Adams and Clay, a *corrupt bargain*," had taken place.

Although there is no evidence that any such bargain was made, the accusation had political traction. Adams had a difficult presidency, during which he faced much opposition, for he held no clear electoral mandate to enact his policies. Henry Clay's reputation had also been hurt. Jackson himself called him the "Judas of the West," and asserted that he had sold his influence for "thirty pieces of silver." The sense of indignation that was widespread among Jackson's supporters fueled an energetic effort to formulate a plan for victory in the upcoming election of 1828. Meanwhile, Adams attempted to put an even more ambitious program of economic and national development in place than that which had existed under Monroe. He put forth proposals for nationally funded canals, roads, education, and other government services. He was able to get little of his agenda enacted, however, as accusations of the corrupt bargain hung over him throughout his presidency, and as Jackson's supporters in Congress blocked his efforts.

By the time of the next presidential election, a new two party system had begun to materialize. Supporters of a strong central government and economic development rallied around President Adams, and they became known as National Republicans. Supporters of Jackson came together in opposition to this block, calling themselves Democratic Republicans. Differences in opinion on economic issues were important in this new division. National Republicans favored a stronger connection between the government and the market economy, while many Democratic Republicans argued that this involvement promoted the interests of the economic elite over that of average Americans. Personality also played into this division, for John Quincy Adams, the wealthy son of a Federalist president, seemed aristocratic in his bearing and unapproachable to the American people. Jackson, on the other hand, seemed to embody the values of the common man.

Americans United, Americans Divided

In the aftermath of the War of 1812, a number of forces had served to knit the nation together. Americans experienced a surge of nationalism, and party divisions fell away with the decline of the Federalist Party. The country was expanding geographically, gaining new respect from foreign nations, and developing a vigorous new industrial economy that was increasingly linked together by improvements in communication and transportation.

At the same time, however, American development would produce ruptures in American society. Sectional difference was exacerbated as the northern and southern economies became ever more distinct, and residents of each region realized that these differences had large political implications as they moved westward, adding new territory to the nation. Questions about slavery thus became infused into American politics in a profound way. Disagreements also arose concerning American economic development. How would Americans deal with the notion of equality in this modern economy? Was the modern economy an agent of uplift for all or for just a few? Should the government help to stimulate the market economy? Americans found that different groups had different answers to these questions, and new political factions arose in order to represent these varied interests.

Ironically then, westward expansion, sectional economic specialization, and demographic change during the first half of the nineteenth century were at the center of both a new sense of unity and new awareness of the differences that divided Americans. As Americans moved forward, they would struggle to find common ground.

Suggested Readings

Stuart Blumin, *The Emergence of the Middle Class: Social Experience in the City, 1760–1860* (1989)

George Dangerfield, *The Awakening of American Nationalism, 1815–1828* (1965)

Daniel Walker Howe, *What God Hath Wrought: The Transformation of America, 1815–1848* (2009)

Dale T. Knobel, *America for the Americans: The Nativist Movement in the United States* (1996)

Gerard Koeppel, *Bond of Union: Building the Erie Canal and the American Empire* (2010)

Bruce Laurie, *Artisans into Workers: Labor in Nineteenth-Century America* (1989)

John Lauritz Larson, *The Market Revolution in America* (2001)

Matthew Mason, *Slavery and Politics in the Early American Republic* (2008)

Ernest R. May, *The Making of the Monroe Doctrine* (1975)

Chapter 10

THE AGE OF JACKSON

Democracy and Individualism

As we observed in the previous chapter, beginning in the 1820s America was undergoing a dramatic transformation. It was an exciting time in which to live. The nation was experiencing rapid geographic changes, economic changes, social changes, and political changes. In particular, many Americans were becoming devoted to the ideals of democracy and individualism. The election of Andrew Jackson in 1828 symbolized this new era in politics, economics, and society, ushering in what historians have come to call "The Age of Jackson."

The population was growing rapidly through both natural increase and heavy foreign immigration. A revolution in transportation was taking place as individuals invested in turnpikes, steamboats, canals, and later the all-important railroad, pushing the frontier westward more rapidly than ever before. The frenzied building and experimenting with new ways of transporting people and products that took place in the Age of Jackson only proved Alexis de Tocqueville's observation that Americans were always on the move. It also produced dozens of new western communities and towns, and with all this rapid movement westward came the requisite American entrepreneur in search of fortune through a feverish land speculation. The nation was taking on an entirely new look.

Economically, the production of manufactured goods was coming increasingly under the control of the merchant-capitalist or the factory owner. This development reduced many skilled artisans to helpless wage earners. In many parts of the country, the reaction to these changes was a labor reform movement. In agricultural production, similar changes were taking place. In the west and north, machinery was becoming increasingly important for farmers as they became businessmen-farmers. In the south, agriculture increasingly relied on the staple crop cotton and on slavery.

American society was similarly in flux, as many native-born Americans became increasingly worried that continued immigration was diluting American culture. For some of these Americans, their solution was a bigoted know-nothing hatred and oppression of immigrants. Societal change often produces tensions that lead to attempts at repression. But repression often produces a backlash, and at this time in American history, the backlash manifested itself in a generalized desire to reform American society to improve not only the life of the immigrants but of all Americans as well. As the century wore on, some in the nation even suggested societal improvements should apply to black Americans as well as white, but the people advocating this kind of restructuring of society were in the decided minority.

In the midst of all this geographic, economic, and social change there were political changes going on; in particular, American society was becoming more *democratic* and more *egalitarian*. These two words are important ideas so we need to have a good understanding of what they represent, both today and to the American people in the Age of Jackson. *Democracy* has a double meaning, one political (in two parts) and the other social. Politically, a democracy is a system in which all adult citizens have an opportunity for an equal share of political power by their ballot. For this definition to work in this period of American history, we must exclude women and non-whites from consideration. Democracy is also a term used to denote a political system in which the machinery of government is responsive to the majority of the voters. You must understand that this system (where government is responsive to the majority of the voters) did not exist at this time in American history (and it may not exist today in the 21ˢᵗ century).

Democracy is also a term used to designate a set of attitudes and convictions that pertain to activities other than politics. In this social definition, democracy means the absence of any hereditary or any other arbitrary class distinctions or privileges. It stands for a belief in human equality, a belief in *egalitarianism*— the conviction that one person is as good as another and that each person should be treated equally, whether in politics, in the law courts, in having access to economic opportunity, or in social relations. (Again, understand that during this period of American history "the people" excluded women and non-whites.) Egalitarianism does not mean that all people are exactly alike, but it does mean that there should be no artificial distinction of position among people based upon one's nation of origin, race, gender, etc.

At the same time that the American people were focusing more acutely on the concepts of democracy, they also remained tied to the idea that the American people consists of self-reliant individuals. Individualism is a theory maintaining the political and economic independence of the individual. It is an idea that stresses individual initiative, individual action, and individual interests. Individualism suggests an antagonism to restraint; it is the conviction that the individual is sovereign and can stand on his own feet without institutions—the "inner-directed" man.

Americans in the Age of Jackson, perhaps more than at any time since the revolutionary era, began to focus on what it meant to be an American. These Americans were beginning to believe that democracy and individualism (as defined above) were the guiding values of

the nation. In other words, broadly construed, democracy means both a political system responsive to the majority and a social egalitarianism, which involves the belief that each man should be free to seek his own political, economic, and social good without interference. Man is important for who he is—not for who his parents, or friends, etc. are. And he can make his voice heard in his own government. Much of the time, democracy and individualism seem to go well together. Democracy in this way implies individualism, but there is also a tension between these two concepts.

Democracy means that the majority will rule, which usually requires some conformity and suppression of individuality. But individualism means to hell with conformity and the majority; I'll do it my way, no matter what anybody else thinks. There exists, thus, a noticeable tug in American life between democracy and individualism. The tension was present in America's past, and it is present today.

Although Americans in the Age of Jackson were beginning to focus on democracy and individualism as the guiding values of the nation, we must be careful to understand that this did not mean that American society was particularly democratic or that the American people was made up of self-reliant individuals. American society in the early 19ᵗʰ century was not as democratic in practice and behavior as people at the time thought it was. Moreover, American society in the early 19ᵗʰ century was not a particularly egalitarian society. As we have seen in the previous chapter, the working classes were probably worse off in the 1820s and 1830s than they had been in the past, and there exists much evidence that Americans then (and now) were (and are) much more conformist than individualistic. But having noted that—that America in the 1820s and 1830s was not as democratic and egalitarian as many then thought it was—it is also true—and equally important to our understanding of this period in American history—that some democratizing changes in politics really were taking place beginning in the 1820s. America was moving toward becoming a political system in which all adult males theoretically possessed an equal share of political power. The machinery of government was becoming more responsive to the majority of the voters.

The most obvious example of the movement toward democracy was the broadening of suffrage by means of the widespread elimination of property qualifications for voting. In other words, during the Age of Jackson, more people were eligible to vote. As the new western states entered the Union, their constitutions usually did not have property qualifications for voting. By the 1820s, many of the eastern states had changed their constitutions to eliminate property qualifications for voting. Restrictions on the vote of adult white males remained in only four states—Rhode Island, Virginia, Mississippi, and Louisiana.

Not only were more people now able to vote, but the process was made more equitable. In most states, the printed or secret ballot replaced voice voting. In addition, more positions became elective that had once been appointive, especially in the constitutions of the new western states. (Incidentally, one of the democratic changes in American political practices that did NOT take place during the Age of Jackson was the popular election of U.S. senators. They would not be elected by popular vote until 1913 with the passage of the 17th Amendment). Political parties began to hold national conventions for the nomination of presidential candidates. And beginning in 1828, those eligible to vote cast ballots for presidential electors. Thus, as a consequence of these (and other) changes, the 1830s and 1840s witnessed greatly increased participation by the "people" in politics and government. As more people began to participate in their political system primarily by exercising their right to vote, politicians began to profess their democratic convictions

Andrew Jackson drawn from life and engraved by J.B. Longacre

and switch their appeal to the "people" instead of to special groups.

Much more important than all these changes, however, was that crucial changes in American attitudes were taking place. The Age of Jackson witnessed both the development of a democratic rhetoric and the development of a democratic ethos (the distinguishing character, sentiment, moral nature, or guiding beliefs of a person, group, or institution). Many Americans in the 1820s and 1830s thought of themselves as egalitarian democrats and individualists (whether they really were or not), and both the practice of and belief in these values have had an enormous and pervasive influence on American life. For a public figure to denounce democracy in America today would be equivalent to denouncing honesty or hard work or virtue and would surely lead to his or her political demise.

It seemed as if democracy and individualism had become the guiding values of the new nation, and, more, Andrew Jackson had become the symbol for this rising ideology. Jackson, more than any of his predecessors, seemed to have embodied the American dream of the rise of "the common man." He was the prototypical "born in a log cabin" "rags to riches" story, except in his case it was true. Unlike his predecessor presidents, he had no college education; he lived in the west, Tennessee, not Virginia or Massachusetts. He represented the new coonskin-capped American—no longer in powdered wigs and silver-buckled knee breeches. And he had led the American yeoman farmers in battle, defeating the best professional soldiers the British Empire had to offer at the Battle of New Orleans in 1815. The political party that formed around him represented him as the champion of the common people, the personification of America's new democratic spirit. Jackson and his supporters now called themselves simply Democrats, having self-consciously dropped "Republican" from their previous name (the Democratic-Republican Party).

The Election of 1828

The presidential campaign of 1828 was exceedingly dirty, with both sides reaching new depths of insults and half-truths. Because of the 1824 election, supporters of Jackson (Jacksonians) called incumbent-President John Quincy Adams a "usurper" of the presidency and labeled the chess set and billiard table, which he purchased with his own money, "gaming tables and gambling furniture." Not to be outdone, Adams's supporters denounced Jackson as a liar, a thief, a drunkard, a bigamist, an adulterer, a gambler, a cockfighter, a slave trader, and a murderer. Jacksonians circulated the story that Adams had introduced a young American chambermaid to Czar Alexander when Adams was ambassador to Russia. The story was true enough, Adams had introduced a young American chambermaid to the Czar and his wife, but that was all. Nonetheless, Jacksonians falsely charged that Adams was a "practicing pimp," and a "procurer" of American girls for the Czar of Russia.

On the other side, a Cincinnati newspaper that supported Adams reported that "General Jackson's mother was a COMMON PROSTITUTE brought to this country by British soldiers! She afterwards married a MULATTO MAN, with whom she had several children, of which General JACKSON IS ONE! [capitalization in original]" The newspaper also reported that Jackson's "older brother was sold as a slave in Carolina."

The slander that most enraged Jackson was the attack on his wife Rachel, whom he had married under the mistaken impression that she was legally divorced from her first husband. When they discovered that her divorce was not yet final, they dissolved their marriage and repeated their vows four months later, after her divorce was obtained. But in the campaign of 1828, Adams's supporters dredged up the story and charged that Jackson had persuaded Rachel to desert her husband and "live with him in the character of a wife." One newspaper editor wrote, "Ought a convicted adulteress and her paramour husband be placed in the highest offices of this free and Christian land? What effect, think you, fellow-citizens, will it have upon the American youth?"

When the race was over between the "pimp" and the "convicted adulterer," Jackson won a resounding victory with 56% of the popular vote and 178 electoral votes to Adams's 83. Because this was the first time presidential electors had been popularly chosen (before they had been chosen largely by the legislatures), Jackson was—in a sense—the first popularly elected president. Jackson appealed to a broad cross-section of voters. Westerners saw Jackson as their candidate, a man who opposed traditional eastern elites. Southerners identified with Jackson the planter and southern slave owner. But Jackson also drew support in the east from laborers and craftsmen who identified with his belief that banking elites had denied workers equal opportunities. Immediately after Jackson's election, one event more than any other seemed to symbolize the arrival of this new age of democracy in America: Jackson's inauguration in March 1829.

Margaret Bayard Smith, a "proper American lady," witnessed Jackson's inauguration and described it this way: "The old man with his grey locks [Jackson], that crown of glory, advances, bows

to the people, who greet him with a shout that rends the air . . . it was grand—it was sublime." Jackson took the oath of office, and then "the marshal presented the Bible. The President took it from his hands, pressed his lips to it, laid it reverently down, then bowed again to the people—Yes, to the people in all their Majesty!"

If Mrs. Smith had gone home then, she might have ended the day filled with the thrills of democracy, but she made the mistake of going to the White House for the reception that followed later that afternoon. "What a scene," she later wrote, "did we witness! The Majesty of the People had disappeared, and a rabble, a mob, of boys, negros, women, children scrambling, fighting, romping. What a pity, what a pity! . . . the whole house had been inundated by the rabble mob. We came too late. The President, after having been literally nearly pressed to death and almost suffocated and torn to pieces by the people in their eagerness to shake hands with Old Hickory, had retreated through the back way . . . and had escaped to his lodging." Jackson had opened up the White House to anyone who cared to attend. Shocked by the impropriety of

Jackson's First Inauguration

it all, Mrs. Smith noted, "Ladies and gentlemen, only had been expected . . . not the people en masse. But it was the People's Day, and the People's President, and the People would rule." Although Mrs. Smith may have been upset by the behavior of the "people en masse," Jackson and his supporters had actively encouraged the democratic impulses that the mob scene at the White House revealed. It was a good image, and they were eager to maintain it for their president and for their party.

The Peggy Eaton Affair

President Jackson, commenting on who should hold public office, said that the duties of governmental officials should be made so "plain and simple that men of intelligence may readily qualify themselves for their performance." He seemed to believe not only that anyone could vote, but also that anyone could fill any public office. He also thought that office-holders should not stay in office too long because power tends to corrupt. Thus, in the early days of his presidency he began replacing former Adams's bureaucrats with his own Jacksonian democrats. He was roundly criticized at the time for his use of the "spoils system" (the practice where the incumbent party gives jobs to its supporters), but only about one-fifth of public office holders changed jobs during Jackson's two terms as President. For the most part, the old bureaucrats stayed on.

Jackson's cabinet was divided into essentially two camps; one supported Secretary of State Martin Van Buren of New York and the other supported Vice President John C. Calhoun of South Carolina. Both men were vying for precedence as Jackson's heir apparent.

Jackson tended to rely more on Van Buren, who resolutely pursued his own ambitions, than his Vice President, who was more determined to use his post to defend southern slavery against the spread of northern industry and against a growing abolitionist movement. A sex scandal, however, rather than political motivations ultimately decided the battle for precedence within Jackson's cabinet.

Peggy Eaton was the wife of Tennessee senator John Eaton, who Jackson made his Secretary of War. Jackson had known Peggy Eaton for some time and liked her, but rumors swirled about an unsavory past. Peggy Eaton was the daughter of an Irish tavern owner, but worse than that lowly background, her first husband had been a Navy purser who supposedly committed suicide overseas because of Peggy's affair with Senator Eaton. Jackson naturally stood by her side against every attack because he had just lost his wife, Rachel. Jackson blamed his own wife's death on the harshness of his presidential campaign, and he was not going to allow Mrs. Eaton to suffer the same fate. Mrs. Calhoun objected to Peggy Eaton's lower class background and untimely marriage to Senator Eaton. With Mrs. Calhoun leading the way, the other cabinet wives pointedly and repeatedly snubbed Peggy Eaton at every social gathering.

Jackson came to Peggy Eaton's aid, announcing her as "chaste as a virgin," and he demanded his cabinet treat her properly. Van Buren, who was a widower himself, did as Jackson asked and thereby strengthened his position with the president. Calhoun, who had never been particularly close to Jackson, suffered due to his inability to get his wife and the other cabinet wives to accept Peggy Eaton. Thus, Van Buren became Jackson's vice president in 1832 and succeeded Jackson to the presidency in 1836, while Calhoun was consigned to Congress, a seat from which he loudly and repeatedly defended southern slavery and states' rights.

Peggy Eaton ultimately withdrew from society because of the scandal. In 1859, the widowed (for the second time) Mrs. Eaton remarried at age 61; her new husband was twenty-one. Seven years later, her new husband fled the United States with the family fortune, taking Mrs. Eaton's 17-year old granddaughter with him. Mrs. Eaton died poverty-stricken in 1879.

The Nullification Crisis

The personal and political rift between Jackson and Calhoun was never more evident than during the Nullification Crisis. The crisis began in 1832, when South Carolina's legislature passed the Ordinance of Nullification, which declared two federal tariffs null and void within the state. During the presidency of John Quincy Adams, Congress passed the Tariff of 1828, which was designed to protect and promote the growth of northern industry by taxing low-priced imported goods. Southerners labeled it the "Tariff of Abominations," because the tariff made it difficult for the British to import goods into the South and thereby raise revenue to purchase southern cotton. With South Carolinian Calhoun serving as Jackson's vice president, southerners expected the incoming administration would significantly reduce the tariff.

When the Jackson administration failed to take action on reducing the tariff, radical leaders within South Carolina suggested they simply declare the tariff null and void within their state. In Washington, Calhoun pursued the constitutional theory of state nullification against the wishes of Jackson. Finally, in

July 1832, Calhoun resigned the vice presidency to run for the Senate to better defend nullification. Jackson, hoping to avoid a larger controversy, signed into law the Tariff of 1832, which reduced the Tariff of 1828. This compromise tariff was too little for South Carolinians, and in November 1832, a state convention declared that both tariffs were unconstitutional and therefore void in South Carolina. At the same time, the state made military preparations to resist expected federal enforcement of the tariff.

At the request of Jackson, the U.S. Congress responded by passing the "Force Bill" that authorized the use of military forces against South Carolina. At the same time, Jackson endorsed a bill reducing the tariff. South Carolina reluctantly accepted the reduced tariff and repealed its Nullification Ordinance on March 11, 1833, ending the crisis and South Carolina's threats of secession. Both sides claimed victory in the crisis. The administration successfully fought off a threat to national sovereignty by clearly rejecting the doctrine of states' rights, but South Carolinians had won for their section a reduction in tariff rates. The issue of states' rights, however, was far from dead. As the nation continued to expand its borders westward, states' rights became even more intricately connected with the issue of the extension of slavery into the territories. An exhausted Calhoun wrote of this crisis, "The struggle, so far from being over is not more than fairly commenced."

The Bank War

As important as the Nullification Crisis was to the nation, it was not the most important concern for the Jackson administration. The central symbolic event of Jackson's presidency was a set of events that has come to be known as the Bank War. The Bank War also represents another example of the surging democratic spirit during the Age of Jackson. When Jackson became president, as we have seen, the nation was becoming transformed from one that was Jeffersonian and agrarian to one that was more Hamiltonian, a nation focused on financial and industrial growth. But the supporters of democracy were still men who had been born and reared on farms in the south and west. The language of democracy was still Jeffersonian, but the basic concepts of democracy had changed almost imperceptibly from the libertarianism of agrarianism to that of laissez faire free enterprise. Many of these southerners and westerners had come to hate the Second Bank of the United States. They saw it as a grant of exclusive privilege to economic special interest groups, primarily easterners and foreign investors.

The bank was being capably run by Nicholas Biddle and was serving a very useful purpose as the financial regulator of the American economy. But the Jacksonians looked on the power of the bank as a restraint on economic freedom. Jackson, who believed rumors that the Second Bank purchased votes for John Quincy Adams in 1828, called the bank "a hydra of corruption." Jackson was determined to end what he perceived to be the bank's uncontrolled power. One solution might have been regulation instead of destruction, but Jackson was too individualistic for that. He rejected regulation and chose destruction instead.

Biddle remained unconcerned about Jackson's dislike for the bank, confident of its purpose and support of the people. Nonetheless, Biddle decided to make the bank a political issue in the 1832 presidential campaign by seeking the bank's recharter, even though the current charter did not end until 1836. Jackson took Biddle's action as a personal attack (which he did with most issues), and announced, "The bank is trying to kill me, but I will kill it." Kill it he did by vetoing the Congressional recharter bill. When a group of bankers complained to Jackson about the economic troubles being caused by his attack on the bank and asked him for some relief, Jackson roared: "Relief sir! Come not to me, sir! Go to the monster [the Bank]. It is folly, sir, to talk to Andrew Jackson. The government will not bow to the monster . . . Andrew Jackson yet lives to put his foot upon the head of the monster and crush him to the dust. Andrew Jackson would never recharter that monster of corruption. Sooner than live in a country where such a power prevailed, he would seek an asylum in the wilds of Arabia." Indeed, Jackson, the overemotional, unreflective, frontier aristocrat had made the bank a personal issue.

Jackson issued his veto message on July 10, 1832. In it, Jackson said the Bank was unconstitutional because it was a monopoly, a grant of exclusive privilege that excluded most of the American people from participation and, therefore, was a menace to the country's liberty and independence. At the end of his veto message, Jackson offered perhaps the most forthright statement of the social philosophy of the entire Jacksonian movement:

"It is to be regretted that the rich and powerful too often bend the acts of government to their selfish purposes. Distinctions in society will always exist under every just government. Equality of talents, of education, or of wealth can not be produced by human institutions. In the full enjoyment of the gifts of Heaven and the fruits of superior industry, economy, and virtue, every man is equally entitled to protection by law; but when the laws undertake to add to these natural and just advantages artificial distinctions, to grant titles, gratuities, and exclusive privileges, to make the rich richer and the potent more powerful, the humble members of society-the farmers, mechanics, and laborers-who have neither the time nor the means of securing like favors to themselves, have a right to complain of the injustice of their Government. There are no necessary evils in government. Its evils exist only in its abuses. If it would confine itself to equal protection, and, as Heaven does its rains, shower its favors alike on the high and the low, the rich and the poor, it would be an unqualified blessing."

Senator Daniel Webster bitterly denounced Jackson for demagogically seeking "to inflame the poor against the rich," but Jackson's veto stood and the effort to re-charter the Second Bank of the United States failed. Webster was wrong. The ideas expressed by Jackson in his veto were not those of a revolutionary engaged in class warfare. Instead, they represented instead the philosophy of the rising middle class. The Jacksonians, like the Jeffersonians before them, did not want to take property away from the rich or reconstruct society along drastically different lines, but they did wage a fight against economic privilege. They wanted to get rid of government-granted privileges to special-interest groups and provide "fair play and an open field" (turning Daniel Webster's phrase against himself) for all Americans: competition, yes; monopoly, no.

In the election of 1832, Jackson did easily win reelection and with that mandate went ahead with his plan to destroy the Second Bank of the United States. In October 1833, after replacing two uncooperative Secretaries of State, Roger Taney obliged Jackson and began to move federal deposits into 22 state banks. By the end of the year, the Second Bank of the United States was essentially insolvent, unable to make loans to anyone. To work around the problem of no cash, under the direction of Biddle, the Second Bank began to call in loans and foreclose on debts in a grim repeat of the conditions that brought about the Panic of 1819. Within months, the nation fell into a deep recession.

In an unprecedented action, the Senate passed a censure resolution against Jackson for removing the funds from the Second Bank, arguing the president had undertaken "authority and power not conferred by the constitution and laws." Jackson was undeterred and simply asserted his position as the first popularly elected president, reflecting his—and many Americans'—belief that democracy was the guiding value of the nation. "The President," he said, "is the direct representative of the people."

Although Jackson's destruction of the Second Bank of the United States turned out to be a terrible economic mistake, Jackson believed the Bank was undemocratic and had to go. Whether Jackson was acting on behalf of the people or on behalf of himself is difficult to delineate. Jackson usually took action only when he felt that he had some personal stake in an argument. In almost every important case where Jacksonian ideas were advanced, Jackson simply used principle as convenient ammunition for his own personal feuds. His selfish motivations are almost always evident. Jackson was a man of strong passions, and he did not try to hide them. Jackson once killed a man in a duel over an insult after himself being wounded; Jackson boasted, "I would have killed him even if he had shot me through the brain." Later in his life he wrote, "I have an opinion of my own on all subjects and when that opinion is formed I pursue it publicly, regardless of who goes with me." He certainly did this when he destroyed the Second Bank. When he left the presidency in 1837, he said he had only two regrets: he said he was sorry that he did not "shoot Henry Clay and hang John C. Calhoun." All evidence indicates he meant it.

Whatever Jackson's real motives—whether they were public considerations or private animosities—he always defended his actions in terms of the will of the majority and the greatest good for the greatest number. And in so doing, he demonstrated the popularity of America's widespread commitment to democracy—or at least the appearance of democracy. The American people during the Age of Jackson had come to consider Andrew Jackson as the symbol for democracy and individualism.

Nonetheless, we must note that at the same time we find democracy espoused and defended by Jacksonians, we can also see that American society was not particularly egalitarian. Urban upper classes with long established wealth clearly separated themselves from the recently rich, and a considerable gulf separated both the old and new rich from the democratic masses. Moreover, working classes were worse off under the factory system. America was not that different from Europe, except perhaps that it was money rather than blood that separated Americans into different classes. Average Americans during the Age of Jackson asserted their own desire for economic and political empowerment.

Although the Age of Jackson was a period of rising democratic ideals, it is important to understand that that there was then (and there is now) a gap between the egalitarianism of democratic values and the inequalities of social conditions and political practices. However, the democratic value that one man should be treated like any other and that each should have an equal share of political power have obviously endured to this day, but so has the gap between value and practice.

Indian Removal

Nowhere was the gap between democratic value and practice more evident than the way in which the Jackson administration dealt with Native Americans. The primary beneficiary of the rising democratic ethos in the Age of Jackson was the "common man," and for Jackson the quintessential "common man" was the western settler, the very same people Jackson grew up with in Tennessee. Native Americans were little more than barbaric peoples impeding territorial expansion and the extension of American power across the continent. At the time of his election in 1828, Jackson was less concerned about building the continental empire than clearing the land east of the Mississippi River for white settlement. Congress obliged the president, who had called for a removal act in his First Annual Message to Congress in 1829, by passing the Indian Removal Act on May 26, 1830. Over the next several years, the administration negotiated dozens of removal treaties with native tribes.

In the north, most tribes were unable to resist the offers of corrupt Indian commissioners who used bribes and alcohol to manipulate tribal chiefs into signing one-sided treaties. In some cases native groups attempted to resist

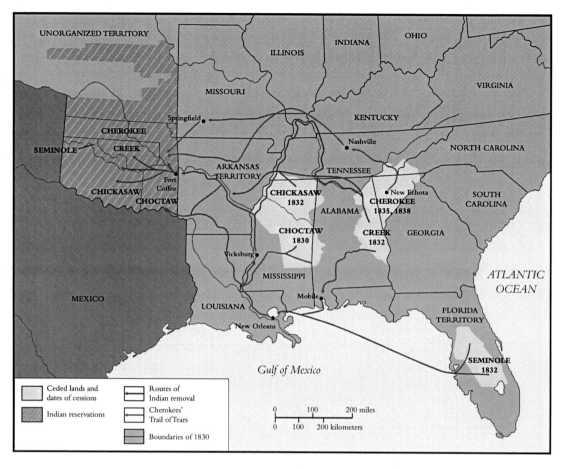

Map of Indian Removal

the removal policy, but most northern and Midwest tribes accommodated the administration and moved west of the Mississippi. In Illinois and the Wisconsin territory, however, members of the Sauk and Fox tribes fought back under the leadership of Chief Black Hawk beginning in 1832. During the previous two years, Chief Black Hawk led a group of tribal members into previously ceded areas in Illinois. The governor of Illinois declared their return an "invasion" and called out the state militia to expel them. The Illinois militia pursued the Indians north into the Wisconsin territory, and when Chief Black Hawk surrendered, native resistance in the Midwest effectively ended. Upon his surrender, dispirited, Chief Black Hawk declared, that his "heart is dead, and no long beats quick in his bosom. [I am] now a prisoner to the white men; they will do with [me] as they wish."

In April 1833, after eight months in captivity, Jackson had Chief Black Hawk sent east; Jackson wanted to meet him. Along the way, he was paraded before huge crowds of gawking spectators. Eventually Chief Black Hawk was reunited with his people who had settled in what is now southeast Iowa. The war produced atrocities on both sides and resulted in approximately 70 dead settlers and soldiers; uncounted hundreds of natives died in the conflict. And although the way was now clear for continuing settlement of Illinois, Iowa, and Wisconsin, in later years the conflict came to be remembered more because of two of its participants: Abraham Lincoln and Jefferson Davis, both of Kentucky.

The Trail of Tears

Jackson's removal policy drew its strongest supporters in the South, where state leaders were keen to acquire land inhabited by the Choctaw, Seminole, Creek, Chickasaw, and Cherokee Indians—the so-called "Five Civilized Tribes." The Choctaw were the first to be removed beginning in 1831, the Seminole followed in 1832, the Creek in 1834, and the Chickasaw in 1837. The last of the Cherokee were removed in 1838; their removal was the most prolonged.

The War Department oversaw the removal of the Choctaws in three phases; the last of the Choctaw left their native lands in 1833. In all, 17,000 Choctaws moved to what would be called Indian Territory and then later the Oklahoma Territory. As many as 6,000 died along what one Choctaw Chief reportedly called the "trail of tears and death." Alexis de Tocqueville, who witnessed part of the Choctaw removal from Memphis, Tennessee, wrote that the removal possessed "an air of ruin and destruction, something which betrayed a final and irrevocable adieu."

The Seminoles fought removal as long as possible—for a full decade—by killing both soldiers and civilians and burning whites' crops and homes. The effort to remove the Seminole from Florida cost the federal government as much as $20 million and left 1,500 dead soldiers. Although most Creeks were forced from Georgia to the Indian Territory, nearly 20,000 remained in Alabama. The Treaty of Cusseta in 1832 ended any hope they had of maintaining their culture. The treaty divided Creek lands into individual allotments, whereupon the Creeks could sell their land and move west or stay and submit to Alabama law. Land speculators defrauded those who chose to stay and war broke out. The administration sent General Winfield Scott to quell the violence and remove the remaining Creeks west. Of all the five tribes, the Chickasaw fared best—of course, they still lost their land—but they Chickasaw received financial compensation of $3 million from the federal government for their land east of the Mississippi River.

The removal of the Cherokees from their lands in the southeastern part of the United States resulted in the deaths about approximately 4,000 people. In 1827, the Cherokee had adopted a constitution that deliberately stated they were an independent nation. The state of Georgia responded to that action by passing a law claiming sovereignty over the Cherokee nation after June 1, 1830. Cherokee leaders brought suit, but in *Cherokee Nation v. Georgia* (1831), Chief Justice John Marshall ruled that the Cherokees were a "domestic dependent nation," rather than a foreign or independent state. At the same time, however, Marshall declared that the Cherokees possessed "an unquestionable right" to their land unless and until they wished to cede it to the United States.

Another Supreme Court case in 1832 furthered the Cherokee claim to their land. In *Worcester v. Georgia* (1832), the court ruled that the Cherokee nation was "a distinct political community" in Georgia, and, therefore, Georgia had no legal jurisdiction within

Cherokee land. With President Jackson's tacit consent, the state of Georgia ignored the ruling. If the president was not going to enforce the law, there was little the court could do. In 1835, a minority group of Cherokee leaders agreed to a treaty, giving up their lands in the southeast in exchange for land in the Indian Territory, $5 million, and additional funds to cover transportation expenses. By 1838, 12,000 Cherokee had followed the "Trail of Tears" traveled by the Choctaws, Seminoles, Creeks, and Chickasaws before them. Only 8,000 Cherokee survived the journey.

Jacksonian Democracy and Race

The treatment of Native Americans is not the only contradiction of the rising spirit of democracy and individualism in the Age of Jackson. As the nation pursued its democratizing changes, the contradiction of the existence of slavery in a free society only became more apparent. Democrats in the North and South were increasingly forced to find justifications for the subjugation and removal of Indians and the inhumanity of human bondage. European visitors to America were shocked by the paradox of nation proclaiming the ideals of democracy while simultaneously enslaving millions. English aristocrat Frances Trollope wrote she was "revolted" by this aspect of American society: "You will see them with one hand hoisting the cap of liberty and with the other flogging the slaves." The best, and most obvious way, to reconcile the contradiction for most Americans was to fall back on the perceived inherent inferiority of natives and blacks—in other words, the deceit was maintained through racism.

Although no one could have predicted its importance, one event during Jackson's first term sounded an early call to arms over the paradox of slavery in America. Abundant evidence exists that most slaves abhorred slavery and never lost their desire for freedom. Former slave turned abolitionist Frederick Douglass argued that thoughts of freedom were present in the minds both of slaves who were well treated as well as those who were mistreated: "Give [a slave] a bad master," he wrote, "and he aspires to a good master; give him [a slave] a good master, and he wishes to become his own master." Runaway slaves numbered in the thousands each year, although the South took elaborate steps to make escape almost impossible. Most runaways were caught and returned within a few days or weeks at most. But still every year a large number of slaves made the vain attempt to escape. Not enough slaves escaped to threaten the institution, but their attempts were an important form of protest against slavery.

For most slaves, running away was little more than an idle dream, so most slaves found countless other ways to express their discontent and unhappiness at their perpetual bondage, ways that exasperated their owners. One method is common today for disgruntled hourly wage employees: slowing down, doing less than they were supposed to do. Slavery was a notoriously inefficient system of labor. In addition to careless work, other slaves demonstrated their discontent by damaging the master's property. Still other's pretended to be ill. Much of the time slaves were simply attempting to avoid work, but it appears that more often than not most slaves engaged in these exasperating and annoying activities as a silent protest against their status.

Some slaves protested by committing various crimes: petty theft, not only to secure things they needed (like food), but also to hurt an owner who was enriching himself from their misery. Next to theft, the most popular crime was arson: burning barns or outbuildings or, even better, the slaveowner's house (better yet with him inside). A few slaves went even further and turned to open violence. Many examples of this exist, but by far the most famous and important example of slave violence is the Nat Turner Revolt (or rebellion or insurrection), which took place in Virginia in August of 1831. No Southerner could forget Nat Turner and his revolt.

Turner was a 30-year-old slave who lived on his owner's farm in tidewater Virginia. He seemed to be as humble and docile as any slave owner could expect. Turner even had some slight education. By all accounts, Nat Turner was the prototypical "good" slave, at least until August 1831. There is no evidence that he had ever been underfed, overworked, or treated with unusual cruelty, but Turner developed a messianic complex and came to believe that he had been chosen by God to deliver his people from bondage.

Turner rounded up as many followers as he could among his fellow slaves and launched his revolt on August 21, first against his own owners and then against other slave owners who lived nearby. His rebellion only lasted about 48 hours, but during that time Turner and his followers—about 70 slaves—killed 60 whites, including the family that owned Turner. At the first sign of armed resistance by local whites, Turner's short but bloody uprising collapsed. The Virginia militia, who quickly put down the revolt, killed 18 blacks including some innocent slaves who were not even involved. Turner was captured, jailed, tried, convicted, and eventually executed. But before he was hanged, he (supposedly) gave his account of the revolt to a white journalist, Thomas R. Gray, who interviewed Turner in prison. In 1832, Gray published *The Confessions of Nat Turner*, which

The Confessions of Nat Turner

"I was intended for some great purpose. . ."

"Accompanied by Will [another slave], I entered my master's chamber; it being dark, I could not give a death blow, the hatchet glanced from his head, he sprang from the bed and called his wife, it was his last word. Will laid him dead, with a blow of his axe, and Mrs. Travis shared the same fate, as she lay in bed. . ."

"There was a little infant sleeping in a cradle, that was forgotten, until we had left the house and gone some distance, when Henry and Will returned and killed it. . ."

"As we approached [another house], the family discovered us, and shut the door. Vain hope! Will, with one stroke of his axe, opened it, and we entered and found Mrs. Turner and Mrs. Newsome in the middle of a room almost frightened to death. Will immediately killed Mrs. Turner, with one blow of his axe. I took Mrs. Newsome by the hand, and with [my] sword . . . I struck her several blows over the head, but not being able to kill her, as the sword was dull. Will turning around and discovering it, dispatched her also. . ."

"I proceeded to Mr. Levi Waller's, two or three miles distant. . . . [I]t was my object to carry terror and devastation wherever we went . . .

"[At the Waller's house] I got inside in time to see the work of death completed, viewed the mangled bodies as

they lay, in silent satisfaction, and immediately started in quest of other victims—Having murdered Mrs. Waller and ten children, we started for Mr. William Williams'—having killed him and two little boys that were there; while engaged in this, Mrs. Williams fled and got some distance from the house, but she was pursued, overtaken, and compelled to get up [on a horse] behind one of the company, who brought her back, and after showing her the mangled body of her lifeless husband, she was told to get down and lay by his side, where she was shot dead. . ."

had an indelible and enduring affect throughout the south.

In addition to Turner, sixteen other slaves who participated in the revolt were hanged. Seven other slaves who had not been a part of the revolt but had expressed sympathy for it were deported out of the area. Despite the punishments, the revolt had a tremendous impact on the mindset of southerners. It immediately caused great fear throughout the South. If a "good" slave like Turner could not be trusted, who could? Equally important, the revolt frightened the South into greatly increasing the severity of its slave codes to prevent any other uprisings from occurring. And in fact, no other slave revolt on the scale of Nat Turner's ever occurred. Most slave revolts never got past the planning stage. Nat Turner's revolt also caused the emancipation movement in the South to collapse completely, and instead, a pro-slavery argument developed that defended slavery as a good thing, not something that should be abolished.

The official Southern interpretation of the Nat Turner Revolt was not that blacks hated slavery and hated those who inflicted slavery on them. The official Southern interpretation was that "outside agitators" caused the Nat Turner revolt. Virginia's Governor Floyd quickly explained that the slave plot was "undoubtedly designed and matured by unrestrained fanatics in some of the neighboring states." And who was the most obvious "unrestrained fanatic" around: abolitionist William Lloyd Garrison. The reaction in the South against Garrison made him and his abolitionist newspaper, *Liberator*, famous. It also helped to produce a crisis psychology in the South which, in turn, helped spread abolitionism. The influential editor of the Richmond, Virginia, *Enquirer*, Thomas Ritchie, admitted after Nat Turner's revolt: "We may shut our eyes and avert our faces, if we please, but there it is, the dark and growing evil at our doors; and meet the question we must, at no distant day. What is to be done? Oh! my God, I do not know, but something must be done."

After Nat Turner's revolt, the Virginia Legislature debated for two weeks a bill to gradually emancipate all the slaves in Virginia. The gradual emancipation plan had the strong support of Virginia's governor, who vowed, "I will not rest until slavery is abolished in Virginia." The plan also had the support of the leading newspapers of the state. But it did not have the support of the citizens. After two weeks of debate, the plan was tabled by a vote of 73 to 58 and never taken up again. With that vote, the plan for the gradual emancipation of slaves in Virginia died. When Virginia decided not to emancipate its slaves, other southern states followed Virginia's lead. The debate in the Virginia legislature was the last major free debate in the South before the Civil War on the issue of freeing slaves.

The Rise of the Whig Party

So influential were the related currents of democracy and individualism during the Age of Jackson that they even influenced the Whig Party, the political party that developed in opposition to the Jacksonian Democrats. The Whigs were the party of respectability and business men, the party of those who did not really care much for the new Jacksonian democracy. But there is no clearer evidence of the power of the democratic ethos at the time than that the members of the Whig Party—the political descendants of the Federalists and ancestors of the modern day Republicans—found it politically necessary to talk and act like democratic individualists, even if they didn't really mean it.

The Whig Party, like Jackson's Democratic Party, was a national party with representation in all sections of the country. Yet, although its members came from all parts of the country, urban and commercial interests dominated, especially the growers of large staple crops: cotton planters of the South, sugar planters of Louisiana, and hemp growers of Kentucky. The Whig Party in the United States grew out of the remnants of the National Republicans, who were strongly opposed to what they considered Andrew Jackson's abuse of presidential power. The Whigs accused Jackson of usurping executive authority and acting much like a king.

In addition to opposing just about anything Jackson wanted to do, most Whigs supported Henry Clay's American System, which called for a protective tariff to encourage the growth of American industry, furnish a home market for the agricultural products of American farmers, and provide revenue for the central government. Tariff revenue would be used

Henry Clay

to fund internal improvements, which would improve the national communications system and thereby facilitate internal trade. Finally, Clay called for a strong national bank, which would insure a stable currency and thereby facilitate trade, foreign and domestic.

Henry Clay and Daniel Webster dominated leadership of the party. Clay was simple and democratic in his own personal demeanor, but had no sympathy with the rough and tumble democracy on display, for example, at Jackson's inauguration. Clay considered democracy reckless of property rights and vested interests. In his speeches and letters, Clay said and wrote little about the common man. He was not concerned with workers and dirt farmers but, rather, with manufacturers and planters. Daniel Webster, like Clay, was of modest birth, but unlike Clay, he was personally aristocratic in his habits as an adult.

He was trained as a Federalist and held to those ideas throughout his career. Webster's central political axiom was that power follows property, and if there was to be a stable representative government, the two—power and property—had to be tied together. In other words, Webster thought those who possessed economic power should also possess political power. "There is not a more dangerous experiment," Webster wrote in 1820, "than to place property in the hands of one class, and political power in those of another." Just as Alexander Hamilton before him believed, the best way to achieve and maintain class harmony in America was for the central government to provide aid to business enterprise.

These attitudes of Clay and Webster and other Whigs were not popular with many Americans in the 1830s. They seemed elitist and anti-democratic. This was a problem for a political party trying to establish itself in an era that for the first time required the support of the voters to win elections and stay in office. Compelled by the revolution in political values, the Whigs started talking as if they were primarily concerned with the common American, whose votes up until then had seemed to belong to Jackson and the Democrats, instead of being mainly concerned with the rich, special interest groups who were their real constituents. The Whigs, to survive in the political arena of Jacksonian America—the America that thought of itself as being democratic and individualistic—felt compelled to adopt the rhetoric of democracy and individualism, even if they didn't really mean it, which they didn't. One Whig writer came right out with it: democracy, he wrote, is "a word of deep meaning and great potency in America. No political party can dispense with it there. Whatever their principles, radical or conservative, their best passport is democracy." In other words, say you believe in democracy, no matter what you really believe. Otherwise, you will never win.

Henry Clay, for example, after the growth of the democratic movement in the 1830s, found that it was to his political advantage to exaggerate his humble origins. In fact, Clay, son of a Baptist preacher, had been born in a frame house in Virginia that was far superior to the homes of most Virginia farmers. When he was five years old, his widowed mother owned eighteen slaves and nearly 500 acres of land. That's not poor. As an adult, Clay prospered. He lived on a large estate in Ashland, Kentucky, that had a 200-acre woodland park and one of the first and finest private horseracing tracks in the country. But in response to democratic developments in America, Clay characterized himself in political campaigns as the "mill boy of the slashes"—another version of a "poor country boy born in a log cabin." He conveniently ignored his estate and the riches he had acquired as an adult.

Daniel Webster, another Whig of modest background, but who became quite wealthy as an adult and who lived like an aristocrat, said this during the 1840 political campaign: "The man that says that I am an aristocrat is a Liar!" And anyone who makes this charge "and then will not come within the reach of my arm, is not only a liar but a coward." Webster also apologized to the voters for not having been born in a log cabin.

The Whigs discovered, early in their campaigns against Jackson that their most effective candidates were backwoods types—whether real or fake—who could steal Jackson's thunder as a democratic figure, candidates who could seem to be just like Old Hickory or, better yet, more like Jackson than Jackson himself. The best example the Whig Party found was Davy Crockett of Tennessee.

Daniel Webster

Crockett first turned up in Washington in 1827 as a Democratic congressman and a member of Andrew Jackson's own party. But by 1832, the Whigs had adopted him and turned him into a Whig version of Andrew Jackson. He was from the West, had fought Indians, and in general was the living incarnation of frontier individualism and democracy, except now he was on the side of the Whigs. The climax of the Whig adoption of democratic rhetoric and appearance, however, came in the presidential campaign of 1840.

The Election of 1840

To no one's surprise, the Democrats selected incumbent President Martin Van Buren as their candidate in the election of 1840. Van Buren had been Andrew Jackson's Vice President and succeeded Jackson as President in 1836—not many Vice Presidents ever do that. In the modern era, only George Herbert Walker Bush (Reagan's Vice President 1980–88) has done it, and he lasted only one term in the White House. In 1836, the Whig Party chose to run four candidates, each one representing one section of the nation. They had hoped that the tactic would throw the election into the House of Representatives, but the strategy failed as Van Buren won a majority of the electoral votes and became the nation's eighth president. The Whigs were determined not to make that mistake in the election of 1840.

The Whig Party nominated William Henry Harrison. Harrison was born into the Virginia aristocracy—his father signed the Declaration of Independence—but the Whigs cleverly packaged him in 1840 for popular taste, not as a Virginia aristocrat, but as a military hero, a Westerner, and a plain man of the people—i.e. he was just like Andrew Jackson, except a Whig. At the Whig nominating convention held in Harrisburg, Pennsylvania, in December 1839, Henry Clay led on the first ballot. He was a veteran politician and well known to the American people. But in the end, the Whigs rejected Clay as their presidential candidate in 1840 for the same reason he seemed to be the obvious candidate. He had taken too many clear positions on important issues for too many years. People knew where he stood and he had made enemies. The Whigs wanted to win and did not want to offend any element in their own party. To avoid offense, they did not even propose a party platform, let alone adopt one.

The campaign of 1840 set a new pattern in American politics, worse even than the campaign of 1828 between the "pimp" and the "convicted adulterer." It was like a circus, a carnival, with much ballyhoo and little substance. Harrison's political managers employed every device they could think of to mobilize the voters in favor of their candidate. The primary focus of the Whig campaign centered on the adopted slogan of "Log Cabin and Hard Cider."

A Baltimore newspaper supporting President Van Buren wrote sarcastically that old General Harrison was a simple soul who would be very happy living quietly on his backwoods farm if he had just three things: a government pension, a log cabin, and a barrel of hard cider. But the attack utterly backfired. General Harrison's advisors turned the sarcastic attack back on the Democrats and claimed

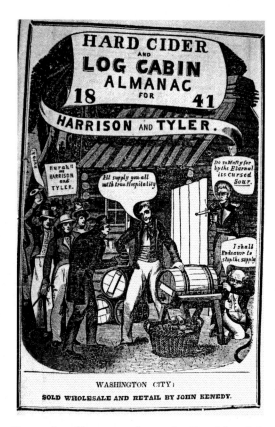

Campaign literature from the Presidential Election of 1840.

that indeed the Whig Party and General Harrison were the party and the candidate of log cabins and hard cider. And the log cabin—a symbol of democratic simplicity and frontier individualism—became the main symbol of General Harrison and the Whig campaign, which was the first to make extensive use of campaign ephemera. All over the country, Whig Party members handed out log cabin badges and log cabin sheet music to the revelers. At various locations, the Whigs put on log cabin raisings, even in New York City, where they built a 50×100 foot log cabin on Broadway. Whenever a log cabin was raised, there would be a parade, a communal feast with aspects of a medieval fair, and lots of eating and drinking. Harrison's supporters wore coonskin caps and offered hard cider to any and all takers.

Emotionalism characterized the entire campaign. The Whigs outdid themselves and even outdid the Democrats in campaigning as small "d" democrats. They held huge rallies, staged massive torchlight parades, sang campaign songs, and chanted campaign slogans. The most notable slogan was "Tippecanoe and Tyler too." To balance the Whig ticket, they chose Senator John Tyler as Harrison's running mate. Tyler was hardly the prototypical Whig, but he was pro-slavery and pro-south so his selection satisfied southerners.

Significant issues got lost in the shuffle of the campaign hoopla. Senator Webster was not amused by the lack of any attention to the serious issues facing the country, noting, "The time has come when the cry is change. Every breeze says change . . . We have fallen, gentlemen, upon hard times, and the remedy seems to be hard cider." The Harrison campaign also marked the beginning of the large-scale manufacture of campaign souvenirs. Examples can still be found today of Tippecanoe shaving soap, Log Cabin emollient, "Tippecanoe and Tyler Too" neckties, and Old Cabin Whiskey in miniature bottles shaped like log cabins, which were produced by the E. C. Booz Distillery of Philadelphia, thus introducing the new slang word "booze" into the American language.

Harrison was also the first presidential candidate to make campaign speeches around the country on his own behalf. He made twenty-three speeches to crowds of over 50,000. His speeches, however, were devoid of any real political positions; he pioneered what was to become an important campaign axiom: "The more you talk, the less you should say." What he did say focused mostly on denunciations of the Democrats, Van Buren particularly. Character attacks were very much in fashion in 1840. Both sides did it, but the Whigs were better at it. They called the President, "Martin Van Ruin" and sang songs with the lyrics" Farewell, dear Van, you're not our man" and claimed more cruelly that "Van, Van is a used-up man."

The Whigs made the presidential election of 1840 a contest between the simple life of their homespun, log cabin candidate, General Harrison, and that of the aristocratic, corset-wearing President Van Buren. Although the popular vote margin was close (1,275,390 to Van Buren's 1,128,854), only about a six per-cent difference separated the two candidates (52.9% to 46.8%), Harrison won an over-whelming victory in the Electoral College (234-60). The dire economic state of nation brought about by the economic policies of Jackson and Van Buren certainly helped Har-rison win, but the Whigs also won in 1840 because they showed that they had learned better than the Democrats the political lessons on how to appeal to the people. "Tippecanoe and Tyler too" had won over "Van, Van, the

used-up man," and in so doing established the two party electoral system in much the way we know it today.

Incredibly, an unprecedented 80 percent of the eligible voters voted in 1840, more than twice as many people (2.5 million) as in 1828 (1.15 million) when Andrew Jackson was first elected. As John Quincy Adams noted about the election in his diary, "Here is a revolution in the habits and manners of the people." The election of 1840 was the first great "image campaign" in American history where the can-didate's image mattered more than the candi-date's issues. A new era had arrived in American society. From this election forward, politics would have a broad popular base. The ideals of democracy and the value of the indi-vidual voter were here to stay. Or, so it seemed. In fact, more often than not, in politics, it was not democracy, but a parody of democracy. Still the democratic ethos had become deeply embedded in American life, if not in American practice. Americans believed they were demo-cratic and believed they were individualistic.

John Quincy Adams, a perceptive observer who did not like what he saw happening to politics in America, raised an anxious question in 1840, "Where will it all end?" Politics had moved from the 1828 campaign based on the charisma of Old Hickory to the cynically-contrived bandwagon campaign in 1840 of "Old Tippecanoe and Tyler too." Just as impor-tant, society had moved toward embracing the ideas of democracy and individualism, which seemed to require an examination of the mean-ing of the declaration that in America "all men are created equal."

Suggested Reading

Freehling, Alison Goodyear. *Drift toward Dissolution: The Virginia Slavery Debate of 1831–32*. Baton Rouge: Louisiana State University Press, 1982.

Freehling, William W. *Prelude to Civil War: The Nullification Controversy in South Carolina, 1816–1836*. New York: Oxford University Press, 1992.

Howe, Daniel Walker. *The Political Culture of the American Whigs*. Chicago: University of Chicago Press, 1979.

Remini, Robert Vincent. *Andrew Jackson and the Course of American Democracy, 1833-1845*. 1st ed. New York, N.Y.: Harper & Row, 1984.

Remini, Robert Vincent. *Andrew Jackson and the Course of American Empire, 1767–1821*. 1st ed. New York: Harper & Row, 1977.

Remini, Robert Vincent. *Andrew Jackson and the Course of American Freedom, 1822–1832*. 1st ed. New York: Harper & Row, 1981.

Watson, Harry L., and Eric Foner. *Liberty and Power: The Politics of Jacksonian America*. 1st ed. New York: Hill and Wang, 1990.

Chapter 11

BUILDING THE CONTINENTAL EMPIRE

Americans living during the first seventy-five years of the United States—1787 to 1853—witnessed the building of a continental empire. From a meager 13 colonies along the eastern coast of North America, the United States expanded with unprecedented speed to form a coast-to-coast commercial and territorial empire. The United States in the early 19th century was an aggressive, expanding country, determined to incorporate large areas of new territory into its boundaries. Successive presidential administrations were extremely successful at doing just that—incorporating large areas of new territory into its boundaries seemingly at will.

Between 1803, when the Jefferson Administration purchased Louisiana, and 1853, when the last piece of the continental empire was added (the Gadsden Purchase in what is southernmost Arizona today), the land area of the United States increased three fold. This expansion was brought about in various ways. The first and easiest was purchase. The second was something similar to the legal process of Eminent Domain—white settlers illegally move into areas held by natives; the government attempts to negotiate for legal acquisition; when that fails (as it often did), the government confiscates the land in the name of the American people and at the behest of American power. In the early part of the 19th century, the process was simply ascribed to "natural expansion," and, later, to the nation's "Manifest Destiny." Finally, and on more than one occasion, building the continental empire was accomplished only through war. Again, to leaders and citizens alike, these conflicts were considered wars of "national liberation," carried out in the interest of the United States but also for the peoples residing in the territories being acquired, whether or not they wanted or appreciated being "liberated."

By definition, the United States is an imperialist nation—imperialism is the advocacy and practice of extending national power and control over other areas territorially, economically, and politically. Imperialism is not unique to the United States, and some do not consider America an imperialist nation at all, especially during the 19th century when the nation was merely expanding "naturally" across the continent. Imperialism can be found in the distant past in the histories of China, Rome, Greece, and Persia. More recently, imperialist practices were utilized by most of the European nations—Great Britain, France, Germany, and Italy—in the late 19th and early 20th centuries, particularly during the so-called "Scramble for Africa" (the period between the 1880s and WWI, when the European nation-states struggled for control over various parts of Africa).

Most historians have become comfortable with including the United States in the list of imperialist nations beginning with the Spanish American War at the end of the 19th century but remain reticent to include the United States as an imperialist nation prior to that time. Part of the explanation for that is historical and the rest is cultural. Imperialism has a negative connotation, and most Americans—American historians included—are disinclined to think of the establishment of the United States disapprovingly. Historically however, the appearance of Vladimir Ilyich Lenin's last book, *Imperialism, the Highest Stage of Capitalism* (1916) explains why many have not considered the United States imperialist in its early decades. In his book, Lenin claimed that capitalist nations turned to imperialism in their final days in an effort to keep their capitalist system going. Lenin also gave a special definition to imperialism. Lenin said for imperialism to occur, people from one nation had to get

American Progress. Chromolithograph, ca. 1873, after **Manifest Destiny** 1872 painting by John Gast. *George A. Crofutt. Popular Graphic Arts Collection. Prints and Photographs Division. Library of Congress.*

into ships and go across oceans to take over another nation and people. So ships and oceans were essential parts.

In the 20th century, Lenin's definition caught on, not only in Europe but in other parts of the world as well, including the United States. It had wide acceptance in many non-European countries, particularly in Africa and the Middle East, because it seemed to describe their own experiences with Europeans, who had gotten into ships and crossed oceans to subjugate them. It also

became an acceptable definition for the Soviet Union and the United States; both were great land powers that did not need to get into ships and cross oceans to expand (at least, for the U.S., not until the end of the 19th century). Many historians, particularly during the first half of the 20th century, adopted Lenin's definition. America's continental growth in the 19th century, therefore, was ascribed to "expansionism"—a policy or practice of territorial growth by a nation. So in the late 18th and 19th centuries, when the United States increased its territorial boundaries, it was expansionism, not imperialism—a process of national growth that was decidedly less repellant or injurious to those peoples being incorporated into the nation.

American expansionism—as many historians and, therefore, many Americans would have it—lasted until the late 1890s when Americans finally got into ships, crossed oceans and acquired territory during the Spanish-American War. For many historians, then, only in the 20th century and after was expansionist America an imperialist nation. But expansionism is too soft a word to describe the actions of the United States in the late 18th and 19th centuries. The history of the United States from its very inception has always been a story of impenitent imperialism, the story of building an empire. Expansionism is merely a subterfuge for those who prefer to defend a so-called American exceptionalism (the idea that America is special; America is unique; the notion that America is divinely ordained to spread is ideals and institutions across the globe).

Simply, if we consider that imperialism is the extension of dominion over an area outside one's own sovereignty, then expansion by the United States in the early 19th century was just as much imperialism as what happened in 1898 and after. But, as some have argued, there is one important difference: In the early 19th century, American imperialism involved taking land that was eventually incorporated into the country. The people living there were not subjected to second-class citizenship as, for example, the British did in India and the British, French, Belgians, Dutch, and Germans did in Africa—nations we traditionally think of when we think of imperialism. In the U.S., people in the newly acquired territory were eventually welcomed into the nation with the same privileges of citizenship that the citizens of the original 13 states had—at least on paper according to the precedent set in the Northwest Ordinance. Of course, one might have a different perspective on this if you were an American Indian or an African American. Put simply, 18th and 19th century imperialistic America was not so different from other imperialistic nations of the time (or of any other time).

One way to understand the story of America is to study it from the perspective of extending power. In this view, the story of the nation is the account of the creation of an empire. In the period up to 1853, it is the story of the building of a continental empire. This chapter traces the fundamental importance of empire to the existence of the American nation and people. In later chapters, we will see how a dispute over the future of the empire led the nation into a civil war. By examining this era of empire building, we will come to understand that the creation of a continental empire brought to the surface an irreconcilable difference over the institution of slavery that eventually split the Union. Equally significant, this chapter shows how American power increased at great cost, both in lives and in contradiction to the nation's stated ideals.

"Manifest Destiny"

The imperial impulse, at least among the American people, reached all new heights during the 1840s. Although the desire for empire had existed among American leaders since the revolutionary era, individual Americans embraced western expansion during this decade in ways they never had before and in ever growing numbers. Most went west seeking a better life for themselves and their families. For these Americans, the West represented all new possibilities for freedom and financial prosperity. Of course, many neglected to consider the reality that hundreds of thousands of people already lived in this imagined land of freedom and opportunity. Moreover, most of these settlers and adventurers in search of land, wealth, and a new life had little knowledge the difficulties of the journey or the harshness of everyday living on the frontier.

These American settler-adventurers represented the physical embodiment of the American will to empire, or, America's "Manifest Destiny," a term first coined in 1845 by American journalist and diplomat John Louis O'Sullivan in an editorial supporting annexation of Texas, in the July-August 1845 edition of the *United States Magazine and Democratic Review*. In short form, "Manifest Destiny" is an ideology holding that the territorial expansion of the United States is not only inevitable but also divinely ordained. Since its first use, expansionists in all political parties have gone on used the phrase to justify the acquisition of California, the Oregon Territory, and Alaska. By the end of the 19th century, American leaders applied the doctrine to the proposed annexation of various islands in the Caribbean Sea and the Pacific Ocean. As we shall see later, Americans didn't just sit back and let this ideology of territorial expansion—"Manifest Destiny"—happen; many worked very, very hard to cause it to happen. Moreover, most Americans felt no need to justify it; they merely sought to explain it.

Several important rationales underlie American's belief in the necessity for the will to empire. Perhaps the most essential rationale is embodied in what we term "The American Sense of Mission." When John Louis O'Sullivan first penned "Manifest Destiny," the

American Sense of Mission was already firmly entrenched in the American psyche. Simply, it is the ideal that America has a mission in the world. However one might like to describe it—negatively or positively—most Americans, then and now, remain convinced that America has a unique mission in the world. Positively, we might say America has a mission to spread freedom and democracy. Negatively, we might say America's mission is—and has been—to spread capitalism and consumerism across the globe to maintain American hegemony—America's economic mastery over the world—and the American people's high standard of living.

Although some Americans (and many other non-Americans) disagree, most Americans are inclined to consider the United States a country with a special purpose or a special destiny. In the 19th century, as we shall examine in this chapter, Americans came to believe the nation possessed a Manifest Destiny, first to California and then across the Pacific all the way to Asia. In the 20th century, this Manifest Destiny became expressed as an "America to make the world safe for democracy (WWI);" as an America to save the world from Fascism (WWII); as an America to save the world from Communism (the Cold War); and, as an America to save the world from terrorism (the War on Terror). So how did it come about that Americans came to see their nation as one with a special destiny?

The American Sense of Mission originated in England with the Puritans and was implanted into America in the early 1600s by and with the first English settlements in New England, long before the United States came into existence. The Puritans have influenced American culture out of proportion to their numbers and in spite of their relatively brief period of dominance on the North American continent. Puritan beliefs were very prominent because they talked and wrote and published much more than other groups at the time; they founded schools and colleges such as Harvard and Yale, which in turn spread and extended the influence of Puritan values; they dominated New England, which was far more important in America from the early 17th century to the middle of the 19th century than it is now.

The Puritans came to New England beginning in 1630 desiring to create a model Christian community that would serve as an example for other people and other nations. No one better explained the purpose of the Massachusetts Bay Colony than its leader John Winthrop. On board his ship, the *Arabella*, on the way to New England, John Winthrop delivered a lay sermon, which he entitled "A Model of Christian Charity," and in that sermon, he explained the purposes of the Puritan colony. "For we must consider that we shall be as a city upon a hill," he said, "the eyes of all people are upon us; so that if we shall deal falsely with our God in this work we have undertaken and so cause him to withdraw his present help from us, we shall be made a story and a by-word through the world." Massachusetts Bay Colony was to be a model of what the true Christian community should be, a beacon for a benighted world, an example for the rest of the Christian world to follow. The American Sense of Mission first appears here in the conception of Massachusetts Bay Colony as a City on a Hill.

This concept has undergone many changes from the 17th century Puritans to the present. The primary alteration is that it has become secularized—concerned more with this world (democracy, free enterprise, anti-communism, and anti-terrorism) than the next (the religious world that promises an afterlife). What has remained constant, however, is the belief that some power—God or nature—outside history is directing America's role to some noble end and purpose. The conviction held by most Americans—not all, to be sure, but most—that this country is a special nation with a unique, positive role to play in world history has endured.

Beginning with the revolutionary generation, Americans have continually touted the nation's secularized mission. American colonists had viewed the British Empire as a climax of liberty and believed they had inherited what was best in the British tradition of liberty. But when Britain became corrupt and proved false to her tradition (so American colonists maintained), the colonists revolted, and the United States of America emerged as the keeper of the tradition. The new national goal was to preserve and perhaps eventually even extend the tradition of liberty to others. To accomplish it, the United States must be a strong nation, and the only certain way to become ever stronger was to expand the geographic limits of the country. As Daniel Webster would later put it, speaking at the 50th anniversary of the Battle of Bunker Hill in 1825, "The last hopes of mankind rest with us [the United States of America]."

Most early American leaders were ardent expansionists. Thomas Paine, arguing for independence in his pamphlet *Common Sense*, wrote of an independent America with all new possibilities for security, prosperity, and unlimited potential to expand. "The cause of America," he noted, "is the cause of all mankind." George Washington was fond of writing and talking about what he called "Our Rising Empire." Thomas Jefferson wrote of and spoke of Americans as "the chosen people of God," a special breed of man "whose breast he has made his peculiar deposit for substantial and genuine virtue." John Quincy Adams agreed with Jefferson and rationalized American territorial ambitions in his memoirs. He wrote that what Europeans thought about America's will to empire mattered little because he knew that "from the time we became an independent people, it was as much a law of nature that [North America was ours as] the Mississippi should flow into the sea."

The views held by Paine, Washington, Jefferson, and John Quincy Adams were those of many other Americans as well. American expansion had widespread popular support. With both God and Nature supporting America's sense of mission, who could argue against the acquisition of a great continental empire, which would strengthen the nation by providing for its security, and make possible the dissemination of American ideals and values to other nations and other peoples. So, the American Sense of Mission was one rationale, a very powerful one at that, used by supporters of empire.

Another rationale, closely associated with the American sense of mission, was what was later called "white man's burden," or, more generously, "the civilizing mission." America had a duty to uplift and civilize the peoples around it, who were obviously primitive and miserable. In the United States, Senator Daniel Dickinson perhaps best expressed this ideology at the close of the Mexican War when he wrote: we have not "yet fulfilled the destiny allotted to us. New territory is spread out for us to subdue and fertilize; new races are presented for us to civilize, educate and absorb; new triumphs for us to achieve for the cause of freedom." At the time, Dickinson was a member of the Committee on Manufactures and the Committee on Private Land Claims. And in 1849, he advanced to Chairman of the United States Senate Committee on Finance.

Dickinson was not the only one to believe that white Americans possessed a duty to spread the power of their nation across the continent and "absorb new races." Earlier, others had asserted that the United States must be a haven for all the oppressed: annex Texas, they said, and make it an asylum for the oppressed (an asylum in the best sense of the word). Often this sentiment took the form of boundless idealism, as one poet of the era penned: "Be thou the guardian of the weak, of the unfriended . . . Be godlike in the will to serve." This sentiment, however, was as often as not a pretense for selfish and arrogant ends. And the professed desire to do good—especially if it was by means of the sword—was not always appreciated by those who were being "uplifted" by the Americans.

Another—and very powerful—rational for the will to empire offered at the time was the need for more living space. Americans thought expansion across the continent was essential so there would be enough land available to take care of the natural growth of the nation's population. Today we call this ideology *lebensraum*, a term most famously connected with the political ideas of Adolf Hitler. Hitler had asserted in *Mein Kampf* that the German people needed living space in the East. This contention served as the primary justification for the Nazi invasion of the Soviet Union in 1941 and the subsequent effort to deport, enslave, and exterminate those peoples considered "inferior"—Jews, Poles, Russians, and other Slavic peoples—to make room for the "superior" Germanic people. To a large extent, in the 19th century, many Americans possessed their own desire for *lebensraum*, and for some, the North American continent was just not large enough.

As Congressmen Andrew Kennedy of Indiana said in 1846: "Go to the West and see a young man with his mate of eighteen; and after a lapse of 30 years, visit him again, and instead of two, you will find twenty-two. This is what I call the American multiplication table. . . . We are now twenty millions strong; and how long, under this process of multiplication, will it take to cover the continent with our posterity, from the Isthmus of Darien (another name for Panama) to the Bering's straits (straits separating Asia and Alaska)?" In other words, the country's population was destined to grow larger and larger (one popular prediction was 250 million by 1945—the nation had achieved approximately half that number in reality), so most Americans remained convinced a need existed to guarantee new lands for future generations where they could live free and unencumbered. To these Americans, the Louisiana Territory never seemed big enough.

It is important to understand that in all these rationales for empire, American expansion was not just something that Americans were causing to happen. And it was not something Americans had just willed to happen. Certain outside forces that were all beyond human control—historical, geographical, and cultural—were generating the quest for land and power. It was America's manifest destiny.

Another rationale (because for most Americans justification was unnecessary) for building the continental empire revolved around certain obvious geographical facts. The United States seemed "destined" by geography to control the North American continent from "sea to shining sea," and even parts of the southern continent as well. Did it make any sense for the Floridas to remain in the possession of Spain? Since the western border of the Louisiana Purchase remained in flux, why shouldn't the United States just extend its territory all the way to the Pacific coast? Didn't that make for geographical sense? And what about the islands near the continental United States?

For much of the 19th century, most Americans considered Cuba rightly belonged to the United States. At the time, it was a possession of Spain. John Quincy Adams, when he was U.S. Secretary of State, told the American minister to Spain in 1824 that "there are laws of political as well as physical gravitation, and if an apple severed by the tempest from its native tree, cannot choose but fall to the ground, Cuba, forcible disjoined from its own unnatural connection with Spain, and incapable of self-support, can gravitate only towards the North American Union, which, by the same law of nature, cannot cast her off from its bosom." In other words, just as an apple must fall from a tree to the ground, Cuba must fall from Spain's control to that of the United States. Gravity required Cuba become a possession of America. It was geographical destiny. By the first third of the 19th century, many Americans seemed to think it was their natural right to populate and control the new world. Most Americans, who thought about empire and power, believed both nature and geography were on America's side, compelling certain natural events to come about.

Perhaps the most obvious explanation for the will to empire was commercial exploitation, or more simply, greed. Americans rarely offered this explanation as a rationale for empire. The American sense of mission, white man's burden, *lebensraum*, and geographical predestination were all considered positive rationales for empire to 19th century Americans; these were good, even noble, reasons to extend American hegemony across the continent. The desire for wealth, both public and private, although it was the most powerful motivation underlying the will to empire, was rarely used as a rationale. Nonetheless, the desire for wealth was clear to Americans then and should be understood today. For example, did the United States really want California to free the oppressed people living there from the domination of a tyrannical Mexico, or did they want California because they wanted to take control of the valuable ports of San Diego and San Francisco? The motive, obviously, was not singular, but in the 1840s and 1850s, it was manifest for American leaders, both business and political, that getting control of the ports would expand American wealth and power.

The profit motive—greed—was never uniquely American. Americans had inherited greed from the Europeans, the English in particular. During the so-called Age of Exploration, the relentless pursuit of profit drove European exploration. The western hemisphere simply became the locus for profit for Spain, Portugal, England, and virtually every European nation. Americans simply continued the process. Land speculation in the 19th century, for example, became a way of life for many. Land speculators hoped, indeed demanded, that national leaders open the west to American settlers, most of whom were hoping to make a quick dollar, no matter at whose expense it came. The importance of this motive for empire is hard to measure, but the influence of land speculation was ever present.

Building the Continental Empire

Americans had inherited their will to empire—and all the rationales for it—from Europeans even before the existence of the American nation. It should not come as any surprise, then, that the desire for a continental empire was an implicit policy of the United States since its founding.

As we have seen in an earlier chapter, the United States declared its independence from Great Britain on July 2, 1776. John Adams, a member of the Second Continental Congress wrote his wife the next day (as he often did), extolling the importance of the day: "Yesterday the greatest question was decided which ever was debated in America; and a greater perhaps never was, nor will be, decided among men. A resolution was passed without one dissenting colony, that these United Colonies are, and of right ought to be, free and independent States." Americans will celebrate July 2, he told his wife, as "the day of deliverance . . . from one end of this continent to the other, from this time forward for evermore." At that moment, the United States was a meager 13 colonies populated by barely 2.5 million people, and yet Adams had the temerity—and confidence—to claim that in time the nation would encompass the entire continent. He was not alone in his belief.

The American will to empire was no less evident in the negotiation of The Treaty of Paris in 1783. The treaty that effectively ended the American Revolution did more than just legitimate the United States. Great Britain conceded a western boundary of the United States along the eastern bank of the Mississippi River. This new boundary immediately more than doubled the size of the original thirteen colonies. No longer could the Proclamation line of 1763 or any other artificial boundary hold back Americans. American revolutionists had won their independence and had acquired the vast western imperial domain they so coveted. It was not just independence; it was independence and empire.

Thomas Jefferson articulated his conception of the will to empire in his famous phrase "Empire for Liberty." In 1780—in the midst of the Revolutionary War—Jefferson asserted

John Adams Letter to Abigail July 3, 1776 (in original)

The Second Day of July 1776, will be the most memorable Epocha, in the History of America. I am apt to believe that it will be celebrated, by succeeding Generations, as the great anniversary Festival. It ought to be commemorated, as the Day of Deliverance by solemn Acts of Devotion to God Almighty. It ought to be solemnized with Pomp and Parade, with Shews, Games, Sports, Guns, Bells, Bonfires and Illuminations from one End of this Continent to the other from this Time forward forever more. You will think me transported with Enthusiasm but I am not. I am well aware of the Toil and Blood and Treasure, that it will cost Us to maintain this Declaration, and support and defend these States. Yet through all the Gloom I can see the Rays of ravishing Light and Glory. I can see that the End is more than worth all the Means. And that Posterity will tryumph in that Days Transaction, even altho We should rue it, which I trust in God We shall not.

As we have seen in a previous chapter, the purchase of Louisiana precipitated a constitutional controversy—nowhere did the Constitution state that the federal government could acquire through purchase new territories. Equally important, however, the Constitution did NOT provide for the incorporation of peoples residing in those territories—in this case more than 50,000 Creoles in the New Orleans area and countless untold numbers of Native Americans throughout the greater Louisiana territory: Crow, Sioux, Mandan, Shoshone, Arapaho, Pawnee, Osage, Kiowa, Apache, Comanche, Nez Perce, Blackfoot, and many others. Nevertheless, Jefferson and most of the country embraced the expansionist thrust. The president envisioned the immense but essentially unexplored Louisiana region as "an empire for liberty," large enough to absorb the flood of Americans westward for many generations to come. He rationalized the dubious legality of his actions by invoking "the laws of necessity, of self-preservation, of saving our country when in danger." When he left office in 1809, Jefferson wrote his successor, "we should have such an empire for liberty as [the world] has never surveyed since the creation . . . I am persuaded no constitution was ever before so well calculated as ours for extensive empire and self-government." He had come to see the Constitution as flexible and dynamic, and, obviously, perfectly suitable for the extension of American power.

The will to empire was equally evident in the motivations behind the War of 1812. This war was ostensibly fought to defend the principles of neutral rights and national honor against the high-handed ways of Great Britain (recall Madison's request of Congress). The expansionist "war hawks," who included the conquest of Canada and Florida as part of

that an independent America could "add to the Empire of liberty" by subverting British hopes for further empire in North America. When he became the nation's third president in 1801, Jefferson pledged at his inaugural a "wise and frugal government," and a strict interpretation of the constitution. In light of this, of course, it is especially ironic that Jefferson doubled yet again the size of the nation's domain in 1803 by the purchase of the Louisiana territory from France.

their goals, supported the war. Despite the exuberant mood of the nation in the aftermath of the perceived victory in the War of 1812, the nation still faced formidable problems in building its continental empire. While the United States would no longer face difficulties like it had before with the British, the United States would still have to deal with Spain.

Since 1803, Spain had disputed the legality of the Louisiana Purchase, particularly the specific boundaries of the Louisiana territory. By 1817, the Spanish government had reluctantly acknowledged the legitimacy of the sale of Louisiana to the U.S. but hoped to define the ambiguous eastern boundary at the Mississippi River (the same boundary agreed upon by the Treaty of Paris 1783). At the same time, the Spanish also claimed that the province of West Florida was not included in the Louisiana Purchase, as claimed by the Americans.

In a larger sense, Spain's continued control of both Floridas troubled many American's imperial desires. From the time of independence, the Floridas seemed a natural appendage to the United States (recall the aforementioned geographic rationale). From a practical standpoint, however, the most pressing concern for America was that the Floridas in Spanish hands were a haven for runaway slaves and recalcitrant Indians, a base from which to launch border raids on Georgia settlements and then flee to safety. After annihilating Indian resistance to white encroachments onto native lands at the Battle of Horseshoe Bend, many Creek Indians fled into Florida to avoid further attacks, capture, and the Indian Removal process that was then underway. Joining with the indigenous Seminole Indians in Florida, these natives became a force that southern whites felt needed to be subdued. Equally alarming to these recent white immigrants to the area, however, was the increasing number of runaway slaves allying themselves with the Creeks and Seminoles in Florida.

In December 1817, in response to the burning of an Indian village (Fowltown) on U.S. territory near the Florida/Georgia border, Seminoles attacked a supply boat on the Apalachicola River, killing most of its 40 to 50 passengers. Six survivors made it to safety including one woman; some reports indicated that possibly four children were killed in the attack. The attack provided the Monroe administration with the pretext it needed. American General Edmund Gaines was given broad authority to pursue the Seminoles into Florida and "adopt the necessary measures to terminate" the Seminole raids. On December 28, 1817, President Monroe's Secretary of War, John C. Calhoun was even more explicit in a message to General Andrew Jackson, "The movement against the Seminoles . . . will bring you on a theatre where you may possibly have other services to perform. Great interests are at issue . . . This is not a time for repose . . . until our cause is carried triumphantly thro[ugh]."

On January 6, 1818, Jackson along with 3000 Tennessee volunteer militiamen was already marching south toward Florida, even before receiving the order. Meeting minimal opposition from Seminoles, Creeks, and runaway slaves, Jackson and his men destroyed villages, food stores, and crops in a calculated attempt to inflict terror and starvation on these Florida inhabitants. By May, Jackson and his men occupied the fort at St. Marks in the East and the fortified town of Pensacola, the center of Spanish rule in Florida. Meanwhile, back in Washington, the Spanish Minister, Don Luis de Onís demanded evacuation of American troops from Florida and "suitable punishment" for Jackson. President Monroe, wavering on just what course to take, followed the advice of Secretary of State John Quincy Adams and opted to defend the actions of Jackson, entrusting the task to Adams.

Secretary of State Adams' reply berated the Spanish for not restraining the inhabitants of the Floridas and included the following: "Spain must immediately [decide] either to place a force in Florida adequate at once to the protection of her territory . . . or cede to the United States a province, of which she retains nothing but the nominal posses-

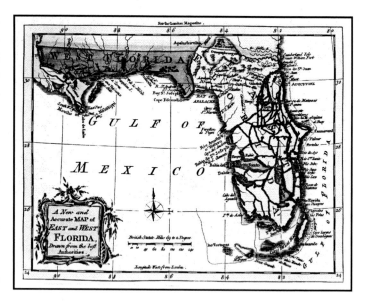

East and West Florida

sion, but which is, in fact . . . a post of annoyance to them." It very quickly became obvious to the Spanish government that the United States planned to seize the Floridas militarily if Spain was unwilling to negotiate a resolution.

Under pressure, the Spanish Minister began negotiations with Secretary of State Adams in late 1818. While Onís knew the United States would demand the cession of the Floridas unconditionally and that Spain would have to give it, he was unprepared for the boldness of Adams' new demand. He told the Spanish Minister that the western boundary of the United States must be extended all the way to the Pacific Ocean. For the first time in the history of the young country, an American administration demanded a European nation concede the American claim to a continental empire. To grant this American demand meant that Spain would have to give up all claim to the Oregon Territory. Not incidentally, the Monroe administration made no

claim to any part of Texas for fear of opening up the debate over the extension of slavery in the territories.

The Spanish government could do little else than give in to American demands. They had few inhabitants in Florida, a limited military force within their reach to fight, and it was clear to the Spanish that no other European country would intervene on their behalf. In February 1819, the Adams- Onís Treaty was signed. It later became known as The Transcontinental Treaty. It defined the western boundary of the United States all the way to the Pacific and provided for the cession of the Floridas to the United States. In addition, the U.S. agreed to pay 5 million to cover southern claims against the Spanish. The British press characterized the treaty as further proof of the ambitious, aggressive, expansionist ways of their former colonies. But to Secretary of State Adams, the treaty was but partial fulfillment of a divine plan. Europe, he had written in his diary, must become "familiarized with the idea of considering our proper dominion to be the continent of North America." Even more revelatory of American motivations, Adams added, "Until Europe shall find it a settled geographical element that the United States and North America are identical, any effort on our part to reason the world out of the belief that we are ambitions will have no other effect than to convince them that we add to our ambition hypocrisy."

With the acquisition of all of Florida and the still rather indefinite resolution of a western border all the way to the Pacific, America was well on its way to building the continental empire. We cannot neglect to notice that America's Florida endeavor resulted in a treaty between Spain and the United States, not a treaty between the United States and the Florida inhabitants. The reality was that there were very few Spaniards in Florida. At the time, Seminoles, Creeks, and runaway slaves populated Florida. But, these inhabitants of Florida were irrelevant to Spanish and American government leaders. If you were a person of color in Florida (or anywhere else in North America), you simply did not count in the world of global diplomacy.

Perhaps no development epitomized the motives and contradictions of America's building of a continental empire than the forced removal of approximately 125,000 Indians who still inhabited the lands of the Southeastern United States. As much as anything else, their removal was a clear indication of the darker side that came with building the assertion of American power. The driving force behind this acquisition of land by southern planters and the consequent removal of the native inhabitants was cotton. The massive and expanding demand for raw cotton was directly responsible for the urgency attached to removing Indians from fertile lands in what would soon become the plantation south. Private greed, justified by appeals to scripture and civilization (recall the aforementioned "white man's burden") had driven Indian Removal.

As we have seen, Indian Removal was accomplished by the federal government at a fearsome cost in human misery and human death. Despite numerous treaties between the federal government and Native tribes and a ruling by U.S. Supreme Court Chief Justice John Marshall upholding the principle of Indian treaty rights, the Jackson administration forcibly removed the native inhabitants from their lands without due process of law, something John Marshall declared could not be done. Treaties between the United States and Native Americans were routinely broken or ignored by successive American administrations. It would remain that way for essentially the entirety of the century. At the time, the Governor of Georgia, George Gilmer, made that openly and abundantly clear when he proclaimed: "Treaties were expedients by which the ignorant, intractable, and savage people were induced without bloodshed to yield up what civilized people had a right to possess by virtue of that command of the Creator delivered to man upon his formation—be fruitful, multiply, and replenish the earth, and subdue it." Almost every rationale listed for empire in this chapter is implied in this one statement: Sense of Mission, "white man's burden," *lebensraum*, and it is not too much of stretch to include geography as well. By 1837, most members of the five southeastern nations—Cherokee, Creek, Choctaw, Chickasaw, and Seminole—had been killed or relocated west, opening 25 million acres of land to white settlement and, significantly, to slavery.

By the 1840s, the two main areas into which many Americans thought the United States should next extend its control and its institutions were the northern possessions of Mexico—particularly Texas, but also New Mexico and California—and the Oregon country. Texas was the first area beyond the Louisiana Purchase where Americans moved in large numbers.

"Gone To Texas"

Following the "acquisition" of Florida from Spain in 1819, Anglo-Americans began to migrate into Texas, which remained (but not for long) part of Spain's dwindling New World Empire. In the wake of the Panic of 1819, indebted Americans, mostly from the upper South, left their homes and headed to what they considered the next and most natural frontier to them. By the end of the 1820s, increasing numbers of Anglo-Americans immigrated to Texas, many in hopes of extending plantation agriculture fueled by slave labor. Some left the phrase, "Gone to Texas" or just "GGT" haphazardly scrawled on their abandoned homes. The phrase remains common today in popular culture—musicals, movies, novels, and television—helping to romanticize what was nothing more than a rebellion of slaveholders in Texas against the government of Mexico into a "revolution." There was nothing "revolutionary" about what happened in Texas.

In 1820, Spain liberalized its immigration policies and gave a land grant to Moses Austin to settle 300 families in Texas. Spain hoped by doing so the increased numbers of settlers might discourage Comanche raids in the territory. At the time, there were barely 3,000 people (almost entirely Mexicans) living in the area. Before he could bring any set-

tlers to Texas, Moses Austin died on June 10, 1821. Initially reluctant, his son, Stephen F. Austin, agreed to fulfill the land grant and begin settling Anglo-Americans—primarily southerners—on the banks of the Colorado and Brazos River beginning in 1821. Before that happened however, Mexico won its independence from Spain, and made the Texas territory part of the state of *Coahuila y Tejas*. The new Mexican government Austin the title of *emprasario*, which allowed him to offer heads of Anglo-American immigrant families a league of land—approximately 4,400 acres. Such a large grant of land was very attractive, so much so that leaving the United States for a foreign nation was not really an issue for most. Austin himself received a grant of 67,000 acres. The Mexican government, for its part, initially encouraged Anglo-American immigrants into the area in hopes that a thriving cotton market might develop in Texas and help economically support the newly independent Mexico.

By 1830, more than 20,000 Anglo-Americans had gone to Texas, including 1000 slaves. These American immigrants bought their culture with them, and a big part of that culture was plantation agriculture fueled by the labor of slaves. As more Anglo-Americans began to move into Texas, the Mexican government put conditions on the land grants. Although the majority of immigrants were Protestant, a provision in the grants required conversion to Catholicism. Mexico had no protections for freedom of religion. These newest Mexican citizens (Texicans) agreed to the stipulation, but the vast majority did not live up to it. More problematic for the immigrants to Texas was Mexico's abolition of slavery in 1829. Given a one-year exemption from the law, most Texicans simply converted their slaves to indentured servants for life. By 1836, a thriving cotton economy dependent on nearly 5,000 lifetime "indentured servants" resided in Texas.

The fundamental issue of the illegality of the institution of American slavery in Mexican culture caused many Texicans to resent and eventually to reject the authority of the Mexican government, which, by the early 1830s, had begun to take steps to limit further American immigration. As early as 1832, Texicans were demanding the right to form their own state within Mexico—one that included the legalization of slavery. As tensions continued to rise, a fortuitous event for the Texicans occurred in 1834. General Santa Anna dissolved the Mexican Congress and became dictator of Mexico. Texicans, who considered themselves the inheritors of Anglo-American republican values, vowed to fight for Mexico's old democratic constitution by drawing up one of their own, which, of course, included slavery. But still they would be part of Mexico. Austin traveled to Mexico to acquire Santa Anna's acceptance, but Santa Anna denied the request for an independent slaveholding state within Mexico. He had Austin jailed when he learned Austin was advocating that Texicans act unilaterally on the statehood issue.

As Anglo-Americans continued to migrate into Texas in increasing numbers, many as squatters, Santa Anna came to believe a plot was underway to make Texas part of the United States and took steps to stop illegal immigration of Anglo-Americans into the region. By 1835, the Anglo-American population in Texas had grown to an estimated 30,000, about ten times as many as the number of Mexicans in the region. As Santa Anna centralized his control and abolished the federal system in Mexico, the Texicans assembled a convention and declared their independence on March 2, 1836. But Santa Anna was already moving north with a large army to subdue the rebelling Texicans.

On March 6, after 13 days of siege at the Alamo in San Antonio, a superior force of 3000 Mexicans soldiers wiped out a Texican force of a mere 186 men who had decided to hold out to the last man. It was a total victory for Santa Anna who ordered wounded men put to death. Only sixteen women, children, and servants who were in the Alamo survived the siege. One thousand five hundred and

Battles of the so-called "Texas Revolution"

forty-four Mexican soldiers were killed in the battle, which Santa Anna called a "glorious" victory. His aide commented in a diary, "One more such 'glorious victory' and we are finished."

Although the Alamo was of no real strategic value, the suicidal attempt to hold the mission slowed the Mexican army. The new Texan government dispatched Sam Houston, a protégé of Jackson, to reinforce the Alamo, but he was too late and began a retreat eastward after learning of the fall of the mission, gathering recruits along the way. On April 21, 1836, just west of the San Jacinto River, Houston and his Texican Army defeated and captured Santa Anna. An injured Houston—shot in the leg—forced Santa Anna to agree to Texas independence. Barely 800 Texican and American volunteers surprised and overwhelmed a larger Mexican force in a scant fifteen-minute battle. A reconstituted Mexican Congress repudiated the treaty, but the war was over.

The residents of Texas hastily drafted a new constitution, made Houston their first president, and sought immediate annexation to the United States. Most Texicans had always longed to be part of the United States. The addition of another slave state to the Union, however, threatened to initiate a sectional quarrel by upsetting the delicate balance of free and slave states. Democrats in Congress avoided the issue of annexation for fear of hurting the chances of Democrat Martin Van Buren in the coming election. Even the President, Andrew Jackson, moved cautiously on the issue, waiting until his last day in office to recognize the Texas Republic. He left the issue of annexation to his successor, Van Buren, who also chose to avoid the issue throughout his presidency. Both France and England chose to recognize an independent Texas in hopes of developing another source for cotton, but also to hinder American expansion across the continent.

Although prospects for annexation to the United States were not good, most residents of Texas, nonetheless, refused to give up on the idea. In the years following the so-called "Texas Revolution," continued fear of British efforts to thwart American imperial desires turned more government leaders toward considering annexation, particularly southern slaveholders, who had always made up the largest number of advocates for annexation. In early 1843, the United States commenced secret negotiations with Texas. By April, Secretary of State John C. Calhoun, an ardent supporter of slavery and its extension, concluded a treaty of annexation and sent it to the Senate for ratification. At the same time, Calhoun unwisely sent a letter to a representative of the British government, which promoted the virtues of slavery. He also suggested that the United States must add Texas as a reminder to abolitionists in Britain (by this time Britain had ended slavery throughout the empire) that slavery in America was not an evil. When the letter was published, any hope was dashed that annexation of Texas might be accomplished without a contentious debate over the institution of slavery. Adding this to the fear that annexation might bring war with Mexico resulted in an overwhelming rejection of the treaty in the Senate.

The Election of 1844

Although the wisest among the Whig and Democratic Party leaders hoped to keep the divisive issue of annexation of Texas out of the 1844 campaign, that desire turned out impossible. Already by 1844, the extension of empire and of slavery had become inseparably intertwined. Consequently, the presidential election of 1844 became nothing less than a national referendum on the question of Manifest Destiny for American voters.

Throughout the campaign, Manifest Destiny was more important than all other issues. The Whigs nominated Henry Clay, "Mr. Whig," who still hoped to avoid the whole controversial question of territorial expansion in the campaign because of the sectional animosities between the North and the South that the question aroused (i.e., would new territories be slave or free?). The Democrats rejected incumbent President John Tyler, as well as former President Martin Van Buren, and instead chose the country's first "dark horse" nominee, James K. Polk of Tennessee. Polk was far from unknown, however. He had served in the House of Representatives for 14 years—two terms as Speaker—and had been governor of Tennessee for one term. Newspapers labeled Polk a "dark horse" candidate only because he had not been considered for the nomination before the Democratic Party's convention.

Polk, who possessed none of Andrew Jackson's charisma, enjoyed being called "Young Hickory." He did share much of the former president's determination and unwillingness to compromise. He also shared Jackson's prejudices. Hardworking and focused, Polk promised to serve only one term. In almost every way, he was very much a Jacksonian Democrat. He did not like abolitionists; he thought they might bring about the destruction of the Democratic Party and even the Union with their unceasing nattering against slavery and slaveholders. In the campaign, he promised to reduce tariffs, reestablish an independent treasury, and acquire vast expanses of territory in the west.

Polk, unlike Clay, made no attempt to avoid the issue of empire; quite the contrary, building the continental empire was a major part of his campaign. Polk made it clear he was an expansionist and was eager to add the territories of northern Mexico and Oregon to the United States. During the campaign, the Whigs, in scornful derision of the "dark horse" Democratic candidate, asked, "Who is James K. Polk?" The Democrats answered that he was the man who would carry out the "re-occupation of Oregon" and the "re-annexation of Texas." The claim was, of course, bogus, but very effective, not too different from today's modern campaign rhetoric. After the election was over, had the Whigs continued to ask, "Who is James K. Polk?" the Democrats could have answered: he was the President-elect of the United States. The vote was close, but Polk won. Although he received only 38,000 more votes than Clay, his margin in the Electoral College was 170 to 105. Despite its closeness, Polk interpreted his victory over Clay to be a popular mandate for expansion. And expand the nation, he did.

The "re-annexation of Texas," much to Polk's delight, was already underway before he took office in 1845. Outgoing President Tyler interpreted Polk's victory in the election as a mandate to act on the issue. It was still not possible to bring Texas into the nation by means of a treaty of annexation, which required a 2/3^{rds} vote in Congress, so instead Texas became a state by a joint resolution, which required only a simple majority. Nonetheless, the debate in Congress was volatile and quite acrimonious. The resolution passed in the House by a margin of 120-98. In the Senate, the vote was even closer, 27-25. On March 1, 1845, President Tyler signed the resolution.

This was the first time Congress used a joint resolution to acquire new territory, and the resolution made no mention of securing Mexico's consent to the annexation. The resolution provided that Texas would become a state immediately without a preliminary period as a territory. It also allowed Texas, after it became a state, to divide itself into as many as five separate states without having to obtain the permission of Congress, the other states, or anybody else. To no one's surprise, Mexican leaders were so angry, having never recognized the Republic of Texas in the first place that the government broke diplomatic relations with the United States and began to beef up its army in preparation for a possible fight with the United States to stop it from annexing Texas. But the annexation occurred anyway. The following October, Texas voters ratified it and the state formally entered the fold—as a slave state—on December 29, 1845. Texas had been "re-annexed," but acquiring other parts of northern Mexico turned out to be much more difficult.

The "Re-occupation of Oregon"

During the campaign of 1844, candidate Polk insisted the only settlement he would accept regarding the Oregon Territory was a northern border along the 54°40′ north latitude line. By later abandoning his insistence on 54°40′ north latitude, the new President was able to add a large part of the Oregon territory to the United States by a treaty with Great Britain, ratified by the U.S. Senate in June 1846.

A long history of dispute had characterized the "ownership" of the Oregon Territory, which included present-day Oregon, Washington, Idaho and portions of Montana, Wyoming and British Columbia. Spain, Great Britain, and the United States had at one time or another made claim to the Oregon Territory (mostly ignoring the rights of the original inhabitants of the area). By the Polk administration, both Spain

and Russia had surrendered their claims to the region, but the United States and Britain remained active claimants. During the 1830s, the American position generally came to favor establishment of the northern border along 49° north latitude, arguing that the nation's Manifest Destiny required no less. But during his inaugural address on March 4, 1845, Polk claimed the United States possessed "clear and unquestionable" title in the area all the way to 54°40′ north latitude. The claim, he knew was spurious, but by making it he believed he would later be in a better position to compromise (demand more than you want or expect, then, as you reduce your claim, you appear magnanimous). The British, wanted to see the southern boundary of British Columbia (and, thus, the northern boundary of the Oregon Territory) established at the Columbia River. They based their claim on the long presence of a British company in the area, the Hudson's Bay Company. So, when Polk later offered to accept less than he had initially demanded—settlement of a boundary at 49° north latitude—the British refused.

In December 1845, in his annual address to Congress, Polk suggested he give the British one-year's notice that continued joint occupation of the area would be terminated. After bitter debate, Congress adopted the resolution. The idea worked. The British were not particularly interested in going to war with the United States over a wilderness area within which few British citizens resided. By the mid-1840s, large numbers of American settlers had poured into the disputed area by travelling the Oregon Trail. Great Britain and the United States entered into diplomatic discussions and in early June 1846, the British government relented to 49° north latitude as the border. On June 18, the U.S. Senate ratified the Treaty of Washington. It was the best

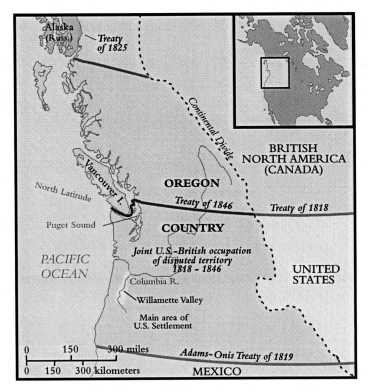

The Oregon Territory

But there also was no doubt that he was ready to resort to war if he could not get them peaceably. President Polk sent his personal emissary, John Slidell, on a secret mission to Mexico City with an offer to purchase New Mexico and Upper California from Mexico for from $15 to $40 million. The Mexican government turned down the offer; in fact, they even refused to meet with Polk's emissary. It was then that President Polk began to realize that since the use of diplomacy and money had failed, the "manifest destiny" of the United States might only be achieved by war.

Encouraging the possibility of war, in January 1846 President Polk sent American soldiers under the command of General Zachary Taylor into an area still disputed between Texas and Mexico along the Rio Grande River. For Mexico, there existed no such thing as the "re-annexation of Texas;" annexation had not been recognized by Mexico nor, obviously, had the Rio Grande been accepted as the border. The border of Mexican Texas (*Coahuila y Tejas*) had always been the Nueces River, not the Rio Grande. Polk simply insisted the territory between these two rivers (like the rest of Texas) was American territory, and, therefore, American troops had a right to be there. But the President knew that Mexico did not consider it American territory and did not believe U.S. troops had a right to be there. And surely Polk knew that Mexico would interpret his move—sending in U.S. troops—as an aggressive act. Polk seemed to be looking for trouble—even hoping for trouble. One

deal Polk could get, so he took it—over the strong objection of some expansionists in his own party. In any case, the United States had "re-occupied Oregon," (at least a large part of it) and one element of Polk's vision for a continental empire had been achieved. For his part, Polk did not want a war with England over Oregon. Throughout the negotiations, Polk was much more concerned about events in in Texas and what would later become the New Mexico and California Territories.

The Mexican War

Polk hoped to acquire the New Mexico and California Territories by peaceful methods—through the use of diplomacy and money.

young officer, Ulysses S. Grant, who would serve in the coming war, later conceded, "We were sent to provoke a fight, but it was essential that Mexico commence it." To Polk's chagrin, however, nearly four months passed by and nothing happened; the Mexican government and military—irritatingly from Polk's perspective—refused to react with any provocative moves of their own.

Finally, on April 25, 1846, a skirmish broke out between Mexican and U.S. troops just north of the Rio Grande. Mexican soldiers killed 11 Americans, wounded five, and captured about 50. Meanwhile, back in Washington, President Polk had already decided to ask Congress to declare war on Mexico on the grounds that Mexico was not honoring its financial obligations and had insulted the U.S. by refusing to deal with the President's emissary, John Slidell. But when word of the skirmish reached Washington, Polk hastily modified his war message to Congress and concluded with these words: "The cup of forbearance had been exhausted even before the recent information from the frontier . . . But now, after reiterated menaces, Mexico has passed the boundary of the United States, has invaded our territory and shed American blood upon the American soil . . . the two nations are now at war . . . notwithstanding all our efforts to avoid it . . . we are called upon by every consideration of duty and patriotism to vindicate with decision the honor, the rights, and the interests of our country."

Not many people questioned Polk's interpretation at the time, and Congress honored the president's request for a declaration of war by huge margins. Most Whig politicians felt they had no choice but to support the military measures, but they showed less enthusiasm for the war than Polk's own Democratic Party. In the House, the vote for war was 174-14, with all the opposition coming from northern Whigs. In the Senate, the vote was 40-2 (both votes against came from Whig Congressmen).

Despite appearing to want war with Mexico, under Polk's guidance the United States did little in preparation for it. At the outset of the war, the American army numbered but 7,000 men, while the Mexican army could field close to 32,000. By the end of the war, however, the U.S. army had grown to 104,000. Food, transportation, clothing, tents, and even weapons tended to remain in short supply throughout much of the war. A then unknown Lieutenant George McClellan noted that when he arrived to the Rio Grande there were no supplies whatsoever: "I have also come to the conclusion that the quartermaster's department is most woefully conducted—never trust anything to that department that you can do for yourself." One regiment sent to Mexico in February 1847 was unarmed for an entire week because the army essentially ran out of muskets; yet another went three weeks without tents. Clothing issues became so bad that General Winfield Scott filed a protest with the Secretary of War, noting that when he should have been conducting operations, he had to detail 1000 of his men to make shoes and pants for his army.

Polk wanted a brief and small war; win early and force a quick surrender. In California, before the war began, the President hoped to cause a Texas-style revolt. Toward the end of 1845, John C. Fremont and a group of about sixty men headed west allegedly to explore the area. After hearing war was imminent between the U.S. and Mexico, Fremont moved into the Sacramento Valley area and endorsed the independent Republic of California, which a group of barely thirty settlers, mostly American, had declared in June 1846. The Republic of California, however, existed for less than a month.

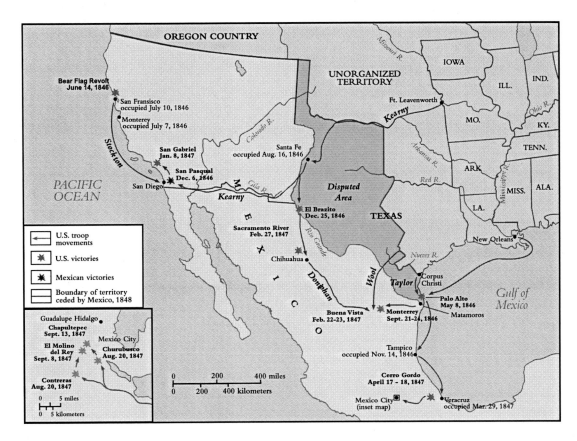

The Mexican War

Intermittent fighting between Mexican and American troops continued in California for the remainder of the year. U.S. Colonel Stephen Kearny with just 300 men, meanwhile, captured Santa Fe. Linking up with Fremont's forces, the remaining Mexican force in California was ousted and armed conflict ended in the area in January 1847. Shortly thereafter, General Scott's army sailed to a landing at Veracruz on the Mexican coast along the southern Gulf of Mexico.

Scott's force of 10,000 captured the city of Veracruz easily in April, carrying out America's first successful amphibious assault. The Mexican commander surrendered the city after only a one-week siege. Scott then moved inland to Mexico City along the same route Spanish Conquistador Hernan Cortez had travelled three centuries earlier. On September 13, 1847, American troops entered the city. A battalion of Marines raised an American flag at the National Palace and occupied what was ever after known in America as the "halls of Montezuma." The war—from an American perspective—had gone so well that many began to think of permanently annexing all of Mexico, not just the northern part of it. An editor of the *New York Herald* spoke for many when he wrote: "We believe it is a part of our destiny to civilize that beautiful country and enable its inhabitants to appreciate some of the many advantages and blessing they enjoy." Even President Polk had begun to think the idea of annexing all of Mexico made a lot of sense. But the State Department official he had sent in with the American troops, Nicholas P. Trist, had already negotiated on February 2, 1848, a remarkably successful treaty with Mexico ending the war and settling most of the outstanding disputes between Mexico and the United States.

By the terms of the Treaty of Guadalupe Hidalgo, the United States secured the Rio Grande as the border for Texas and obtained New Mexico and California. In return for all this, the United States agreed to pay Mexico some $15 million for all the territory taken away and also agreed to assume all claims of U.S. citizens against Mexico (up to a total of $3.25 million). Paying Mexico $15 million was a strange provision to end a war that had supposedly begun because Mexico had unjustly attacked U.S. troops on American soil, or as Polk put it, had "shed American blood upon the American soil." Polk was furious with Trist for negotiating the treaty prematurely. He labeled him "an impudent and unqualified scoundrel" and fired him immediately upon his return from Mexico because he let the entire nation of Mexico slip out of American hands. Polk eventually decided it would not have been prudent to pursue more territory, writing in his diary that he thought "Congress would not grant either men or money to prosecute the war" further. The U.S. Senate ratified the Treaty of Guadalupe Hidalgo in March and the last American troops left Mexico by the end of July 1848.

The newly acquired territory (including the present states of Arizona, Nevada, California, and Utah, and parts of New Mexico, Colorado, and Wyoming) when combined with Texas added nearly 1.2 million (1,193,061) square miles to the national domain, an area 40% larger than the Louisiana Purchase, which had added some 828,000 square miles to the country back in 1803. Most Americans regarded the war against Mexico as a great American victory. Most Americans were satisfied that the United States had realized its Manifest Destiny, as the nation now assumed most of its present continental boundaries (only the Gadsden Purchase was still to be added in 1853).

Not everybody in the United States was happy with the war. Public satisfaction with the war was not unanimous from the very beginning. Not all Americans viewed the Mexican War as some divinely conceived battle to fulfill America's national destiny and bring the benefits of civilization and democracy to many blighted peoples beyond American borders. As the war continued and as costs and casualties began to mount, opposition in Congress intensified to what some opponents began to call "Mr. Polk's War." Opposition was especially strong among the Whigs, while most Democrats resolutely defended the war as a just one. Many Whigs attacked the war as an expansionist drive for territorial spoils, and accused the president of having initiated the war in violation of the Constitution.

Abraham Lincoln, then a first-term Whig Congressman from Illinois, privately expressed his fears over the growing power of the president to lead the nation into war in a letter to his law partner, William Herndon on February 15, 1848. Publicly, this same Whig Congressman had shown a distressing lack of patriotism by introducing a resolution in Congress demanding that the President identify the exact "spot" on which American blood had been spilled on American soil. His resolution came to be known as the "spot resolution." For his lack of patriotism, Lincoln lost

Abraham Lincoln Letter to William Herndon February 15, 1848

DEAR WILLIAM:

Your letter of the 29th January was received last night. Being exclusively a constitutional argument, I wish to submit some reflections upon it in the same spirit of kindness that I know actuates you. Let me first state what I understand to be your position. It is that if it shall become necessary to repel invasion, the President may, without violation of the Constitution, cross the line and invade the territory of another country, and that whether such necessity exists in any given case the President is the sole judge.

Before going further consider well whether this is or is not your position. If it is, it is a position that neither the President himself, nor any friend of his, so far as I know, has ever taken. Their only positions are—first, that the soil was ours when the hostilities commenced; and second, that whether it was rightfully ours or not, Congress had annexed it, and the President for that reason was bound to defend it; both of which are as clearly proved to be false in fact as you can prove that your house is mine. The soil was not ours, and Congress did not annex or attempt to annex it. But to return to your position. Allow the President to invade a neighboring nation whenever he shall deem it necessary to repel an invasion, and you allow him to do so whenever he may choose to say he deems it necessary for such purpose, and you allow him to make war at pleasure.

Study to see if you can fix any limit to his power in this respect, after having given him so much as you propose. If to-day he should choose to say he thinks it necessary to invade Canada to prevent the British from invading us, how could you stop him? You may say to him,—"I see no probability of the British invading us"; but he will say to you, "Be silent: I see it, if you don't."

The provision of the Constitution giving the war making power to Congress was dictated, as I understand it, by the following reasons: kings had always been involving and impoverishing their people in wars, pretending generally, if not always, that the good of the people was the object. This our convention understood to be the most oppressive of all kingly oppressions, and they resolved to so frame the Constitution that no one man should hold the power of bringing this oppression upon us. But your view destroys the whole matter, and places our President where kings have always stood. Write soon again.

Yours truly,

A. LINCOLN.

the support of the voters back home in Illinois and decided not to run for reelection in 1848. Lincoln found that it is difficult to oppose a president when he is leading the country in a war—not impossible, of course, but exceedingly difficult especially for a politician. Thus, Abraham Lincoln left Congress after one term and returned to a life he expected of obscurity and quiet desperation as a small-town lawyer in Illinois.

Lincoln was not the only one to oppose the Mexican War. Many Northern abolitionists and Northern intellectuals, most of whom saw the war only as an effort to extend slavery and strengthen the political power of the South in Congress, bitterly opposed it. Henry David Thoreau even spent a night in jail because he would not pay his taxes. He was afraid his tax money would be spent to support what he considered an unjust war in the name of the extension of slavery. Against his wishes, he was freed after only one day when a relative paid his taxes. In 1847, the Massachusetts legislature passed a resolution stating that the war was "unconstitutionally commenced by the order of the President" and that it was being waged for "the triple objects of extending slavery, of strengthening the slave power, and of obtaining the control of the free states." But opponents to the war were a decided minority of the American people. The majority of Americans believed that America had a destiny and that an important part of that destiny was geographic—a destiny which could only be achieved, at least in this instance, by war.

Relocating West

Although the majority of Americans supported the will to empire and many helped to make it a continental reality, most settlers of the west travelled there for very different and mostly personal reasons. In the second quarter of the 18th century, the largest number of these western pioneers came from the Midwest and upper South. They were mainly American-born whites, although a few blacks joined in the journey west. Between the Van Buren and Lincoln administrations (1836–1865), approximately 350,000 men, women, and children left areas east of the Mississippi to settle remote western lands, traveling the Overland Trail to the Oregon and California Territories. Tens of thousands more settled in Arkansas, Colorado, Utah, New Mexico, and Texas. This massive influx of people to the west often resulted in conflict and death, as the western pioneers encountered the indigenous inhabitants, many of whom who had lived there for centuries.

Some of the first migrants west traveled the Santa Fe Trail, which begin in the central Missouri town of Franklin (although many settlers began the journey from Independence on the western edge of Missouri) on the bank of the Missouri River and split into a northern and southern branch on the way to Santa Fe. After Mexico achieved its independence from Spain in 1821, the new nation encouraged trade and commerce with Americans (something Spain had prohibited), and hundreds of Americans then forged the trail to Santa Fe in hopes establishing their futures as businessmen and traders. Although traders taking the route were often under attack by Native Americans, the trail became so active that the Mexican silver peso became a primary currency in Missouri during the 1830s. With Mexican control over its northern borderlands weak and with more Americans seeking their fortunes by using the Trail, some began to settle in Santa Fe, although they were few in number compared to traders. Nonetheless, these settlers over time successfully asserted a U.S. presence in the area. Equally important, the traders who forged the Santa Fe Trail had developed the pioneering techniques that even greater numbers of Americans traveling along the California and Oregon Trails would use over the next several decades.

Using what they learned on the Santa Fe Trail, American migrants traveled in wagon caravans first to Oregon the then later to California. But unlike what happened with the Santa Fe Trail, most of the people traveling on

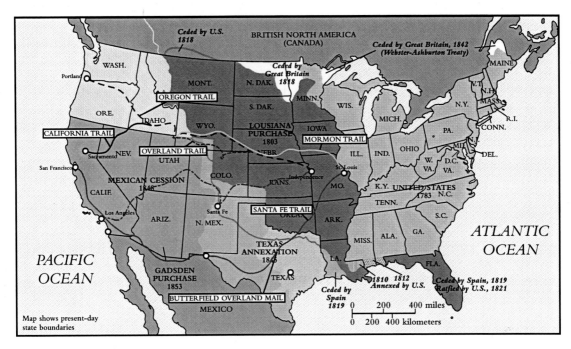

Overland Trails Network

Overland Trail were settlers—families from all over America seeking a new life in the west—not traders. And while many were believers in America's manifest destiny, their primary motivation for heading west was seeking their own personal destiny separate from that of their nation.

Families traveling west left Independence, Missouri, moving into what is now Wyoming on the Overland Trail. The wisest of the migrants left in early spring in order to complete the arduous 2,000-mile trek before winter set in—the journey took most about six months. The first pioneers departed in 1841, heading for the fertile Willamette Valley in the Oregon territory in ox-drawn, canvas-covered wagons, which quickly became known as "prairie schooners." By the middle of the 1840s, nearly 5,000 settlers per year were attempting the crossing. At Fort Hall in present

day Idaho, the Overland Trail split into its northern and southern branches. The southern branch was the California Trail and the northern, the Oregon Trail. By the late 1840s, settlers simply traveled either the Oregon or California Trail from Missouri, depending upon the final destination. Prior to discovery of gold in California in 1848, only about 2,500 settlers had traveled to California, but those settlers were instrumental in helping California become part of the United States during the Mexican War. In 1850, the peak year for migration, nearly 55,000 settlers headed west along the Oregon and California Trails. The journey, however, remained fraught with danger no matter how many attempted it.

Few were prepared for the hardships of the journey, to say nothing of the difficulty of establishing a life on the frontier. Over 20,000 people are estimated to have died during their journey west, many from disease—primarily cholera, caused by a bacterial infection that attacks the small intestine producing profuse diarrhea, vomiting, and ultimately death. Although Native Americans attacked some caravans, it was actually a rare occurrence. Most settlers travelled along the trail unmolested. In some cases, Native raiding parties demanded payments, usually goods or supplies. In other cases, Native peoples aided struggling settlers. Conflict between Native Americans and settlers heading west as portrayed in movies and television in the 20th century was simply invented for popular consumption.

In 1851, U.S. government officials and representatives of Native tribes in the Plains agreed to the Ft. Laramie Treaty. The Treaty promised annual cash payments to Native peoples as compensation for any damages caused by settlers traveling west across hunting grounds. In exchange, Native Americans agreed to discontinue any harassment of wagon trains, to acquiesce in construction of U.S. forts in the west, and—significantly—to restrict themselves to land areas "of limited extent and well-defined boundaries." Initially, these areas were immense. The government only asked for a corridor through which the Overland Trail passed. This agreement, reluctantly agreed to by most of the Native tribes, was just the first of many treaties to come which would restrict Native Americans to increasingly smaller areas, inaugurating the "reservation" concept employed in the post-Civil War era.

The most tragic story of hardships faced by migrants along the Overland Trail involved a group of settlers known as the Donner Party. George Donner, a wealthy Illinois farmer led his family and a group of other settlers west in 1846. Making every possible error, they began too late in the year; they overloaded down the wagons with unnecessary items; and, significantly, they recklessly attempted a shortcut to California across the Wasatch Mountains in the Utah Territory. They had arrived at Truckee Pass too late and remained trapped there beginning in November 1846. As food supplies ran low, a group of 17 set out on foot in hopes of finding help. The remaining 70 settlers—half of whom were children—were trapped with food enough barely to last for a month. When the first rescue group arrived in mid-February 1847, they discovered a grisly scene. Thirteen members of the Donner Party had died and the survivors had taken to eating their bodies. Of the 87 members of the Donner Party, only 48 survived the journey.

A Counter Destiny

Whether or not American settlers considered their journeys and settlement of the west as part of America's divine destiny to build a continental empire, their actions, nonetheless, helped it become a reality. Certainly, the American government's thuggish behavior toward Mexico was the most blatant example of ignoring the rights of other peoples and nations in its quest for empire. The Mexican War had achieved a part of the nation's manifest destiny. But it also opened the door to a terrible, seemingly insoluble problem regarding the future of the country. Would slavery be allowed in the new territories? Would a political conflict develop between the sections of the country over the issue?

By the decade of the 1850s the United States had expanded across a continent—America had built its continental empire—America had achieved the potential for strategic supremacy in the Western Hemisphere as foretold in the Monroe Doctrine.

America had also established the foundations for a future 20th and 21st century global empire. The dreams of the nation's founders—Washington, Jefferson, Hamilton, Adams, and so many others—had been realized and in many respects surpassed. And although so many destroyed and murdered lives lay in its wake, America did seem to have achieved a divine destiny. Yet, a counter-destiny now awaited fulfillment.

Almost from the start, the threat of secession—even the possibility of civil war—had been a common discourse in American politics. Toward the end of the 1850s, William Seward, a leader of the newly formed Republican Party—the free-soil party opposed to the extension of slavery in the territories—plainly described the developing battle this way: "It is an irrepressible conflict between opposing and enduring forces, and it means that the United States must and will, sooner or later, become either entirely a slave-holding nation, or entirely a free-labor nation . . ."

Although the American nation began simply as a compact among the states, the unrelenting will to empire transformed it into much more than a loose confederacy of states. America had achieved its manifest destiny, but that destiny produced a growing political crisis in the nation over the extension of slavery in the territories. American slavery could no longer remain merely a moral crisis over good and evil behavior; it was a political problem dividing the nation into sections, one in favor of slavery and its extension, and the other opposed to its extension. The will to empire in a very short time had dramatically extended American power, but at the same time, that accomplishment forced the nation to come to grips the inherent problem in the definition of the American people—namely, the existence of slavery in a society of citizens espousing freedom and equality as the guiding values of their nation.

Suggested Readings

Bauer, K. Jack. *The Mexican War, 1846–1848*, Lincoln: University of Nebraska Press, 1974.

Campbell, Randolph B. *An Empire for Slavery: The Peculiar Institution in Texas, 1821–1865*. Baton Rouge: Louisiana State University Press, 1989.

Kluger, Richard. *Seizing Destiny: How America Grew from Sea to Shining Sea*. 1st ed. New York: A.A. Knopf, 2007.

Merk, Frederick. *Manifest Destiny and Mission in American History; a Reinterpretation*. 1st ed. New York,: Knopf, 1963.

Pletcher, David M. *The Diplomacy of Annexation; Texas, Oregon, and the Mexican War*. Columbia: University of Missouri Press, 1973.

Weeks, William Earl. *Building the Continental Empire: American Expansion from the Revolution to the Civil War*, American Ways Series. Chicago, Ill.: Ivan R. Dee, 1996.

Chapter 12

DIVERGENT SOCIETIES: SLAVERY, ANTI-SLAVERY & ANTEBELLUM REFORM

Because of the different nature of their geography, economy, and culture, a sense of distinction had existed between the northern and southern portions of the United States since before the founding of the nation. While the South relied heavily on staple crops, the plantation system, and slavery; Americans who lived further north developed a more diverse economy, eliminated slavery in favor of a wage labor system, and lived very different kinds of lives than southerners. During the *antebellum era*—the decades preceding the Civil War—this sense of difference became even more profound; for the economic changes of the early 19th century had strengthened southern dependence on slavery at the same time that it brought a new order based on wage labor to the northern portion of the nation.

In reaction to the changes of the times, northerners increasingly became involved with various reform movements aimed at mediating the changes they saw going on around them. The religious impulses of the era also encouraged them in efforts to perfect American society and make it more godly and moral. While southerners, like northerners, experienced a rise in religious enthusiasm in the early 19th century, it did not translate to the same reformist type of impulse in the slave states. In fact, northern reform efforts widened the sectional breach even further, as southerners resisted northern prescriptions for change. Why such resistance? One of the most prominent reform efforts of the era was the movement to abolish slavery—a movement that threatened the underpinnings of southern society. Between 1830 and 1850 Americans in the North became increasingly critical of the southern commitment to slavery, and Americans in the South became increasingly defensive about that commitment. During these decades, then, Americans experienced a rise in sectional tensions that caused northerners and southerners to see themselves, more and more, as societies that functioned in opposition to one another.

The Reform Impulse in the North

As discussed in Chapter 9, the northern economy underwent profound change during the antebellum era as a result of the rise of industrialization, the creation of new transportation and communication networks, and the development of a more interconnected market economy. While the South became more dedicated to plantation agriculture, the North was increasingly becoming more urban, more committed to industry, and more dependent on wage labor. Economic change brought cultural change throughout the region—especially the northeastern part of the United States—as Americans adjusted to the separation of the workplace and the home, the growth of cities, and the uncertainties of the emerging capitalist economy. An expanding middle class took notice of the problems associated with change, and many became involved in reform movements in an attempt to solve them.

Between 1820 and 1850, a numerous variety of reform movements flourished in the northern section of the United States as northerners organized societies in an attempt to solve societal ills. Among the causes they took up were health reform, anti-dueling campaigns, attempts to curb alcohol use, the promotion of public education, prison reform, the creation of asylums for the mentally ill, attacks on prostitution, societies to promote peace and discourage war, attempts to provide bibles and religious writings to new audiences, and, most significant all—a movement to end slavery in the United States.

This reform impulse emerged in the North for a number of reasons. First, and most important, reformers were reacting to the rapid economic growth of the era. The economic and social change that occurred during the early 19th century produced both a sense of hope and a sense of anxiety about America's future. On the one hand, many Americans were optimistic that economic development would make Americans prosperous and the country strong. On the other hand, the competitive spirit that accompanied industrial capitalism, the stresses that the system placed on the individual, and the disruption of the social order that came with change worried many Americans. Reformers were anxious about the turmoil that seemed to accompany rapid economic development, but they also were optimistic about the ability of mankind to create a perfect society. Efforts at reform would arise out of both of these outlooks.

A drive for *perfectionism* was an important element of the reform spirit. Reformers of the era truly believed that they could rid American society of all of its evils, and the religious mood of the times contributed to this ideology. In addition to economic change, a great wave of religious excitement had spread through the United States during the first half of the 19th century. Beginning in the 1820s and continuing into the 1850s, Protestant Americans experienced what has become known as the *Second Great Awakening*. Throughout the nation, preachers and church lay leaders responded to the increasing materialism and growing secularism of American society with sermons and *revivals*, long religious meetings aimed at reviving religious enthusiasm and bringing new converts to the church. Central to this wave of revivalism was a belief in the perfectibility of mankind. Religious leaders of the Second Great Awakening emphasized that

individuals had it within their power to make both themselves and the larger society they lived within perfect in God's eyes. Many church leaders preached that the *millennium,* a period when they believed that Jesus Christ would return to earth and reign for a thousand years, would come only after mankind had reached this state of perfection. Revivalist ministers thus emphasized the necessity for Christians to try to reform their society in order to achieve this goal of godly perfection.

One of the most influential religious leaders of the Second Great Awakening was Charles Grandison Finney. Finney was an English Presbyterian minister who visited the United States during the 1820s and 1830s and led revivals throughout the north. He appealed to a breadth of individuals, and he preached that everyone was individually in charge of their own salvation. He thus rejected the Calvinist ideal of predestination, as did many other evangelical leaders of the time. Finney emphasized that mankind had the capability of working towards bringing about the millennium through active involvement in societal reform movements, and he promoted an emotional type of worship that centered on the individual conversion experience—a moment when one committed him or herself to Christ and to the creation of a godly society. He preached his message in the towns along the Erie Canal that connected New York City to the western states. So many were converted as a result of these efforts that the region around the canal in western New York became known as the *Burnt Over District*—as the place had been "burnt over" by evangelical Christianity.

Finney's influence, however, extended beyond the number of conversions for which he was personally responsible. He popularized methods that would be copied by many other ministers as they recognized their effectiveness in generating religious enthusiasm. Finney appealed to the emotions of his audience. He was democratic, and he preached that any person—not just the religious elite—could have a personal relationship with God and could participate in spreading the Christian message in society. He held long revivals, some of which lasted several days, and he pushed participants to share their conversion experiences with one another. He appealed to women and encouraged them to use their moral influence on the men in their household. As Finney gained more and more converts, others copied these techniques, and they helped to energize American religion throughout the United States and evangelical reform movements throughout the North. The revivals had an impact on a wide variety of Americans, crossing regional, racial, class and gender boundaries.

As revivalism spread, voluntary associations were formed throughout the North to serve as agents through which to spread the evangelical message and attack social problems in the nation. Missionary societies came together with the goal of spreading Christianity both abroad and within the United States. Bible and tract societies were formed in order to provide Christian literature to Americans who might not have easy access to those materials (such as western settlers and the urban poor). As these voluntary associations became increasingly well-organized, new moral reform organization emerged in order to attack vice and promote Christian values.

Perfectionism was not just a religious impulse, however. The possibility of perfecting society also imbued the ideals of influential thinkers outside of the realm of the church. At the same time that the Second Great Awakening was taking place, Europe and then the United States experienced an intellectual and artistic movement known as *Romanticism*.

The Romantic Movement began as a reaction against the Enlightenment ideology that encouraged a dedication to scientific knowledge and to reason over emotion. Many thinkers of the 19th century felt that this dedication to fact and to what could scientifically be proven was uninspired. Like the evangelicals of the time, they emphasized a spirit of individualism and a dedication to emotion. They lifted up the natural world as superior to the urban environment created by mankind, and they rejected the materialism of their age.

In America, Romanticism found its clearest expression in *Transcendentalism*. The Transcendentalists were a group of influential New England thinkers and writers who lifted up the natural world, asserted the sanctity of the individual, and promoted the idea that imagination and intuition could lead to a higher level of understanding than the accumulation of facts and data. The Transcendentalist movement was not an organized movement per se; it was more a collection of individuals with similar ideals. They were united by a desire to go beyond, or to transcend, enslavement to both reason and the material world.

Among the most influential Transcendentalists were Ralph Waldo Emerson and Henry David Thoreau. Emerson was a former Unitarian minister who left the ministry in order to become a writer and lecturer. His most famous essays include *Nature* (1836) and *Self Reliance* (1841). In them he argued that the individual was sacred, and he encouraged a spiritual connection between the individual and nature. Henry David Thoreau's work put forth similar ideals. His most famous work, *Walden* (1854), recounts his attempt to retreat from society and materialism in order to commune with nature, where he could find a greater connection to God. Thoreau is also famous for his opposition to the Mexican War and slavery. He went to jail because he refused to pay taxes that would support a war that he felt was wrong. In his essay *Civil Disobedience* (1849), he urged individuals to reject conforming to society's expectations and the laws of the state if the values they lifted up violated one's own conscious.

Like the Great Awakening, the spirit of Romanticism promoted a desire to recreate and perfect American society. The Transcendentalists were concerned about the materialism that had arisen in American society and the move that mankind had made away from nature and away from the exercise of individual conscience. Their anxiety was paired with optimism, however, for they believed that mankind could perfect itself by tapping into the individual conscience and turning away from the competitive materialist mindset that had emerged during the antebellum period.

The shifts that occurred in the early 19th century thus helped to encourage a spirit of reform in both the secular and in the religious arenas of American society. The mixture of anxiety about change and hope for the future caused many Americans to work towards creating a more moral society. This spirit of reform generally took two directions. While most reformers worked to bring about change among the general public, others withdrew from the larger society in order to create a different kind of social order that could serve as an example to mankind.

Utopian Communities

Some Americans coped with the changes of their era by retreating from society and creating experimental communities where members established new types of social structures within which to live. These social experiments are referred to as *utopian communities*— a name that references a book by English philosopher Sir Thomas More, *Utopia* (1519), which described an island on which inhabitants created a perfect society. Utopian communities could be religious or secular in nature, but they all sought to create a social order separate from immoral influences and the chaos that seemed to characterize American society during their times. Although they separated themselves from the rest of American society, members of these communities were still interested in widespread social reform; for many were immersed in the perfectionist ideal. They wanted to organize a perfect society that would serve as an example for others to imitate.

In response to the competitive market economy that was emerging, some reformers sought refuge in master-planned cooperative communities—societies where all members would share equally in work and its rewards. Two of the more famous communities of this type were *Brook Farm*, a Transcendentalist community established by George Ripley in West Roxbury, Massachusetts and *New Harmony*, a community that was developed in Indiana by Scottish socialist thinker and industrial reformer, Robert Owen. Neither of these communities was successful in the long term, but they illustrate attempts to create alternatives to a competitive capitalist system.

Brook Farm, which was created in 1841, lifted up both the ideology of individualism that characterized Transcendentalist thought as well as the importance of community. At Brook Farm all members would share in the work of the community, choosing jobs that would suit them as individuals; and all would reap the rewards of work equally. Ripley believed that this communitarian philosophy would free members of society to have the leisure to pursue their own path to self-realization. In reality, however, the individualist mindset of the society's members often conflicted with its communitarian organization, and Brook Farm did not run smoothly. Although many who lived at Brook Farm found their lives there to be satisfying, the community was never financially successful, and in 1847 a fire in one of its main buildings led to the abandonment of the experiment.

New Harmony, founded in Indiana, was Robert Owen's attempt to build a "Village of Cooperation" where all members of society would live and work in equality. In Scotland, Owen had become concerned with the poverty that accompanied the rise of industry in Great Britain, and he spent time trying to formulate a plan of reform that would alleviate the hardships of industrialism. He believed that one's environment was central to one's character and experience of the world. Thus, he believed that by changing the environment in which community members lived, he could help to elevate individuals and society at large. In 1824, he came to the United States, and he established his master-planned community in Indiana. He sought volunteers to come live in New Harmony where all would work in equality and where there would be no private property. Owen's experiment was not long lived, as the community disintegrated into factions within a few years of its founding.

These secular communitarian societies did not easily take hold in America because of the strong spirit of American individualism that conflicted with the communitarian ethos. In addition, the lure of western lands and the desire for wages that might allow for upward mobility prevented most Americans from committing themselves to these types of experiments long-term. In fact, utopian communities tended to prosper in the United States during times of economic depression when the market-place provided few opportunities, and they declined when prosperity returned.

While Brook Farm and New Harmony were founded out of secular impulses, many of the utopian societies of the time were religious in origin. These religious societies were, in general, more long-lived than the secular societies in America, for religious beliefs helped to cement the societies together and encourage a greater commitment to individual sacrifice for the larger community.

One of the earliest religious utopian communities to take shape in the United States was that of the *Shakers*, or the United Society of Believers in Christ's Second Appearing. The Shakers were an offshoot of the Quakers, so named because of a shaking motion they performed as they danced during worship. The founder of the Shakers was a woman named Ann Lee, who migrated with a small number of followers to America, settling in Massachusetts in 1774. Ann Lee was the daughter of an English blacksmith, and she believed that she had experienced religious visions that revealed that she was a female version of Jesus Christ. She also believed that there was a great need to reform society in order to prepare for the millennium, and she sent her followers out through New England to spread the word.

The Shaker following grew after her death in 1784, and during the time of the Second Great Awakening Shaker communities attracted many of the converts of the evangelical revivals of the era. The Shakers established around twenty settlements in the United States, and they formed a distinctive type of community. Following the practices of "Mother" Ann Lee, they practiced celibacy. Because the millennium was at hand, they believed, procreation was no longer necessary. The sexes lived separately in Shaker communities, sleeping in different quarters and eating and working separately. They did come together to worship, however, and their worship was characterized by the shaking dance they performed while singing religious songs. In Shaker communities, women had more power than they did in mainstream American society. Although there was a gender division in the type of work done—with women looking after the household and men providing the field labor—the sexes lived in relative equality, sharing in leadership roles. The Shakers were known for their hard work and for the orderliness and the simplicity of their lives. Shaker communities flourished up until 1850, as many new converts came into the communities, but their numbers began to decline in the late 19th century. Even so, Shaker communities persisted in small numbers through the end of the 20th century.

Another religious community that held alternative ideas about the relationship between the sexes was the *Oneida Community*, founded in 1848 by John Humphrey Noyes. Noyes had been one of the many converts that adopted a perfectionist ideology during the revivals of the Second Great Awakening.

A portrayal of the way in which Shakers incorporated dance into their worship.

Unlike most perfectionists, however, Noyes believed that perfection was not something that Christians had to strive for. He believed that the state of perfection already existed within the individual. He preached that the millennium had, in fact, already arrived and that it was the Christian's job to recreate heaven on earth. In order to do this, community members should live in complete equality and live to support the community as a whole.

According to Noyes, there was no marriage in heaven, for marriage was a preferential institution that kept individuals from treating all members of society with the same regard. Thus, he preached that all men should be married to all women. In the Oneida community this element of his belief, that of *complex marriage*, became the most radical and controversial elements of the Oneida practices. The doctrine of complex marriage allowed members of the society, after obtaining permission from community leaders, to have sexual relations with multiple partners within the community. This reordering of gender relations was shocking to mainstream American society, and Noyes was widely criticized for his encouragement of "free love." The Oneida Community prospered for a time, until 1879, and then Noyes was removed from power in the community due to internal disputes. The Oneida Community declined without his leadership, and in 1881 the community was transformed into a business enterprise, Oneida Ltd., which still exists today and is most well-known for producing silverware.

The most enduring of the religious utopias of the time was the Church of Jesus Christ of

Latter-day Saints, or, as they have become more popularly known, the *Mormons*. The Mormon religion was founded in upstate New York by a young man named Joseph Smith. In 1827, Smith, who was 22 at the time, claimed that he discovered a set of golden tablets that were inscribed with the *Book of Mormon*, which told the story of an ancient American civilization that Jesus Christ visited after he arose from the grave. Smith, who said he received a visitation from an angel, believed he was charged with the duty of spreading the word about this book and establishing a "community of saints." This community would live a perfect life and provide an example to the wider world, helping to usher in the millennium.

Although the Mormons were evangelical and were born out of the enthusiasm of the religious revivals of their era, Smith's church was more conservative than many of the other utopian religious communities. Troubled by the chaotic nature of society, Smith said that he sought to go back to the "ancient order of things," and the church he established was a *theocracy* that combined church and state authority and observed old fashioned hierarchies. Smith believed that all could be saved, however, and he preached to the middle class values of the early 19th century, emphasizing hard work, self control, thrift, and material success. Thus, the Mormon religion was very much a product of its time. While it exhibited a concern with the problems brought by modernity and a desire to go back to older, less fluid social structures; it also tapped into the values of the new market economy and urged behavior that would encourage one's material success.

Smith's Mormons met with much persecution wherever they attempted to settle because of the unconventional nature of some of his teachings. The rigid social hierarchy in the Mormon community and the secrecy practiced by the church leaders made some suspicious, but many Americans were particularly concerned with the practice of *polygamy*, plural marriage, that emerged among the early Mormons. Smith first settled his followers in Ohio, then Missouri, and finally in Nauvoo, Illinois—moving as his people met with hostility wherever they settled.

In Nauvoo, the Mormons set out to establish a permanent "community of saints," and the church gained a great amount of economic and political power in the region. Reacting to this, many who resided near Nauvoo called for a check on the growth of the Mormon community. Smith and his followers were harassed and urged to leave town. The end result of the conflict was that an angry mob attacked and killed Joseph Smith. The Mormons decided to abandon Nauvoo. After Smith's death in 1844, Brigham Young assumed leadership over the community and led the Mormons west to establish a new settlement in Utah, where they would be far from those who might harass them. Here, the Mormon Church prospered, and, because of the evangelical nature of the religion, the church today has a world-wide presence.

In addition to the above utopian societies were a plethora of others, all with a different twist on how they should organize their version of utopia. While there were differences in the kinds of societies they established, the religious utopians of the antebellum era were driven by many of the same impulses. They believed that they had a special duty to God to live a morally sound life that would serve as an example to the rest of mankind. They believed that they must create separate communities from the rest of society in order to live this kind of life, and they believed that they must sacrifice for the good of this community so that it would succeed and be worthy of imitation.

Institutionalization & Rehabilitation

Another reform impulse that emphasized the need to separate oneself from the larger society was the movement to create more asylums and institutions for those who were unable to cope with the challenges of American society. During the antebellum era, numerous special institutions were created in order to deal with the social problems of the times. Beforehand, individuals who had problems fitting into or surviving in American society had been seen as burdens that simply must be removed from mainstream society and confined, but the antebellum belief in the perfectibility of the human character encouraged reformers to develop institutions that were aimed at rehabilitation and reform. Thus, penitentiaries, orphanages, poorhouses, schools for the blind and deaf, and mental asylums were erected in large numbers during the first half of the 19th century.

The isolation provided by the new institutions was instrumental to the effort to rehabilitate. Reformers believed that many of the problems that people coped with were a result of the inability to function in the chaos of modern society. Removal from the mainstream would allow for recovery. If prisoners were taken away from the temptation of the cities or the psychologically disturbed were removed from the stresses of modern living, reformers of the era believed, they could be rehabilitated or cured.

Prisons were thus transformed into *penitentiaries* during the antebellum period, so named because they were intended to be places where an inmate could do penance. Instead of just removing criminals from the streets, the penitentiary system imposed rigid schedules upon the prisoners and established various levels of solitary confinement in order to encourage the inmates to concentrate on what they had done wrong and to develop the habits of a moral citizen.

For their part, asylums were erected as places of refuge, usually built in rural settings, where patients could be cured of their psychological disorders. The ideal was for asylums to emphasize peacefulness and orderliness and provide a safe haven for those distressed by the chaos of modern society. Many asylums, however, fell short of the ideal. Beginning in the 1840s, Dorothea Dix, a Boston school teacher, reported on the neglect and at times the horrific treatment of the mentally ill—who had theretofore been seen primarily as burdensome individuals. They were often kept chained and, sometimes, were beaten in order to keep them compliant. Dix encouraged a widespread reform of the treatment of the mentally ill. The reformed asylums of the era aimed not just to remove the burden of such individuals from society, but to cure them. Living conditions improved, but the new institutions also imposed a rigid routine on inmates, as this was seen as key to psychological rehabilitation.

Other institutions also appeared during the antebellum era. Institutions for the deaf and blind, for orphans, and for the poor appeared beginning in the 1820s, replacing older, more informal forms of caring for those in need. All of these caretaking institutions were similar in that they emphasized the need for orderliness, exhibited a desire to inculcate morality, and were founded upon a belief that human nature could be improved. Although these institutions reflect the optimism of the time, they also reflect the sense of anxiety concerning the maintenance of social order that was widespread during the early 19th century. Motivating the creation of new institutions was not only the desire to rehabilitate individuals for their own individual improvement but also a desire to promote an orderly society free from the burdens of those who found it difficult to conform and might be disruptive.

Public Education

Institutions were not just created for rehabilitation. Antebellum reformers also created new educational institutions, and during the antebellum era, the *common school movement* promoted the first comprehensive public education system for children in the United States. Before the antebellum era, American schooling was disorganized and haphazard. Most American children in the Northeast attended school only a few months of the year, attendance was not required, and many who did attend ceased once they learned to read and gained basic math skills. (In the South and the newly settled western areas of the nation, few attended school at all.) The schools of the time consisted primarily of private schools for those who could afford them, a smattering of charitable schools for the poor, and many rural one room school houses.

During the 1820s, laborers in the Northeast began to call for public schools that would democratize access to education, but it was not until the late 1830s that reform would take place. Middle class Americans had resisted tax-supported public education until this time because of its costs, but the reform spirit helped to change their minds. The spirit of perfectionism motivated northeastern reformers to promote publicly supported schools that would not only educate American children but also help to instill the moral values necessary to uplift American society. Middle class Americans began to

recognize the role schools could play in producing moral citizens, and dedicated workers, in American society.

The common school movement revolutionized American education in the Northeast. The father of this movement was Horace Mann, a Whig representative in Massachusetts who, in 1837, promoted a law that would create a new state school system. When that law was passed and a state school board was created, he became the state's first secretary of education. The new school system had rules for compulsory attendance, requirements for strict discipline and order, and standards for professionally trained teachers. Students used standardized textbooks, they were segregated by age, and they were graded competitively.

Behind Mann's plan for state schools was the optimism about human improvement that was characteristic of his time. He firmly believed that society could be improved through educating the young. Education would allow for increased upward mobility for all classes of Americans and would provide for a more moral and self-controlled populace. Mann became a vigorous promoter of the establishment of common schools throughout the nation, and by the 1850s all of the American states outside the South provided free public elementary schools and had instituted schools for training teachers. Although states varied in the quality of education provided, by 1850 more children were enrolled in school in the United States than in any other nation in the world and the nation had one of the world's highest literacy rates.

In addition, the common school system brought with it another major change. With its spread, teaching increasingly became a women's profession. According to the domestic ideal of the 19th century, working with children was a natural job for women. Also, as Mann pointed out, women teachers could be paid less than men. Those managing new schools thus sought out women teachers, and teaching became the first vocation, albeit a low paying one, that was widely open to American women.

Voluntary Associations & Moral Reform

While some sought reform through the establishment of new state institutions like prisons, asylums and schools; many more American reformers worked through *voluntary associations* to encourage moral reform. Instead of retreating from American society, like the utopians, volunteers who participated in the many reform associations of the era sought to improve society by working together through a network of organizations to encourage change. Instead of seeking to create a perfectionist model apart from society, they wanted to improve mainstream American society. Many voluntary associations arose in the 1820s among evangelicals who had been touched by the revivalist spirit, and a cross-denominational evangelical network of reformers emerged that became known as the *benevolent empire.*

The early evangelical associations that made up the benevolent empire included such groups as the American Board of Commissioners for Foreign Missions, the American Bible Society, the American Sunday School Union, the American Tract Society, and the American Home Missionary Society. In order to spread their message, they used the techniques that had been so successful for ministers during the Great Awakening, sending out speakers who appealed to the emotions of the audience and played upon their consciences in order to gain converts for their cause. Reformers also harnessed the changes that came with the communications revolution. Improvements in the speed and efficiency of printing allowed them to produce pamphlets that could be distributed cheaply to the American masses in order to get word of their cause out, and millions of religious tracts were printed by religious presses and distributed each year. Finally, reformers developed organized networks to give coherence to their cause. National societies arose as umbrella organizations that oversaw numerous local societies, which were formed after agents and speakers from the national society visited and aroused support for the cause. The national society would then provide literature and publicity that the local societies could use to promote the reform effort further.

As these early evangelical associations experienced success, new voluntary associations emerged that modeled their organization and methodology upon the earlier ones. Numerous moral reform organizations were created in order to attack the various vices that reformers targeted in their efforts to eradicate sin: gambling, drinking, profanity, the breaking of the Sabbath, prostitution, dueling, slavery and other activities that Christian reformers saw as an impediment to godly perfection in society.

As the name implies, voluntary associations were made up of volunteers who gave their time, money, and effort to the cause of the organizations that they joined. Many members of the rising middle class were attracted to voluntary associations. Business owners and managers saw them as a way to maintain order in the workplace by encouraging moral behavior among their workers. Upwardly mobile men in America who wished to demonstrate their respectability and their roles as social leaders joined the associations in large numbers. Middle class women were also active in the reform associations. Although women were generally expected to refrain from public expression and confine themselves to the domestic sphere in the early 19th century, reform was a way for women to extend their domestic talents into the public sphere. Because women were seen as having a special moral sensibility, involvement in moral reform associations was acceptable. Women not only participated in but founded and led a number of associations. They sponsored missionaries and speakers, visited the poor, distributed literature, circulated petitions, raised money, and took on many other roles in the moral reform associations of the period.

The Temperance Movement

One of the most influential moral reform movements of the time was the *temperance movement*, the movement to limit alcohol use in American society. Beginning in the 1820s, reformers attacked alcohol abuse as one of the most dangerous moral vices in the nation, believing that drunkenness was one of the major causes of immorality, crime, and disorder in American society.

Up until this time, there had been little stigma placed on drinking alcohol in the United States. American consumption of alcohol had steadily been increasing since the time of the American Revolution, and by 1830 it had reached an all-time peak of an average of approximately 7 gallons of pure alcohol consumed annually for each American over the age of 14. (This amount is around three times the estimates for present-day alcohol consumption.) Alcohol was inexpensive and plentiful at this time. It was cheaper than many other beverages, and it was safer from contamination than 19th century water supplies. Whiskey, in particular, was readily available.

Farmers who planted corn in the west found it cheaper to distill their product and transport it as whiskey than to ship the product whole; so whiskey flooded the American markets. Rum, shipped in from the West Indies, was also in good supply in the eastern cities. By the antebellum era, the consumption of alcohol had become integrated into the American culture. Wages were sometimes paid in alcohol, and workers often took work breaks throughout the day to imbibe with one another. Americans drank with most of their meals, and alcohol was sure to be present at celebrations, gatherings, and other public events.

In the 1820s, however, reformers began to connect alcohol abuse with many of the evils in American society. In particular, they blamed problems associated with the growth of American cities—poverty, vice, violence, and crime—on the prevalence of alcohol use. Other issues were also at stake. Not only was widespread drinking disruptive of the social order, but constant imbibing did not fit well with the industrial culture that was rising in the northeastern United States. Wage laborers who were impaired by alcohol, or by its lingering effects, were not efficient workers. Its use did not fit with middle class values like self-control and hard work that were increasingly emphasized in the North. Finally, reformers—especially the women reformers who were involved in the movement—pointed to the way in which alcohol abuse could affect American families. Men who drank heavily might neglect their duties to provide for their loved ones, or worse, become abusive towards them. For all of these reasons, the move to limit alcohol consumption rose as one of the most visible reform movements of the antebellum era.

At the forefront of the temperance crusade was evangelical Boston minister Reverend Lyman Beecher. "Intemperance is the sin of our land," he preached, "and if anything shall defeat the hopes of the world, which hang upon our experiment of civil liberty, it is that river of fire." During the 1820s, Beecher spoke out in favor of temperance in many sermons, and his ideas were published and distributed in Christian tracts that were distributed by benevolent associations. Following the wake of these pamphlets, voluntary associations were formed in order to promote temperance, and in 1826, a national organization, the American Temperance Society, emerged.

Many of the early temperance crusaders were not prohibitionists. As the name of their crusade implies, they simply wanted Americans to "temper"—practice more moderation in—their drinking. Their concern was essentially with drunkenness and not alcohol itself. Most of the early temperance reformers also did not advocate legal restrictions on alcohol production or its use. Instead, they relied on the idea of *moral suasion*, using education and rhetoric to convince individuals to voluntarily change their behavior. In time, however, most of the temperance advocates would urge abstinence from drinking altogether, and many also became more comfortable with pushing for governmental legislation that would restrict alcohol production.

Still, even as abstinence became the goal, during the antebellum era most temperance reformers advocated the use of moral suasion. They wanted to convince Americans to voluntarily give up alcohol, and so massive publicity campaigns were launched by temperance organizations in order educate the public on the personal, social, and

spiritual dangers of alcohol abuse. In their propaganda, alcohol use was depicted as a sin that ruined both the individual and American society. Intemperance was connected with the many problems of American society that was keeping it from progressing towards perfection. Temperance, on the other hand, was connected with the middle class traits that were valued in American society such as industry, self-control, obedience, and godliness.

The temperance crusade was one of the more effective of the antebellum reform

TREE of TEMPERANCE
BY A. D. FILLMORE.

Temperance advocates circulated literature that extolled the positive traits that were encouraged by abstaining from alcohol.

movements. By the 1830s the American Temperance Society had over 5,000 local affiliates, and more and more reformers were encouraging voluntary discontinuance of all alcohol use. Ministers and temperance reformers gave rousing speeches, printed millions of tracts, and urged Americans to sign a pledge of abstinence. While white middle class Americans dominated the movement, by the 1840s other groups had joined in. Working class Americans formed Washington Temperance Societies, named in honor of the first president, to encourage workers to take the temperance pledge. These *Washingtonians* helped to make temperance a cause that crossed class boundaries. Portions of the African American and Irish American communities also took temperance pledges and promoted the movement. During the 1840s, some state governments got involved. *Maine Laws*, named after the first state to adopt statewide prohibition legislation, were passed throughout the Northeast during the decade, conscribing the production of alcohol in various states. These laws were soon overturned, however, as most Americans remained uncomfortable with the idea of government mandated social reform. Even so, their passage shows the enormous influence of the temperance movement during the antebellum period. By 1850, per capita alcohol consumption had dropped to around 2 gallons a year, and millions of people had signed temperance pledges.

The Movement to Abolish Slavery

One of the most visible, and most divisive, reform movements of the era was the abolition movement. Antislavery sentiment was not new during the antebellum period; Americans had expressed moral disapproval of slavery since the revolutionary era, but the movement to end slavery entered into a different phase beginning in the 1830s.

Before this time, those who held antislavery ideals promoted ending slavery gradually and with compensation to slave owners. This was the way that emancipation had taken place throughout the northern states. Early antislavery activists also widely promoted the *colonization movement*, an effort to transport freed blacks to Africa or the Caribbean; for while Americans had increasingly become uncomfortable with the notion of slavery, they were also uncomfortable with the idea of the large free black population that would result from widespread *manumission*, the freeing of slaves, throughout the South.

Antislavery activism evolved during the antebellum era, however, with the rise of the *abolition movement*. Those involved with this movement, *abolitionists,* promoted the unconditional, immediate emancipation of all slaves and the acceptance of African Americans as equal members of American society. William Lloyd Garrison, a white reformer from Massachusetts is often credited with the birth of movement. In truth, however, free blacks in the North had already been speaking out against gradualism, compensation, and colonization before Garrison arrived on the scene. Northern black leaders asserted that the nation owed nothing to the slave owners and that attempts to colonize African Americans to areas outside the nation robbed them of their birthright as Americans whose labor had been essential to the building of the nation. In 1829 one such black leader, David Walker, wrote an influential pamphlet, *David Walker's Appeal to the Coloured Citizens of the World*, which denounced slavery in the United States and called on all people of African descent throughout the world to use any means necessary

Abolitionist literature emphasized the humanity of the slave.

and he was involved with the American Colonization Society. In 1830, however, influenced by the arguments of northern black leaders, Garrison went through a change of heart. He left Lundy's moderate antislavery journal and founded his own newspaper, *The Liberator*, in 1831 to advocate for the immediate, unconditional, universal abolition of slavery and the extension of citizenship to all African Americans. His paper gained much attention due to its uncompromising tone, and it attracted other reformers to the cause. In 1832 he founded a voluntary association to promote abolitionist goals, the New England Antislavery Society. During the next year he helped to create a national organization, the American Antislavery Society, with fellow abolitionists Lewis Tappan and Theodore Dwight Weld. By 1835 hundreds of local antislavery organizations had been created, and by 1838 over a thousand existed. It is estimated that as many as 200,000 northerners joined some sort of antislavery society during the antebellum era.

to work against slavery and other forms of racial oppression.

It was when William Lloyd Garrison began to push for unconditional emancipation and black equality, however, that white Americans began to support these goals and it became a bi-racial movement. Garrison began his career in antislavery reform during the 1820s advocating, as did most white antislavery activists of the day, gradual emancipation and colonization. In the late 1820s he worked with Quaker antislavery spokesman Benjamin Lundy on the leading antislavery newspaper of era, which promoted gradual emancipation,

Most white Americans who were attracted to the abolitionist movement in the 1830s were young adults who had been aroused by the religious energy of the Second Great Awakening. They believed that the sin of slavery was one of the largest impediments to their millennial hopes. America could never truly be a moral example to the rest of the world as long as it was corrupted by the existence of this institution. Women as well as men became involved, and many—like Southern transplants Sarah and Angelina Grimké—took on leadership roles. Free northern blacks were also active in the movement. They made up the majority of subscribers to the *Liberator*, and many became prominent spokesmen for the cause. Frederick Douglass, an escaped slave who gave rousing public speeches and who wrote a moving biography depicting his experience as a slave, was the most famous of the black abolitionists; but there were many others who made great contributions, including Charles Lenox Remond, Sojourner Truth, William Wells Brown, William Still, Jermain Loguen and Martin Delany.

Like the temperance advocates of the day, the early abolitionists relied on the technique of moral suasion. They believed that they could convert others to their cause in much the same way as the revivalists had converted the masses to evangelical Christianity. They published pamphlets, produced antislavery newspapers, sponsored lectures, and collected names on petitions. In the 1830s, most of their energy was aimed at the southern population. They sent pamphlets and abolitionist literature through the mails to the southern states, hoping that by educating southerners about the evils of slavery they could convince slaveowners to voluntarily emancipate their slaves. Their hopes were dashed, however, as southerners reacted to their campaign with hostility. Thus, during the late 1830s and early 1840s, abolitionists searched for other ways of furthering their cause.

It was during this time that the abolition movement began to fracture. Disagreements arose among abolitionist leaders over the proper methods through which to attack slavery and promote black equal rights. Some more conservative abolitionists wanted to work through churches or through the political system, while more radical abolitionists

like Garrison argued that these institutions themselves had been corrupted by their tolerance of slavery and thus needed to be replaced. Also, as more women emerged as leaders within the abolitionist movement, some of the more conservative abolitionists questioned the appropriateness of their involvement, while Garrison and other radicals actively promoted it. With time Garrison became ever more confrontational in his views. Although he was devoutly religious, he condemned churches as proslavery institutions and urged Christians to "come out" of them in order to encourage change. He also was increasingly critical of the American government and the compromises the founders and subsequent politicians had made concerning slavery. Because it had allowed for slavery, he called the Constitution "a covenant with death and an agreement with Hell," and at one antislavery meeting he publicly burned a copy of the document.

In 1840, the American Antislavery Society split up because of the disagreements that had arisen within the movement. Radical abolitionists who agreed with Garrison remained in the society. Evangelical abolitionists, who objected both to Garrison's critique of American churches and to his support for women leaders in the movement, withdrew from the American Antislavery Society and became involved in alternative associations like the American and Foreign Antislavery Society and the American Missionary Association. Others, who hoped to effect change through political institutions, joined an antislavery political party, the *Liberty Party*, which was organized in 1839.

Despite the dissent that arose within the movement, abolitionism did not fade away. Supporters of immediate emancipation remained active throughout the 1840s and

1850s. Using their various methods they continued to agitate against slavery and racial oppression in the United States. They experienced limited success, however. In addition to internal differences, abolitionists faced challenges from outside their organizations. Southern slave-owners were predictably hostile to the movement, but the abolitionists also faced widespread northern opposition to their cause. Abolitionism threatened the livelihood of businessmen and factory owners who were dependent on southern cotton, and many, therefore, had economic reasons for opposing the movement. Others were antagonistic towards the movement because it not only attacked slavery but also the racial status quo in the North. Finally, many northerners were hostile to abolitionists because they believed they were dangerous fanatics whose activities threatened the ties of union between the northern and southern states. Thus there were economic, social, and political reasons why many northerners rejected the abolitionist call.

At times anti-abolitionist sentiment could fuel violence. Throughout the 1830s especially there were many episodes of mob aggression against abolitionists throughout the northern states. In 1835 Garrison was attacked by a mob at an antislavery meeting in Boston, and he barely escaped with his life. In 1837 Elijah Lovejoy, a publisher of an antislavery newspaper in Alton, Illinois, was murdered when he tried to defend his printing headquarters from an attack by an angry crowd. In 1838 Pennsylvania Hall, a building that had just been erected in Philadelphia to serve as an abolitionist meeting place, was burned to the ground. Free blacks were also attacked by those who were hostile towards granting them equal rights. During the antebellum era white mobs attacked black neighborhoods in many northern cities, including Philadelphia,

Boston, Cincinnati, Hartford, New York, Pittsburgh, and Utica.

Thus, although the abolitionist movement attracted many northern followers during the antebellum era, it failed to gain universal support. Even so it was one of the most influential movements of the era. In addition to their attack on slavery, abolition leaders were also prominent supporters of many other reforms, and they rose to the forefront of the antebellum reform culture of the North. And while their efforts did not bring an end to slavery, they forced the American public to confront an issue that had long been avoided. This confrontation would help to ignite a bitter sectional dispute between the free states of the North and the slave-holding states of the South. In addition, out of abolition was born another important movement that would have far-reaching consequences—the movement for women's rights.

Women's Rights

The women's rights movement grew in general out of women's participation in the reform movements of the antebellum erra and in particular out of the abolition movement. The view of women as the moral center of the home that was prevalent during the early nineteenth century allowed them to participate in the reform movements of the era. Because reforms promoted moral uplift, participating in them was seen as a respectable activity for women. This involvement in reform gave antebellum women a rare opportunity to have a public voice. With time, however, as the public activity of some women reformers increased, new debates arose concerning women's place in American society. In particular, debates over the proper place of women rose to the forefront of the abolition movement when women rose to leadership positions within antislavery societies and began to speak to mixed audiences of men and women.

Among the conflicts concerning women's role in the abolitionist movement was one surrounding the activities of Sarah and Angelina Grimké. The Grimké sisters had moved from their homes on a slave-owning plantation in South Carolina to Philadelphia, where they became outspoken critics of slavery. (Angelina would become the wife of abolitionist leader Theodore Dwight Weld.) Both of these women wrote letters to newspapers, published tracts, and spoke to audiences in their service to the abolitionist cause. In 1836, a group of northern ministers published an indictment of the two women for their willingness to speak in front of audiences that were not confined to women only. Their actions were seen as an affront to the proper role of Christian women, which was, of course, subordinate to men. The Grimké sisters responded to the critique with their own interpretation of the proper role of women, and in these they included assertions of the equality of the sexes. Sarah Grimké's *Letters on the Condition of Women and the Equality of the Sexes* was published in 1838, and it became an important tract that fueled feminist arguments as the woman's movement percolated.

In 1840, another episode within abolitionist circles provided further fuel for a women's rights movement. In that year, delegates from the American Antislavery Society travelled across the Atlantic to attend a World Antislavery Convention hosted by British abolitionists. Among the American delegates were Elizabeth Cady Stanton and Lucretia Mott. When they arrived at the meeting, however, British abolitionists refused to allow them to attend the gathering as delegates, relegating them to a gallery where they could view the proceedings but not participate. This event prompted the two women's decision to launch a formal movement to promote the equality of women when they returned to the United States. By 1848, they had gathered enough support to do so. They held a meeting in the town of Seneca Falls, New York that was attended by approximately 70 women and 30 men. At the meeting they presented the *Declaration of Sentiments and Resolutions*, a document that embellished upon the wording of the Declaration of Independence in order to outline the purpose of their new organization. "We hold these truths to be self evident," it stated, "that all men and women are created equal." It then outlined the "sentiments," or grievances held by women, and presented their "resolutions," or demands, which included measures that would provide for equality under the law including the right to vote. While it would be decades before women achieved many of these demands—the right to vote, for example, was not constitutionally guaranteed until 1920—the Seneca Falls meeting was an important beginning point in the institution of new ideas about the relationship between the sexes in the United States.

Reform and the South

While the reform spirit permeated the northern states during the antebellum era, it was not so widespread in the South. Some of the reform efforts that existed in the North did take place in the South—asylums were constructed, temperance societies were established, and utopian communities existed—but the reformist impulse generally remained weak throughout the slave states. There are a number of reasons for this.

One, as we have seen, the reformist impulse was largely a result of the many changes the North underwent as a result of the rise of industrialism. The economic changes of the 19th century produced a very different society in the South than in the North, and many of the elements that encouraged reform were lacking there. The problems of industrialization, the rise of wage labor, and rapid urbanization were less prevalent. The society remained more hierarchal in the South than the North, and in the slave states a large middle class—which was the engine of northern reform—did not exist. The society was also more rural, and so connections between organizations that were formed were more tenuous. In the North, as Americans became connected to a larger market economy and increasingly moved away from older communal institutions, voluntary associations arose in order to deal with social ills that in the past had been tended to on a community level. In the South, many of these communal hierarchies remained in place.

Second, while Southerners did experience the religious fervor of the Second Great Awakening, revivalism did not feed reformist energy as it did in the North. Evangelical religion spread through the southern states in the early 19th century attracting large numbers to southern *camp meetings*, revivals that attracted huge numbers of participants from rural areas around the South. Southerners journeyed to these revival meetings, set up camps, and stayed for days. They were just as much a social as a spiritual outlet for rural southerners, who experienced much isolation from one another. The evangelical spirit that spread through the South was based on many of the same beliefs as those that were prevalent in the North. White southerners, however, had to reconcile the religious teachings of the evangelical revivals with their commitment to the institution of slavery. They did this by stressing humanitarian treatment of the slaves and by using biblical teachings to justify the racial hierarchy that existed in the South. Although all were equal in God's eyes, southerners argued, hierarchies existed in all human societies—not just those that included slaves. Thus, to many white southern thinkers, spiritual equality did not translate to equality in human relationships.

This concern about slavery leads to a third reason why the reformist impulse did not take hold in the South. After 1830, reform was increasingly associated with the abolition movement. Many abolitionists, who criticized slavery and the southern way of life, were involved in other reform movements of the era, and southerners became suspicious of northern reformist rhetoric in general as more and more causes, like the peace movement and the women's movement, became interconnected with the abolition movement. The abolitionists were deemed to be dangerous fanatics throughout the South, and after the rise of abolitionism in the 1830s, southerners became increasingly defensive about slavery and the plantation system. Southern leaders and thinkers reacted to the rise of the abolition movement with the development of a more elaborate defense of southern slavery and society and a parallel critique of northern society. They pointed to the many problems associated with the rise of industrialism in the North and asserted that the southern culture was superior and less in need of reform.

The Antebellum South & "King Cotton"

While the economic changes of the early 19th century resulted in the rise of industry, capitalism and wage labor in the North, the changes of the era had affected the South in a profoundly different manner. Because of the innovation of the cotton gin and the enormous demand for cotton in the textile factories of New England and Europe, cotton production exploded throughout the South during the first part of the 19th century, and during the antebellum period southern society and its economy was dominated by *King Cotton*.

As new states were added to the Union in the Southwest, cotton production expanded. By the 1850s, the American South produced around 70% of all of the world's cotton, and cotton plantation owners became the wealthiest group of men in the United States. Farmers throughout the South rushed to capitalize on the profitability of the crop, establishing new plantations on the southern frontier and investing in slave labor to produce the crop. Cotton became absolutely essential to the southern way of life.

The expansion of cotton production brought with it a concurrent expansion of southern reliance on slave labor. After the American Revolution, slavery had been gradually abolished throughout the northern states. In the *Upper South*—the northernmost slave states—many were becoming less reliant on plantation agriculture and slavery, and discussions about gradual emancipation even took place. Opinion in the nation seemed to be turning against the notion of slaveholding, and many Americans in both the North and South believed that the institution of slavery would wither away as economic change came to the new nation. King Cotton changed all of this. The plantation system was revitalized, and the slave states of the southern United States became increasingly committed to protecting the institution of slavery.

Thus, while the North was experiencing the rise of industry and was becoming more urban, the South remained decidedly agricultural and rural. This was a conscious choice made by southerners, who knew that there was big money to be made in investing in cotton. They tied up most of their wealth in land and slaves for their plantations, and few saw any reason to make investments in industry or in the type of infrastructure that was growing throughout the North. Because of cotton, southerners recommitted themselves to the plantation system and to the institution of slavery. Because of this commitment, older notions of social hierarchy prevailed in the South at the same time that Americans in other regions began to express an increasing commitment to *free labor*—labor that is freely contracted rather than coerced—and to a vision of equal opportunity for upward mobility for all.

The Antebellum Slave

King Cotton had profound implications for the southern slave. A vigorous domestic slave trade arose as the plantation system expanded westward. In older slave states like Virginia and North Carolina, there was a decreased need for slaves as the plantation system declined in those areas, and plantations were supplanted by smaller farms that produced wheat, corn and livestock. There was thus a surplus of slaves in the Upper South at the same time that there was rising demand for them in the states of the *Lower South*—the southernmost slave states—where the cotton plantations were taking hold. Between 1820 and 1840 an estimated 2 million slaves were sold from the states of the Upper South to the cotton growing regions of the nation.

The internal slave trade led to the uprooting of many slaves from their homes in order to fuel the expansion of King Cotton. Families were separated as slaves were sold in the slave markets of cities like Charleston or Richmond

A scene from a southern slave market.

1860 there were around 4 million. During the antebellum period, the majority of these slaves lived on cotton plantations in groups of ten or more. These living conditions helped to encourage the development of a distinctive slave community, albeit an unstable one that could be broken up by the internal slave trade or by planter migrations westward.

At the center of slave culture was the notion of family. Although the southern states did not recognize slave marriage, slaves committed themselves to one another and had children. They usually resided together in family units in slave cabins, and the slave family served as an important vehicle for the transmission of a value system from one generation to another. Slave

or to slave traders in the interior, who would transport them down the Mississippi River ("down the river") to New Orleans slave markets. The specter of being sold was a constant threat to slaves throughout the antebellum era.

This did not stop slaves from developing strong community ties and a distinctive African American culture. The legal international slave trade had been abolished in the United States in 1808, and so most of the slaves were American born (although a small number of African-born slaves came into the South through an illegal slave trade that brought slaves into ports like New Orleans and Galveston). Despite the ending of the legal slave trade, the American slave population grew. In 1790 there were approximately 700,000 slaves in the United States, and by

owners permitted these relationships because they believed that family ties would decrease the desire of slaves to run away or rebel and because children meant more wealth for the slave owner. Although the nuclear family was important for slaves, the notion of family extended beyond their immediate blood relatives. Extended family ties and informal notions of kinship existed within the slave community, giving slaves a larger support network when they might lose their immediate relatives to the slave trade or death.

Christianity was an important element within the slave community as well. Slaves combined older, African ways with Christian beliefs in order to produce a unique form of Christianity. During the Second Great Awakening, slaves were drawn to the enthusiastic forms of worship that prevailed and by the message of equality under God's eyes that was part of the evangelical message. While white slave owners generally encouraged slaves to worship at white services, where sermons emphasized obedience and acceptance of one's station in life; slaves often held their own, separate services in late-night gatherings where they focused on Christian teachings about equality and liberation. At these gatherings, they combined an observance of Christian beliefs with elements of African culture like circle dancing, singing, and call and response activities, producing a distinctive African American form of Christian worship. Many of the great African American spirituals originated in such gatherings.

The slave's experience of daily life was very much shaped by the type of work they were expected to do. Because of the expansion of the plantation system, most slaves during the antebellum era were field workers who provided the labor needed for staple crops, especially cotton. In the decade before the Civil War, approximately 75% of the slaves were field workers. Field workers generally worked within one of two systems. The *task system,* most often used on the rice plantations of the southeastern coast, required slaves to finish the tasks required to cultivate the crop each day. After these tasks were complete, they could work on their own gardens and do other things. Most antebellum slaves, however, experienced the *gang system* of slave labor. Under this system, slaves worked from sun-up to sun-down six days a week in gangs, usually of around 20, to provide the labor needed to cultivate crops like tobacco and cotton. By the antebellum era, most slaves worked on cotton plantations. Cotton was a labor intensive crop that required year-round work. Slaves were used

for the planting, hoeing, cultivating, and picking of cotton. Their work was arduous and often painful, as they labored in the hot and humid areas of the South all day with no respite and overseers used whips to keep the slaves moving.

While most antebellum slaves were field laborers, some did have different roles. House servants helped to clean and run the elaborate plantation households that were erected by prosperous planters. House servants generally experienced less harsh working conditions than field workers, but they were also more isolated from their fellow slaves. In addition, unlike the field workers who lived in slave quarters, house servants experienced little relief from the oversight of their white owners. Slaves who lived in urban areas also had a different experience from field workers. A small number of slaves were skilled artisans in the southern cities, working as blacksmiths, carpenters, seamstresses, or participating in other trades. These urban slaves were frequently hired out by masters, and the masters collected the wages they made.

Among the biggest fears of southern plantation owners was that of a slave uprising. Episodes like the Nat Turner Rebellion of 1831 filled their minds with dread. Large scale uprisings, however, rarely happened as there was so little chance of success. White slave patrols were ever-present throughout the South, especially after the Nat Turner incident. They stood their watch, returning runaways and discouraging rebellion. A failed rebellion would result in death for the slave, and runaways who were returned home were subjected to harsh punishments. Because reprisals were so brutal, uprisings seldom took place, but running away was much more common. Some slaves sought to make their way north to the free states or to

Canada through the network that became known as the *underground railroad*, secret routes along which sympathetic individuals would provide shelter and aid to runaways. Relatively few slaves accomplished such escapes, however. Most runaways went to nearby swamps or forests for short periods when tensions might arise on the plantations, returning home to what they hoped would be light punishments when their resources ran out. Slaves who voluntarily returned were generally treated more leniently than those who were returned by force.

Slavery & the Social Structure of the White South

Just as antebellum slave culture was shaped by expansion of the plantation system in the South, so was white southern culture. Because of the importance of cotton to the economy, large plantation owners in the South dominated social and political life in the region. They held a large share of the political offices, and their economic power gave them an enormous amount of social clout. They saw themselves as an elite ruling class, and most of the rest of southern society saw them that way as well. Before the expansion of the cotton kingdom, the most powerful planters lived in the southern states along the Atlantic seaboard. It was in this region where they developed many of the cultural ways that are associated with the southern plantation culture. The wealthiest planters lived as a sort of aristocracy, building elaborate mansions and spending money in lavish displays of wealth. Plantation mistresses were expected to reflect the status of the planter by exhibiting refined manners, charm, and hospitality in all her relationships. Members of the southern plantation household were preoccupied with displaying a gentile lifestyle.

As cotton spread west, aspirations to live this kind of lifestyle spread with it. The opportunities of King Cotton allowed new men to enter into the planter ranks. The acquisition of land and slaves was the surest path to upward mobility in the South, and savvy businessmen and other men of the professional class built up their capital and bought into the system, establishing small plantations. If they were lucky, they too ascended to the ranks of the plantation elite. Less wealthy southerners also saved up their earnings and invested in slaves, land, and cotton, hoping to climb the southern social ladder. Most of these men would never hold more than 5 slaves, but some were able to accumulate more wealth and establish their own plantations. Cotton, land and slaves were central to the aspirations of many southern whites during the antebellum era.

The cotton plantations of the Old South were self-contained communities, where cotton was grown and processed in order to ready it for the market. Slaves were used to work the fields and provide domestic labor, but plantation owners also hired less well-to-do relatives and neighbors to perform some tasks and often allowed them to use their grist mills and cotton gins. In doing so, they tied them to their interests. The southern planter oversaw the workings of both the plantation and the larger community that held ties to it, and he held authority over all of his dependents.

The philosophy of *paternalism* was central to the structure of southern plantations. The idea behind paternalism was that there was a reciprocal relationship between the master of the plantation and his subordinates. A planter had the duty to provide for the material needs and ensure the well-being of all of his dependents. In return, the duty of his dependents—including his wife, children, employees and slaves—was to be obedient and submit to his authority.

Despite their dominance, the plantation elite made up a small minority of southern white society. In fact, the majority of southern whites were non-slaveholding yeoman farmers, and most of those who did own slaves lived on relatively modest farms with less than 5 slaves. The southern slave-owning population was itself around 1/3 of the total white population of the South. Members of the *planter class,* those who held over 20 slaves, made up less than 15% of the slave-owning population and the *plantation elite*, those who owned over 50 slaves and held most of the power in the South, made up less than 2.5% of the slave-owning population. Slave-owners were a diverse lot; nevertheless, they were all united by their commitment to the cotton economy and to slavery. Upward mobility and social power in the South was directly connected to the ownership of slaves, and these planters all hoped to increase the number of slaves they owned and protect their "property" investments once they owned them.

While planters held land in the most productive areas of the South, many southerners of the antebellum period lived on land that was less suitable for growing cotton. On these lands, *yeoman farmers*, most of whom did not own slaves, grew corn and raised hogs on smaller plots of land. They also might dedicate a small percentage of their acreage to tobacco or cotton to sell in the marketplace. These farmers, often referred to as the "plain folk" of the South, lived simple lives and were fiercely independent. Although yeoman farmers did not own slaves in large numbers, most did not attack the slave system of the South.

As was true of those who had already bought into the slave system, their hopes of upward mobility were framed within the construct of slave-owning.

In addition to the economic value it represented, the subordination of the slaves was accepted · throughout the white South for another reason. It elevated the status of all whites; for in the antebellum South, even the poorest white was higher on the social ladder than the slave. As in the northern states, poverty was a problem throughout the South during the antebellum era. Many white southerners remained landless or lived on land that was unproductive. Many lived subsistence lifestyles in log cabins, growing what they could on their lands and relying heavily on hunting and fishing to supplement their diets. There was limited opportunity for wage labor in the rural areas of the South because slaves provided so much of the labor, and urban job opportunities were limited because the South remained mostly rural. Many poor whites moved frequently, living transient lives that kept them searching for work. Nevertheless, despite the fact that they did not benefit economically from the existence of slavery in the South, most poor whites supported the system of slavery because the racial hierarchy it came with enhanced their own status.

Although the antebellum South was primarily rural, there were some cities in the region, and in these cities the social structure more closely mirrored the North. Even so, the existence of slavery throughout the rest of the region affected southern urban culture. A small commercial middle class lived in the urban areas of the region, most of them dependent in some way on the cotton economy. Even in the urban areas of the South, therefore, the planter's interests dominated.

Because of their dependence on cotton, many urban southerners held pro-slavery views.

There was thus widespread support for plantation culture and the institution of slavery throughout the South. Most southerners, however, saw themselves as living lives consistent with the democratic values of the American republic. In the antebellum southern mind, white liberty was connected to black slavery. One of the freedoms held by white Americans was the freedom to protect their property, and because slaves were defined as property, the liberty of white Americans rested on their freedom to hold slaves. In the South, the ability to hold slaves was an essential component of the 19th century ideal of equality of opportunity and the ability to achieve upward mobility. These possibilities, of course, only existed for white southerners.

The Southern Defense of Slavery

It wasn't until the 19th century that southerners developed an elaborate defense of their commitment to the institution of slavery. Until the revolutionary era, slavery had been accepted by most white Americans, and so there had been little reason to defend it. The mood changed, however, with the spread of Enlightenment era thinking about individualism and opportunity and with the Northern Emancipations that took place after the American Revolution. As Americans formed their new nation, concerns about how slavery fit into a society that proclaimed republican ideals were widespread not just in the North but in the South. While these concerns led to the gradual abandonment of the practice of enslaving human beings in the North, however, it did not in the South. Southerners were more economically dependent on slave labor, and leaders of the region clung to the institution.

Even so, during the early years of the republic, many Southern leaders recognized that the practice of slavery was inconsistent with the ideals upon which the republic had been founded. They felt defensive about their continued commitment to slavery, and they justified this commitment by proclaiming it to be a "necessary evil" that they had inherited from their colonial predecessors. This inherited institution had become so intertwined with the southern economy and culture, they argued, that it could not easily be abolished. Some southerners expressed a belief that the institution would eventually fade away with time. As southern society modernized and diversified, they said, slave labor would cease to be profitable. If southerners tried to end the system too early, however, the southern economy would collapse and the influx of freed slaves would upset the racial boundaries of the South, causing chaos. Thus, southerners of the early republic who wanted to end slavery advocated that it be done gradually and voluntarily by slaveowners, and they supported the practice of colonization.

During the antebellum period this type of thinking changed. As King Cotton expanded throughout the South, southerners became increasingly committed to the institution of slavery. In the 1830s, southern rhetoric shifted from a defensive stance of characterizing slavery as a "necessary evil" to a more aggressive one. Slavery, antebellum southern leaders now asserted, was actually a "positive good," and southern social structures, including that of slavery, were in fact superior to those developing in the free North. Slavery should not be attacked, they argued. Instead, it should be allowed to expand.

What triggered this change? First, by the 1830s, the cotton boom had thoroughly revitalized the plantation system and the commitment of the South to the institution of slavery. By the mid-1830s there was no longer much desire to consider the possibility of emancipation. Second, the rise of the abolition movement in the North in the 1830s shifted the tone of discussions concerning slavery in a more antagonistic direction. In response to abolitionist criticisms of the sinful nature of southern society, southerners responded with justifications for their commitment to slavery and their own critique of northern society. Southerners abandoned their apologies for slavery, denied that it was evil, and characterized the South as a superior society.

Many southerners focused on religious teachings in their proslavery defense, asserting that, contrary to what the abolitionists proclaimed, slavery was not inconsistent with Christianity. In fact, ministers throughout the South were active in constructing proslavery arguments. They stated that slavery was not condemned in the Bible, and that, in fact, biblical teachings taught slaves to obey their masters. In addition they argued that slavery had helped to spread Christianity, as slaves had been exposed to the religious system through their enslavement. Ministers in the South thus emphasized the duty of masters to encourage Christian practices among their slaves and the duty of slaves to obey their masters, a reciprocal relationship that was consistent with the idea of paternalism.

A more vehement racial defense of slavery also took place as southerners sought to justify the institution. Southerners asserted that slaves were racially inferior due to their African descent, and that they would not be able to care for themselves should they be freed. Some married the racial argument to a biblical one, arguing that people of African ancestry were the descendants of Ham, Noah's son who was cursed for looking upon his father while he was naked when his other sons looked away. Because of this sin, they believed that Ham's descendants were cursed to be the servants of the descendants of his other sons—who made up the rest of humanity. In addition, many southerners feared racial warfare should slaves be set free; they asserted the need to keep the black population of the South under the control of the plantation system to avoid such a fate.

Some of the most influential proslavery theorists of the era used economic and social theory to justify slavery. Among the prominent proslavery intellectuals of the time were South Carolina political leader John Calhoun, South Carolina planter and politician James Hammond, and Virginia planter, lawyer, and sociologist George Fitzhugh. According to their arguments, all of the greatest societies in history—Greece, Rome, Egypt, and Israel for example—had incorporated slavery. Calhoun, who was one of the most outspoken defenders of slavery, made this point in his writings. "There has never yet existed a wealthy and civilized society in which one portion of the community did not live on the labor of others," he said. Hammond built upon this idea in his own writings. He argued that all societies required a class of people to perform the labor necessary to keep society going. This laboring class he called the "mud-sill" of society because their work supported the activities of higher levels of society much as a mud-sill—the portion of a building closest to the ground—supports higher levels of that structure. According to Hammond, the workings of this *mud-sill class* allowed others to go about the business of achieving higher levels of civilization. In the South, he asserted, slaves made up the mud-sill class that allowed white southerners to pursue "progress, civilization, and refinement." Fitzhugh also accepted the notion that some people would naturally rise above others in society. In his writings, he asserted that it was expected for those who had the talents to escape a life of labor to rise to "more respectable and lucrative employments," while those who did not have these talents were relegated to the more arduous jobs in life. These theorists all contributed to a southern mindset that held that a hierarchal society was the natural state of things and that such a structure helped to promote human progress—thinking that was very much in opposition to that of most Americans living in the northern states.

A critique of northern society also played into the arguments of proslavery thinkers, especially that of Hammond and Fitzhugh. Hammond, for his part, characterized the plantation as a model society and condemned the wage system of the North as inferior. Lifting up the paternalistic ideal, he argued that slaves were better cared for than those left to the uncertainties of the free market. George Fitzhugh made a similar argument. Free labor, he said, had actually created masses of *wage slaves* among whites living in industrial societies. Despite their position as "free laborers," they had very little independence, as their lives were dominated by the ups and downs of the new industrial economy. Wage workers, he argued, were forced to work just as hard in the factories of the North as the slaves did in the South; but,

unlike slaves, they had no protection from starvation when they became too old or weak to work or when they were unable to find a job. He compared the slave-owning South to the industrial societies of the North and of Europe, and he found the industrial societies to be wanting. To support this argument he pointed out that the South did not experience the same level of class conflict among whites, incidents of mobbing, trade union agitations, or crime. Fitzhugh believed that it was preferable for the laborers of society to be slaves rather than free workers.

Slavery & the Southern Attack on Free Speech

Southerners defended slavery not only by developing their own proslavery arguments but also with attempts to silence the voices of their critics. The abolitionist critique

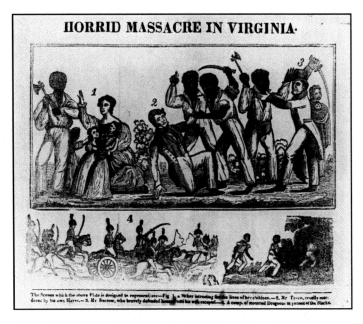

The Nat Turner Rebellion of 1831 enflamed Southern fears of slave insurrection.

contributed to a siege mentality among southerners, who felt that their way of life was under attack. Also contributing to this feeling was an intensification of the fear of slave rebellion after the Nat Turner Insurrection of 1831. Southerners connected this rebellion, which took place in the same year that Garrison began to publish the *Liberator,* with the abolition movement; and they increasingly felt that to allow any discussion of emancipation in southern society would be to encourage instability of the slave system and the social order of the South.

In response to the abolitionist threat, southern leaders pushed for new limitations on freedom of speech regarding slavery. Most of the southern states passed laws that prohibited abolitionist speech, doling out stiff penalties for publications or speeches that criticized slavery. In some areas "Committees of Public Safety" were formed in order to expose and punish anyone who may hold abolitionist views or who might attempt to provoke a slave rebellion. Those suspected of being supporters of abolition were driven out of town, tarred and feathered, subjected to mob violence, and in some cases, lynched.

Southerners also aimed to suppress expressions of dissent concerning slavery that came from outside of the South. At the behest of southern congressmen, a *Gag Rule* was adopted in the US Congress in the 1830s in order to prevent the discussion of the slavery issue in the federal legislature. As their movement took shape in that decade, abolitionists had begun submitting antislavery petitions to Congress in order to introduce the taboo topic into political discussions. Southern congressmen insisted that the petitions not be considered, but northern congressmen pointed out that the First Amendment of the Constitution guaranteed the right "to petition the government for a redress of grievances." Southern representatives found a way to prevent the petitions from being discussed in Congress, however, by insisting on the establishment of a gag rule. While antislavery petitions could not be rejected, they could be *tabled*—set aside and not discussed. The gag rule required that all antislavery petitions be treated in such a manner. In 1836, the first such gag rule was implemented, and it was reinforced with stricter versions passed by later congresses. The gag rule remained in place until 1844, when former president John Quincy Adams, who was serving the House of Representatives, convinced congressmen to rescind the rule.

Another interference with freedom of speech had to do with the delivery of abolitionist literature through the federal mail service. During the early years of the movement, abolitionists spent much of their energy on

Burning abolitionist literature in Charleston.

producing and sending abolitionist literature into the southern states in an attempt to convince the South to voluntarily end slaveholding. Southerners were incensed by the inundation of abolitionist literature, however, and they sought to prevent its distribution. Throughout the South, states passed laws prohibiting the circulation of "incendiary" literature, and postmasters refused to deliver the mail. In 1835, an angry mob seized abolitionist literature from a Charleston post office and publicly burned it. President Andrew Jackson, himself a southern slave-holder, denounced mob action, but he was even more critical of the abolitionists whose "fanaticism" incited such action. He called on Congress to pass laws that prohibited the using of the federal post office system to circulate abolitionist literature, but his proposal was shot down. In fact Congress responded by reorganizing the post office and inserting a provision that interference with delivery of the mail was not to occur. Jackson did not enforce this provision however, and the southern laws against the circulation of abolitionist mails stayed on the books and southern postmasters complied with them.

Antebellum Sectionalism

As northern and southern society increasingly diverged in their economic structures and in their sentiments concerning slavery, strong feelings of sectionalism exploded within the American republic. The North and the South seemed to be following separate paths, and Americans in both sections began to believe that they held interests that were fundamentally in opposition with one another. This sense of divergence played into the sectional crisis that would emerge in the 1850s as Americans debated the extent to which slavery would be allowed to expand into the new areas of the nation added by the Mexican War. Southerners argued that slavery must expand in order to continue as a viable system and in order for the superior social structure of the South to endure. Northerners increasingly believed that the existence of slavery was a blot on the nation. While some accepted the abolitionists' arguments that it was sinful and prevented Americans from achieving a morally sound society, others were more concerned with the way in which the expansion of slavery affected white opportunities for upward mobility. Slavery, they argued, inhibited the growth of free labor. Thus a contest between slave labor and free labor would dominate the politics of the 1850s.

Suggested Readings

John W. Blassingame, *The Slave Community: Plantation Life in the Antebellum South*, 1979.

Nancy, Isenberg, *Sex and Citizenship in Antebellum America*, 1998.

Lacy K. Ford, *Deliver Us from Evil: The Slavery Question in the Old South*, 2009.

Steven Mintz, *Moralists and Modernizers: America's Pre-Civil War Reformers*, 1995.

James Brewer Stewart, *Holy Warriors: The Abolitionists and American Slavery*, 1975.

Ian R. Tyrrell, *Sobering Up: From Temperance to Prohibition in Antebellum America*, 1800-1860, 1979.

Chapter 13

THE PATH TO WAR

The expansion of American power across the North American continent helped fuel increasing tensions over the meaning of that power and over the very identity of the United States. After Mexico surrendered the territory that now makes up New Mexico, Arizona, Colorado, Utah, Nevada, and California to the U.S. in the treaty of Guadalupe Hidalgo in 1848, American citizens immediately began to argue about the status of the new territory, focusing primarily on the question of whether or not the new states created would allow slavery. This reinvigorated a cultural battle that had been simmering since colonial times and had erupted in the 1820s during the debates over Missouri's status. Indeed it was the issue of slavery in the new territories that would lead the nation into civil war. As William Seward warned in 1858, an "irrepressible conflict" had emerged "between opposing and enduring forces"—a conflict that would force the nation to "become either entirely a slaveholding nation, or entirely a free-labor nation."

Missouri and the Rise of "Free Soil" Ideology

While more and more Americans would come to oppose slavery in the years leading up to the Civil War, most opposition was actually to the spread of slavery into new territories rather than to human bondage itself. Only a small minority joined the movement for immediate abolition in calling for an end to slavery in the South. Indeed, most who adopted anti-slavery ideas in the antebellum years came to believe in ideas of *"free soil"* and "free labor." Instead of opposing slavery out of moral concern for the slave, most who challenged the spread of slavery did so out of concern for white Americans. They wanted to ensure a level playing ground in the new territories so that whites of little means could afford to buy the new land and farm it without having to compete with wealthy planters who sought to bring slaves into the new lands. The tension over the spread of slavery began just after the turn of the 19th century with the Louisiana Purchase.

The first major controversy involved Missouri in the 1820s, as we have already seen. When the land in that area came up for grabs, southerners moved there and wanted to take their slaves with them. However, by this point there was a group of people who believed in a concept known as "free soil." This was not abolition, but it was against slavery in one sense. Basically, the idea was that slavery should not be allowed to spread into the new territories and that the new lands should be reserved for whites only. What resulted from the Missouri crisis was the Missouri Compromise, which allowed Missouri to become a slave state but created Maine as a free state to balance it all out. The Missouri Line was drawn into the West, and everything south of the line was to be slave territory, while everything north of the line was to be free territory.

The decade of the 1830s only saw growth in the tension over slavery. It was during the 1830s that Calhoun and other southerners argued for "states' rights" by insisting that states could nullify tariffs that did not benefit them, as we saw before. This decade also saw the "Gag Rule" controversy described earlier. Finally, Texas became a major issue in the 1830s, especially after it gained independence in 1836. The problem was that slavery was legally sanctioned in the independent Texas republic, and those who supported this idea of free soil already feared that it would be annexed and join the union as another slave state. They were right, and Texas was indeed

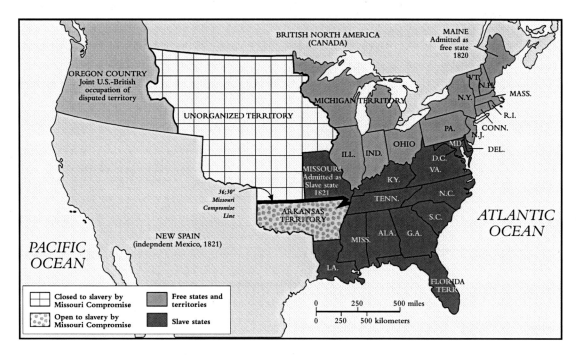

Under the Missouri Compromise, an agreement had been reached that would have limited slavery to future states and territories below the Missouri Compromise Line. After reaching this agreement, lawmakers hoped to put the slavery issue to rest, but the Kansas Nebraska Act and the Compromise of 1850 would essentially nullify this agreement.

annexed as a slave state in 1845. This was seen as another victory for southern slave interests. After Texas was annexed the U.S. went to war with Mexico and ultimately acquired a great deal more new territory, as we saw earlier. Right away arguments erupted over whether the new territory would become slave states or free states.

Tension over the status of the land acquired from Mexico actually emerged before the war's end. Indeed, the War with Mexico was a very unpopular war in the North because a wide range of the northern public saw immediately its potential to lead to the expansion of slave territory. Of course, more slave states would also mean more power for slave interests in Congress since each new

state would have representation in both the House and Senate. Remember that the Three Fifths Clause in the Constitution stacked the balance of power in favor of slave states by allowing slaves to be counted as three-fifths of a person when determining the number of representatives each state would be allowed in Congress, even though slaves would, of course, never be allowed to vote. More and more northerners began to cry out against the hypocrisy of using slave population numbers to grant slaveholders more power that ultimately allowed them to fight harder for the perpetuation of that very system. Abolitionists of all types cried out against this expansion of slave holders' power, and more and more Americans began to enlist in the antislavery cause. It is important to remember, however, that the average American viewed abolitionists with suspicion and feared that their radical movement would split the United States apart. Thus, instead of supporting any idea of universal abolition, a growing number of Americans began to embrace the type of antislavery that focused on limiting slavery to the South, where it already existed. Antislavery though not "abolitionist," free soil supporters argued that the Constitution protected slavery in the South but that the institution should not be allowed to spread into the West because the new territories should be open to all Americans on an equal basis. They did not want slave owners to be able to use their slaves to monopolize the new land.

Diverging Agendas for the West

As we have already seen, the northern and southern sections of the United States had been different from the beginning, but those differences had really started to show by the Jacksonian Era. Industrialization played a large role in the divergence, as did the growth of the cotton industry after the invention of cotton gin. At this point, the North had come to rely primarily upon free labor, while slavery, once a dying institution in the tobacco areas of the "Upper South," once again began to thrive as it spread westward throughout the "Deep South." As the nation acquired new westward land, each side had a different vision for the new states that would emerge.

Northerners generally saw the West as a land where surplus workers from the cities of the Atlantic seaboard could go to find an independent living. Theirs was an idea of "free soil, free men, and free labor" which celebrated the idea that wage laborers could

earn enough money to travel west, buy a moderate sized farm, and then work the land and enjoy an independent livelihood. This ideal, of course, was more a dream than a reality for most. The simple fact is that most laborers were not paid nearly enough to subsist comfortably while working in the North, much less to put money aside to purchase land. Even so, the very idea of available land open to free settlers remained the ideal to many northerners, and they began to see this possibility of independence and land ownership as a sacred right—the "American dream." They had visions of expanding the canals, roads, and railroads they had been building in their section into the new western land to encourage just such settlement.

For southerners, it was a different type of property right altogether that was at stake. As the revival of slavery through the cotton boom had shown, bound labor could thrive in much of the new western territory. From the cotton fields of Texas, to the wheat fields of Kansas, to the mines of the far West, southerners held out great hope that, through the work of their slaves, they could find much wealth in the new lands. The Texas Revolution had been a large victory to their cause, and they continued to insist on their constitutional right to take their property wherever they chose to settle. Because slaveholders generally had more resources than the northern freehold settlers, they were able to buy the best land with the best market access, clear that land, and set up homesteads quickly, effectively shutting out the idealized "independent" northern settlers.

For the most part, politicians hoped these competing interests would continue to work things out on their own with as little strife as possible. Trying to downplay the tensions between the North and the South, both major political parties—the Democrats and the

Whigs—kept public debates about slavery and its expansion out of the foreground. The acquisition of land following the war with Mexico and the California Gold Rush combined to force the issue back into prominence in the late 1840s.

The Wilmont Proviso and the Free Soil Party

The first attempt to exclude slavery from the new territories came in August of 1846 when a Pennsylvania congressman David Wilmont (a Democrat) attached a special amendment to an appropriations bill. This amendment would ban slavery from all of the territories that had been acquired as a result of the war with Mexico. Wilmont's goal was to preserve the new land for independent settlement by "free white men." He argued that slavery had come to an end in Mexico and, thus, in the new territories the U.S. had just acquired. He agreed to the annexation of Texas as a slave state because Texas had gained independence from Mexico on its own, but he insisted that both slavery and involuntary servitude be excluded from territories taken from Mexico by the U.S. Though the *Wilmont Proviso* was ultimately defeated, it reopened the fury of the Missouri controversy, and the issue of expanding slavery into the territories came to dominate American politics until the end of the Civil War.

In response to Wilmont's proviso, a new coalition of free soil supporters emerged. This coalition included people who saw immediate abolition as too radical but still opposed slavery, such as anti-slavery Whigs and some dissident Democrats. They argued that slavery should be excluded from the territories altogether. Most Whigs had long opposed slavery mostly because they saw it as a threat

to their modernizing *"American System"* agenda. Put simply, they believed that slavery was holding the South back by preventing southern leaders from building roads, canals, and railroads and investing in other important internal improvements. For these leaders, the best example of which was Henry Clay, the solution was to end slavery and allow the federal government to fund the colonization scheme supported by the American Colonization Society. Others who opposed slavery for various reasons, including the racist idea that the U.S. should be a "white man's country," could easily support this free soil idea, even if they could not support the idea of freeing the slaves and making room for free blacks in the U.S. A final group that was drawn toward the new *Free Soil Party*, which formed in 1848 in Buffalo, New York, was made up of those who had joined another third party, the anti-slavery Liberty Party. For these abolitionists, the only realistic way to end slavery was to compromise and work with these other opponents of slavery, even if their focus and overall belief system varied in many ways. (See the chapter on antislavery for more details about the specific beliefs and tactics of the Liberty Party.)

Even as Wilmont's efforts galvanized the free soil movement, it also created a backlash that saw the emergence of a faction of southern extremists, known as *"Fire Eaters."* Led by *John C. Calhoun*, this group demanded that slavery not only be protected in the South, but also that it be allowed to expand to the new territories. They insisted that Congress could not interfere with property rights and could not regulate what slaveholders took with them into the territories. They even went so far as to threaten secession and war if their demands were not met. They also threatened the lives of abolitionists.

Popular Sovereignty

In light of the growing tensions, two compromise positions emerged. Some, including President James K. Polk, argued that the solution was to extend the Missouri Compromise line all the way to the Pacific Ocean, making everything north of it free territory and everything south slave territory. Others supported an idea known as *"popular sovereignty,"* which argued that citizens in the territories should decide the fate of those territories by voting on whether or not slavery would be allowed.

All of these ideas influenced the presidential election of 1848. In the North, the Democrats and the Whigs both lost supporters to the new Free Soil coalition, which earned 14 percent of the northern vote. In the South, the Democrats lost support to the Fire Eaters, who maintained they were not doing enough to support the interests of slaveholders. Whig candidate Zachary Taylor, known for his efforts in the Mexican war, won the presidency but the tension continued to grow.

As the politicians tried to work through the growing sectional tension, westward settlement continued to complicate matters. In addition to the Mormon settlement in the Great Salt Lake region of modern-day Utah, enough settlers had reached New Mexico and California that they were in need of territorial governments. Congress left it to the new President to decide what to do in the territories, and despite his own southern origins he put national unity first by proposing that New Mexico and California skip territorial status and be made states immediately. What this meant was that the question of slave or free territory, which would have been a Congressional matter for territories, went straight into the hands of the people through popular sovereignty. Taylor hoped this would bypass

bitter debate and deny further fuel to the sectional battle that was growing daily. California immediately applied for admission as a free state, and New Mexico soon followed.

Fire eaters responded by calling a convention in Nashville, Tennessee to come up with "some mode of resistance to Northern aggression." The North had done nothing aggressive; the people of California and New Mexico had simply chosen to seek admission without slavery. This posed a threat to the slave interests, however, because at the time there were 15 slave states and 15 free states, leaving a balance of power in the Senate. Two new free states would upset this balance and take away the South's ability to block legislation that threatened southern interests, foremost of which was slavery. Slave interests feared that it would only be a matter of time before such an unbalanced Congress would abolish slavery completely. Of course, very few Americans, politicians or the general public, wanted to end slavery in the South. Most who cared at all only wanted to block its extension. Blinded by fear and rage, however, southern leaders did not see it that way. As the debate raged on, fistfights broke out in Congress, and elected officials challenged each other to duels.

The Compromise of 1850

There was a clear sense of imminent danger, as there had been during the Missouri Crisis of 1819–1820 and the Nullification Crisis of 1832–33, but once again Henry Clay stepped in with a compromise to avert war. He suggested that California be admitted as a free state and New Mexico broken into two territories with the status determined by popular sovereignty. He also proposed a clear border between Texas and New Mexico, suggested that the national government pay Texas's debt, and called for a banning of the slave trade in Washington, D.C. Finally, to counter resistance to the latter he proposed a stronger federal fugitive slave law.

John C. Calhoun, dying of tuberculosis, made his last stand, leading the opposition to Clay's proposals and demanded that the North not only enforce fugitive slave laws but also allow slavery in the territories and stop attacking slavery. Finally, Massachusetts Senator Daniel Webster delivered a plea for moderation, begging both proslavery and antislavery extremists to put the Union above sectional interests. Even so, tensions grew to the point where Mississippi Senator Henry S. Foote threatened Missouri Senator Thomas Hart Benton with a pistol. Clay's compromise bill was eventually voted down, and these three legendary leaders faded into the background as a new generation, which included New York's William H. Seward and Illinois's "Little Giant," Stephen A. Douglas, took the lead.

Douglas played a large role in rescuing Clay's omnibus compromise bill, but he was aided by the unexpected death of President Taylor. What Douglas realized was that the bill as a collective entity was doomed to fail, but that smaller parts of the bill appealed to enough congressmen to pass on their own. To get past this problem, he broke the large bill into five separate bills, collectively known as the *Compromise of 1850*. As Douglas was ushering the bills through, President Taylor died of a gastrointestinal illness caused by tainted food or water. This had a large impact on the fate of the bills because while Taylor saw the new territories as unsuited to slavery anyway and thus pushed for the admission of California and New Mexico without compromise, his successor, Millard Fillmore, had different ideas. Ironically, Taylor, a Louisiana

slaveholder had put the union above sectional animosity and was unsympathetic to slave interests in the expansion debate. Fillmore, a New Yorker assumed to be antislavery, was actually more sympathetic to southern interests and more eager to compromise.

The individual bills made it through Congress, and each of Clay's original proposals was eventually enacted. California was indeed admitted to the union as a free state, but New Mexico and Utah territories were created under the agreement that their status would be decided by popular sovereignty when they were ready to apply for statehood. (Nothing was said about the status of the territories before they were ready to apply, however.) Texas was required to give disputed western territory to New Mexico, and this appealed to the opponents of slavery because it reduced the size of a slave state. In exchange for ceding the territory, Texas was allowed to transfer debts it had incurred while a republic to the federal government. Since southerners held most of this debt, this provision was seen as a victory for southern interests. Abolitionists, on the other hand, secured a small victory by the provision that banned the slave trade (but not slavery itself) from the nation's capital.

Of all of the separate bills that made up the compromise, the *Fugitive Slave Law of 1850* caused the most backlash. Many states in the North had passed personal liberty laws to guarantee the rights of blacks accused of being runaways, and they made slave catchers prove that the person they were trying to take into custody was indeed a runaway slave. The 1850 fugitive law denied northern states their rights at such regulation. Under this new law, the national government agreed to hire officials to capture slaves in the North and return them to their masters. This was a change from the original law, the Fugitive Slave Law of 1793, because it meant that the government, rather than the master who lost a slave, would do the dirty work of capturing the fugitive. Federal marshals were also given the power to deputize private citizens to help capture fugitives, and citizens who refused to help faced fines of $1,000 and up to six months' imprisonment. Suspected fugitives had no right to trial by jury, instead having their fate decided by a federal commissioner who would earn a ten dollar fee if he found the accused guilty and only a five dollar fee if he released the accused.

The new law made it almost impossible for someone without papers to prove his or her innocence. For African Americans born free in the North this was a real problem, because they did not have free papers. (Only those who had been slaves but were then freed would have free papers.) Some blacks began to talk about armed defense, and within three months of the law's passage, more than 3,000 African Americans fled to Canada. Others, like Martin R. Delany, Henry Highland Garnet, and Alexander Crummell, began to consider the idea of going "back" to Africa.

Black and white abolitionists both became more radical after the passage of the new law, sometimes even helping fugitives escape and hiding them from slave catchers. The most famous instance occurred in Boston when *Anthony Burns*, a runaway slave from Virginia, was almost rescued by 2,000 abolitionists who stormed the jail to free him after he was arrested and set to be returned to his owner. A federal marshal was killed and Burns was ultimately returned, but 50,000 people lined the streets of Boston in protest as the fugitive was marched to the docks and put on a southbound ship. A number of demonstrations followed throughout the North with men like the transcendentalist writer Henry David Thoreau speaking out against the Fugitive

Slave Law and abolitionists like William Lloyd Garrison burning not only copies of the law but copies of the U.S. Constitution as well. Though these incidents were highly publicized at the time and have gained much attention historically, they were not typical. Overall very few runaways were rescued from slave catchers and relatively few (around 200) were returned to bondage in the South under this law. Burns was ultimately freed by the efforts of Boston free blacks, who raised the money to purchase him.

Besides Garrison's inflammatory demonstrations, the most famous reaction by a white abolitionist to the Fugitive Slave Law was Harriet Beecher Stowe's novel, "Uncle Tom's Cabin." Published in 1852, this best seller was written in protest to the law and it emphasized the ways that slavery broke families apart thanks to the domestic slave trade. It also highlighted the brutality and inhumanity of the system and made heroes of characters who broke the law by helping the main character, a slave named Eliza, escape the pursuit of a master who planned to sell her and her child to different buyers. Stowe's husband, brother and father were all Congregationalist ministers, and like many abolitionists she was influenced by a strong religious background. Even so, she did not necessarily embrace the type of immediate abolition supported by William Lloyd Garrison. Instead, her novel actually supported the idea of colonization.

Backlash

Ultimately the Fugitive Slave Law of 1850 gave abolitionists an emotional rallying point. It led more and more people who had previously been indifferent to slavery to question the system, if not for what bondage did to the slave, then for what the power held by slave owners

Uncle Tom's Cabin for Children—The success of Harriet Beecher Stowe's novel *Uncle Tom's Cabin* led to a cultural phenomenon throughout the northern reform community that would seem familiar to 21st century Americans. In addition to selling over 300,000 copies in its first year and over two million copies in 1856, the book was translated into 13 different languages and was the best-selling book of the 19th century. Some of the characters, especially a white child named Little Eva, reach the status of cultural icons. As this illustration shows, the book was so popular that children's editions were created. In fact, children were not only able to read the story, they were soon able to play out the drama with dolls and other toys that were made based on the characters. Board games based on the story were also popular among reform-minded consumers. Of course, Stowe's characters were based on simplistic notions that perpetuated stereotypes of African Americas, from the "happy darky" Sam to the maternal figure of Mammy. In fact, the very name Uncle Tom became a derogatory term for blacks who were too eager to please whites.

and, by extension, slave states, did to the freedom of all citizens from non-slaveholding states. This led to growing resentment from many everyday people in the North toward the South. In many ways they saw the law as an infringement of their states' rights to pass laws to protect citizens within their own borders.

The Fire Eaters became as angry as the northern public and abolitionists toward the compromise and the fugitive law, but for different reasons. They said the law did not go far enough to protect slavery. They wanted a guaranteed protection of slavery and an assurance that it would be allowed to spread. They said the abolitionists were calling for radical measures that were dangerous to white society and encouraging racial mixing, and they insisted that slaves were better off than the workers who suffered under the evils of industrial capitalism. They argued that at least slaves were taken care of when they got old, while workers were just left to die, and they added that slaves were fed adequately while workers were allowed to starve. (Historians have found that slavery was different from plantation to plantation but that in most cases these arguments were not necessarily true.) Fire Eaters also said that blacks were not smart enough to take care of themselves so freeing them would create a public burden.

This bickering over the Fugitive Slave Law shows that the Compromise did not solve the problems in the long term. Indeed, the voting on the separate bills showed an ominous pattern that revealed growing sectional animosity and supported Seward's warnings that an "irrepressible conflict" was on the horizon. While northern Whigs had supported the admission of California as a free state and opposed the Fugitive Slave Law, southern Whigs had opposed California but supported the fugitive law. Only about 20 percent of Congress supported all five bills. Clearly the issue had not been resolved.

The Election of 1852

The Democrats and Whigs again tried to regain control in the election of 1852, and they did manage to take back some of the Free Soil votes. Indeed, the Free Soilers gained only half as many votes in 1852 as they had in 1848. Still, the two main parties were clearly facing a number of problems of their own.

The Democrats chose Franklin Pierce of New Hampshire as their candidate and rallied behind the slogan "We Polked you in 1844, we shall Pierce you in 1852." Pierce, a veteran of the Mexican War, had little experience in politics, but he managed to gain the support of Van Buren Democrats and the southern rights' faction. One way the party managed to gain southern support was by making enforcement of the Compromise of 1850, including the Fugitive Slave Law, the centerpiece of its platform. This alone allowed the party to remain a national force.

The Whigs had no such luck. Unable to find a similar point of unity, they lost much southern support because southerners had come to believe that the party harbored antislavery advocates. On the other hand, northerners resented the party's endorsement of the Compromise of 1850. Indeed, Henry Clay, perhaps the strongest Whig of all, had written the Fugitive Slave Act, and Daniel Webster, another main Whig leader, had supported it. To please the southern Whigs, the party endorsed the Compromise at its convention that year. To please their northern supporters they chose General Winfield Scott as their presidential candidate. What this meant was that their candidate appealed to one section and alienated the other, and their platform did the opposite.

Despite their hopes that Scott's military reputation would win support, it was not enough to overcome his reputation for anti-slavery. Ultimately the party lost enough southern support to assure their loss that November.

In the end, Pierce won the election with 254 electoral votes to Scott's 42. Pierce, however, was soon labeled a failure by his own party. In fact, he lost favor before the end of his first year in office. During this year, sectional tensions were heightened as efforts were made to build a transcontinental railroad.

The Kansas-Nebraska Crisis

Congress considered a number of proposals for a transcontinental railroad route in 1852 and 1853. Pushing for a southern route, Secretary of War Jefferson Davis promoted the *Gadsden*

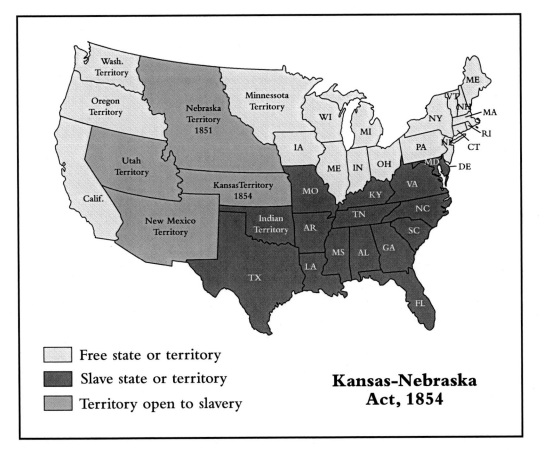

Free state or territory

Slave state or territory

Territory open to slavery

Kansas-Nebraska Act, 1854

The Kansas-Nebraska Act of 1854 nullified the Missouri Compromise by allowing people in the Kansas and Nebraska territories to vote on whether or not slavery would be allowed in their future states. This set off a firestorm of both pro- and anti-slavery agitation that led to the events collectively known as "bleeding Kansas" and ultimately to the caning of Senator Charles Sumner.

Purchase, convincing the federal government to buy a stretch of land from Mexico (in present-day New Mexico) for $10 million. At the same time, Illinois's senator *Stephen A. Douglas* pushed for a northern route that would run through present-day Nebraska. To achieve this goal he needed to secure southern support for granting Nebraska territorial status, and that meant making concessions on the issue of slavery in the territories. His solution was to suggest popular sovereignty for the territories of Kansas and Nebraska so the settlers could decide the fate of each future state. This required repeal of the Missouri Compromise, since it excluded slavery north of the Missouri Line. While Douglas preferred that slavery be excluded from these territories and believed that it would be kept out simply because the climate and geography of the area was not suited to plantation agriculture, his support of popular sovereignty opened the new territory to the possibility of slavery. Douglas's *Kansas-Nebraska Act* was thus a clear victory for slave interests and a defeat for free soilers and abolitionists.

After the passage of this act the Whig party basically disintegrated. Most northern Whigs joined new parties that were emerging during this period of instability. Many joined the anti-slavery coalition we have already discussed, coming to agreements with independent Democrats and Free Soilers to oppose the spread of slavery. Others were attracted to various specialized third parties such as the Anti-Nebraska Democratic Party, the Fusion Party, the American Party, and finally, after 1854, the new Republican Party.

The Growth of Nativism

As if the tensions over slavery were not enough, a growing current of *nativism* also seeped its way into American culture and politics. The American Party, also known as the *Know-Nothing Party*, emerged in 1852 in the wake of the demise of the Whig Party and gained support during the 1854 midterm elections. (The party began as a secret organization and, when asked about their group, members would claim to "know nothing" about it.) This short-lived group appealed primarily to middle class Protestants who viewed with fear and disdain the growth of the immigrant population. Much of their concern stemmed from the fact that many of the immigrants were Catholic. They also saw the Irish and German immigrants as drunken rabble rousers who lived in slums and had low aspirations, and they did not like that many of these working-class immigrants bolstered the strength of the Democrats by voting in large blocks for that party. The American Party gained 25 percent of the New York vote and 40 percent of the Pennsylvania vote. They actually managed to win control of the state legislature in Massachusetts.

Some saw these results as evidence that nativism would take the spotlight away from slavery as the main political issue in the United States. For many supporters, however, the two issues went hand in hand. Slavery and Catholicism were both seen by many white American Protestants as antiquated and authoritarian systems that were incompatible with modernism and individualism. With the growth in nativism, immigrants were drawn increasingly into the Democratic fold.

Irish immigrants especially were attracted to the Democratic Party. For one thing the Democrats appealed to working-class voters in general. Their appeal to white workers went hand in hand with another characteristic often associated with antebellum Democrats—their resistance to abolition. Basically, they argued that if the slaves were freed they would head north in search of employment. This, of course, would lead to job competition that would put the livelihoods of white workers in jeopardy, according to Democratic leaders, who were no fans of free labor or free soil.

Bleeding Kansas

After the Kansas-Nebraska Act passed, settlers began to migrate to the new territories. It was generally agreed that Nebraska would be a free state, and the House of Representative passed a bill prohibiting slavery from that territory because it was above the Missouri Compromise line. The bill died in the Senate and Stephen Douglas offered a bill that would have brought popular sovereignty to the area. To gain support for this bill, he added a provision that split the territory in two, creating Nebraska above the Missouri Compromise line and Kansas below it. Repealing the Missouri Compromise of 1820, the new bill placed the fate of both territories in the hands of residents who would vote for slavery or free soil, but it was universally assumed that Kansas would become a slave state and Nebraska a free state.

Groups emerged in both the North and the South that sought to influence the outcome of the vote on whether or not slavery would be allowed in the Kansas territory. Northern groups funded the moves of settlers that would vote against slavery, and southern groups paid the way for those who would vote in favor of slavery in the new state. It is important to note, however, that these opponents of slavery's spread into Kansas were, for the most part, not abolitionists. They were people who wanted to keep all blacks, whether enslaved or free, out of the territory. At any rate, Kansas's first territorial governor

arrived after thousands of settlers had already staked their claims and started to build their homesteads. Arriving in 1854, the governor set to work preparing for a census, and he scheduled elections to determine the fate of the future state.

On the day of the election several thousand men from Missouri crossed state lines to illegally vote for slavery. These *"border ruffians"* also threatened to kill abolitionists. Though he admitted the fraudulent nature of the election, the governor did nothing about the situation because he feared being murdered. The few antislavery members who had been elected to the territorial legislature were expelled and the remaining legislators adopted a very harsh slave code and declared it a capital offense to assist fugitive slaves.

Of course, those who wanted Kansas to be a free state refused to accept the fraudulently-elected government and formed one of their own. They met in Topeka and drafted a state constitution that excluded all blacks—enslaved and free. After drafting their constitution, this second state government applied for admission to the union as a free state.

By 1856 Kansas had two governments, one governing as a free state and one as a slave state. Both sides were armed and ready to fight. That May a gang of about 700 proslavery men ignited an all-out dressed rehearsal for the Civil War by attacking the free soil stronghold of Lawrence, destroying newspaper presses and other property in the town and setting the free state governor's home ablaze. This attack, known as the *"sack of Lawrence,"* only led to one death but it is most famous for arousing the ire of a mentally unstable antislavery man named *John Brown.* After the attack upon Lawrence, Brown and four of his sons (he had 20 children) joined forces with a handful of other locals to exact vengeance upon proslavery settlers, where they dragged five men from their homes and butchered them in front of their families in what is known as the *Pottawatomie Massacre*. This act of retribution led to what was essentially guerilla warfare in the territory, and the end result included the death of Brown's son Frederick and the near death of Brown himself at a raid upon the free settlement of *Osawatomie*. By the end of the year millions of dollars of property had been destroyed and the deaths of about 200 settlers had been recorded in the territorial civil war that is known as *"Bleeding Kansas."*

Both sides, pro and anti slavery, were guilty of the violence, but the newspapers in each region wrote about the events in a very biased manner. Essentially, the northern press portrayed free soil settlers as innocent and proslavery settlers as brutal, while the southern press made the free soilers and antislavery settlers appear to be the aggressors and proslavery settlers the victims. The result was an increase in the sectionalism that was already polarizing the nation.

The Caning of Sumner

The polarization entered a new phase when violence spread to the Senate floor in late May of 1856—within days of both the Sack of Lawrence and the Pottawatomie Massacre. In response to these events, Massachusetts Senator *Charles Sumner* blamed southerners for the lawlessness in Kansas, targeting especially South Carolina senator Andrew Pickens Butler. Taking aim at the elderly southerner's sense of honor, Sumner accused him of dishonesty and of keeping a slave mistress. He even went so far as to poke fun at a speech impediment Butler had developed following a stroke. Perhaps this last action would have

hurt Sumner's image in the public eye, but another South Carolina congressman and relative of Butler, *Preston Brooks*, stole the scene. After simmering for a few days, Brook's anger exploded when he approached Sumner at his desk on the Senate floor to accuse him of slander against Butler, South Carolina, and the South in general. As his rage grew he began assaulting Sumner by hitting him on the head with his cane. Wedged into his desk, Sumner was not able to defend himself from the attack, and he sustained a beating that left his Senate seat vacant for two and a half years.

The reaction to the *caning of Sumner* varied by region. In the North, Brooks' actions produced an antislavery martyr as northerners in general reacted to the beating with disgust and fear, calling him "Bully Brooks." At this point, abolitionists and free soilers made up a very small part of the northern population, but the caning of Sumner made more northerners join these two antislavery groups. They began to see the South as violent and the North as the victim of southern aggression, and they began to argue that the slaveholders were so accustomed to controlling the slaves with violence that they had started to try to control other whites that way as well. They started to use the term *"Slave Power"* to describe the brutal nature of southern white behavior. This was significant because it led many who had been neutral before to side with the opponents of slavery. The reaction in the South was quite different. There Brooks was seen as a hero who had put a trouble maker in his place. Though the House censured Brooks and he resigned, he was promptly reelected. Many of his supporters sent him new canes, and there were many calls for him to use the canes to put another abolitionist in his place.

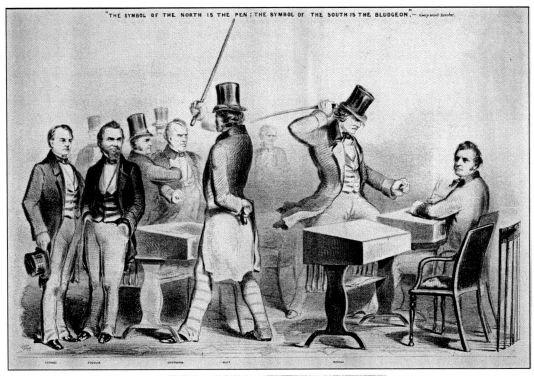

"THE SYMBOL OF THE NORTH IS THE PEN; THE SYMBOL OF THE SOUTH IS THE BLUDGEON." — *Henry Ward Beecher*

ARGUMENTS OF THE CHIVALRY.

After commenting on the violence in Kansas and publically insulting pro-slavery senators Stephen A. Douglas and Andrew Pickens Butler, antislavery senator Charles Sumner of Massachusetts was brutally attacked on the senate floor by Butler's cousin, South Carolina senator Preston Brooks. In this drawing Sumner sits at his desk unsuspectingly while Brooks prepares to beat him with his cane. This attack led many northerners who had previously felt no concern over the slavery debates to fear the idea that a southern "Slave Power" sought to beat the rest of the nation into submission as part of their drive to spread slavery throughout the country.

After May of 1856 American politics reached a new level of bitter sectional strife as neither party could continue to push the slavery issue into the background. Northerners rallied behind the fear of slave power and focused on the violence of "Bleeding Kansas" and "Bleeding Sumner" to argue that it was even more important than ever to keep slavery bottled up in the South. Southern attacks upon northern liberties, they argued threatened the freedom of whites as well as blacks in both the North and the South. Southerners, meanwhile continued to insist that any efforts to restrict the spread of slavery amounted to an attack upon the institution overall and their way of life in general.

The Emergence of the Republicans as a National Force

Once slavery was at the forefront of American politics the parties underwent further realignment. The Whigs basically fell apart. The new Republican Party held its first national convention, choosing military hero and western explorer John C. Fremont as its 1856 presidential candidate. Following in Whig footsteps the new party developed a platform that included internal improvements such as a transcontinental railroad. Borrowing also from free soilers and taking a clear stand against the expansion of slavery, they rallied behind the slogan "Free soil, free speech, and Fremont." This was the first time a national party had included antislavery as part of its platform, but note that their platform did not address slavery in the South, only the spread of slavery into the territories. Thus, the Republican Party was an "antislavery" party but *not* an "abolitionist" party.

The Democrats now faced a party with a clear stance on slavery and a resulting regional appeal. Even so, they faced a number of problems of their own. For the only time in history they rejected an incumbent President, refusing to nominate him for re-election. Many thought Stephen Douglas would have been a logical nominee, but his Kansas-Nebraska Act had seriously harmed his political reputation. Instead they turned to a former senator and secretary of state from Pennsylvania, James Buchanan. Their platform endorsed the Kansas-Nebraska Act and called upon Congress not to interfere with slavery in either the states or the territories. They reached out to those who had been alienated by the Know-Nothings, namely the Irish and German Catholics, by coming out in support of religious liberty and against nativism.

This presidential campaign demonstrated the depth of the sectional chasm. Republicans understood the futility of seeking southern support, and only a handful of border state voters were brave enough to chance disunion by supporting the new party. They did manage to gain the support of all of the states along the northern border of the U.S. and gain 114 electoral votes, but Buchanan managed to gain 174 electoral votes by adding five free states to his southern support bloc. Millard Fillmore, running as the candidate for the American Party, managed to gain Maryland's eight electoral votes.

Buchanan's election postponed the complete splitting of the Union for a few more years. With experience in Congress, as an ambassador to Britain and Russia, and as the Secretary of State under Polk, he had a great deal of political experience, and he was known for believing that the way to save the Union was to make peace with the South. For Republicans, the fact that Buchanan chose four cabinet members from slave states and three from free states showed from the beginning that he would pander to southern interests. Within a year of his election three key events proved them right.

Dred Scott v. Sandford

The first of these major events occurred in 1857 when the Supreme Court ruled that blacks could not be citizens of the United States. This happened after a slave named *Dred Scott*, who had lived in the North with his master, sued for his freedom based on a law that any slave who lived in the North for more than 6 months would be declared free.

Dred Scott was born into slavery around 1800 in Virginia but through sale had been relocated to St. Louis, Missouri by 1830. His owner, a surgeon with the Army, then took him into the territory that is now modern-day Minnesota. While there Scott married Harriet Robinson, and the couple had two daughters. Even so, Scott and his master returned to St. Louis in 1842, and the master died the next year. Three years later Harriet Scott convinced Dred to sue for their freedom in Missouri and base the claim upon their residence in Illinois and the Wisconsin Territory. Initially a jury ruled in their favor but the state supreme court overruled that decision, arguing that once the Scotts were back in a slave state they were no longer free. When the case reached the national Supreme Court, the question being decided was whether freedom granted to those who lived in free states could be retained if the freed returned to a slave state.

The answer, according to the Supreme Court, was that the Scotts had resumed their slave status once they returned to Missouri. The court went even further by ruling that Scott, and by extension all blacks, could not appeal to the courts to decide such matters at any rate because they were not citizens of the United States. According to Chief Justice Roger B. Taney, all blacks, slave or free, were regarded as inferior to the point that they "had no rights which the white man was bound to respect." While he was on a roll, Taney went on to tackle another related issue—the status of slavery in the territories. He concluded that the Missouri Compromise had violated the constitutional property rights of citizens by prohibiting slavery in any of the territories. This was the first

time that the Supreme Court had deemed a congressional act unconstitutional since the 1803 case of *Marbury vs Madison*. Furthermore, through this overruling of the Missouri Compromise the Court was challenging the very concept of popular sovereignty. What this all means is that, essentially, instead of declaring Scott free, the court ruled that he would remain a slave, that all slaves were property and could be taken anywhere by their owners, and that free blacks were not citizens and thus were not equal under the Constitution.

This was a huge victory for proslavery interests and a heartbreaking loss for the black community, abolitionists, and even free soilers. At the same time, it also created another backlash in the North and boosted the popularity of the free soilers even more. Remember, though, most whites who were coming around to the antislavery side were doing so not because of what slavery meant for slaves or free blacks, but because of what slaveholders' power was

Dred and Harriet Scott. Dred Scott's famous case led to the Supreme Court ruling that not only would slavery be allowed in the territories but that black Americans would not be accepted as citizens of the United States.

doing to white liberty throughout the nation. They simply did not like that the Dred Scott ruling was going to allow slavery to expand. They also pointed out that all but one of the Supreme Court justices were southerners.

Dred Scott did manage to gain his freedom, but it was short-lived. His new owner, the widow of his previous owner, freed the Scotts after marrying an abolitionist from Massachusetts in 1857. The next year, however, Scott died of tuberculosis.

Lecompton Constitution

Matters remained unsettled in Kansas, which by this point had an antislavery legislature but a proslavery constitutional convention that was meeting at Lecompton. The constitution drawn up by this group, the *Lecompton Constitution*, would have made Kansas a slave state, and it was put to popular vote in an election set for December of 1857. Free soil advocates argued that the election was rigged in favor of the slave interests, so they refused to participate. The result was over 6,000 votes for the constitution with slavery. Only about 550 voted for the constitution under the condition that slavery be taken out. The antislavery legislature, which had been called to action by the acting governor, called for another election on this constitution. This time the proslavery interests refused to participate. Of course, the results were quite different this time: over 10,000 voted against the Lecompton Constitution, 138 voted for the constitution with slavery, and fewer than 25 voted for the constitution if slavery were to be taken out. President Buchanan supported the Lecompton Constitution as it was (with slavery) and fought to push it through Congress so that Kansas would be accepted into the Union as a slave state. This

led to turmoil in the Democratic Party, but the President's supporters in the Senate managed to get the constitution passed in 1858. Even so, there was enough resistance in the House that they managed to get an amendment added that called for yet another vote in Kansas on the issue of slavery, this one to be carefully supervised to prevent fraud. The result of this final election, much to the surprise of southerners, was a large antislavery referendum of 11,300 votes against Lecompton and only 1,788 for it. This meant that the antislavery legislature was the legitimate governing body, that statehood would be postponed until the territory reached a population of 90,000, and that Kansas would likely end up being a free state. It also meant that the matter of Kansas was settled for the time being.

Financial Panic

As the nation's sectional crisis heated up, a financial panic added fuel to the fire. Starting in August of 1857, Europe's demand for American grain dropped, leading to over production in the agricultural sector just as the U.S. experienced significant growth in manufacturing that led to over production in the industrial sector. In both cases, production exceeded consumption and prices of goods dropped. Adding to this problem was a railroad boom in which construction outpaced the financial resources to fund it, as well as a confusing system in which state bank notes meant decentralization of currency. The resulting economic slump did not begin to lift until 1859.

This troubling economic state added to sectional tensions and appeared to tilt the balance in favor of the South. Basically, the South weathered the economic storm better because of its agricultural base—especially cotton. Even though cotton prices fell, the drop in value was slow and the rebound was quick. While the markets for grains suffered, the markets for cotton recovered quickly, and this led to a heightened sense of the importance of cotton to the world financial system. Many southerners saw this as a vindication of their slave-based labor system and their section's importance to the national economy. Businessmen in the North, on the other hand, argued that the low tariffs put in place by the Democrats in 1857 had caused the problems by failing to protect American manufactures.

John Brown's Raid

As the nation began to recover from the financial crisis, sectional tensions reached a fever pitch. Southern fears reached an apex and abolitionists gained a martyr in late 1859 beginning with a failed raid upon the federal arsenal at *Harper's Ferry*, Virginia (now West Viriginia). The leader of this raid was *John Brown*, one of the key figures on the antislavery side of "bleeding Kansas." On October 16, 1859, he led a band of approximately 20 men, five of whom were black, in an attempt to seize and occupy the arsenal with the hope of using the weapons there to arm slaves throughout Maryland. Once armed, he hoped, blacks would follow him to the mountains of western Virginia where they would set up a base of operations. From that base he wanted to support slave insurrections throughout the southern states.

The plan failed. Brown did manage to surprise officials at the arsenal and seize a few hostages. He and his followers, however, were soon surrounded by local residents and militia who were so incensed that they shot two members of Brown's group,

including Brown's son Watson, as they tried to surrender the next morning. Gunfire resulted on both sides and another of Brown's sons was injured. U.S. Marines, led by Lieutenant Colonel Robert E. Lee and Lieutenant J.E.B. Stuart arrived and, on October 18, managed to

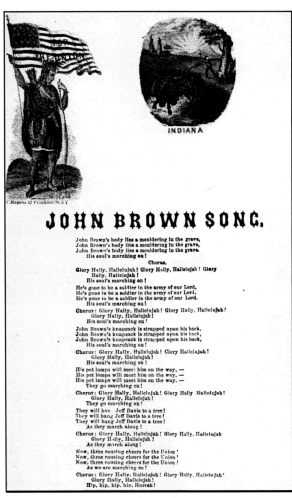

John Brown's execution gave the antislavery community a valuable martyr. After his death Brown became for many a hero in a glorious cause, and the song "John Brown's Body" (sung to the tune of the "Grapes of Wrath") provided a rallying cry for the antislavery community.

break down the barricaded doors of the fire engine house where Brown and his men were keeping the hostages and arrest Brown and his men. The raiders had killed four people, one of whom was a marine, and wounded nine, but they lost ten, two of whom were sons of Brown. Five escaped, and seven tried to escape but were captured.

Realizing the importance of his martyrdom to the antislavery cause, Brown, who was convicted of treason and sentenced to hang, met his end unflinchingly. After pointing out that he was "worth inconceivably more to hang than for any other purpose," Brown said that ". . . if it is deemed necessary that I should forfeit my life for the furtherance of the ends of justice, and mingle my blood further with the blood of my children and with the blood of millions in this slave country whose rights are disregarded by wicked, cruel, and unjust enactments, I say, let it be done." His death and the way he approached it became a rallying point for the antislavery cause. Transcendentalist Ralph Waldo Emerson referred to him as a "saint," and abolitionists from across the North celebrated his contribution to the cause through a new anthem, "John Brown's Body."

Of course, southerners did not share the abolitionist admiration for this would-be revolutionary. Instead, they saw him as a terrorist representative of the new Republican Party. There was no connection, but they saw antislavery of all sorts and immediate abolition as one in the same. They also became increasingly terrified of the idea that, although Brown had failed, someone somewhere could be organizing a successful insurrection. Throughout the fall and winter of 1859 and 1860 this specter haunted the South as rumors of slave insurrections and suspicion of all northern visitors, travelers and immigrants spread.

Conclusion

The 1840s and 1850s were a tumultuous time in the United States. The acquisition of new lands bolstered the geographic strength of the United States, stretching the nation "from sea to shining sea," but at the same time this growth brought tremendous tensions over the issue of slavery. The question was never whether or not slavery should be abolished in the South, where it had been long entrenched by law and was both a crucial economic system as well as the bedrock of social relations. Rather, what came under intense debate was the question of whether or not slavery should be allowed to spread into the new territories. Antislavery sentiment began to grow, and it spread further and wider with each conflict over territorial status, but this opposition was based on ideas of free soil, not abolition. Feeling increasingly under attack as more and more people came to question their labor system, southerners began to hold more and more tightly to that very system and became enraged at any questioning of their way of life. Seeing the resistance as abolition itself, they became determined to protect their economic and social interests. John Brown's raid on Harper's Ferry left them in no mood for further compromise, and the political atmosphere would only deteriorate from there.

Suggested Readings

Fergus M. Bordewich, *Bound for Canaan: The Epic Story of the Underground Railroad, America's First Civil Rights Movement* (2006)

Victoria Bynum, *The Long Shadow of the Civil War: Southern Dissent and Its Legacies* (2010)

Eric Foner, *Free Soil, Free Labor, Free Men: The Ideology of the Republican Party Before the Civil War* (1970)

William E. Gienapp, *The Origins of the Republican Party, 1852–1856* (1987)

Bruce Levine, *Half Slave, Half Free: The Roots of the Civil War* (1992)

James Oakes, *The Radical and the Republican: Frederick Douglass, Abraham Lincoln, and the Triumph of Antislavery Politics* (2007)

David Potter, *The Impending Crisis, 1848–1861* (1976)

James A. Rawley, *Race and Politics: "Bleeding Kansas" and the Coming of the Civil War* (1969)

Leonard Richards, *The Slave Power: The Free North and Southern Domination, 1780–1860* (2000)

Albert J. von Frank, *The Trials of Antony Burns: Freedom and Slavery in Emerson's Boston* (1999)

Eric Walther, *The Fire-Eaters* (1992)

Eric Walther, *The Shattering of the Union: America in the 1850s* (2003)

Douglas Wilson and Rodney O. Davis, eds., *The Lincoln-Douglas Debates* (2008)

Chapter 14

THE CIVIL WAR

The Election of 1860

The election of 1860 occurred in an atmosphere of national crisis. For much of the previous decade the Democratic Party had been able to withstand the sectional animosity that had demolished the Whigs and created the Republican Party. But in April at Charleston's South Carolina Institute Hall, Democrats were unable to nominate a candidate for the coming presidential election. The early favorite had been the nationally known and popular Illinois Senator, Stephen A. Douglas, but Douglas had alienated southern "fire-eaters" because of the stance he had taken in his 1858 campaign against Republican challenger Abraham Lincoln. The savvy Lincoln had cornered Douglas into repudiating the *Dred Scott* decision. *Dred Scott* had been enormously unpopular in the North. By reaffirming his faith in popular sovereignty, Douglas was able to retain his seat in the Senate narrowly, but he had alienated himself in the South, essentially ending any real chance he had at becoming president in 1860.

At the Democratic convention in Charleston, southern fire-eaters pressed for the endorsement of *Dred Scott* and the adoption of a pro-slavery platform, which called for federal protection of slavery in the territories. Blocked by Northern Democrats from getting any of the measures adopted, Southern Democrats bolted out of the hall in protest, gathered at Charleston's nearby Military Hall, and declared themselves the real convention, trusting that the move would force some sort of reconciliation and the adoption of their ideas. Back at Institute Hall, however, Douglas's supporters saw the walkout as an opportunity to realize the nomination of their candidate.

Neither faction accomplished their goals. Northern Democrats rejected any compromise and the fire-eaters therefore refused to participate in the activities at Institute Hall, where the remaining delegates had begun voting to select a candidate. Although Douglas led on the first ballot and every ballot thereafter, including the final one, the fifty seventh, he never attained the required two-thirds majority, and the delegates voted to adjourn the convention on May 3 without selecting a candidate.

A little more than a month later on June 18, Northern Democrats convened in Baltimore and finally succeeded in nominating Douglas, but Douglas was unacceptable to the South. So one week later, also in Baltimore, Southern Democrats nominated the current Vice President, John C. Breckenridge of Kentucky, a steadfast supporter of slavery. With the Democratic Party split in two, the last remaining national political party had itself become sectional, assuring that whoever won the 1860 election would be a sectional president from a sectional party.

Further dividing the electorate, a group of former Southern Whigs and Know-Nothings, who were disinclined to join up with either faction of the Democratic Party or the new Republicans, formed the Constitutional Union Party. The Constitutional Union Party nominated pro-Union slaveholding John Bell of Tennessee as their candidate for president. Bell foolishly assumed he and his party could simply ignore slavery and the issue of its expansion into the territories. Given the events of the previous decade, most understood that was impossible. Bell took the Liberty Bell as his party's symbol, which at the time seemed very appropriate and caused some to say that the candidate, like the famous bell, was also a little "cracked."

The Republicans passed over the more extreme leaders of their party, including frontrunner New York Governor William Seward,

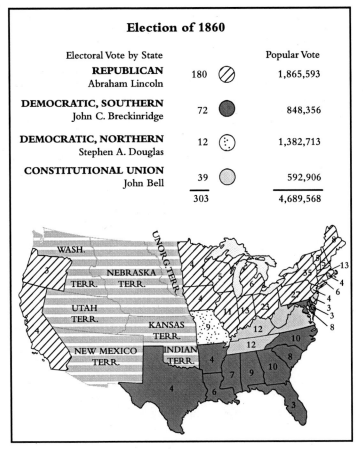

Election of 1860

Electoral Vote by State			Popular Vote
REPUBLICAN Abraham Lincoln	180		1,865,593
DEMOCRATIC, SOUTHERN John C. Breckinridge	72		848,356
DEMOCRATIC, NORTHERN Stephen A. Douglas	12		1,382,713
CONSTITUTIONAL UNION John Bell	39		592,906
	303		4,689,568

Congress nor local legislatures can give legal existence to slavery in any Territory." Republicans were not willing to compromise on the issue of slavery in the territories. They rejected Douglas's popular sovereignty. They rejected the pro-slavery stance of Breckenridge. And they were not about to ignore the issue of slavery as Bell proposed.

The crises of the 1850s had produced a full slate of four presidential candidates for the election of 1860, but none of them appealed to the entire country. It was a full slate of candidates, but a full slate of sectional candidates, each representing one part of the nation and one approach to the issue of slavery in America. The very thing leaders feared, the very thing they had been working to prevent throughout the series of crises following the end of the Mexican War, now seemed all too likely: disunion.

and nominated a moderate with few political enemies, former Whig Congressman Abraham Lincoln, who, like Stephen A. Douglas, was also from Illinois. Lincoln won on the third ballot, but the Republicans adopted a party platform that offended the South. The Republicans supported the ideas of free labor and the passage of a homestead act. When it came to slavery, the party considered itself moderate, opposing only the extension of slavery into the territories. According to the Republican platform, on which Lincoln ran for president: "The normal condition of all the territories of the United States is that of freedom. Neither

Republican Lincoln won the 1860 election with the majority of the electoral votes—180 of 303, or 59.4%—but he received only 39.8% of the popular vote (1,865,593), almost one million fewer votes than the combined total of his three opponents. Lincoln had swept all the northern states, plus the western states of California and Oregon (see map and chart of election). Northern Democrat Douglas finished second in popular voting (29.5%/1,380,201), but he won only Missouri and its 12 electoral votes. Breckenridge won the entire Deep South states and finished second to Lincoln in electoral votes (72) but behind both Lincoln and

Douglas in popular voting with 18.1% (848,019). Bell finished last with 590,901—popular votes, giving him 39 electoral votes from Kentucky, Tennessee, and Virginia.

For the first time in the nation's history a wholly sectional party, the Republican Party, had won the presidency. What so many had feared had finally come to pass. And for southern fire-eaters, it was the scenario that they suggested would surely lead to secession. In the immediate aftermath of the election, that possibility overshadowed everything. Would the South accept the election of Republican Lincoln as president? The South's answer came even before the inauguration of the new president.

Secession

Seven southern states—South Carolina, Georgia, Florida, Alabama, Mississippi, Louisiana, and Texas—seceded following the election of Lincoln in November 1860 but before he was inaugurated in March 1861. These southern states made it clear that they believed what southern fire-eaters had expounded, that the election of the Republican Lincoln meant the destruction of their entire way of life; the Republicans, they argued, did not merely oppose the extension of slavery, they intended to end slavery everywhere.

The voices of Southern Unionists, like Sam Houston, had long since been drowned out. The recurring crises of the 1850s and the resulting growth of a Southern nationalism, separate and apart from American nationalism, had triumphed. Southern nationalists, like fire-eaters South Carolinian William Lowndes Yancey and Virginian Edmund Ruffin, had come to regard secession as a necessity, not just some constitutional right

that they might invoke to bring about some sort of compromise, as had been the practice in so many earlier crises.

By late 1860, it was the fire-eaters, who spoke for the South. For southern fire-eaters, the election of 1860 precluded any new thoughts about threatening disunion in hopes of forcing a compromise. To them, secession had become a positive good, something that must be accomplished as soon as possible, preferably before the inauguration of the new president. Fire-eater rhetoric had convinced a large number of Southerners that there remained no benefits to them in maintaining the Union, that secession was the right thing to do. And if the South were to leave the Union, it had better do it as soon as possible rather than wait and get weaker under further Northern attacks. Why postpone the inevitable?

Southern nationalists wanted to create their own new nation, their own "more perfect union," because they believed it was no longer possible to protect the institution of slavery within the framework of the old Union led by a Republican president who was pledged to prevent the spread of slavery everywhere—a Republican who seemed, by his own admission, opposed to the existence of slavery everywhere.

Back on June 16, 1858, Lincoln gave what his law partner, William Herndon, and other colleagues considered and overly extremist acceptance speech for the nomination as Republican challenger for Stephen Douglas's Illinois Senate seat. Lincoln attacked Douglas's popular sovereignty policy, arguing that since it had been instituted in the Kansas-Nebraska Act in 1854, it "augmented" rather ended the crisis over slavery. But Lincoln did not stop there. The "agitation" over slavery would not cease, he announced, until "a crisis shall have been reached and passed." Paraphrasing Jesus, Lincoln offered a sentiment that was ever after repeated and used by southern nationalists to support secessionist sentiment:

"A house divided against itself cannot stand."
I believe this government cannot endure, permanently half slave and half free.
I do not expect the Union to be dissolved—I do not expect the house to fall—but I do expect it will cease to be divided.
It will become all one thing or all the other.

When news of Lincoln's election reached South Carolina, the state legislature called a state convention, which met on December 20, 1860. At the convention, representatives unanimously adopted a resolution that stated "that the Union now subsisting between South Carolina and other states his hereby dissolved." By February 1, 1861—still more than a month before the inauguration of Lincoln— six other states had followed South Carolina's lead and seceded—Mississippi, Florida, Alabama, Georgia, Louisiana, and Texas. Delegates from these seceded states then met in Montgomery, Alabama, and established the Confederate States of America (CSA). The southern government and its constitution, which was unanimously adopted on March 11, 1861, differed little from the one they had just left. The new southern constitution, however, explicitly protected slavery and declared it legal everywhere. Jefferson Davis of Mississippi was elected President of the Confederacy and Alexander Stephens of Georgia as his Vice President.

In an attempt to forge a southern claim as the inheritors of the traditions of the founding father, they created a Confederate Seal, which featured George Washington at its center. Not only was Washington the most famous American, but he was also a Virginian and a slave owner. Southern secessionists selected his birthday, February 22, as the official "birth" for the CSA to establish a connection between their new nation and the one that had been created in 1776 in an attempt to legitimate secession as a successful minority tactic.

Southern nationalists had established a new nation based upon states' rights and a legal theory of secession, a nation which they hoped was no less legitimate than that of the one that began when the thirteen colonies had broken away from England nine decades earlier. This time the seven southern states had left because of the election of a president who had once talked of a "house divided," and the growing strength in the United States Congress of the Republican Party, a party which was led by men who had talked about "irrepressible conflicts" and which was dedicated to the philosophy of "free soil." All of these developments had seemed to be a clear signal to many southerners that they should abandon all hope of compromise with the North and get out of the Union. But in February 1861, even after the creation of the CSA, eight southern slave states were still not yet ready to leave the Union.

North Carolina, Virginia, Tennessee, and Arkansas did not secede until after the first shots of the war were fired at Fort Sumter and after Lincoln had called for 75,000 volunteers to put down the rebellion. The soldiers, Lincoln said, were essential "to cause the laws to be duly executed" and because the crisis in the nation was "too powerful to be suppressed by the ordinary course of judicial proceedings." Secessionist sentiment in these four states was apparently not sufficiently strong enough until

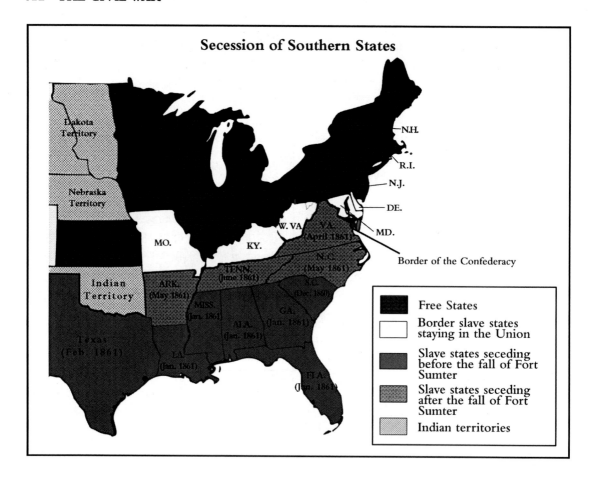

Secession of Southern States

Border of the Confederacy

Legend:
- Free States
- Border slave states staying in the Union
- Slave states seceding before the fall of Fort Sumter
- Slave states seceding after the fall of Fort Sumter
- Indian territories

warfare broke out. Their secession came between mid-April and mid-May.

Four other slave states—Maryland, Delaware, Kentucky, and Missouri—never did secede. The Confederate battle flag, the stars and bars, contained fifteen stars, but that was hopeful thinking on the part of secessionists. Only eleven states ever joined the CSA. More important than the reality that the south never achieved its confident expectation that all slave states would join the Confederacy was the enormous reality that eleven states did secede. The so-called new world's experiment in democracy, the United States of America, that had begun as a "more perfect union" in 1789 was facing the most severe test of its existence only seventy-one years later. Could the nation that had promised "to establish justice, insure domestic tranquility, provide for the common defense, promote the general welfare, and secure the blessing of liberty to ourselves and our posterity" live up to its original promise, or, worse yet, was it unwilling? In late 1860 and early 1861, the answer was not all that clear.

To Jefferson Davis and southern secessionists, the answer to the first part of the question was obvious. On February 18, in Montgomery, Davis asserted in his inaugural address that the old Union "had ceased to answer the ends for which it was established," and, therefore, the states which created it had the right to leave it. Southern states were but victims of "wanton aggression" on the part of the North. The South had always been "devoted to agricultural pursuits" and interested only in "the export of a commodity required in every manufacturing country," he said. They were dedicated to "peace" and "the freest trade." But what about the rise of the Republican Party and the threat they posed to the extension of slavery in the territories? What about the election of Lincoln and his announcement that the "government cannot permanently endure half-slave and half-free?" And, more to the point, what about slavery? President Davis's explanation for the secession of the southern states did not focus on slavery. Why did the southern states secede? What was the real reason?

The reasons stated by the southern states in their secession resolutions made it clear that the real reason the southern states seceded was to preserve and protect their peculiar institution of slavery. On November 30, 1860, the Mississippi legislature passed a secession resolution prior to the state's actual secession on January 9, 1861.

"The people of the Northern States have assumed a revolutionary position towards the Southern States . . . they have . . . interfered with slavery as it prevails in the slaveholding States . . .

They have enticed our slaves from us . . . they continue their system of agitation obviously for the purpose of encouraging other slaves to escape from service . . .

They claim the right to exclude slavery from the Territories . . . they thus seek by an increase of abolition States 'to acquire two-thirds of both houses' for the purpose of preparing an amendment to the Constitution of the United States, abolishing slavery in the States . . .

They have elected a . . . President and Vice-President on the ground that there exists an irreconcilable conflict between the two sections of the Confederacy . . . thus declaring . . . that the powers of this Government are to be used for the dishonor and overthrow of the Southern Section of this great Confederacy . . .

Mississippi legislators were afraid that Lincoln and the Republicans were not simply working to stop the spread of slavery in the territories; they were going to eliminate slavery everywhere, including the southern states where slavery, they assumed, had long been protected by the Constitution. Looking back, it is clear to us today that southern fears were exaggerated. But their perception was their reality, and they perceived a real threat to the existence of their peculiar institution. They did not know then that their fears were exaggerated. To Mississippi legislators, and southerners in every state, Lincoln and the Republicans represented that part of the North that threatened slavery everywhere.

The Confederate States of America had been created to preserve and protect slavery everywhere. The political philosophy underlying that new government was promulgated by Confederate Vice President Alexander Stephens in a speech to an audience in Savannah, Georgia, on March 21, 1861. Not only did Stephens lay bare the core philosophy of the Confederacy, but he also exposed in the most obvious manner the fundamental contradiction that had existed in American society

Declaration of the Immediate Causes Which Induce and Justify the Secession of South Carolina from the Federal Union

[The 14 northern free states] have assumed the right of deciding upon the propriety of our domestic institutions . . . have denounced as sinful the institution of Slavery; they have permitted the open establishment among them of societies, whose avowed object is to disturb the peace of and eloign [in law, eloign means to remove beyond the jurisdiction of the local sheriff, etc.] the property of the citizens of other States.

They have encouraged and assisted thousands of our slaves to leave their homes; and those who remain, have been incited by emissaries, books, and pictures, to servile insurrection . . .

A geographical line has been drawn across the Union, and all the States north of that line have united in the election of a man to the high office of President of the United States whose opinions and purposes are hostile to Slavery . . .

He has declared that "Government cannot endure permanently half slave, half free," and that the public mind must rest in the belief that slavery is in the course of ultimate extinction . . .

[The Republican] party . . . has announced that the South shall be excluded from the common territory, that the Judicial tribunal shall be made sectional, and that a war must be waged against Slavery until it shall cease throughout the United States . . .

We, therefore, the People of South Carolina, by our delegates in Convention assembled, appealing to the Supreme Judge of the world for the rectitude of our intentions, have solemnly declared that the Union heretofore existing between this State and the other States of North America, is dissolved, and that the State of South Carolina has resumed her position among the nations of the world, as a separate and independent State; with full power to levy war, conclude peace, contract alliances, establish commerce, and to do all other acts and things which independent States may of right do.

since the nation's founding. The American *Declaration of Independence* had put forth the proposition that certain "self-evident" truths existed, that all people "are endowed by their Creator with certain unalienable rights, that among these are Life, Liberty, and the pursuit of Happiness." But just who exactly constituted the "American People?" Alexander Stephens put forth an answer to that question in no uncertain terms.

> The Confederate Constitution has put at rest forever all the agitating questions relating to our peculiar institutions—African slavery as it exists among us—the proper status of the negro in our form of civilization. This was the immediate cause of the late rupture and present revolution . . .

> The prevailing ideas entertained by Jefferson and most of the leading statesmen at the time of the formation of the old Constitution were, that the

enslavement of the African was in violation of the laws of nature; that it was wrong in principle, socially, morally, and politically . . .

These ideas, however, were fundamentally wrong. They rested upon the assumption of the equality· of races . . .

Our new Government is founded upon exactly the opposite ideas; its foundations are laid, its cornerstone rests, upon the great truth that the negro is not equal to the white man, that slavery, subordination to the superior race, is his natural and moral condition. This, our new Government, is the first, in the history of the world, based upon this great physical, philosophical, and moral truth . . .

So racism was at the core of the philosophy of the government of the Confederate States of America. If Southern secessionists meant what they wrote and meant what they said, they left the Union to protect and perpetuate their institution of slavery, an institution based upon a racist ideology, against Northern abolitionist assaults. Talk of secession had been around a very long time, but prior to 1860 it had always been no more than that—talk, a way to force the North into further compromise. No state had ever seceded. None seceded over the Alien and Sedition Acts in 1798. None seceded over the War of 1812. None seceded over the so-called Tariff of Abominations. And none had seceded over the Mexican War.

Growing sectional tension between North and South does not explain the Civil War. Sectional conflicts preceded the events leading to the Civil War and there was some sectional tension after the Civil War, but in no other instance did sectional tension and conflict lead to war. By 1860, the moral issue of slavery had made the sectional conflict difficult to settle amicably. Slavery involved questions of moral principle, which are not easily compromised. The uncompromising positions taken by both the anti-slavery faction—located almost entirely in the North—and the pro-slavery faction—located entirely in the South—made the sectional chasm nearly unbridgeable. But it did not automatically mean that secession was inevitable.

The South seceded because the election of Abraham Lincoln to the presidency. Southerners' fear as to what his election meant to them in the near future created virtual panic among Southern leaders. By the fall and winter of 1860–1861, Southern leaders had come to the conclusion that anyone who was not pro-South and pro-slavery was an abolitionist who hated the South and Southerners. The very sudden and seemingly irretrievable loss of political power to the Republicans in the North caused Southern leaders to conclude that all was lost and that some dark and regrettable fate awaited the South. We may look back now and conclude that it was an exaggerated and irrational response, but it was a response based on the Southerners' perception of reality. They believed they had no future in a Union controlled by an anti-Southern political party, the Republican Party of Abraham Lincoln.

In the winter of 1860–61, one momentous issue remained: would the North accept southern secession, or, rather, would the North be willing to fight to save the Union? Given the enormous threat secession posed, the furtherance of American power weighed in the balance. And although northern leaders were not yet ready to face it, secession and war would force a fundamental redefinition of the American people.

Southern Justification for Secession

Although southern secession declarations made clear their belief that secession was necessary for the protection and perpetuation of slavery, southern leaders justified their action on the principle of extreme state sovereignty, not on the right of revolution. They could have cited the Declaration of Independence which had asserted that "Governments are instituted among Men, deriving their just powers from the consent of the governed. That whenever any Form of Government becomes destructive of these ends, it is the Right of the People to alter or to abolish it and to institute new Government." But the right of revolution was a dangerous principle to use to justify secession for southern slave states. Jefferson's theory of revolution applied to all people at all times. Other groups of people in the South might also have cited the same justification—poor whites, even slaves—and demanded a new government to protect their rights. So instead of using the principle of revolution, Southern secessionists justified secession on the principle of extreme state sovereignty.

Southern leaders argued that each state had retained its complete sovereignty, that the Constitution was a mere compact between the states, not, as Lincoln was shortly to argue, a compact between the people of the United States. Southern leaders maintained that the Federal Union was a mere league and that it had always been a mere league, from which any state might withdraw at its pleasure. This—this principle of extreme state sovereignty—found its way into the Constitution of the CSA, which argued that "each State" had acted "in in its sovereign and independent character." But the principle of extreme state

sovereignty was both historically and logically unsound.

No one knows for certain what the intentions of the framers of the Constitution were concerning secession. There's no mention of secession in the Constitution itself or in the record of the Founding Fathers' debates. But the contention that the Founding Fathers intended the Constitution to be nothing more than a treaty or that the new national government created in 1787 was nothing more than a league or a loose confederation

---

The United States Constitution Preamble

We, the People of the United States, in Order to form a more perfect Union, establish Justice, insure domestic Tranquility, provide for the common defence, promote the general Welfare, and secure the Blessings of Liberty to ourselves and our Posterity, do ordain and establish this Constitution for the United States of America.

Constitution of the Confederate States Preamble

We, the people of the Confederate States, each State acting in its sovereign and independent character, in order to form a permanent federal government, establish justice, insure domestic tranquillity, and secure the blessings of liberty to ourselves and our posterity invoking the favor and guidance of Almighty God do ordain and establish this Constitution for the Confederate States of America.

was manifestly absurd. No government could be expected to run for very long under the perpetual threat of peaceful dissolution. Logically there was no built-in right of secession in the Constitution. Nevertheless, even though the Southern states may not have had the right to secede, they did it, at least in the months between Lincoln's election and inauguration seven states had taken that momentous step; they declared their separation from the no-longer United States, and they had established a new government. Right or no right, that was the reality of the moment. That was the situation that the government of the United States faced in late 1860 and early 1861.

Northern Reaction to Secession

Initially, the northern public reaction to secession was one of disbelief. Some Southerners had been talking about secession for many years. Most people in the North had come to look on all such talk as political gamesmanship. Threats didn't really mean what they seemed to mean. Brash words were not meant to be taken at face value. They never had been in the past. But once it became obvious in late December 1860 that this time the Southerners really meant it, that they were serious about disunion, disbelief in the North began to be replaced by relief. Horace Greeley, influential editor of *The New York Tribune,* spoke for many northerners when he wrote in January 1861, "Wayward sisters, depart in peace!" It was almost as if the North were saying goodbye and good riddance.

As important as public reaction in the North was, most looked to President Buchanan to solve the growing crisis before it was too late. Remember that Lincoln was

elected in November 1860, but was not inaugurated until March 1861, so the country had a lame duck president during that awkward four-month period during which the first seven Southern states seceded. Buchanan was a timid and weak man with Southern sympathies who tended to vacillate and drift. Moreover, he was surrounded by conflicting advice. Three of his cabinet members were Southern secessionists. Consequently, he did almost nothing to solve the crisis; if anything, he exacerbated it.

In his annual message to Congress in early December 1860, a little more than two weeks prior to South Carolina's secession from the Union, Buchanan implied that no state had a right to secede, but if one ever did, the federal government had no power to stop it. Secession, Buchanan told Congress was "wholly inconsistent with the history as well as the character of the Federal Constitution." "The question fairly stated," he went on, is whether the Federal government has "the power to coerce a State into submission which is attempting to withdraw." However, "after much serious reflection," he announced, "I have arrived at the conclusion that no such power has been delegated to Congress or any other department of the Federal Government." Buchanan would have fit right in with strict-constructionism of the Jeffersonians in the 1790s. Prominent Republican and Secretary of State-elect William Seward paraphrased the President's vacillation on secession this way: "It is the duty of the President to execute the laws . . . unless somebody opposes him; and no state has a right to go out of the Union . . . unless it wants to."

In fairness to Buchanan, his policy of watchful waiting may have been the wisest one at the moment. In his own way, Lincoln followed the same policy for nearly a month

Lincoln's First Inaugural Address

Apprehension seems to exist among the people of the Southern States that by the accession of a Republican Administration their property and their peace and personal security are to be endangered. There has never been any reasonable cause for such apprehension . . .

I have no purpose, directly or indirectly, to interfere with the institution of slavery in the States where it exists. I believe I have no lawful right to do so, and I have no inclination to do so . . .

The Union of these States is perpetual. . . . No state upon its own mere action, can lawfully get out of the Union . . . I shall take care, as the Constitution itself expressly enjoins upon me, that the laws of the Union be faithfully executed in all the States . . .

The power confided to me will be used to hold, occupy, and possess the property and places belonging to the Government . . . In your hands, my dissatisfied fellow-countrymen, and not in mine, is the momentous issue of civil war. The Government will not assail you. You can have no conflict without being yourselves the aggressors. You have no oath registered in heaven to destroy the Government, while I shall have the most solemn one to "preserve, protect, and defend it."

I am loath to close. We are not enemies, but friends. We must not be enemies. Though passion may have strained it must not break our bonds of affection. The mystic chords of memory, stretching from every battlefield and patriot grave to every living heart and hearthstone all over this broad land, will yet swell the chorus of the Union, when again touched, as surely they will be, by the better angels of our nature.

after his inauguration in March 1861. Buchanan hoped that Congress might be able to work out some sort of last minute compromise as Congress had always done before. And Buchanan knew that moderate Democrats in Congress from both the North and the South were already working desperately to do just that.

The most significant effort to find some compromise were a series of resolutions—the so-called Crittenden Compromise—that were to be submitted to the people as amendments to the U.S. Constitution. If accepted, the amendments that made up the Crittenden Compromise would have extended the Missouri Compromise line (36°30') all the way to the Pacific and prohibit slavery in the territories north of that line and guarantee slavery in all territories south of that line, including any territories that might be acquired later. Another called for all new states carved out of the territories to enter the union on the basis of popular sovereignty regardless of whether they were north or south of the Missouri Compromise line. Still another denied Congress the power to abolish slavery in states where it already existed or in the District of Columbia. Finally, the Crittenden Compromise proposed these amendments to the Constitution be made forever un-amendable.

Unlike earlier compromise efforts in 1820, 1833, 1850, and 1854, these compromises were too little, too late for the Southern fire-eaters. And they were far too much for the Republicans. Although President-elect Lincoln expressed a willingness to compromise, even protect slavery in the states where it already existed, he was unwilling to compromise on the issue of the extension of slavery into the territories. "On the territorial question," he said, "I am inflexible." For his part, Confederate President Davis rejected any compromise that did not recognize the legitimacy of the new southern nation, even if it ultimately meant war.

Once in office, President Lincoln reiterated his unwillingness to compromise on the extension of slavery into the territories, but he assured the South that he had no intention to interfere with slavery where it already existed; moreover, he announced it his belief that he had "no lawful right" as President to do so. About the continued existence of slavery in the Old South, Lincoln seemed absolutely clear. Lincoln hoped—vainly it would soon turn out—that the voices of pro-Union Southern moderates might drown out the secessionist demands of the fire-eaters. Even as Lincoln spoke his inaugural address, eight slave states still remained in the Union.

Still, Lincoln also made it plain that he rejected outright southern theories of secession. The Constitution was not a mere league from which any member state may choose to secede. And he pledged to use all his powers as President to preserve the Union of the states. Lincoln believed in the maintenance of American power. The American nation, as Union Captain Philip Sheridan stated, "Is too great and good to be destroyed." Most northerners, and especially Lincoln, agreed. The Union must be preserved.

Fort Sumter

When Lincoln promised in his inaugural address to use all his presidential power "to hold, occupy, and possess the property and places belonging to the Government," the main pieces of property to which he was referring were two harbor forts in the south. One was Fort Pickens in Pensacola, Florida, and the other was Fort Sumter in Charleston harbor, South Carolina. Both were manned by a small U.S. Army force. By March 1861, the South had come to regard the continued presence of "Yankee" troops at Fort Sumter and Fort Pickens as northern aggression.

In the immediate weeks after his inauguration, President Lincoln, like Buchannan, was slow to take action against the South. Lincoln did not want to do anything that might cause more states to secede, especially Virginia and Maryland, which surrounded the District of Columbia. He also hoped that the leaders of the seceded states might come back into the Union when they learned that neither he nor the Republican Party intended to get rid of slavery in the Southern states. As the prospect dimmed for the return of the seceded states, Lincoln soon came to believe that surrendering Fort Sumter or Pickens to the Confederates would only further strengthen secessionist zeal.

As supplies began to run low at Fort Sumter, Lincoln decided he could delay no further. Although Fort Sumter in Charleston harbor had no strategic value, it had great symbolic value. To the South, it had become a symbol of a Federal threat to Southern independence. To the North, it had great psychological value as a symbol of Federal authority in the South. To yield Fort Sumter without a fight, Lincoln understood, would fatally compromise the principle of Union. Yielding Fort Sumter to the Southerners would be tantamount to giving official recognition to the CSA and would established secession as a successful minority tactic. Lincoln was not about to permit state sovereignty to triumph by default over national sovereignty.

Lincoln hoped for a peaceful settlement of the Fort Sumter crisis, but was willing to risk war in the name of the Union. Rather than give tacit consent to secession, Lincoln sent word to the South Carolina government in mid-April 1861 of his intention to resupply the fort with non-military provisions. With much forethought, Lincoln had acted to preserve the Union. If there was to be war, the South would have to fire the first shots.

Things were not going well for the CSA during these early months of 1861. President Jefferson Davis, like his counterparts in the North, first Buchanan and now Lincoln, was pursuing a do-nothing policy. And that was making many in the South angry, especially Southern fire-eaters. Allowing Yankees to remain in Southern forts was becoming more intolerable by the day. As the *Mobile Mercury* expressed it: "If something is not done pretty soon [by the Davis government to get the Federal troops out of Fort Sumter], the whole country will become so disgusted with the sham of southern independence that the first chance the people get at a popular election they will turn the whole movement topsy-turvy so bad that it never on earth can be righted again." The new southern nation's prospects were deteriorating; something had to be done and soon.

Southern leaders thought that any attempt to get the Yankees out of the Southern forts might lead to war, but to them war was not necessarily the worst of all possible evils. In fact, many in the South thought war might be a good thing. They believed the outbreak of war would enlarge and solidify the Confederacy. For the South to survive, the other slave states must join the CSA. War, southern leaders thought, would cause Virginia to secede and then the remaining slave states would fol-

low. If all seven followed Virginia, the CSA would consist of fifteen states. They also believed that the outbreak of war would cause European nations to extend official recognition to the CSA in order to guarantee continued access to Southern products, especially to King Cotton. ·

Others in the South did not think a Southern attack on Fort Sumter would provoke a war at all. It was incomprehensible to them that the North would be willing to fight a war to save the Federal Union—yet another example of the gross misunderstanding that had come to exist between the South and the North. Moreover, in the overconfident heady days of the creation of the new Confederate nation, everybody in the South knew that even if that "nation of shopkeepers" did decide to fight, one Southerner could lick five Yankees with one hand tied behind him. Like every other war in history, no one yet knew how horrible it would all turn out. Nonetheless, faced with all these pressures, assumptions, and myths, Confederate President Jefferson Davis decided it was in the best interest of his government to force the evacuation of Fort Sumter and to do it soon before Lincoln had re-supplied it.

On April 11, 1861, Confederate General P. G. T. Beauregard sent three representatives to meet with the Union commander of Fort Sumter, Major Robert Anderson. Beauregard demanded that Anderson surrender the fort. Anderson refused. At 4:30 a.m. the next day, Confederate batteries opened fire. By that afternoon, Anderson accepted the terms of surrender and marched his garrison out of the fort. A Confederate flag now flew over Fort Sumter. The bombardment was a visible sign that the war had begun, a thunderous announcement to the whole world that the so-called New World's experiment in democ-

The Confederate Flag flying over Fort Sumter, South Carolina, April 4, 1861.

racy had taken a strange new turn. Three days later, Lincoln called for 75,000 volunteer militiamen to put down the "insurrection," and on April 19, Lincoln ordered the blockade of all southern ports. The American Civil War had begun.

The Northern public seemed strangely relieved that war had come. As Lincoln wanted it perceived, despite Southern arguments to the contrary, the South had started the conflict and it was clear now that the North had to respond to this Southern aggression. When Lincoln called for 75,000 volunteers, thousands more than that answered his call; there was a rash of enthusiastic recruiting all across the North. Nobody yet knew how horrible the war would be. It, like most wars, seemed glamorous and heroic at the beginning. That would all change, of course, but it would take time.

Lincoln had hoped for peace but had willingly risked war to send supplies to symbolic Fort Sumter. And why did he do it? Lincoln willingly risked a war to save the Union. Over and over again, he made it clear that he had risked war to save the union. In his July 4, 1861, message to Congress, he said: "Our popular government has often been called an experiment. Two points in it our people have already settled—the successful establishing and the successful administering of it. One still remains—its successful maintenance against a formidable internal attempt to overthrow it. It is now for them to demonstrate to the world that those who can fairly carry an election can also suppress a rebellion . . ." Lincoln and the North did not go to war to end slavery.

One year later Lincoln made this abundantly clear in his response to Horace Greeley,

To ABRAHAM LINCOLN,
President of the United States

DEAR SIR: I do not intrude to tell you—
for you must know already—that a great
proportion of those who triumphed in
your election . . . are sorely disappointed
and deeply pained by the policy you
seem to be pursuing with regard to the
slaves of the Rebels . . .

. . . On the face of this wide earth,
Mr. President, there is not one disinter-
ested, determined, intelligent champion of
the Union cause who does not feel that all
attempts to put down the Rebellion and at
the same time uphold its inciting cause
are preposterous and futile—that the
Rebellion, if crushed out tomorrow, would
be renewed within a year if Slavery were
left in full vigor . . . and that every hour of
deference to Slavery is an hour of added
and deepened peril to the Union . . .

Yours,

Horace Greeley
New York, August 19, 1862

Executive Mansion,
Washington, August 22, 1862.

Hon. Horace Greeley:
Dear Sir.

I have just read yours of the 19th.
addressed to myself through the New-
York Tribune . . . As to the policy I "seem
to be pursuing" as you say, I have not
meant to leave any one in doubt . . .

. . . My paramount object in this struggle
is to save the Union, and is not either to
save or to destroy slavery. If I could save
the Union without freeing any slave I
would do it, and if I could save it by free-
ing all the slaves I would do it; and if I
could save it by freeing some and leav-
ing others alone I would also do that.
What I do about slavery, and the colored
race, I do because I believe it helps to
save the Union; and what I forbear, I
forbear because I do not believe it would
help to save the Union . . .

I have here stated my purpose according
to my view of official duty; and I intend
no modification of my oft-expressed per-
sonal wish that all men everywhere
could be free.

Yours,

A. Lincoln.

---

who had publicly urged him to make abolition of slavery the chief aim of the war. Lincoln and the North fought to save the Union. But while the North fought to save the Union, we must remember that the only thing threatening the Union was the issue of slavery. The South was demanding of the North what the North was less and less willing to give: theoretical and, as far as possible, practical equality for slavery, for its "peculiar institution." To get that, the South was willing to break up the last unifying force in the country, the Democratic Party. To prevent the extension of slavery, Lincoln and the Republicans were willing to risk Southern secession. And to preserve the Union, which was threatened by the moral crisis over slavery, Lincoln was willing to risk war. And the South, to preserve slavery, was willing to fight a war and destroy the Union. As Lincoln himself later put it: "Both parties deprecated war, but one of them would make war rather than let the nation survive; and the other would accept war rather than let it perish. And the war came."

Considering the circumstances in 1860–61, first secession and then armed conflict at Fort Sumter, war had likely become inevitable. Despite sharing so much: a common heritage, a common language, customs, and traditions—both political and social—contentious problems had driven North and South to disunion and, finally, war. During the Jacksonian era, the American people had come to see democracy and individualism as the guiding values of the nation. This growing devotion to the spirit of egalitarianism served to accentuate the great contradiction of the existence of slavery in a nation so dedicated, producing a moral crisis, a crisis over good and evil behavior that ultimately tore the nation apart.

For a time, the desire to extend American power and build a continental empire had united the various sections of the country behind the belief in the nation's world redeeming mission. The achievement of America's "manifest destiny," however, created a vexing and ultimately insoluble conflict over slavery in the territories. Republican leader William Seward in 1858 called it "irrepressible." "The United States," he noted, "must and will. . .become entirely a slave-holding nation, or entirely a free-labor nation." Throughout the growing political crisis over slavery in the 1850s, the divisions between North and South only grew larger. The growth of American power had not united the American people. As Northern editor Horace Greely had put it, "We are not one people. We are a people for Freedom and a people for Slavery." And the war came.

Choosing Sides

As Southern leaders had hoped, the outbreak of war and Lincoln's call for volunteers led four additional slave states to secede from the Union—Virginia, Arkansas, Tennessee, and North Carolina. Slavery in these upper Southern states was scarcer than that of the Deep South and tended to be concentrated in specific sections; consequently, Union sentiment was strong in many areas. With the help of a Union army from Ohio, citizens in the western section of Virginia broke off and formed a new state in 1862, becoming the only state to secede from the Confederacy during the war. Secession, apparently, was an acceptable minority tactic if used against the Union's enemy—power, in America, as it did here, usually comes before principle. Lincoln issued an enabling act that admitted the state on the condition of gradual abolition of slavery, and West Virginia officially joined the Union in June, 1863.

The remaining slave states—Delaware, Maryland, Kentucky, and Missouri, collectively known as the Border States—with the exception of Delaware, underwent bitter battles over allegiance. To stave of secession in Maryland, an action that would have surrounded the Union capital, Lincoln suspended the writ of habeas corpus—individuals were then unable to seek through legal action relief from unlawful detention—and pro-southern leaders in the state were jailed and, thus, silenced. In state elections that fall, pro-Union politicians wrested control of the state for the remainder of the war, notwithstanding the southern sympathies of many of the people in Maryland.

In Missouri, Union sympathizers outnumbered secessionists but that did not stop conflict within the state throughout the war. During the siege of Vicksburg in 1863, thirty-nine Missouri regiments saw combat:

seventeen for the Confederacy and twenty-two for the Union. Similarly, opinions were divided in Kentucky, birthplace of both Lincoln and Davis. Initially, state legislators hope to remain outside the fight, declaring "neutrality" in the conflict, but warfare in the state precluded any such foolish expectation. After Union General Ulysses S. Grant captured Paducah and control of much of the western part of the state, Kentucky remained in the Union.

As states were forced to choose sides, obviously, citizens within them were forced to do the same. The choice facing Mexican War veteran Robert E. Lee at the outbreak of the conflict typified the problem for many of the American people. Lee was the son of a Revolutionary War hero ("Light Horse Harry Lee) and had married a great-granddaughter of Martha Washington (Mary Custis). His estate was just across the Potomac River in Virginia, facing the Union capital. Lee had even accepted a promotion to Colonel in the Union army in March, at the height of the secession controversy. Union general-in-chief Winfield Scott, who was also a native Virginian, wanted Lee for a top command (and with it would come another promotion to Major-General), but when Virginia seceded Lee determined that he could not take up arms against what he called his "country," meaning Virginia. Lee, like many others in the South was against secession, but local loyalties were stronger than national. In June 1862, Lee assumed the command of the Army of Northern Virginia.

Still others in the South found ways to remain loyal to the Union. Every Confederate state except South Carolina, for example, had citizens who formed entire regiments and fought for the Union. Some southerners, particularly poor whites, many of whom were recent German and Irish immigrants and had no affinity for slavery or the planter elite, attempted to wait out the war, some even helping the Union cause when northern armies moved into southern states. Above all, however, the war divided the allegiances of almost everyone.

The Civil War pitted families against each other. Senator John J. Crittenden of Kentucky had two sons who became major generals during the Civil War: one for the North and one for the South. Jefferson Davis's wife had relatives in the Union army and Lincoln's wife had three brothers who died fighting for the CSA. Confederate armies contained men from every Northern state; the Union army and navy contained men from every seceded state. Years later, Theodore Roosevelt recalled during his boyhood in New York City listening to prayers in church for Union soldiers while his mother feared for her brothers fighting for the Confederacy in Georgia. And so it went; the war divided families in ways none had before. The bitter divisions among the American people would not soon, if ever, be forgotten.

Predicting a Winner of the "First Modern War"

Both sides entered the conflict with the presumption of victory, each possessing a confidence in the surety of their section's ability to triumph over the other as well as ignorance about just how horrible the war would be. Still, many in the South understood their minority status in America—in fact, that knowledge had convinced many upon Lincoln's election of the necessity of secession before the disparity grew even larger. The North possessed numerical advantages in just about every category except textile production. [see chart]

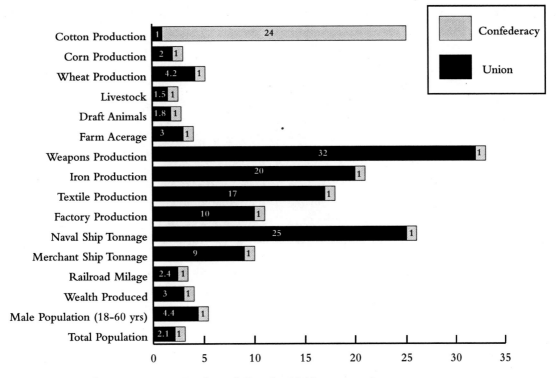

| | Confederacy |
| | Union |

Cotton Production — Confederacy: 24, Union: 1
Corn Production — Confederacy: 2, Union: 1
Wheat Production — Confederacy: 4.2, Union: 1
Livestock — Confederacy: 1.5, Union: 1
Draft Animals — Confederacy: 1.8, Union: 1
Farm Acerage — Confederacy: 3, Union: 1
Weapons Production — Union: 32, Confederacy: 1
Iron Production — Union: 20, Confederacy: 1
Textile Production — Union: 17, Confederacy: 1
Factory Production — Union: 10, Confederacy: 1
Naval Ship Tonnage — Union: 25, Confederacy: 1
Merchant Ship Tonnage — Union: 9, Confederacy: 1
Railroad Milage — Confederacy: 2.4, Union: 1
Wealth Produced — Confederacy: 3, Union: 1
Male Population (18-60 yrs) — Confederacy: 4.4, Union: 1
Total Population — Confederacy: 2.1, Union: 1

Economies and Manpower, North and South, 1860

Consequently, many in the North entered the war reassured. The North would not only win easily but quickly. Nonetheless, many Southerners remained steadfast in the belief in the destiny of their nation. They were fighting for independence, after all, and that sense of purpose they hoped would sustain their cause throughout.

Larger population was perhaps the North's most obvious advantage. The Union possessed approximately 23 million citizens versus only 9 million in the Confederacy of which close to 3.5 million were slaves (about .5 million slaves resided in the Border States). The nearly 4 to 1 advantage meant the Union had the potential to put significantly more men in the field of battle. By 1864, the Confederacy had put 90% of its men age 18–60 into uniform, while in the Union the number was just 44%. Almost a third of the Confederacy's men in uniform would never return from battle. The disparity in numbers also made it possible for the Union to put more men to work in factories.

In terms of industrial output, the Union was well-equipped to face war. In addition to possessing the bulk of America's clothing and shoe production facilities, Northern industries produced almost all the weapons manufactured in America. The only iron producer of any size in the Confederacy was the Tredegar Iron Works in the Confederate capital of Richmond, Virginia. More than 95% of all iron production was located in the Union. The production of adequate weaponry would trouble the Confederacy throughout the war. The North also possessed large advantages in transportation (wagons, horses, rail mileage, and merchant and naval vessels) and farm production, as well as banking and financial resources.

Perhaps the Confederacy's greatest advantage was geographical. To win the war, the South simply needed to survive. Outlast the willingness of the North to fight and Southern independence would be assured. The Confederacy was a vast territory and the Southern army merely needed to fight a defensive war. Survive long enough, and the Confederacy might acquire the help of a European nation. England, which depended heavily on Southern cotton, might want to intervene and end the war if textile production in England was interrupted for long.

Another advantage the Confederacy possessed, although Southern leaders probably did not know it at the beginning of the war, was superior military leadership. Years of expansion across the Deep South and fighting off Native Americans in the process had developed a military tradition. Fear of slave uprisings as well had furthered a Southern predilection and comfort with violence. The South had a long-standing belief in the prestige of military careers. In the prewar years, The Citadel and Virginia Military Institute produced a cadre of skilled military professionals. Others had gone north and attended West Point. With the outbreak of war, a sizable proportion of officers (29%) shed their Union uniforms and joined the Confederate army.

Southerners also believed they possessed clear advantages at the top. Confederate President Davis seemed exceptionally prepared to serve as a wartime president. Davis came from a family of military men; his father had served in the Continental Army during the Revolutionary War and three older brothers saw battle in the War of 1812, two of them alongside Andrew Jackson at the Battle of New Orleans. Davis himself attended the United States Military Academy, graduated in 1828 with a second lieutenant's commission and served until 1835. After years of intense private study of history and politics, Davis was elected to the U.S. House of Representatives in 1844, but he resigned just two years later to raise a regiment of Mississippi volunteers for the Mexican War. Davis and his men participated bravely in the siege of Monterrey and the Battle of Buena Vista. After the war, the governor of Mississippi appointed Davis to complete the term of the late Jesse Speight, and in 1853 Davis became Secretary of War for President Franklin Pierce. In 1857, Davis returned to his seat in the Senate, serving until January 1861 when Mississippi seceded.

Lincoln, on the other hand seemed ill-prepared to lead a nation at war. He had never seen combat (although he had served as a captain in the Illinois militia during the Black Hawk War), had served but one term in the Illinois legislature, and one term in the U.S. House of Representatives (1846–1848). Consequently, no one anticipated the success with which the relatively inexperienced Illinois lawyer would adapt to his task. Many of his cabinet members expected that they would have to lead the nation, not Lincoln.

Most military historians have come to assert that the American Civil War was the world's first modern war. The war was not contained to the battlefield and professional armies. It was contested by and against entire societies. Enormous armies (one in twelve Americans served) marched across the country armed with some of the newest technology made available by the Industrial Revolution. Consequently, the casualty figures were staggering; most estimates place the number dead at just over 620,000, ten times more than all the previous American wars combined. Most of the dead, however, were brought down by disease, which took two for every one battle death.

Technology made the war increasingly impersonal. Many of the men killed on the battlefield never knew what hit them. Rifled weaponry (the barrels are grooved for greater accuracy) took men down from ever greater distances, repeating rifles increased the firepower on the field, and a new array of the instruments of war appeared: "ironclad" ships, observation balloons, submarines, and even wire entanglements, which would be made famous later during WWI in "no man's land." Technology had also dramatically improved communication and transportation making it possible for armies to fight for extended periods and, thus, absorb tremendous numbers of casualties.

As important as advances in technology, communication, and transportation were in making the Civil War the first modern war, these advances did not automatically predetermine the war's outcome. Robert E. Lee explained the South's loss this way: "After four years of arduous service marked by unsurpassed courage and fortitude, the Army of Northern Virginia has been compelled to yield to overwhelming numbers and resources." Lee's assessment has endured among many. For popular consumption, author Shelby Foote echoed a similar sentiment in Ken Burn's Civil War documentary; the North, he said, fought the war "with one hand behind its back . . . if there had been more Southern victories . . . the North simply would have brought that other hand out from behind its back. I don't think the South ever had a chance to win that war." Most historians are much less secure in that interpretation and continue to debate why the North won and the South lost the American Civil War.

Although the Union possessed an overwhelming advantage in manpower and industry at the outset of the war, southerners remained steadfastly confident in victory, believing superior leadership combined with a supportive populace and the expectation of European allies would make all the difference. Northerners remained confident in the power and patriotism of their section. The Union must be preserved. How long northerners would remain faithful in their desire to uphold the Constitution and fight to save the Union no one knew. Similarly, how long Southerners would persevere in their desire to create a new nation to preserve, protect, and extend slavery could not be predicted. And further, what would happen if Lincoln and the Union changed the aim of the war? What if the abolition of slavery everywhere rather than simply stopping its extension became a part of the Northern war effort? Would northerners still support the war? Would Southerners fight to the bitter end to preserve their "peculiar institution?" Would internal strife, even guerilla warfare, dominate the continent for years to come? None of the answers to these questions were predictable at the beginning of the war.

The Early Conflict— 1861–1862

In the early years of the war, the Confederacy won repeated victories, beginning with the first major battle, Bull Run in July 1861. Thirty-thousand Union soldiers led by General Irwin McDowell moved south from Washington, DC, toward the small farming community of Manassas, Virginia, where Confederate General P.G.T. Beauregard had gathered his forces.

Lincoln hoped for a quick victory followed by a march on to Richmond, the Confederate capital, and a swift end to the war. Both sides anticipated a gallant victory. Literally hundreds of expectant Washingtonians followed the Union army to the battleground with picnic baskets, hoping to take in what they thought would be the first and only battle of the war.

The two generals, who had attended West Point together, followed similar battle plans, each trying to turn the other's left flank. The Union nearly won the day by the afternoon of July 21, but Confederate reinforcements held the line and then counterassaulted, resulting in an all-out retreat of the Union army in first confusion, then chaos, and finally in panic. This first Confederate victory did much to bolster confidence in the new southern nation, but in the North the shocking and humiliating defeat ended any hopes for a short and bloodless war. In defeat, Lincoln turned to General Winfield Scott's Anaconda Plan and called for the enlistment of one million volunteers who would serve a three-year term of service. He also turned to the young General George B. McClellan to organize the inexperienced men of the Army of the Potomac into a legitimate fighting force.

The Anaconda Plan consisted of three parts. First, the Army of the Potomac would put constant pressure on the Confederate capital. The Union Navy would blockade all southern ports, thereby cutting Confederate access to foreign supplies and weapons. Finally, naval gunboats would divide the Confederacy by conquering the main water routes: the Cumberland, Tennessee, and Mississippi Rivers. Northern newspapers attacked the plan as a relic of bygone days, old and tired like the man who created it, the 75 year-old Scott, but in the end, the strategy would do much to ensure Northern victory.

The Confederate strategy was far simpler: survive—defend borders as much as possible but outlast the Northern will to fight. The longer the Confederacy survives, Southern leaders believed, the more likely it would become that England or even France might join their cause. And when public sentiment in the North turned against Lincoln due to the length of the conflict, they believed, Lincoln would be forced to negotiate an end to the war, an end that would recognize the legitimacy of the Confederacy.

After the defeat at Bull Run and as the Army of the Potomac regrouped under the leadership of McClellan, the Union concentrated on its naval strategy during the remainder of 1861 and early 1862. The Union Navy grew from 90 to 650 vessels in its attempt to blockade the South. Although unable to completely cut off the South, it became increasingly difficult for blockade runners to get through as war dragged on. In the west, the then virtually unknown Ulysses S. Grant brought the Union two desperately needed victories when he seized Fort Henry on the Tennessee River and Fort Donelson on the Cumberland River in February 1862. In addition to a much needed morale boost for northerners, militarily the victories gave the Union control of both the Tennessee and Cumberland Rivers, making it virtually impossible for the Confederate army to operate in Kentucky or Tennessee. News of Grant's victories and his demand of "immediate and unconditional surrender" turned him into an early Union hero. The veneration of Grant would not last long.

After these victories, Grant moved south along the Tennessee River, capturing railroads along the way. Encamped near Shiloh Church near the Tennessee and Mississippi border in early April 1862, Grant's forces were surprised and nearly routed. Shiloh, a Hebrew word meaning "place of peace," turned out anything but that. Confederate General Sydney Johnston was mortally wounded and Beauregard took command, but he called off the Confederate assault, giving Grant time to reinforce and rally his men. Grant counterattacked the next day and the Confederates left the field. One-hundred thousand men took to the field for both sides and more than 20,000 were killed and wounded; the number exceeded the total casualties of the Revolution, the War of 1812, and the Mexican War combined. Grant's second in command, General William Tecumseh Sherman commented, "The scenes on this field would have cured anybody of war."

Northern newspapers vilified Grant and suggested that he had been drunk on the first day of the battle. The commander of the western theatre for the Union, General Henry Halleck, relieved Grant of his command for several months, but Lincoln refused to sack the General, famously commenting, "I can't spare this man; he fights." Despite the carnage of the battle on both sides, Lincoln seemed to understand that winning the war required the defeat of the Confederate armies and that required a willingness to endure high casualties. Perhaps if he knew the war was to last three more long and bloody years, including eight larger and deadlier battles to come, he might have thought differently.

But while Lincoln was singing the praises of Grant for his willingness to fight, he was simultaneously disappointed in McClellan's lack of it. Not much had happened in the East in the nearly nine months following the Union defeat at Bull Run. Even with the loss, Lincoln still desired a march on Richmond, but McClellan was reluctant to risk defeat and spent his time drilling his men and restoring their morale.

Tired of his General who, Lincoln said, "has got the slows," the President ordered him to begin moving no later than February 22, 1862 – the anniversary of Washington's birthday. So finally, nearly a month later, McClellan headed south, boldly proclaiming that he would be in Richmond in ten days. His plan was to travel down the Chesapeake Bay and then attack Richmond from east moving between the York and James rivers. But McClellan dug in much of his 110,000 man army at Yorktown, believing – erroneously – that he faced an enemy of vastly superior numbers. A Confederate army under the command of Joseph E. Johnston struck back against a divided Union army at Seven Pines beginning on May 31. Both sides took heavy losses, including the Confederate commander, Johnston. The Army of Northern Virginia was then Lee's to command for the rest of the war. Lee, like Johnston however, was unable to dislodge McClellan's forces at an even bloodier conflict on the same battlefield.

Confident in his own abilities (and McClellan's unwillingness to go on the offensive), Lee turned his attention northward and struck a Union army at the Second Battle of Bull Run at the end of August 1862. The Union commander, General John Pope, retreated to defensive positions around Washington after being defeated by Lee at Bull Run. McClellan, ordered to abandon his Peninsular campaign by Lincoln, took command and once again began to reform and organize the troops. The failure of the campaign against Richmond and yet another loss at Bull Run crushed any hopes in the North that the war would be a short one. General Pope, disgraced, was dispatched to the Minnesota frontier to do battle against the Dakota.

The Dakota War

Lincoln's war to preserve the Union was not the only military conflict of his presidency. At the same time Union and Confederate armies were fighting it out east of the Mississippi River in a war that would do much to begin a fundamental redefinition of the American people, Lincoln committed a portion of his troops to southwestern Minnesota to round up several bands of Native Americans—peoples who had never been considered part of the "American experiment"—and reassert American power in the region.

By the time Minnesota became a state in May 1858, various groups of Dakota had given up more than 24,000,000 acres of their territory in exchange for goods and annuity payments from the U.S. government. The Dakota had agreed to live on a reservation about twenty-five miles wide that stretched westward along the Minnesota River for 150 miles. With more than 150,000 white settlers having moved into Minnesota and boundaries difficult to delineate, encroachment onto Dakota land was inevitable. Making the situation more problematic, government annuity payments were habitually late or redirected by Indian agents to traders who charged the Dakota exorbitant repayment rates.

Tensions between white settlers and the Dakota continued to grow in Minnesota into the early 1860s. Most of the land that remained in Dakota hands was not suitable for agriculture. In addition, unrestricted hunting by white settlers had dramatically reduced the game necessary for the survival of the Dakota people. Beginning in 1861, with the U.S. increasingly preoccupied with the Civil War, annuity payments became even more unreliable. Although many Dakota blamed Chief Little Crow for signing away all their land, nonetheless, discontented they turned to him.

Back when Minnesota became a state, Little Crow went on a tour of American cities, including Washington to meet "the Great Father," President Buchanan. Little Crow had come to believe resistance to American power was futile. He joined the Episcopal Church, adopted white dress, and when he returned home attempted to farm like white men. By 1862, with his people growing hungry and promised annuity payments still missing, he led several thousand Dakota to Upper Agency to demand their payments and to purchase food and other supplies.

Little Crow suggested Indian Agent Thomas Galbraith issue food to his people in lieu of annuity payments. Galbraith refused the request and called in U.S. soldiers to protect government supplies. But those soldiers, outnumbered, only stood by and watched as more than 500 Dakota took foodstuffs and other supplies from storehouses in Upper Agency in early August. Little Crow then demanded that Galbraith release more supplies from storehouses in a neighboring settlement, Lower Agency. "We have waited a long time," Little Crow told Galbraith. "The money is ours, but we cannot get it. We have no food, but here are these stores, filled with food. We ask that you . . . make some arrangement by which we can get food from the stores . . . or else we may take our own way to keep ourselves from starving." Buoyed by Galbraith's refusal and the presence of Union troops, a local storekeeper Andrew Myrich responded, "So far as I am concerned, if they are hungry let them eat grass or their own dung."

Unable to get government representatives to live up to their agreements, Little Crow was losing what little control he had over his own people. Near Acton, Minnesota, on August 17, four Dakota on a hunting trip attacked and killed a group of five white settlers. Unable to deter the desires of a war council to act swiftly, Little Crow reluctantly agreed to lead a war to force the white settlers from Minnesota, but not before warning those in attendance what the result of such action would be. The whites, he said, would come like "locusts when they fly so thick that the whole sky is a snowstorm . . . kill one—two—ten, and ten times ten will come to kill you. Count your fingers all day long and white men with guns in their hands will come faster than you can count."

The next morning, Little Crow led his people in an attack at Lower Agency. Storekeeper Myrick was among the first whites killed. He was later found with his mouth stuffed full of grass. Little Crow had ordered all whites in the settlement killed, including women and children. With much of the settlement in flames, over forty white settlers managed to escape, fleeing toward Fort Ridgely. On the same day Minnesota militia and members of Company B of the Fifth Minnesota Voluntary Infantry Regiment were defeated at the Battle of Redwood Ferry, resulting in the deaths of twenty-four soldiers. For the next month and a half, open warfare raged across Minnesota and became front-page news back East.

The Dakota War in Minnesota was an especially undesirable problem for President Lincoln. Beset by defeats in the Civil War, he could little afford the ongoing disaster in Minnesota. Lincoln ordered General Pope to put down the uprising in Minnesota. Pope wanted to "badly punish" the Dakota for what he deemed unwarranted attacks on civilians, which he said demanded "punishment beyond human power to inflict." There was nothing vague about Pope's plan in Minnesota. "It is my purpose," he announced, "to utterly exterminate the [Dakota] if I have the power to do

so and even if it requires a campaign lasting the whole of next year."

By the end of September 1862, hundreds of Dakota had surrendered, and the government established a five-man Court of Inquiry to try the prisoners. The trials were so summary that they could hardly be called trials. No defense was put forth for the defendants; most of the Dakota had no understanding of the trial proceedings, some of which lasted fewer than five minutes. General Pope was enthusiastic about the speediness of the trials and refused any reduction of the charges. Believing he had sufficient troops by then on hand to control any further uprisings, he warned he would "exterminate them all, if they furnish the least occasion for it."

By early December, 303 Dakota had been convicted of murder and in some cases rape and sentenced to death. Pope wrote the Union's Western Theater commander, General Henry Halleck, for authorizations to proceed with the executions. Before the authorization arrived, however, President Lincoln sent a dispatch ordering that no executions take place until such time as he had personally reviewed each death sentence. The legality—or, rather, the illegality of the convictions—was not at issue. The execution of so many Dakota, as Lincoln well understood, was a political matter. What was the proper number of executions that would reestablish and advance American power in the region? Execute too few and whites in the region might resort to vigilante violence, their revenge not having been satisfied. Execute too many and the Dakota—indeed, all native tribes—might wage an all-out war against the United States.

On December 6, 1862, just a few weeks shy of the issuance of his Emancipation Proclamation, the former circuit lawyer turned President made public his decision:

"Anxious not to act with so much clemency as to encourage another outbreak on the one hand, nor with so much severity as to be real cruelty on the other," Lincoln made a distinction between those convicted of participating in massacres or of "violating females" from those who had participated in battles. This delineation reduced the number of death sentences from 303 to 38.

On December 26, the largest mass execution in the history of the United States took place. Over 3,000 settlers witnessed the event. They were closely watched over by more than a thousand soldiers. Both soldiers and settlers cheered when the rope was cut that sent the condemned to their deaths. The next year, the state of Minnesota began offering a bounty of $25 for Dakota scalps, and on July 3 Little Crow met his end. Two white settlers out hunting shot him. Little Crow's corpse brought them a bounty of $500 in addition to the standard $25. After numerous mutilations, his skull and scalp were put on display in St. Paul. There they remained until 1971, when they were returned to Little Crow's grandson.

In the end, the executions did little to bring peace to Minnesota in the short term or to solve the problems of a people standing in the way of the extension of American power. More than that, the events on the Minnesota prairie in 1862 reiterated what was clear from even before the creation of the United States; native peoples were clearly not included in the definition of the American people.

Antietam and Fredericksburg

After his victory at the second battle of Bull Run, General Lee was determined to go on the offensive, hoping another victory deeper in northern territory might bring European recognition of the Confederacy and deal yet another blow to morale in the North. When a Union soldier accidently discovered a battle order wrapped around a bundle of cigars, McClellan miraculously was handed an opportunity to deal a severe blow to the Confederacy; the note revealed that Lee had dangerously divided his army. True to form, McClellan delayed attacking, ever fearful that Lee's Army of Northern Virginia possessed superior numbers, divided army notwithstanding. Finally, on September 17, 1862, the leading parts of McClellan's forces attacked Lee near Sharpsburg, Maryland, beginning the Battle of Antietam. Outnumbered nearly two to one, Lee's army fought the Union to a stalemate in what became not just the bloodiest single day of the Civil War—23,000 casualties—but the bloodiest single day ever in American military history.

In addition to his general unwillingness to fight, McClellan, horrified by the losses, failed to press his advantage, and Lee secured his men back across the Potomac River. Disgusted over McClellan's explanation for the failure, Lincoln wired his general, "I have just read your dispatch about sore-tongued and fatigued horses. Will you pardon me for asking what the horses of your army have done since the battle of Antietam that fatigues anything?" In a second message, Lincoln asked, "If you don't want to use the army, I should like to borrow it for a while." To no one's surprise, Lincoln sacked his general for the last time. McClellan never again led troops into battle for Lincoln. Before long, however, the general would do battle with Lincoln for the highest office in the land.

Still, because of his failure to win an outright victory in the North, Antietam was a loss for Lee and the Confederacy. Any hopes of European recognition were sunk. McClellan's failure to destroy the Army of Northern Virginia, though, meant the war was no closer to its end. Lincoln appointed Ambrose E. Burnside as McClellan's replacement. It was obvious to Burnside that Lincoln wanted the war taken to Lee. Burnside was willing to fight, and fight he did, ordering six direct assaults on nearly impenetrable Confederate positions at the battle of Fredericksburg in Virginia in December 1862. The bloody carnage at this battle caused General Lee to observe, "It is well that war is so terrible—we should grow too fond of it." Suffering more than double the losses of his enemy—more than 12,000—a weeping Burnside ordered the withdrawal of his forces. With the war in an apparent stalemate, Lincoln then moved to alter the course and meaning of the war.

Emancipation

From the beginning of the war, abolitionists had been demanding that Lincoln make the Civil War not only a war to save the Union but also a war to abolish slavery in the South. Lincoln hesitated because he feared that to make freeing the slaves a war aim would cause one or more of the five slave states that had not seceded (Delaware, Maryland, West Virginia, Kentucky, and Missouri) to leave the Union. And that, in turn, might cause the North to lose the war; so, Lincoln hesitated. But there were other pressures on Lincoln to end slavery besides those of the abolitionists. In Europe, for example, public opinion was disgusted with Lincoln for refusing to use the war to free the slaves and concluded that the American Civil War was simply a political squabble, not a moral struggle. Consequently, many in Europe felt free to buy Confederate bonds and sell arms to the Confederacy. In England, Queen Victoria was openly sympathetic with the South, causing some in the North to fear that, unless Lincoln enlarged the war aims to include freeing the slaves, major European nations like France and England would extend diplomatic recognition to the CSA.

Finally, Lincoln acted on January 1, 1863, issuing his famous Emancipation Proclamation. The proclamation freed all slaves in the rebel states not under U.S. control, but it did not free any slaves in the states not in rebellion or under U.S. control. So, in reality, it really did not free any slaves. Lincoln's Emancipation Proclamation actually freed no slaves because it applied only to areas over which the federal government exercised no control and specifically exempted all regions under federal military occupation. A member of the London press observed caustically, "The principle is not that a human being cannot justly own another, but that he cannot own him unless he is loyal to the United States."

Lincoln issued the Emancipation Proclamation as a compromise document—a halfway measure—but a valuable document nevertheless, to win the political support of the abolitionists, to win the moral support of public opinion in Europe and prevent the diplomatic recognition of the CSA by any European nations, and to avoid alienating the slave states that had not seceded. Even though the Emancipation Proclamation did not free a single slave, it is significant because it challenged the institution of slavery in the South where it had long been assumed that the federal government had no power to mess around with the South's "peculiar institution." The Emancipation Proclamation set the stage for the enactment and ratification of the Thirteenth Amendment to the U.S. Constitution, which did free all slaves everywhere. Passed by Congress on January 31, 1865 (but not ratified until December of that year), the amendment ended human bondage in the United States and thereby swept away without compensation a $2 billion investment belonging to almost half a million Americans. Lincoln deserves much of the credit for pushing that Amendment through Congress.

Black Troops

Lincoln's Emancipation Proclamation further encouraged Blacks to enlist in the military. The previous year, on July 17, Lincoln had signed the Militia Act of 1862, which authorized the enlistment of African-Americans into the military. By the end of the war, some 180,000 Blacks joined the service, ten percent of the Union total. Lincoln hoped that Black men in arms might help turn the tide, even win the war. By placing weapons in the hands of men who arguably had the most to gain by a Northern victory, particularly the emancipated slaves from the rebellious states, Lincoln sought to inflame "the South's worst fears," as he put it. Any psychological advantages Southerners could claim by fighting a war for independence was thus counteracted, as Black soldiers fought for personal freedom.

Within the ranks, Black troops had to first overcome inherent racism of whites. They did so primarily by proving themselves in battle. By mid-1863, Black troops were widely used in every theatre of the war, and by the war's end, they had participated in 449 engagements. Nearly 38,000 lost their lives in the cause. Black Civil War soldiers proved themselves in every battle. The institution of slavery—among its other destructive facets—served to destroy self-esteem. Service in the military for many Black soldiers restored it in a way that nothing else could. Despite unequal pay, continuing racist treatment within the ranks, service of Black troops helped to validate the Emancipa-

tion Proclamation and, later, the Thirteenth, Fourteenth, and Fifteenth Amendments. As Frederick Douglass best said, "Once let the black man get upon his person the brass letters US; let him get an eagle on his button and a musket on his shoulder and bullets in his pocket, and there is no power on earth which can deny that he has earned the right to citizenship in the United States."

1863

Following the debacle of Fredericksburg, Lincoln yet again made a change at the top, replacing Ambrose Burnside with one of his lieutenants, Joseph E. Hooker, known to his men as "Fighting Joe." But Hooker had no more success than did any of his predecessors. In May 1863 at Chancellorsville, Virginia, possessing one of the largest armies to date in the U.S., Hooker was outclassed by Lee. Flush with this latest victory, Lee again attempted to invade the North, in part to counter military problems out in the west; General Grant had surrounded and laid siege to the city of Vicksburg, Mississippi. In the absence of Lee's army, Hooker wanted to take the lightly defended Confederate capital of Richmond, but Lincoln ordered him to pursue Lee's army. Impulsively, Hooker offered his resignation, and Lincoln without delay accepted it, placing General George Meade in command of the army just three days before the beginning of the Battle of Gettysburg.

Although neither side had purposely chosen Gettysburg, Pennsylvania, as the site to fight what many military historians consider the turning point in the war, nonetheless, approximately 160,000 Americans fought there for three days—July 1–3, 1863. Both sides suffered a similar number of casualties, more than 23,000 each. On the first day of the battle, Confederate forces pushed Union troops from the town. Importantly, Union troops were then able to reform their lines along higher ground to the south of the city. With his cavalry missing, on the second day of the battle Lee ordered attacks on both flanks of Meade's army, to no result. Inexplicably, the next day Lee ordered an all-out assault on the center of the Union position.

At about 2:00 pm in the afternoon, on July 3, 15,000 plus Confederates left their lines and began a slow advance across open fields toward the Union line. Pickett's charge, named after the Confederate General who led the attack, General George Pickett, was a disaster for the South. Barely half the attackers returned from the assault. A distraught Lee blamed himself: "All this has been my fault," he said. Utterly dispirited, Lee ordered a full retreat back to the relative safety of Virginia on July 4.

General Meade, in a repeat of Antietam, failed to take advantage of the victory and allowed the Confederate army to escape. Nonetheless, the battle was a much needed victory for Lincoln's Union. That same day Vicksburg fell, and the Confederacy was then torn in two. Beginning in the fall, the Union achieved other important victories in Tennessee. By the end of the year, Tennessee was effectively in Union hands. In March 1864, Lincoln turned to General Grant, bringing him to Washington and making in general-in-chief of all Union armies.

Total War

With Grant now firmly in command of the Union military, northern strategy to conclude the war changed. Rather than attempt to win climactic battles, the conflict became a war of attrition—attack, attack, and attack some more. Both Lincoln and Grant, through his service in the western theater, had come to understand that not only must Confederate armies be destroyed, so, too, must the Southern will to fight be destroyed. Rather than attack just southern armies, the Union military under Grant waged war against all southern society. Issuance of the Emancipation Proclamation the previous year was only the first indication of the newly evolving strategy. To win the war, the Union must destroy the entire southern culture, which was built upon a pro-slavery ethos and cotton production. As one Union officer put it, "The only possible way to end this unhappy and dreadful conflict . . . is to make it terrible beyond endurance."

Beginning in May 1864, using the Army of the Potomac, Grant pursued Lee across Virginia. And although the Northern army suffered heavier casualties, Grant was undeterred and relentless in continuing the attack. In early June, for example, at the Battle of Cold Harbor, Virginia, 7,000 Union men were killed or wounded in one twenty minute assault. Following the devastation at Cold Harbor, Grant moved his army to the south of Richmond and laid siege on Lee's men at Petersburg. With the numbers of battle deaths on the rise, a veteran Confederate soldier later noted that it was not really a war of attrition; it was worse than that, much worse: the war had "become nearly a war of extermination." In the context of persistent death and destruction—and with no end of the war in sight—Lincoln faced his own battle to retain the presidency.

The Election of 1864

Lincoln's chances for reelection were not good as late as the summer of 1864. The war was not going well, and the country's economy was beset by inflation. To the Democrats,

Lincoln was a target for much rhetorical abuse. They called him an "awful woeful ass," a "dictator," a "grotesque baboon," and "a third-rate lawyer who once split rails and now splits the Union." Even some of Lincoln's Republican friends thought he was a misfit in the presidency. Lincoln's Secretary of War, Edwin Stanton, even went so far as to refer to the president in public as "a low, cunning clown." Lincoln himself despaired of winning reelection, but he was determined not to go down without a fight, because he thought his Democratic opponent, General George B. McClellan, would compromise with the South, end the war, and thereby destroy the Union.

Lincoln was nominated, not by the Republicans, but by an alliance of his supporters in the Republican Party and Northern members of the Democratic Party who supported the war—the War Democrats, as they were called (as opposed to the Peace Democrats). This alliance of Republicans and Democrats was called the National Union Party. Lincoln was the presidential nominee and his vice-presidential running mate was a War Democrat from Tennessee, Senator Andrew Johnson.

The campaign of 1864 was fiercely fought and extremely dirty. McClellan kicked off the Democrats' campaign with the statement: "The President is nothing more than a well-meaning baboon. He is the original gorilla. What a specimen to be at the head of our affairs." Other Democrats were equally unkind. One popular description of the time claimed Lincoln's "anatomy is composed mostly of bones and when walking he resembles the offspring of a happy marriage between a derrick and a windmill." Despite these attacks from the Democrats, Lincoln won reelection in 1864.

What turned the election was the drastic improvement in Union fortunes in the war. But before Union victories assured Lincoln's reelection, Lincoln took some dramatic—even illegal—steps to help his own cause. In the key border state of Kentucky, for example, the Republicans had won only 1,364 votes in 1860 compared to the combined Democratic vote of 143,000 (Douglas and Breckenridge). In 1864, Lincoln hoped to do much better. Three days before the election, Union troops arrested the leading Democratic candidates for office. Lincoln still lost the state, but he came much closer than he had in 1860, winning 27,000 votes to McClellan's 63,000.

Indiana was another key state, which was also in doubt. Just before the Atlanta campaign, Lincoln wired that General Sherman should let his Indiana soldiers return home to vote, adding wryly that "this is not an order." In case that was not enough, members of the 19th Regiment of Vermont Volunteers were allowed to vote in the Indiana election, while at the same time, many Indiana Democrats were barred from voting. Lincoln won Indiana with a 20,000 majority, but smaller than his margin of victory in 1860.

In Pennsylvania, state leaders authorized the soldiers to vote in the field. Although the governor sent a bipartisan commission to supervise the voting, as the commissioners were en route, Secretary of War Stanton had the Democratic members of the Commission jailed without any charges being filed. For insurance, Lincoln ordered some non-Pennsylvania soldiers into Pennsylvania to vote there. Finally, Postmasters appointed by the Republicans "corrected" ballots mailed home by soldiers. Lincoln won Pennsylvania by 19,000 votes, 296,000 to 277,000. Lincoln and Johnson won every state (outside the Confederacy) except Kentucky, New Jersey, and Delaware.

Unchecked executive abuses of power continued throughout the war years. In 1864, Lincoln told a Michigan Senator Zachariah Chandler, "I conceive that I may in emergency do things on military grounds which cannot be done constitutionally by Congress." After the war was over, most of Lincoln's "emergency" powers—legal and otherwise—disappeared. During the war, however, Lincoln had tested the pool of presidential power and found it almost bottomless.

The Atlanta Campaign and Sherman's March to the Sea

With Grant doing battle with Lee in the Eastern theater, battle tested General William Tecumseh Sherman was pursuing a Confederate army under the command of General Joseph Johnston in Georgia. After a series of defeats in May and June, Confederate President Davis replaced Johnston with General John Bell Hood. Under Hood, the Confederate army fought back fiercely rather than simply fight a retreating campaign, but the results changed little, except for higher casualties. When Sherman's army encircled Hood's headquarters of Atlanta and cut off communication and supplies, Hood was forced to evacuate the city. Sherman thereupon sent a letter to the mayor of Atlanta, demanding the surrender of the city. It was reflective of his acceptance of Lincoln's and Grant's new strategy to win the war: "War is cruelty, and you cannot refine it, and those who brought war into our country deserve all the cures and maledictions a people can pour out." The fall of Atlanta was a terrific blow the Confederacy, and, as important as that was, Sherman's victory there made the reelection of Lincoln possible.

In mid-November 1864, Sherman began the Savannah Campaign, or what has become commonly known as "Sherman's March to the Sea." The campaign effectively ended on December 21, when Sherman's army captured the port city of Savannah. After ordering the burning of Atlanta, Sherman sent his men toward Savannah. Along the way, they cut a swath of devastation and destruction 250 miles long, giving new meaning to the doctrine of "total war." From Savannah, Sherman's men moved north, continuing their work of bringing the war to the civilian population, this time through the state of South Carolina. By mid-February 1865, several cities had been captured, including the South Carolina capital, Columbia. For Lincoln and so many others in the North, the war that just a year earlier had seemed so far from an end, was nearly over.

Andersonville

If Sherman and his army had headed south rather than east, they would have come across perhaps the most dramatic result of the decision to conduct a total war on the South. Andersonville prison camp had been designed to hold a maximum of 10,000 men, but by August 1864 over 33,000 men, many new captives from Sherman's army, populated the camp. By the summer of 1864, under the leadership of Grant the earlier policy of prisoner exchange had ended. Secretary of State William Seward confirmed the policy by writing, "We have got to fight on until the whole South is exhausted, and if we release or exchange prisoners captured, it simply becomes a war of extermination." In all too many ways, certainly for the men of Andersonville, the decision to end prisoner exchanges meant nothing less than extermination.

Conditions of prison camps in the South were generally well-known in the military and civilian leadership of Lincoln's administration. Inmate rations by the last year of the war were little more than a few spoonful's of beans and cornmeal per day. The cornmeal was of such poor quality it often produced internal bleeding among many inmates. The primary water source was a stream, which was contaminated with urine, excrement, and often corpses. By this point in the war, it had become difficult for the South to feed its own men; consequently, rations for prisoners were awful and sometimes nonexistent.

A southern woman who observed the camp in Andersonville wrote, "My heart aches for these poor wretches. Yankees though they are, I am afraid God will suffer some terrible retribution to fall upon us for letting such things happen. If the Yankees should ever come . . . and go to Anderson and see the graves there, God have mercy on the land." Dozens of Union soldiers in Andersonville were dying daily from gangrene, scurvy, dysentery, and starvation.

Of some 45,000 prisoners held at Andersonville during the war, nearly 13,000 died—nearly one in three. After the war, the commander of the camp, Henry Wirz, was put on trial for conspiracy and murder. Several former inmates testified to the horror of the camp, some even accusing Wirz of specific acts of criminality. Later investigations by historians have shown that much of the testimony was exaggerated. One witness has even been shown not to have ever been to the camp. And Wirz produced evidence that he had attempted on several occasions to improve the conditions for the inmates and provide more food. In the months following the assassination of President Lincoln, the nation wanted vengeance, and Wirz was found guilty of murder and sentenced to

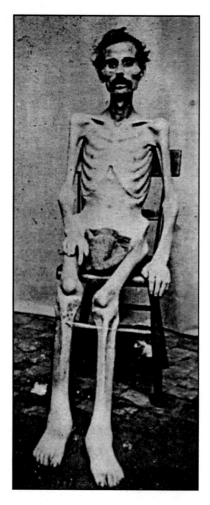

Survivor of Andersonville prison

death. He was hanged on November 10, 1865. Wirz was the only Confederate ever tried for war crimes.

Lee Surrenders

Having been under siege by Grant at Petersburg, Virginia, for months, finally, Lee made the decision to leave Petersburg and attempt to join with another Confederate Army under the command of Joe Johnston in North Carolina in late March 1865. In Richmond, the Confederate President gathered what records he could and fled the city, still determined to carry on the fight. What was left of value in the city was put to the torch as the last Confederate troops left the capital on April 2, 1865. President Lincoln took the opportunity (and risk) to tour the city with his young son, Tad, in hand, following a meeting in Petersburg with his two most important Generals, Grant and Sherman.

With Richmond smoldering and Lee in flight, the Union Army followed, just as they had done since Grant was put in command the previous year. When Union cavalry cut off his escape route, the duration and the enormity of the destruction finally caused Lee to call an end to it all. With his army surrounded and outnumbered, Lee put on his best uniform and met the disheveled and mud-splattered Grant in the McLean home in Appomattox on April 9, 1865. This time, "unconditional surrender" Grant was willing to compromise, allowing, at Lee's request, Confederate officers to keep their sidearms and the enlisted men to keep their horses and mules. Three days later the Confederate troops assembled for the last time and formally surrendered, marching in near silence before Union troops at full salute. Lee's Army of Northern Virginia had long been the embodiment of the Confederate cause. The surrender of his army had been unthinkable to most southerners and signified the end. The sustained pressure of the Union Army had finally brought it down, and with it, the Confederacy.

Although the nation's bloodiest war had effectively ended (the offi-

cial last battle took place in Palmito Ranch, Texas, on May 13, 1865), one momentous casualty remained. Actor and southern sympathizer John Wilkes Booth assassinated Lincoln on April 14, 1865, as the President and his wife attended "Our American Cousin" at Ford's Theater in Washington. The President, who had willingly led the nation in a war to save the Union and who had hesitantly come to the decision to destroy slavery to accomplish it, was now gone. It would be left to other leaders, consequently, to direct the nation's reconstruction.

President Lincoln, taken by Alexander Gardner on February 5, 1865

Consequences

The Civil War was a turning point in American history. After it, Americans lived in a very different nation, one in which freedom and equality now applied to all men—at least constitutionality—one in which the union of the nation was beyond dispute, and one in which the power of the national government was more nearly supreme than ever before. Lincoln had led a nation torn by the tensions between nationalism and sectionalism into a war, and what emerged were a nation and a people convinced of the value of nationalism and the continued extension of American power as a supreme goal. Consequently, one significant change brought on by the war was an increase in patriotism, certainly in the victorious North, if not in the vanquished South. Ralph Waldo Emerson asserted, "Before the war our patriotism was a fire-work, a salute, a serenade for holidays and summer evenings. Now the deaths of thousands and the determination of millions of men and women show that it is real . . . Now we have a country again. Sometimes gunpowder smells good."

When the Civil War began, most northerners accepted it and its goal of saving the Union. The war had widespread support in the North, at least until it became evident how horrible war really can be. The Civil War was a people's war; it directly touched thousands of men, women, and children who never forgot its effect on their lives and on the lives. Almost 3 million men fought in the war—about 15% of the total population. This war not only took so many from their homes, it also caused the deaths of tens of thousands. Two percent of the population died in it, more than 620,000 men; so many never returned that it was a new kind of war—the first modern war full of incomprehensible death.

During one day at the Battle of Antietam, 23,000 men fell. As many as 7,000 men fell at Cold Harbor in Virginia in twenty minutes. The war might also be properly called a "Boys War." Seventy-four percent of the Union soldiers were twenty-one or under; close to a million men were eighteen or under. One hundred thousand were fifteen or under and could hardly be called men.

One out of every three homes in the nation had been touched in some way by death before the war was over. The deep feelings people on both sides had about the war were intensified by the terrible choices of loyalties they had to make. The war—a Civil War—pitted families against each other. Confederate armies contained men from every Northern state; the Union army and navy contained men from every seceded state. The initial Commander of the Union forces, General Winfield Scott, was from Virginia, a slave state that seceded. So was the commander of the Army of Northern Virginia, General Robert E. Lee. Senator John J. Crittenden of Kentucky had two sons: one was a major general in the Union army; the other was a major general in the Confederate army. Mrs. Lincoln had three brothers who died fighting for the CSA. Mrs. Jefferson Davis, wife of the President of the CSA, had near relatives in the Union army. It was not a war soon forgotten by most Americans who were alive at the time. Twenty years after he left the Union army, Oliver Wendell Holmes wrote: "Through our good fortune in our youth, our hearts were touched by fire. It was given us to learn at the outset that life is a profound and passionate thing."

The Civil War had profound effects on both the Democratic Party and the Republican Party. It was no surprise that all the elected presidents between Abraham Lincoln and

Theodore Roosevelt—that is, between 1865 and 1901—with but one exception—had served as officers in the Union army. The one exception was Grover Cleveland, who purchased a substitute so he did not have to fight (the procedure was legal at the time). Cleveland was also the only Democrat elected president between Lincoln in 1860 and Woodrow Wilson in 1912. The Republican Party—the Party of the Union—became the party for a majority of Americans. The War for the Union shattered the once-popular Democratic Party—the party of Jefferson and Jackson—and also the party of the president of the Confederate States of America, Jefferson Davis. It would take another equally profound event—the Great Depression of the 1930s—to displace the Republicans and make the Democratic Party the majority party in America again.

The Civil War sped up the process of partial assimilation by immigrant groups into Northern society. Many of the men who fought in the Union armies were recent immigrants to the United States from Europe. Not since the Thirty Years War in 17th century Europe had so cosmopolitan a group of Europeans been assembled in one army as in the Union army during the Civil War. Natives and immigrants, especially Germans and Irishmen, were thrown together in a way that emphasized their common loyalty. Often the military service of the immigrant marked his transition from alien to citizen, and, more importantly, from rejection to acceptance by his fellow Americans. Irish-Americans were astonished that the war and their service in it had turned them into "damned Yankees."

The war also strengthened nationalism in general in the North. Men from different states of the North and even from some parts of the South mingled with one another in the common cause of fighting for Union, fighting for their nation's survival. Their commitment to the United States of America only grew stronger as a result of their fighting for their country. If you're willing to die for something, it's almost always very important to you.

Incidentally, the living monument to the profound nationalistic influence of the Union Army was an organization of veterans established after the war was over, the Grand Army of the Republic (GAR). Several hundred thousand veterans joined together in this self-proclaimed incarnation of the cause of the Union. Its subsequent political activities proved a measure and a symbol of the deep well of national feeling which the war had revealed. In subsequent political races, the GAR actively supported candidates who'd been "right" on the issue of union v. secession and opposed those whose commitments to the Union had not been as strong as their own.

The Civil War also destroyed forever the political theory of secession as a legitimate act. Lincoln said the sole reason for conducting the Civil War was NOT to abolish slavery (though it did that), NOT to discredit the doctrine of states' rights (though it did that, too), NOT even to settle the issue of the expansion of slavery into the Mexican territories (though it also did that), BUT TO SAVE THE UNION, or, in other words, to establish the illegality of secession. The North fought the Civil War to save the Union. When the war ended in 1865 and the South surrendered, the Union had been saved, and the doctrine of secession constructed by southern fire-eaters had been laid to rest. The U.S. Supreme Court correctly understood the meaning of the South's loss and the North's victory, and, in 1869, incorporated the legal consequence of that victory into the supreme law of the land when it declared the Union to be "indestructible" in *Texas v. White*.

Never again—or at least not so far—has any state (or any sensible politician) seriously imagined that secession was a constitutional remedy for state grievances.

The Civil War broadened and strengthened the powers of the central government. It built a bigger and stronger central government. The sheer magnitude of the emergency that confronted the Lincoln administration in 1861 and throughout the war produced a permanent transformation of the powers of the federal government. In part, this was an inevitable result of the war.

To fight the war, Lincoln needed an army, but at the beginning of the war in 1861, the regular army of the United States was woefully inadequate—only 15,000 men and 1,000 officers—and of the latter, one third of the officers left for the Confederacy. State militias were also inadequate to deal with the magnitude of the conflict, and the result was the need to create a large, strong national army under the central control of the federal government. Draft laws were passed by Congress in 1862 and again in 1863 and were enforced, despite widespread opposition, even riots.

Fighting the war was an expensive proposition. Federal expenditures increased almost 20 fold (from $66.5 million in 1861 to approximately $1.3 billion in 1865), and the financial powers of the government expanded accordingly. The federal government printed more than $400 million in paper money—"greenbacks"—during the war and passed legislation—the National Banking Act—that allowed the central government in effect to tax all state and local bank notes out of existence. Never again would state bank notes be of any significance in the American economy. From the time of the Civil War onward, currency affairs were firmly in the hands of the more powerful national government. In addition,

new and heavier excise taxes appeared, and, for the first time in American history, the federal government levied a tax on personal income.

A second important cause of the strengthening and broadening of the powers of the federal government during the war years was the attitude of the Republican Party toward the proper role of the central government. The Republicans were believers in American power. They envisioned a stronger central government with more power and more authority than ever before. Much of their activity was made possible by Southern secession. Because the South had seceded, its representatives were no longer in Congress to block the enactment of measures long supported by the North but successfully opposed by the South. So Congress, under the leadership of the Republicans, was able during the war years to pass several measures that served to strengthen the power of the central government, among them: the Homestead Act (20 May 1862), which offered citizens 160 acres of public land after five years of continuous occupancy and a small registration fee ($24–36); and the Morrill Act (2 July 1862), which provided public land for agricultural colleges (over 70 land-grand colleges have been established under its provisions).

The central government also embarked on a program of generous subsidization of the great national railroads (1862 and 1864) that would link all parts of the nation together. The long-term effect of these railroads, when combined with other Republican measures sympathetic to business, such as new banking legislation and high protective tariffs, would not only link the nation geographically, but also link it economically as well. During and immediately after the Civil War, actions by the central government set the stage for the growth of a truly national economy that would go far toward erasing—at least symbolically—the arbitrary lines on a map that distinguished states or regions.

Not only did the central government in general grow stronger during the war, but also the presidency in particular grew stronger, thanks in large measure to the actions taken by President Lincoln. The Civil War saw the creation of a new sort of American presidency. Lincoln, who was a strong leader and a committed nationalist, used the conditions produced by the war to create a far stronger presidency than the nation had ever known before. In the course of the war, Lincoln stretched his presidential war powers to the limit. He suspended the writ of habeas corpus (a legal measure to protect a person from unlawful restraint), suppressed free speech and press, declared a blockade of the southern ports without a declaration of war by Congress (four justices of the Supreme Court thought this to be unconstitutional), spent money in the early months of the war without Congressional authorization, raised federal troops without an enabling act by Congress, abolished slavery in some parts of the country, but not in others, and undertook to reconstruct the rebellious states and provide for their return to the Union.

During the war, Lincoln had tested the pool of presidential power and found it almost bottomless. And this was a lesson not soon forgotten by presidents who followed him, especially in the 20th and 21st centuries. The old, limited federal government which Lincoln inherited in 1861 was overthrown in the course of the war and its place was taken by a United States government truly supreme over the states that once called themselves sovereign.

Certainly, the most important effect of the Civil War on American culture was that the war "settled" the issue of slavery. Even though the war had begun as a war to save the Union, it also dramatically affected the institution of slavery. How the Republicans and Lincoln handled the issue of slavery may be the most dramatic example of how the war and the nationalist ideology of the Republican Party continuously created opportunities and the necessity for enlarging the powers of the federal government at the expense of the states.

For decades, almost everybody (except the anti-slavery advocates, the abolitionists) had agreed that slavery where it already existed was protected by the U.S. Constitution. Even the Republican Party began by denying any intention of interfering with slavery in the South, but all that changed during the war. Lincoln clearly and insistently made the point that the purpose of the war was to save the Union, not to end slavery in the South. But, as the war progressed, he and others in the North realized that to save the Union, the Confederacy would have to be defeated. In the South, Alexander H. Stephens and many other leaders of the CSA said repeatedly that slavery was the "cornerstone" of the Confederacy. So it followed logically that one way to defeat the Confederacy and save the Union would be to destroy slavery in the South. At first, Lincoln was very reluctant to use his extensive presidential war powers against slavery.

When two Union generals (John C. Fremont and David Hunter) proclaimed that the slaves of disloyal masters in Missouri, Georgia, South Carolina, and Florida were free, Lincoln revoked their proclamations primarily. In 1861, Congress passed a confiscation act that freed those slaves put to military use by the CSA, and in 1862, passed another confiscation act that declared "forever free" all slaves whose owners were in rebellion whether or not the slaves were being used militarily. While Lincoln did not veto the laws, he did not execute them either.

On January 1, 1863, Lincoln issued his Emancipation Proclamation. All slaves in the rebel states not under U.S. control were henceforth forever free, which set the stage for the Thirteenth Amendment, ending slavery everywhere in the United States. Although the question of slavery was settled by the Civil War and the Thirteenth Amendment to the U.S. Constitution, white racism did not disappear; white racism still existed after the war was over. The Civil War had ended slavery, but blacks were not made equal. The question of the future status of blacks in America was NOT settled by the Civil War. Much of what came to be called "Reconstruction" dealt with the question of what the proper status of black people should be in the United States after the Civil War.

After the Civil War, a subtle difference appeared when the American people talked about the nation in which they lived. Before the war, they had referred to THESE United States. After the war, without even knowing it, they said THE United States. Lincoln fought a war to save the Union, but the Union he saved was different from the one he set out to save in 1861. Of necessity, born of war, Congress and the president gained power at the expense of the states. Precedents were set and the American people had become more comfortable than ever before with the idea of American power.

Suggested Readings

Catton, Bruce. *The Coming Fury.* A limited ed. Franklin Center, Pa.: Franklin Library, 1980.

Gallagher, Gary W. *The Confederate War.* Cambridge, Mass.: Harvard University Press, 1997.

Glatthaar, *Joseph T. General Lee's Army: From Victory to Collapse.* 1st Free Press hardcover ed. New York: Free Press, 2008.

Glatthaar, Joseph T. *The March to the Sea and Beyond: Sherman's Troops in the Savannah and Carolinas Campaigns,* The American Social Experience Series 1. New York: New York University Press, 1985.

McPherson, James M. *Battle Cry of Freedom: The Civil War Era,* The Oxford History of the United States V. 6. New York: Oxford University Press, 1988.

Chapter 15

RECONSTRUCTION

One of the greatest paradoxes in United States history was the Civil War. For forty years (1820-1860), white Americans debated slavery, often violently and never without acrimony. Yet, rarely if ever, did their arguments reflect any genuine humanitarian concern for the plight of the millions of African Americans in bondage. Even many abolitionists worried more about the sin and stigma of slavery upon the nation's image than about the institution's barbarity. In short, white Americans divided not on the morality of slavery but on the institution's political and economic ramifications. Such little regard for the slaves' condition reflected an inherent and prevailing racism among the majority of Northern whites, including a good number of even the most zealous of abolitionists. As will be seen in this chapter, such Northern white attitudes toward African Americans significantly impacted the course of Reconstruction.

Since the nation's beginning in 1787 and over the course of the next 73 years, the political elite avoided confrontation and the potential disruption of the Union by promulgating a series of compromises on the slavery expansion issue. However, by the late 1850s, the political leadership at that time (Abraham Lincoln's generation, and sadly one of the worst generations of political leaders in the history of the Republic) proved incapable of finding common ground to forge another compromise. By 1860, Southern whites, led by the "slaveocracy," concluded that their inalienable right to "property" (their slaves) was no longer secure in the Union and thus seceded, declaring that the Union that had been created in 1787 had been subverted by a "black Republican" party determined not only to abolish slavery but to abrogate as well states' rights, which to Southern slaveowners meant the right to own slaves and to take their property anywhere they deemed essential for their "pursuit of happiness." Therein lies part of the paradox of the Civil War: it was a conflict caused by slavery yet became the nation's greatest bloodbath ignited by secession. In the end, the United States convulsed in bloody conflict, not to end the blight of human bondage but to preserve the Union; for an abstract entity rather than for the liberation of human beings.

Secession, however, united Northern whites, for in the Northern white mind secession and slavery were mutually exclusive issues: the former tied to the sanctity of nationhood, with the latter associated with a race of inferior people, not worth a blood sacrifice. Nonetheless, an interesting coalition formed in the North during the war years that helped to guarantee a Union triumph. Unionists and antislavery men put aside their differences and joined forces, for both knew they could not obtain their respective objectives without the other. Both opposed secession and agreed that the Union must be preserved. Unionists, however, did not see the abolition of slavery and the preservation of the Union as symbiotic. Yet, the Unionists knew they could not defeat the secessionists without antislavery support and abolitionists knew they would not see the end of slavery without unionist support, nor without defeating the Confederacy. Thus an uneasy alliance formed between the two groups. The Union victory put an end to the coalition, for the two allies no longer needed one another. Most important, the Confederacy's defeat transformed the issue of union into a question of race, and, as will be seen in this chapter, the freedmen (ex-slaves) had few Northern supporters, and thus were doomed almost from the beginning of Reconstruction to a life of continued servility, oppression, poverty, illiteracy, terror, and all too frequently an early death.

Whenever a successful coalition dissolves after a war because of dissension among the victors, the vanquished, if shrewd and united, almost always find an opportunity to reassert or reclaim their power, often in a greater, more dominating form than before the conflict. That was precisely what the white South was able to accomplish by the end of Reconstruction.

Reconstruction's Overarching Issues

Without question, the emancipation of four million African Americans from bondage presented both white and black Americans with Reconstruction's most pressing issue. There was simply no consensus among whites and even among some blacks about the possible place of freed people in a reconstructed United States. Both black and white leaders, including Lincoln, wondered, if not doubted, whether different races could ever peacefully coexistence, let alone be willing to accept each other as equal citizens. Also vexing, especially for white Northerners, was the question of how Southern whites, particularly those who had aided and encouraged the slaveholders' rebellion, were to be treated. Should they be punished—executed or imprisoned, their property confiscated, or permanently disenfranchised? On what terms should the Confederate or rebellious states return to the Union? And finally, what would be the powers of the states and of the national government in a reconstructed Union?

Although Reconstruction would affect every aspect of Southern life, it's most dramatic and enduring impact was social—the daily working out by black and white, male and female, rich and poor, of how they were to treat each other in these changed times. In some instances these social dramas reflected old ties sundered or renewed, as when former slaves drifted back to the plantation after having enjoyed freedom for a few weeks, looking for work or someone to provide for them as "old massa" had for years. Some times the bonds were reversed, as when freedmen brought food to a former master who was now steeped in poverty. On another occasion, a white man would be hauled before a black judge; African Americans defending their homes with rifles; a black militia instead of a white slave patrol. Other transformations were smaller: freedmen driving newly bought buggies, poor black and white children attending school together. Of such seemingly insignificant changes revolutions are made; against such dread reordering the forces of reaction launch their strongest battalions. So it would be in the Reconstruction South.

As this chapter will reveal, Reconstruction unleashed unforeseen conflicts that propelled events along a startling revolutionary path. The dialectic between conservatism and revolution, the desire for order and for freedom defined Reconstruction in both its successes and failures. At Reconstruction's start only one certainty prevailed: thousands of black Southerners eagerly awaited its advent while thousands of their white counterparts dreaded its inaugural.

Abraham Lincoln and Wartime/Presidential Reconstruction

No history of Reconstruction is complete or accurate without discussion of Lincoln's views and policies, no matter how ambiguous, conflicting, inconsistent, and half-hearted they might have been. Although Lincoln is considered to be the nation's greatest president, successfully holding the country together through its most perilous ordeal, he nonetheless had "flaws," especially when it came to the issue of race, which as noted above, became Reconstruction's most critical dynamic. Perhaps the first question that must be asked regarding Lincoln and race was Lincoln a racist himself? The answer is a "qualified" yes. As he declared during the 1858 Illinois senate race in one of his debates with Stephen Douglas, "I am not, nor ever have been in favor of bringing about in any way the social and political equality of the white and black races; that I am not, nor ever have been in favor of making voter or jurors of Negroes, nor of qualifying them to hold office, nor to intermarry with white people;. . . .there is a physical difference between the white and black races which I believe will forever forbid the two races living together on terms of social and political equality. And

Abraham Lincoln, *ca. 1860–ca. 1865*

inasmuch as they cannot so live, while they do remain together there must be the position of superior and inferior, and I as much as any other man am in favor of having the superior position assigned to the white man."

Abraham Lincoln, President, U.S, ca. 1860–ca. 1865

If the above statement is taken at face value, then Lincoln was indeed a "white supremacist," holding the same racial attitudes at that time as the majority of his fellow white citizens. But was Lincoln's racism simply "political;" that is, was he expressing such views in order to win votes? Four years earlier a different Lincoln is revealed, one who recognized that color prejudice was a totally irrational basis for determining race relations. "If A can prove conclusively that he may of right enslave B—why may not B snatch the same argument, and prove equally, that he may enslave A? You say A is white and B is black. It is *color* then; the lighter having the right to enslave the darker? Take care. By this rule, you are to be the slave to the first man you meet with a fairer skin than your own. You do not mean *color* exactly? You mean the whites are *intellectually* the superiors of the blacks, and therefore you have the right to enslave them? Take care again. By this rule, you are to be slave to the first man you meet with an intellect superior to your own. But you say, it is a question of *interest;* and if you make it your interest, you have the right to 'enslave others. Very well. And if he can make it his interest, he has the right to enslave you."

Unfortunately for posterity, Lincoln never publicly stated this lean and muscular bit of reasoning. Had he, the "racist" label would have been expunged, especially when coupled with his public declaration that both he and his party (the Republicans) considered slavery as "a wrong. . . a moral, social, and political wrong." Thus, at best, Lincoln, like many of his white contemporaries, was ambiguous about race in America. Lincoln without question believed black folk to be people, human beings, albeit "inferior," but nonetheless members of the human race entitled to their freedom. To enslave them and strip them of their humanity and reduce them to property, was, as he publicly announced, morally, socially, and politically wrong, particularly in a country that proclaimed to the world in 1776 that "all men are created equal." To Lincoln this included "men of color" as well.

Although publicly condemning human bondage and acknowledging the slaves' humanity, Lincoln nonetheless was not willing to engage in a clash of arms to rid the nation of chattel slavery. From the moment the first salvos were fired, the Civil War to Lincoln was unequivocally about preserving the Union, and thus the slavery issue became of secondary importance. Lincoln made this point very clear in a letter to newspaper publisher Horace Greeley in August 1862. "My paramount objective is to save the Union, and is not either to save or destroy slavery. If I could save the Union without freeing any slave, I would do it; and if I could save it by freeing all the slaves, I would do it; and if I could save it by freeing some and leaving others alone, I would also do that. What I do about slavery and the colored race, I do because I believe it helps to save this Union." Interestingly, the Emancipation Proclamation, though unannounced, was already in his desk, the result of his conclusion that such an act would help the Union cause by giving Yankee soldiers and Northern whites in general hopefully something more tangible to fight for than an abstraction—the Union—while simultaneously crippling the Confederate war effort by depriving it of valuable labor. Thus for reasons political and strategic, Lincoln "freed the slaves" in the states still in rebellion against the United States on January 1, 1863. Thus "forever free" were slaves in North Carolina, South Carolina, Georgia, Florida, Alabama, Mississippi, Arkansas, Texas, parts of Louisiana, (those parishes under Union control), and Virginia. Not included in the proclamation were the border states—Missouri, Kentucky, Maryland, Delaware, and Tennessee, which had come under complete Union control by that time. Thus in five states slavery still existed legally, and would so until the end of the war. Although a potentially sweeping declaration, promising freedom soon to come to all slaves, regardless of where they resided, the document could also be interpreted as a bid to the seceded states to end their resistance before January 1, and thus keep their slaves. The proclamation's various caveats and "qualifications" did not escape notice. Particularly critical of the document was the foreign press, which as the London *Spectator* acerbically observed, "The principle is not that a human being cannot justly own another, but that he cannot own him unless he is loyal to the United States." Despite such criticism, the Emancipation Proclamation and the later Thirteenth Amendment, passed by Congress on January 31, 1865 (but not ratified until December of that year), which abolished slavery forever, were the two fundamental measures in the overthrow of human bondage in the United States.

Joint Resolution Proposing the Thirteenth Amendment to the United States Constitution, 01/31/1865

As the man who issued the Emancipation Proclamation and as the key leader in securing Congressional adoption of the Thirteenth Amendment, Lincoln could certainly be called the "Emancipator," albeit a reluctant one. Indeed, no sooner did the Emancipation Proclamation go into effect, than Lincoln initiated "phase two" of his manumission agenda—the colonization of freedmen outside the United States—in Haiti, in Panama, or elsewhere in the Western Hemisphere in which could be found countries with all-black populations. Could such an initiative be further proof of Lincoln's inherent racism? Perhaps, for it appears that Lincoln had thought about this idea for quite some time as part of his overall emancipation plan. He tested black receptivity to his scheme in August 1862 when he invited to the Oval Office a group of already free African Americans, some of whom had been interested in colonization, to confer with him about such a prospect. Usually a man with great sensitivity to others' feelings, Lincoln on this occasion seemed hard-hearted and obtuse. Observing that whites and blacks were of different races, he said further, "your race suffers greatly and we of the white race suffer from your presence. Even when you cease to be slaves, you are yet far removed from being on an equality with the white race. On this broad continent, not a single man of your race is made the equal of a single man of ours. I cannot alter it if I would. It is a fact. It is better for us both to be separated." He then proceeded to describe to them the attractions of an area in Colombia (the future country of Panama) made available for such purposes by the Colombian government, which at the time needed to populate the isthmus. Lincoln urged them to emigrate there as soon as possible.

Again, if Lincoln's words are taken at face value, then he most definitely was a racist. However, Lincoln's racist rhetoric and callousness could also be interpreted as an awkward attempt at humanitarianism. By painting such a bleak and cruel picture of post-emancipation for freedmen, perhaps Lincoln was trying to impress upon African Americans a harsh reality few could envision. In effect, what Lincoln was trying to say to his black audience was that America was for whites only, and that the overwhelming majority of white Americans, including himself, subscribed to that racist premise and thus a post-Civil War United States would be anything but a save haven for freedmen. By encouraging emigration, Lincoln hoped to save black folk from the oppression, violence, and anguish that would become part and parcel of their every day life in the South for the next 100 years.

Entirely separate from the harshness of telling African Americans that they were to pursue their new life as a free people in some place other than the land of their birth, Lincoln's plan was completely unrealistic: the United States had neither the facilities to colonize four million human beings nor a place to which it could send them. At the existing procreation rate, no less than 500 hundred black Americans were being born in the United States every day, it would thus be logistically impossible to "colonize" (deport) the African American population as rapidly as it was increasing. Moreover, increasing numbers of black leaders, abolitionists, and many Republicans objected to Lincoln's policy, rightly arguing that such action would punish the victims of racial prejudice rather than its perpetrators. Black folk were Americans. Why should they not have the rights of American citizens instead of being urged to leave the country?

Nonetheless, Lincoln actually got a colonization experiment into operation in April 1863, when a group of 453 freedmen settled on Cow Island (Ile a Vache), off Haiti. Predictably, they suffered and died from smallpox, malaria, and poisonous insects. They were unable to sustain themselves because of infertile soil and thus in March 1864 a Navy transport arrived and took back to the United States 368 survivors. Despite the dismal failure of the Cow Island experiment, Lincoln, down to his death, continued to believe that African American emigration was the solution to the "Negro issue" if the nation hoped to avoid generations of bitter, vicious, and tragic race relations. Lincoln's dream of colonization prevented any significant public discussion about the hard question of the position of former slaves in American society.

Although addressing the freedmen issue, Lincoln made the re-assimilation of Southern *whites* his priority, especially those white Southerners whose loyalty to the Confederacy had been lukewarm. He believed these folk would become the foundation for his overall objective for as rapid a restoration of the Union as was possible. As will be seen later in this chapter Lincoln's desire for leniency for Southern whites became a divisive issue not only within the Republican party but among Northern whites as well, many of whom believed *all* Southern whites were guilty of secession and should be punished accordingly. For the moment, however, Lincoln prevailed on this issue with the promulgation of his Proclamation of Amnesty, which offered a presidential pardon to all Southern whites (excluding Confederate government officials and high-ranking military officers) who took an oath of allegiance to the United States and accepted the abolition of slavery. More important, in any state where the number of white males aged 21 or older who took this oath equaled 10 percent of the number of 1860 voters, that group could establish a state government, which Lincoln promised he would recognize as "legitimate" and thus that state could reenter the Union, as if it had never left.

Lincoln's so-called "ten percent plan" outraged many Republicans, who rightly claimed that Lincoln's amnesty policy favored former Confederates at the freedmen's expense. To this opposition, Lincoln's plan smacked of betrayal and hypocrisy, for it rewarded "traitors" to the country with a complete restoration of their political rights while denying such rights to black men who had fought *for* the Union. Further incensing these Republicans was Lincoln's Proclamation of Reconstruction, which in effect, allowed ex-Confederate landowners and former slaveholders to establish labor regulations and other measures to control the freedmen's labor, so long as they recognized manumission and made minimal provisions for their ex-slaves' education.

The freedmen issue was not the only source of conflict between Lincoln and some

Republicans. Also causing rancor was the percolating question of which branch of government—executive or legislative—should have authority and control over the reconstruction process. In Lincoln's mind, it should be the president. Lincoln based this prerogative on his belief that he had been engaged for fours in suppressing an insurrection, which according to Lincoln's interpretation of the Constitution, was clearly an executive, not legislative responsibility. Moreover, Lincoln never asked Congress for a "declaration of war," only the right to use force to suppress an internal rebellion, the exact term he used in April 1861 when he called for 75,000 volunteers to join the United States Army for six months. Thus in Lincoln's mind no state of war existed between North and South because a "war" can only be fought between two "legitimate" nations. In Lincoln's view, the Confederate States of America, another "country," never existed because no state has the right to secede from the Union. Based on such an interpretation of his executive powers, Lincoln assumed the right to reorganize the South and guide it back into the Union largely on his own authority as commander-in-chief.

Many Congressional Republicans thought otherwise. They interpreted Lincoln's call for volunteers to suppress rebellion not to be an executive order but a declaration of war, which only Congress can approve. By sanctioning Lincoln's call for troops, Congress believed a state of war existed between the United States of America and another political entity, the Confederate States of America. If that were the case, then the legislative branch, not the executive branch, should have authority over reconstruction, for only Congress can declare war not the president; he can only ask for such a proclamation. Disturbing these Republicans most was Lincoln's apparent states' rights disposition. By insisting that secession was illegal, that the Southern states had never actually left the Union, Lincoln appeared to be asserting that the Southern states thus maintained their right to govern their own affairs. Such a rendering was completely unacceptable to hardline Republicans, who rejected any notion that the rebellious states had the right to immediately reclaim their antebellum status without retribution for their "treason." Congressional Republicans believed that the only way to avoid such an insult to the Union dead was to challenge Lincoln's interpretation of the "crisis" by defining the Civil War as a war rather than a rebellion. If that conception prevailed then they, not the president, would have the Constitutional right of jurisdiction over reconstruction, thus guaranteeing punishment of Confederate Southerners for their treasonous acts. This controversy coupled with the debate over the status of the freedmen destined the two branches of government for a showdown for power. Such a confrontation, however, would not occur until the ascendancy of Andrew Johnson to the presidency.

Radical Republicans and Reconstruction

Those Republicans who opposed Lincoln's agenda became known as the "radicals." These men, led by Charles Sumner of Massachusetts in the Senate and Thaddeus Stevens of Pennsylvania in the House, believed, contrary to Lincoln, that not only must the white South be punished for secession and rebellion but for the sin of slavery as well. To the radicals it was quite obvious and simple what should be done in the South in the war's aftermath: all white Southerners, regardless of status, should be punished for their treason, either by their property confiscated or disfranchisement, or both. Appropriated rebel land should then be given to freedmen to help them to establish themselves as an independent yeomanry. The Radicals feared that Lincoln's lenient policies would result in the old ruling class being restored to power. To prevent that possibility the radicals proposed that freedmen be given the right to vote, which, they believed, would ensure a genuine nucleus of loyal supporters in the South.

The Radicals countered with their own plan, the Wade-Davis bill (named for Senator Benjamin Wade of Ohio and Representative Henry Winter Davis of Maryland), which required white Southerners to take a much more stringent loyalty oath (the "iron clad oath" to be discussed later in the chapter) as well as requiring 50% rather than Lincoln's 10% of the population to swear allegiance to the Union. Surprisingly the Wade-Davis bill made no provision for black enfranchisement, the result of the radicals being a minority within the Republican party at that time (1864). The majority of Congressional Republicans were moderates and conservatives, cool to the idea of black voting rights and thus were more inclined to support Lincoln's agenda rather than that of the radicals. With such a coalition behind him, Lincoln killed the Wade-David bill with a pocket veto (whereby a bill passed at the end of a congressional session fails to become law if it is not signed by the president).

Lincoln's action enraged the radicals, who issued a blistering "manifesto' denouncing the president. However, the radicals' outrage failed to rally much support for their cause. By the fall of 1864, especially after the fall of Atlanta, a Union victory seemed imminent and with such a prospect Lincoln's popularity ascended, guaranteeing his reelection. Although upset

with Lincoln, the radicals were loyal Republicans and thus united with their more moderate comrades to ensure Lincoln's and their party's victory and control of both the White House and Congress. By the spring of 1865, the Confederacy's collapse was only a matter of weeks, setting the stage for a compromise between Lincoln and Congress on a policy 'for the postwar South. Two day's after Lee's surrender at Appomattox to Ulysses S. Grant, Lincoln promised that he would soon announce a more thorough reconstruction agenda, which he intimated would include provisions for black enfranchisement and stronger guarantees to protect their civil rights.

Tragically for the entire nation, no one will ever know what Lincoln had in store for the South or for 4 million African Americans. On April 14, 1865 as Lincoln and his wife watched a play at Ford's Theater in Washington, a rebel fanatic and failed actor named John Wilkes Booth, shot Lincoln at close range in the back of the head, leaped to the stage and escaped. Lincoln never recovered consciousness; he died early the next morning.

Booth was part of a larger conspiracy of rebel zealots which almost succeeded in beheading the national executive branch in one, coordinated fatal blow. While Wilkes murdered Lincoln, his two compatriots, Lewis Powell and George Atzerodt, were to kill Secretary of State William Seward (Powell's target) and Vice-president Andrew Johnson (Atzerdot's assigned victim). Powell came close with his knife, but Seward fought his attacker off and the Secret Service (the Pinkerton Detective Agency) arrived in time to save Seward and kill Powell. Atzerdodt got drunk and backed down. After a long and frantic search, Booth was captured and killed in a burning barn. Wilkes' bullet lost the North its hero; African Americans a potential ally for fair and equal opportunity; and Southern whites a leader who called for "charity toward all" and "malice toward none."

Andrew Johnson and Reconstruction

Between 1865 and 1868, the United States confronted one of the greatest political crisis of its history—the battle between President Andrew Johnson and Congress over Reconstruction. The struggle resulted in profound changes in the nature of citizenship, the structure of constitutional authority, and the meaning of American freedom

Booth's bullet elevated to the presidency a man who still thought himself a Democrat and a Southerner: Andrew Johnson of Tennessee. Originally from North Carolina, of poor white heritage, Johnson rose to power in Tennessee politics as a Jacksonian populist, championing the cause of the small, non-slaveholding farmers, shopkeepers, and artisans of East Tennessee against the planter elite of the state's central and western regions who controlled Tennessee politically. Indeed, Johnson was a Jacksonian to the core (his middle name was Jackson), sharing his namesake's suspicion of banks, corporations, bondholders and New Englanders. He fervidly opposed the Whig/Republican policy of government participation in, and promotion of, the nation's economic development. Johnson's enemies list included not only the plantation aristocracy but the "bloated, corrupt aristocracy" of the commercial-industrial economy emerging in the Northeast. A devoted Unionists Johnson was the only senator from a seceding state not to support the Confederacy. For his loyalty, the Republicans in 1864 rewarded him with their party's vice-presidential nomination, hoping that his presence on the ticket would

attract the votes of Northern pro-war Democrats and upper-South yeoman Unionists.

Although many radicals believed that Johnson would be too "soft" on his white Southern brethren, such concerns faded quickly as the new president displayed an enmity toward "the stuck up [slaveholding] aristocrats" that shocked at times even the most passionate of radicals. In Johnson's mind it was clear from the start that it was the South's slaveholding elite who had been responsible for secession and war. Thus the time had come to punish these "traitors. Treason must be made odious. Traitors must be impoverished; they must not only be punished, but their social power must be destroyed."

Suffice it to say, the radicals delighted in Johnson's harsh and proscriptive rhetoric. His rantings against the slaveocracy seemed to convey that he was in agreement with the radicals on the type of reconstruction policy to be pursued—one that would disenfranchise ex-Confederates but would enfranchise the freedmen. With Johnson's support, the radicals envisioned the creation of a coalition between the freedmen and the small minority of Southern white Unionists. Together they would become the basis for a new Southern political order; naturally they would become Republicans, the party of Union and emancipation. Once such a coalition took power in the Southern states they would pass laws to provide civil rights and economic opportunity for African Americans. Not incidentally, these new Republicans would also strengthen the party nationally by ending the Democracy's hegemony over the Southern states.

Much to the dismay of the radicals and even some moderate Republicans, Johnson proved hostile to the party's vision of the freedmen's place in society. Although earlier proclaiming to be black Tennesseans "Moses," leading them out of bondage, Johnson never embraced the liberal tenets of the antislavery ideology. Indeed, Johnson had owned slaves himself. The Civil War to Johnson was about secession and destroying the power of those responsible—the slaveholders; it was never a crusade to end slavery. In 1866 a black delegation led by Frederick Douglass visited with Johnson to urge the president to include provisions for black suffrage in his reconstruction agenda. Johnson parried their arguments and afterwards remarked to his secretary: "Those damned sons of bitches thought they had me in a trap! I know that damned Douglass; he is just like any other nigger, and he would sooner cut a white man's throat than not."

Johnson clearly was a racist, sharing with his white brethren North and South a firm belief in white supremacy. Johnson and other non-slaveholding white Southerners may have despised the slaveocracy, but it was not because they owned slaves; it had been their possession of disproportionate political power that had caused such antipathy. Not all Southern whites owned slaves (only about 20% of the total antebellum white population were classified as slaveholders; even if one owned a single slave), but they all owned white skins. To all Southern whites slavery was not only a system of labor exploitation but a method of racial control as well in which all whites had a vested interest in preserving. Even those white Southerners who disliked slavery did not believe in emancipation. The sociologist Pierre L. van den Berghe describes this rationalization for slavery and white supremacy as "Herrenvolk democracy"—the equal superiority of all who belong to the Herrenvolk (master race) over all who do not.

This ideology even took hold in the North, which saw the Democratic party aggressively champion white supremacy, resulting in the party's ability to attract to its camp the Irish, southern Midwest "Butternuts" (white Southerners who migrated to the southern areas of free states such as Indiana, Illinois, and Ohio) and unskilled laborers. All believed blacks to be inferior, and that no matter how poor they might be they were still better than blacks. Like their Southern nonslaveholding counterparts, they feared emancipation because it would render their whiteness meaningless. As one Butternut politician declared, "Break down slavery and you would with one blow destroy the democratic principle of equality among [white] men." Here was the central paradox of American history in 1860: slavery became for many whites the foundation of liberty and equality. Andrew Johnson was a hardcore believer in such tenets and thus vehemently opposed political and civil rights for black folk.

To the further consternation of many Republicans, Johnson, like Lincoln, believed reconstruction (which he preferred to call "restoration) to be primarily an executive function. He also believed in Lincoln's theory of "indestructible states"—that the rebellion had been one of individuals, not states, and although the individuals might be punished, the states retained all their constitutional rights. Given such conflicting views about who should control the reconstruction agenda and what the priorities were to be, it would only be a matter of time before the inevitable occurred: a nasty showdown between the president and a Republican-dominated Congress.

Johnson's Policy

Johnson fired the opening salvo in his war with Congressional Republicans when in May 1865 he issued two proclamations on his own initiative. The first provided for a blanket amnesty and restitution of property (except slaves, of course) to all who would take an oath of allegiance. Excluded from Johnson's general pardon were, Confederate civil and diplomatic officials; army officers above the rank of colonel; Confederate state governors; and all persons owning taxable property valued at $20,000 or more. Johnson was true to his word that he would punish those most responsible for having caused the war—"the stuck-up aristocrats." In his second edict, beginning with North Carolina, Johnson personally appointed provisional governors for the former Confederate states, directing them to call elections for delegates to draft new state constitutions. Only those white men who had received amnesty and had taken the oath of allegiance could vote. The state conventions were to draft constitutions that abolished slavery, nullified secession, and repudiated all debts incurred by the state when it was a member of the Confederacy (on the grounds that, secession being illegal, all indebtedness acquired in its behalf were null and void). Johnson's policy was clear. He would exclude both the freedmen and upper-class whites from the reconstruction process. The new political foundation for the "restored South" would be those yeomen and artisans who had remained loyal Unionists in alliance with those who now proclaimed themselves loyal.

Johnson outraged the radicals by his complete disregard for the freedmen and by his blatant slight of Congress. It appeared that Johnson was not only a dedicated white supremacist but intent on usurping power as well by arrogating to the executive branch complete control of reconstruction. In hopes of rallying Northern opinion to their side, the radicals organized a "Universal and Equal Suffrage Association" through which they bombarded Northern whites with speeches, pamphlets, and editorials, all declaring that the president's policies would inevitably lead to the restoration of the old power structure in the South, minus only slavery. Johnson responded to the radicals' railings against him, but not in a manner which eased their anxieties. He asked the provisional governors whom he had appointed, such as William L. Sharkey of Mississippi, who presided over the first state convention to meet under Johnson's plan, if Sharkey would ensure that his state's new constitution enfranchised literate blacks and those who owned property worth $250. Johnson knew that very few Mississippi freedmen would be able to meet this criterion. As the president told Sharkey, the stipulations were designed to "completely disarm the adversary [the radicals] and set an example the other states would follow. This you can do with perfect safety, and as a consequence, the radicals, who are wild upon negro franchise, will be completely foiled."

Johnson's message to Sharkey revealed a president who already viewed the radicals as "adversaries" to be "foiled." At best one in nine adult black males in the South could have qualified to vote under Johnson's mandates. Such a small number of black voters thus posed no immediate threat to white supremacy. Interestingly, if enacted the conditions would have put the South on a higher plane than the North, where only six states allowed African American males to vote on any terms. Unfortunately for Johnson's future, Southern whites paid no attention to his suggestion. None of the conventions made any provision for black suffrage in their new constitutions. The provisional governor of South Carolina declared why: "This is a white man's government, and intended for white men only. The Supreme Court of the United States has decided [in the Dred Scott case] that the negro is not an American citizen." Johnson made no more gestures in the direction of black enfranchisement. He stated that voting qualifications were a state matter and that it was beyond his constitutional right to interfere. Johnson's refusal to push any further for even a limited black suffrage not only alienated moderate Republicans but encouraged Southern defiance on other issues as well.

The Black Suffrage Issue in the North

The radical cause for black enfranchisement in the South received a devastating blow in the fall of 1865 when Connecticut, Minnesota, and Wisconsin, held referendums on whether or not to amend their respective constitutions to allow the few black men in their states the right to vote. Everyone knew, that in some measure the referendums' outcome would reveal much about white Northern racial attitudes. The Democrats in the three states engaged in their usual race-mongering and black-baiting, with the result that the amendments were defeated in all three states. In Connecticut the vote was 33,489 against to 27,717 for; in Minnesota, 14,840 against and 12,170 for; and in Wisconsin, 55,591 against to 46,588 for. Republicans in those states voted overwhelmingly for allowing black men the right to vote. Most contemporaries interpreted the election outcomes as a Northern white mandate against black suffrage. Southern whites were delighted with the results, for in their mind the amendments' defeat was confirmation that their Northern white brethren were just as determined to keep the United States "a white man's country." Perhaps more important, the defeat of black suffrage in the North only further emboldened Southern whites to flagrantly defy Johnson's reconstruction mandates.

Southern Defiance

Not only did the Southern state constitutional conventions reject black enfranchisement in any capacity, but some even balked at ratifying the 13th Amendment and at repudiating the Confederate debt. Once again, throughout the South, could be heard disparaging anti-Yankee rhetoric and deprecating and mocking of all things "Yankee." It sounded and felt like 1861 all over again. White, neo-Confederate paramilitary units appeared which terrorized blacks and their white sympathizers. Johnson seemed to encourage such activities by his own rhetoric and refusal to address such reprisals.

Compounding Johnson's troubles with white violence perpetrated on freedmen was the issue of presidential pardons. Indeed, this particular matter caused more immediate acrimony between the president and Congressional Republicans than any other controversy. After all his bluster about punishing Southern "traitors," by the fall of 1865 Johnson had reversed himself, issuing special pardons to 13,500 ex-Confederates, restoring to them all property and political rights. The majority of these individuals were the "stuck-up aristocrats" he had vowed he would "impoverish and destroy" only a few months earlier. What had caused this transformation in Johnson's attitude and behavior, from one who spoke menacingly about the crime of treason to one who now spoke of forgiveness? For one, Johnson was a Southerner and thus had no more liking for the radical Yankee ethos than the majority of his Southern brethren. Moreover, his exchanges and encounters with the radicals during the summer and fall of 1865 convinced him that his real friends were his Southern white compatriots, including the very individuals he once personally despised and publicly lambasted. They praised his policy and flattered his ego, while the radicals chastised him openly and moderates expressed their "concerns" in private. Reveling in his power over these once-haughty aristocrats who had deprecated him as a humble tailor, Johnson waxed eloquent on his "love, respect, and confidence" toward Southern whites, for whom he now felt "forbearing and forgiving." Perhaps more important was the outpouring of support by Northern Democrats, many of whom disingenuously whispered in his ear that he would be their party's choice in the 1868 election if he could manage to reconstruct the South in such a way that would maintain the Democratic majority there.

To the Republicans further apoplexy, under the new state constitutions established by Johnson's policy, southern voters were electing hundreds of ex-Confederates to state offices. Northerners were even more outraged by the election of nine ex-Confederate congressmen, seven ex-Confederate state officials, four generals, four colonels, and even former Confederate Vice-President Alexander H. Stephens, to Congress. To Republicans it appeared that the rebels, unable to capture Washington in war, were about to do so in peace.

The Black Codes

As many radicals feared, no sooner did Southern whites reclaim their governments than they passed the infamous "black codes," reflecting not only devotion to white supremacy but a determination as well to reduce the freedmen to a condition of virtual reenslavement. In effect, the codes relegated the freedmen to second-class citizenship; they were excluded from juries and voting and could not testify against whites in court. Also forbidden was interracial marriage and for certain crimes blacks suffered much harsher punishment than whites. Most states passed vagrancy laws, subjecting to forced labor on a plantation any unemployed freedmen. Blacks could not lease land and any black youth whose parents could not adequately provide for his care, was "apprenticed" to a white man.

Suffice it to say, the black codes outraged Republicans, who could not believe this latest manifestation of Southern white arrogance and brazenness. For many Republicans the codes were the last straw in their war with Andrew Johnson, whom they held responsible for this latest insult to the Union dead. As the *Chicago Tribune* declared, "We will tell the white men of Mississippi that the men of the North will convert the State of Mississippi into a frog pond before they will allow such laws to disgrace one foot of the soil in which the bones of our soldiers sleep and over which the flag of freedom waves."

Land and Labor in the Postwar South

Although blatantly racist and oppressive, the black codes were designed to address a legitimate problem. Emancipation plunged black-white relations into a world of uncertainty, fear, and hostility, with whites especially bitter toward their former slaves. In much of the South, the Yankee army had physically destroyed the Southern landscape and antebellum economy. Burned-out plantations, fields gone to seed, railroads without tracks, bridges, or rolling stock marked the effects of total war visited upon the South by the invading Federal army. Over half of the South's livestock was gone as well as much of its sustainable land, compounding already serious food shortages; possible starvation loomed for both white and black Southerners. Lawlessness was rampant as well, with roaming bands of hungry ex-rebel soldiers and black vagabonds, looking for food and shelter, often engaging in acts of violent crime to survive. The war ended early enough in the spring to allow the planting of at least some crops but who would plant and cultivate them? The South had lost one-quarter of its white farmers killed in the war and slaves were slaves no more.

Despite such travail, life went on. Soldiers' widows and their children plowed and planted; masters without slaves and their wives calloused their hands for the first time. Former slaveowners now had to "ask" their former chattels if they would be willing to work the land for wages or shares of the crop and many freedmen readily agreed to such a changed capital-labor relationship; plantation life and economy was all they had known for generations. Many freedmen, however, wanted nothing to do with their former masters, choosing instead to get as far away from the old plantation as possible. Thousands migrated to the nearest city or town in search of work there rather than return to the painful memory of bondage. Some wandered aimlessly, simply enjoying freedom as long as they could until getting hungry or "disciplined" by roaming white vigilante groups. Nonetheless, for the majority of freedmen, true emancipation meant never returning to the plantation. As a black preacher told his congregation, "You ain't, none of you, gwinter feel rale free till you shakes de dus' ob de ole plantashun offen yore fee an an' goes ter a new place why you kin live out o'sight o' de gret house." (dialect in original source).

The Freedmen's Bureau

Attempting to bring a semblance of order and stability to the South was the United States Army and the Freedmen's Bureau. Tens of thousands of United States troops remained in the South as an occupation force, establishing martial law in the ex-Confederate states until civil government could be restored. Perhaps more important to the history of Reconstruction, was the Freedmen's Bureau (the agency's official name was the Bureau of Refugees, Freedmen, and Abandoned Lands), created by Congress in March 1865. This particular federal initiative marked the first time in the history of the Republic the establishing by the national government of an agency to protect and promote the socio-economic welfare of its citizens. Although the bureau's primary purpose was to safeguard the freedmen from white reprisals, whether legal, physical, or from whatever form such retaliation might take, white Southerners too benefited from this program. The bureau issued food rations to 150,000 people daily in 1865, one-third of them to whites.

The Bureau's commissioner, General O.O. Howard had his headquarters in Washington. In each former slave state, an army general was assigned as assistant commissioner and directed his field operatives from the state's capital or largest city. The majority of the Bureau's 550 local agents were junior officers from middle class Northern backgrounds. Some took genuine interest in their charges' well-being, displaying a sincere belief in equality, while others were simply marking time until something better in the civilian world came along. Sadly, the officers of the latter disposition often displayed toward the freedmen the same racist attitudes and general disdain for blacks as their Southern white counterparts. The Bureau also appointed some civilian agents, including a few African Americans. Although the number of agents was too few to reach every corner of the South, these agents—backed by the army's occupation troops—nevertheless had considerable potential power to transform postwar Southern labor relations.

Once it became clear that the federal government intended no massive land redistribution for the freedmen's benefit, the Bureau then focused its energies on trying to forge a new relationship between planters and freedmen. The agents' main objective was to encourage (or require) planters and laborers to sign written contracts that specified the amount and kind of work to be done, the wages to be paid, and other conditions of employment. Wages agreed upon ranged from eight to fifteen dollars a month, plus room and board, and sometimes work clothes and equipment and even medical care. Freedmen were paid either in cash or a share of the crop. Because of a shortage of money, planters preferred to pay laborers with a percentage of the crop, which would not be paid until after harvest. Such a contract ensured worker loyalty by creating a relationship in which both planter and freedmen had a vested interest in getting the crops out of the ground. Thus, one of the Bureau's principal tasks was to protect freedmen from potential exploitation as its agents adjudicated thousands of complaints registered by black workers against their employers not only for abuse but for violation of contracts as well. Because Southern state courts would never give freedmen a fair hearing, General Howard urged Congress to revise the original bill to empower the Bureau to establish special courts to function as military tribunals until Congress declared the rebellious states restored to the Union. Johnson vetoed the new mandate but the increasingly radically-controlled Congress would not be deterred and overrode the president's rejection. With usually only one agent acting as judge and jury, these "special courts" remained in existence until 1868.

Not surprisingly, Southern whites, particularly the antebellum elite, came to despise the Bureau, denouncing it as "a curse," a "ridiculous folly," a vicious institution." Interestingly, such aspersions reflected not so much a hatred of the Bureau for what it did, but rather, for what it symbolized—conquest and emancipation. Ex-Rebel General Wade Hampton of South Carolina wrote in 1866: "The war which was so prolific of monstrosities, new theories of republican government, new versions of the Constitution, gave birth to nothing which equals in deformity and depravity this [the Freedmen's Bureau] 'Monstrum horrendum informe ingens.'" Planters insisted they could "make the nigger work" if meddling Bureau agents would only leave them alone. In reality, such complaints and denunciations were unfounded. More often than not, the Bureau proved to be more of a planter ally than a manifestation of emancipation and alleged white degradation. Agents got idle freedmen back to work and by enforcing contracts whose terms favored employers rather than workers. Reflecting sensitivity to criticism in both the Northern and Southern press that the Bureau was promoting a welfare ethic among freedmen, many Bureau officers would cut off rations to able-bodied blacks to force them to work. While publicly vilifying the Bureau, privately planters admitted that without it the postwar labor situation would have been even more chaotic. Indeed, in late 1865, the Bureau helped to suppress a possible "Christmas insurrection" among freedmen when they learned that they were not going to receive their anticipated "forty acres and a mule." In response to the news, thousands of freedmen throughout the South refused to sign contracts for the next year. To the Bureau fell the unhappy task of disab using the freedmen about land redistribution and compelling them to sign contracts.

In 1867, a Bureau official assessed the contract system: "It has succeeded in making the Freedman work and in rendering labor secure & stable—but it has failed to secure the Freedman his just dues or compensation."

The Issue of Land for the Landless

Naturally freedmen wanted land for themselves rather than having to work for former masters or other white folk. The majority of freedmen believed that only ownership of their own land would make them truly free. "What's de use of being free if you don't own land enough to be buried in?" asked one black man. "Might juss as well stay slave all yo' days." A black army veteran said: "Every colored man will be a slave, & feel himself a slave until he can raise his own *bale of cotton* & put his own mark upon it & say dis is mine!" For most slaves however, purchasing land was impossible; few of them had money, and even if they had, even the most destitute of whites often refused to sell or even rent land to them for fear of having African Americans other than subservient and dependent. Thus, freedmen looked to the federal government to help them gain true independence from continued white control. The hope for "forty acres and a mule" was no delusion of ignorant minds. By June 1865, the Freedmen's Bureau had appropriated along the Georgia and South Carolina coastal areas almost 500,000 acres of plantation lands and had settled in those areas nearly 10,000 black families. Also given to these freedmen by Army General William T. Sherman, were captured horses and mules so freedmen could work the land. Elsewhere in the South, Freedmen's Bureau agents took it upon themselves to reallocate to freedmen nearly a million acres of abandoned or confiscated land in their respective areas.

Such initiatives by Union generals and Bureau agents raised expectations throughout the South that all freedmen would soon be given their own land by a massive confiscation and redistribution plan being formulated in Washington. That was precisely the agenda envisioned by Radical Republicans such as Thaddeus Stevens of Pennsylvania, who advocated the appropriation of land owned by wealthy ex-Confederates and allocating forty acres of this land to each adult freedman. The remainder was to be sold to finance war pensions and repay the war debt. As Stevens declared in a congressional speech, "Strip a proud nobility of their bloated estates; send them forth to labor, and teach their children to enter the workshops or handle the plow, and you will thus humble the proud traitors." Thus in 1865, freedmen seemed to have good reason to hope for government assistance in obtaining land.

Unfortunately Andrew Johnson and Congress dashed such hopes. As noted earlier, Johnson's amnesty and pardon proclamation restored all property to their original owners and Congress failed to pass effective legislation that would have allowed for even abandoned land to be turned over to freedmen. Commissioner Howard however, refused to comply with Johnson's edicts. Howard considered the amnesty proclamation inapplicable to abandoned or confiscated property, which he interpreted as being "set apart [for use] by refugees and freedmen." Johnson believed otherwise, ordering Howard to restore property to all pardoned Confederates. But Howard ordered his agents to stall and delay as long as possible property restoration to rebels, hoping to retain as much land as possible until Congress met in December.

Howard hoped Congress would challenge the president on this issue and allow for the freedmen's possession of at least some of the land under Bureau control.

In February 1866 Congress passed an addendum to the Freedmen's Bureau bill that allowed for those freedmen given land along the Georgia and South Carolina coastal areas to keep the land for three years. But Johnson vetoed the bill and Congress failed to pass it over the veto. In July 1866 Republicans finally managed to pass a revised bill over the president's veto but the new law called for the displacement of freedmen from Georgia and South Carolina proper to those states' respective offshore islands! Worse, the dispossessed freedmen now had to purchase the government-held land on those islands, albeit at a price below market value. Only about 2,000 displaced black families were able to purchase the offshore land. The new policy marked a sad denouement to the high hopes of 1865. By the end of 1866, nearly all the arable land once controlled by the Freedmen's Bureau had been returned to its ex-Confederate owners.

Perhaps to atone for such betrayal, Congress passed the Southern Homestead Act soon after its earlier measure had displaced Georgia and South Carolina freedmen. Similar in design and purpose to the 1862 Homestead Act for the Great Plains area (the former "Great American Desert"), this law set aside 44 million acres of public land in five Southern states (Alabama, Arkansas, Florida, Louisiana, and Mississippi) to be parceled out in 80 acre allotments, to black settlers. If they improved the land over a five-year period, then, as stipulated in the 1862 act, it was theirs for the keeping, free of charge. In order to ensure that the land designated in these states went to freedmen and Unionist whites, the law forbade anyone who had supported the Confederacy from settling in

the specified areas. Generous in conception, the Southern Homestead Act was largely a failure in practice. Typically, most of the remaining public land in these states was marginal at best and few freedmen possessed enough money to purchase seed, tools, livestock, and building materials in order to improve the land. Consequently, fewer than 7,000 freedmen relocated to these states and only 1,000 of these homesteaders were able to fulfill the requirements for final ownership. Thus, meaningful land reform did not become part of Reconstruction, and with such a failure came the inevitable return of the majority of freedmen to a status of quasi-bondage (debt peonage) in the form of share-cropping and tenant farming.

The Origins of Radical Reconstruction

It was only a matter of time before the growing schism between Andrew Johnson and the Republican-dominated 39th Congress would escalate into an outright power struggle over who should control the Reconstruction process and dictate its agenda. However, not until the radicals gained dominance within the party did a full-fledged assault on the president become a certainty. As long as Republicans divided along radical, moderate, and conservative alignments, Johnson's reconstruction policies would prevail. However, once Republicans put aside their differences and united in a determination to oppose Johnson and agree on the course reconstruction should take, then the president's days as an effective leader would indeed be numbered.

Conservative Republicans were generally satisfied with Andrew Johnson's policies, although some wished the president would do more to protect the freedmen from violence and discrimination. Some moderates agreed with the radicals that the president's policies failed to safeguard the fruits of the Northern victory. Yet, they were unwilling to support the radicals' call for black suffrage, fearing that such action would alienate Northern voters, driving them into the Democratic fold. They also feared breaking with Johnson, believing such a rupture would also benefit the Democrats. All Republicans, however, united in opposing the seating of the newly-elected Southern representatives to Congress, for all agreed that the election of so many ex-Confederates was an insult to the Union dead and a mockery of the Northern cause. To the radicals' chagrin, Johnson did not contest the Republicans on this issue, conceding that Congress had the right to judge the qualifications of its own members.

What good will existed between Republicans and the president began to evaporate when Johnson vetoed two bills to protect the freedmen. The first extend the life of the Freedmen's Bureaus, expanded its legal powers, and authorized the agency to build and support schools. The second bill defined the freedmen's civil rights and gave federal courts appellate jurisdiction in cases concerning these rights. Moderates, who believed that they had Johnson's support for these measures, felt duped and betrayed by the president, who declared in his veto message that he never contemplated a "system for the support of indigent persons"— the freedmen. As the moderate leader Lyman Trumbull of Illinois declared to the Senate, "I thought in advocating [the bill], that I was acting in harmony with the views of the President. I regret exceedingly the antagonism his message presents to the expressed views of Congress. He believes the freedman will be protected without it; I believe he will be tyrannized over, abused, and virtually reenslaved without some legislation by the nation for his

protection." Trumbull wanted his Republican colleagues to pass the measure over Johnson's veto, but five conservatives voted against it and the motion fell short of the required two-thirds majority.

Johnson knew his veto would alienate the moderates and move him toward an alliance with the Democrats, who held mass rallies in support of the president's veto. After one such gathering, the celebrants marched to the White House where Johnson feted the crowd with one of the most remarkable presidential speeches ever delivered. Johnson denounced the radicals as traitors who did not want the Union restored. He also told the crowd that the radicals were plotting his assassination, comparing them to Judas and himself to Christ. "If my blood is to be shed because I vindicate the Union and the preservation of this government in its original purity and character, let it be shed; let an altar to the Union be erected, and then if it is necessary, take me and lay me upon it, and the blood that now warms and animates my existence shall be poured out as a fit libation to the Union."

The president's behavior mortified many Americans. "Was he drunk?" they asked. Radicals could now declare to their moderate colleagues that "I told you so!" Even some Republican conservatives such as Senator William Pitt Fessenden of Maine admitted privately that, "the President's recent exhibitions of folly and wickedness" had disillusioned him. "He has broken the faith, betrayed his trust, and must sink from detestation to contempt." The final straw for moderate and radical Republicans came with Johnson's veto in March 1866 of a civil rights bill for freedmen, initiated by Trumbull. The measure defined freedmen as United States citizens and guaranteed their rights to own or rent property, to make and enforce contracts, and to have access to the courts as parties and as witnesses. In effect, it affirmed the rights of African Americans to "the full and equal benefit of all laws and proceedings for the security of person and property as is enjoyed by white citizens." Interestingly, Trumbull's initiative did not call for black enfranchisement, nor mandate that African Americans sit on juries, nor require integrated schools and public accommodations. Republicans therefore expected Johnson to sign this moderate bill despite his states' rights convictions. Even his cabinet was unanimous in urging the president to sign the measure.

Like his earlier veto, this one also provoked Democratic euphoria and Republican condemnation. Democratic editors rejoiced that Johnson did not believe "in compounding our race with niggers, gipsies [sic], and baboons." If Congress could declare African Americans citizens, said another party organ, "how long will it be before it will say the negro shall vote, sit in the jury box, and intermarry with your families? Such are the questions put by the President." If Johnson's objective with his vetoes had been to isolate the radicals while forging a moderate/conservative coalition in support of his policy, he had badly miscalculated just how far moderates were willing to go to obtain at least a modicum of rights for the freedmen.

The Fourteenth Amendment

Johnson had thrown down the gauntlet with his veto of the Freedmen's Bureau and Civil Rights bills and congressional Republicans, led by the radicals did not hesitate to pick it up, pushing through Congress in June 1866 the Fourteenth Amendment to the Constitution. (It would take an additional two years before the requisite

two-thirds of the states ratified the amendment). The measure defined all native-born and naturalized person, including African Americans, as American citizens and prohibited the states from denying any such individual from the "privileges and immunities" of citizenship and from depriving "any person of life, liberty, or property without due process of law." The initiative further mandated that states enfranchise black males or they would forfeit a proportionate number of congressional seats and electoral votes. Another section barred a significant number of ex-Confederates from holding federal or state offices while repudiating the Confederate debt. All of the bill's stipulations were to be enforced by Congress by "appropriate legislation."

White Southerners and Democrats naturally denounced the bill as one more manifestation of radical vengeance on men who had already suffered enough for their sins. Radicals countered by declaring the measure did not go far enough to punish traitors and prevent their political resurgence. Radicals and abolitionists also decried the bill for not making fiat in all states black enfranchisement. The bill penalized Southern states from denying black suffrage but allowed Northern states to do so with impunity because their black population was too small to make a difference in the basis of representation. Abolitionists condemned the bill as a "swindle," a "wanton betrayal of justice and humanity." It was "only fitted to protect the North and the white race, while it leaves the Negro to his fate," declared the American Antislavery Society. "It is the blighted harvest of the bloodiest sowing the fields of the world ever saw."

For the moment the radicals accepted the amendment as the best they could get while hoping that future events would move the country toward universal African American male suffrage. Despite radical and abolitionist lamentations, the Fourteenth Amendment had far-reaching consequences; the initiative became the most important Constitutional provision for defining and enforcing civil rights in the nation. Unlike the first 10 amendments (the Bill of Rights), which imposed restrictions on federal power, the Fourteenth Amendment greatly expanded federal authority to prevent state violations of civil rights. To the radicals' joy the bill also greatly expanded African American rights (at least on paper), while curtailing ex-Confederates' political power. That is why Johnson and his Democratic supporters, with their states' rights, proslavery mentality, opposed it.

The 1866 Congressional Elections

In many ways the 1866 congressional elections were a referendum on the Fourteenth Amendment, which the Republicans made the centerpiece of their party's platform. Since moderates still held sway in the party, they offered Southerners a carrot: any ex-Confederate state that ratified the amendment would be declared "reconstructed" and its representatives and senators could then take their respective Congressional seats. Tennessee accepted this overture, ratified the amendment and its representatives and senators were duly seated. Johnson, believing he could still stem the Congressional/Republican tide against him by rallying Southern and Northern Democrats to his position, unwisely counseled other Southern legislatures to reject the amendment and they did so. Johnson then prepared for an all-out campaign to gain a pro-administration Northern majority in the congressional elections by cobbling together a coalition of a few conservative Republicans,

border-state Unionists, and Democrats. The "new" party called itself the National Union Party and had the backing of such notables as old New York Whigs Henry Seward, Thurlow Weed, and Henry J. Raymond, editor of the New York *Times*. These men along with other conservative Republicans hoped they could keep Democrats from overwhelming the party but that proved delusional. No sooner was the coalition formed than the Democratic tail soon began to wag the National Union dog, thus dooming from the outset the party's chances of victory at the polls. Northern voters remained suspicious of Democrats, many of whom still believed the party had betrayed the country by opposing the war. Also adversely affecting Johnson and his coalition was the ongoing violence against freedmen, which resulted in vicious race riots in New Orleans and Memphis, where white mobs rampaged against freedmen and their white allies, killing 80 blacks, among them several former Union soldiers. The endemic violence against African Americans only served to confirm the Republican contention that without greater federal protection and intervention in the South, African Americans were doomed to a life of perpetual fear, proscription, and terror.

Perhaps the National Union Party's greatest liability was Andrew Johnson, who in a speech in St. Louis soon after the melees in New Orleans and Memphis, blamed Republicans for provoking the white mobs while expressing no regret for the victims. In a whistle-stop tour of the North (a "swing around the circle," Washington to Chicago and St. Louis and back to Washington), Johnson engaged in shouting contests with hecklers and traded insults with hostile crowds. The substance of his speeches never varied: the South was loyal; the real traitors were the radicals, who were bent of revenge, further polarizing the nation, and he, Andrew Johnson, was willing to give his life if necessary for the Union's and the Constitution's salvation. In virtually every speech Johnson closed by comparing himself to Jesus and his Republican adversaries to Judas. Johnson reminded audiences that Jesus had come to earth to forgive men rather than to condemn them. "He died and shed His own blood that the world might live. If more blood is needed, erect an altar, and upon it your humble speaker will pour out the last drop of his blood as a libation for his country's salvation." Johnson had clearly lost control of himself and the country as well. The National Union Party was embarrassingly routed at the polls, with the Republicans sweeping the election and gaining a 3-to-1 majority in the next Congress. The party gained ascendancy in every Northern state as well as in West Virginia, Missouri, and Tennessee. As one moderate-turned-radical Republican declared, "The [Southern Democrats] would not cooperate in rebuilding what they destroyed, so we must remove the rubbish and rebuild from the bottom. Whether they are willing or not, we must compel obedience to the Union and demand protection for its humblest citizens." Southern intransigence and the condoning of the wanton, often violent persecution of the freedmen coupled with Johnson's tacit if not blatant approval of both actions, accomplished what the radicals alone could not achieve: the conversion of moderates to black suffrage and the congressional takeover of the reconstruction process.

The Reconstruction Acts of 1867

No sooner did the Republicans gain control of Congress with the radicals in the ascendancy, than the history of the post-war South took yet another turn, one which many Southern whites to this day, would come to despise. As far as the radicals and many of their once-moderate allies were concerned, the South had yet to be "properly" reconstructed; nor had Southern whites sufficiently atoned for their sins of slavery and secession—treason. Until that reformation occurred, the South would have to be placed under martial law, for not only the freedmen's protection but for those white Southerners who had remained loyal to the Union. Thus the 1867 Reconstruction act divided the 10 Southern states into five military districts under the authority of a Union general and whose sub-commanders in the states in his district were to register voters for the election of delegates to new constitutional conventions. *All* adult males over the age of 21 were to be enfranchised to vote in those elections. However, the act disenfranchised (for these elections only) those ex-Confederates who were disqualified from holding office under the not-yet-ratified Fourteenth Amendment, which translated to fewer than 10 percent of all eligible white male voters. The act further stipulated that all new state constitutions had to ratify the Fourteenth Amendment as well as guarantee equal civil and political rights to all citizens, regardless of race; until that occurred, the state's congressional representatives would not be seated.

The radicals believed that the reduction of ex-Confederate states to the status of "conquered territories" would bode well for their larger vision and agenda for Southern reconstruction. They hoped that such a condition would allow time for the Freedmen's Bureau, freedmen's aid societies, Northern soldiers and settlers, and Northern money to flow into the South to help elevate and educate the freedmen and protect them from white reprisals. The radicals believed that until the Southern rebels felt the heavy hand of national power and presence, they would continue to resist all attempts at reformation. In many ways the radicals hoped to rebuild a "new" South in a Northern image, in which, as historian David Donald described, would be a land of "small farms, thrifty tillage, free schools, closely-associated communities, social independence, respect for honest labor, and equality of political rights." In effect, the radicals hoped to remake the South within the context of the free-labor ideology that had come to inform the Republican party since its inception in 1856.

The 1867 Reconstruction acts reflected a true revolution—"the maddest, most infamous revolution in history," according to many Southern whites. Just a few years earlier white Southerners had been masters of 4 million slaves and leaders of an independent Confederate nation. Now they had been stripped of political power and their former slaves not only freed but politically empowered as well. The "Old South" was (temporarily) vanquished and the radicals could not have been more delighted, for as they argued correctly, the revolution that began in 1863 with emancipation would never be realized as long as the old master class retained economic and social preeminence.

Despite radical hopes that all would go smoothly with the presence of federal troops Southern whites continued to breathe defiance and refused to cooperate. Although white reprisals on the freedmen somewhat abated, thousands of white Southerners who were eligible to vote refused to do so, hoping that their non-participation would delay the process long enough for Northern voters (the majority of whom were as racist as their Southern brethren) to come to their senses and elect Democrats to Congress to reverse this "mad revolution."

Literate freedmen, white Southern unionists, and northern white emigrants organized Union leagues to inform and mobilize new black voters into the Republican party. Southern Democrats contemptuously labeled southern white Republicans as "scalawags" and northern migrants as "carpetbaggers." It was obvious to the Southern "loyalists" (to the Lost Cause) that the radicals intended to use the new black registrants and their white allies to gain control of the upcoming constitutional conventions. Since white Republicans were a minority in the South, the key to establishing such regimes in the Southern states was the black vote. Thus, in order to prevent blacks from registering and voting, whites engaged in all manner of terrorists activities against freedmen, officially sanctioning such reprisals with the organization of the Ku Klux Klan in Pulaski, Tennessee in 1867. Although the Klan's terrorizing of blacks and whites who supported the radical agenda would not become a serious problem until the early 1870s, the fact that such an organization emerged rather early in Reconstruction reflected white determination to resist any changes in the socio-political order that the war had brought.

With their huge majority, congressional Republicans were confident that could stymie the President's capacity to thwart the enactment of the new reconstruction mandates. However, as commander in chief of the army and as head of the branch of government charged with executing the laws, Johnson still retained great power to frustrate the implementation of congress's stipulations. Johnson made clear his intention to do so. Indeed, the President did all he could to try to stop the radical momentum. He replaced several Republican generals in command of Southern military districts with Democrats; he had his attorney general issue a ruling that interpreted the Reconstruction acts so narrowly that Congress had to hold a special session in July 1867 to pass supplementary measures, "clarifying" and specifying exactly what the previous acts had decreed. And in the process, decided to impose even harsher mandates on the South. For instance, Southern provisional governments became subordinate in all respects to military rule, and a district's military commander had the "discretion" (power) to remove any civilian officials they considered "disloyal." The new act also empowered voter registration boards to reject a voter's oath if they believed it "suspect" (falsely sworn), as well as determine more broadly the categories by which ex-Confederates could be disfranchised.

Johnson meanwhile encouraged Southern whites to obstruct and delay voter registration and the election of convention delegates. Never in the history of the Republic had these two branches been more bitterly at odds.

Johnson's plan in obstructing the congressional agenda was to retard the process until 1868, in the hope that northern voters would repudiate the radicals' program and elect him president on a Democratic ticket. Encouraging Johnson in this direction were the off-year state elections, held in the fall of 1867, which saw Republicans take a beating at the polls in several Northern states, especially where they endorsed referendum measures to enfranchise black males. After the elections results, one gleeful pro-Johnson supporter declared that, "I almost pity the radicals. After giving ten states to the negroes, to keep the Democrats from getting them, they will have lost the rest. Any party with an abolition head and a nigger tail will soon find itself with nothing left but the head and tail." Such Democratic euphoria, however, was destined to be short-lived; there

was no way the radicals would allow Johnson to prevail on these crucial issues. Many were willing to go to any extreme necessary to defeat the president, even if it meant removing him from office. In short, increasing numbers of radicals concluded that the South's "proper" reconstruction would never come about as long as Andrew Johnson was president of the United States. They thus put forth a concerted effort to impeach the president and remove him from office, hoping to replace him with the radical president pro tem of the Senate, Benjamin Wade of Ohio.

The Impeachment of Andrew Johnson

The radicals' drive to rid themselves of the "Johnson nuisance" began with the passage of the 1867 Tenure of Office Act, which required Senate approval of the president's removal of any cabinet members. Johnson naturally vetoed the bill, rightly declaring it to be unConstitutional. In Johnson's view, the act violated presidential authority and prerogative: the right of presidential appointment of cabinet members. Although all such individuals selected by the president had to be approved by the Senate, once confirmed, the president could remove them at his discretion. Thus, in many ways, the conflict between Johnson and the radicals reflected a much larger struggle between the executive and legislative branches for supremacy; in this instance the right to determine national policy relative to Southern reconstruction.

Adding to the "sensitivity" of this particular showdown was the fact that through the course of the war, Lincoln greatly expanded presidential power, ranging from the unprecedented issuance of executive orders to the suspension of the writ of habeas corpus, all in the

Andrew Johnson, *ca. 1921–ca. 1921*

they contended Johnson, (not Lincoln), had so egregiously upset. In reality, however, the radicals simply used such arguments to mask their own personal antipathy toward Johnson's "copperheadeness" and obvious pro-Southern and anti-freedmen sentiments. Although Johnson brought upon himself much of the radicals' scorn and opposition with his arrogance, self-righteousness, and general personality flaws, he nonetheless did not warrant impeachment; constitutionally none of his actions could be considered "Treason, Bribery, or other high Crimes and Misdemeanors." The radicals, however, asserted that impeachment was not a criminal proceeding but rather a means of punishing a public official for "grave misuse of his powers, or any mischievous nonuse of them—for any conduct which harms the public or perils its welfare." In the radical view, Johnson's obstructionist policies and his consorting with rebels to oppress the freedmen and restore the political status quo antebellum had most definitely harmed the public welfare. To substantiate their position, radicals pointed to Johnson's wholesale pardons of ex-Rebels,, his open defiance of Congress, his intimation that Congress was an illegal body, his disgraceful public speeches, and his complicity by inaction in the New Orleans and Memphis riots. As one moderate Republican warned: "If Johnson fails to execute the laws, in their spirit as well as in their letter, if holding the South in his hand, either by direct advice or personal example he shall encourage them to such resistance to progress as may tend to defeat the public will, the President may, may after all, come to be regarded as an 'obstacle' which must be deposed."

name of national security and crisis. Indeed, Lincoln perhaps became the most notorious executive violator of civil liberties and other usurpations of Constitutional authority. As a result, during Lincoln's presidency, Congress increasingly found itself becoming subservient to the executive branch. In the eyes of many radicals, Johnson's obstructionism provided the perfect opportunity (or excuse) to reverse such an imbalance in national power, which

Andrew Johnson

The radicals believed Johnson had demonstrated no intention of enforcing the law in good faith and thus wanted to begin impeachment proceedings immediately. Moderates, however, still hoped to avoid such a controversy, fearing that impeachment might make Johnson a martyr. Unfortunately for Johnson, he allowed his petulance and arrogance to get the better of him, and to the radicals' delight, he took their "bait" (the Tenure of Office Act), and fired the last member of his cabinet, Secretary of War Edwin Stanton, who supported congressional reconstruction. In order to try to stave off a full-fledged radical assault on his administration, Johnson attempted to mollify Republicans with the appointment of General Ulysses S. Grant as interim Secretary of War. Grant was the most popular man in the country, and despite a personal aversion to politics, Republicans were determined to make him their standard-bearer in 1868. However, some radicals worried that Grant's acceptance of the position reflected his support of the president's policies; to their great relief it did not. Indeed, Grant had urged Johnson not to remove Stanton and he only accepted the position so he could serve as a buffer between Johnson and the army to prevent Johnson from doing more mischief. Grant, for example, refused Johnson's request to replace the more zealous, "radically-inclined" commanders of the military districts, such as Grant's best friend, General William T. Sherman, of the Louisiana-Texas district, with more "compliant" individuals. Grant refused and eventually resigned from the office, turning the reigns of power back to Stanton! In the meantime, Johnson took the initiative to replace Sheridan and a whole host of other generals with men of a more moderate disposition, especially toward Southern whites. As predicted, these moves outraged the radicals, for Johnson's actions further encouraged the growing Southern resistance to reconstruction. By February 1868, both moderate and radical Republicans had had enough; the Republican-controlled House voted to impeach Johnson by a vote of 126-47. All 47 opposition votes were Democratic. The official reason for impeachment was Johnson's violation of the Tenure of Office Act; the real reason was Johnson's stubborn defiance of three-quarters of Congress on the most important issue before the nation—Reconstruction.

Under the Constitution, impeachment by the House does not remove an official from office. The process is more like a grand jury indictment that must be tried by a petit jury—the Senate, which sat as a court to try Johnson on the impeachment charges brought by the House. If convicted by a two-thirds majority of the Senate, Johnson would be removed from office and president pro tem of the Senate, Benjamin Wade, a radical, would become president.

Tension filled the Senate chambers as Johnson's impeachment trial began on March 4, 1868. The trial proved to be long and complicated, which boded well for Johnson by allowing passions to cool. Also a plus for Johnson was his defense counsel, which included some of the best lawyers in the country: Henry Stanbery, the attorney general; William M. Evarts, a future secretary of state; and Benjamin R. Curtis, a former Supreme Court justice, who had written the principal dissenting opinion in the Dred Scott case. During the trial these men demonstrated greater legal acumen than their opponents. These counselors argued that a government official can be impeached only for criminal offenses that would be indictable in ordinary courts; Johnson had committed no crime by seeking to test the constitutionality of the Tenure of Office Act. In short, they exposed the act's technical ambiguities that raised doubts about whether Johnson had actually violated it.

To counter these assertions, the "impeachers" argued that to allow a president to disobey a law in order to test it in court would set a dangerous precedent; and regardless of whether Johnson was guilty of any crime, impeachment was a political rather than a criminal process. In short, to the radicals and their supporters, Johnson had been impeached and was now on trial for two years of relentless opposition to the Republican reconstruction vision and agenda. As one congressman observed, Johnson's "crime" was "the one great overshadowing of reconstructing the rebel States in accordance with his own will, in the interests of the great criminals who carried them into the rebellion." Perhaps most important, Johnson's impeachment reflected the culmination of the long power struggle between Congress and the executive, which as alluded earlier, began with the Lincoln administration. As one advocate of impeachment declared, "The great question to be decided is whether the National Legislature is to be as omnipotent in American politics as the English is in English politics. May we not anticipate a time when the President will no more think of vetoing a bill passed by Congress than the British crown thinks of doing?" This particular remark was absurd, not only at the time but will be forever in American politics, for relegating the executive branch to such a status would be a blatant contravention of the sanctity of the checks and balance system, which would not only cause the Founding Fathers to rise from the dead, but more important, would be totally unacceptable to the American people. In effect, in many ways, Congress, not Johnson, had become the abusers

and usurpers of power. Many moderates and the American public feared the creation of a precedent by which a two-thirds majority of Congress could remove any president who happened to disagree with them. In short, despite public and partisan disgust with Johnson, neither moderate Republicans nor the American people wanted to emasculate or disgrace the executive branch.

Thus, behind the scenes moderates and other anti-impeachment coalitions worked to get Johnson to concede on some of the key reconstruction issues that had caused the crisis. Apparently, the president understood the gravity of his predicament, and responded positively to such overtures. He conducted himself with dignity and restraint during the trial; he gave no more self-righteous, emotionally-charged, irrational speeches or interviews; and most important, he promised to enforce the Reconstruction acts. As a further sign of conciliation (even capitulation), Johnson appointed General John M. Schofield as Secretary of War, an individual acceptable to all factions. Johnson's willingness to reach such accords with Congress portended well for his acquittal. However, such a prospect remained in doubt until the very end. The final roll call took on the dimensions of high drama; not until West Virginia's Senator Peter G. Van Winkle, near the end of the alphabet, voted nay, did it become clear that Johnson had been acquitted by one vote short of the necessary two-thirds majority. The final tally was 35-19; had Van Winkle voted yes, Andrew Johnson would have become the first president in United States history to have been removed from office. Johnson remained on his good behavior for the rest of his term; Congressional (radical) reconstruction proceeded without any further presidential hindrance; and a crisis that had shaken the constitutional system to its foundation ended without any fundamental altering of that system.

The Southern Response to the Reconstruction Acts

Much to the surprise and disappointment of many radicals, prominent ex-Confederates advised their white compatriots to accept the inevitable—defeat and the end of slavery—and comply with the laws. The thinking of such members of the antebellum elite was that cooperation with the congressional mandates would allow them to influence the process in a moderate direction, especially when it came to the freedmen issue. Many of these individuals still possessed their sense of pre-war paternalism and thus saw themselves as the freedmen's "natural" protectors and benefactors, who knew what was best for their "people." They certainly believed they knew their "negroes" better than any alien Yankee intruders, whom they believed (somewhat correctly) were only using the freedmen as political pawns to remake the South into a Republican majority. The old elite thus organized interracial political meetings and barbecues at which they urged the freedmen to vote Democratic with their fellow white Southerners in order to keep out the Yankees. This "convergence" approach became known as the New Departure, and it became part of a persistent effort in postwar Southern politics, led mainly by former Whigs, to create a moderate third force independent of both Democrats and Republicans. These New Departure advocates believed in enfranchising the freedmen as well as guaranteeing them their full civil rights. That is not to suggest such individuals believed in equality; to a man they were all

committed racists but they nonetheless believed that it was wrong to wage aggressive war on the freedman, strip of his basic Constitutional rights, ostracize him, humiliate him, and rob him of elemental human dignity. In short, to the proponents of convergence, African American degradation was not a necessary corollary of white supremacy. As prominent antebellum attorney William Pitt Ballinger of Texas told a friend, although freedmen were "in our power," whites, particularly those of Ballinger's class, were their "custodians. We should extend to them as far as possible, all civil rights that will help them to be decent and self-respecting, law-abiding, and intelligent citizens. If we do not help elevate them they will surely bring us down." As far as Ballinger (and other New Departure proponents) was concerned it was time for white Southerners "to bury the past and move forward." Southern whites had to accept "the fact of the negro's right to vote," and thus white reprisals of "intimidation & violence" toward freedmen must end. Indeed, Ballinger believed it was time for all white Southerners to "gracefully and magnanimously acquiesce in accomplished facts," by "acknowledging the negro's legal status" and accept them as "full citizens." By downplaying the issue of race, Ballinger and his compatriots hoped convergence would attract black votes, for African Americans would realize that their true "guardians" were patricians, like himself and not the radicals. The New Departure movement also hoped to win the support of moderate and conservative white Republicans once they became convinced that the postwar South's "true" leaders had accepted "the accomplished facts of the war."

Unfortunately, Ballinger's and others' pleas for moderation and accommodation went unheard. The majority of white Southerners rejected the legitimacy of Reconstruction or the permanence of black suffrage. Even among many of its supporters, the New Departure was less of a genuine commitment to the democratic revolution manifested in Reconstruction, than a strategy for mollifying Northerners about the Southern Democratic party's intentions. Most Northern whites knew that in their hearts few of their Southern brethren accepted black civil and political equality. As a Mississippi editorial declared in 1871, "We are led to this course, not through choice, but by necessity—by the stern logic of events."

Not only did the insincerity of many convergence advocates hurt the New Departure movement but so did the imperatives of the two-party system, just as they had doomed the National Union movement in the North. Moreover, the Republicans demonstrated an ability to mobilize black voters en masse under their banner, reflecting that the party of Lincoln and emancipation had an unbeatable advantage in this respect. Equally important, much to the chagrin of New Departurites, no matter how sincere in their commitment to black civil and political rights many may have been such as William Pitt Ballinger, the majority of African Americans simply could not bring themselves to trust that their former masters would, in the end, be willing to extend such privileges as fully as they had claimed.

Assisting Republicans in mobilizing black voters was the Freedmen's Bureau and the Union League, which together were capable of overwhelming any efforts by the "convergers" to draw black voters away from the Republican party. Indeed, some Bureau agents served simultaneously as Union League officials and, in their military capacity, as supervisors of voter registration under the Reconstruction Acts. These partisan activities gave white Southerners another reason to condemn the Bureau—not only did it intervene in their labor relations with the freedmen but now it was helping to rally these workers into an alien political party. A Republican success in wooing black voters to the Grand Old Party became clear, many Southern whites, including some "convergers," began to change their tune about "accommodation." Yet, many remained sanguine that somehow or other, Andrew Johnson or the Northern Democrats could reverse the process and overthrow the radicals. All such hopes, however, were dashed with Johnson's impeachment proceedings, which in effect, turned Johnson into one of the "lamest of duck" presidents in the Republic's history. The way was now clear for the completion of congressional reconstruction.

The Completion of Formal Reconstruction

Under the mandates established by the Reconstruction Acts of 1867, the Southern states held their constitutional conventions during the winter and spring of 1867-68. Hostile whites, especially those who had been disenfranchised by the "iron-clad oath," derisively referred to the gathering as the "Bones and Banjoes Conventions" and the Republican delegates, many of whom were black, as "ragamuffins and jailbirds, baboons, monkeys, and mules." In a typical denunciation, Louisiana conservatives labeled the new charter written by the state convention as a "base conspiracy against human nature. It is the work of ignorant negroes cooperating with a gang of white adventurers." No doubt the Republican party dominated the assemblages, comprising 75% of the delegates attending the 10 state conventions. About one-quarter of those Republicans were relocated Northern whites ("carpetbaggers"); 45 percent were native Southern whites ("scalawags"); and about 30 percent were African Americans. Only in South Carolina were blacks in the majority. In Louisiana 50% of the attendees were African American, while in Texas, only 10% of the delegates were freedmen. Regardless of their number, the black delegates constituted the elite of their race. At least half of them had been free before the war, and most those who had been slaves belonged to the upper strata of the slave community. About four-fifths of all the black delegates were literate. Their predominant occupations were clergymen, teacher, artisan, and independent yeoman farmers. Contrary to white backlash propaganda, very few were former field hands or unskilled, illiterate laborers.

Much to the consternation of the white backlash, the delegates produced some of the most progressive state constitutions in the nation. In all ten states of the ex-Confederacy, universal male suffrage was enacted, putting the South ahead of most Northern states in this most controversial issue. Some of the constitutions disfranchised certain classes of ex-Confederates for several years more, but by 1872 all such restrictions had been lifted. Ironically, as will be seen later in this chapter, the removal of such disqualifications allowed for Southern whites by the early 1870s to "redeem" their states; that is, a return to white supremacy and political control by the antebellum elite. For the first time in Southern history a mandated public school system was established for both races. However, the constitutions permitted segregated schools but formal education of any kind for African Americans represented a great step forward. Most of the constitutions expanded the state's responsibility for social welfare beyond anything previously known in the South. Some constitutions established state boards of public charities and several of them enacted badly needed prison reforms and reduced the number of capital

crimes. Such welfare expansion naturally had to be paid for and thus property taxes increased significantly. As will be seen later in this chapter, alleged exorbitant taxation became the initial rallying cry of the "redeemers."

Despite the increases, most states provided homestead exemptions that assisted small landowners by exempting from taxation real and personal property up to $2,000 or $3,000 from attachment for debts. Although some of the radical attendees urged confiscating the land of disfranchised ex-Confederates, no convention promulgated such a decree. Only the South Carolina convention made any gesture in this direction, authorizing the state land commission to buy abandoned property at market value and resell it in small tracts (mostly to freedmen) on liberal terms.

Suffice it to say, reactionary whites opposed these new charters and worked assiduously to defeat ratification. Most Southern whites could not believe that their Northern brethren would abandon them at this crucial hour, allowing the radicals to impose "Negro rule" on the South. So determined were Southern whites to defeat ratification that they resorted to all manner of violent intimidation and terrorizing of black voters, whom they believed were the key to Republican ascendancy. Naturally leading this crusade was the KKK, which made it first serious appearance and forays during these elections. However, the main conservative tactic was to boycott the polls; if enough whites could be persuaded or coerced to stay home, the vote in favor of ratification might fall short of a majority of registered voters. Although in some states such as Alabama such a ploy initially worked, by the close of 1868 seven ex-Confederate states had ratified their constitutions and elected new legislatures that also ratified the Fourteenth Amendment, which became part of the Constitution the following summer. The newly elected representatives and senators from those seven states took their seats in the House and Senate.

Despite having "neutralized" Andrew Johnson and establishing (at least for the moment) Republican rule in the South, many party members were reluctant to take the final step of readmission. Causing them the greatest uneasiness was the reduction of federal troops, which would result as soon as self-government had been restored. Moreover, it would only be a matter of time before disfranchised whites regained the ballot, and once they had, the days of Republican control would end soon thereafter. Moreover, the various Republican coalitions that had written the state constitutions and subsequently took control were fragile at best, and during the ratification process, the vulnerability of its black constituents to intimidation became apparent. With troop presence on the decline, what would prevent a Democratic resurgence in the South and the certain dismantling of the new constitutions, black suffrage, and all the other reforms established? As one radical Senator warned, "Beware of hastening back States where rebelism is pervading from end to end. There are not ten men who believe it is a safe thing [the readmission of the states] to do at this time." But political necessities and realities dictated readmission and whether the radicals liked it or not, those Southern states which had complied with all congressional mandates had to be readmitted to the Union. Northern voters would not countenance continued uncertainty and "bayonet rule" in the South come the 1868 election; they wanted an end to such contention, for the majority no longer wanted to think about nor cared about "the Negro problem." Thus, in the minds of most Northern whites,

"Reconstruction" appeared to be completed. Events, however, would soon demonstrate that it had barely begun.

The First Grant Administration: The Election of 1868

Just as the 1864 presidential election had been a referendum on Republican war policies, so the 1868 contest reflected yet another plebiscite on reconstruction. Initially however, it appeared that the "financial question" might supersede reconstruction as the central campaign issue. The origins of this issue went back to the wartime legislation promoted by Lincoln which made legal tender paper money called "greenbacks" while simultaneously creating a host of national banks through which this currency flowed through the Northern economy. Inflation resulted during the war because of the flood of greenbacks into the economy, causing an 80 percent cost of living increase in the North from 1861–1865 but such an acceleration fell gradually but steadily after the war was over. With the suspension of specie payments and the adoption of greenbacks in 1862, the United States in effect went off the gold standard, though it still used gold for international trade.

After the war, Secretary of the Treasury Hugh McCulloch, a "hard-money" (a believer in specie/gold as the only legitimate currency for a nation to circulate), pursued a policy of returning the nation's monetary system to the gold standard by retiring slowly greenbacks while bringing the remainder in circulation to par with gold. By 1867 McCulloch had reduced the value of greenbacks in circulation to $319 million and the gold premium stood at 140 ($140 greenbacks were required to buy

$100 in gold). McCulloch's policies however, caused deflation and a postwar recession and those economic sectors hurt by the secretary's agenda blamed the contraction of greenbacks for their plight. Alarmed, Congress in 1868 forbade further greenback reduction. The issue created a new sectional alignment: East against West (the West was still an overwhelmingly rural and agrarian region) as both Western Democrats and Republicans opposed contraction, which hit the Western states' economy harder than the Northeast, where bankers, financiers, and industrialists all favored contraction and the return to the gold standard. Western farmers and other "debtors" favored soft money, for they would be repaying debts with depreciated currency if the greenbacks continued in circulation. Moreover, such individuals favored greenbacks as legal tender because it was "cheap money" that inflated prices for farm goods. A return to a strict gold standard would negate such a boon for farmers and other debtors.

Led by Ohio party leader, Senator George H. Pendleton, Western Democrats attempted to make the monetary question a major campaign issue. Pendleton, a leading candidate for his party's presidential nomination, favored making greenbacks the nation's legal tender, replacing gold but keeping the new currency on a gold standard. The Pendleton Plan found its way into the Democratic platform but when the party turned to New Yorker Horatio Seymour, a "gold bug" as its standard bearer, this plank became a dead letter as reconstruction and the candidates' war records took center stage. The monetary debate was not dead; indeed as will be seen in later chapters, once Reconstruction had ended, this particular issue reignited, rivaling at times in intensity and partisanship, the North-South slavery debate of the antebellum period.

As the 1868 election neared, the Republican nominee became a foregone conclusion: General-in-Chief of the Army and Union war hero, Ulysses S. Grant. For a while, Supreme Court Chief Justice, Salmon P. Chase, a perennial candidate, appeared to be a contender, but he committed political suicide when during Andrew Johnson's impeachment trial he made it clear he favored acquittal; a "blasphemous" declaration as far as the majority of Republicans were concerned. Grant, by contrast, became the Republican darling because he had opposed Johnson's 1866 reconstruction policy and openly broke with the president by 1868. The Republican convention unanimously nominated Grant on a platform that declared with pride that the general's presence "assured the success of the reconstruction policy of Congress."

Only one issue continued to mar Republican unanimity: the problem of black suffrage in the Northern states. Radicals insisted it must be a central feature of the party's platform while moderates believed it essential to downplay the crusade for fearing of alienating Northern white voters, the majority of whom had made it clear in various state elections that they adamantly opposed black enfranchisement. As one moderate editorial declared, "Discreditable as the fact may be, it is pretty evident that the enfranchisement of the colored race in the Northern States will have to wait. The more immediate interests of reconstruction might be jeopardized by forcing the issue at this juncture." In the end the moderates agreed to impose black suffrage on the ex-Confederate states while allowing the "question of suffrage in all the loyal [Northern] States to properly belong to the people of those States." Moderate hypocrisy and duplicity outraged abolitionists and radicals, who denounced this "mean-spirited, foolish, and

contemptible" plank. Charles Sumner predicted accurately that "the Democrats will
have a great opportunity in exposing its Janus-
faced character."

In contrast to the Republicans, the Democrats initially had a plethora of candidates,
including Andrew Johnson, whom, it was
quickly realized possessed too many political
liabilities to become a viable contender. The
other possibilities—Pendleton of Ohio, Thomas
Hendricks of Indiana, and General Winfield
Scott Hancock—all had supporters but as the
convention progressed and ballot after ballot
had been cast, one by one they all fell by the
wayside, ultimately leaving the "dark horse,"
Horatio Seymour of New York as the last man
standing, whom party officials had to hustle out
of the hall to prevent him from the declining the
nomination! In the end, Seymour reluctantly
accepted his party's dubious honor of running
against Grant.

The Democratic platform naturally condemned the Reconstruction Acts as "a flagrant usurpation of power, unconstitutional,
revolutionary and void." The platform also
demanded "the abolition of the Freedmen's
Bureau, and all political instrumentalities
designed to secure negro supremacy." It was
clear the Democracy hoped to win by engaging in all manner of race-baiting, negropho-
bia, and the promotion of white solidarity and
supremacy with its Southern colleagues. In
this approach, vice-presidential candidate
Frank Blair of Missouri became the party's
mouthpiece. In his famous "Brodhead letter,"
Blair set his party's campaign agenda. "There
is but one way to restore the Government and
the Constitution, and that is for the President-
elect to declare these [Reconstruction] acts
null and void, compel the army to undo its
usurpations at the South, disperse the Carpetbag governments, and allow white people to

reorganize their own governments." Implicitly
Blair and his party was calling for a counter-
revolutionary movement to overthrow the
Southern Republican governments and the
only way to achieve such a goal was to terror-
ize and suppress Southern Republican voters.
The Klan naturally heard Blair's and the
Democrats' clarion call to arms and during the
election the Klan and similar white backlash
terrorist organizations unleashed upon both
white and black pro-Republican supporters
and voters all manner violent mischief and
murder. In Louisiana alone between April and
November, 1868, more than a 1,000 persons,
mostly blacks were killed. Such intimidation
by the Klan and other white paramilitary
organizations did help the Democrats carry
Louisiana and Georgia but their activities hurt
the party in the North by lending substance to
Republican charges that Rebels and Copper-
heads were trying to achieve by terrorism
what they had failed to accomplish by war.

In the end, Grant won handily, receiving
55% of the northern vote, virtually the same
proportion as Lincoln had in 1864. Seymour
carried only 3 Northern states—Oregon, New
Jersey, and New York as well as three border-
slave states (Delaware, Maryland, and Kentucky), and two of the eight reconstructed
Confederate states, Georgia and Louisiana,
giving him 80 electoral votes to Grant's 214.

The Fifteenth Amendment

During the year after Grant's election, Congress focused on the unfinished task of reconstruction by working assiduously on a
constitutional amendment to enfranchise
African American males in every state, not just
the Southern freedmen. Without such an
amendment, the future of black suffrage would

become a farce, especially in the Southern states where the Democrats were destined to regain control. Moreover, the inequity of mandating black suffrage in the South while allowing Northern states the option disturbed many Republicans, for their party's lassitude on the issue smacked of racism and hypocrisy. "We have no moral right to impose an obligation on one part of the land which the rest will not accept," wrote a radical. "We can have no peace until this right is made national."

With such sentiments motivating their efforts, the Republican-dominated Congress passed the Fifteenth Amendment on February 26, 1869, marking the high-point of Reconstruction's constitutional achievements. The amendment prohibited states from denying the right to vote on grounds of race, color, or previous condition of servitude. Its purpose was not only to prevent any future revocation of black suffrage by the reconstructed states, but also to extend equal suffrage to the border states and to the North. Within four months of Congressional passage, 17 Republican legislatures then in session ratified the amendment and the four Democratic counterparts in session predictably rejected it. It remained uncertain where enough votes could be won among the eleven more states when their respective legislatures met in the fall. Fortunately the Republicans had an opportunity to mitigate the chances of defeat by mandating in the still unreconstructed states of Virginia, Mississippi, and Texas, that if they hoped to be readmitted their legislatures had to ratify both the Fourteenth and Fifteenth Amendments. All three states complied and were restored to the Union in 1870. Georgia remained the lone ex-Confederate state still unreconstructed. However, after several months of interesting maneuvers and behind-the-scenes deals, Georgia rejoined the Union and "promptly"

ratified the Fifteenth Amendment, giving the cause the two-thirds majority required. With Georgia's ratification the Fifteenth Amendment became part of the Constitution on March 30, 1870. Many Republicans believed the amendment represented "the last great point that remained to be settled on the issues of the war." Now the nation can focus on the other issues long neglected because of preoccupation with sectional strife. Even since Texas' annexation a quarter-century earlier, the Republic had scarcely a moment's respite from this tension. "Let us have done with Reconstruction," pleaded the *New York Tribune* in April 1870. "The Country is tired and sick of it. LET US HAVE PEACE."

Another motivating factor for many politicians to support the Fifteenth Amendment was to silence the outcry among Northern white women, the "suffragettes," who had been lobbying for the right to vote for decades. Congress never anticipated the suffragette outrage when the Fourteenth Amendment passed, not only making citizens of ex-slaves, but automatically giving them the right to vote at 21. Even black females allegedly had this right, for the amendment made no specific mention of gender. Suffice it to say, such legislation outraged the suffragettes, for not only were they white (a good number of these men were racists) but had never been property (chattel) in the same sense as the freedmen. To give an ex-slave such privileges while white women continued to languish as non-citizens in this capacity was simply unacceptable to the suffragettes. Thus, in many ways the Fifteenth Amendment was a sort of "throw-away" piece of legislation, designed to "clarify" who was "specifically" eligible to now vote in this country: all adult *males*, 21 one years or older, regardless of *race, color, or previous condition of servitude.* Since *gender* was not mentioned it was to be *naturally* assumed that women, regardless of color, were to be excluded from the franchise. No doubt suffragettes felt duped and betrayed, especially by the radicals, whose talk of supposed equality for all, smacked of hypocrisy and political opportunism, especially at the expense of white women. Thus the promulgation of the Fifteenth Amendment reflected that when it came to the extension of full-fledged citizenship to white women, few if any white males were ready to go that far; even in the most revolutionary of times, American white male chauvinism continued unabated.

Grant in the White House

Few presidents in American history entered the White House with more prestige and good will than Ulysses S. Grant. Now that reconstruction was supposedly over, Republican supporters were eager to focus on other pressing issues such as the currency and related financial problems, civil service reform, and foreign policy, an area that had particularly neglected because of sectional strife and civil war. Unfortunately, rather than solving or ameliorating these problems, Grant's inexperience and errors in judgment coupled with the venality of some of his associates, not only worsened many of these issues but created a whole new set of troubles for the president as well. Compounding these vexing domestic difficulties was the ongoing insolvable problems of reconstruction, all of which ultimately dashed the hopes of many Americans that the hero of the War of the Rebellion would be the nation's messiah. In short, from beginning to end, the Grant years were plagued by scandals, corruption, and graft; a

general avariciousness that seemed to pervade his administration from top to bottom from the moment he took office.

Within months of his first term, Grant had to deal with an attempt by two of the Gilded Age's most notorious Wall Street buccaneers, Jay Gould and Jim Fisk, who attempted to corner the gold market. Prompting Gould and Fisk to try such shenanigans was Congress's passing of the Public Credit Act, which allowed for the redemption of all government bonds in gold or its equivalent and the pledging to bring greenbacks to par with gold "at the earliest practicable period." In the meantime, the price of gold fluctuated, creating the perfect opportunity for speculators such as Gould and Fisk, both of whom had previously made a killing in a showdown of among capitalist titans Gould and Fisk, against Cornelius Vanderbilt for control of the nation's most important railroad line, the Erie. With their profits from this venture, Gould and Fisk hoped to corner the gold market by buy as much gold as possible when the market price reached its lowest point, which they were certain it would soon because of the uncertain, fluctuating nature of the nation's overall financial system.

However, much to their chagrin, the government (the Treasury) sold only specified amounts monthly, which greatly limited the amount of the bullion Gould and Fisk could buy at one time. Not to be deterred, the corsairs found an ally in the White House in Abel R. Corbin, the president's brother-in-law, who introduced Grant to Gould and Fisk, who convinced the president to suspend the monthly sales allotment and simply let as much gold be sold on the open market as possible. Gould told the president that such a free-wheeling policy of allowing the price of gold to rise would benefit the nation, especially the farmers by

Inauguration of President Grant, *ca. 1860–ca. 1865*

lowering the dollar price of wheat in European markets, thereby increasing exports. Grant was noncommittal but his brother-in-law assured Gould that the government would suspend restricted gold sales. No sooner did the Treasury lift the limitations on gold sales than Gould and Fisk began buying every ounce of gold in sight, driving up the premium to 144. By late September 1869, the price of gold had risen to 162. Grant saw that he had been hoodwinked by Gould and Fisk and immediately ordered the Treasury to stop gold sales and then only sell $4 million each month thereafter.

Grant's action caused a quick tumble in the gold market, which settled at 133, leaving scores of brokers and speculators ruined. Gould avoided disaster by selling at the top of the market and his sidekick Fisk simply repudiated several of his contracts. Although acting promptly upon learning the truth of Gould's schemes, the gold fiasco nonetheless tainted Grant's image as being an individual susceptible to nepotism and cronyism.

Sadly for Grant, the Gould-Fisk escapade was only the beginning of a wave of scandals and corruption that sullied his White House years. The president's private secretary, Orville Babcock, became involved in the infamous "Whiskey Ring," a network of distillers and revenue agents that deprived the government of million of excise tax dollars on whiskey while amassing fortunes. In one scandal, it was proved that Grant's Secretary of War, William Belknap (who was subsequently impeached) had been accepting bribes from men whom he had appointed as agents on Indian reservations—in effect selling government posts at a price which the agent would recover by cheating the Indians.

Although honest himself, Grant appeared to have an indiscriminate reverence for wealth, and he seemed quite blind to the effect of associating as President with rich, unscrupulous looters and market manipulators such as Jay Gould and Jim Fisk. Grant was also too trusting of subordinates. He appointed many former members of his military family, as well as several of his wife's relatives to offices for which they were scarcely qualified. However, not all of era's scandals emanated from the White House; this was an era notorious for corruption at all levels of government, with the infamous Tammany Hall "Ring" of Democratic "Boss" William Marcy Tweed of New York City leading the way. Tweed and his associates may have stolen more money from New York City taxpayers than all the federal agencies combined, and the New York legislature was famous for the buying and selling of votes. The Tweed Ring used the simple device of taking whatever funds they wanted from the municipal treasury, on the pretext of paying for goods and services which were never ordered and never received. In one day they helped themselves to $14 million by this uncomplicated method. It was said of the Ohio legislature that the only thing the

Standard Oil Company could not do with it was to refine it!

Perhaps the most notorious and widely publicized scandals of the era, was the Credit Mobilier affair, which, much to Grant's relief, involved Congress and not members of his administration. This particular gambol pertained to the building of the Union Pacific railroad. When the railroad company was organized, it did not manage the construction of its own road; rather it farmed out the line's building to a construction company named somewhat fancifully and pretentiously, the Credit Mobilier of America. Although such an arrangement was not unusual, quite legitimate in fact, what made this particular deal suspect was the fact that the railroad company's directors had organized the construction company. Then in their capacity as railroad directors they awarded themselves, as contractors, the contracts to build a cheaply constructed road at exorbitant prices. In this way they could easily siphon off government grants, leaving the railroad company almost bankrupt but themselves wealthy. Now all these "rapscallions" had to do was avoid any government inquiry into their shenanigans, which they did by distributing shares of construction company stock to targeted, susceptible, influential members of the House of Representatives, including its Speaker-soon-to-be Vice-President, Schuyler Colfax, to keep them from becoming "too vigilant"—from doing their job. The influence-peddling was eventually exposed and became the first clear illustration which the public received of what may happen when a group of insiders gains control of a wealthy enterprise which they do not own. The separation of ownership and control marked a new trend in American capitalist development and would become over the next several decades an unfortunate hallmark of Gilded Age politics and economics.

What accounted for this explosion of corruption in the postwar decade, which one historian has called "The Era of Good Stealings?" The expansion of government contracts and the bureaucracy during the war created new opportunities for the unscrupulous, compounded by a general relaxation of tensions and standards following the intense sacrifices of the war years. In other words, for four long, bloody years, white Americans (especially those in the North) seemed to have adhered to a comparatively rigid moral and ethical code, one that placed a premium on the virtues of self-sacrifice, frugality, and altruism, all for the good of a greater cause. Now that that cause had ended, with the Union preserved and slavery abolished, so ended four years of pent-up emotional and material self-deprivation. Americans were now eager to embrace the new industrial order the war had wrought, especially in the North, and with such change came all manner of opportunities for one to not only enjoy a life of material abundance but in the process become rich as well. Enterprises such as railroad construction became the consummate symbolic example of the get-rich-quick mentality and greed that took hold of many post-war Americans, satirized by Mark Twain and Charles Dudley Warner in their 1873 novel *The Gilded Age*, which gave its name to the era. In many ways, post-Civil War American culture produced attitudes, behaviors, and values not unfamiliar to Americans of the late 20th and early 21st centuries: an ethos of crass materialism, hedonistic self-indulgence, and a passion to accumulate monetary wealth regardless of how ethical the endeavor or how detrimental the affects on others.

Civil Service Reform

As a result of the endemic corruption, a civil service reform movement emerged to try to cleanse an inefficient government bureaucracy that had become rife with malfeasance, cronyism, and nepotism; in many ways the inevitable result of decades of the spoils system initiated by Andrew Jackson's administration of the late 1820s. Beginning with Jackson and through Grant (and beyond, unfortunately), the victorious party in an election rewarded party loyalists with all manner of federal appointments, usually at the lower bureaucratic level such as postmasters, customs collectors, and the like. Interestingly, even when a party was out of power, the possibility of appointment helped to maintain party faithful. The spoils system politicized the bureaucracy and staffed it with unqualified personnel who spent more time working for their party than for the government. Such were the realties and conditions on which reformers focused a harsh light; into the dark corners of corruption previously obscured by the sectional conflict, war, and reconstruction. Although much of the corruption may have been exaggerated by reformers for publicity purposes, plenty was nonetheless there to warrant serious investigation and rectification.

Reformers were mainly well-educated Northeastern professionals and many came from some of the nation's most pedigreed families. Most of them were Republicans, "cut" from the old Conscience Whig cloth of the party. They admired the incorruptible efficiency of the British civil service and wanted to emulate that system. Professional politicians on both sides of the aisle, however, looked askance at such notions. To them, patronage was the lifeblood of democracy, and had been since the days of the

"Jacksonian revolution." They accused the reformers of being elitists, and ridiculed them as dilettantes trying to play at the serious business of nitty-gritty American politics.

Civil service reformers wanted to separate the bureaucracy from politics by mandating competitive examinations for the appointment of civil servants. This movement gained momentum during the 1870s and finally achieved success in 1883 with the passage of the Pendleton Act, which established the modern structure, system, and procedure for positions within the civil service. When Grant took office he appeared to share the sentiments of the civil service reformers; several of his cabinet officials—Secretary of the Treasury George Boutwell, Secretary of the Interior Samuel D. Cox, and Attorney General Rockwood Hoar, inaugurated examinations for certain appointments and promotions in their respective departments. Grant also named a civil service commission headed by the editor of *Harper's Weekly* and a leading reformer, George William Curtis. Unfortunately too many of Grant's contemporaries opposed reform; they simply found the spoils system too personally beneficial to do away. Patronage was the grease of the political machines that kept them in office and all too often enriched them and their political chums. They managed to subvert reform, sometimes using Grant as an unwitting ally and thus turning many reformers against the president. Thus, much to the disappointment of the reformers, a thoroughgoing reform of the spoils system was not achieved in the 1870s.

Foreign Policy Issues

Although the Grant administration's priorities were domestic rather than foreign, there were significant foreign policy developments and issues during these years, some of which added to Grant's woes. One such setback was the Santo Domingo affair, an attempt by the Grant White House to annex the island nation of Santo Domingo (present-day Dominican Republic). Such a move by the administration reflected a resurgent American nationalism which the war had fomented and with such a sentiment, a concomitant revival of Manifest Destiny. Ironically, post-war Republicans, not Democrats as had been the case in the past, were in the vanguard of a rejuvenated expansionist spirit. Secretary of State William Seward's purchase of Alaska (to be discussed later in this section) from Russia in 1867 set a precedent for the acquisition of noncontiguous territory. Seward had also earlier attempted to purchase the Virgin Islands from Denmark, for the Civil War had demonstrated the need for a US naval base in the Caribbean. The Senate killed this treaty but not the idea of US expansion into the Caribbean.

Interestingly, the initial overture for annexation came from the wily Dominican dictator, Bonaventura Baez, who wanted the United States to acquire his country as a means to bolster his power against insurgent movements. No sooner did the news of Baez's entreaties reach Washington, than a "Dominican lobby," formed, attracting to the cause a variety of unsavory land speculators, commercial developers, mercenaries, promoters of fabulous gold and silver mines, and naval officers who wanted a Caribbean base and dreamed of an Isthmian canal. There were less unscrupulous and self-interested individuals, including Grant, who believed that American ownership would bring peace and stability to a country of chronic revolutions, develop its rich resources, open the gateway for the extension of beneficent American influence throughout the region, and initiate the Isthmian canal project.

Grant hoped to make annexation the show-piece foreign policy achievement of his administration. But his lack of political savvy and experience betrayed him. His military background got the better of him; he simply "ordered" the scheme into effect without first lining up key political support among his cabinet and Congress. Without consulting either group, Grant sent his private secretary Orville Babcock to the island nation in July 1869 to open negotiations. The overzealous Babcock did more than discuss the possibilities of acquisition; he brought back a treaty of annexation. After the "irregularities" of the procedure had been pointed out by Cabinet members, Grant, determined to have Santo Domingo, regardless of having violated a multitude of diplomatic protocols, sent Babcock back to Santo Domingo with State Department authorization to renegotiate the agreement properly. Baez agreed to the terms and Babcock returned with a treaty that made Santo Domingo a US territory and declared her 120,000 people to be American citizens, all at a bargain price of $1.5 million. In a plebiscite Santo Domingans unanimously approved annexation. In January 1870, Grant proudly submitted the treaty for Senate ratification; in effect he handed the Senate an unwelcomed, distasteful fait accompli, which incensed Senate leaders of both parties.

Leading the anti-annexation movement in the Senate were Charles Sumner of Massachusetts and Carl Schurz of Missouri. Along with others senators from both sides of the aisle, Schurz and Sumner castigated the corrupt promoters who had bought up land in expectation of windfall profits from annexation. Schurz and Sumner invoked the traditional Whig/Republican hostility to expansion with Schurz questioning the wisdom of incorporating a new mixed-blood Catholic population into a polity that already had more than enough trouble with racial issues. Sumner feared that the acquisition of Santo Domingo would threaten the independence of Haiti, which except for Liberia on the West Coast of Africa, was the only self-governing black republic in the world. "These islands by climate, occupation, and destiny belong to the colored people," Sumner declared. "We should not take them away. No greed of land should prevail against the rights of this race."

Outraged by Sumner's and Schurz's opposition as well as by their criticism of his high-handedness, Grant went on a personal rampage, dismissing or sending out to "political pasture" as many of Sumner's and Schurz's allies as fast as he possibly could, such as Attorney General E. Rockwood Hoar of Massachusetts. Grant's counterattack yielded little favorable results except to alienate a growing number of Republicans from the administration. On June 30, 1870, the Senate defeated the treaty by a tie vote of 28-28, with 19 Republicans joining 9 Democrats in opposition. Open warfare now erupted between Grant and Sumner, becoming increasingly savage as the months wore on. Sumner excoriated the president in a Senate speech, likening Grant's arrogance, petulance, and general bulliness and imperiousness to James Buchanan and Andrew Johnson. James Buchanan had forced the removal of Stephen Douglas from his chairmanship of the Committee on Territories at the time of the Lecompton Contest. Such epithets proved too much for proadministration senators who deposed Sumner as Chairman of the Foreign Relations Committee. These are the only two occasions in history when the chairman of a Congressional committee has been removed by his own party while continuing a member of the party.

The Santo Domingo affair seriously divided the Republican party. Both president and senators had demonstrated traits of petty vindictiveness. Sumner's vain ego and righteous moralism seemed to grow more excessive with age. To many of the senator's friends however, Grant's vendetta seemed to be an attack on the idealism that had made the Republican party great. They feared that the party, under Grant's lack of leadership and general personal fortitude, was fast falling into the hands of spoilsmen and opportunists such as Senator Roscoe Conkling of New York and the equally ambitious and opprobrious Benjamin Butler of Ohio, men who had no roots in the antislavery movement and no commitment to moral ideals. To these "old" Republicans, it looked as if the President was sacrificing the best elements of the party to its worst elements. By 1871, a new noun, "Grantism" had entered Washingtonian verbiage. It became a catch-all term for all the things the old Republicans believed were wrong with postwar America: spoilsmanship and corruption in government; crude, vulgar taste and anti-intellectualism in culture; dishonesty in business; and a boundless materialism and a get-rich-quick acquisitiveness that was becoming more and more to define a new American creed. This breach between "old" and "new" Republicans would split the party in the 1872 election, giving rise to the Liberal Republican movement.

The Grant administration also had to reckon with Great Britain and Mexico over events that were in a sense unfinished business from the war itself. One involved the French-supported empire of Austrian archduke Maximilian in Mexico; the other, United States claims against Great Britain for having permitted the construction and outfitting as well as a safe haven for the Confederate commerce raider, the *Alabama*, which ravaged the US merchant marine during the war.

At the beginning of the US Civil War, the Mexican government had defaulted on its debts to Britain, Spain, and France. All the nations agreed to use force if necessary to collect what they were owed but they also agreed that none would attempt to gain "peculiar advantage" from the situation. The French emperor, Napoleon III, however, had no intention of fulfilling his pledge, for he saw a grand opportunity to begin the resurrection of his uncle's empire (Napoleon I, the "real" Napoleon), which he believed he was "destined" to achieve. In secret negotiations with the ruling Habsburgs of the Austro-Hungarian empire, Napoleon III arranged for the archduke Maximilian to become "emperor" of Mexico with French support. Great Britain and Spain knew nothing of this "deal." In 1862, the creditor nations invaded Mexico, driving into exile in the northern Mexican mountains and deserts, its president Benito Juarez. By 1863 England and Spain had grown weary of the whole affair and withdrew their troops, leaving France in charge of future operations. Napoleon could not have asked for a more perfect scenario to implement his scheme. French armies occupied Mexico City a month before the Battle of Gettysburg, and shortly afterward a hand-picked group of wealthy, conservative, anti-Juarez Mexican landowners, Catholic clergy, and military officers "offered" Maximilian the throne as Emperor of their country, which the Austrian accepted in 1864. In reality, Maximilian was barely the emperor of Mexico City, for all around him were the Juarista republican insurgents, who for the next three years waged a guerrilla war against Maximilian's French-supported regime as well as against those Francophile Mexicans who had betrayed their country.

Suffice it to say, the Lincoln administration was greatly upset by this blatant violation of the Monroe Doctrine and Congress responded by voting angry resolutions. But there was little the United States could do at the moment, embroiled as Secretary of State William Seward stated, "in a struggle for our own life." Both Lincoln and Seward knew however, that the French invasion portended ill for national security. Indeed, the French invasion, occupation, and the establishing of an empire represented the most serious direct threat to American security since the War of 1812. Both Lincoln and Seward were biding their time. After Lee's surrender, and with Lincoln killed, the job of getting the French out of Mexico fell to Seward, who began to pressure Napoleon, gently at first, to leave Mexico. When such nudging failed, Seward became more aggressive and bellicose, demanding in February 1866 that France set a date to get out of Mexico or US troops would be sent into Mexico to drive them out! Napoleon knew Seward was serious. Moreover, all of Europe knew, after having watched Americans butcher each other for four years, that the Union Army had "fought" itself into being one of the best armies in the world at that moment and could have easily crushed the French forces in Mexico, which would have become a most humiliating defeat for a supposed great European power, France. Thus in April 1867, Napoleon agreed to begin the withdrawal process. Aside from US pressure, by that time Napoleon had found his venture more costly and unpopular than he had anticipated.

On a somewhat tragic note, Maximilian remained in Mexico, for he regarded himself as a Mexican and a "legitimate" ruler. For such delusion he paid with his life at the hands of a Mexican firing squad in June 1867. Apparently the Mexican did not see Maximilian in the same light as he saw himself. Interestingly, during all these developments, Seward never invoked the Monroe Doctrine, but Napoleon's withdrawal from Mexico was perhaps the most important victory it ever scored.

The second piece of war-related unfinished business were the damage claims against Britain caused by the C.S.S. *Alabama* and other Confederate commerce raiders (the *Florida* and the *Shenandoah*), built in British shipyards. It ought to have been possible to settle this matter quickly, for the British were in a conciliatory mood, convinced that the building of such ships had violated the principles of neutrality. Such altruism however, disguised a fear that if they became involved in a war, American shipyards might allow the building of commerce raiders for England's enemy to be let loose against the British merchant marine. Complicating negotiations were a cluster of other issues as well: a dispute about possession of the San Juan islands off Vancouver; questions about Canadian-American fishing rights; Irish-American aid to Irish revolutionists; and most of all a lingering American desire for the United States to annex all or part of Canada. Because of these issues negotiations did not begin until 1869.

Unfortunately, no sooner did talks begin than Senator Charles Sumner blasted the negotiations, declaring Britain financially accountable not only for destroyed American merchant ships but also for prolonging the war by two years, for according to Sumner (and some others), after Gettysburg and Vicksburg, it was only British support that enabled the Confederacy to continue fighting. He proposed astronomical damages—far greater, in fact, that Germany would soon impose on France at the end of the Franco-Prussian War. Sumner's tirade caused negotiations to break off and for two years strained relations existed between the US and Great Britain. Newspapers on both sides of the Atlantic traded bellicose threats.

Thanks to the adroit handling of Secretary of State Hamilton Fish, the impasse was finally broken when the Grant administration agreed to the Treaty of Washington (1871), which called for submitting the dispute to an international arbitration tribunal comprised of the United States, Britain, Switzerland, Italy, and Brazil. By a 4-1 vote (Britain dissenting) the arbitrators declared that the British government had failed to exercise "due diligence" to prevent the building and arming of the Confederate raiders and awarded the United States $15.5 million for the damages done by these ships.

The events leading to the Treaty of Washington also resolved another long-festering issue affecting relations between Britain and the United States: the status of Canada. The seven separate British North American colonies were especially vulnerable to US desires for annexation. Indeed, so angered were many Northerners toward Britain for the Confederate raiders' depredations, that they demanded that England relinquish her Canadian provinces as payment for these damages. Such bellicosity strengthened Canadians' loyalty to Britain as a counterweight to American aggression. In 1867 Parliament passed the British North American Act, which united most of the Canadian colonies into a new and largely self-governing Dominion of Canada.

Pro-British Canadian nationalism was further strengthened by the actions of the Irish American Fenian Brotherhood, a secret society organized during the Civil War dedicated to the overthrow of British rule in Ireland. For that purpose, the Fenians believed that a US invasion and acquisition of Canada would go far toward achieving an independent Ireland. Three times from 1866 to 1871, Fenians, composed mainly of Irish American ex-Union army veterans, crossed the US-Canadian border, only to be driven back after comic-opera skirmishes. The Fenian invasions intensified Canadian anti-Americanism, complicating the negotiations leading to the 1871 Washington Treaty. However, the successful conclusion of that treaty cooled American-Canadian tensions, leading to resolutions of disputes over American commercial fishing in Canadian waters. US troops prevented further Fenian raids and American demands for annexation of Canada also dissipated as well. These events gave birth to the modern nation of Canada, whose 3,500 mile border with the United States remains the longest unfortified frontier in the world.

The other major event in the field of foreign affairs during these years was not recognized at the time of having any significance: the purchase of Alaska from Russia, the result of Secretary of State William Seward's perspicacity to take advantage of a financially hard-pressed Russian government, which had over-extended himself in the far Pacific Northwest. Through diplomatic "back-channels" Seward found out that Russia would be interested in selling Alaska to the United States. Seward jumped at the possibility, settling on the negotiated price of $7.2 million. When the public found out about "Seward's folly," the secretary was chastised in the press and in government circles for having purchased this "frozen waste." Some congressmen even had to be bribed to vote for the appropriation. Despite the criticism, Seward persevered, certain that some day his "folly" would be worth far more than the purchase price to the United States. The treaty was ratified in 1867, the payment voted in 1868, and then Alaska was put away and forgotten, unexplored and unknown, until the 1897 Klondike Gold Rush, which turned out to be the greatest in American history, yielding more gold than all other such finds combined. No doubt from his grave William Seward smiled and said to his fellow Americans, "I told you so!"

The White Backlash Continues

No sooner did Republican regimes come to power in the South than Southern whites were determined to bring them down. Ready and willing to help in this crusade was the Ku Klux Klan, whose activities rose to a crescendo in 1870 and 1871. Although part of the Klan's purpose was social control of the black population, its main objective during the decade of the 1870s was political: to destroy the Republican Party by terrorizing its voters, and if necessary, murdering its leaders. No one knows the number of politically motivated killings that occurred in the South during Reconstruction but it was certainly in the hundreds, if not in the thousands, with African Americans easily comprising the lion's share of victims. In one notorious incident, the "Colfax Massacre" in Louisiana (April 18, 1873), a confrontation between black militia and armed whites left three whites and nearly 100 blacks dead, with the majority of the latter shot down in cold blood after they had surrendered. In some states, most notably Arkansas and Tennessee, Republicans formed state militias to protect themselves and successfully suppressed Klan raids and other terrorist activities. But in most of the Southern states the militias were outgunned and outmaneuvered by ex-Confederate veterans who had joined the Klan. Some Republican governors were reluctant to use black militia against white guerrillas, fearing that such an encounter could spark a racial bloodbath as happened at Colfax.

No matter what the Republican governments did they appeared to be losing the battle with the Klan, whose popularity among white Southerners seemed to be increasing daily. It was time to seek federal help. In 1870 and 1871 Congress enacted three laws intended to enforce the Fourteenth and Fifteenth Amendments with federal marshals and troops if necessary. Interference with voting rights became a federal offense, and any attempts to deprive another person of civil or political rights became a felony. The third law, popularly called the Ku Klux Klan Act, gave the president the power to suspend the writ of habeas corpus and send in federal troops to suppress armed resistance to federal law.

Although virtually handed by Congress carte blanche to deal with the Klan as forcefully as warranted, Grant showed restraint, sensitive to charges of being a "military despot." He suspended the writ of habeas corpus only in nine South Carolina counties. Nevertheless, there and elsewhere federal marshals backed by troops arrested thousands of suspected Klansmen. Federal grand juries indicted more than 3,000 and several hundred defendants pleaded guilty in return for suspended sentences. To clear congested court dockets so that the worst offenders could be tried quickly, the Justice Department dropped charges against nearly 2,000 others. About 600 Klansmen were convicted; most of them received fines or light jail sentences, but 65 went to a federal penitentiary for terms of up to five years.

The 1872 Presidential Election

The crack-down on the Klan helped to bolster Grant's image, especially among the radicals and even among a still strongly supportive

Northern white majority, many of whom remained in a vindictive mood toward white Southerners. However, within the GOP a dissident group had emerged to challenge Grant's reelection. Disillusioned with his record on civil service reform, and disgusted with the scandals and corruption that seemed to have afflicted his White House from top to bottom, and his consorting with Robber Barons such as Jim Fisk and Jay Gould, and his turning over of the party to "hacks" such as Roscoe Conkling and Benjamin Butler, all served to alienate the more high-minded, righteous purists within the party. These disgruntled Republicans broke with the party and organized a splinter group, calling themselves the Liberal Republicans, who believed that in alliance with the Democrats they could defeat Grant. Indeed, their slogan became "Anything to beat Grant." With Democratic approval and support, this "fusion" party nominated Horace Greeley, the famous editor of the *New York Tribune*, who, ironically, had been a Democratic nemesis for decades. The Liberal Republican-Democratic coalition called for a new policy of conciliation of Southern whites rather than continued military intervention as the only way to achieve peace in the region. The party's platform thus denounced Grant's supposed "bayonet rule" in the South and Greeley urged fellow Northerners to put the issues of the Civil War behind them and to "clasp hands across the bloody chasm which has too long divided" North and South.

Much to the party's chagrin, most Northern voters were still not prepared to trust either Democrats or Southern whites. Powerful anti-Greeley lampoons by political cartoonist Thomas Nast showed Greeley shaking the hand of a Klansman dripping with blood of a murdered black Republican. Nast's most famous cartoon portrayed Greeley as a pirate captain bringing his craft alongside the ship of state while Confederate leaders, armed to the teeth, hid below waiting to board it. Few voters were surprised that on Election Day Grant swamped Greeley by over a million popular votes. Republicans carried every Northern state and 10 of the 16 Southern and border states. In the Electoral College, Grant received 286 votes to Greeley's 66. Southern Blacks enjoyed more freedom in voting than they would enjoy again for a century. But this apparent triumph of Republicanism and Reconstruction proved to be short-lived.

The Panic of 1873

President Grant had but one year to bask in the rays of his resounding victory over Horace Greeley. The following September, the worst economic declension in the Republic's history to date rocked both the Grant administration and the American people, ushering in close to a decade of hard times for millions of Americans. Perhaps most important, the panic proved to be the death knell for Reconstruction. Northern whites, now distracted and consumed by a more pressing economic crisis, simply lost what little interest or passion they had left for Reconstruction and turned away from the cause, wanting an end to issues and concerns that had never really affected their daily lives in the first place. Economic survival now became the order of the day for the majority of Northern whites, and with such preoccupation came the abrupt end of what little interest they might have had left for sustaining either the freedmen's rights or for the Republican regimes established to defend those rights and reform the South.

The U.S. economy had grown at an unprecedented rate since recovering in 1867 from a mild postwar recession. As many miles of new railroad track (35,000) were laid down in eight years as in the preceding 35. The first transcontinental railroad had been completed on May 10, 1869, when a golden spike was driven at Promontory Point, Utah Territory, linking the Union Pacific and Central Pacific. But it was the construction of a second transcontinental line, the Northern Pacific that precipitated a Wall Street panic in 1873 and plunged the economy into a five-year depression and a ten-year general downturn.

Ironically, the hero of Civil War finance, Jay Cooke, was the main culprit. Cooke's banking firm, fresh from its triumphant marketing of Union war bonds, took over the Northern Pacific in 1869. Despite government land grants and loans, the company had not yet laid a single mile of track. Cooke pyramided every imaginable kind of equity and loan financing to raise money to begin laying rails west from Duluth, Minnesota. Other investment firms did the same as a fever of speculative financing swept the country. In September 1873 the pyramid of paper collapsed. Cooke's firm was the first to go under. Like dominoes, hundreds of banks and businesses also collapsed. By 1875, over 18,000 railroad related enterprises had failed. Northern unemployment rose to 14 percent and hard times set in across the region.

Retreat from Reconstruction

It is almost a given in American politics that the party responsible or blamed for economic hard times will most certainly lose, and usually big, in the forthcoming election. That axiom proved true in the 1870s as the Democrats made large gains in the 1874 congressional elections, winning a majority of House seats for the first time in 18 years. Compounding Republican woes, the Panic of 1873, as noted above, caused Northern public opinion to turn against Republican policies in the South, believing continued support for the Republican governments "at the South" to be a waste of valuable money and effort that could be put to better use trying to ameliorate the Northern economic crisis. When the Liberal Republican/Democratic coalition in 1872 clamored against "bayonet rule" and "carpetbag corruption" in the South, their braying at the time fell mostly on deaf ears. However, by 1874 those charges found increasingly receptive Northern audiences. Intraparty party battles among Southern Republicans enabled Democratic "Redeemers" (along with the use of terror and violence) to regain control of several Southern state governments by 1874. As noted earlier, that became an almost inevitable outcome once Southern whites regained their right to vote; no sooner did that occur than they simply voted the "scalawags," "carpetbaggers," and freedmen out of office and if they resisted, they would be visited by the Klan or one of the many other white backlash organizations that had emerged to overthrow "negro rule" and restore white supremacy.

Well-publicized corruption scandals, especially in Louisiana, also discredited Republican leaders. Although malfeasance was probably no worse in Southern states than in many parts of the North, Southern postwar poverty made waste and extravagance seem worse and gave the reform impulse an extra impetus. Southern white Democrats pointed to the corruption as confirmation of the "Negroes" alleged inherent depravity, incompetence, and ignorance; their complete unfitness to participate in political life. The only reason that had gained political office was because they had been placed there by the "scalawags" and "carpetbaggers," who, in reality, had only used them for their own political aggrandizement.

Northerners grew increasingly weary of what seemed the endless turmoil of Southern politics. As noted earlier, from the beginning of Reconstruction, most Northern whites had never had a very strong commitment to racial equality, and they were increasingly willing to let white supremacy restore itself to the South. Also motivating many Northern whites to allow the return of white supremacy was the fact that beginning in the 1870s and over the course of the next four decades, the North would be inundated with millions of Southern and Eastern European immigrants. Indeed, about 30 million of these people would come to the United States from 1870–1910. Never before had so many from Europe come to the United States, and more importantly, few if any had come from southern and eastern Europe. The United States had always been for White Anglo-Saxon Protestants, and now WASP America was about to be overwhelmed by Italians, Poles, Czechs, Slovaks, Greeks, and a whole host of swarthy individuals, whom white Americans believed to be ethnically if not racially inferior to them and thus a threat to the "American way of life." Moreover, these new immigrant not only represented an ethnic/racial menace, but a religious "problem" as well, for the majority were Catholic, many were Orthodox and "horror of all horrors," many were Jews! Not only was the United States a "white man's country" but it was Christian as well, and to most Anglo-Saxon Americans, that meant Protestant. As a result of immigration, a peculiar bond of white solidarity began to take shape between Northern and Southern whites, with the former now declaring they understood Southern

whites' "negro problem," for now Northerners had a similar "immigrant" problem. In the mind of many Northern whites they could not in good conscience continue to force black equality upon their Southern brethren if they were unwilling to accept immigrant equality. Thus, by the mid-1870s, as Northern whites became increasingly obsessed with their immigrant problem, they were no longer willing to support Republican governments in the South that forced "negro rule" on their poor, beleaguered white comrades. As one Northern Republican confessed, "our people are tired out with this worn out cry of 'Southern outrages'!! Hard times & heavy taxes make them wish the 'nigger' 'everlasting nigger' were in hell or Africa."

With the loss of Northern white support, it was no surprise that by 1875 only four Southern states remained under Republican control: South Carolina, Florida, Mississippi, and Louisiana. In those states white Democrats had revived paramilitary organizations under various names: White Leagues (Louisiana); Rifle Clubs (Mississippi); and Red Shirts (South Carolina). Unlike the Klan, these terrorist squads operated openly. In Louisiana they fought pitched battles with Republican militias in which scores were killed. When Grant sent troops to Louisiana to quell the violence, both Northern and Southern whites cried out against military rule. The protest grew even louder when soldiers marched into the Louisiana legislature in January 1875 to expel several Democratic legislators after a contested election in which voter fraud was committed along with the terrorizing of black voters away from the polls. Liberal Republicans such as Carl Schurz were delighted by events such as the Louisiana episode, for such Republican reprisals only helped fuel the fires of Northern discontent with Republican rule in the South, which Schurz and others wanted to end. "Was this America?" asked Schurz in a widely publicized speech. "If this can be done in Louisiana, how long will it be before it can be done in Massachusetts and Ohio? How long before a soldier may stalk into the national House of Representatives, and pointing to the Speaker's mace, say, 'Take away that bauble!'" It was obvious that Schurz and the Liberal Republicans along with their Democratic allies were trying to paint the Grant administration and its supporters as military despots, "Negrophiles," and scandalous, self-serving political hacks and placemen. Sadly, their propaganda was working and thus the days of the last Republican regimes in the South were numbered.

Southern resistance leaders were quick to sense that the tide was turning in their favor. By 1874 the "Redeemers" had regained control of Texas, Arkansas, and Alabama, leaving as noted above radical control of only four states—Florida, Louisiana, South Carolina, and Mississippi. Only the first three had black majorities, which allowed the Republican regimes to hang on by a thread for a few more years. In Mississippi however, whites did not hesitate to institute a reign of terror on black Mississippians in order to regain power. Indeed, that became the key to their return to control of the state, for even with all whites voting Democratic, the party could still be defeated by the 55 percent black majority. Economic coercion against black sharecroppers kept some freedmen away from the polls but overt violence became the most effective means. Democratic "rifle clubs" (code for terrorist paramilitary groups) showed up at Republican rallies, attended mostly by black voters, provoked riots and then shot down in cold blood as many freedmen as possible in the ensuing melees. Governor Adelbert Ames, a native of Maine, Union general and congressional medal of honor winner and one of the ablest of Southern Republicans, dared not to call out the black militia; instead he appealed to Washington for support but the Grant administration rejected his plea for help. "The whole public," responded the Attorney General, "are tired of these annual autumnal outbreaks in the South, and the great majority are now ready to condemn any interference on the part of the government. . . . Preserve the peace by the forces in your own state, and let the country see that the citizens of Mississippi who are largely Republican have the courage to fight for their rights."

The Attorney General's message to Ames made it clear that the Grant administration had "washed its hands' of Reconstruction; that it had finally succumbed to the anti-federal intervention sentiment of the majority of Northern whites, thus dooming one of the last Republican regimes in the South to being violently overthrown. With such reassurance, all Mississippi Redeemers had to do now was "persuade" the 10 to 15 percent of white voters still calling themselves Republicans to switch to the Democrats. Only a handful of "scalawags" and "carpetbaggers" could resist the economic pressures, social ostracism, and threats that made it "too damn hot for [us] to stay out," wrote one white Republican who changed parties. "No white man can live in the South in the future and act with any other than the Democratic party unless he is willing and prepared to live a life of social isolation and remain in political oblivion." With such overwhelming forces arrayed against him and with the Grant administration's abandonment, Ames had no choice but to let reality run its course. Ames was reluctant to use the black militia to stay in power, fearing that if he called them out he would provoke a race war worse than anything yet experienced in Reconstruction. "No matter if they [the Democrats] are going to carry the State," declared a weary and resigned Ames, "let them carry it, and let us be at peace and have no more killing." The "Mississippi Plan" worked like a charm. In five of the state's counties with large black majorities, the Republicans polled 12, 7, 4, 2, and 0 votes, respectively. When the Democratic legislature met the following January 1875, Governor Ames resigned and the Democrats took complete control of the state.

The 1876 Presidential Election

The various scandals of the Grant administration along with those that had occurred in cities such as New York City and Northern states such as New York and Ohio as well as in many of the Southern states under Republican rule ensured that reform would be the leading issue in the year's presidential race. In this centennial year of the nation's birth, highlighted by a great exposition in Philadelphia, Americans wanted to present their nation as the beacon of virtue, justice, righteousness, and morality for all to behold. Although the reality of the last two decades could not have been further from the truth, Americans nonetheless believed they could find their way back to such an image if they chose the right president to lead them in the right direction. Thus, both major parties give their presidential nomination to governors who had earned reform reputations in their respective states: Democrat Samuel J. Tilden of New York and Republican Rutherford B. Hayes of Ohio.

Democrats entered the campaign as the favorites for the first time in two decades. They based their optimism on the belief that they could put together an electoral majority of "solid South" Democrats, disaffected Northern Republicans, (Liberal Republicans) and by carrying New York and two or three other "big" Northern states, hopefully Ohio and Indiana or Illinois where "Grantism" and radical Reconstruction had caused Republican party splits. So desperate for victory, the Democrats even openly supported the "Mississippi Plan" in the South, encouraging their Southern white counterparts to continue their violent rampages against blacks and the use of other terrorist tactics to keep freedmen from the polls and voting Republican.

When the returns were in, Tilden had won the popular vote by 252,000 but had lost in the electoral college by one vote, 185-184, the result screamed the Democrats, of fraudulent "Negro-Carpetbag-Scalawag" voting in the three "unredeemed" Southern states of Florida, Louisiana, and South Carolina. Tilden had carried all the rest of the Southern states, including all the border states, as well as West Virginia, and in the North, he captured New York, New Jersey, Indiana, and Connecticut. Unfortunately for the Republicans, the Democratic accusations of fraud were more than likely correct; obvious voter "irregularities" popped up in several Louisiana parishes and in other districts in both Florida and South Carolina, where two years earlier many of those same districts and parishes and returned sizeable Democratic majorities and now they had miraculously "gone Republican," or the opposite had occurred: in 1874 a Louisiana parish had recorded 1,688 Republican votes but in 1876 only one, the result of obvious voter intimidation by whites of both black and white Republicans. The Democrats refused to yield, continuing to shout "fraud" and even threatened an armed march on Washington. The country now faced a serious constitutional crisis because the document offered no clear guidance on how to deal with such a scenario. The only point of clarity was that a concurrence of both houses of Congress was required to count the electoral votes of the states but with a Democratic-controlled House and a Republican-dominated Senate an impasse would surely be the result. To break the deadlock, Congress created a special electoral commission consisting of five House members, five senators, and five Supreme Court justices split evenly between the two parties.

The commission discovered that even in three disputed Southern states Tilden had won a majority but an estimated 250,000 Southern Republicans had been terrorized away from the polls. Thus in a genuinely fair and free election, the Republicans might have carried Mississippi and North Carolina, as well as the three disputed states. After three months of wrangling, threats, and outright nastiness among partisans of both parties, the electoral commission issued its ruling. By a strict party vote of 8-7, the commission awarded all the disputed states to Hayes but the Democrats refused to accept the decision and began a House filibuster to delay the final electoral count beyond the inauguration date of March 4. Such a move would throw the election into the House, an eventuality that threatened to bring anarchy. To avoid such a cataclysm, behind the scenes less partisan Democrats and Republicans (many of Whig or neo-Whig heritage and used to solving sectional rancor with conciliation) were negotiating a compromise. To these individuals preventing another North-South showdown was essential so the country could get on with the business of economic recovery and development. Thus Hayes promised his support as president for federal appropriations to rebuild war-destroyed levees on the lower Mississippi River and federal aid for a Southern transcontinental railroad. Hayes' lieutenants also hinted at the appointment of a Southerner as postmaster general, who would have a considerable amount of patronage at his disposal. Most important, Hayes signaled that he fully supported the end of "bayonet rule," which meant he would withdraw from South Carolina, Florida, and Louisiana, and anywhere else in the South federal troops still resided, thus allowing a return of complete power to Southern whites. In return for his pledge, Hayes asked for and received "promises" from white Southerners and their respective Democratic state government officials that freedmen would receive fair treatment and respect for their constitutional rights. Such promises were easier to make than to keep as future years would reveal.

As a result of the backroom negotiation, the Democratic filibuster collapsed and Hayes was inaugurated on March 4, 1877. No sooner did he take office than ex-Confederate David Key of Tennessee became postmaster general; the South received more federal money in 1878 for improving its infrastructure than it had ever received before; and federal troops left the capitals of South Carolina and Louisiana. Old abolitionists and radical Republican warhorses denounced Hayes as a traitor to his party as well as having sold out the freedmen. As William Lloyd Garrison declared, Hayes' actions represented a policy "of weakness, of subserviency, of surrender;" a move that sustained "might against right; the rich and powerful against the poor and unprotected."

But cries of protest fell on deaf ears; sighs of relief that the crisis was over drowned out such outrage. Most Americans, including most Republicans, wanted no more military intervention in state affairs. "I have no sort of faith in a local government which can only be propped up by foreign bayonets," wrote the editor of the *New York Tribune* in April 1877. "If negro suffrage means that as a permanency then negro suffrage is a failure."

Conclusion

From the beginning of the Republic to the Civil War most Americans viewed a powerful central government as a threat to individual liberties. That was the principal reason for the promulgation of the Bill of Rights (the first 10 amendments to the Constitution); to impose strict limits on the powers of the federal government. However, during the Civil War and its aftermath, Reconstruction, it became clear that the national government had to exert unprecedented power in order not only win a war but to free the slaves and subsequently secure their equal rights as free citizens. Thus the imperative for the passage of the Thirteenth, Fourteenth, and Fifteenth Amendments to the Constitution, and the including in all three amendments, clauses granting Congress the full power to enforce these provisions for liberty and equal rights.

Much to the consternation of Southern whites and their Northern Democratic supporters, during Reconstruction, the Republican-dominated Congress passed civil rights laws and enforcement legislation to accomplish this purpose. Federal marshals and troops patrolled the polls to protect black voters, arrested thousands of Klansmen and other white terrorists of black civil rights, and even occupied state capitals to prevent Democratic paramilitary groups from attempting coups to overthrow by violent means the Republican governments.

Unfortunately white Northern public opinion began turning against Reconstruction in the early 1870s, largely because of the distractions and preoccupations caused by the Panic of 1873 and European immigration. The eventual withdrawal of the last federal troops in 1877 reflected this changed opinion and constituted both a symbolic and substantive end of the 12-year postwar era known as Reconstruction. Although a dismal and disheartening failure in many key areas, especially the guaranteeing of black civil rights and equality, Reconstruction nonetheless achieved the two great objectives inherited from the Civil War: the reincorporation of the former Confederate states into the Union and to establish a process (albeit haphazard and often lacking in sincerity and commitment) by which the slaves could transition to freedom in the South. That passage, however, was marred by the economic inequity of sharecropping and the social injustice of white supremacy. Reconstruction's third goal, the enforcement of equal civil and political rights promised in the Fourteenth and Fifteenth Amendments, was betrayed by the Compromise of 1877. In subsequent decades the freedmen and their descendants suffered repression into segregated second-class citizenship. Not until another war hero-turned-president sent troops into Little Rock, Arkansas 80 years after they had been withdrawn from New Orleans and Columbia, South Carolina, did the federal government launch a second Reconstruction to fulfill the promises of the first.

Suggested Readings

Benjamin Quarles. *Lincoln and the Negro.* (1962). A judicious account of the evolution of Lincoln's policies regarding slavery, emancipation, and African American rights and presence in the United States.

Heather C. Richardson. *Greatest Nation of the Earth: Republican Economic Policies during the Civil War.* (1997). Examines the far-reaching economic impact policies adopted during the war had on the nation's overall economic development both at the time and in the post-war years.

Willie Lee Rose. *Rehearsal for Reconstruction: The Port Royal Experiment.* (1964). Presents many of the key issues that will come to define much of the Reconstruction era and its policies relative to black folk first manifested on the Sea Islands of South Carolina in the midst of the war.

Dan T. Carter. *When the War Was Over: The Failure of Presidential Reconstruction in the South, 1865–1867.* (1985). A through analysis of the failure of presidential reconstruction in the South.

W.E. B. DuBois. *Black Reconstruction in America.* (1935). The first comprehensive refutation of the traditionalist view of Reconstruction as an ear of misgovernment, oppressive and incompetent "Negro Rule," and white victimization at the hands of lecherous Negroes and their white affiliates. DuBois affirmed that nothing of the sort happened and that it was all part of the white-backlash propaganda to overthrow the radical governments and return power to Southern whites and usher in the ear of Jim Crow.

Laura Edwards. *Gendered Strife and Confusion: The Political Culture of Reconstruction* (1997). Considers how issues relating to gender affected the course of Southern Reconstruction.

Barbara J. Fields. *Slavery and Freedom on the Middle Ground: Maryland during the 19ᵗʰ Century.* (1985). A study of emancipation in a key border state.

Eric Foner. *Reconstructon: America's Unfinished Revolution, 1863–1877.* (1988). The most comprehensive analysis of Reconstruction to date; a seminal study of the era.

Steven Hahn. *A Nation Under Our Feet: Black Political Struggles in the Rural South from Slavery to the Great Migration.* (2003). A detailed study of black political activism, stressing nationalist consciousness and emigration movements.

Harold Hyman. *A More Perfect Union: The Impact of the Civil War and Reconstruction on the Constitution.* (1973). Hyman analyzes how the laws and the constitutional amendments of the Reconstruction era changed the Constitution and the rights of all Americans.

Leon F. Litwack. *Been in the Storm So Long: The Aftermath of Slavery.* (1979). A detailed look at the immediate aftermath of the end of slavery and the variety of black and white responses to emancipation.

George C. Rable. *There Was No Peace: The Role of Violence in the Politics of Reconstruction.* (1984). The only in-depth study of one of the nation's most violent era's, Reconstruction.

Roger L. Ransom and Richard Sutch. *One Kind of Freedom: The Economic Consequences of Freedom.* (1977). Two economic historians examine the transition from slavery to sharecropping in the South among black folk and even looks at southern whites who also had to become sharecroppers in the post-war South.

Heather C. Richardson. *The Death of Reconstruction: Race, Labor, and Politics in the Post-Civil War North.* (2001). An examination of the numerous causes of the North's retreat from Reconstruction by the early 1870s.

John C. Rodrigue. *Reconstruction in the Cane Fields: From Slavery to Free Labor in Louisiana's Sugar Parishes, 1862–1880.* A study of how an often-neglected part of the South experienced the aftermath of slavery.

Mark W. Summers. *Railroads, Reconstruction, and the Gospel of Prosperity: Aid under the Radical Republicans, 1865–1877.* (1984). A detailed look at the southern governments' efforts to promote economic development, and the political corruption that sometimes accompanies such efforts.

Hans L. Trefouse. *The Radical Republicans: Lincoln's Vanguard for Racial Justice.* (1969). An account of the political history of the Radical Republicans, from the pre-Civil War period through the end of Reconstruction.